AF248654

To Nick, Uccia and Johnny C.

sante d'orazio

a private view
photographs & diary

edited by **david fahey**
designed by **isabelle salmon**

a melcher media book

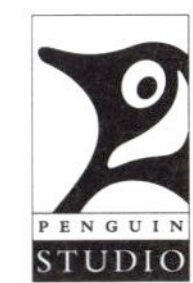

PENGUIN
STUDIO

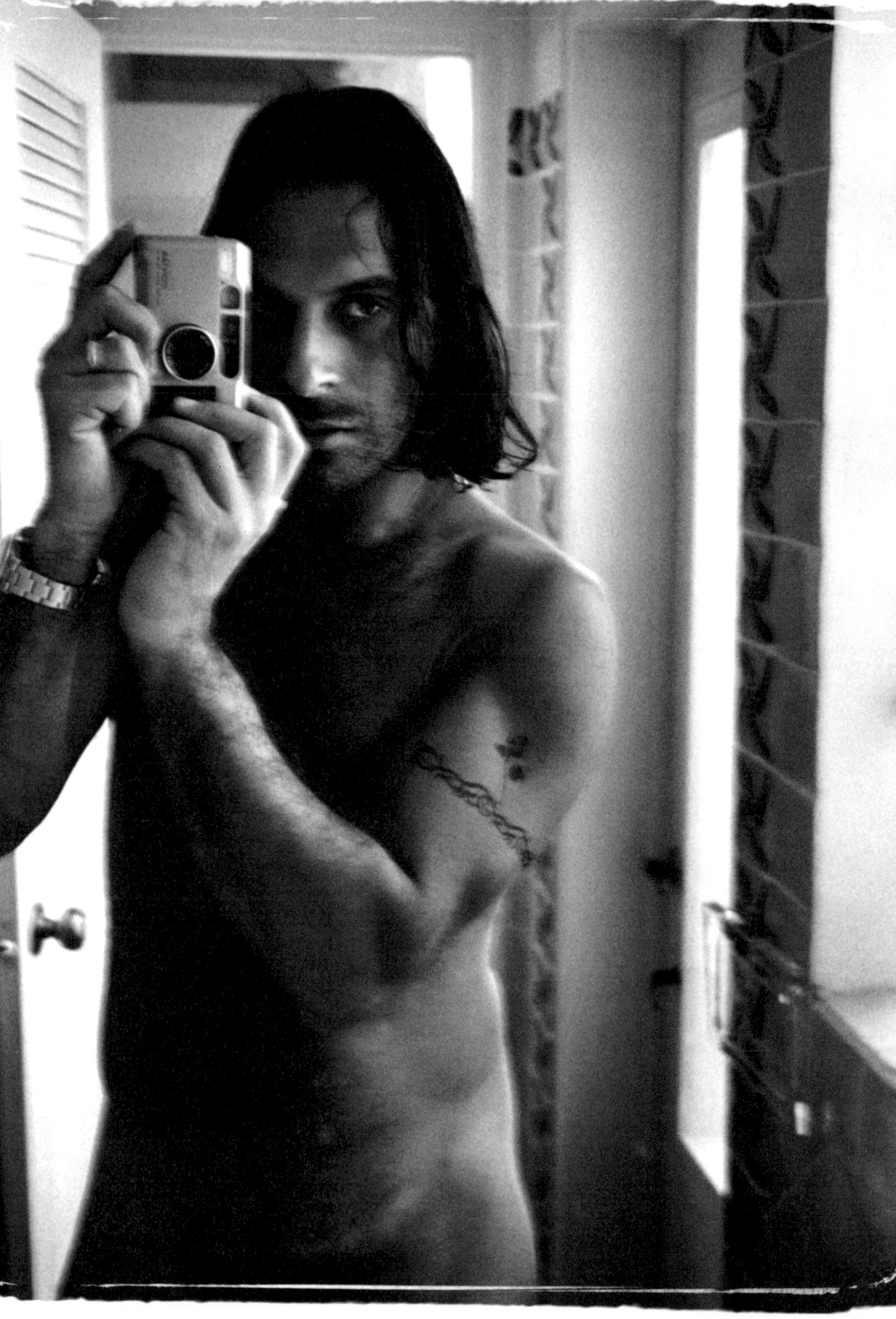

a very red cherry

foreword by francesco clemente

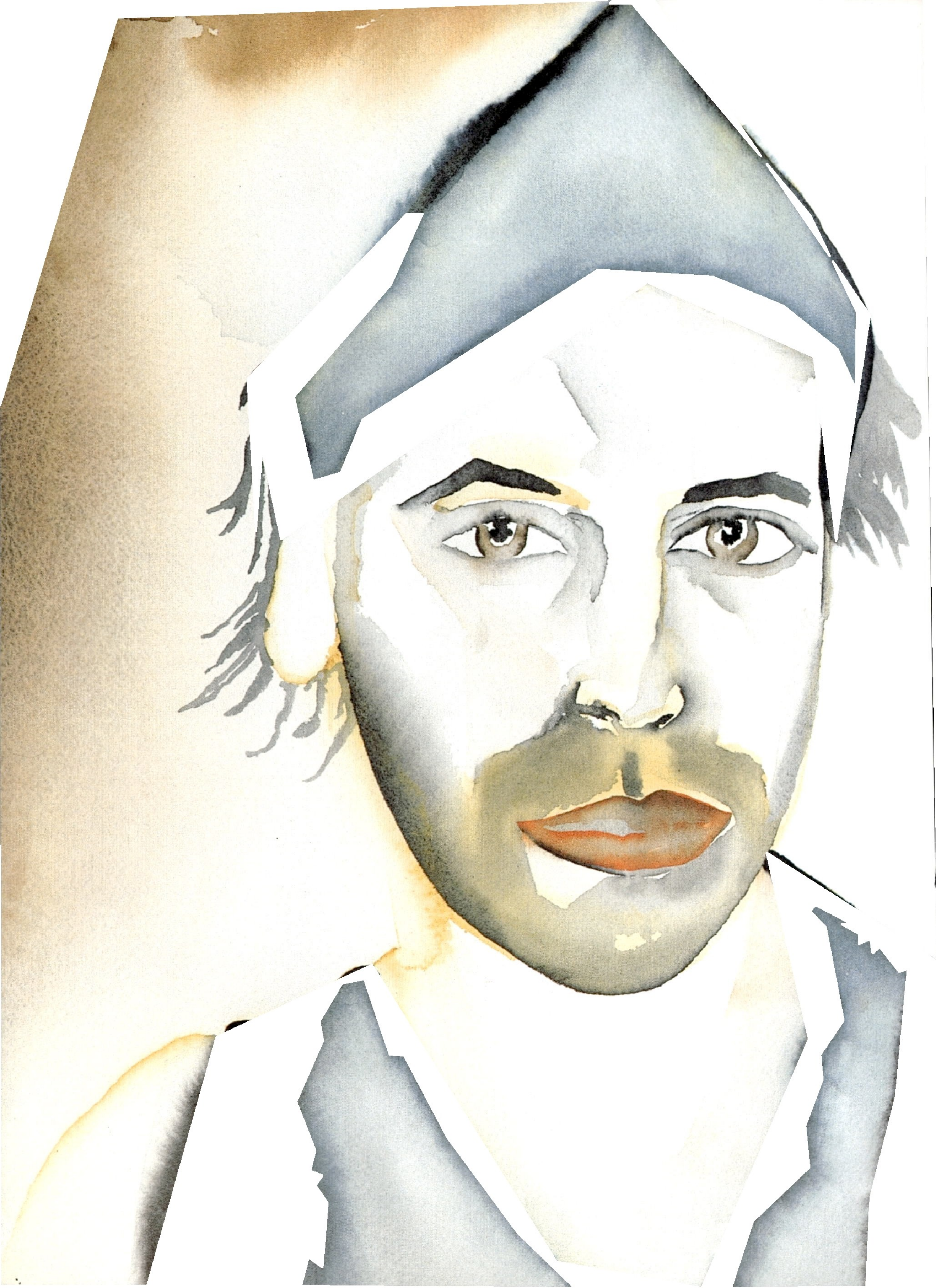

Sante's father. Italian immigrant, barber,
'50s pinups hanging from the mirror at the shop.
Sante, 17, a small room in Brooklyn, drawing
his father's face, obsessively, minutely, lead pencil,
two laborious months to finish the tiny drawing,
photolike resemblance. He hangs it over his bed.

Sante, 19, solitary spring months in
Coney Island. Camera on a tripod, set in front
of the great aquarium. Seminal wait for
the white whales mating time. Large brush strokes
of white, the great bodies touching each other,
a sense of achievement, belonging to a craft
and to a moment.

Sante, fashion photographer, American-Italian.
More Italian than American. Unafraid of
excessive, complacent prettiness. Catholic
celebration of the flesh. Still, the ripeness
of a very red cherry shall imply a melancholic
acknowledgment of fragility. Sante's acceptance
of his subjects' good looks is without apology,
faithful as he is to the essence of photography

as vanitas, a ghostly reminder that the sole
beauty we know is fleeting beauty.

Sante, older, successful, working at the vast
magazine icon factory. After the job is done,
not knowing whether to feel skeptical or sentimental,
he pastes methodically on his diary's pages
the backstage sweat of unreachable beauties,
actors, models, rock stars, who, unpackaged,
reveal at times an endearing anxiety, slipping
unawares through the brittle surfaces of fragility.

Sante, 40, disenchanted with the '60s, easy
recipes of self-destruction, and yet looking out
through the '90s for the people who express
a sense of danger, a friction if not a break
with the ever-growing mantle of hypocrisy.

Sante, a friend, a photographer, no explanation
really needed. Restless, unpretentious, photographs
are entertainment too, to catch the moment.
The picture will compose itself, speak for itself.

Francesco Clement

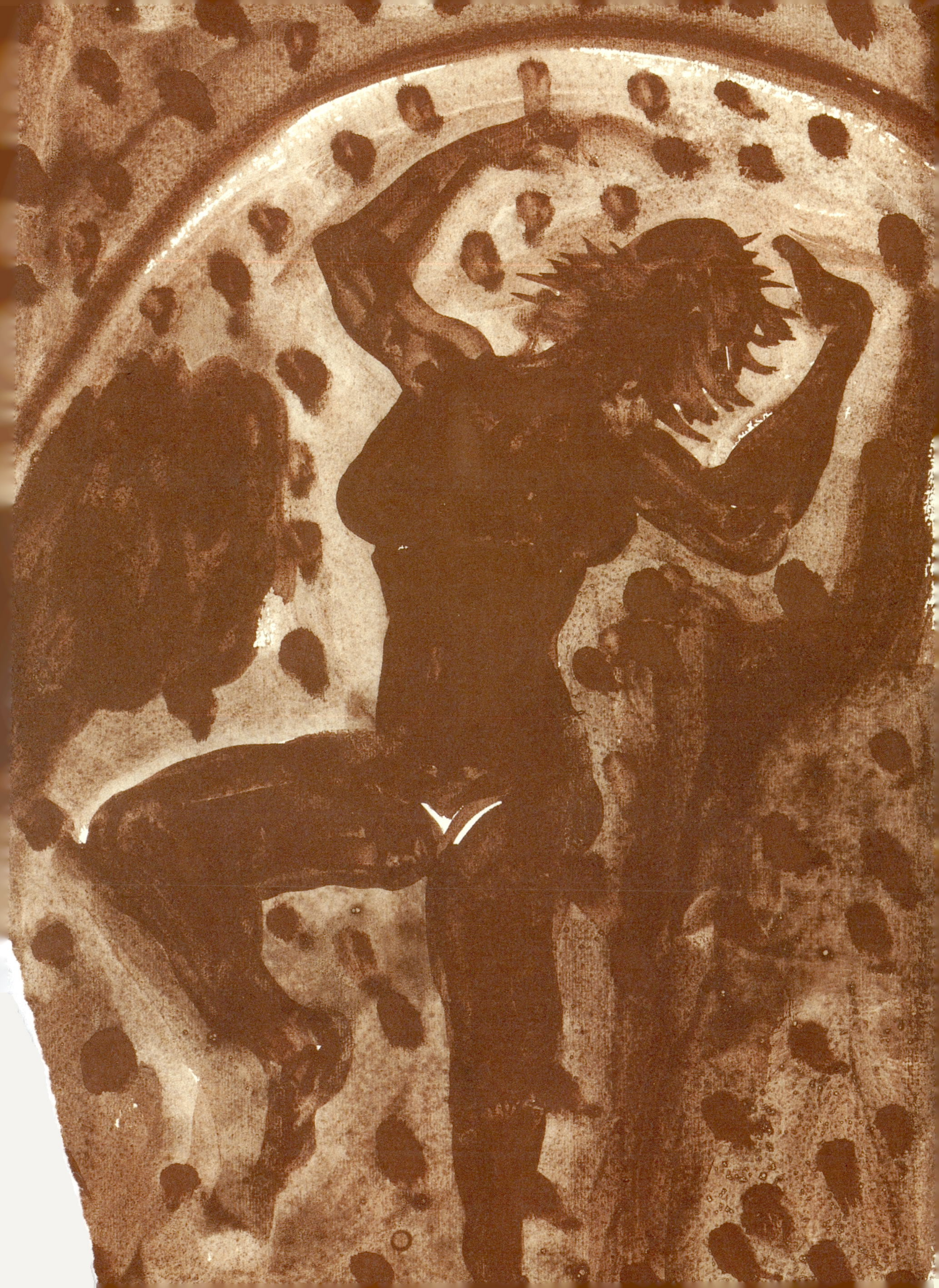

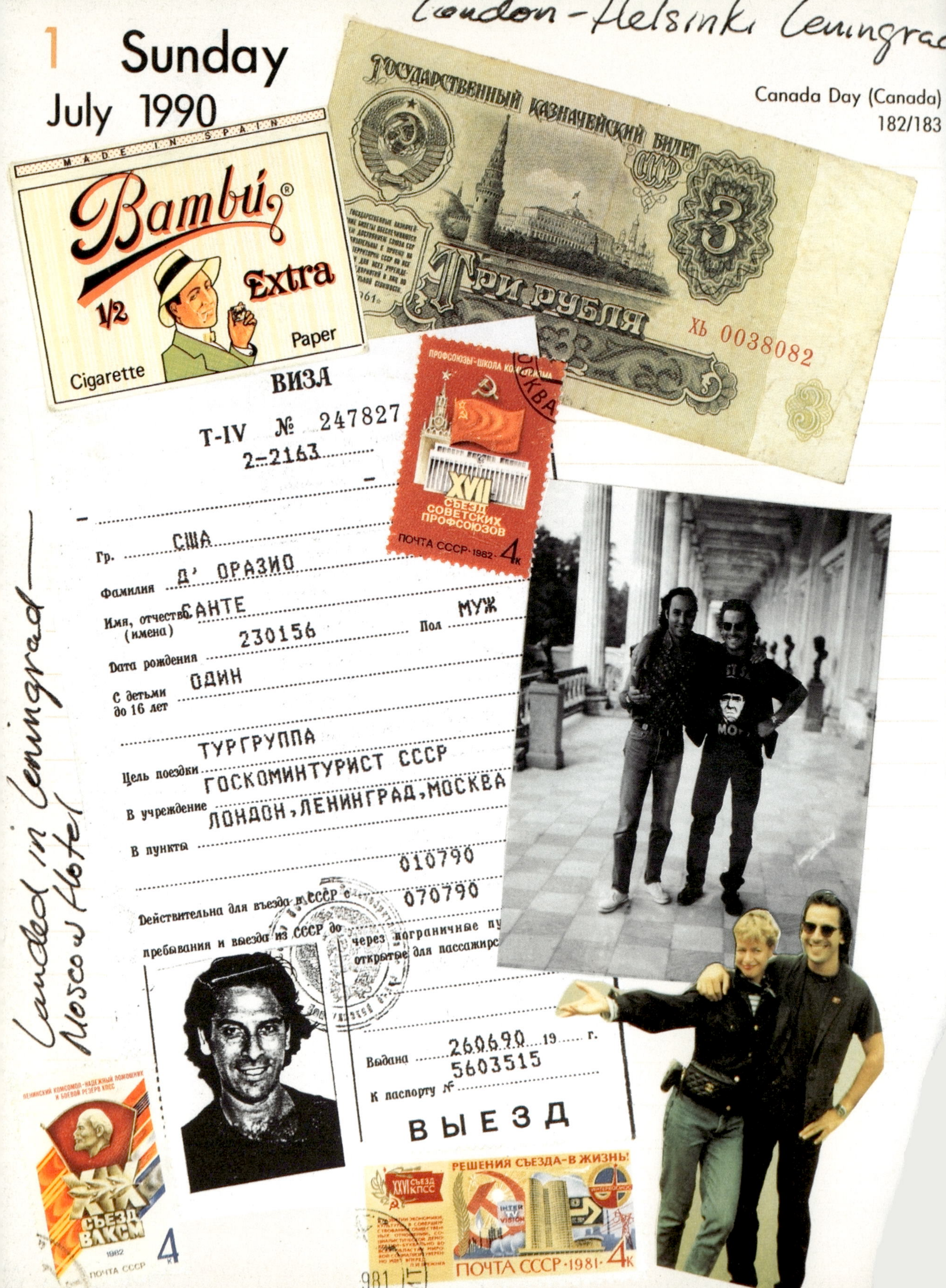
1 Sunday
July 1990
Canada Day (Canada)
182/183
London-Helsinki Leningrad
MADE IN SPAIN
Bambú
Extra
1/2
Paper
Cigarette
ГОСУДАРСТВЕННЫЙ КАЗНАЧЕЙСКИЙ БИЛЕТ СССР
ТРИ РУБЛЯ
3
Хь 0038082
ВИЗА
T-IV   № 247827
2-2163
Гр.   США
Фамилия   Д' ОРАЗИО
Имя, отчество   САНТЕ   МУЖ
(имена)
Дата рождения   230156   Пол
С детьми   ОДИН
до 16 лет
ТУРГРУППА
Цель поездки   ГОСКОМИНТУРИСТ СССР
В учреждение   ЛОНДОН, ЛЕНИНГРАД, МОСКВА
В пункты
010790
070790
Действительна для въезда в СССР с
пребывания и выезда из СССР до   через пограничные пу
открытые для пассажир
260690   19   г.
Выдана
5603515
к паспорту №
ВЫЕЗД
ПРОФСОЮЗЫ-ШКОЛА КО
XVII СЪЕЗД СОВЕТСКИХ ПРОФСОЮЗОВ
ПОЧТА СССР-1982 4к
ЛЕНИНСКИЙ КОМСОМОЛ-НАДЕЖНЫЙ ПОМОЩНИК
И БОЕВОЙ РЕЗЕРВ КПСС
XIX СЪЕЗД ВЛКСМ
1982
ПОЧТА СССР 4к
РЕШЕНИЯ СЪЕЗДА-В ЖИЗНЬ!
XXVI СЪЕЗД КПСС
INTER VISION
ПОЧТА СССР-1981 4к
Landed in Leningrad
Moscow Hotel

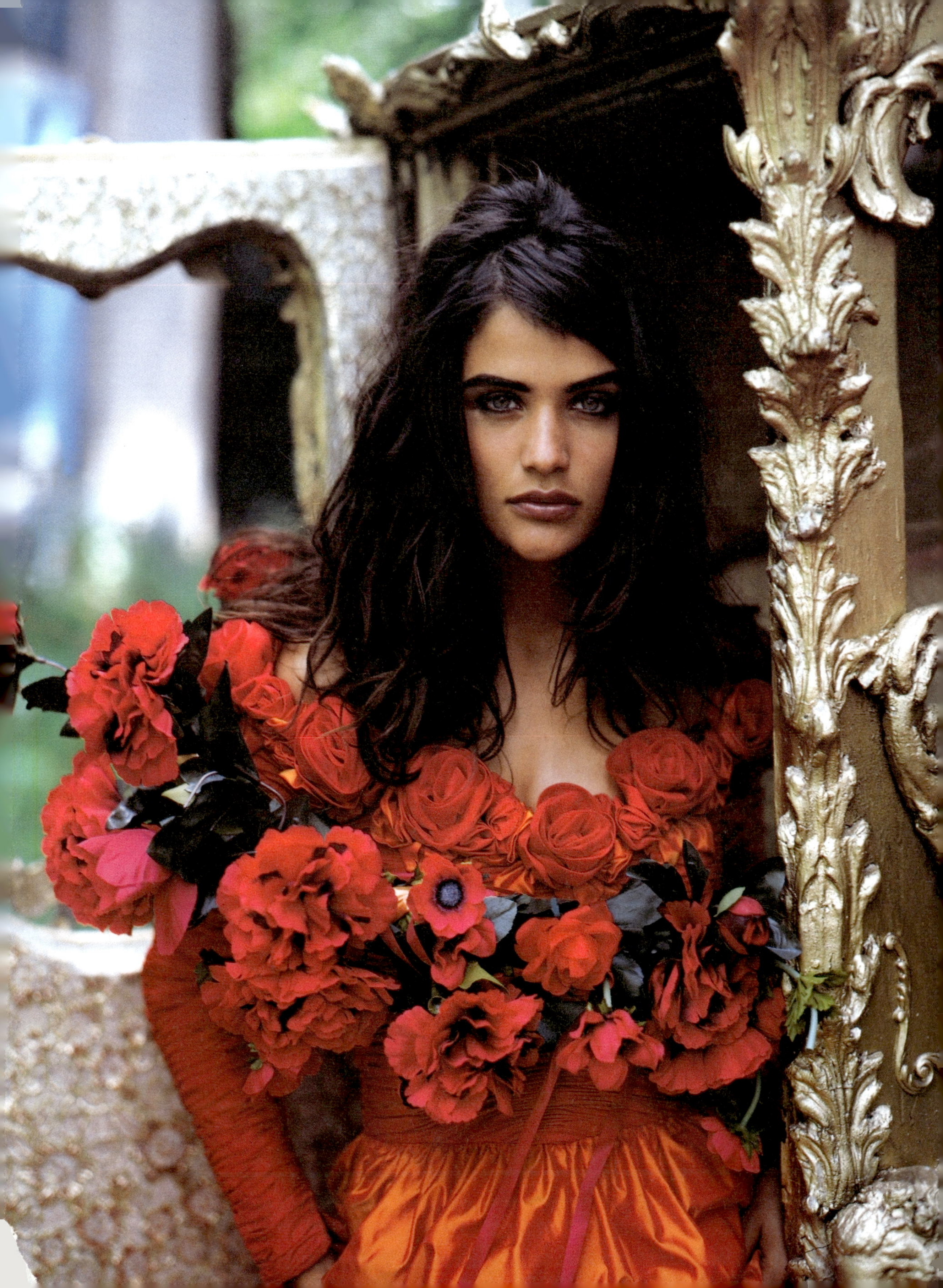

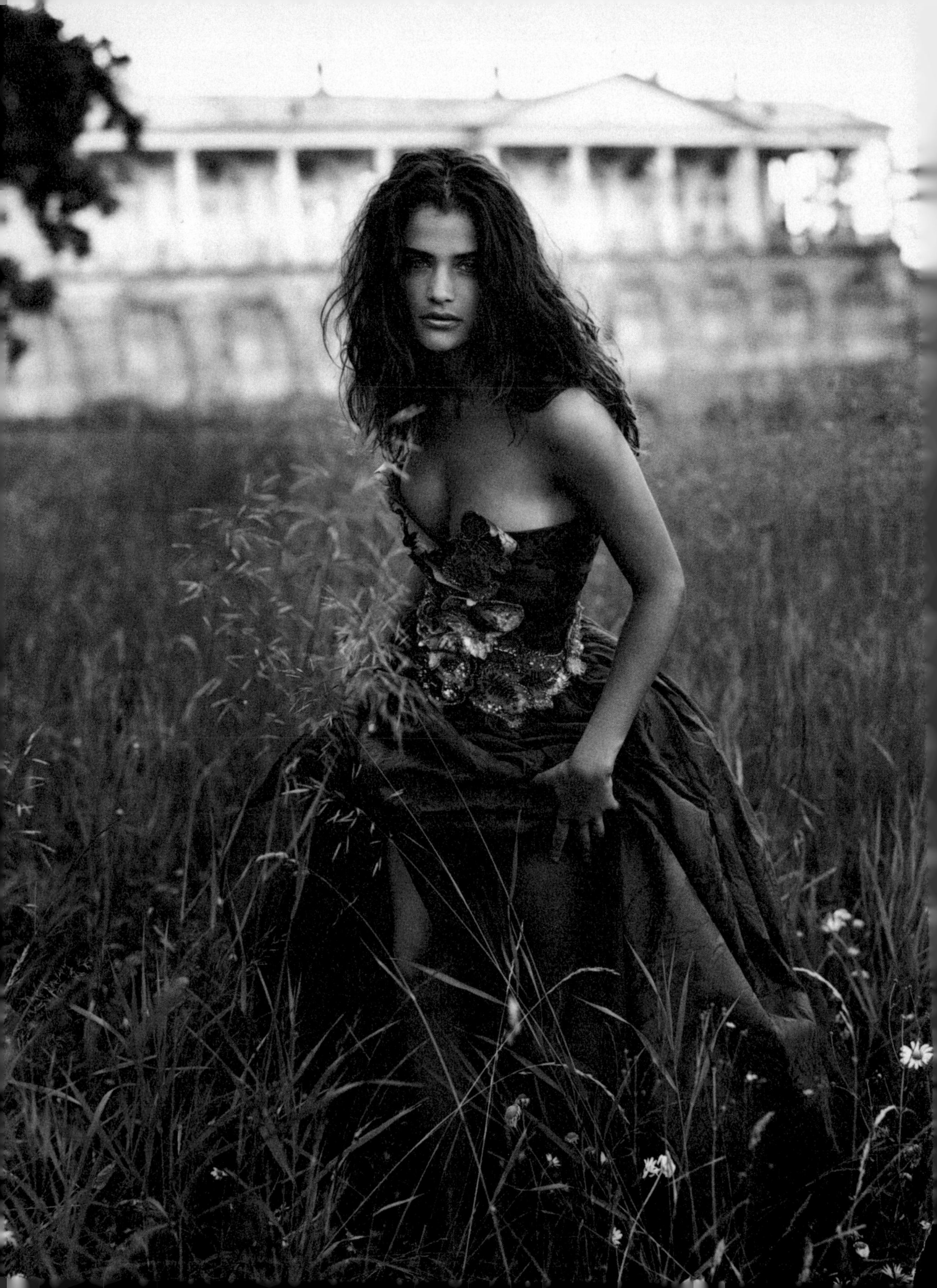

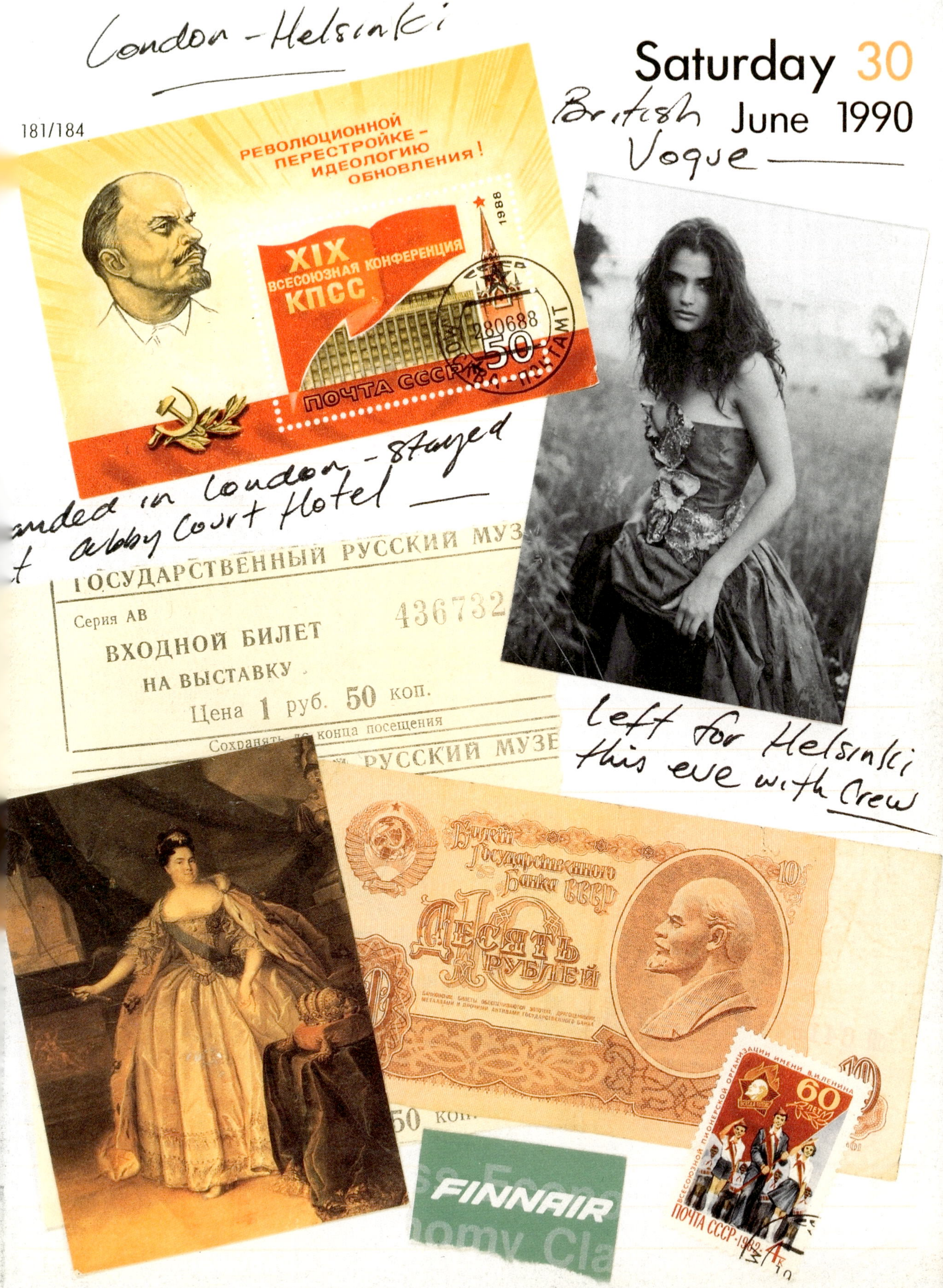
London - Helsinki
181/184
Saturday 30
British
Vogue
June 1990
РЕВОЛЮЦИОННОЙ
ПЕРЕСТРОЙКЕ -
ИДЕОЛОГИЮ
ОБНОВЛЕНИЯ !
1988
XIX
ВСЕСОЮЗНАЯ КОНФЕРЕНЦИЯ
КПСС
280688
50
ПОЧТА СССР
...nded in London - stayed
t Abbey Court Hotel —
ГОСУДАРСТВЕННЫЙ РУССКИЙ МУЗ...
Серия АВ
436732
ВХОДНОЙ БИЛЕТ
НА ВЫСТАВКУ
Цена 1 руб. 50 коп.
Сохранять до конца посещения
РУССКИЙ МУЗЕ...
left for Helsinki
this eve with crew
Билет
Государственного
Банка СССР
ДЕСЯТЬ
РУБЛЕЙ
Всесоюзной пионерской организации имени В.И.Ленина
60
ЛЕТ
ПОЧТА СССР·1982·
FINNAIR

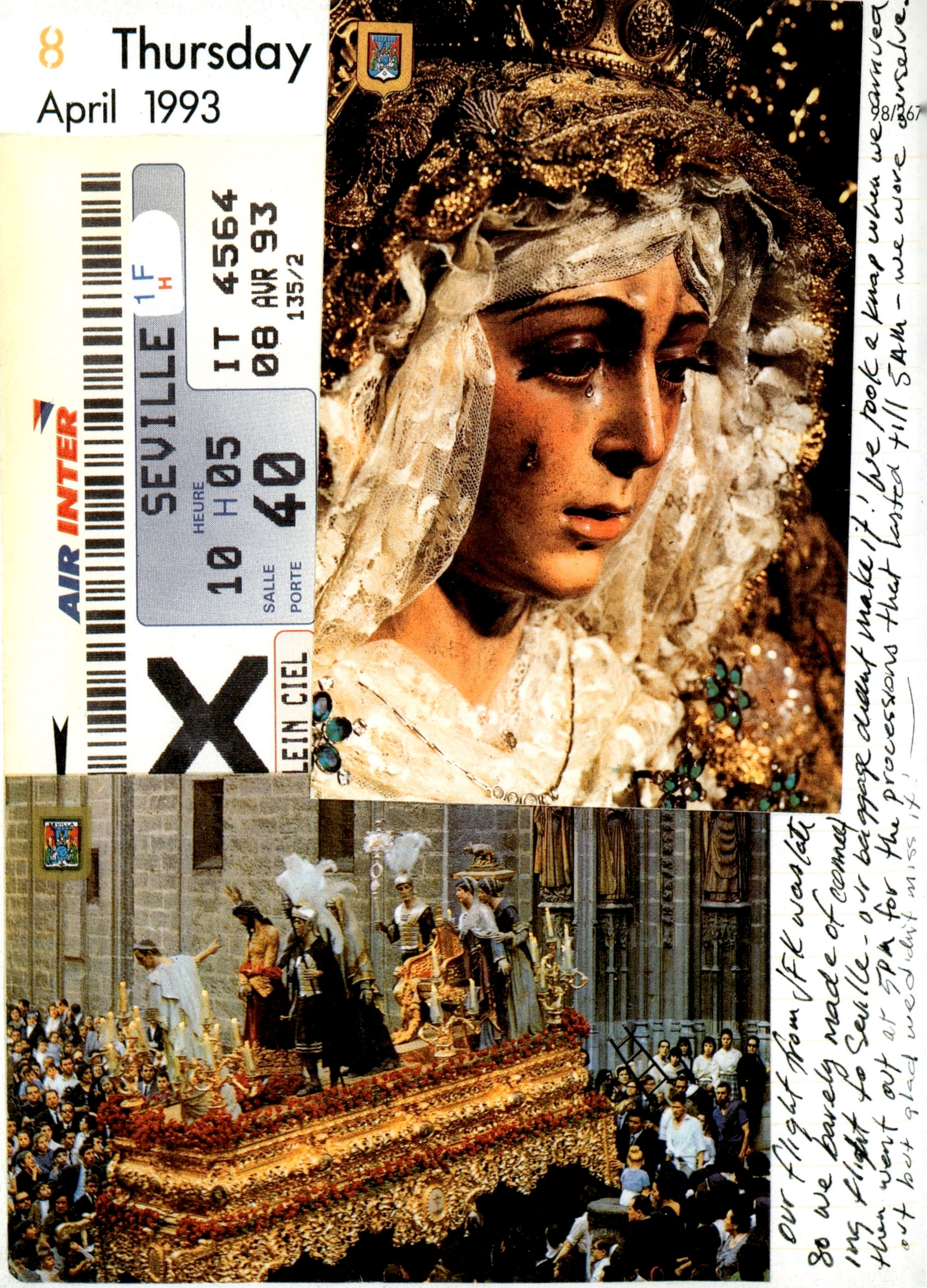

8
Thursday
April 1993
AIR INTER
SEVILLE
1F
H
IT 4564
08 AVR 93
135/2
HEURE
10 H 05
SALLE
40
PORTE
X
PLEIN CIEL
SEVILLA
Our flight from JFK was late so we barely made of connecting flight to Seville — our baggage didn't make it! We took a knap when we arrived then went out at 5PM for the processions that lasted till 5AM — we were out but glad we didn't miss it!
8/267

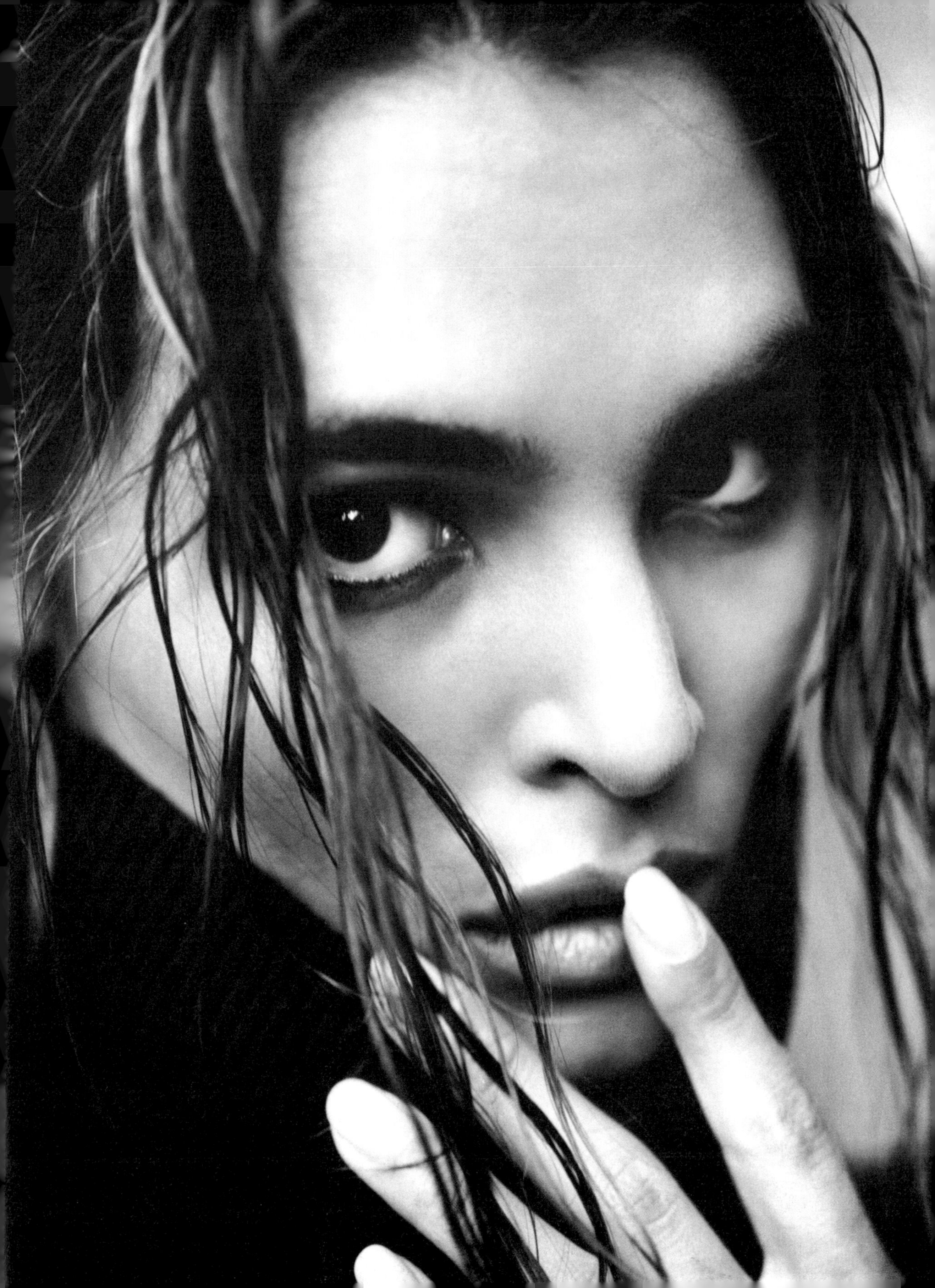

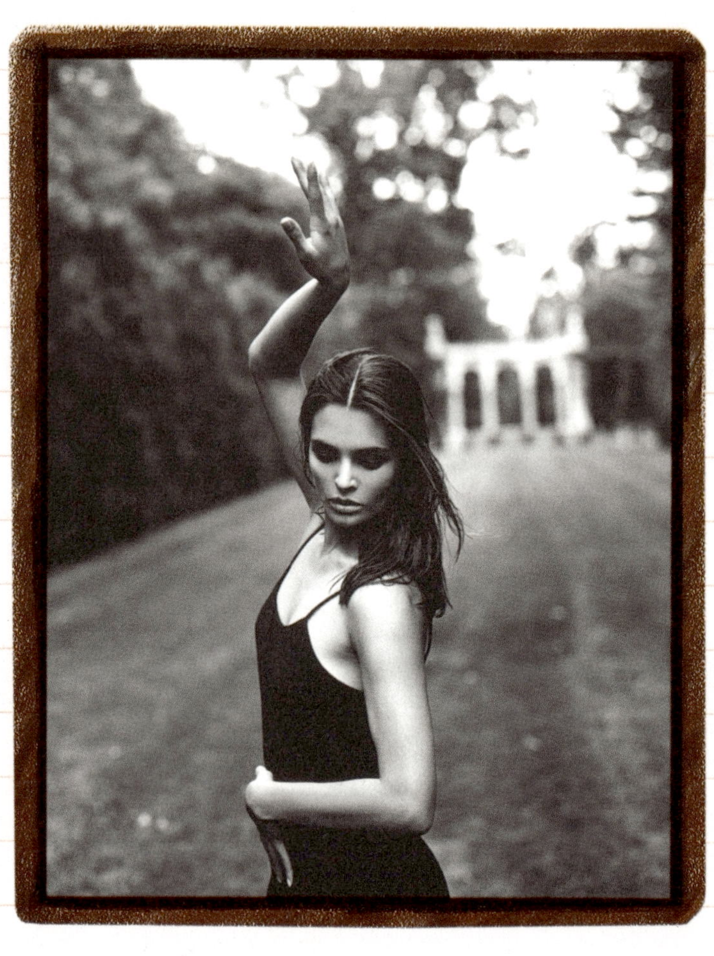

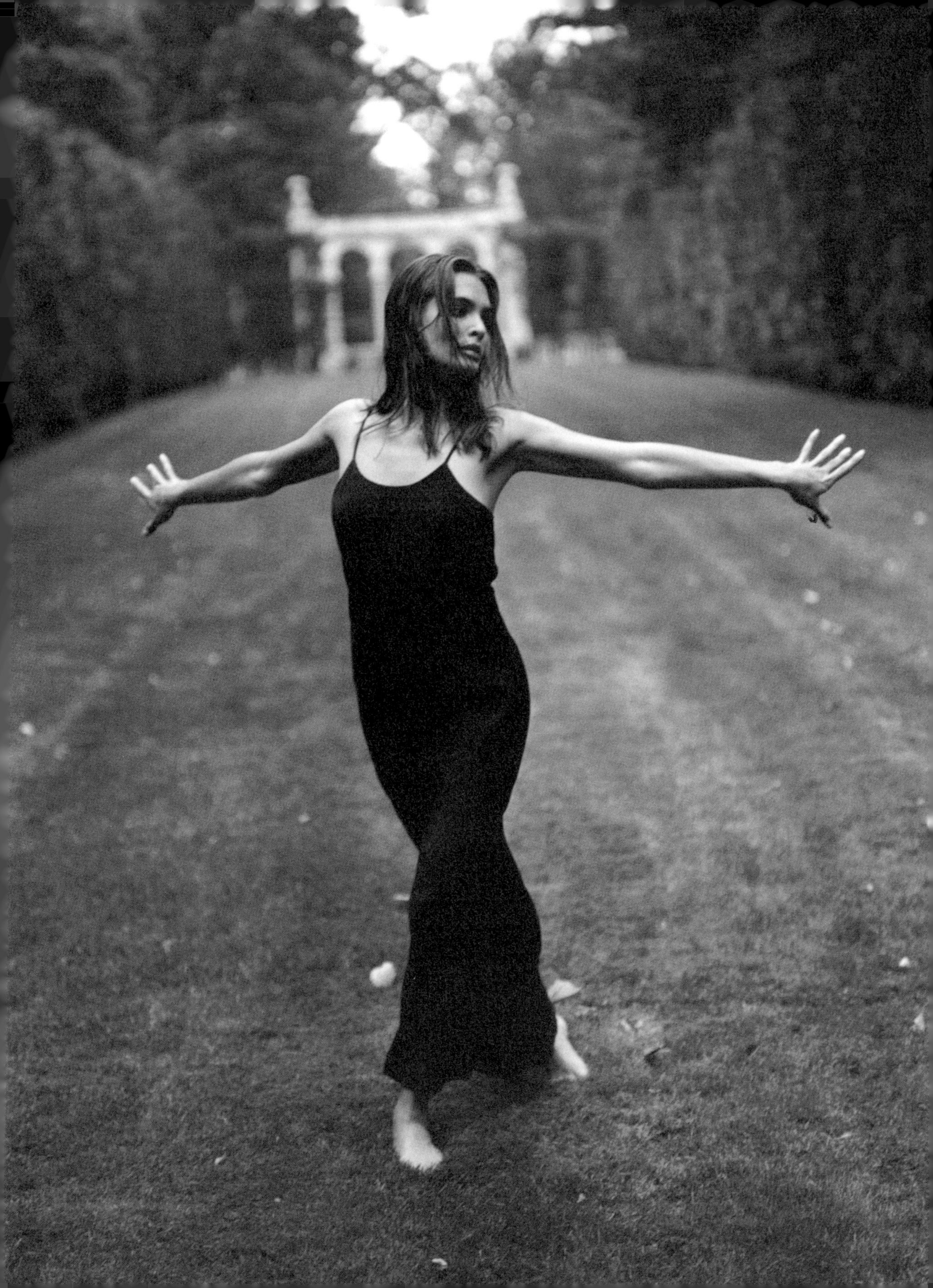

4205

192/174

Allure —

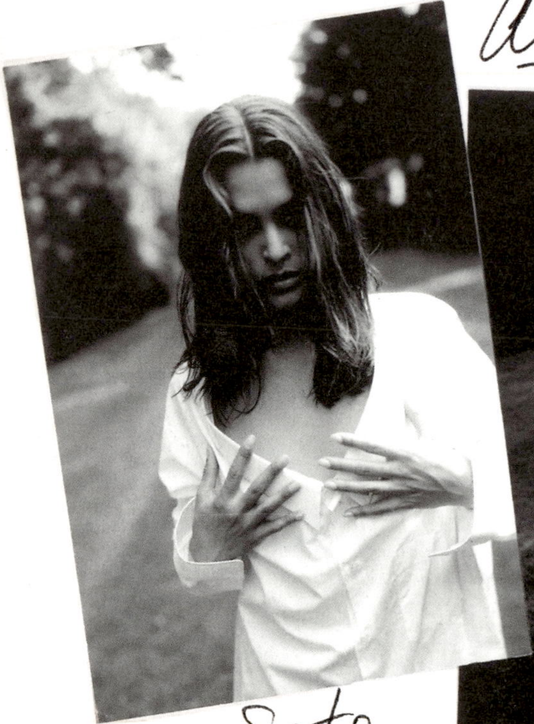

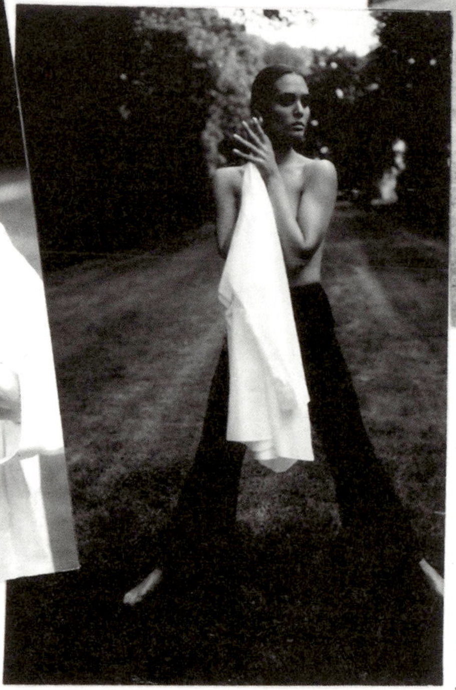

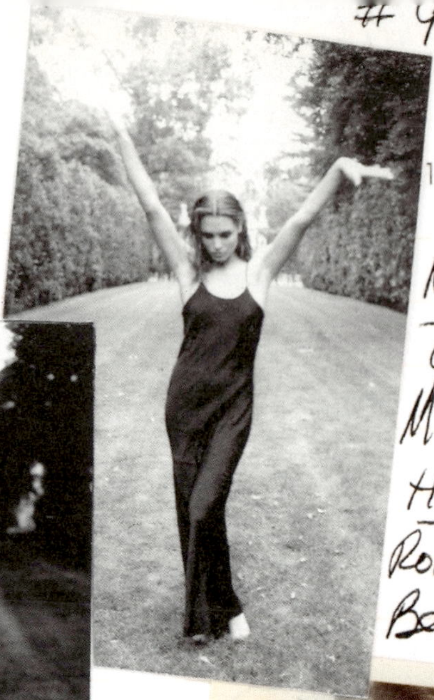

M.K. Up
Glenn
Marsia
Hair:
Rolando
Beauchan

Talisa Soto

Edtr: Polly Mellen

Knoll Estate - Westbory

Assist: Audre +
Alexandra

Film: 24 EPT135
13 CIPS
5 Fuģi Pola
12 Pola665/54 TX 220

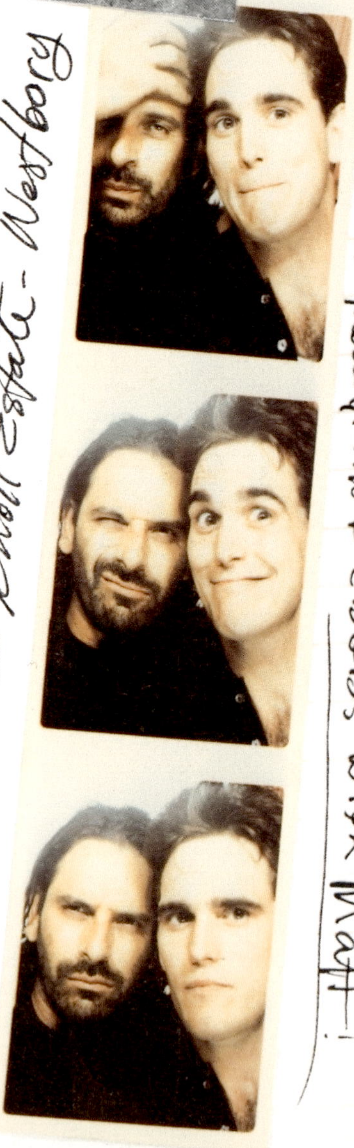

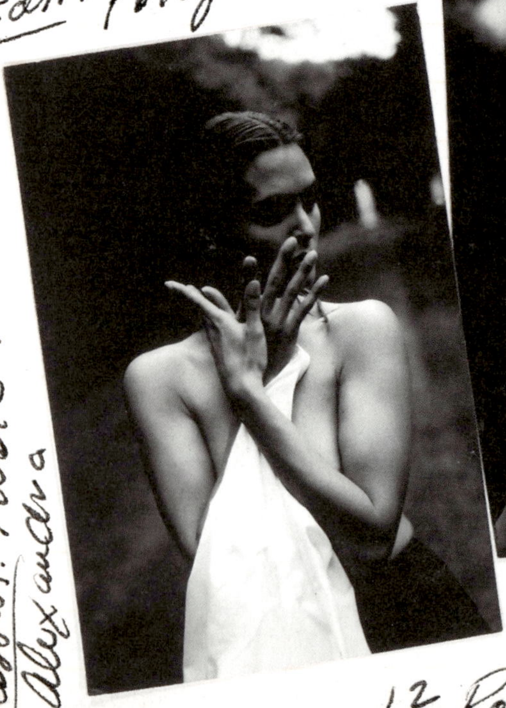

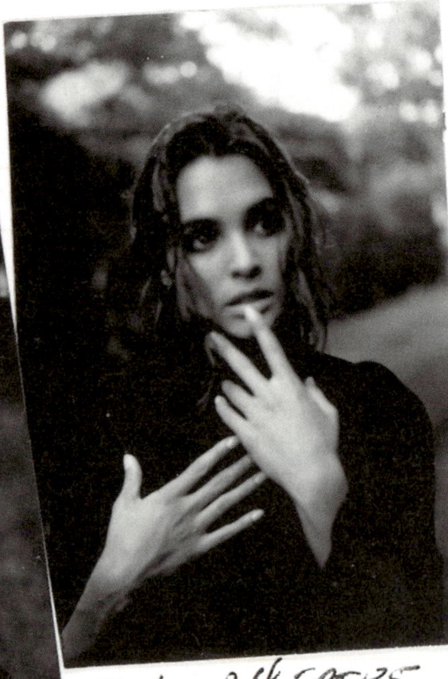

Dinner at Mezzogiorno + COGOS with Matt

Edited Talisa

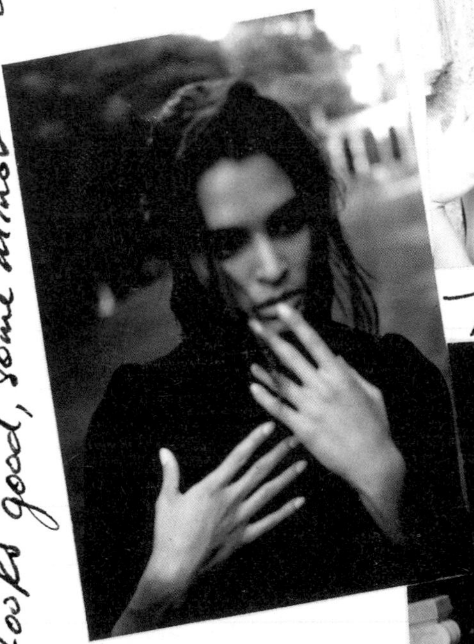

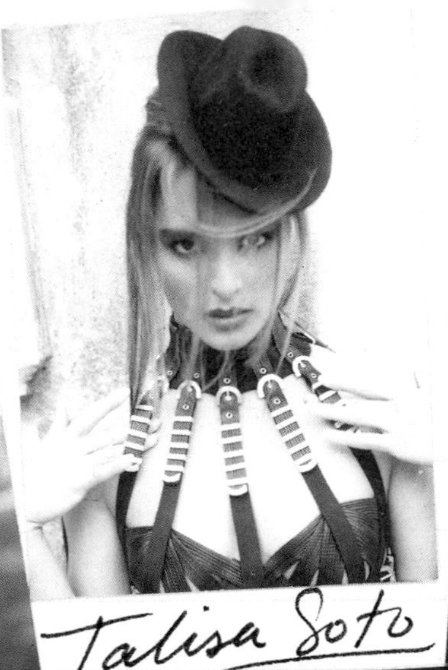

Talisa Soto

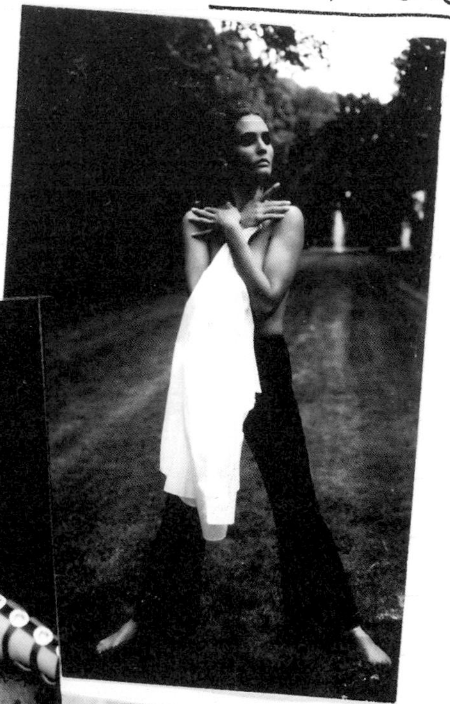

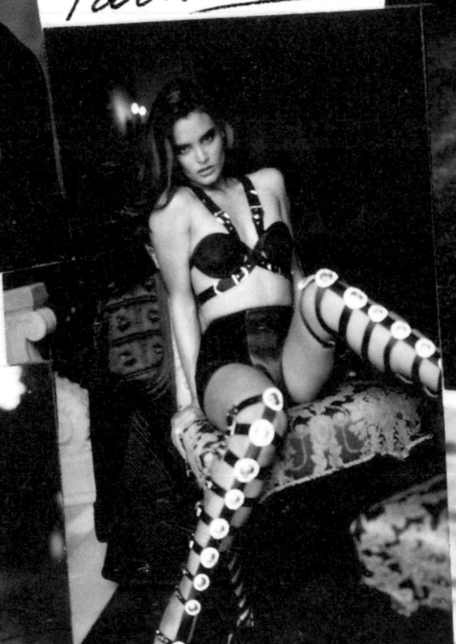

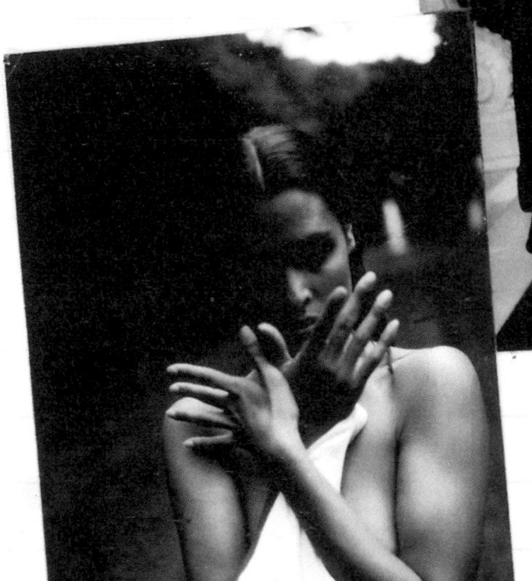

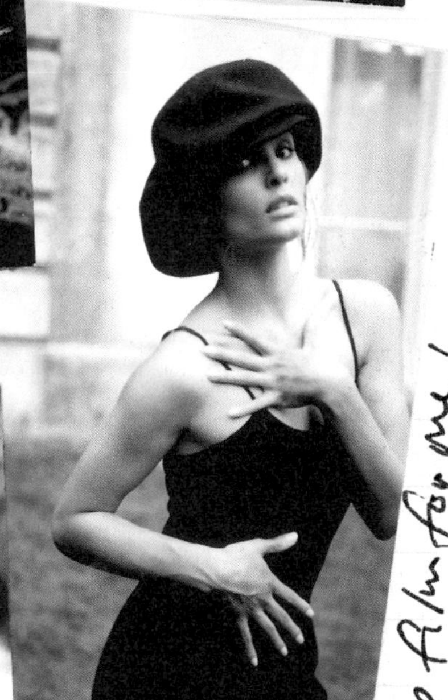

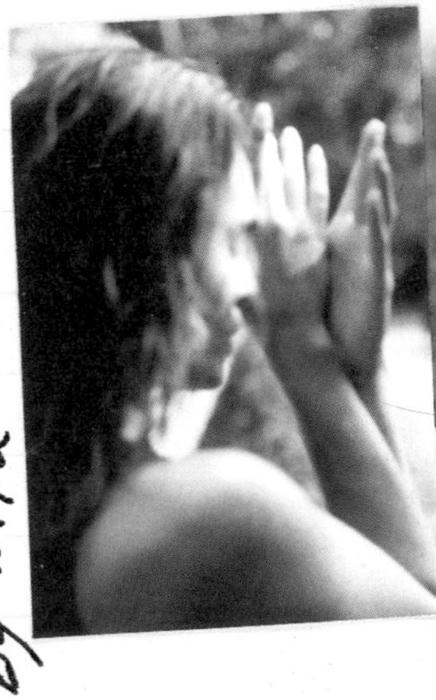

to look at first print of "Sammy". Looks good, some minor adjustments. Working thru my hangover. Spent rest of the day editing 'Allure'. Uccia came by with

Some food + we ate together. Hubie + Alexandra helped out by setting up film for me!

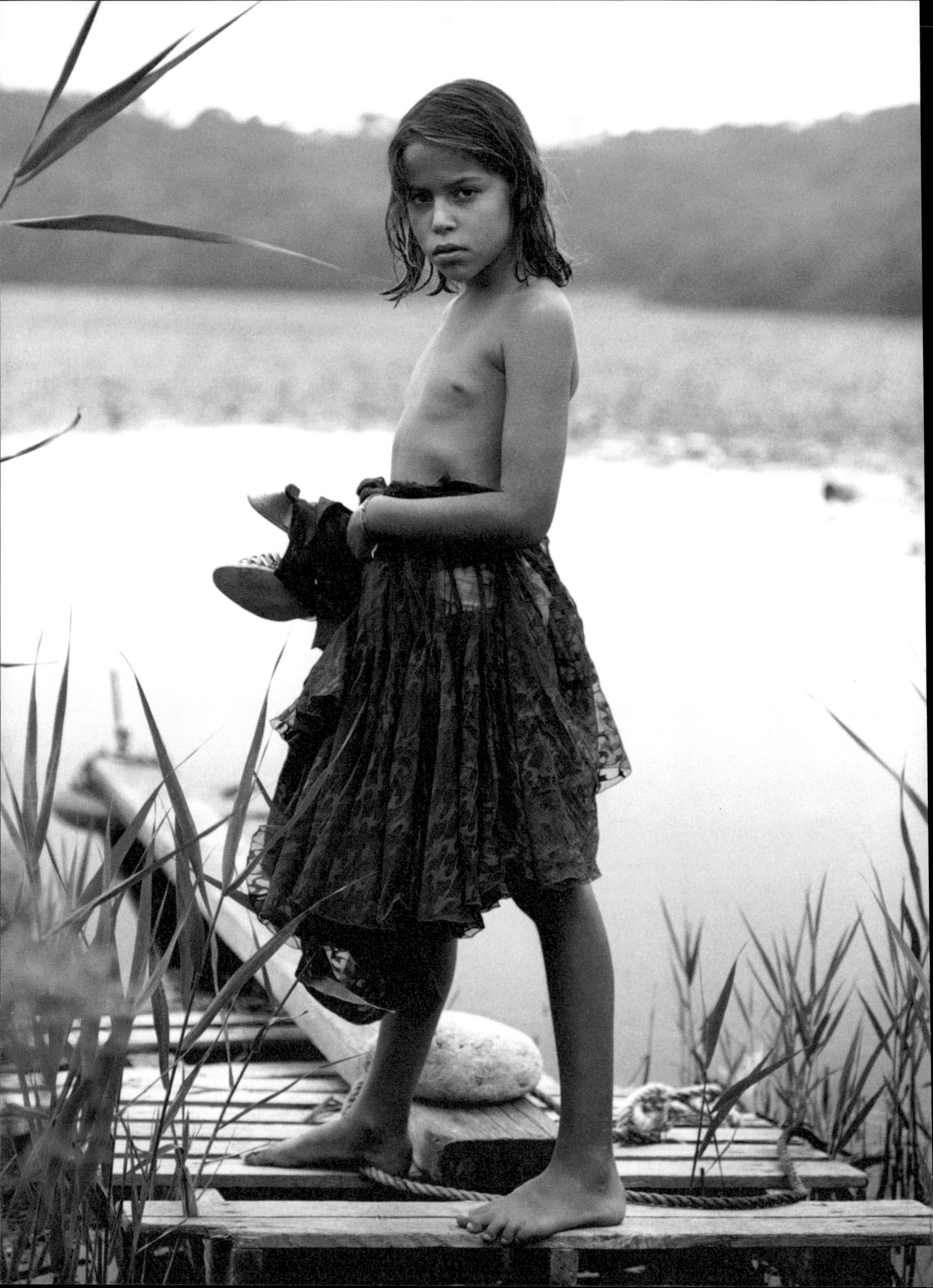

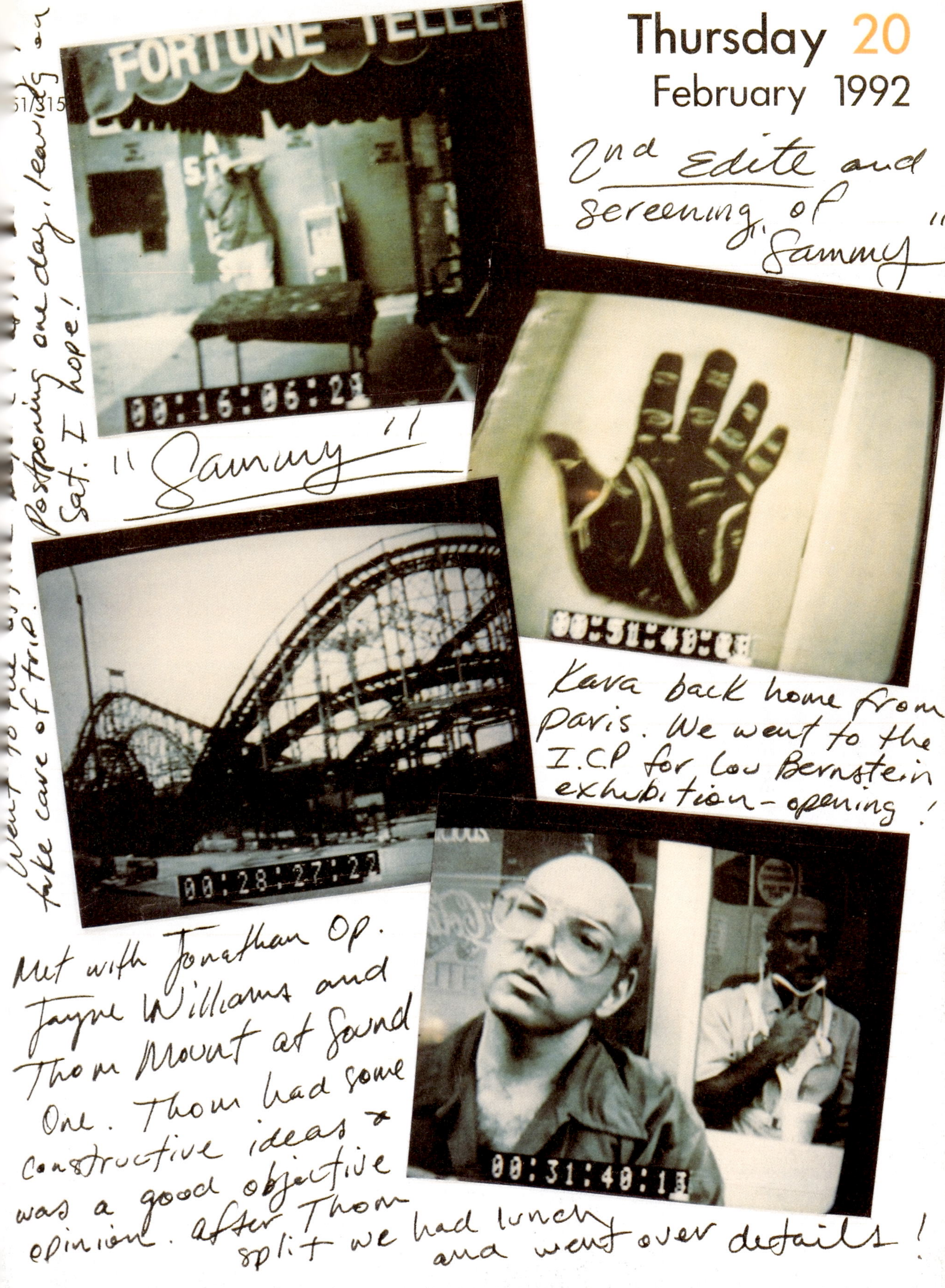

51/315

Postponing one day. Leaving on Sat. I hope!

Went to the ...ite ... with ... take care of trip.

2nd _Edit_ and screening of "Sammy"

" Sammy "

Met with Jonathan Op. Jayne Williams and Thom Mount at Sound One. Thom had some constructive ideas + was a good objective opinion. After Thom split we had lunch

Kava back home from Paris. We went to the I.C.P for Lou Bernstein exhibition - opening!

and went over details!

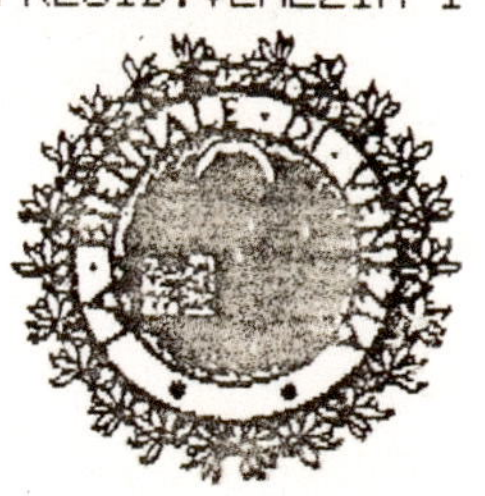

Tazio Secchiaroli (with camera) and partner on their Ves[pa]

). '92 15:44 LA BIENNALE SEG.PRESID.VENEZIA I

LA BIENNALE DI VENEZIA
Ente Autonoma

SANTE D'ORAZIO STUDIO INC.

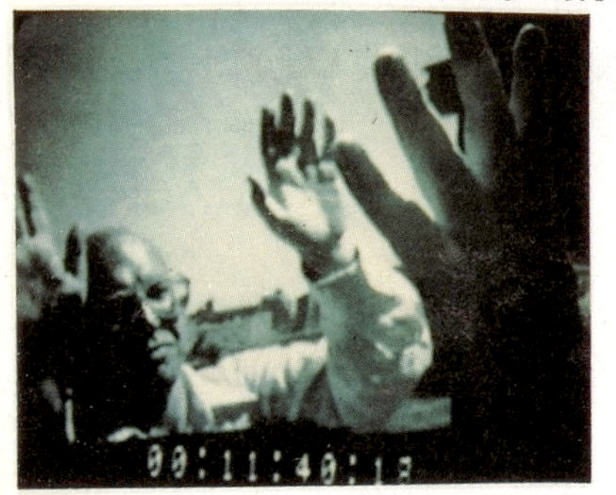

VENICE, 14TH AUGUST 1992

ON BEHALF OF THE BOARD OF DIRECTORS I HAVE THE PLEASURE OF INVITING
THE FILM   " SAMMY "   TO PARTICIPATE IN THE SECTION
" FINESTRA SULL'IMMAGINE " TO THE XLIX MOSTRA INTERNAZIONALE D'ARTE
CINEMATOGRAFICA TO BE HELD IN VENICE FROM 1ST TO 12TH OF SEPTEMBER
1992.
THE DIRECTOR MR. SANTE D'ORAZIO,   THE LEADING ACTOR OR ACTRESS ARE
INVITED AS GUESTS FOR ONE DAY FOR THE PRESENTATION OF THEIR FILM.
PLEASE CONFIRM YOUR PARTICIPATION TO FAX N° 041/5267892.

BEST REGARDS

PAOLO PORTOGHESI
PRESIDENT BIENNALE VENICE

S. Marco, Ca' Giustinian
30124 Venezia
Telefono 041/5218711
Telefax 041/5236374
Telex 410685 BLE-VE-I
Cod. fisc. 00330320276

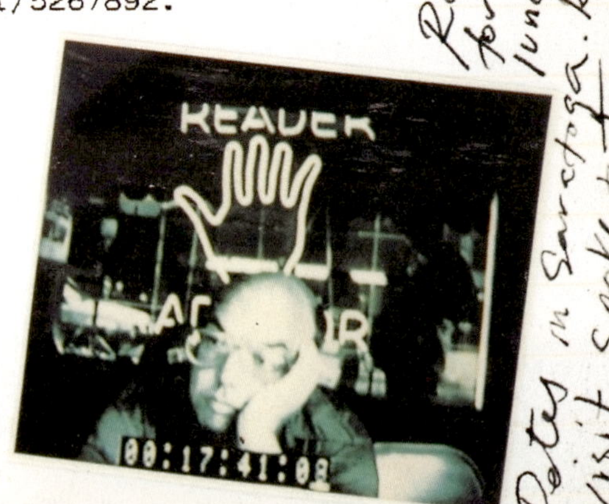

Rain, rain, rain! It's been raining for a week! Went to E. Hampton for lunch+ to develop color plates. Ramona + Cleon & came by for a Peter in Saratoga. Visit. Spoke to Jayne about Venice, read some translation

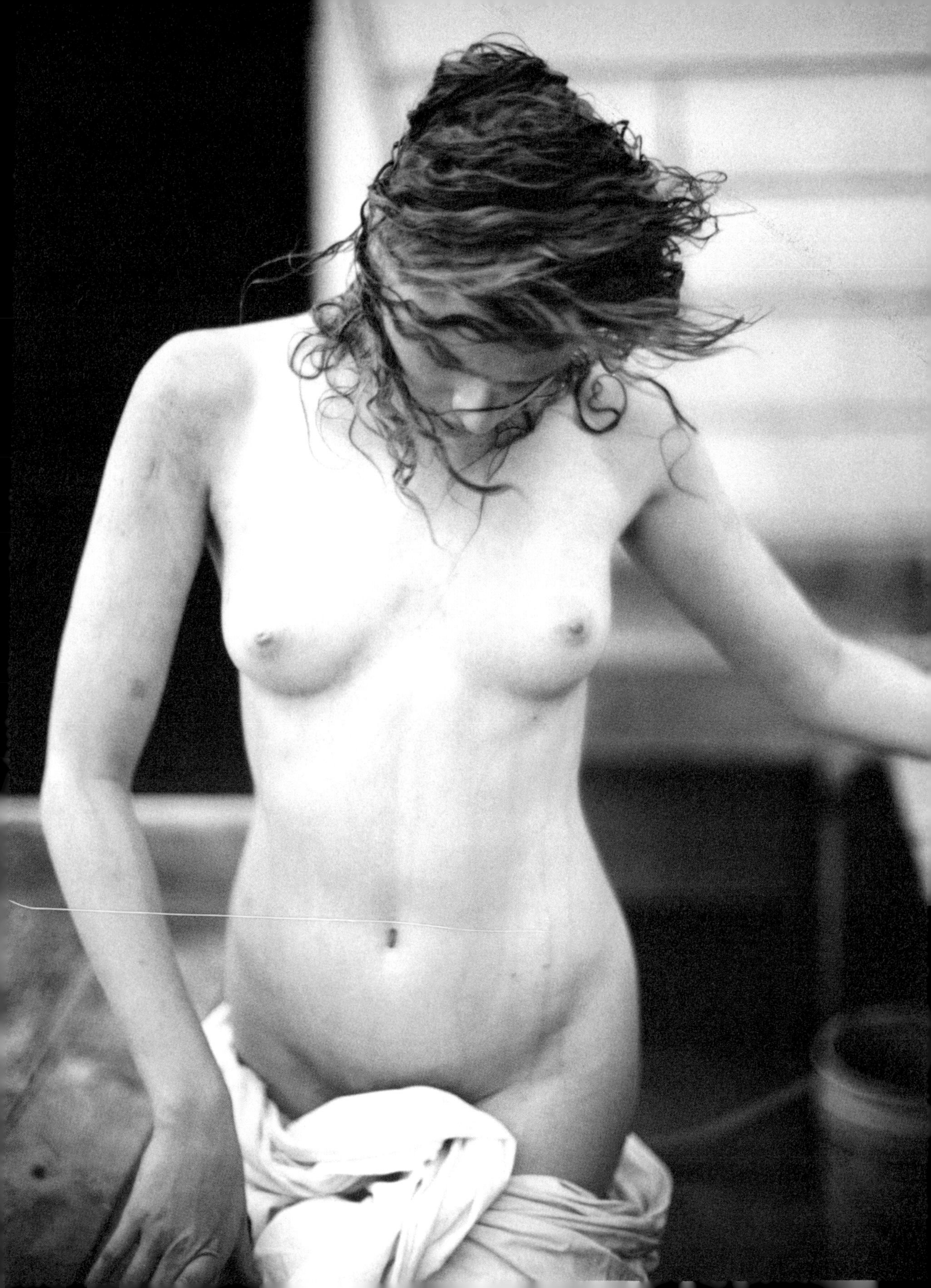

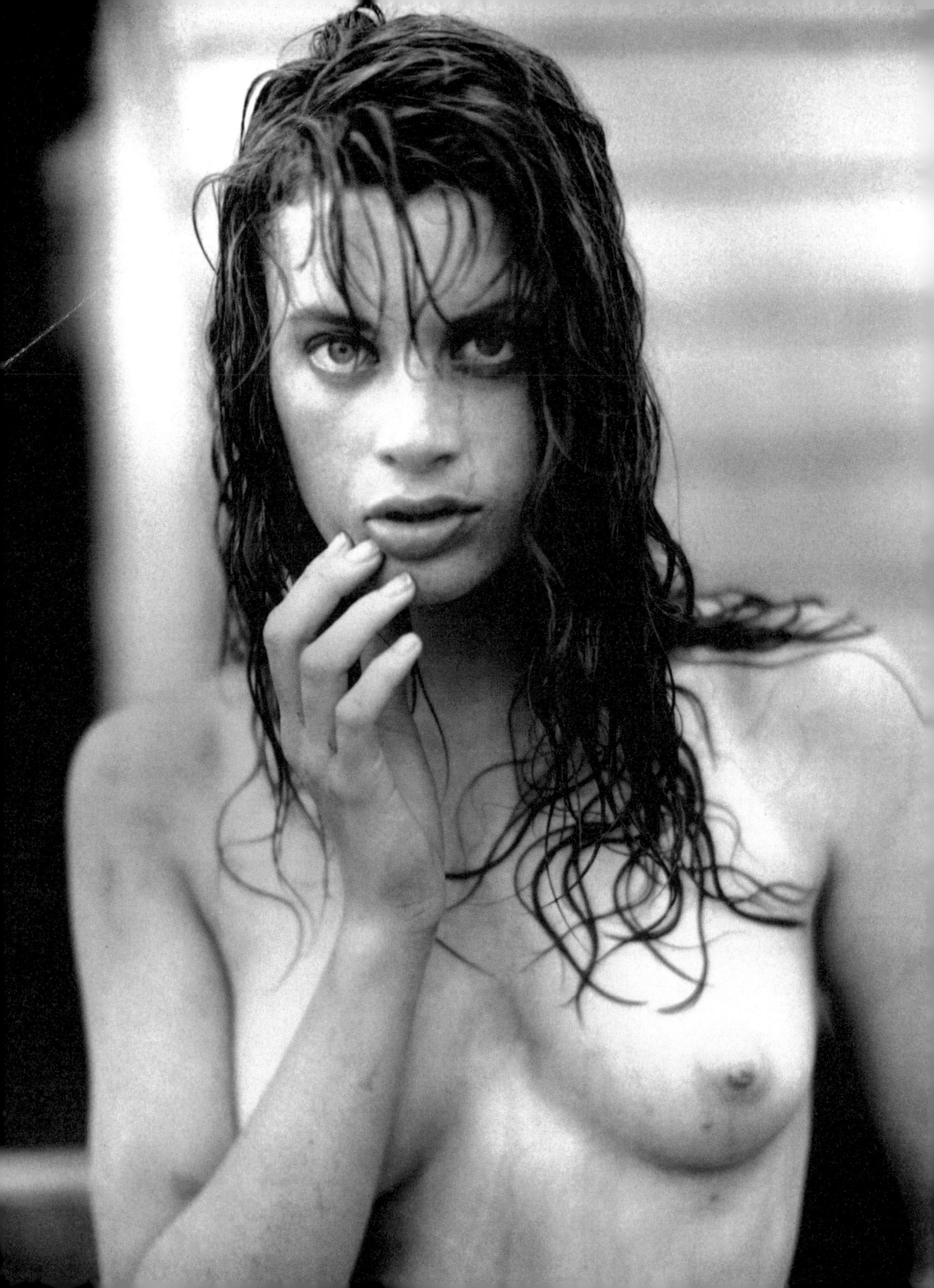

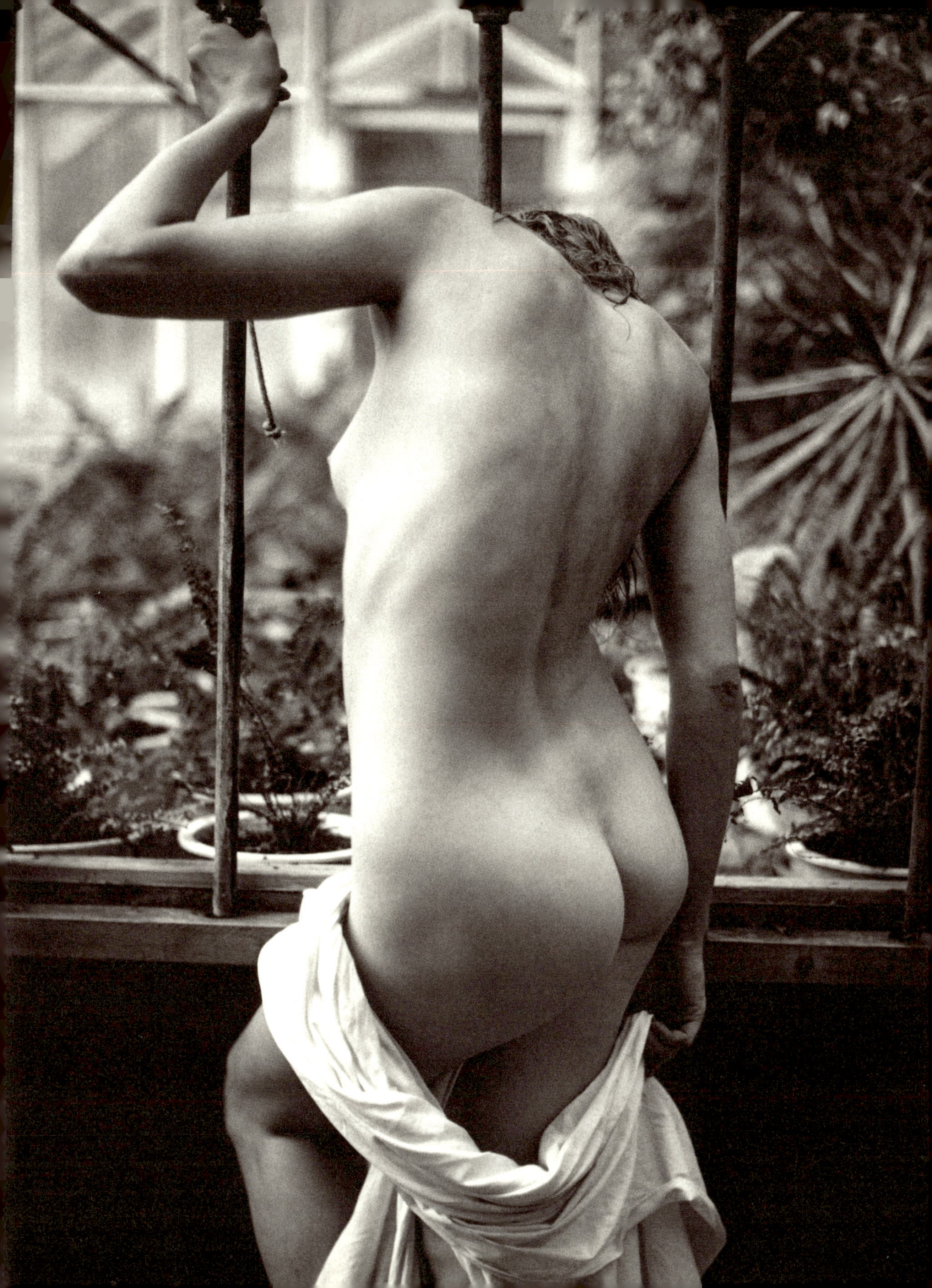

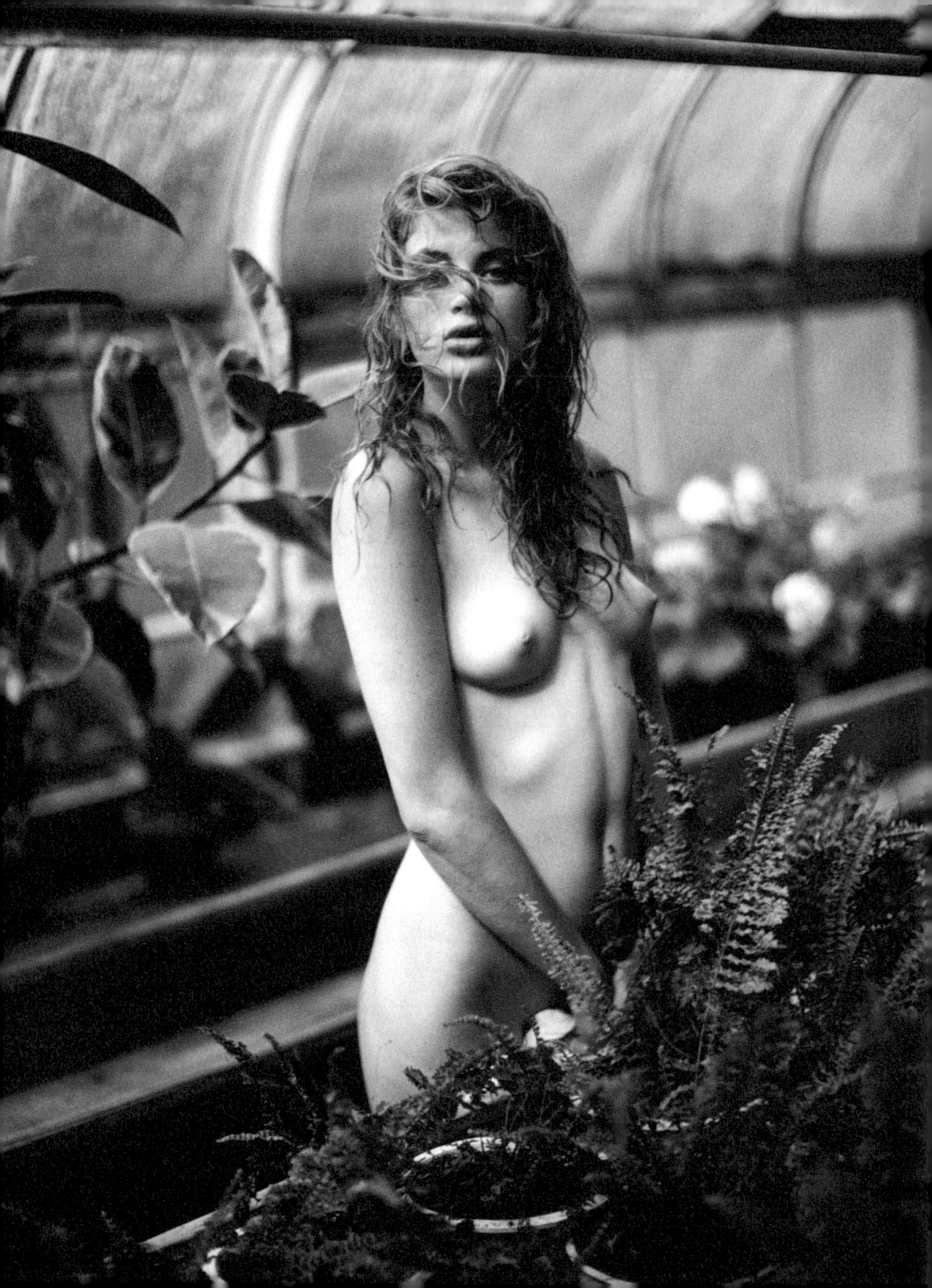

Tuesday 27
April 1993

Sante D.

went to the office then to opt with Dr. Vane, for
medicine. She's goin fit me up with herbs. Went to Chinatown for
ed early dinner with Kara + Tony at Merzegorno then we went
back to loft. Anabella Sciorra stopped by too + ate some pasta fagioli, with me

8 Saturday
May 1993

Italian Vogue

#93025

128/237

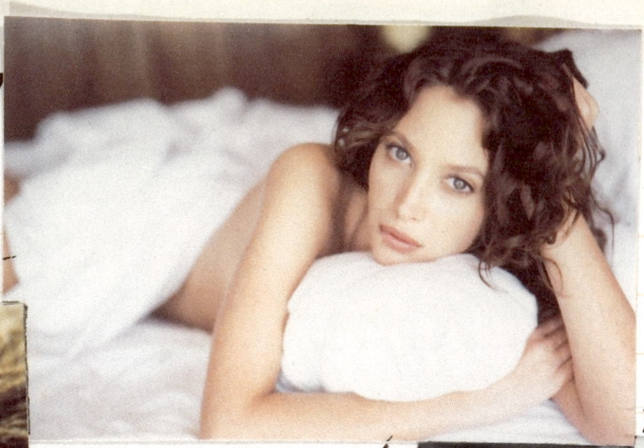

Stylist:
Marianna

Panoramic
view

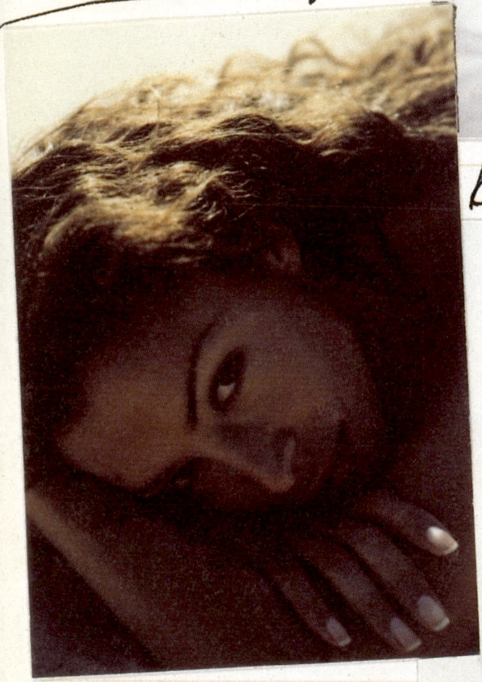

Kara + Christie

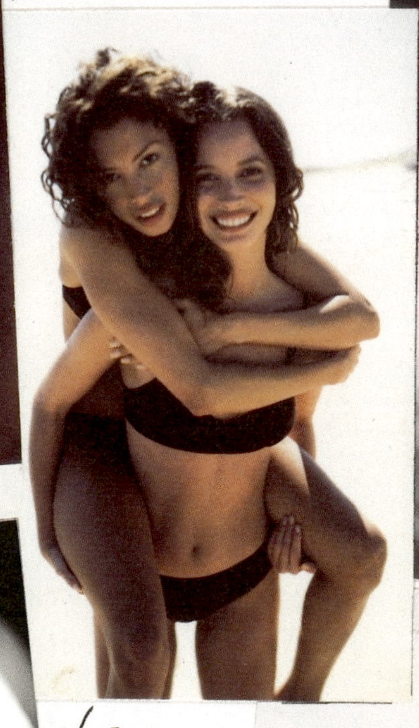

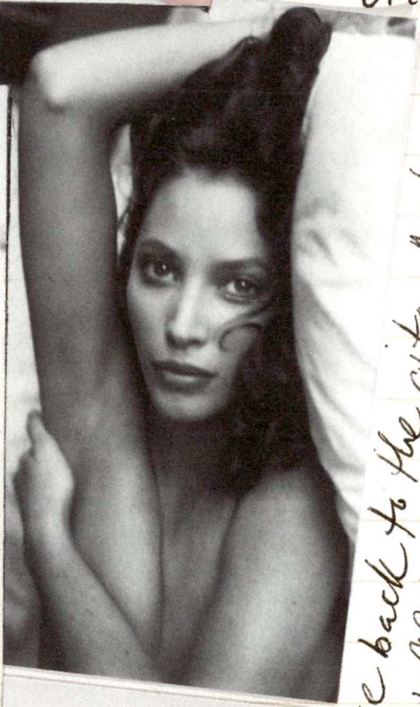

Hair:
Bob.
Recine
Mk. Up:
Patti
Dubroff

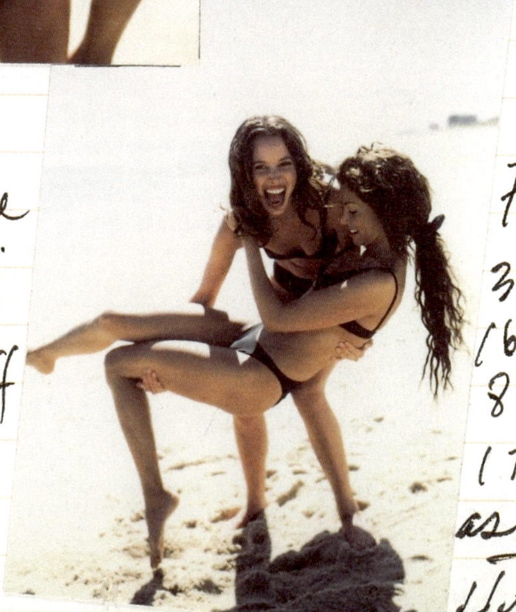

drove back to the city. Met with
Naomi + Alexandra + Paulo + partied!

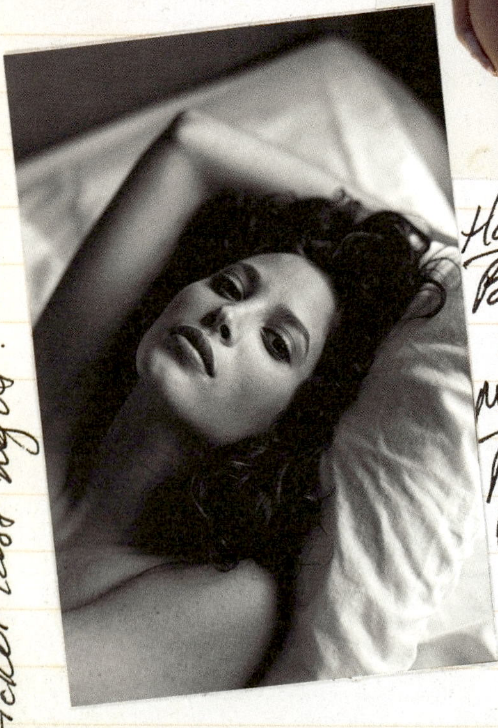

Film
39 Fuji 220
16 Clips
8 Fuji Pola
1 TX B35
assist:
Hubie

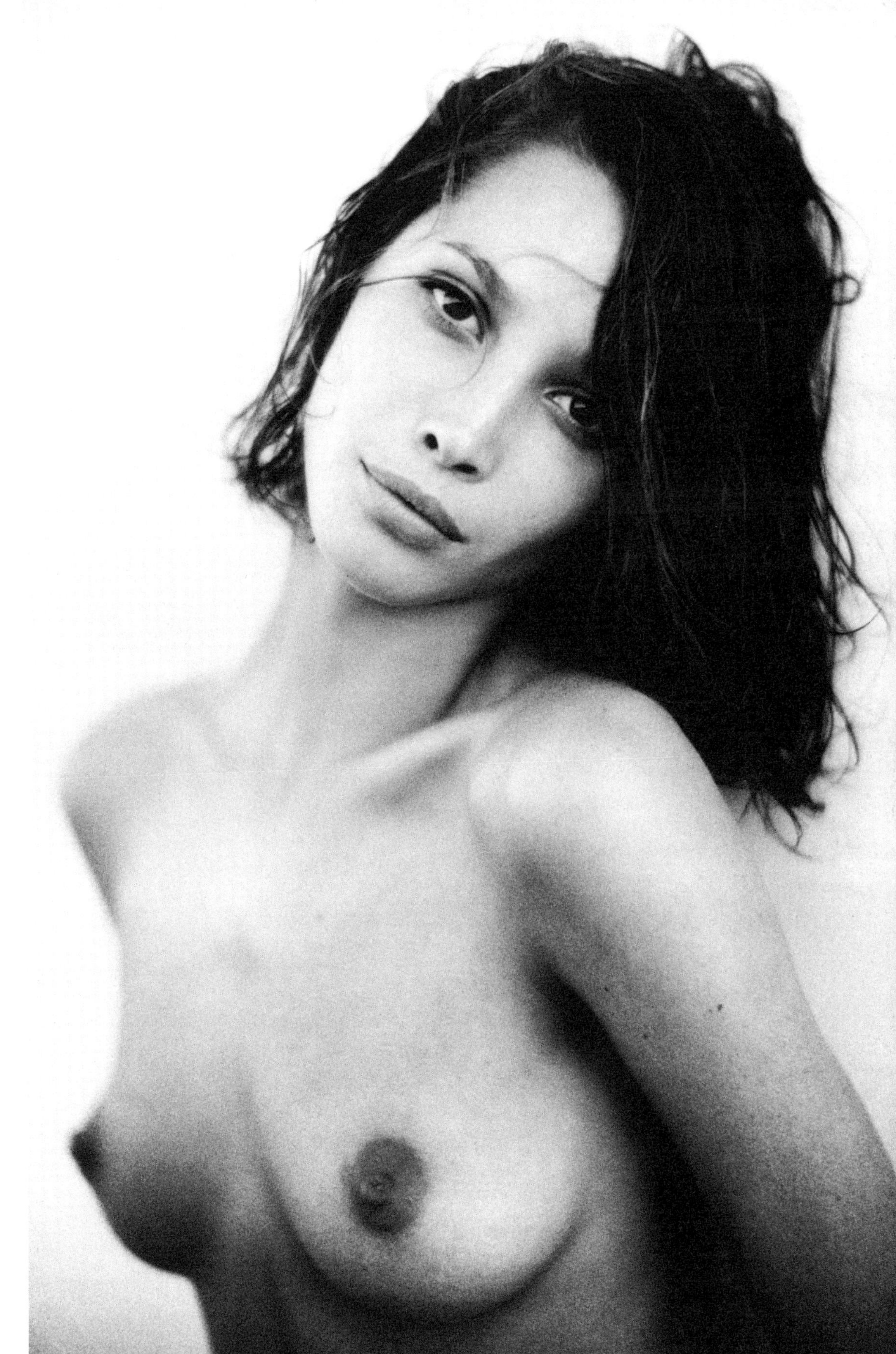

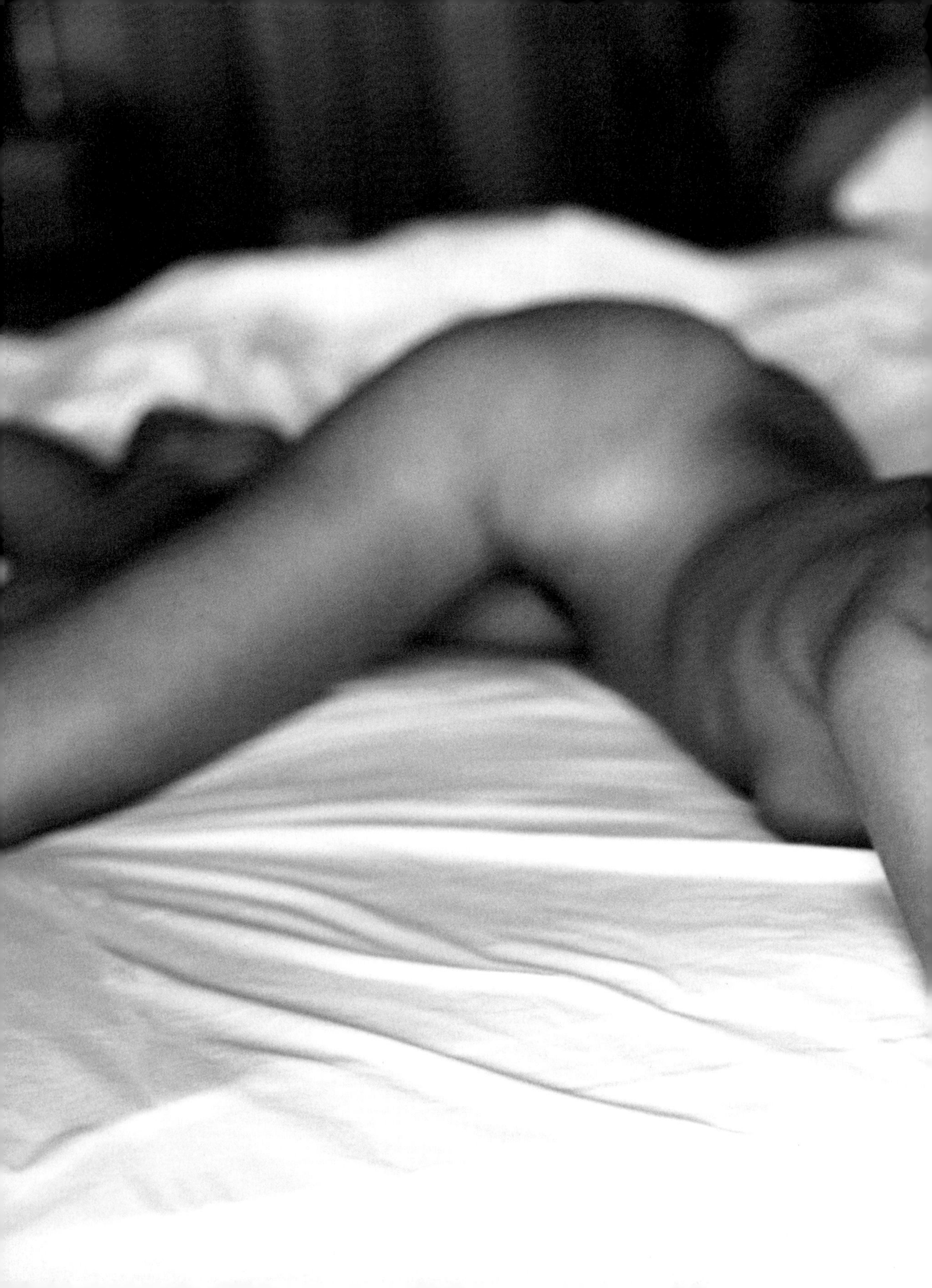

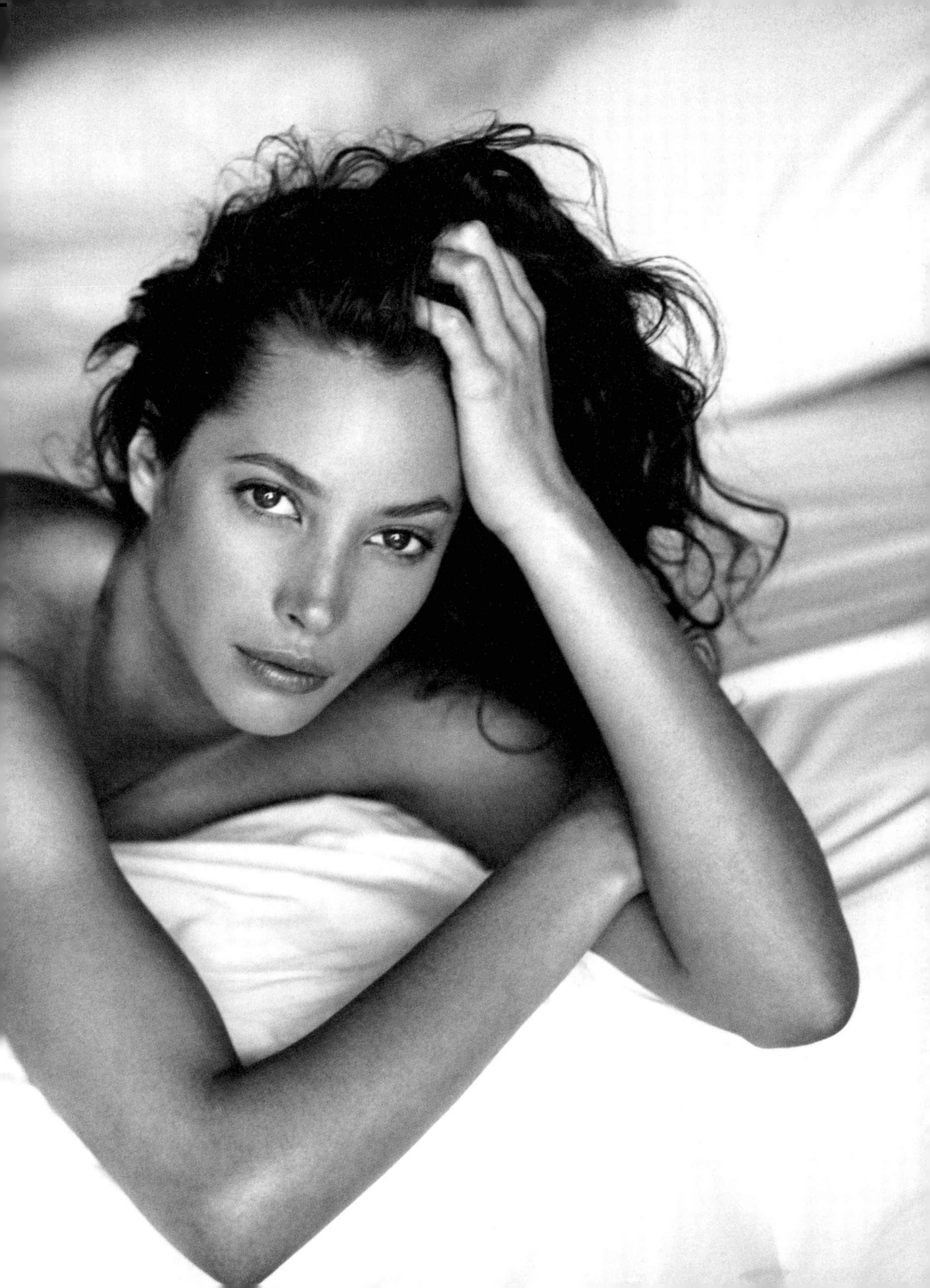

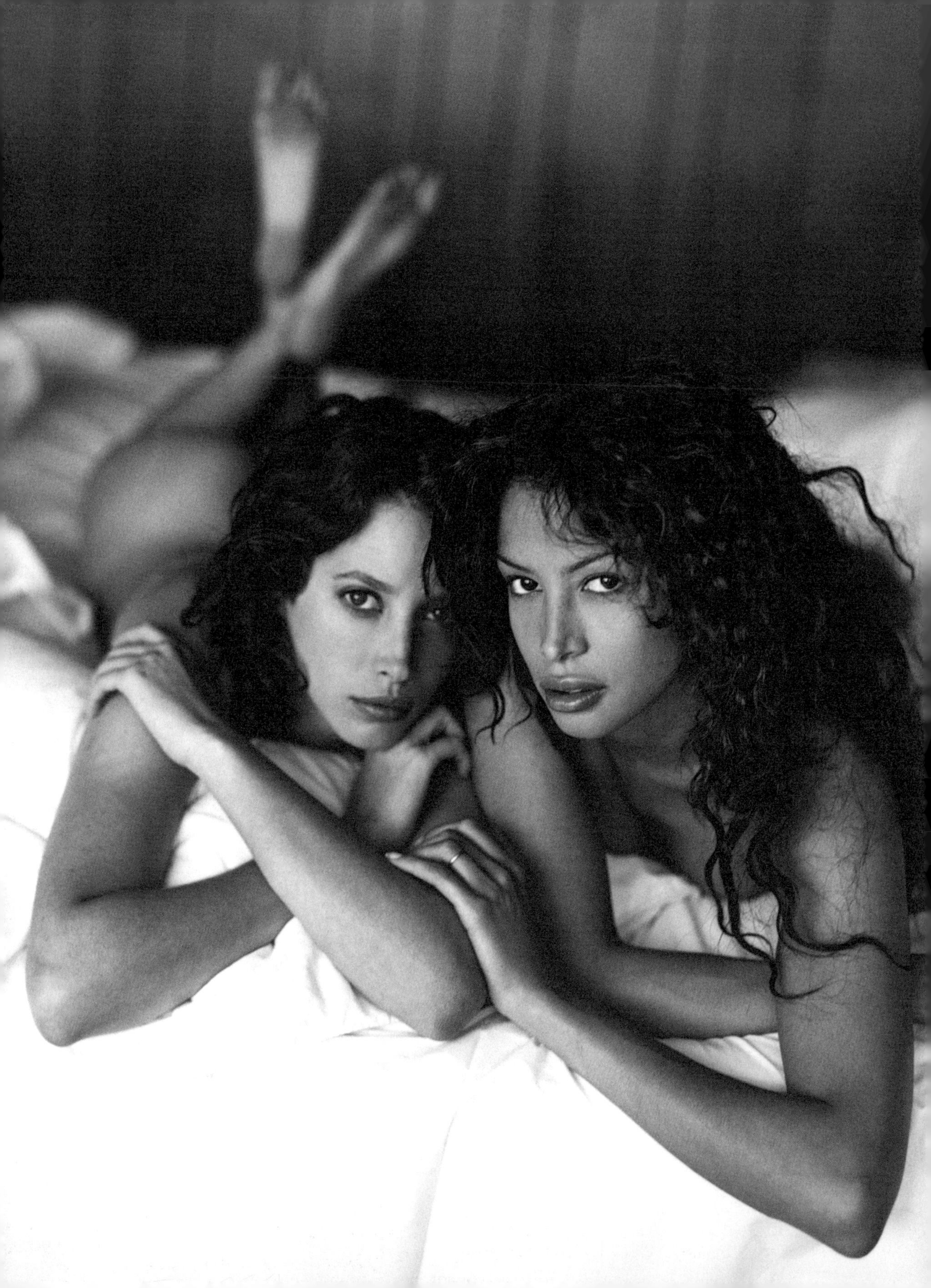

Sunday 9
May 1993

Mother's day

Kava + Christie for Vogue

thing out of us! Uccie came over + we all ate at Barolo's for Mother's day! Pam Pierre + Paul joined us for coffee!

Went to the movies tonite to see "Who the Man"! Kava, Christie Naomi, cousin Paul + Alexandra! Then everyone went home and I got some time with my baby!

M

Augus

Tetu & Maj B.
HOG RANCH
Kenya
E.afr

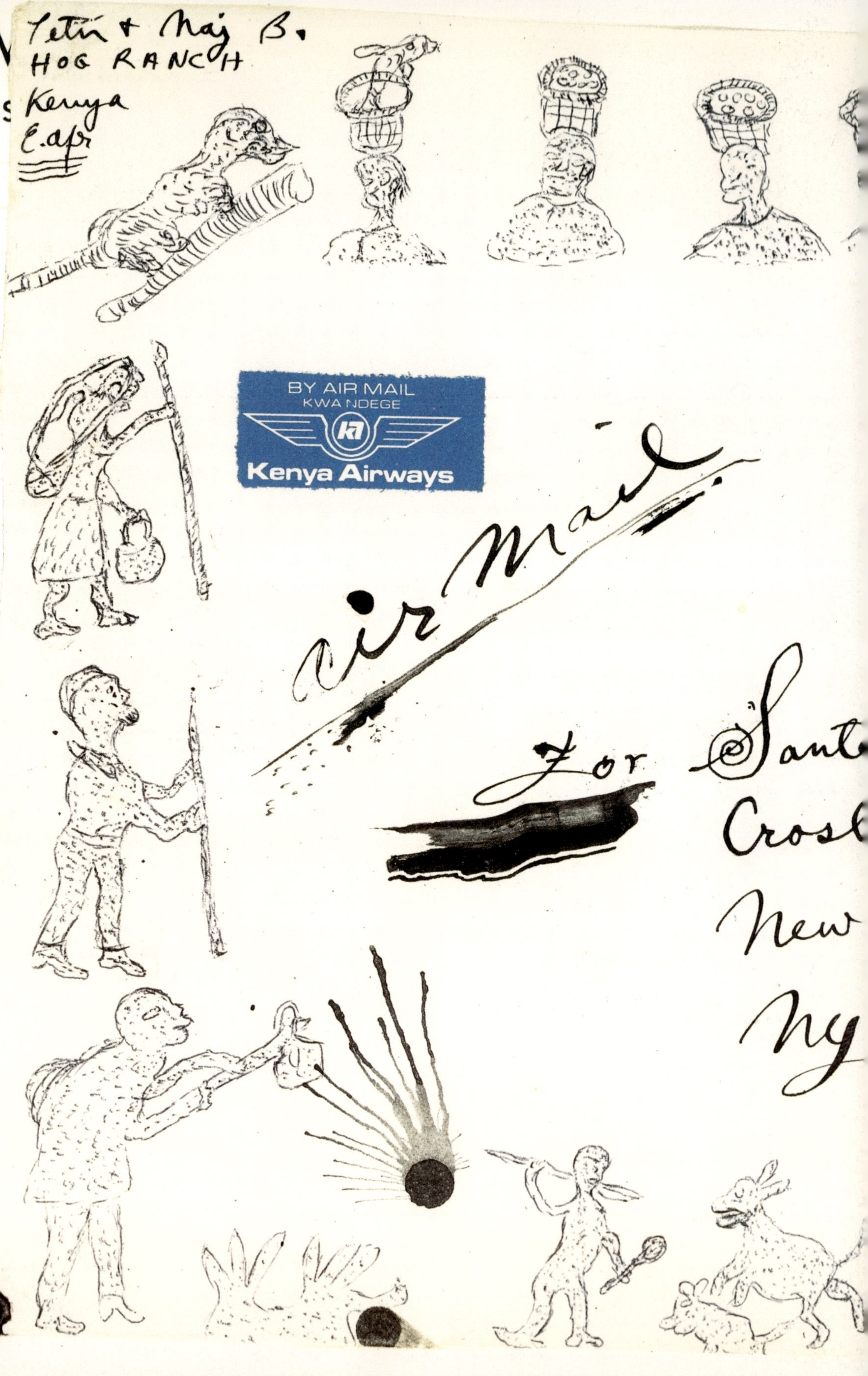

gay back in the office

air Mail

For Sant
Cros
New
Ny

7
1990

Kenya 3/
Papilio desmondi teita
KIPEPEO TAITA

Kenya 20/
Papilio dardanus
KIPEPEO MCHEKI

Kenya
Charaxes druceanus teita
MFUNDA FEDHA TAITA

L'Orazio
Street
York City
10012 USA.

Drawn with Julian + Paul Marciano

10 Friday
August 1990

Montauk with Julian

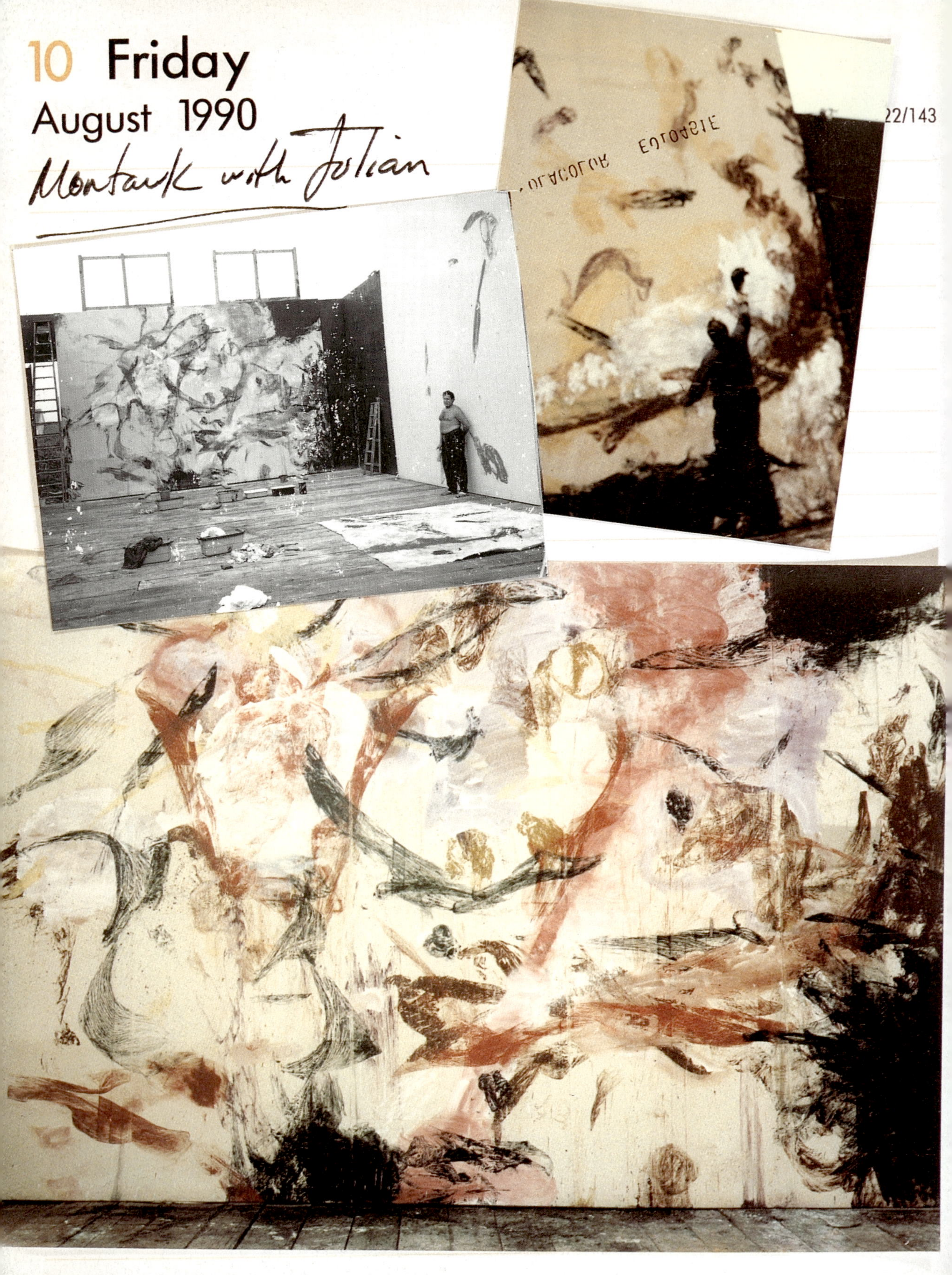

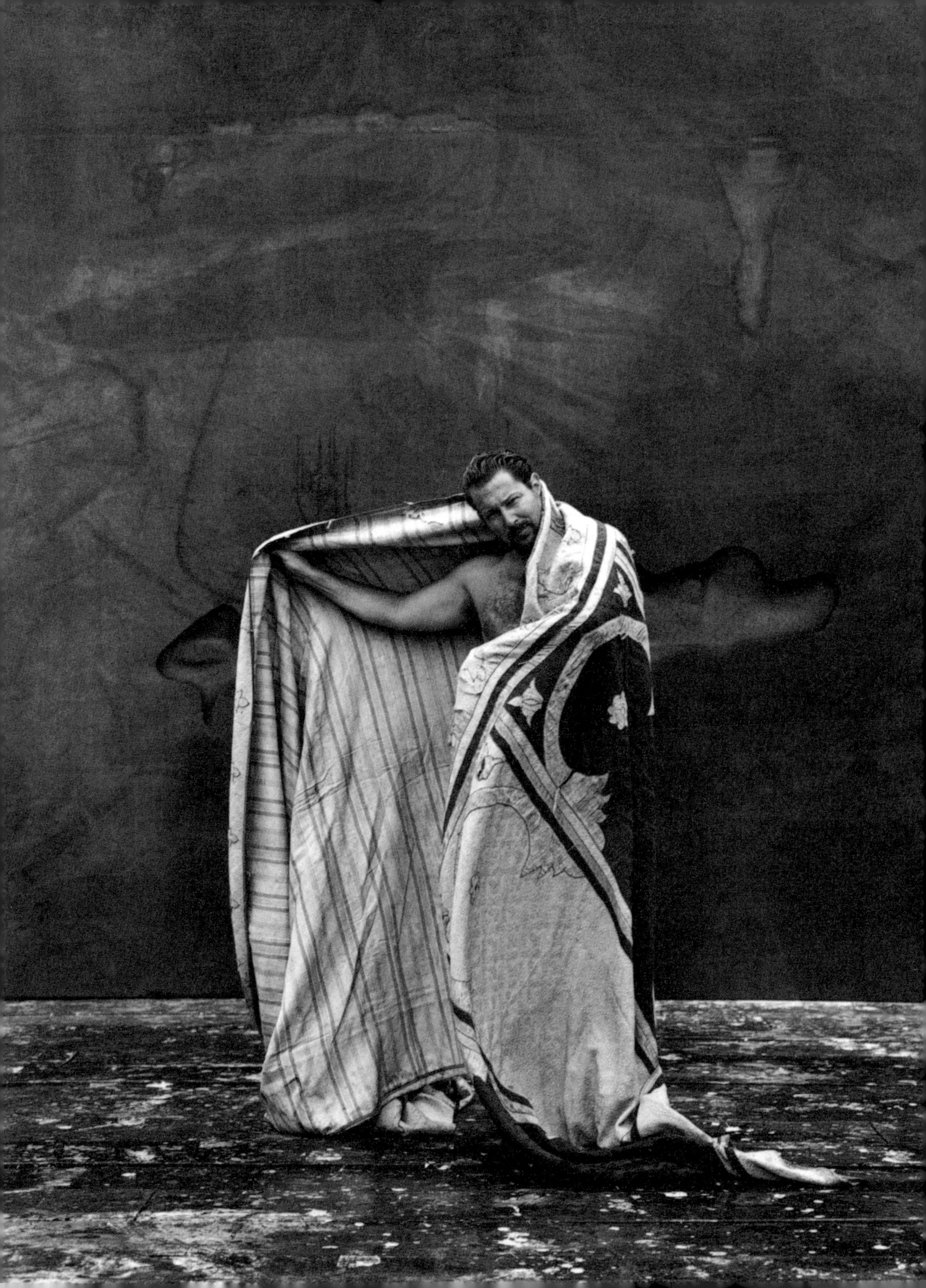

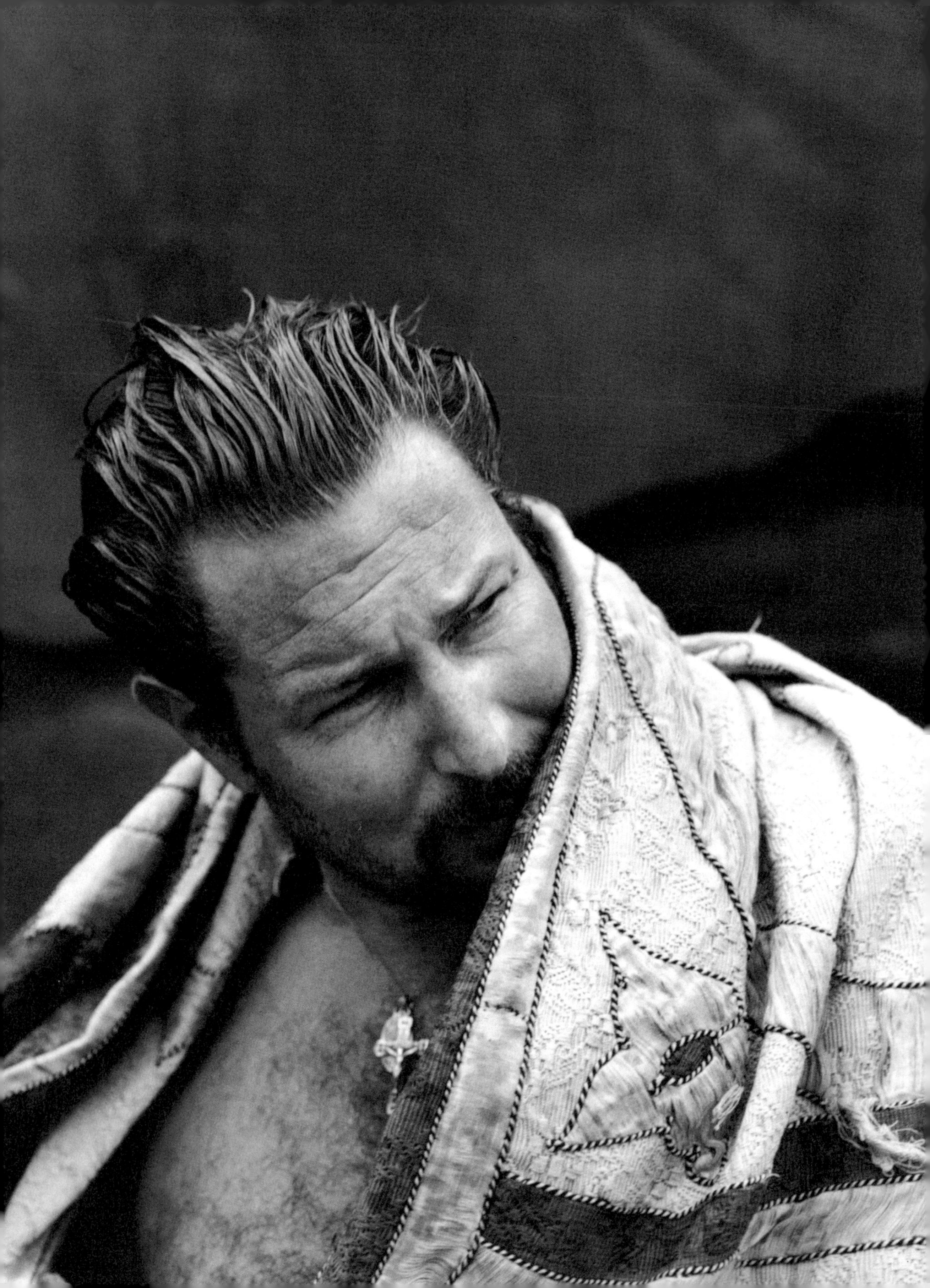

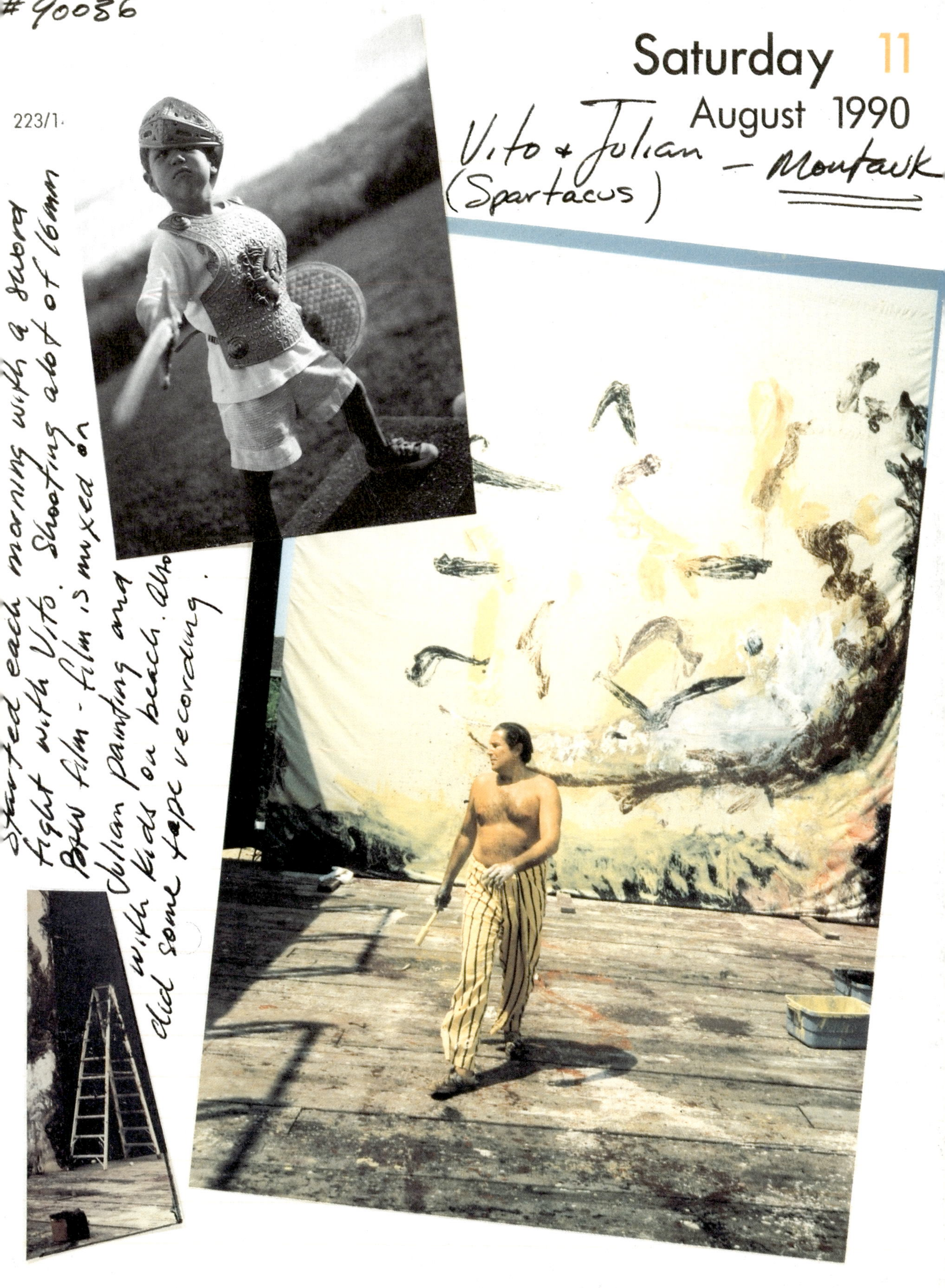

223/1.

#90086

Saturday 11
August 1990
Vito & Julian — Montauk
(Spartacus)

Started each morning with a sword
fight with Vito. Shooting a lot of 16mm
B&W film - film is mixed on
with Julian painting and
with kids on beach. Also
did some tape recording.

12 Sunday
August 1990

did alittle surfing #40036
today with julian — took my first
ride in on my belly

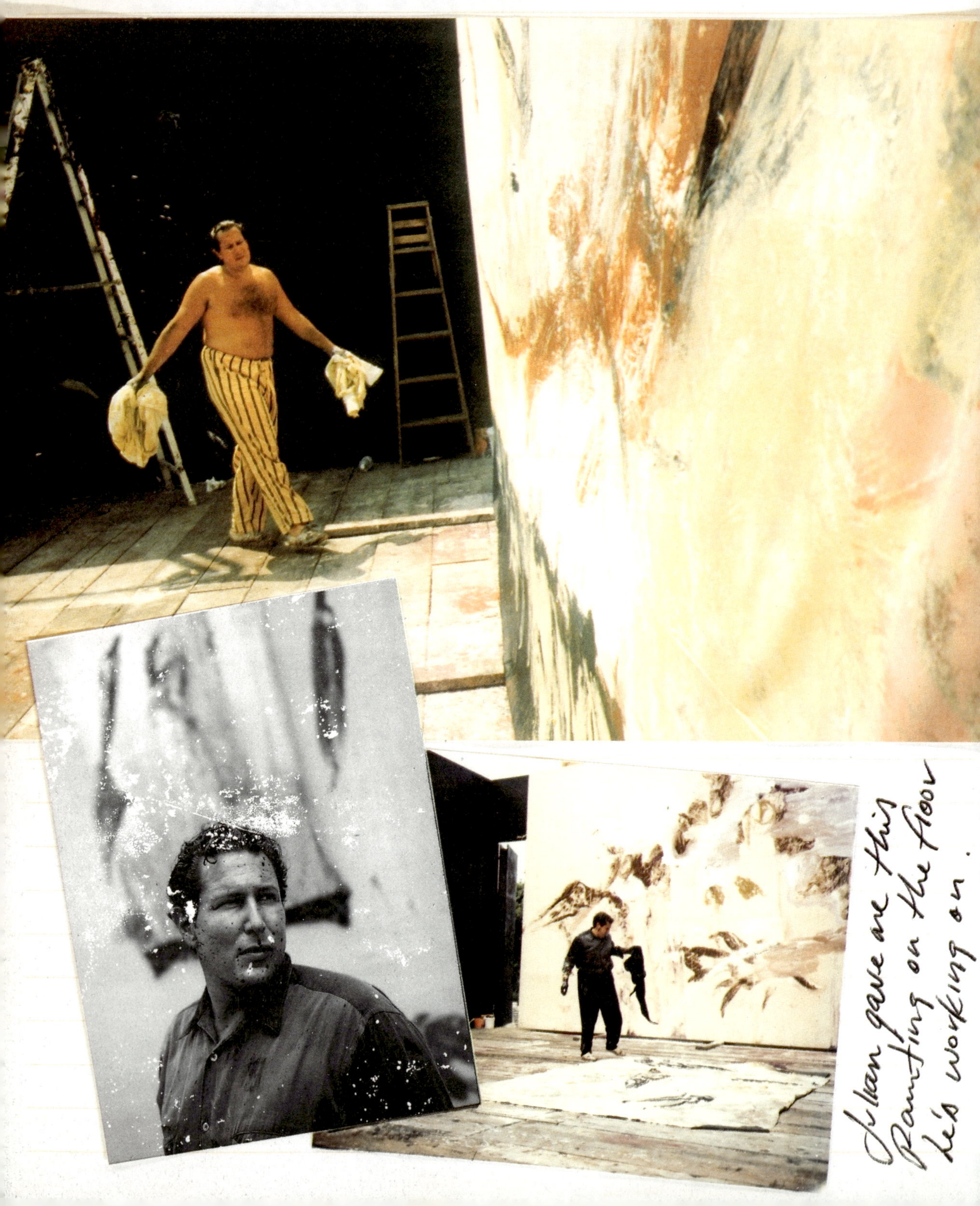

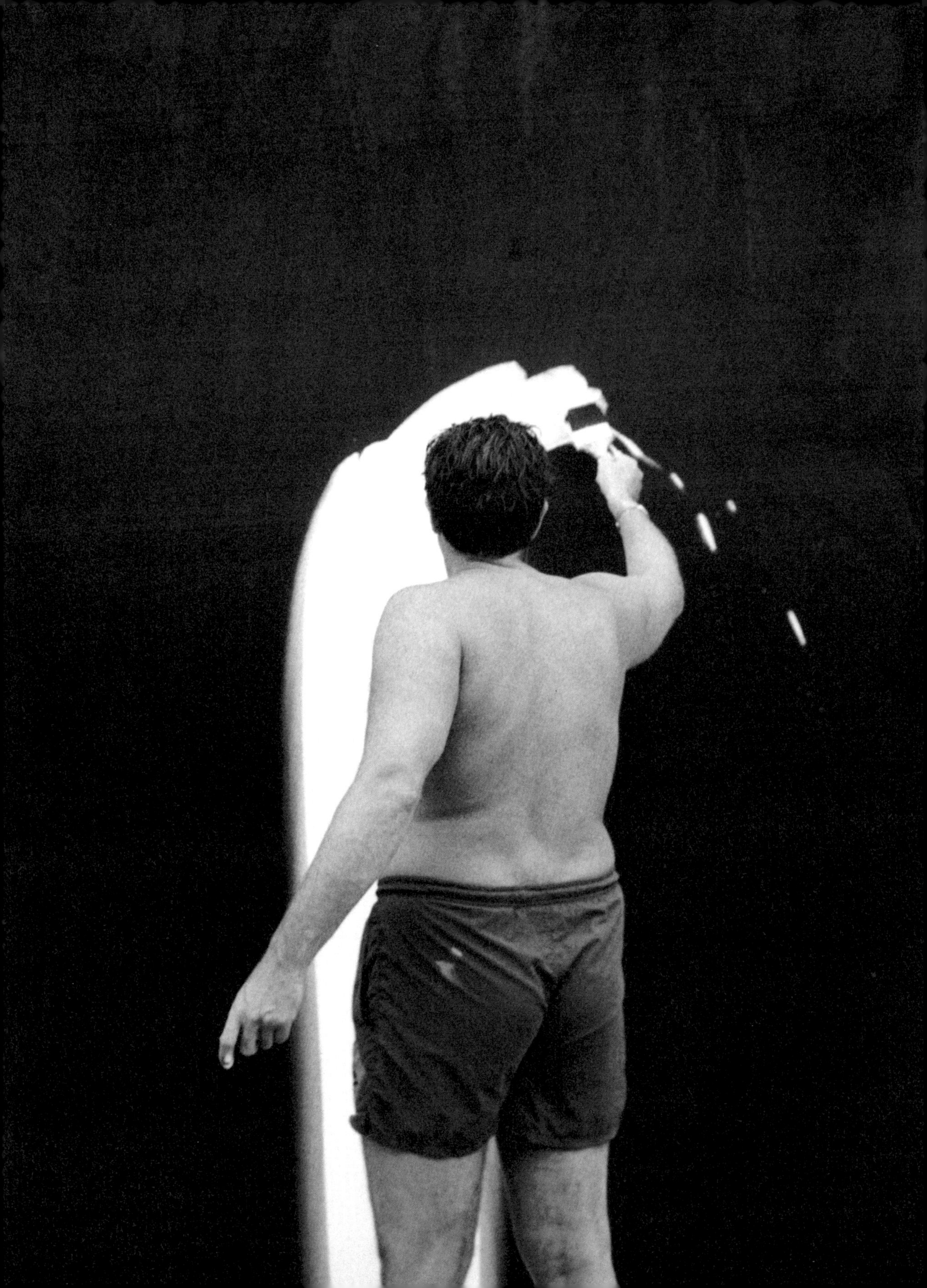

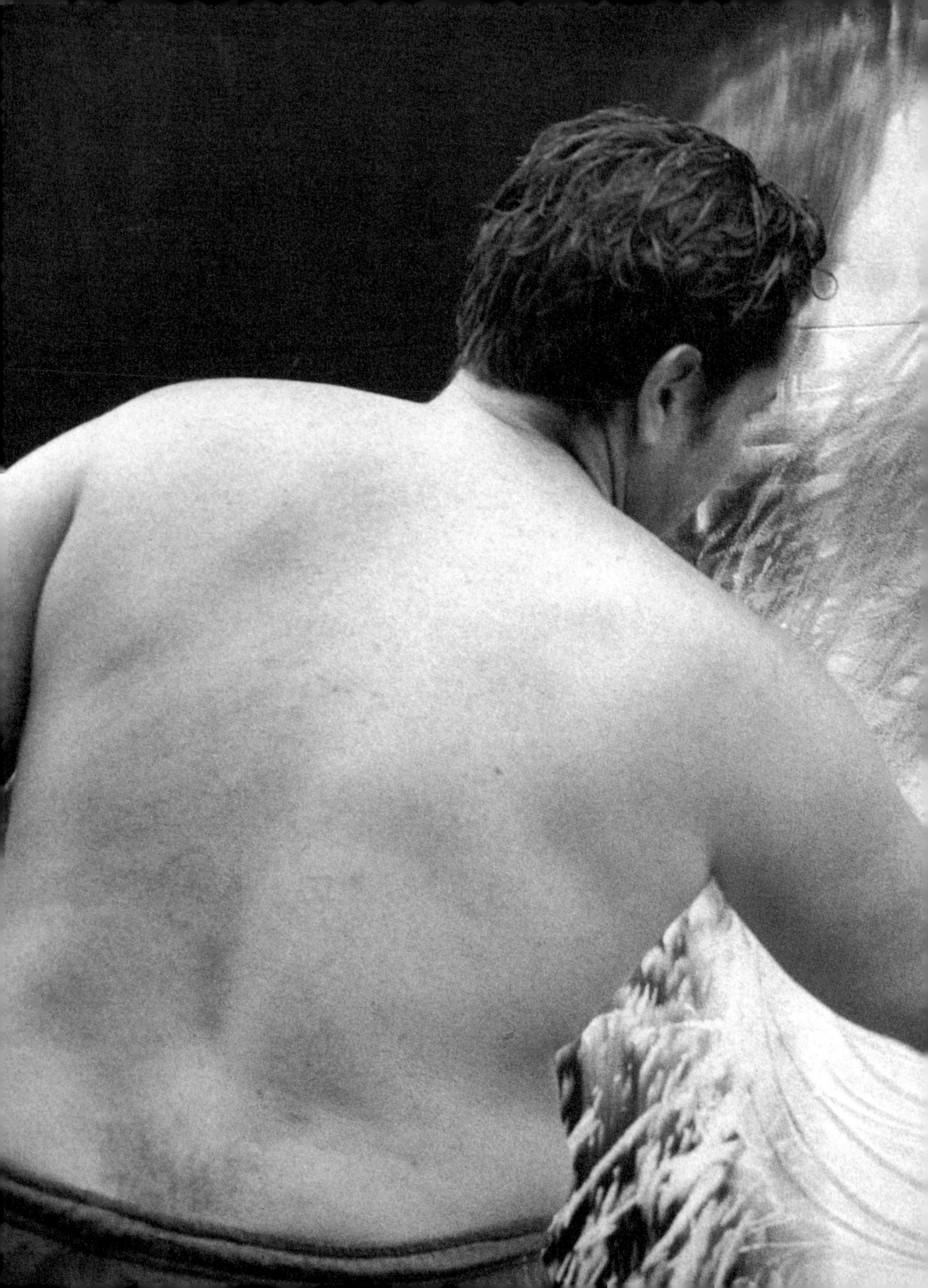

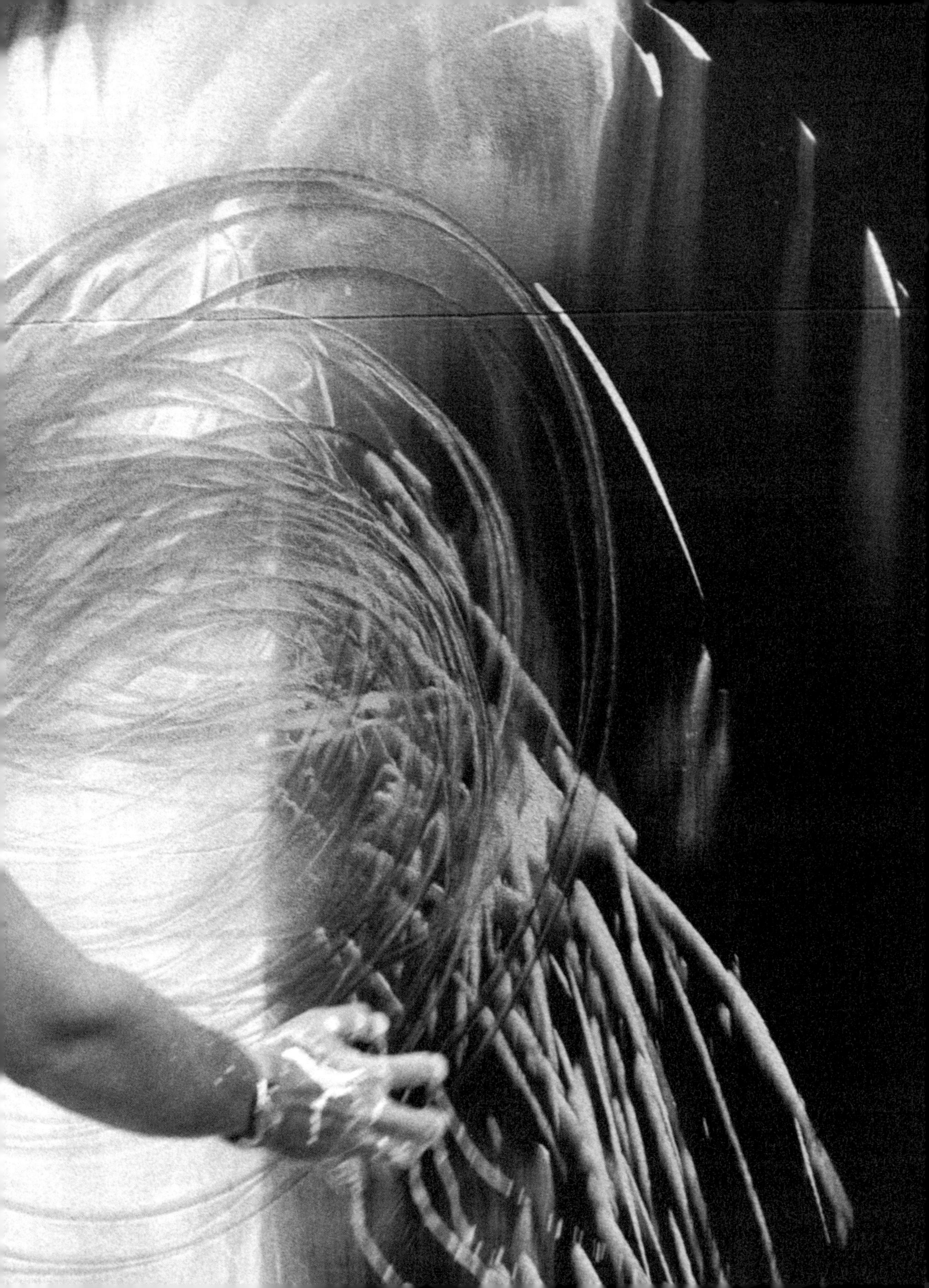

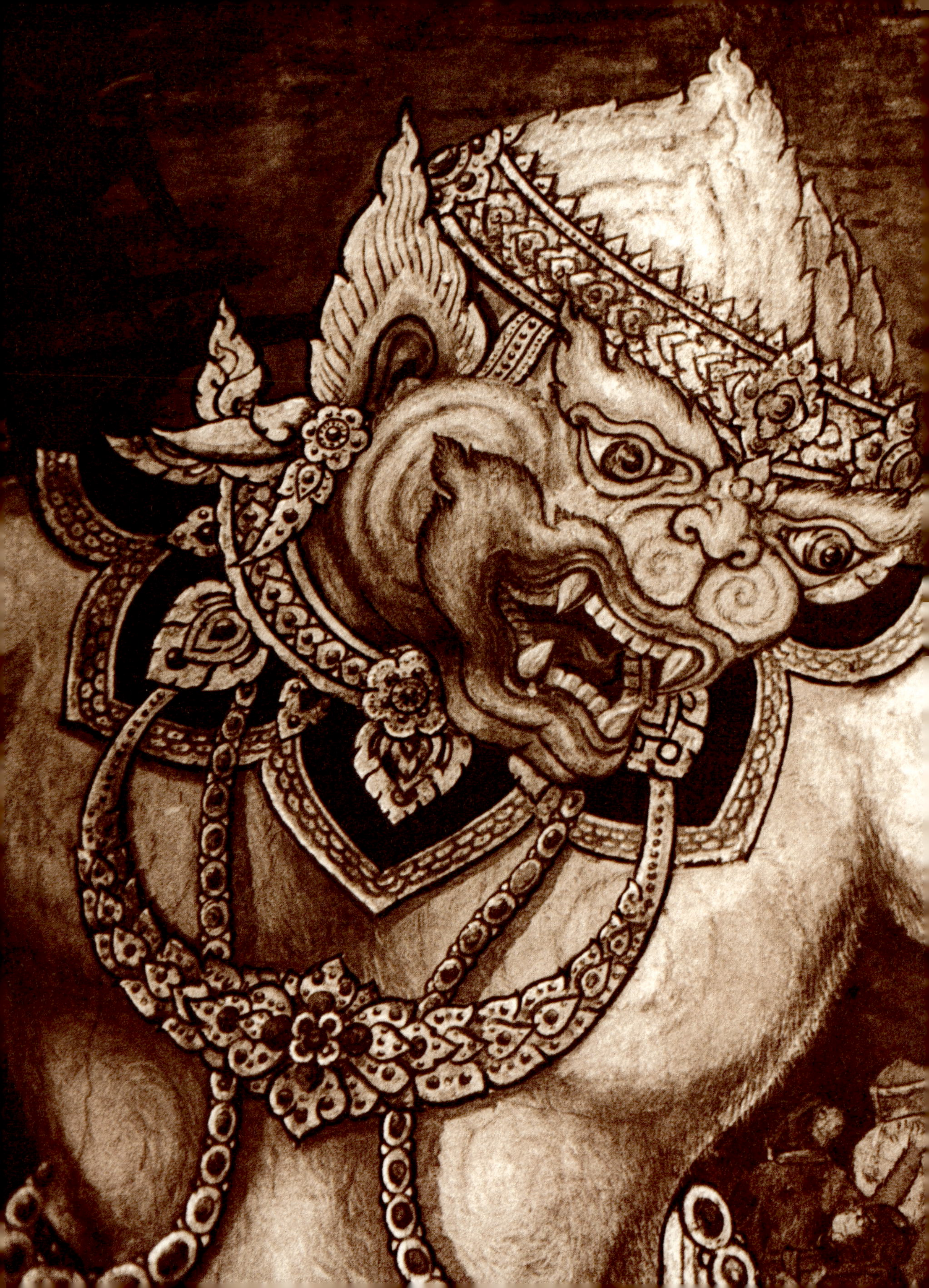

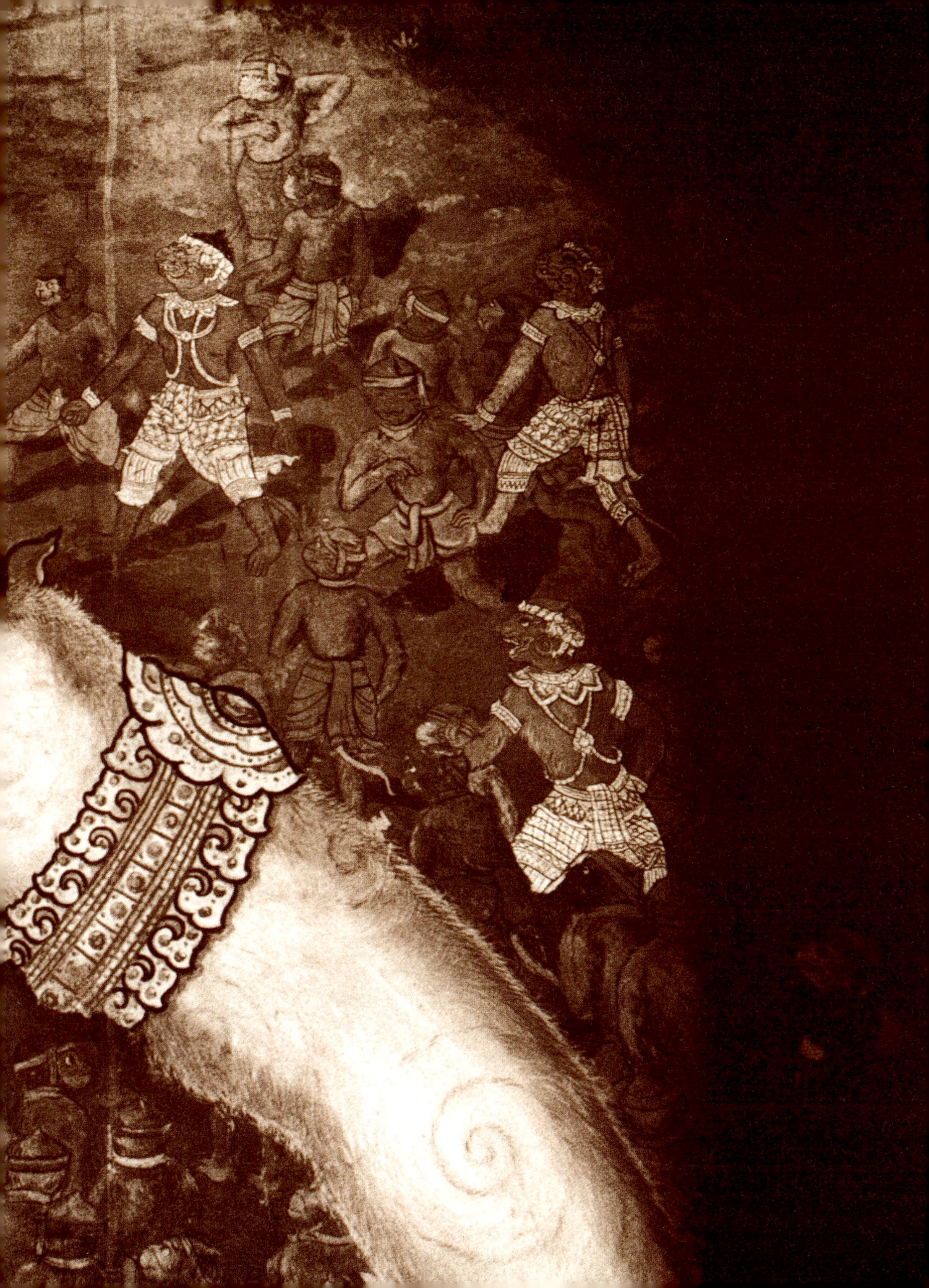

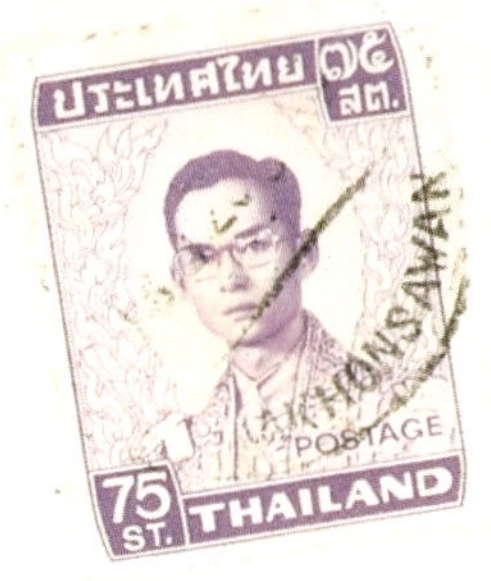
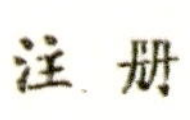
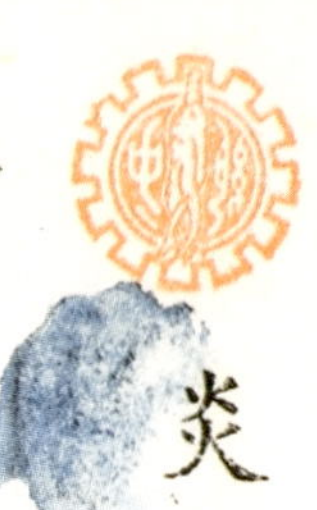
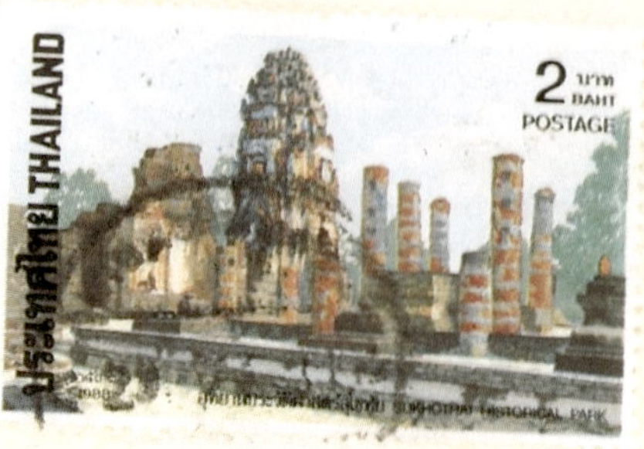

注　册

鼻　炎

鄂卫药准字（81）1138号

处　　方：苍耳子　45%　甘　草　13%　桔
　　　　　辛夷花　　　　　　　　　　　五味
　　　　　连　翘　13%　知　母　8.3%　防
　　　　　白　芷　　　　野菊花　　　　荆

概　　述：急性慢性鼻炎，副鼻窦炎，是五官科
　　　　　病，若不及时治疗，会严重的影响身
　　　　　涕，鼻腔阻塞，分泌物增多，呈脓样
　　　　　有头痛、头昏、失眠、耳鸣、耳聋、
　　　　　用本品治疗。

药效简介：苍耳子　通鼻窍，发汗，祛风湿。
　　　　　辛　夷　鼻塞流浊涕，鼻窦蓄脓，青
　　　　　连　翘　清热解毒，消肿，散结，抗
　　　　　白　芷　发表祛风，胜湿，活血排脓，
　　　　　甘　草　补脾胃，润肺止咳，清热解
　　　　　知　母　滋阴降火，除烦止渴，润燥
　　　　　野菊花　清热祛风，明目解毒，有清
　　　　　桔　梗　排脓，宣肺气，散风寒，镇
　　　　　五味子　补肺，滋肾，生津，敛汗涩
　　　　　防　风　发表祛风，胜湿，解痉。
　　　　　荆　芥　发表祛风，利咽喉，消热散

　　　上述各项药物，相互有协同作用，能增强其
促使鼻炎消除恢复功能，而奏治疗效果。
功能与主治：祛风宣肺，清热解毒。用于急，慢性
用法用量：口服，一次3—4片，一日三次。
规　　格：每瓶100片装
贮　　芷：密封

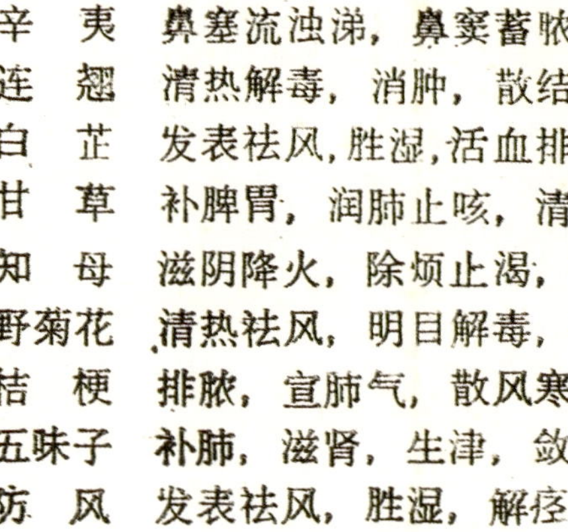

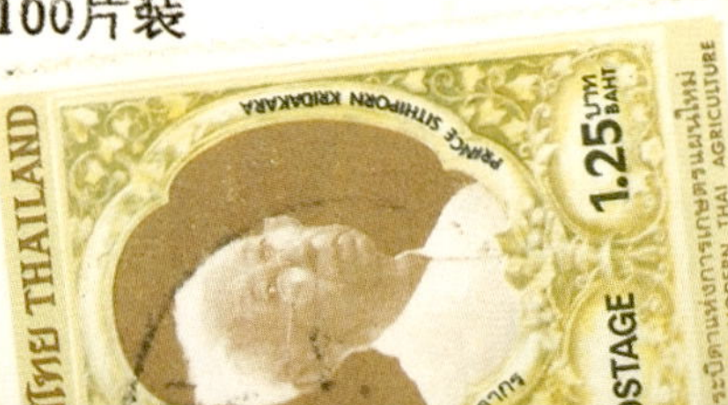

TO WHOM IT MAY CONC

I, THE UNDERSIGNED,
OF THE CONDE NAST P
CERTIFY THAT MISS
D'ORAZIO, AMERICAN
PHUKET ISLAND IN OR

THIS FOLLOWS THE AB
PRACHUABMOH AND MYS
20 PAGES PROMOTION
IN WHICH APPEARED A
QUEEN SIRIKIT AND O

ACCORDING TO THIS C
WOULD GO TO PHUKET
TO BE PUBLISHED AT
COULD BE REINFORCED

I CAN CERTIFY THAT
IS TOTALLY PROFESSI
IN A HOLY AND FORBI
OF THEIR PART. IT '
WERE COMMITTING AN

I WANT TO HOPE THE
SINCERITY AND OF TH
THE THAILAND COUNTR
THE BEST RELATIONSH

JEAN PONIATOWSKI

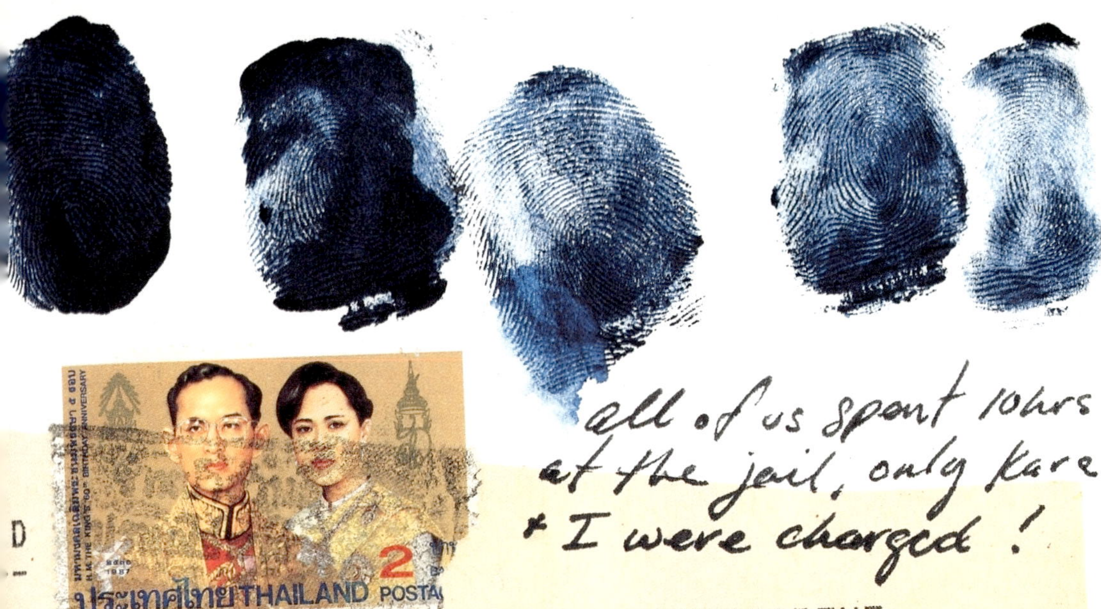

all of us spent 10 hrs
at the jail, only Kare
+ I were charged!

N PONIATOWSKI (DEPUTY VICE - PRESIDENT
ICATIONS S.A., PARIS VOGUE PUBLISHER)
YOUNG, AMERICAN TOP MODEL AND MR SANTE
TOGRAPHER, HAVE BEEN SENT BY VOGUE TO
TO REALIZE A FASHION REPORT.

MENT SIGNED BETWEEN MR GOVERNOR DHARMNOON
ON JUNE 15TH 1988, IN ORDER TO PUBLISH A
THAILAND IN OUR VOGUE DECEMBER ISSUE NO692.
RTRAIT AND INTERVIEW OF HER MAJESTY THE
ER ROYAL HIGHNESS THE PRINCESS CHULABHORN.

RACT, IT WAS AGREED THAT A VOGUE TEAM
FEBRUARY 1989 TO REALIZE A FASHION REPORT
RING 1989 SO THAT THE IMPACT OF THIS PROMOTION

R TEAM, LEAD BY BARBARA BAUMEL, EDITOR,
AL AND THAT IF THIS PICTURE HAS BEEN TAKEN
EN PLACE, IT WAS WITHOUT ANY BAD INTENTION
ONLY BECAUSE THEY REALLY DID NOT KNOW THEY
FENCE AND WE ARE VERY SORRY.

UKET AUTHORITIES WILL BE AWARE OF OUR
FACT THAT OUR ONLY PURPOSE IS TO PROMOTE
THAT WE LOVE AND WITH WHICH WE HAVE ALWAYS

FREEDOM

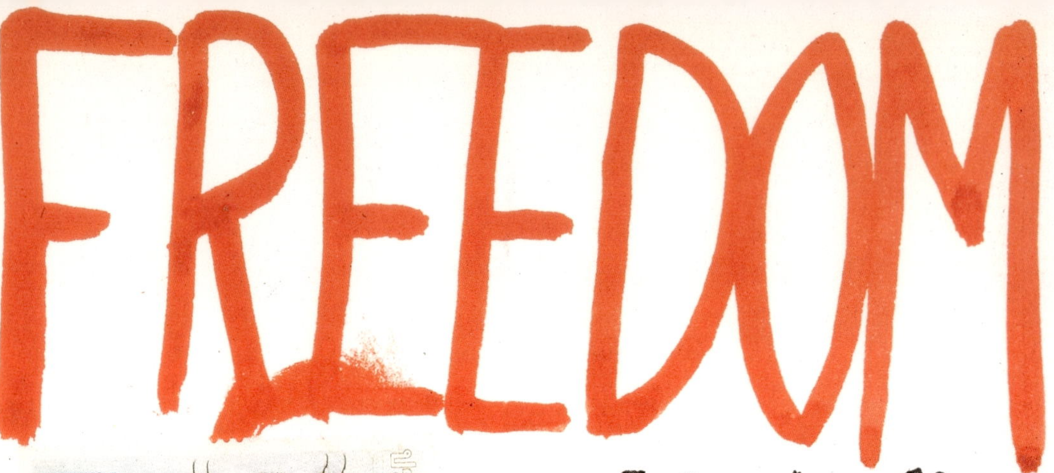

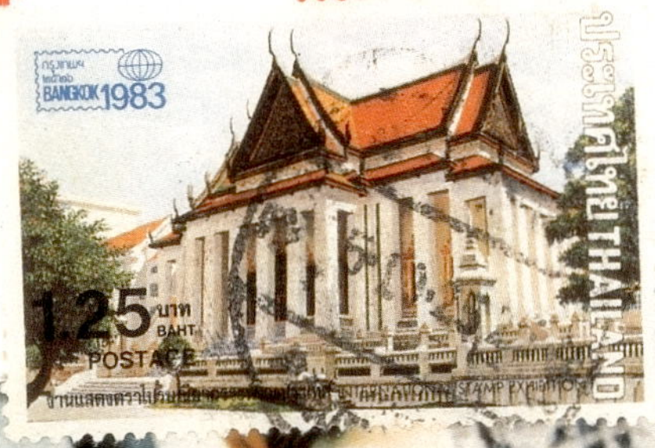

FEB. 24, 1989
COURT FOUND US
GUILTY, SUSPENDED
2 YEAR SENTENCE
AND FINE. OFFICER
ESCORTED US OUT
OF THE COUNTRY

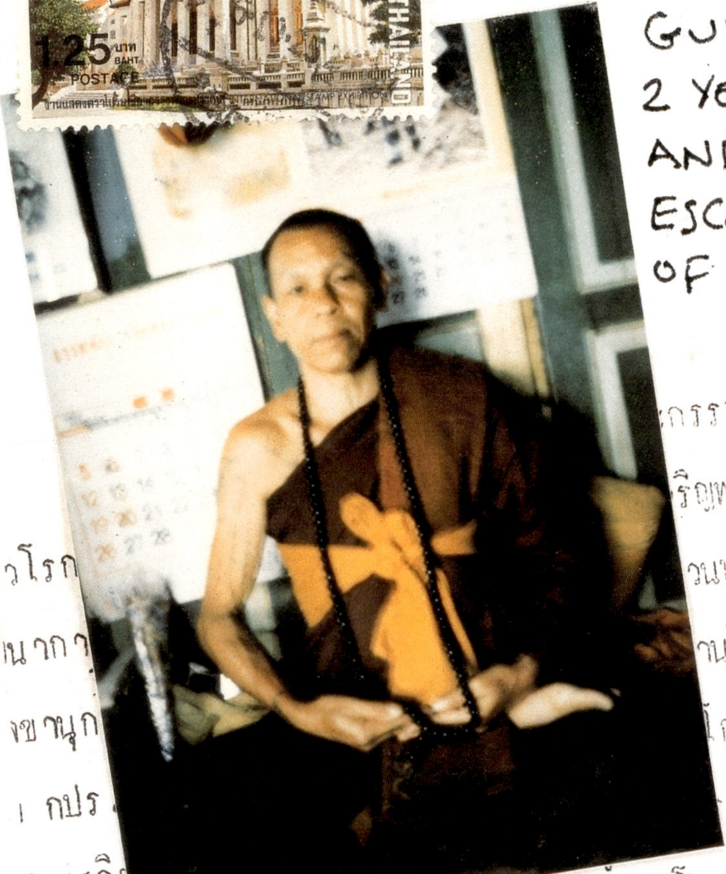

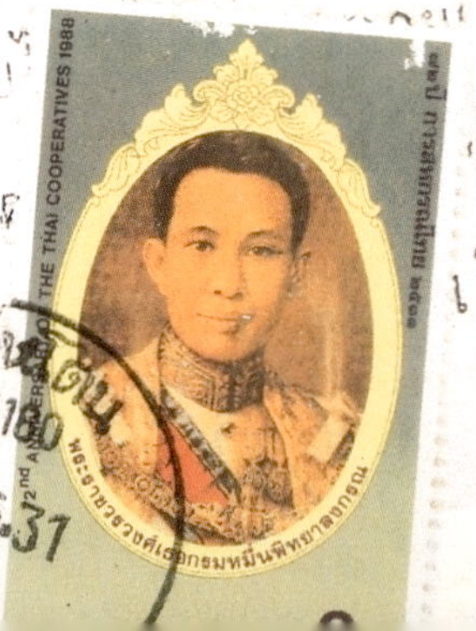

CARTE D'ACCÈS A BORD
BOARDING PASS
AIR FRANCE
56
SANTEDORAZIO
TG 01-61-46
To
CDG
PARIS
NEW YORK
BAGAGES
BAGGAGE
IDENTIFICATION
CORRESPONDANCE
CONNECTING FLIGHT
25 FEB NYC Y
TG 01-61-47
To
CDG
PARIS
FLIGHT
TG 932
DATE
24FEB
SEAT
DG
NAME
DORASIO.S
CARRIER
THAI AIRWAY
BOARDING GATE
Home to N.Y.
then Sricaçai met us at airport CDG
had coffee + gave us our
tickets !
Thai
Thai Airways International Limited
TG 34-0-647
TG 294
ไป/TO
BKK
กรุงเทพ
BANGKOK
BKK
กรุงเทพ
BANGKOK
POSTAGE
2 BAHT
NATIONAL COMMUNICATIONS DAY AUG.4.1986
THAILAND
NAL
POSTAGE
ASEAN SUBMARINE CABLE SYSTEM

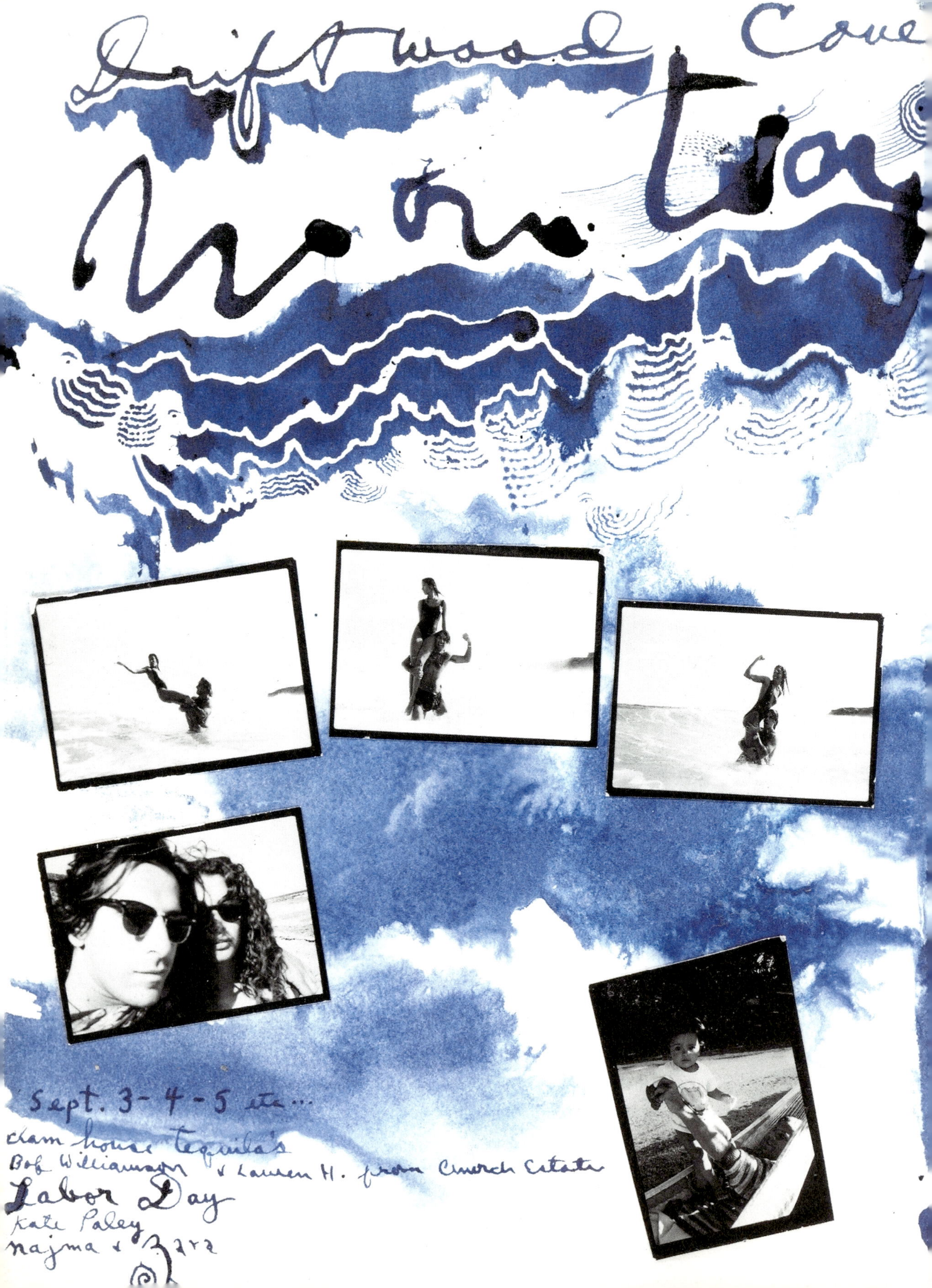

Driftwood Cove
motion
Sept. 3 - 4 - 5 etc...
clam house tequila's
Bob Williamson & Lauren H. from Church Estate
Labor Day
Kate Paley
najma & Zara

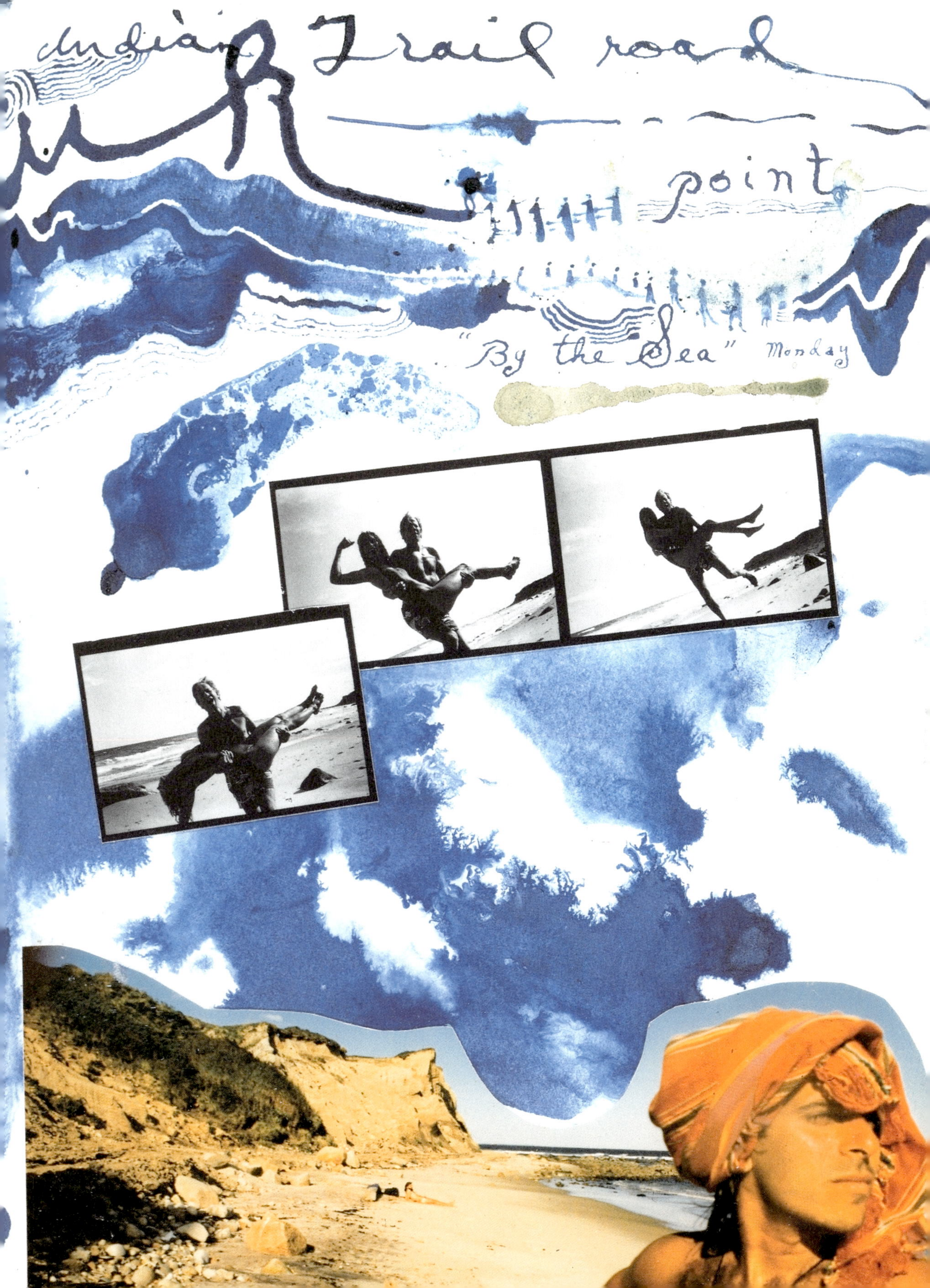

Indian Trail road
point
"By the Sea" Monday

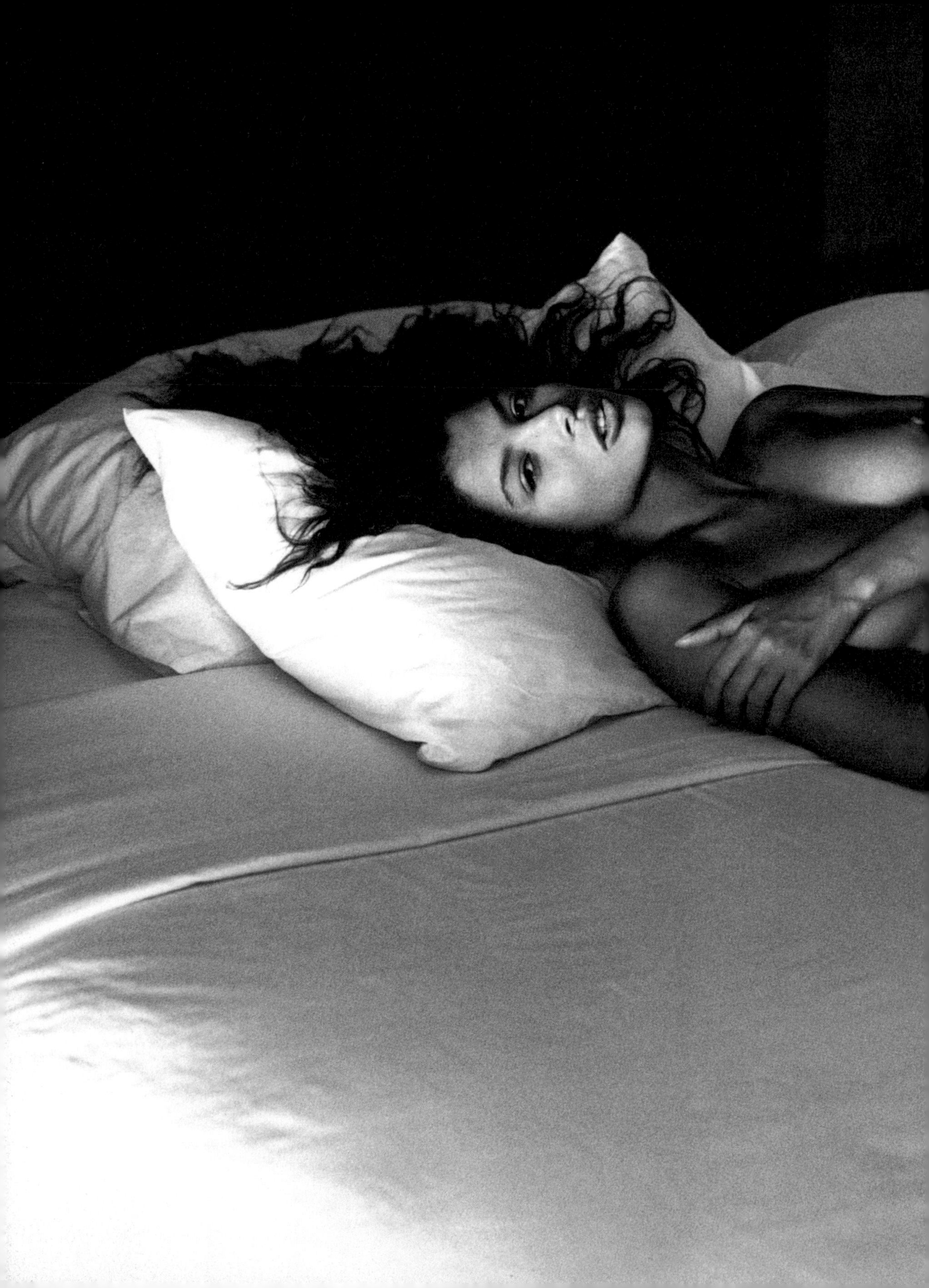

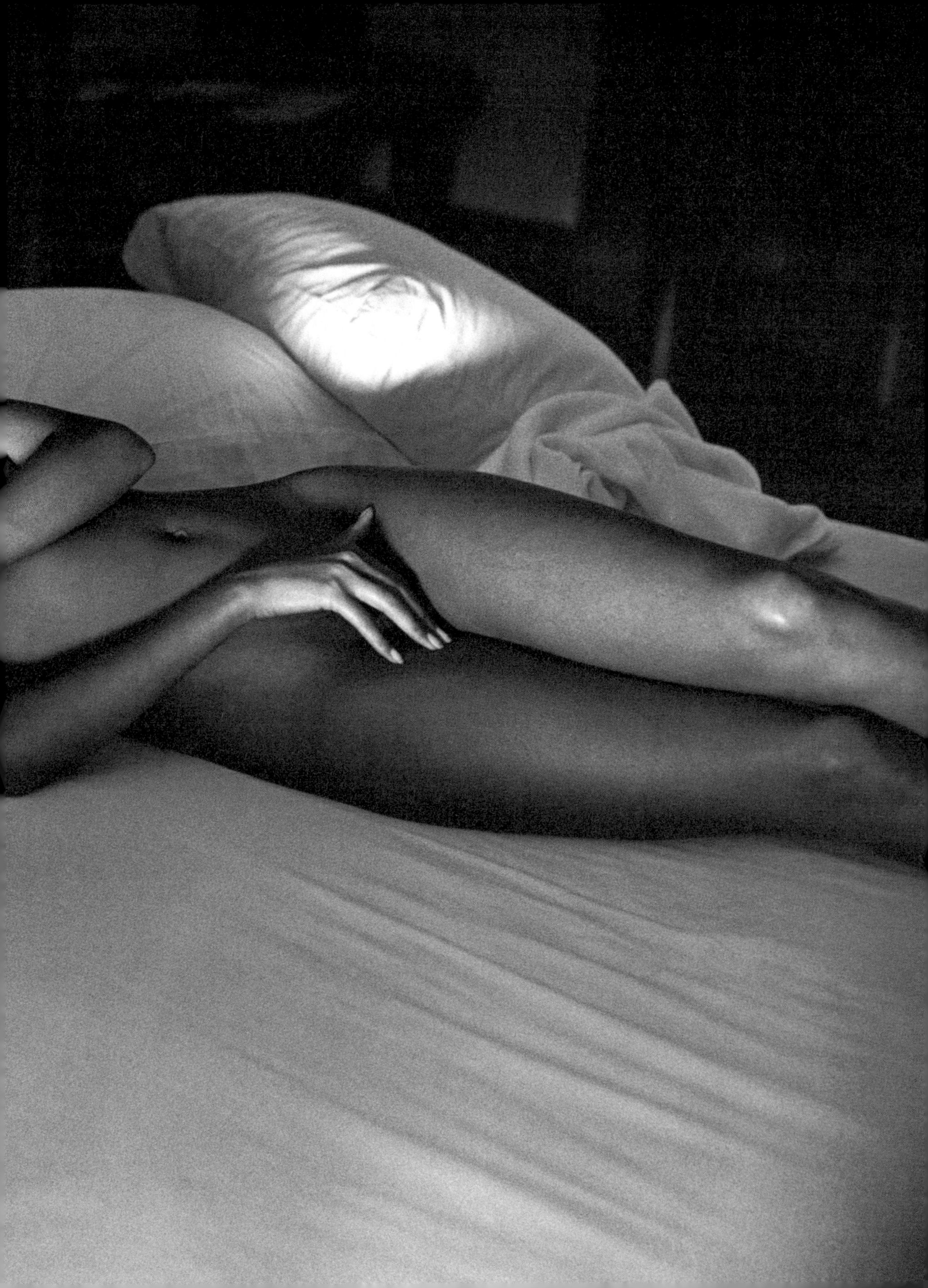

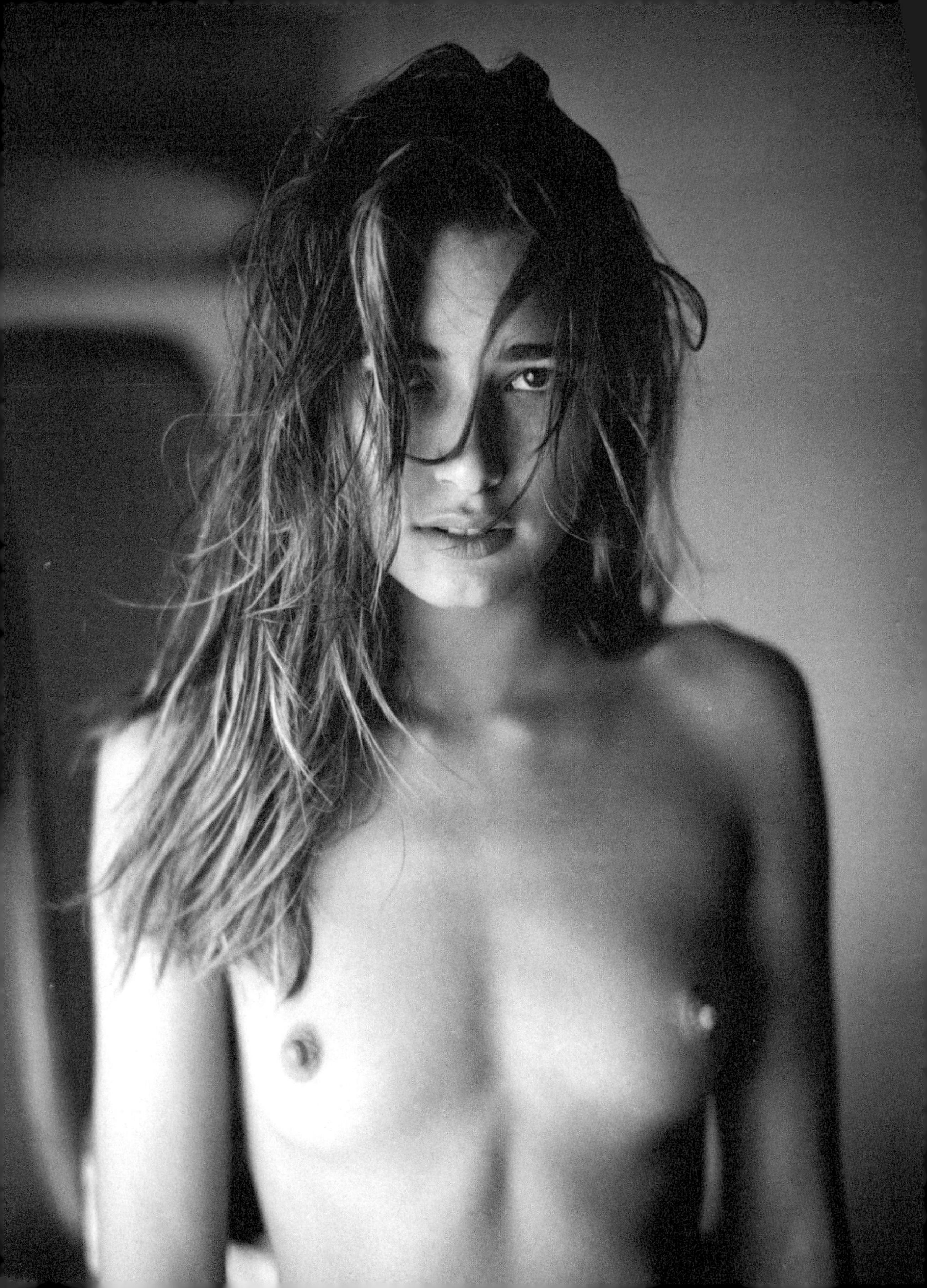

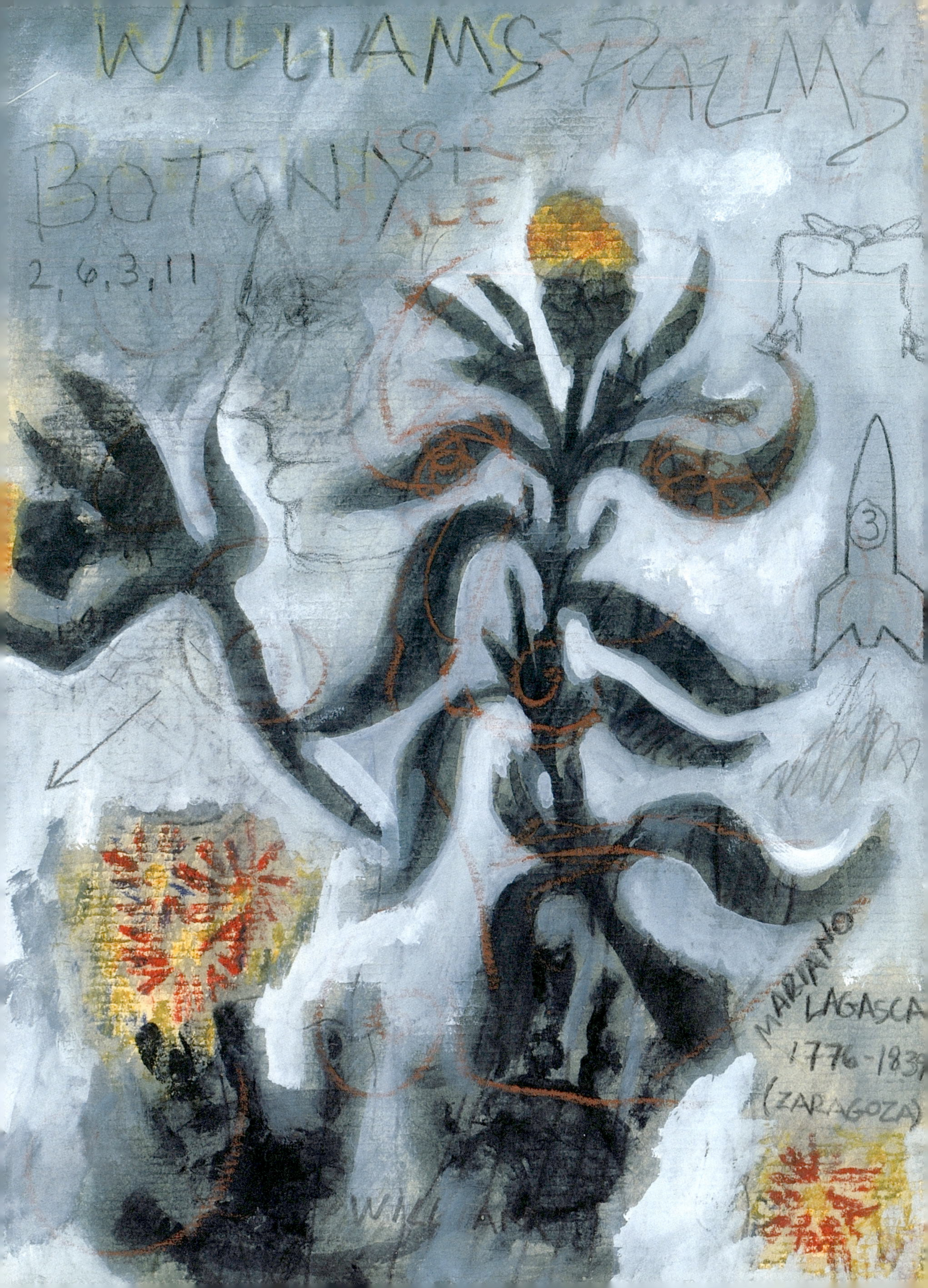

WILLIAMS PSALMS
BOTONYST
2, 6, 3, 11
3
MARIANO LAGASCA
1776 - 183
(ZARAGOZA)

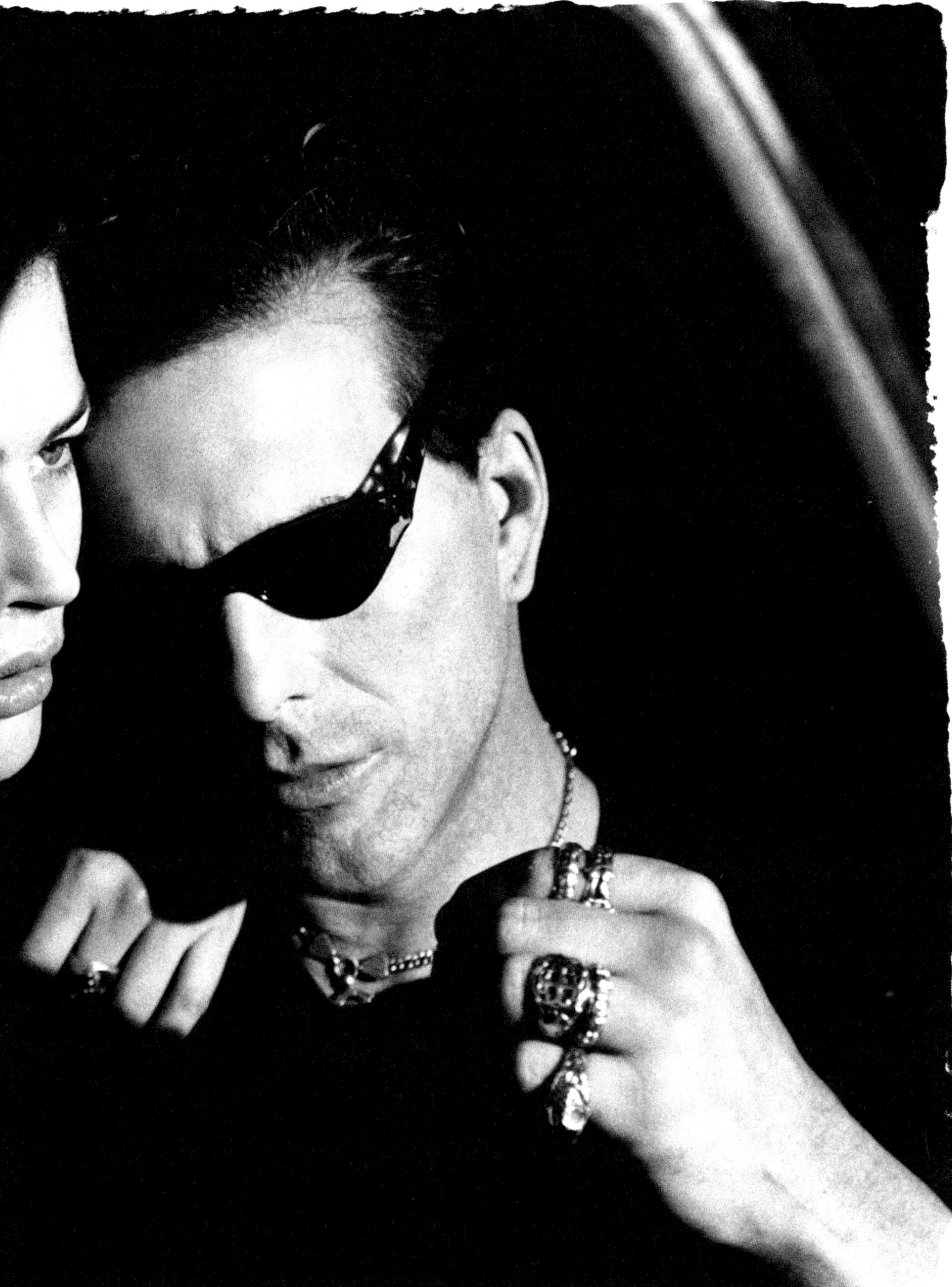

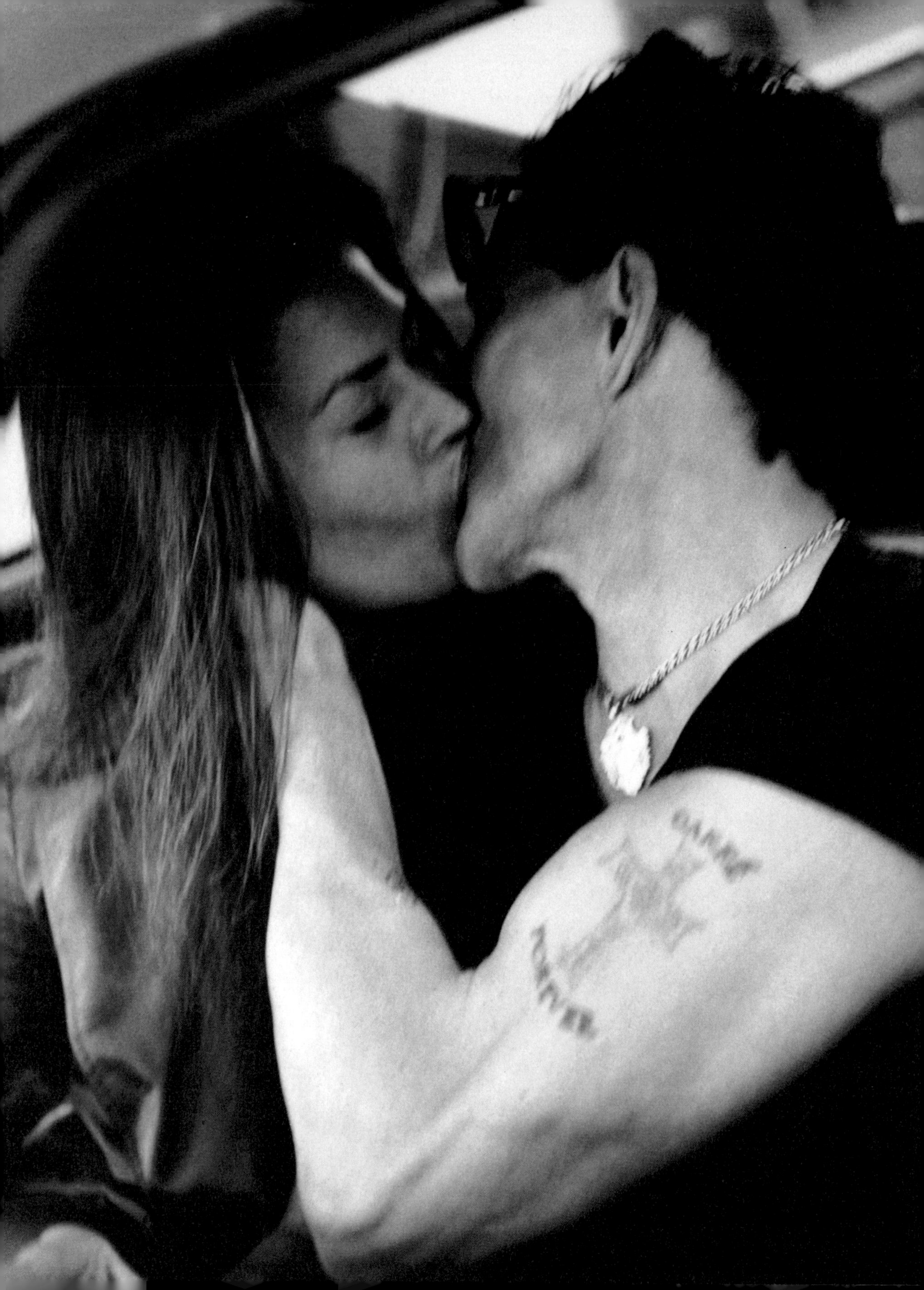

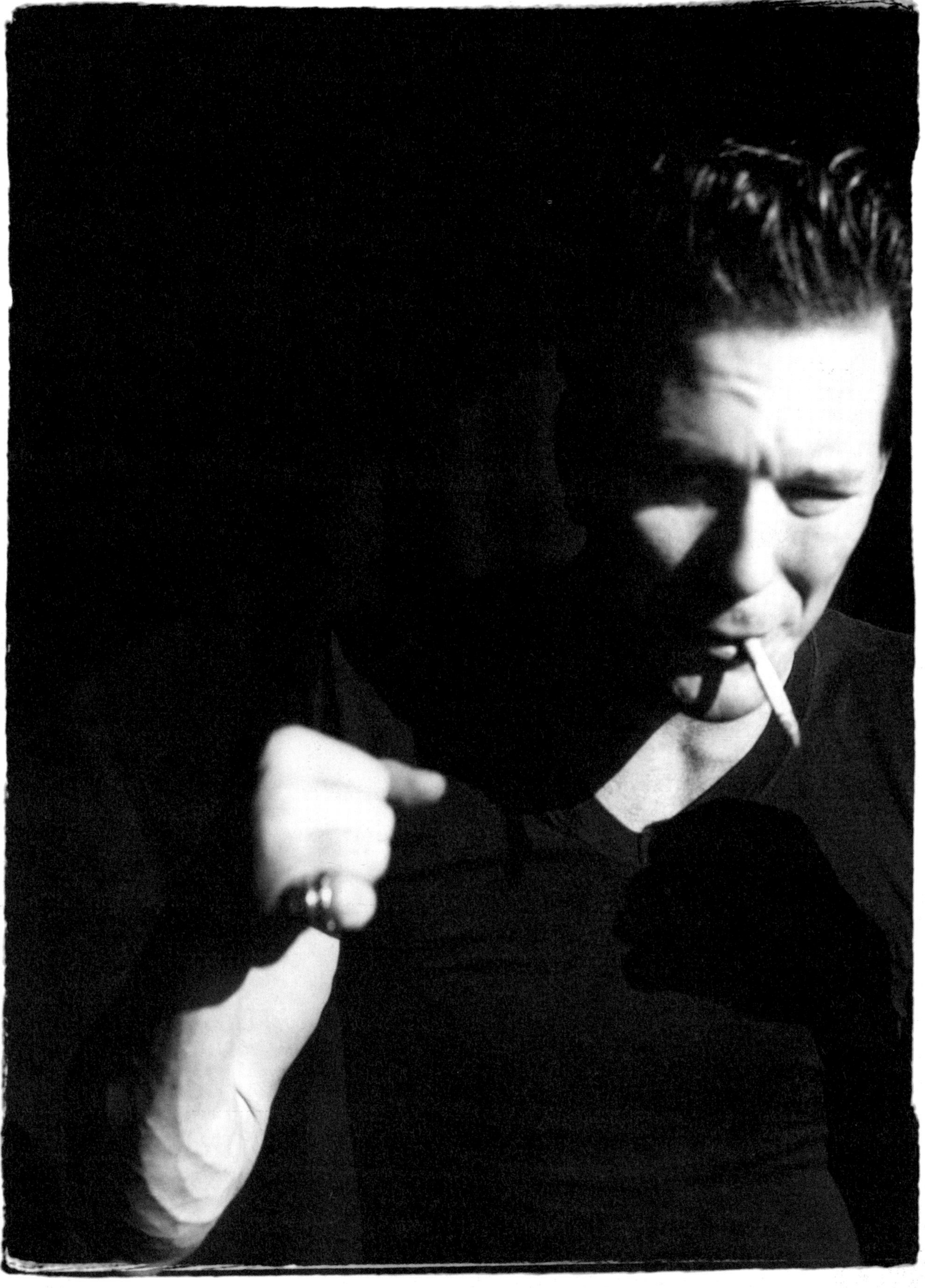

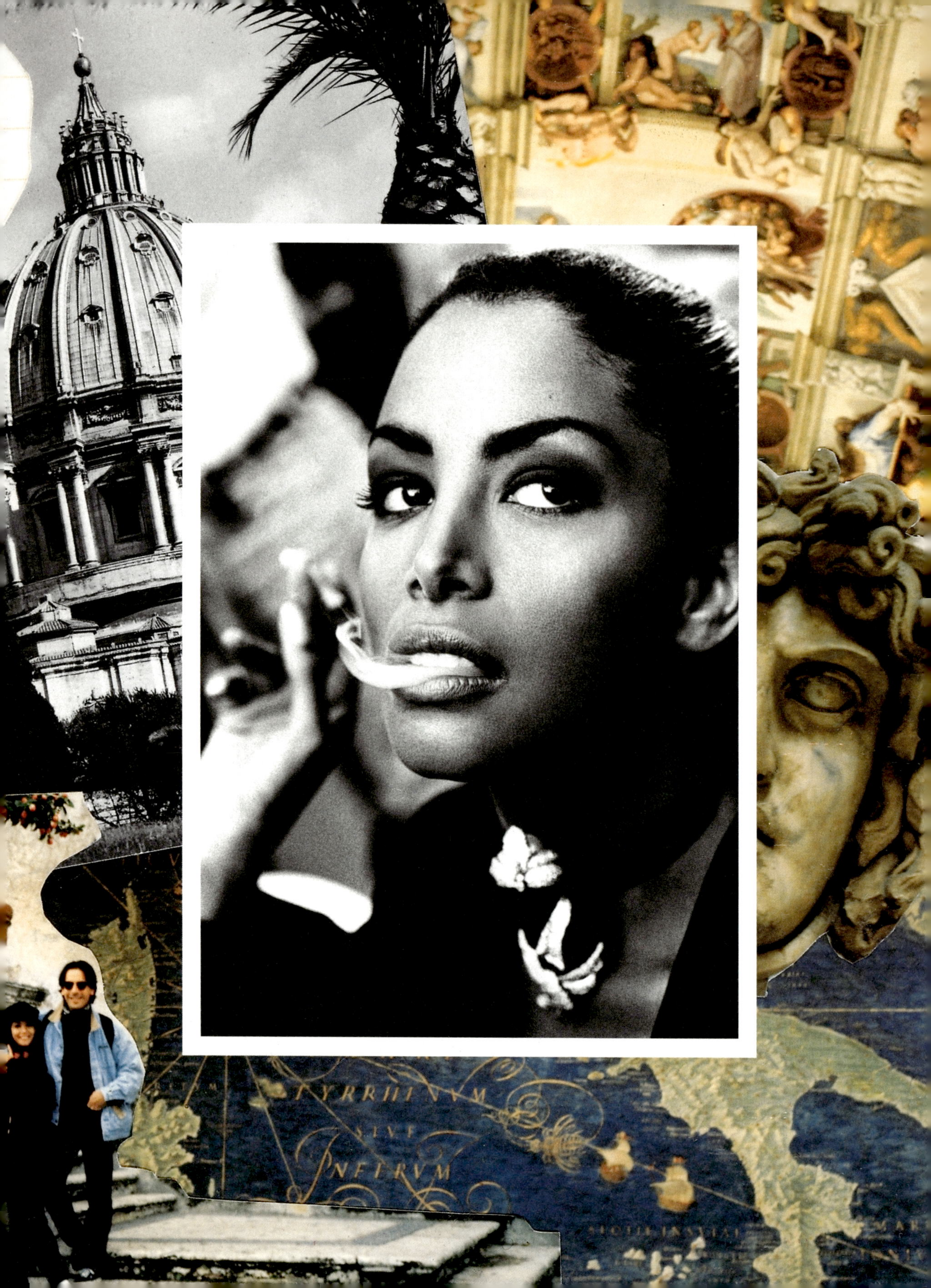
TYRRHENVM
SIVE
INFERVM

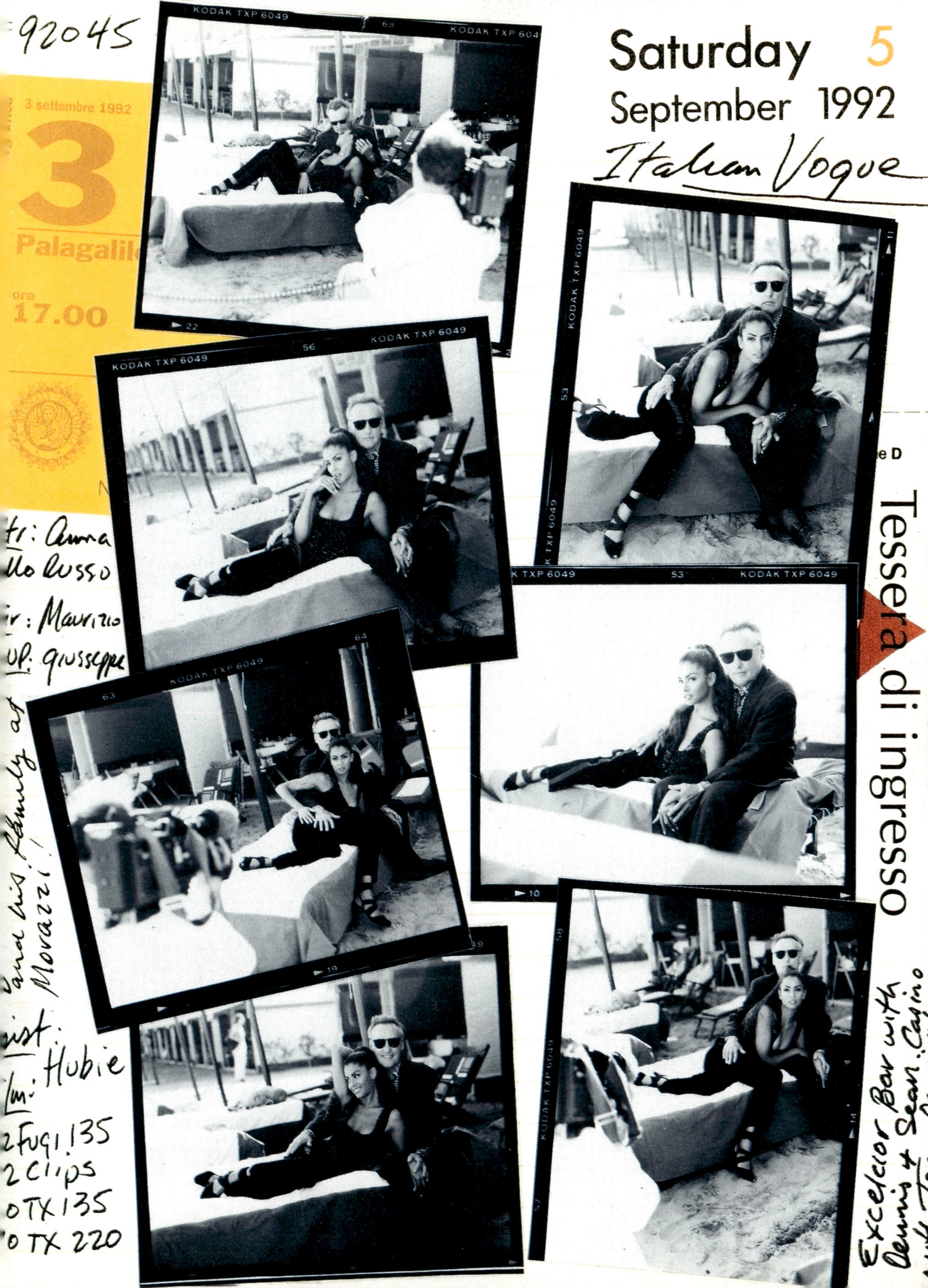

92045
3 settembre 1992
3
Palagalile
ore
17.00
Saturday 5
September 1992
Italian Vogue
Tessera di ingresso
Ti: Anna
llo Russo
ir: Maurizio
UP: Giuseppe
and his family ag
Movazzi!
ist:
lm: Hubie
2 Fuji 135
2 Clips
0 TX 135
0 TX 220
Excelsior Bar with
Denny + Sean Cajino
KODAK TXP 6049

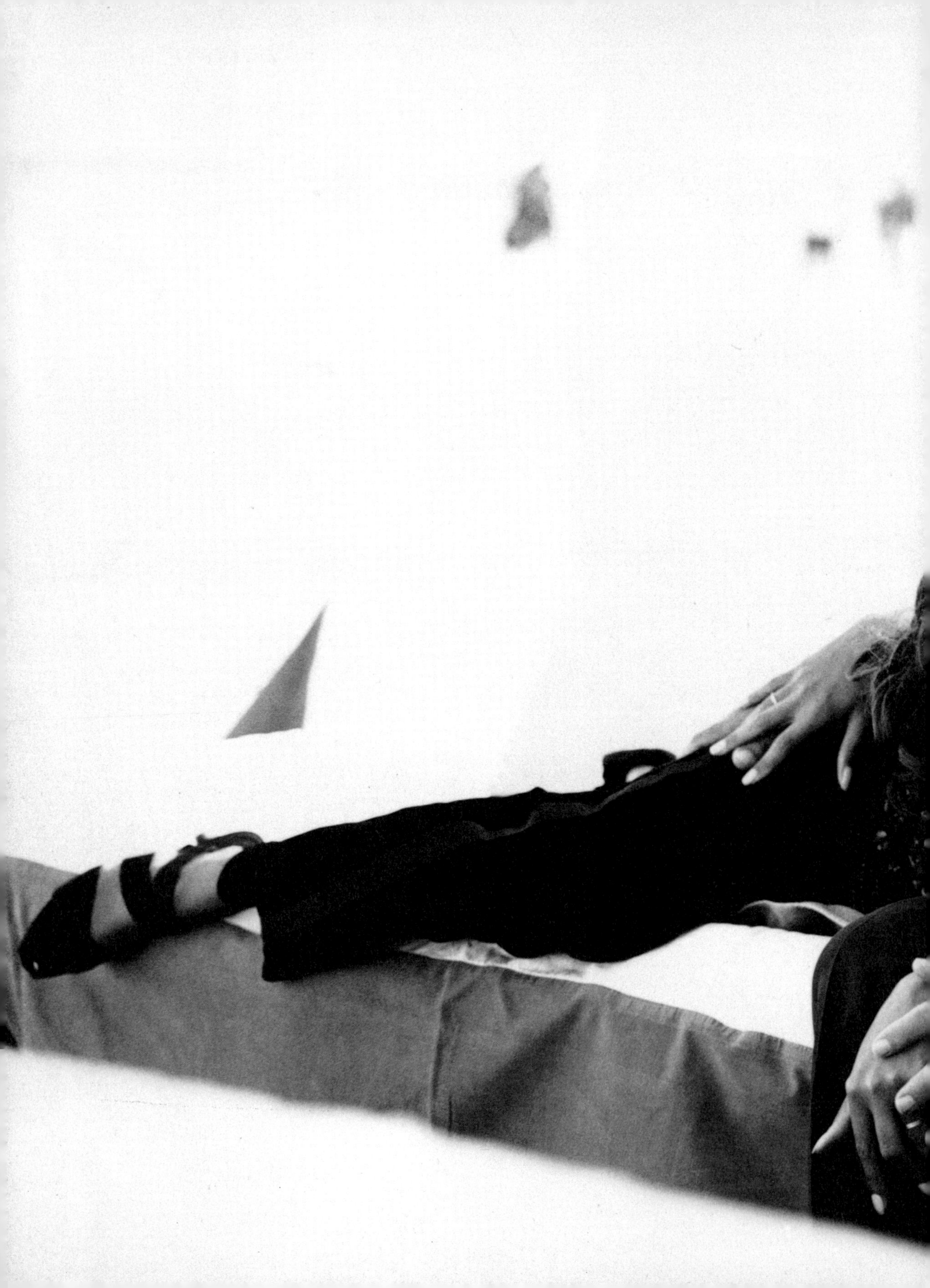

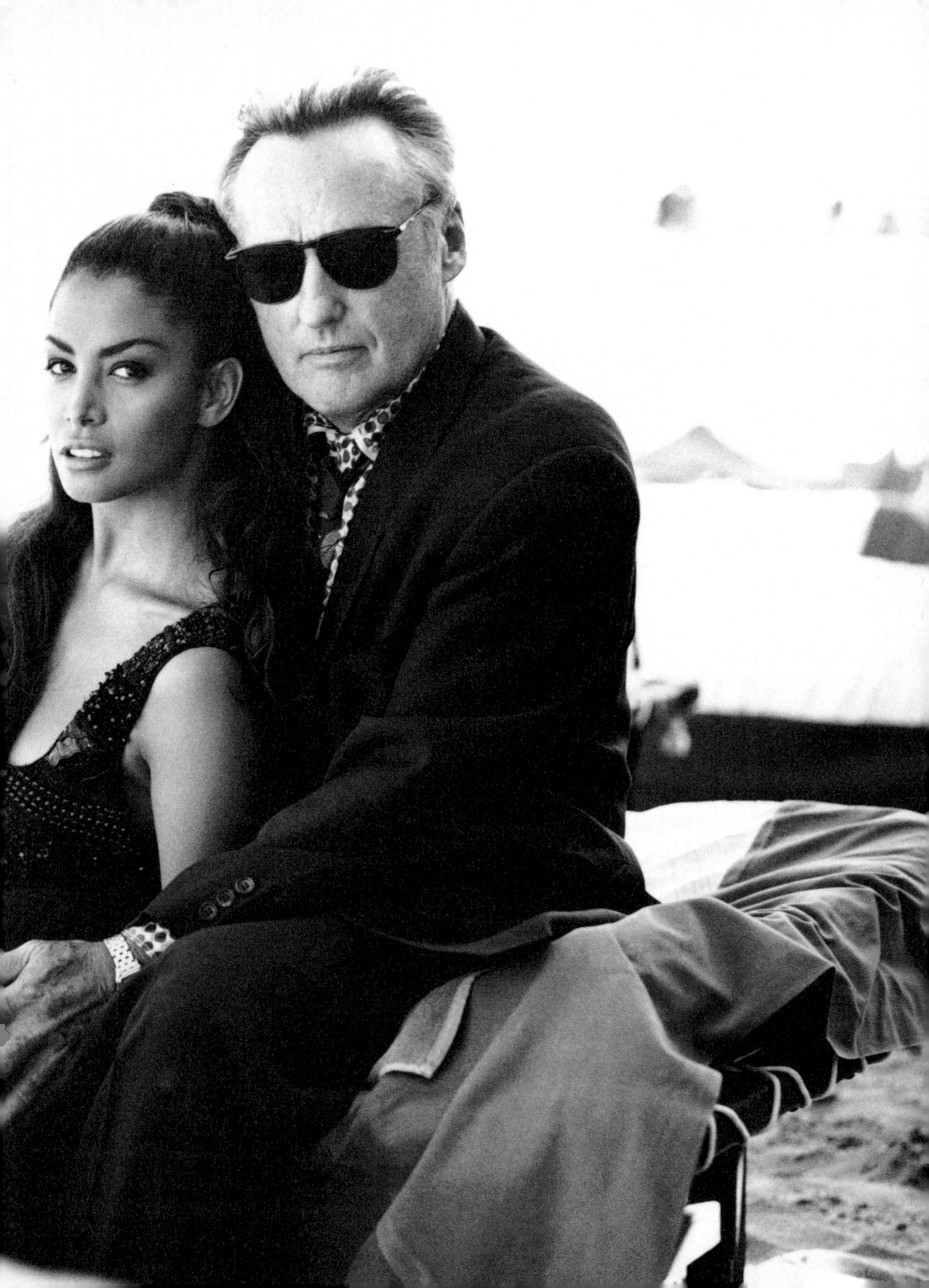

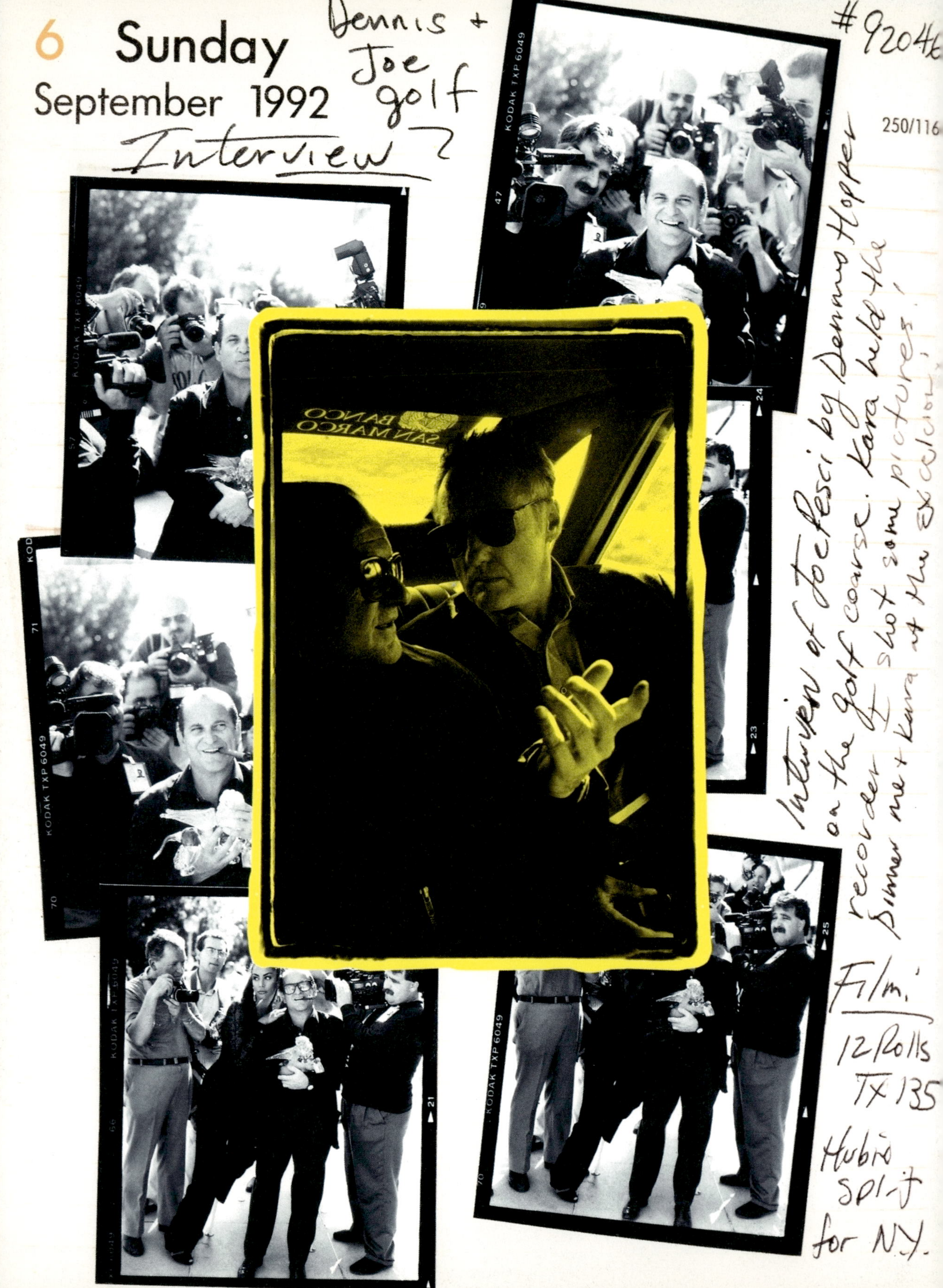

6
Sunday
September 1992
Dennis + Joe golf
Interview
#9204b
250/116
KODAK TXP 6049
BANCO SAN MARCO
Interview of Joe Pesci by Dennis Hopper on the golf coarse. Kara held the recorder & I shot some pictures! Dinner me + Kara at the Excelsior!
Film.
12 Rolls
TX 135
Hubio split
for N.Y.

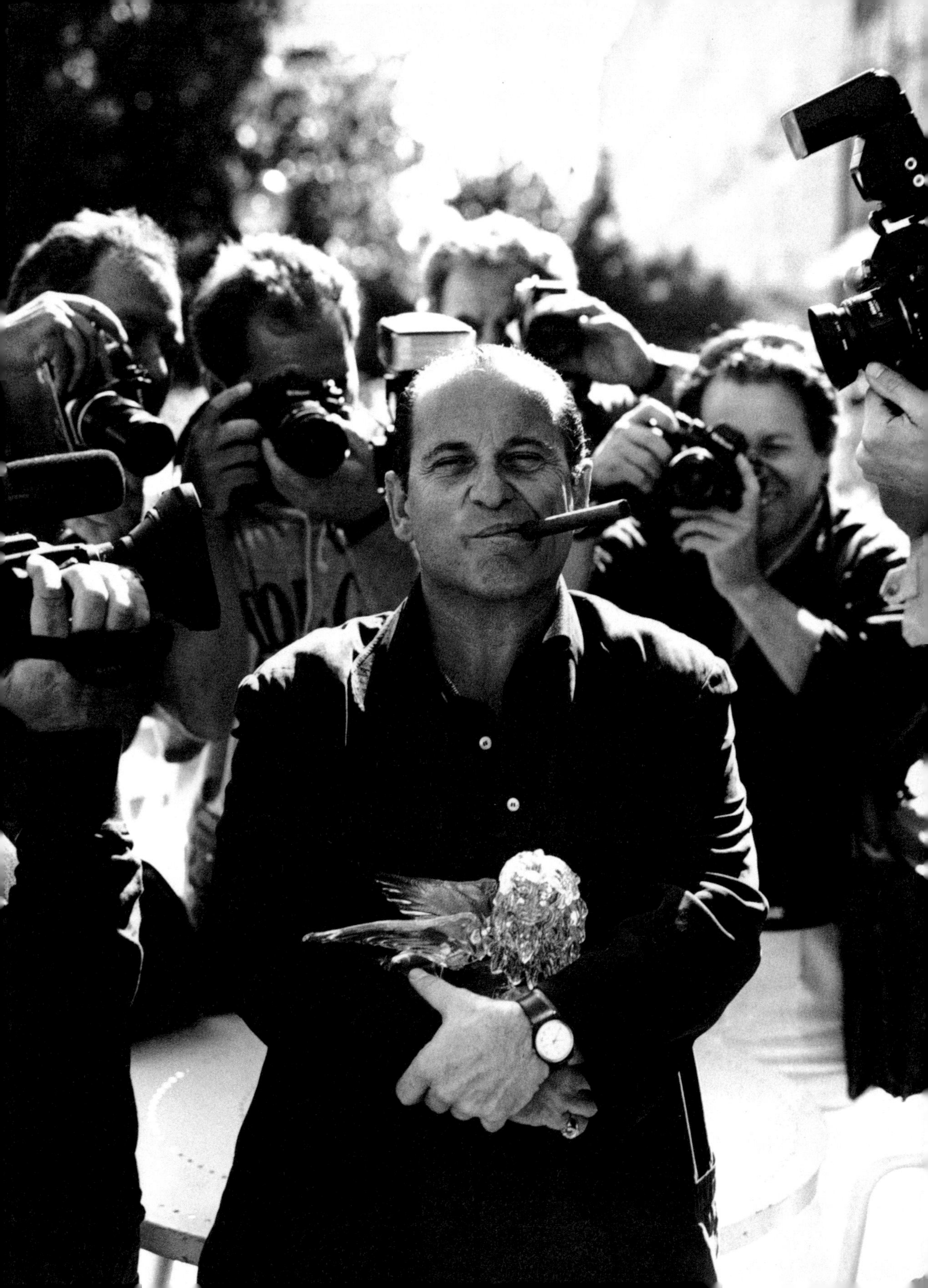

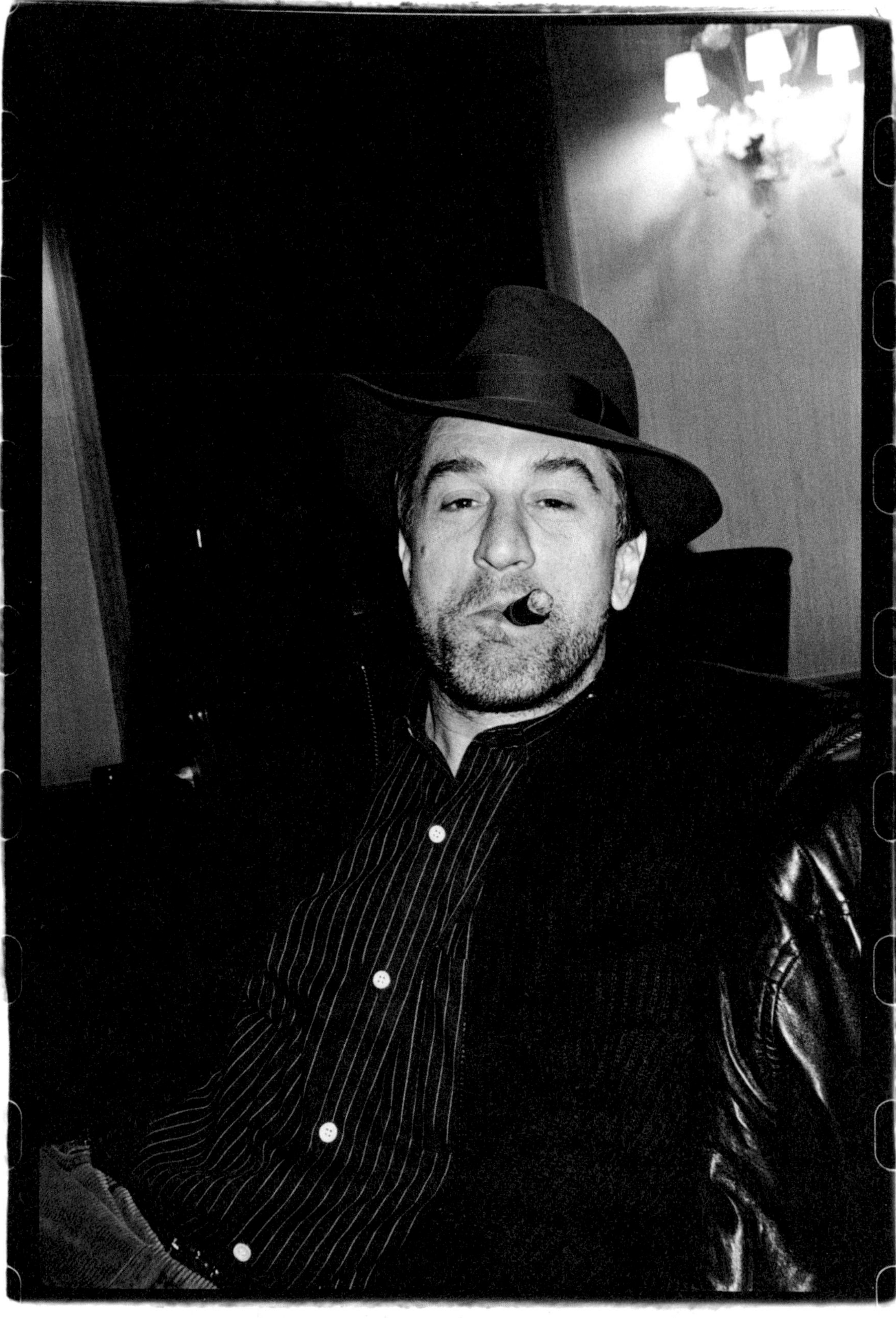

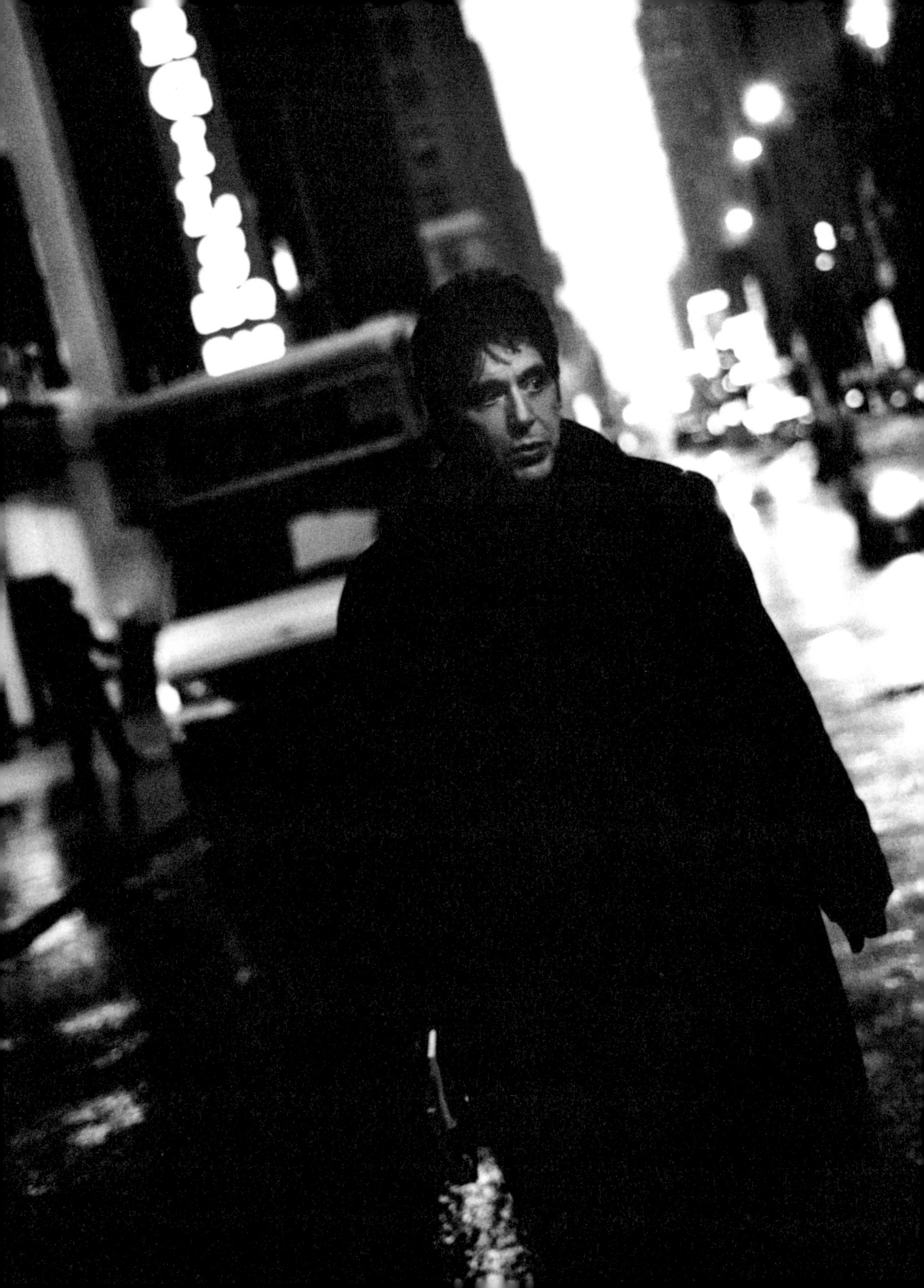

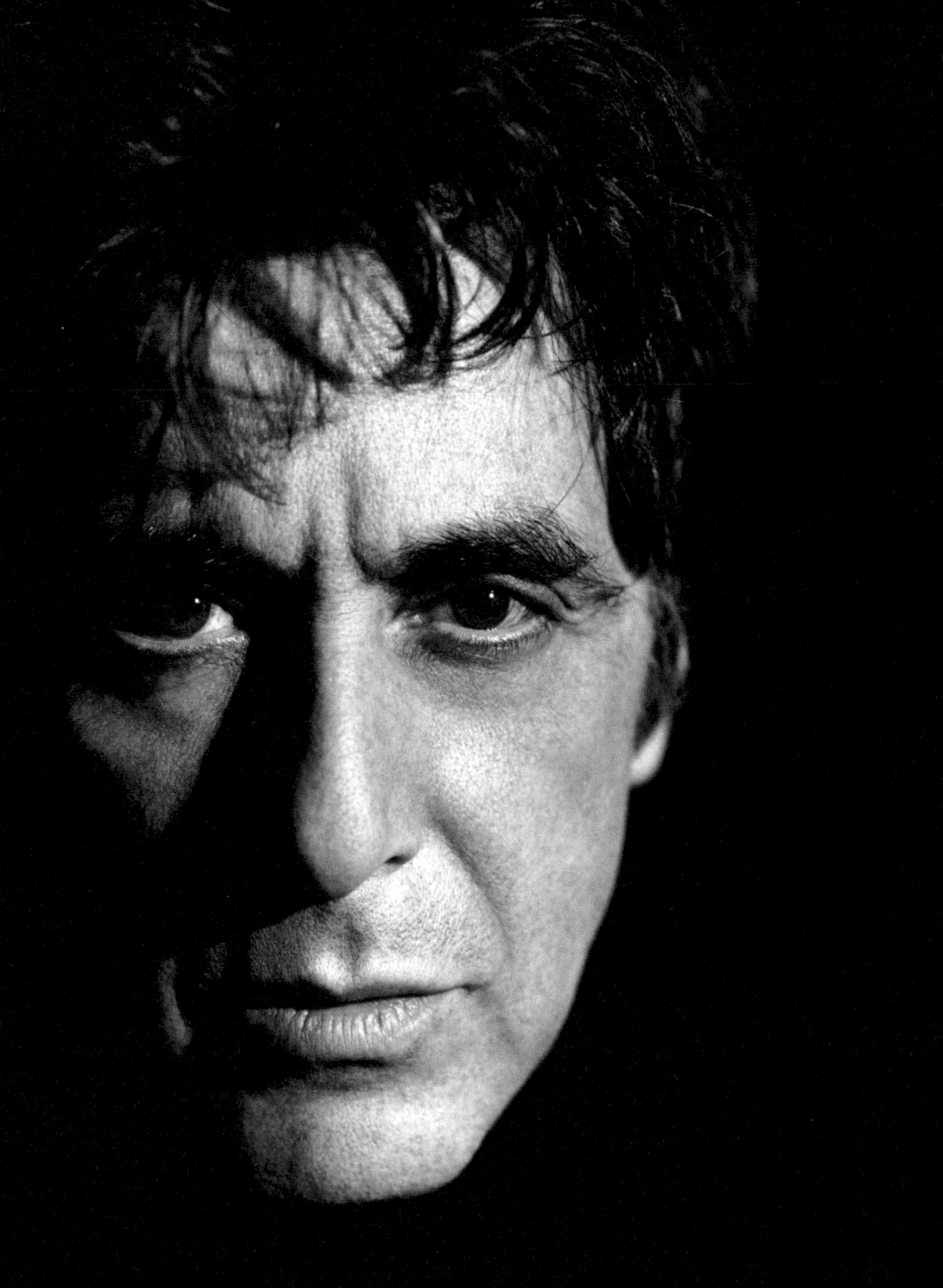

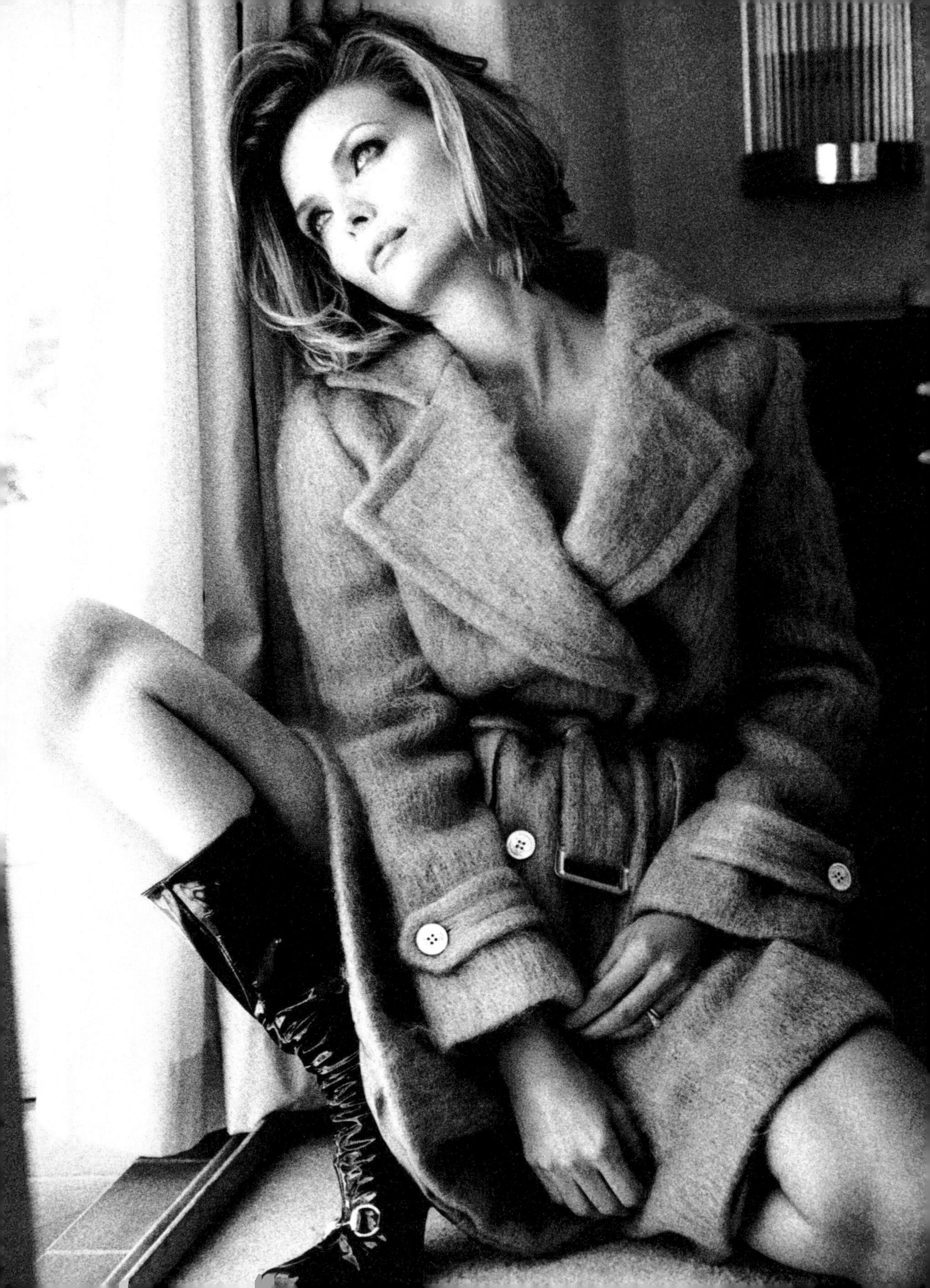

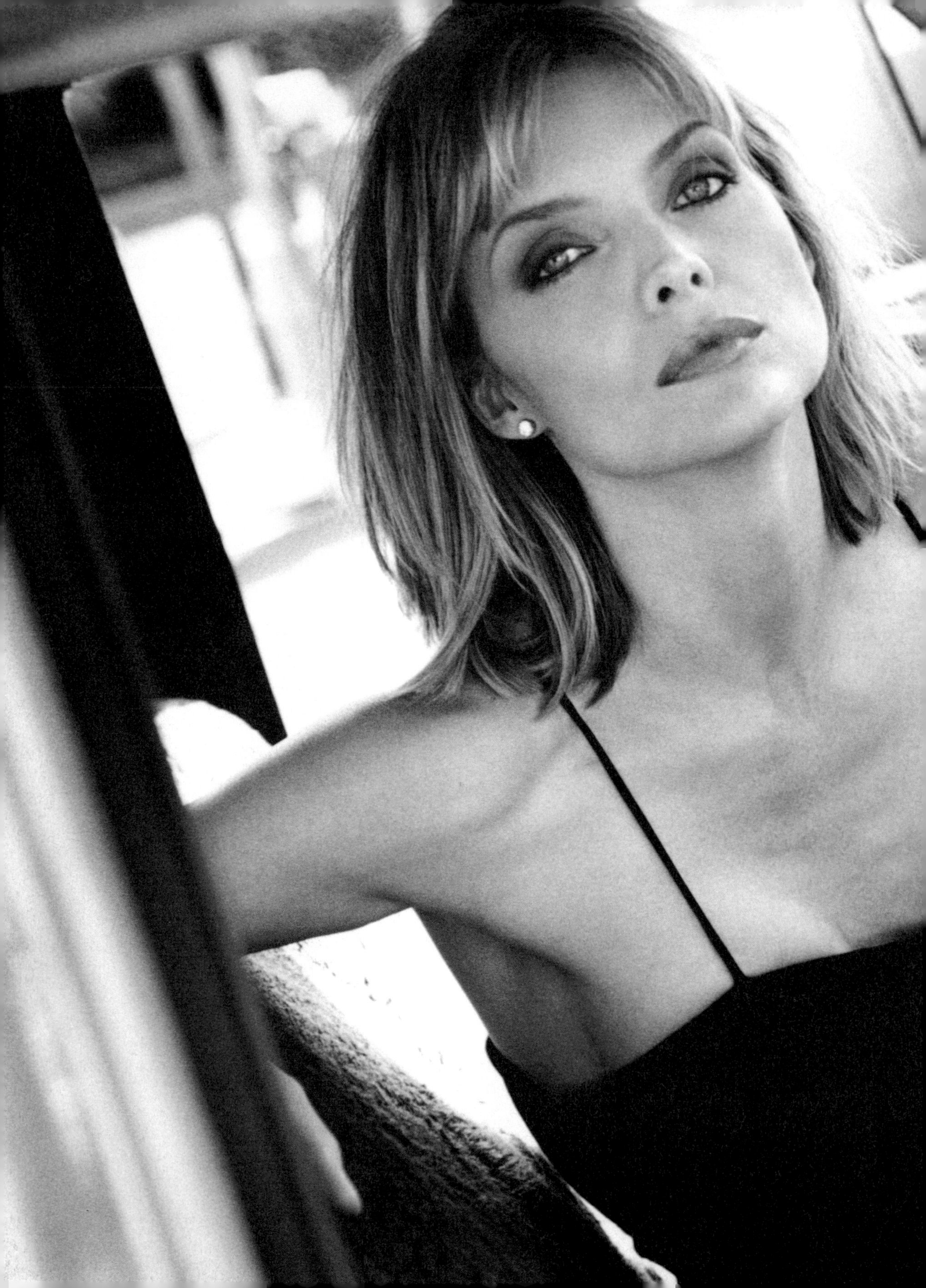

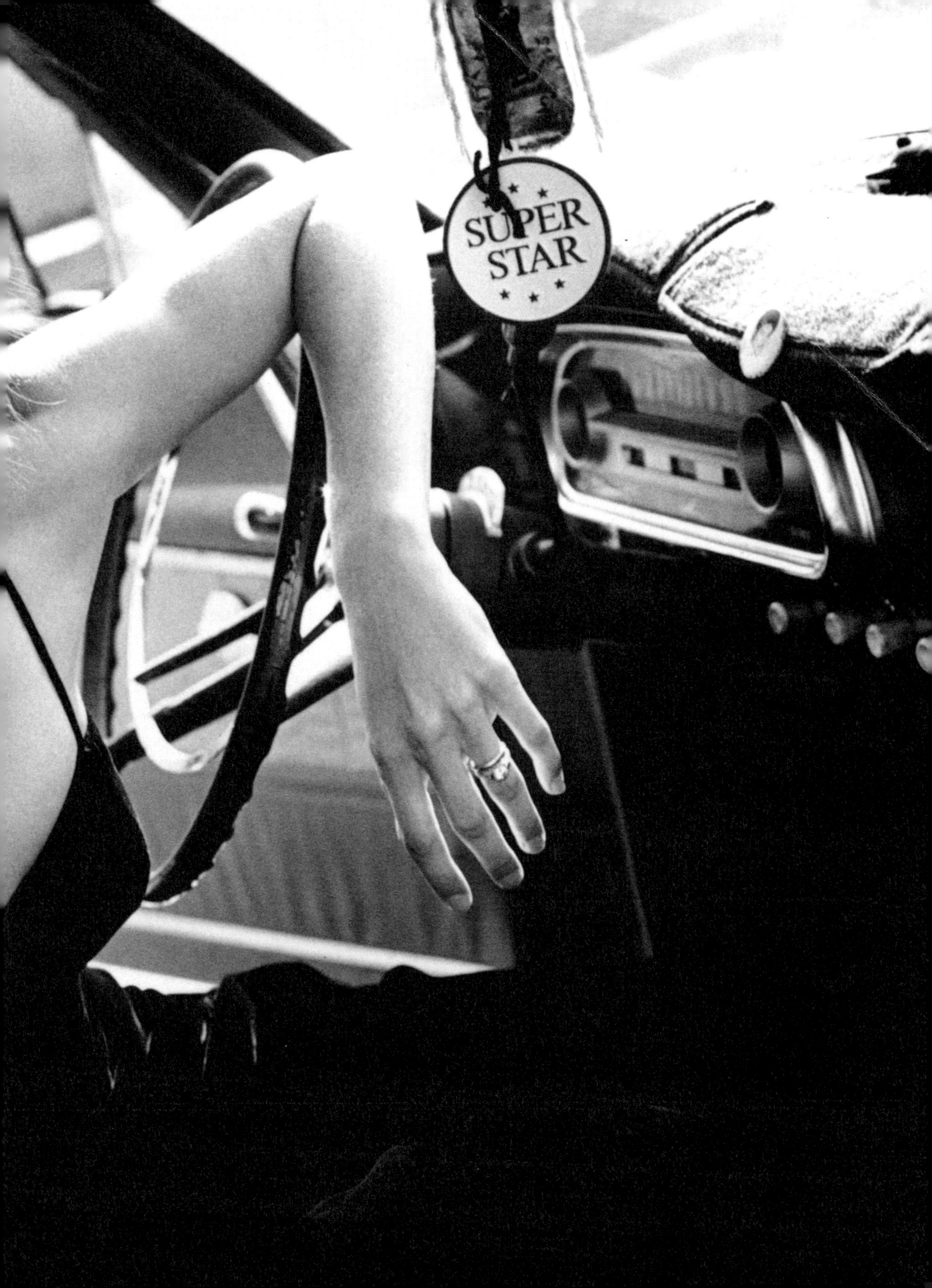

SUPER
STAR

Had some breakfast with Victor at the house, went to Saline beach. Lunch at ToTo Burgers. Picked up Georgine at airport, Victor went to beach. Dinner at Lascale the 3 of us + partied late!

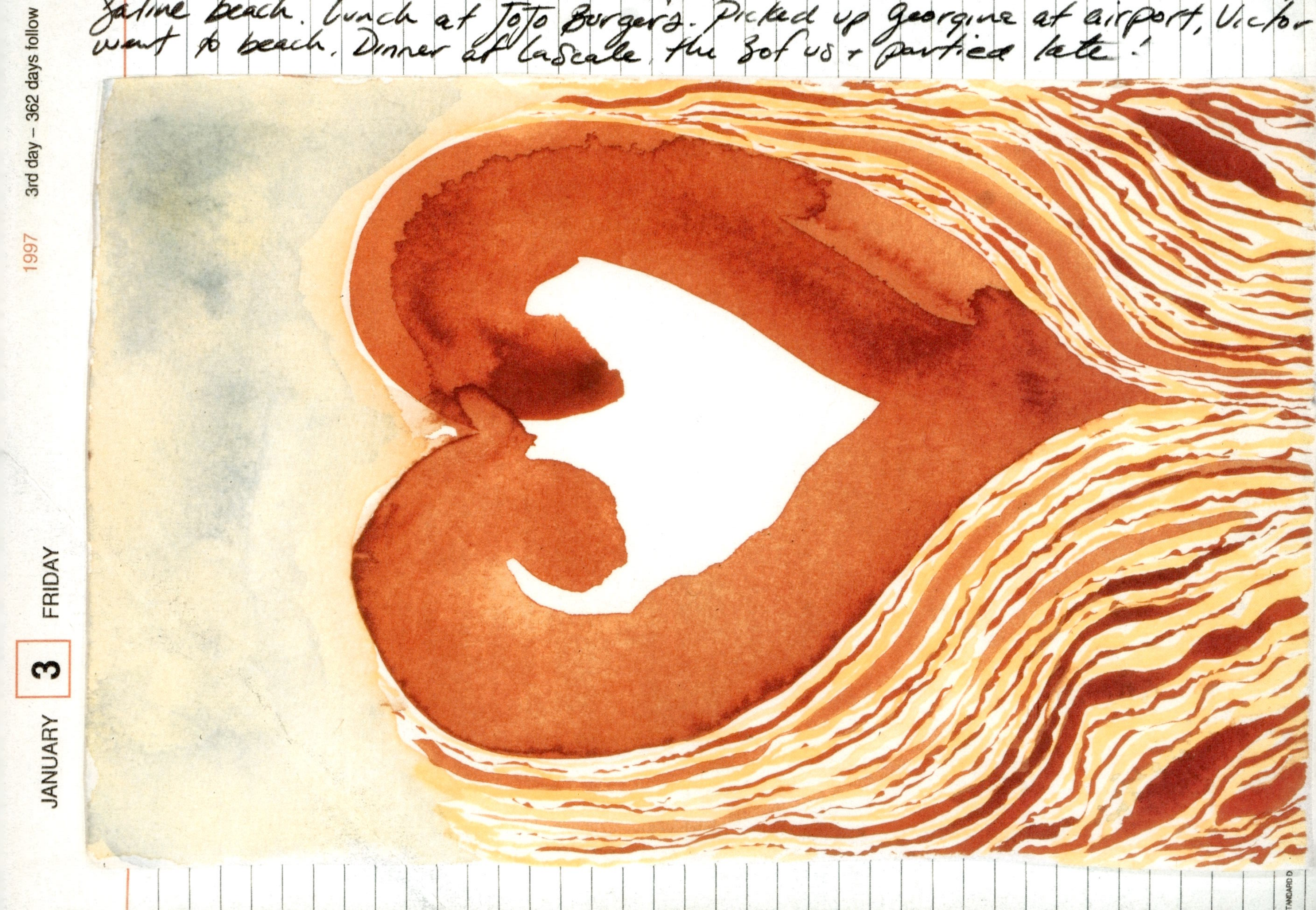

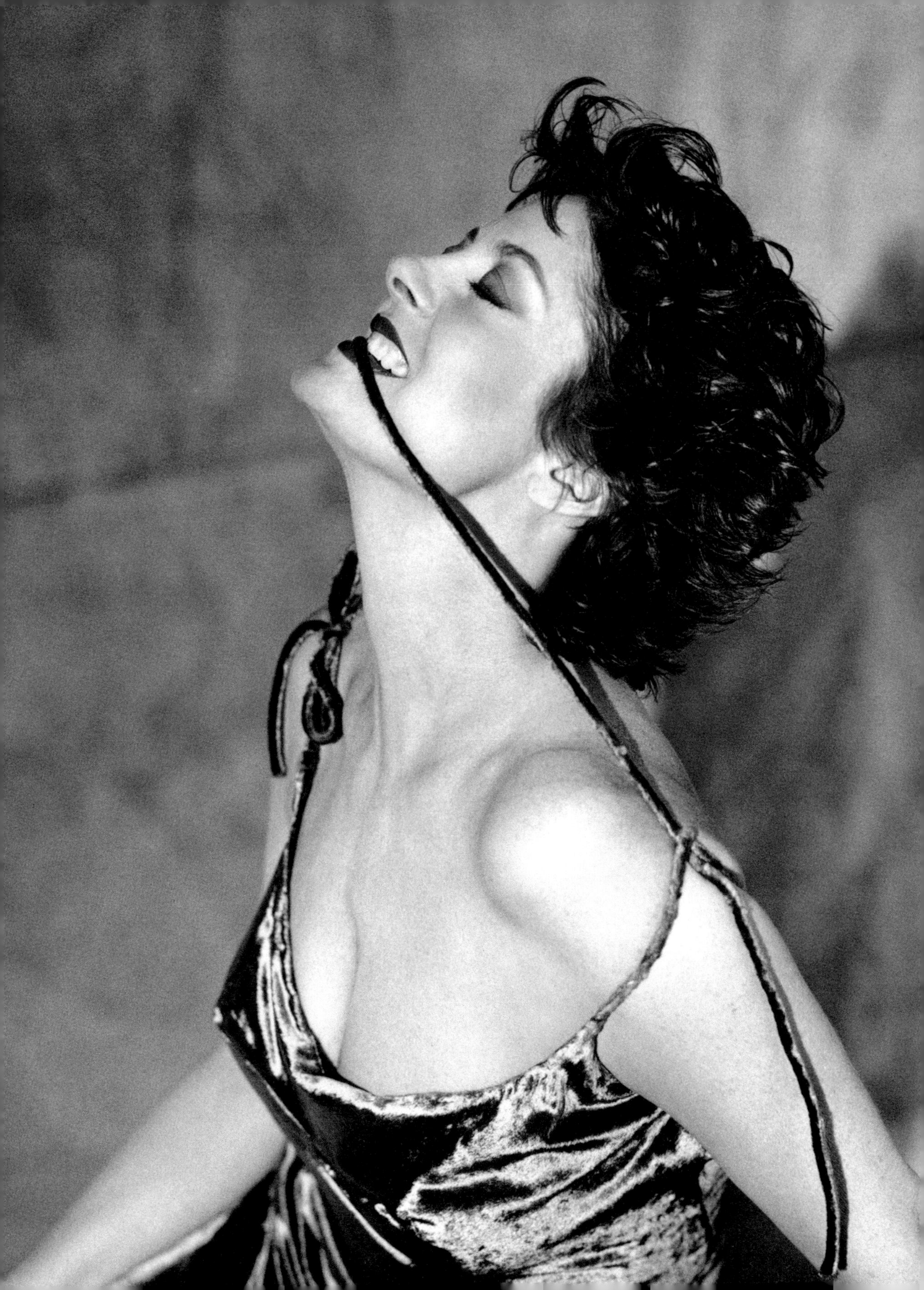

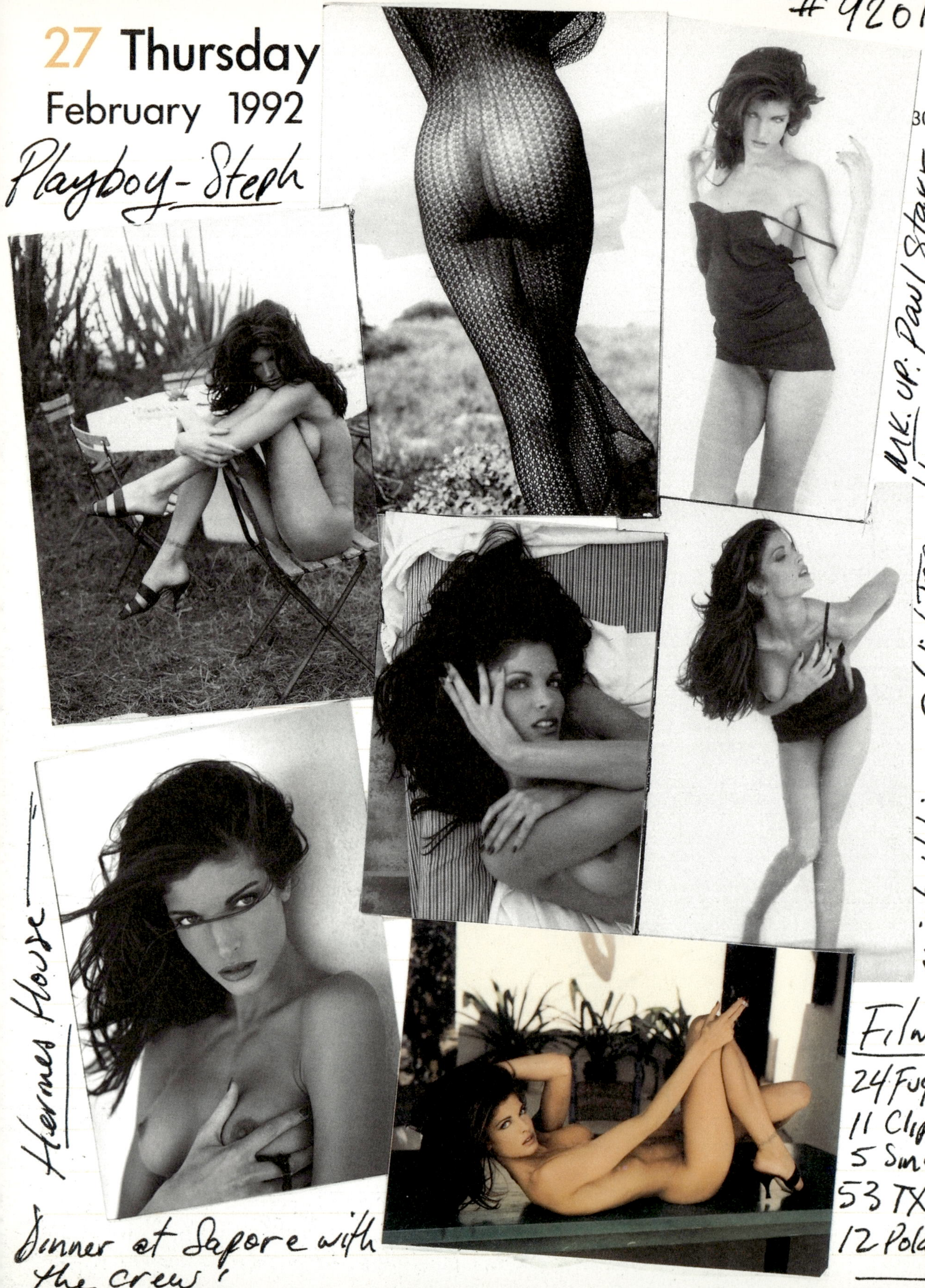

27 Thursday
February 1992
Playboy - Steph
#92013
308
Hermes House
MK. Up: Paul Starr
Stylist: Joe
Film.
24 Fuji
11 Clips
5 Sing
53 TX2
12 Polab
Dinner at Safore with
the crew!

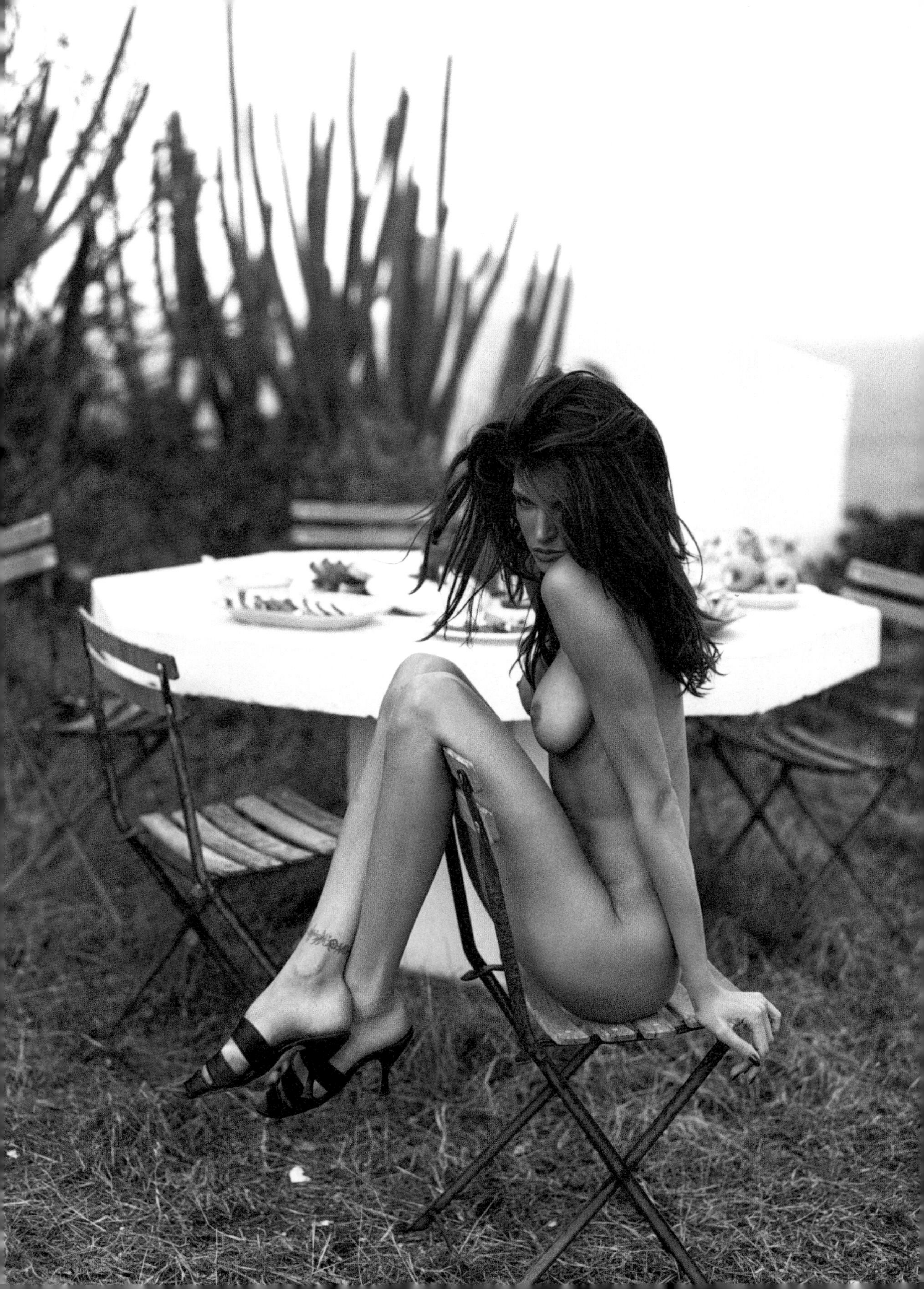

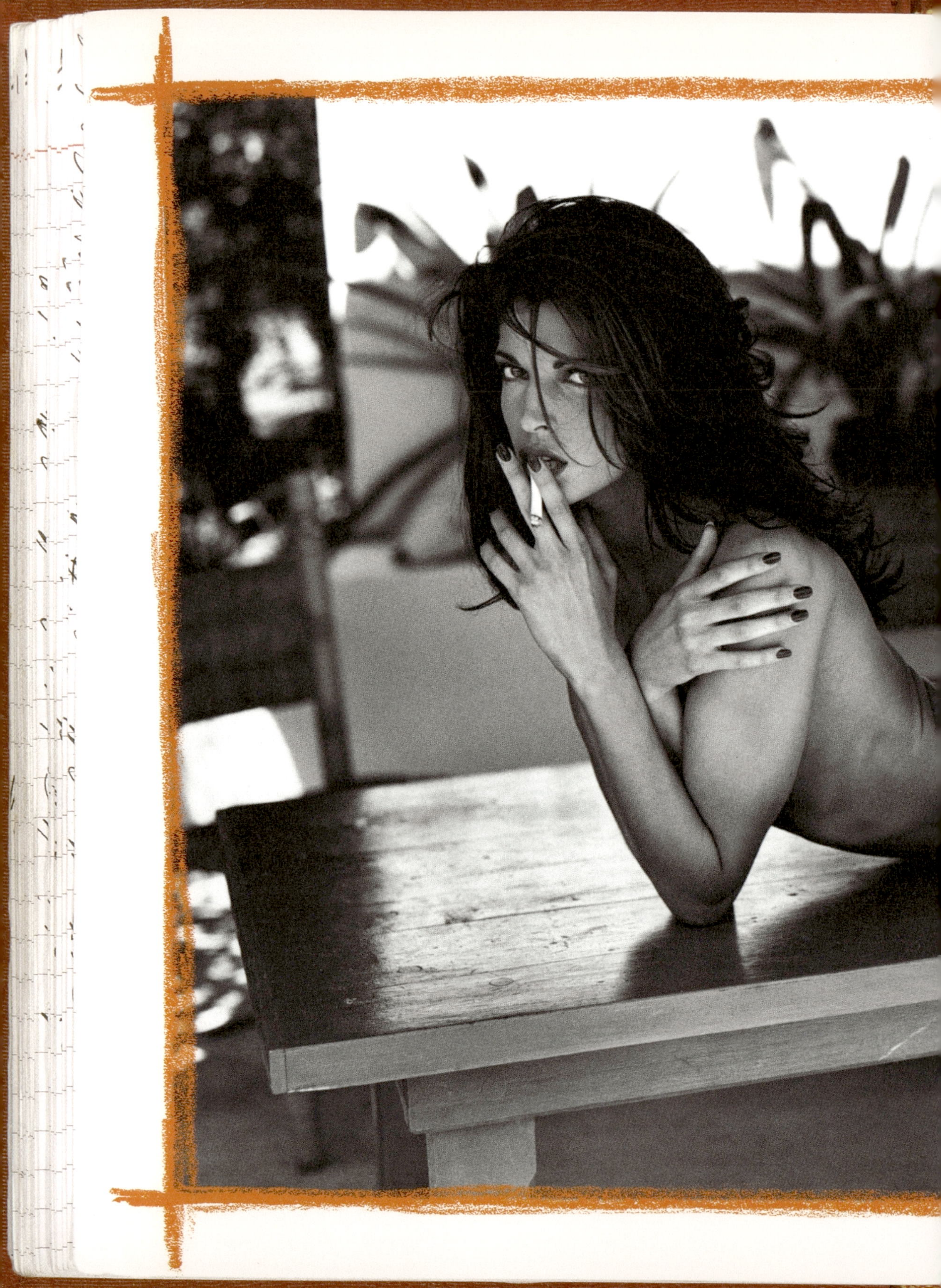

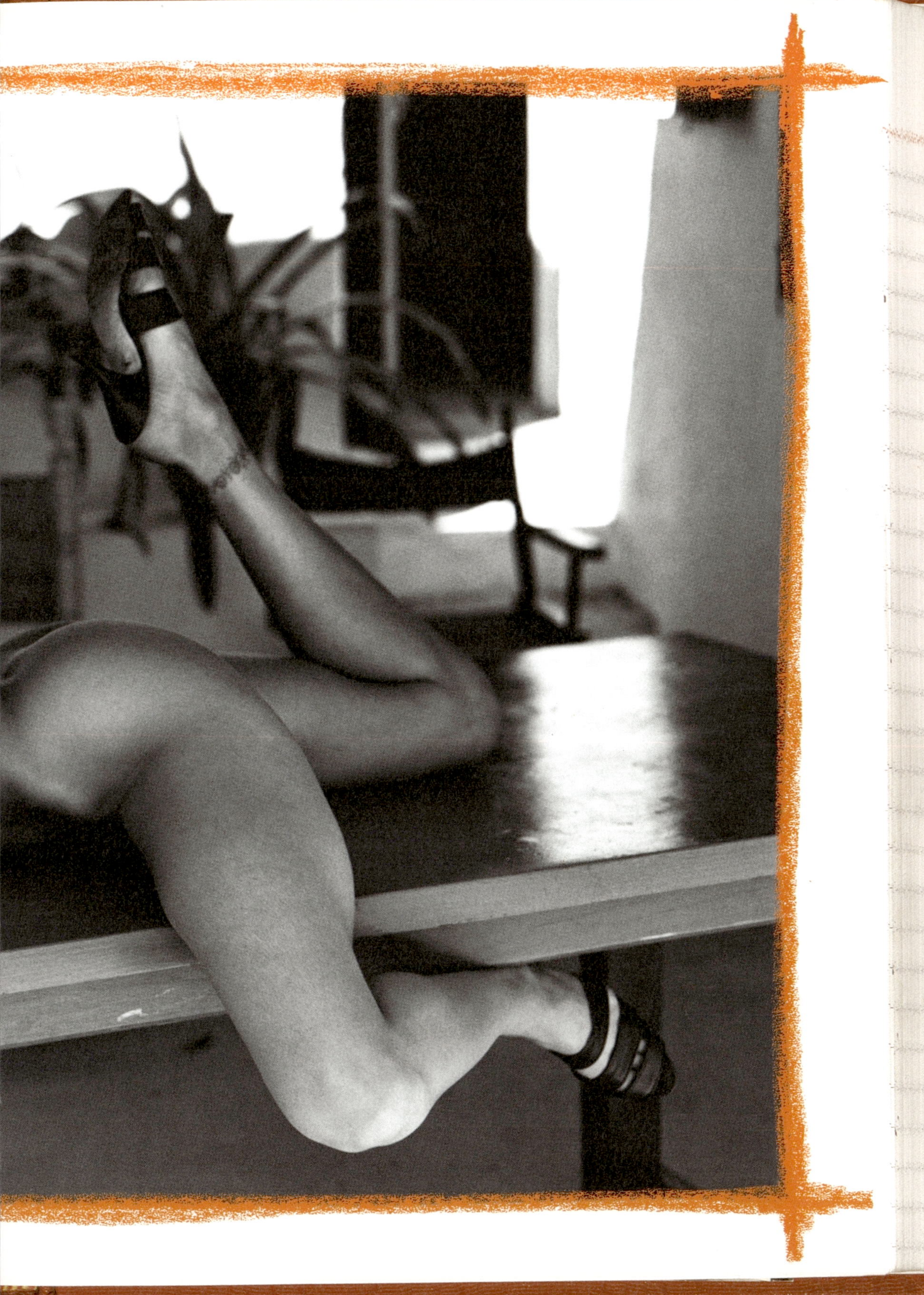

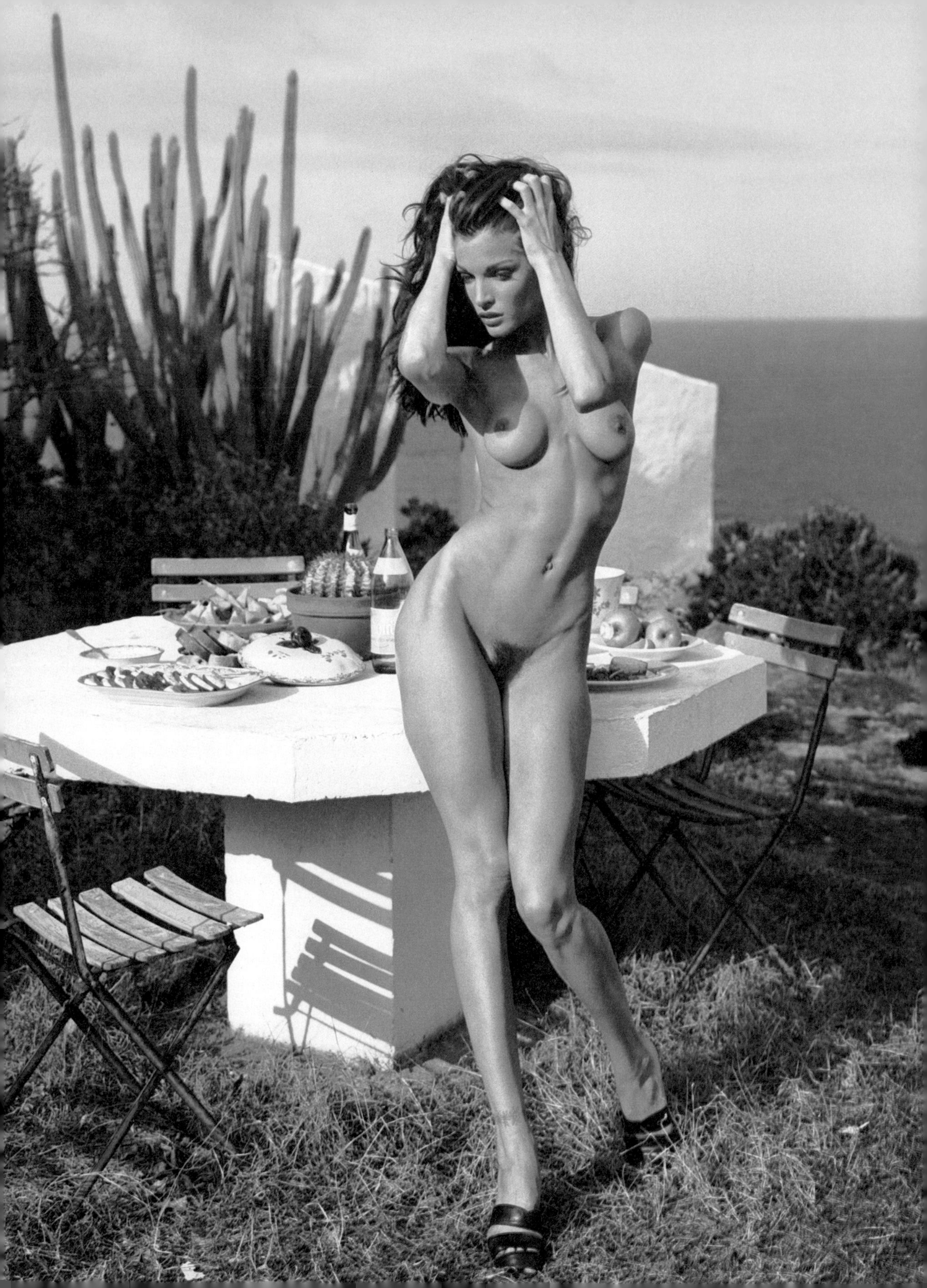

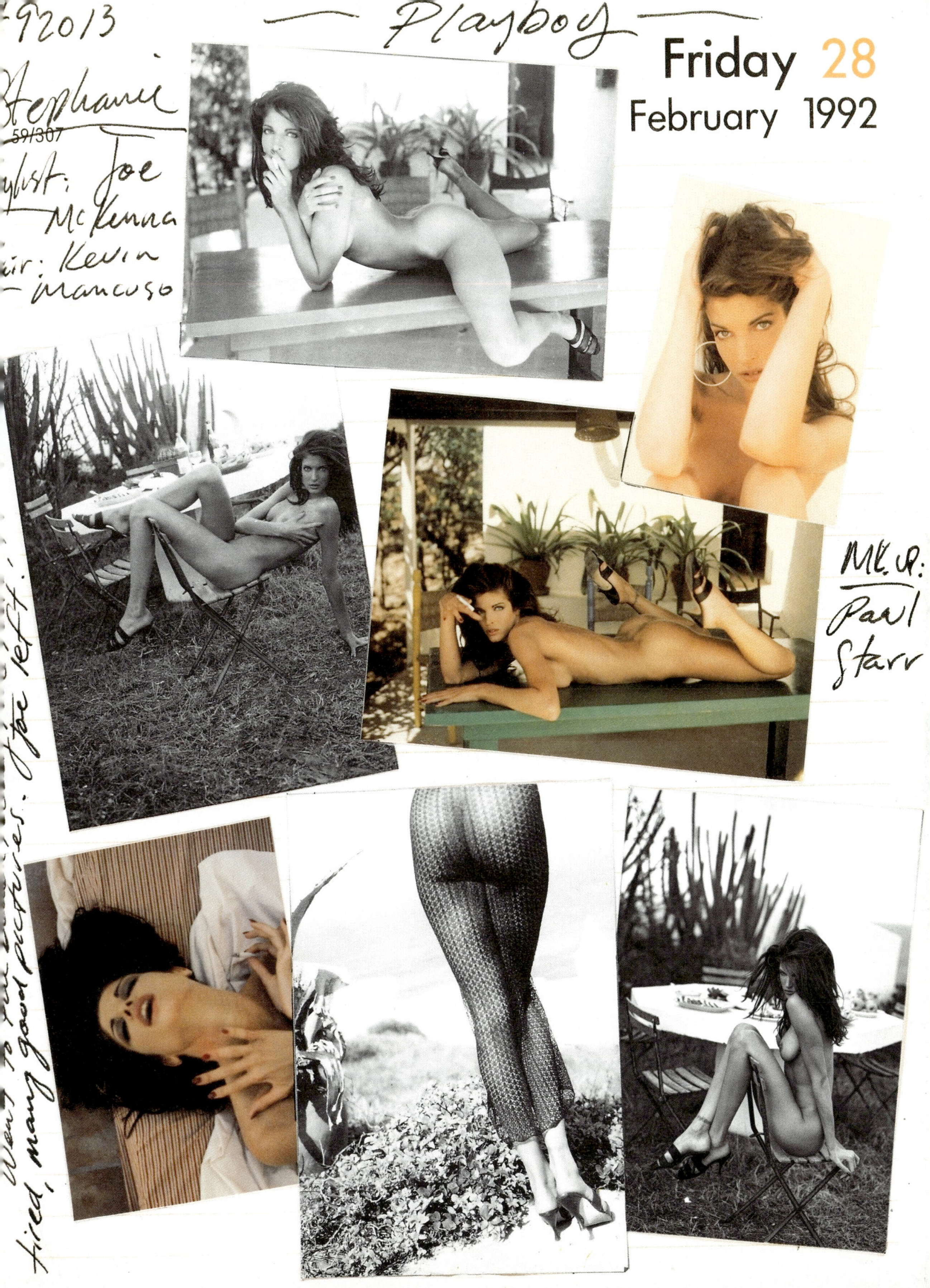

92013
Stephanie
59/307
Stylist: Joe
McKenna
Hair: Kevin
Mancuso
Playboy
Friday 28
February 1992
MK.UP:
Paul
Starr

16 Saturday
January 1993

Slept till noon then went and had late lunch with Tahnee at Mezzogiorno. Felt kinda washed out. Sharon Simanaire invited me to Saturday Nite Live show. I brought Tahnee and we went there around 10:30pm Harvey Keitel + Madonna as musical guest. Went to party at Paramount afterwards then came home to eat Tagliolini! Playboy came out today!

BROADCAST TICKETS

47

PLAYBOY

PL
ENTERTAINMENT

349

COAT ROOM
IN CASE OF
CLAIM BEFORE
Not Respo
Contents of
anything lef

New York City

NBC

DOROZZIO

Name SIGNORELLI, JIM
Program SNL AIR
Program date 1-16-93 2
No. Tickets
From

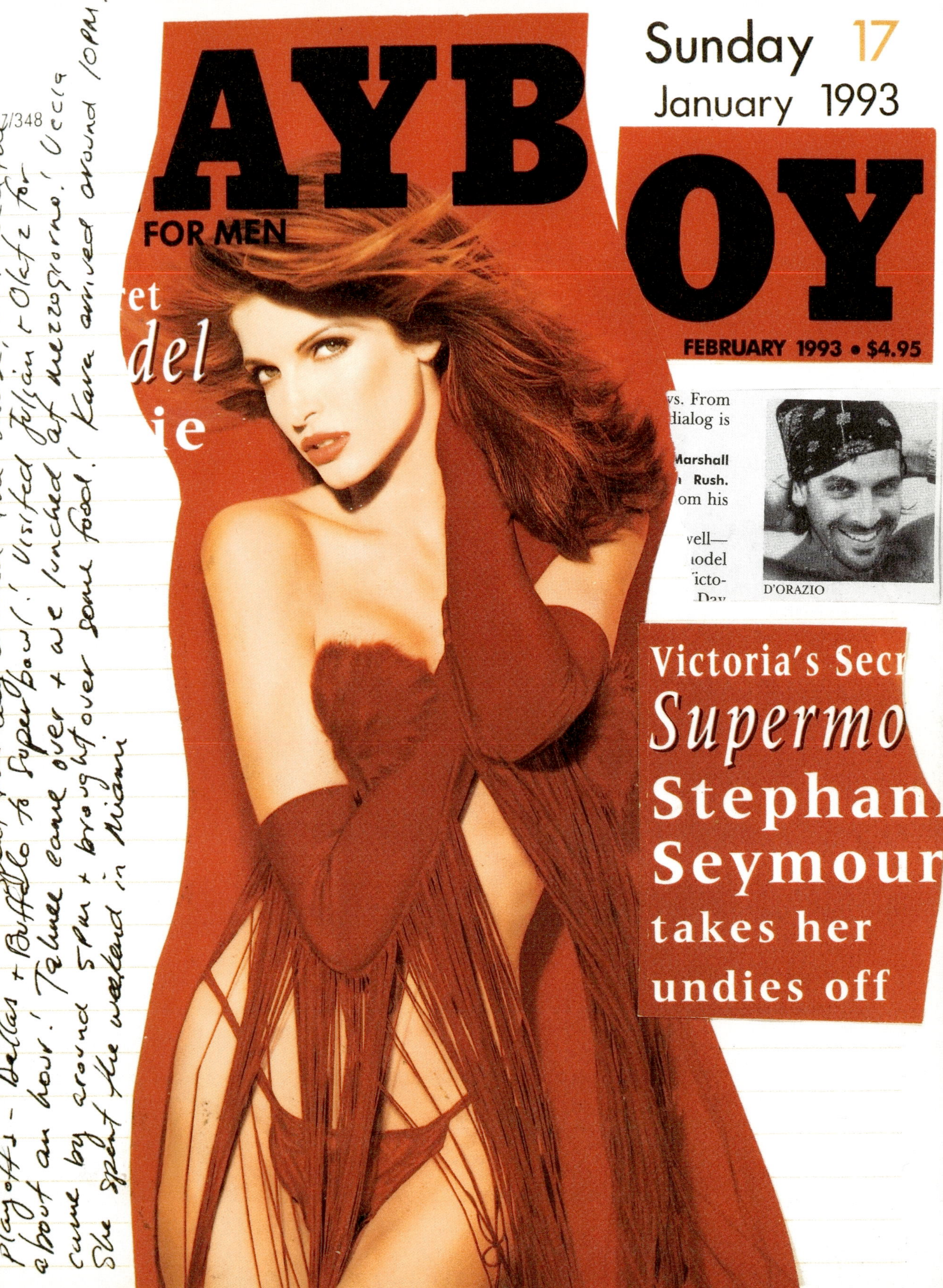

17/348
Playoffs - Dallas + Buffalo to Superbowl! Visited Julian + Okatz for about an hour! Talmee came over + we lunched at mezzogiorno. Uccia came by around 5PM + brought over some food! Kara arrived around 10PM! She spent the weekend in Miami.
AYB
OY
FOR MEN
Sunday 17 January 1993
FEBRUARY 1993 • $4.95
D'ORAZIO
vs. From
dialog is
Marshall
Rush.
om his
vell—
odel
icto-
Day
Victoria's Secr
Supermo
Stephan
Seymour
takes her
undies off

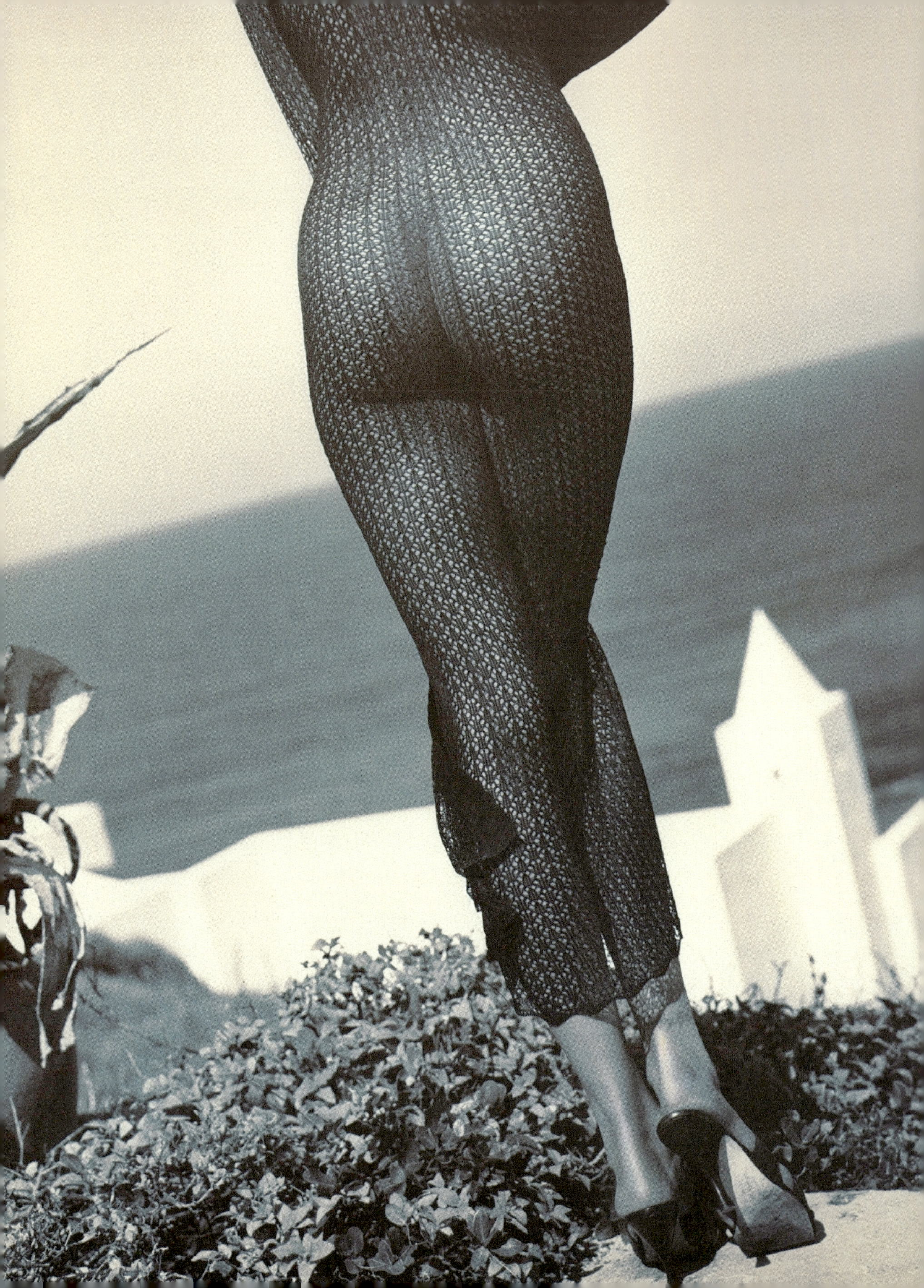

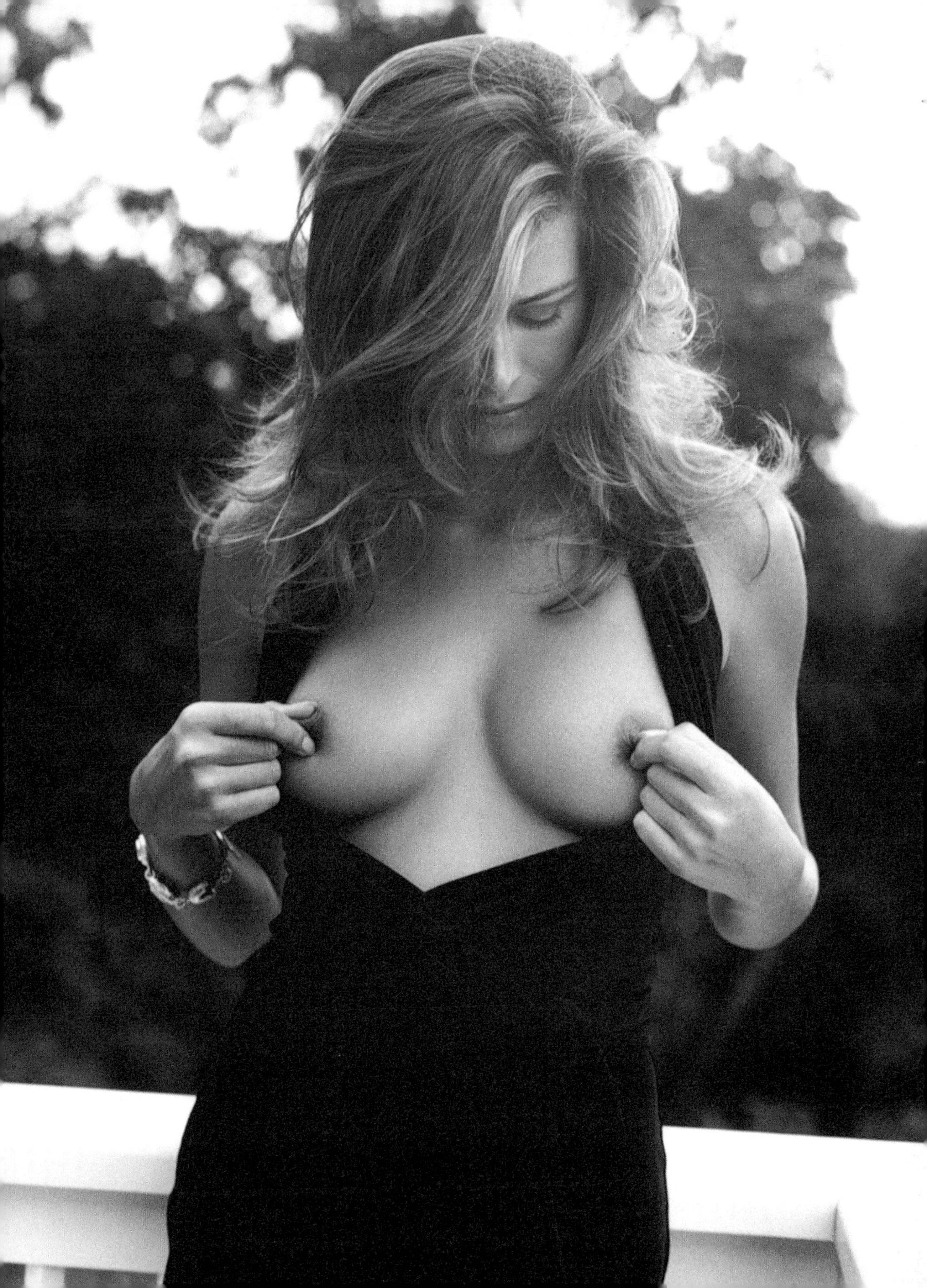

31 Saturday
July 1993
Allure

#93043
Kim Basinger
212/1.

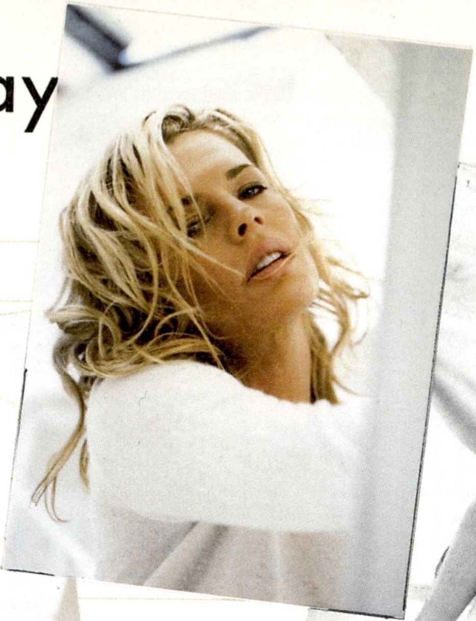

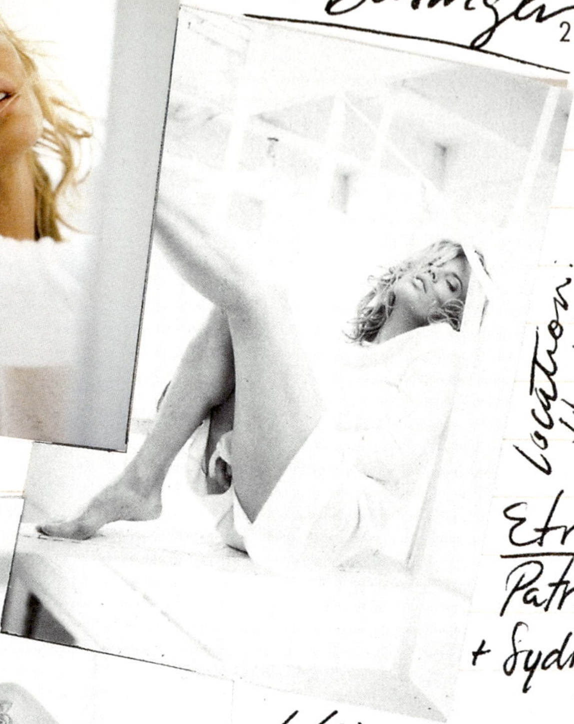

Location: Herbs Studio 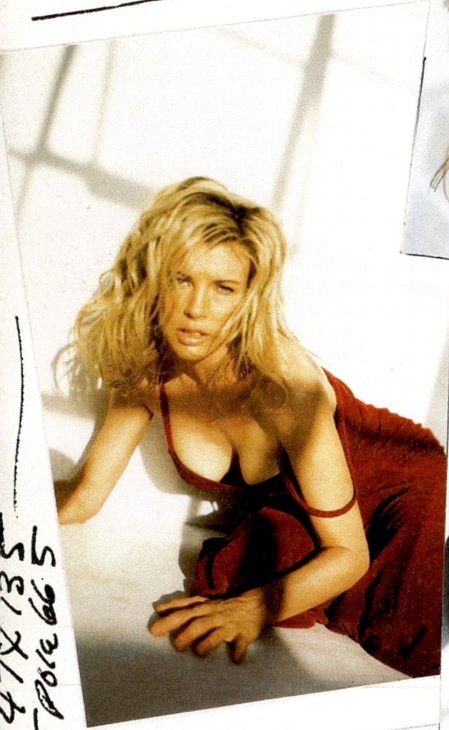
Etr:
Patrice
+ Sydney

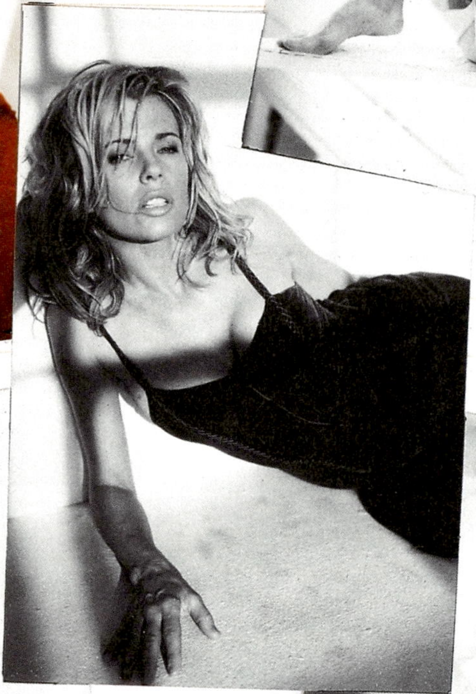

Hair: Peter Savic
MK.UP: Joanne
Garre

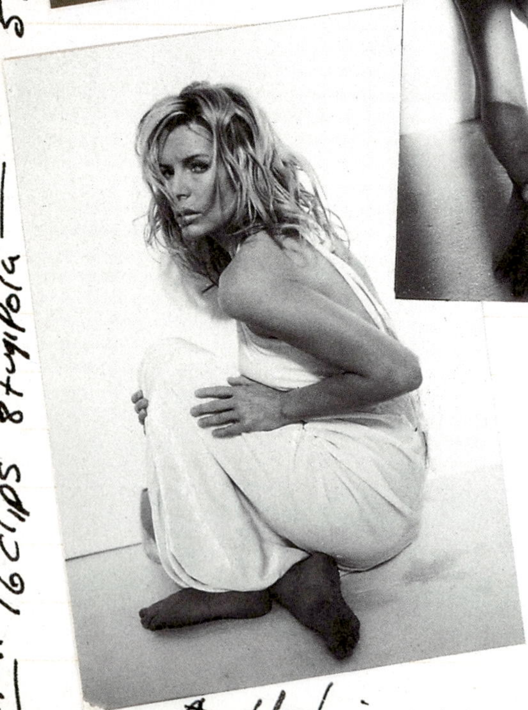

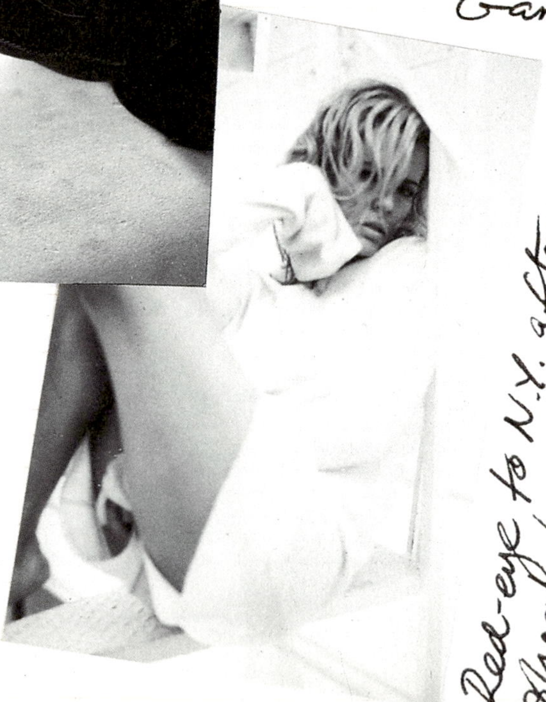

Red-eye to N.Y. after
shoot!

Film: 35Tugi 220   4 1/4 135
16 Clips   8 TugiPola
5 Pola 665

asst. flubie

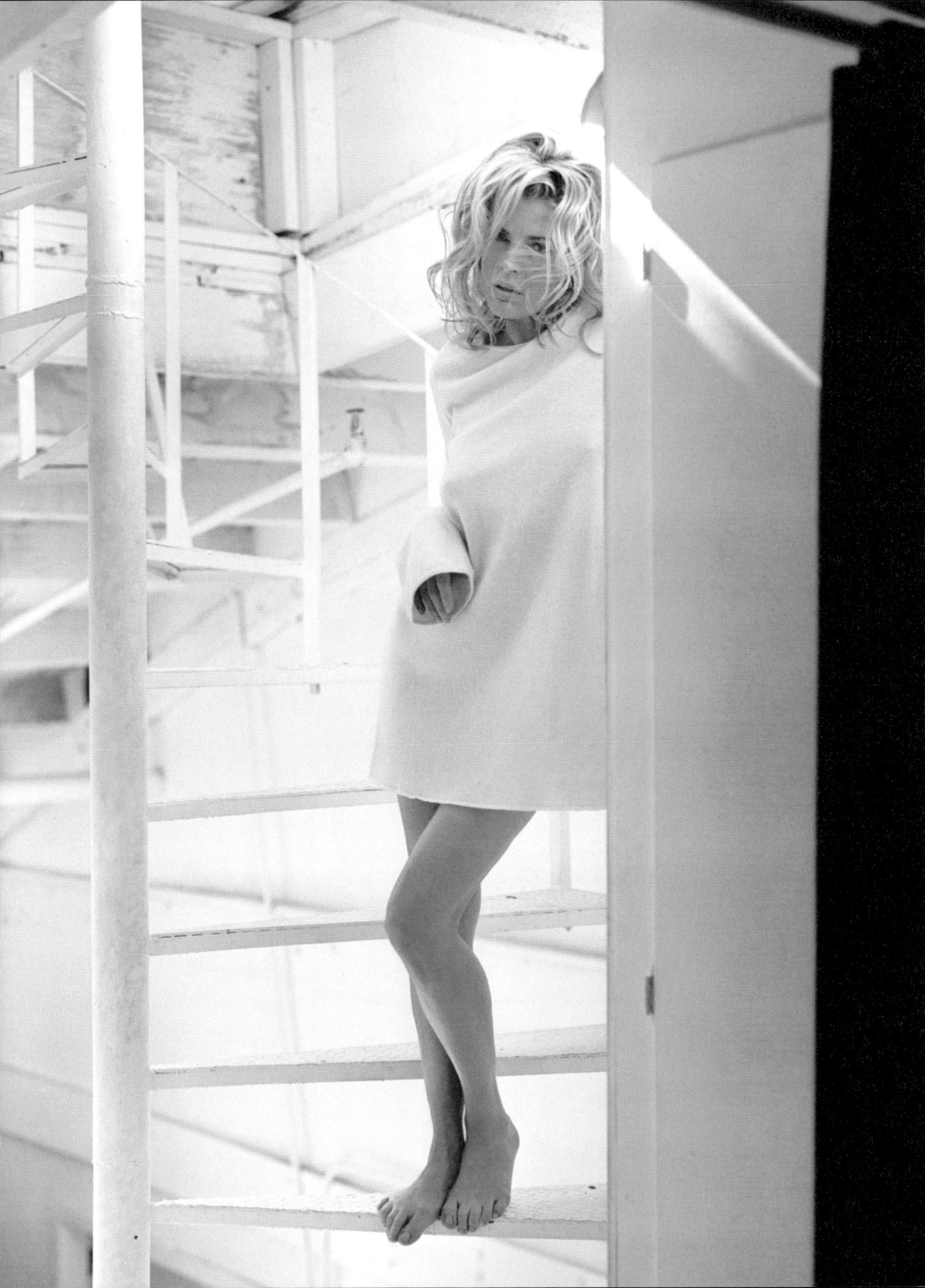

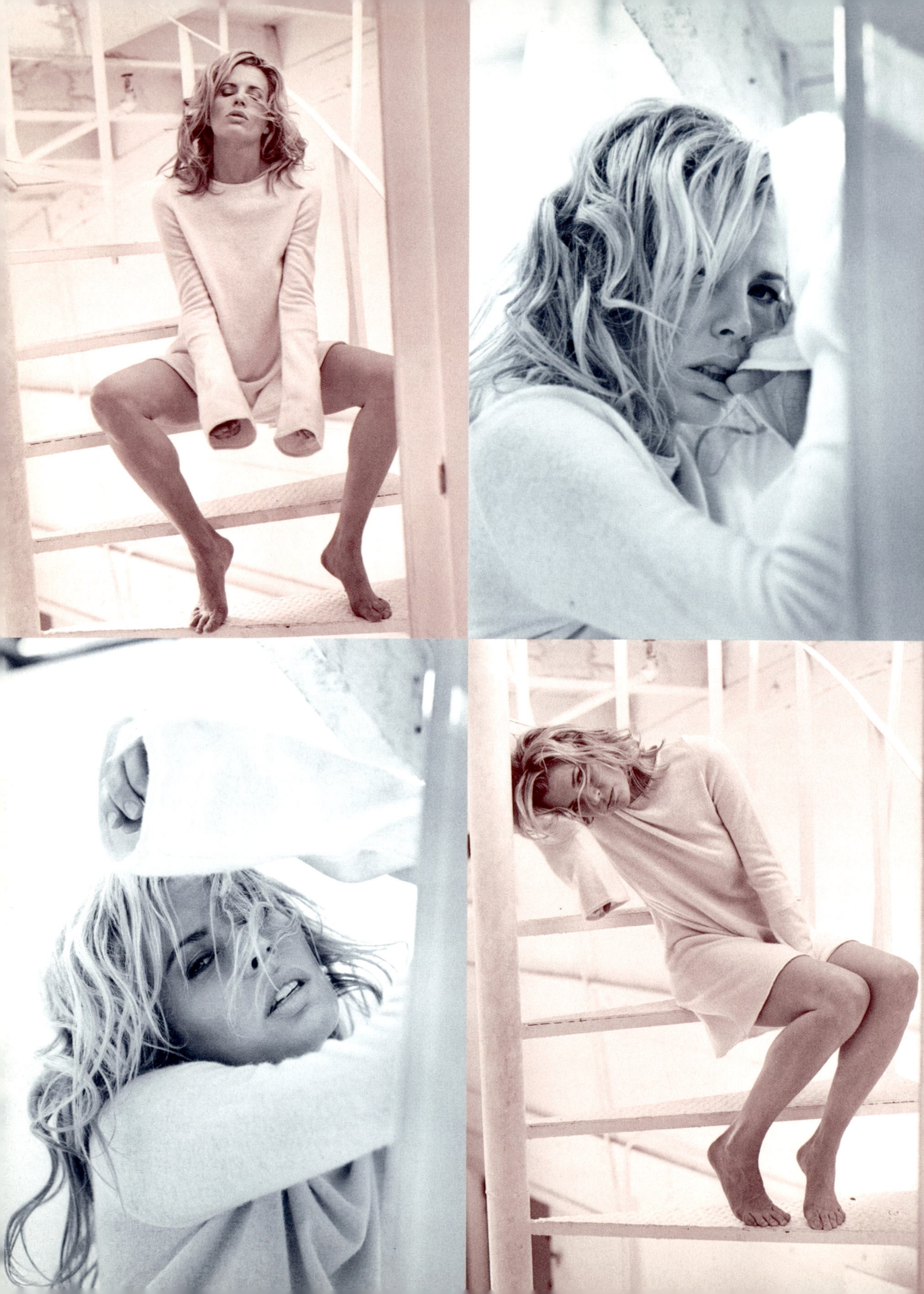

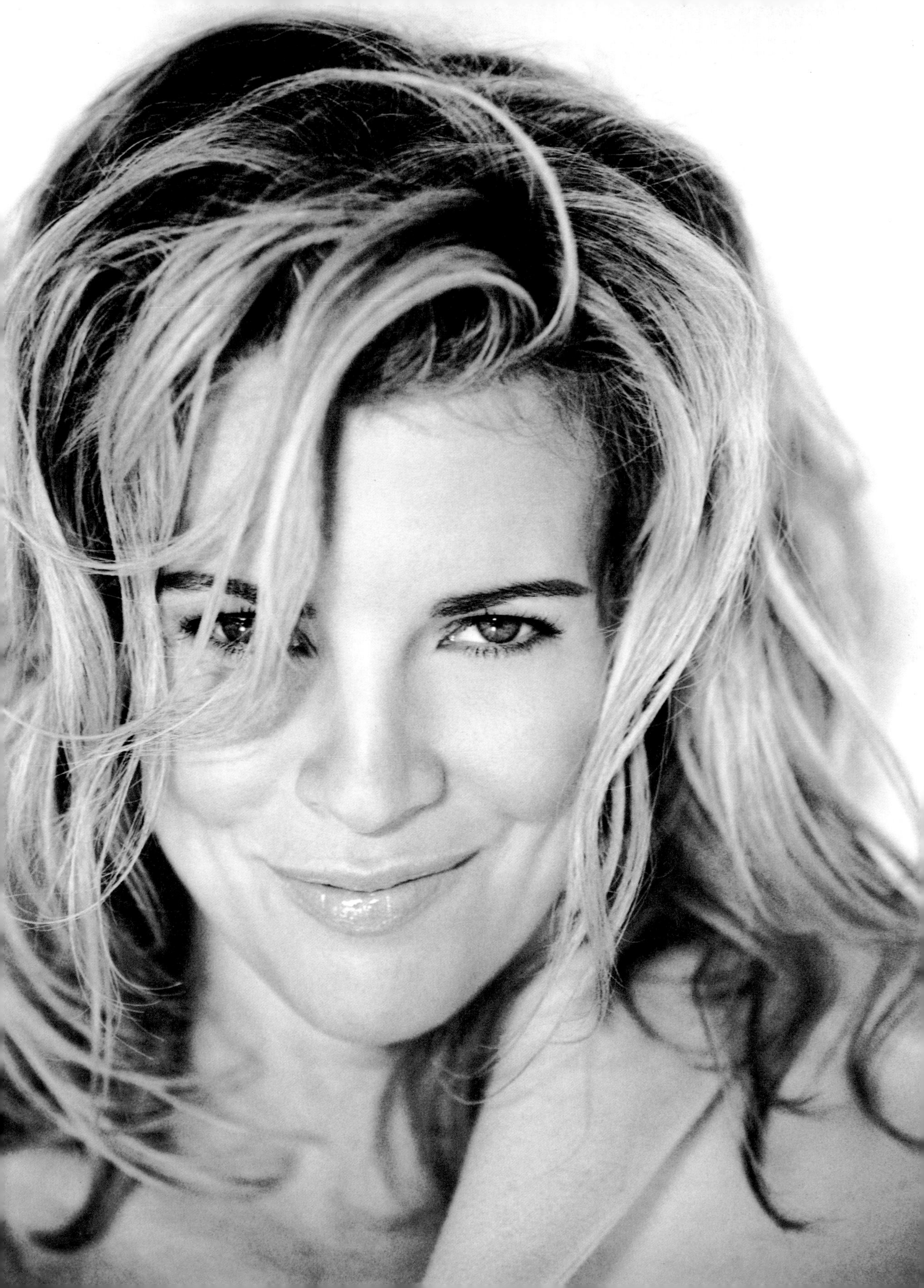

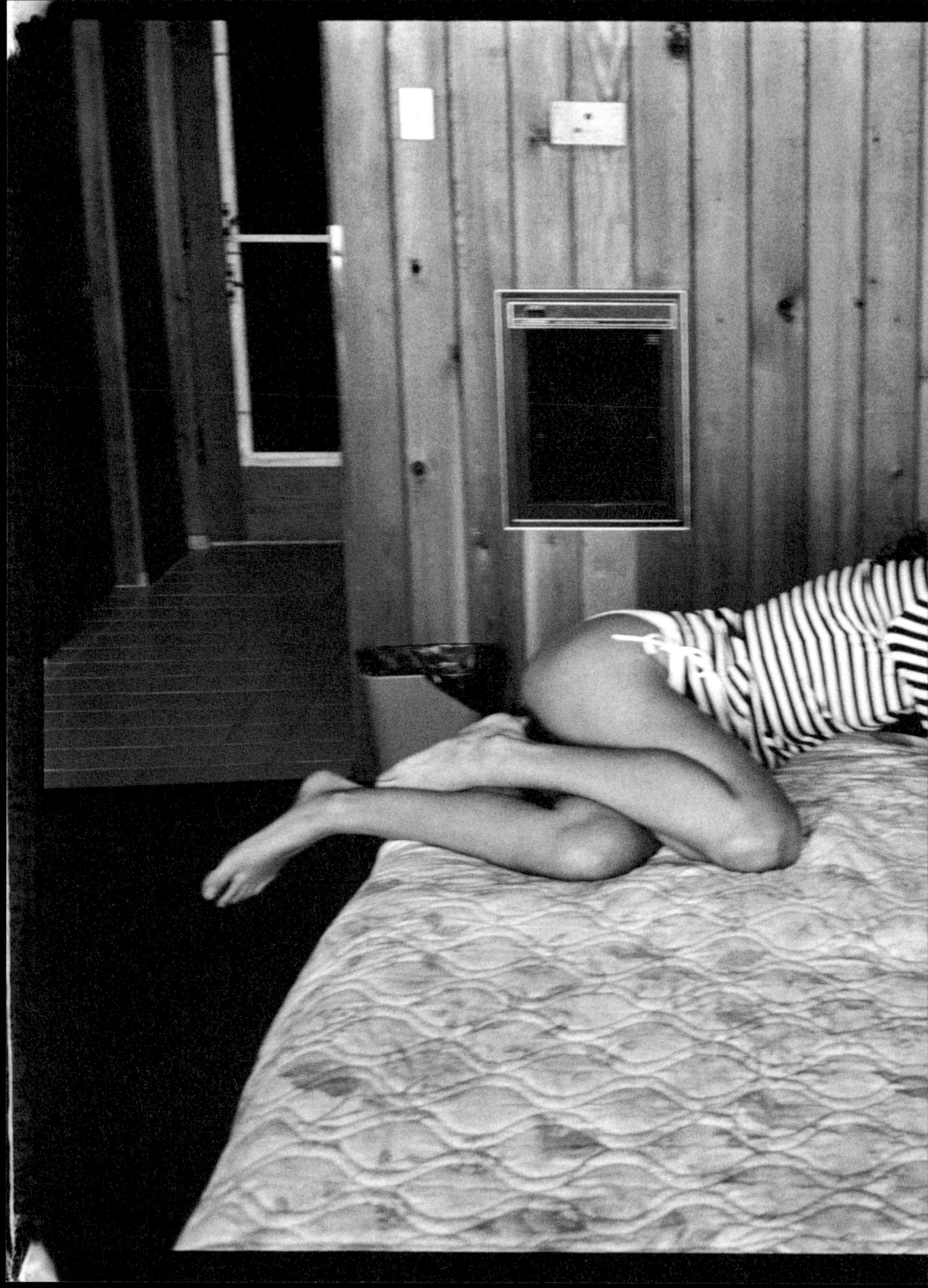

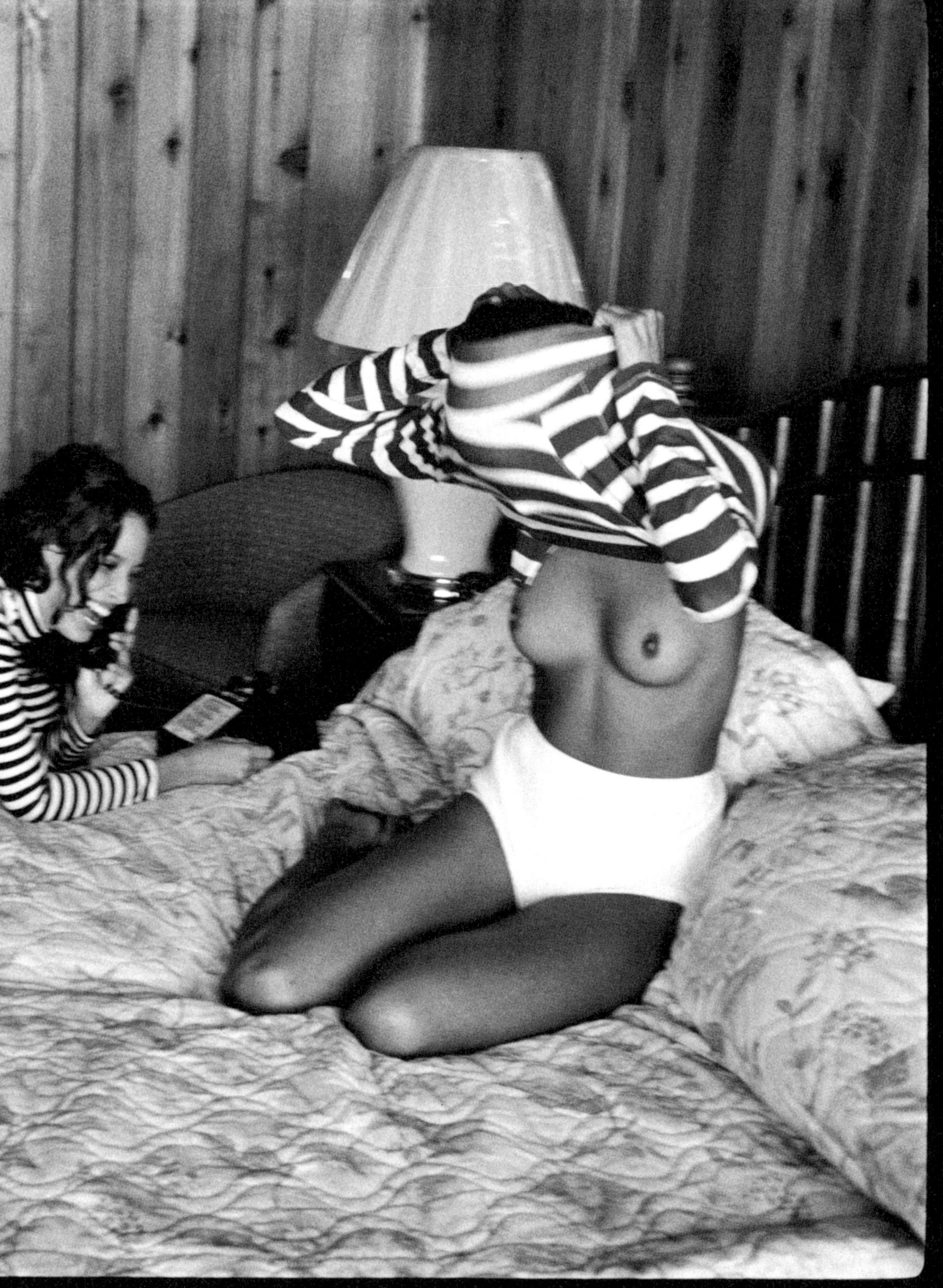

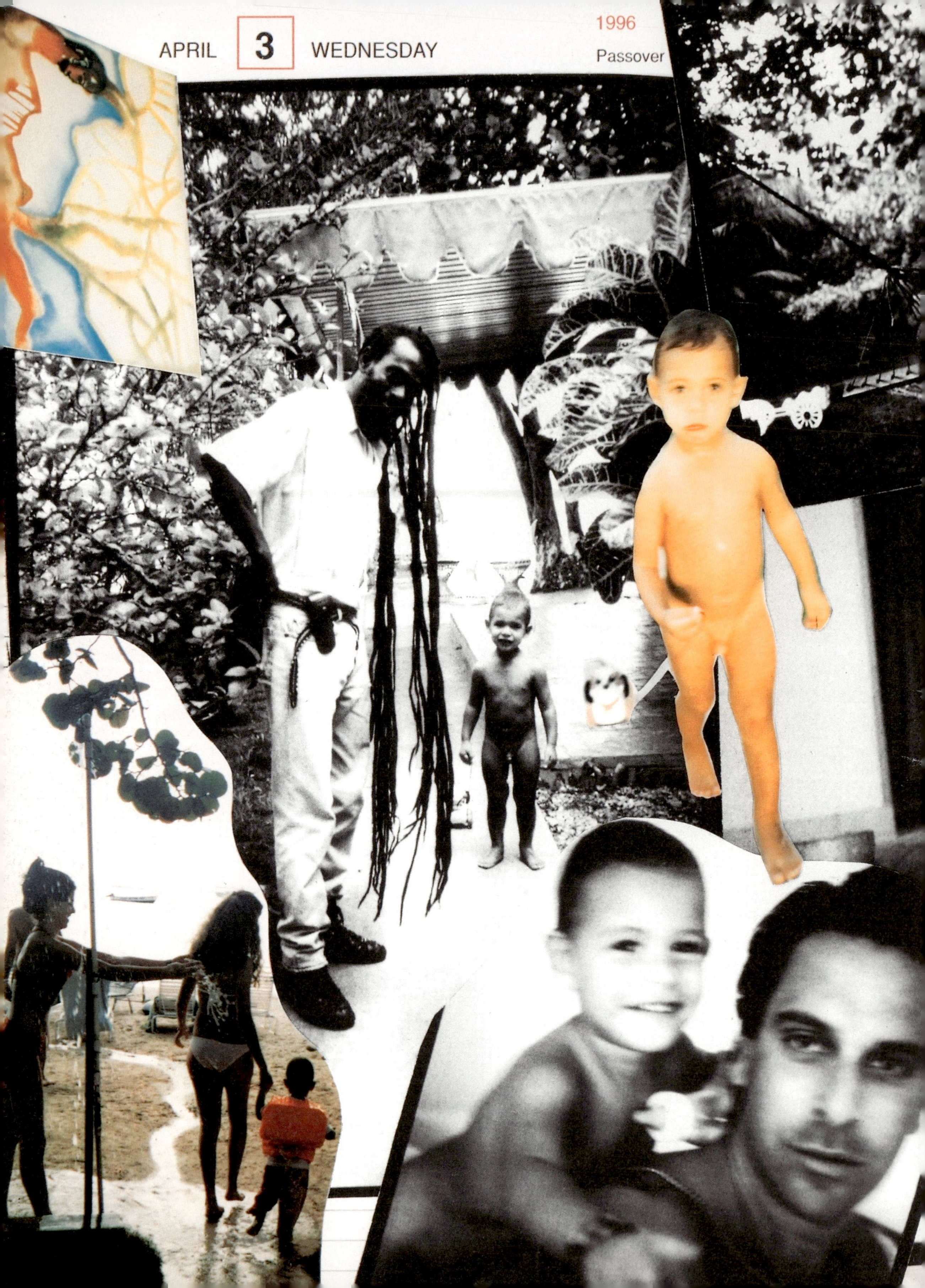

APRIL 3 WEDNESDAY
1996
Passover

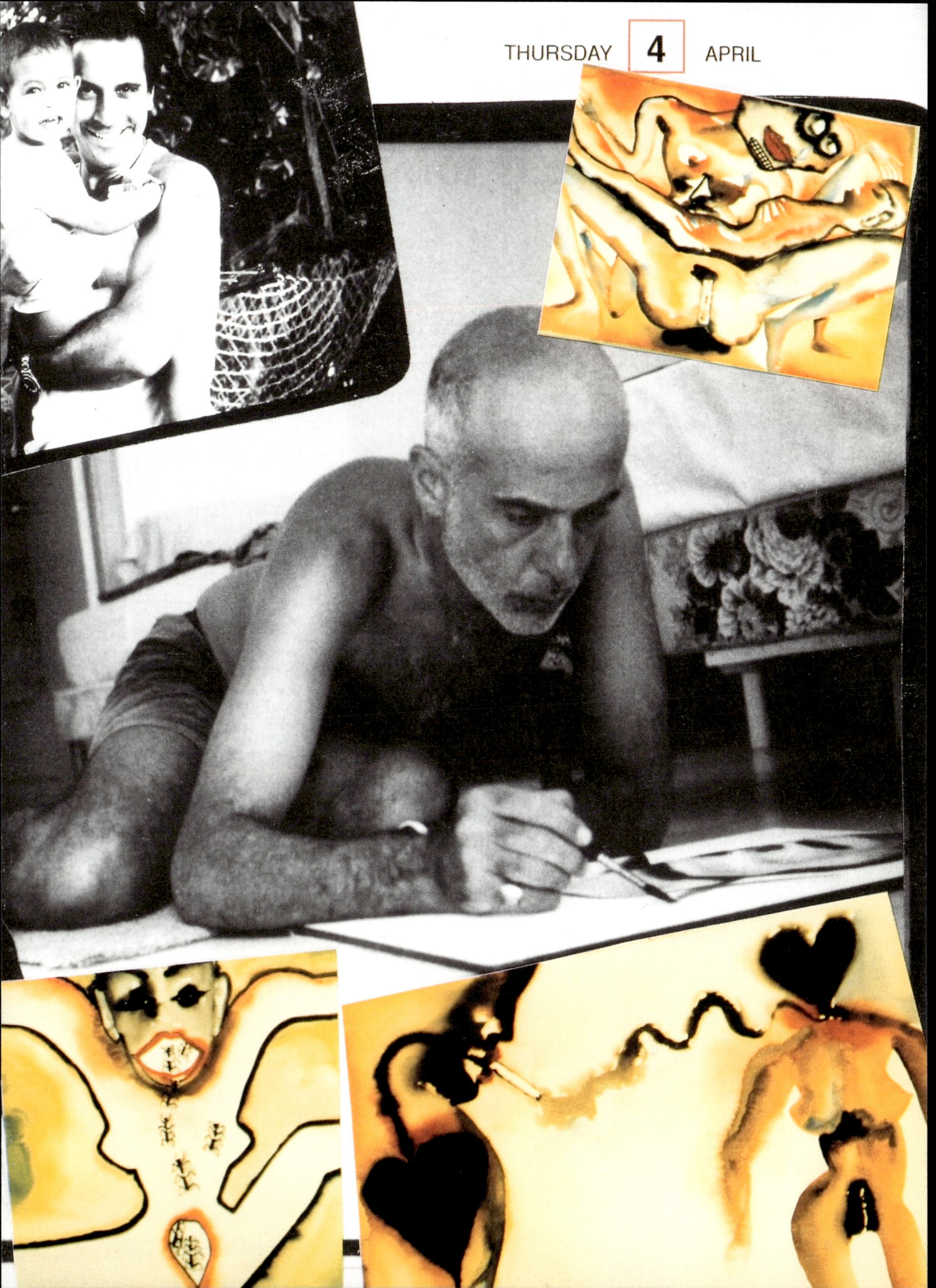

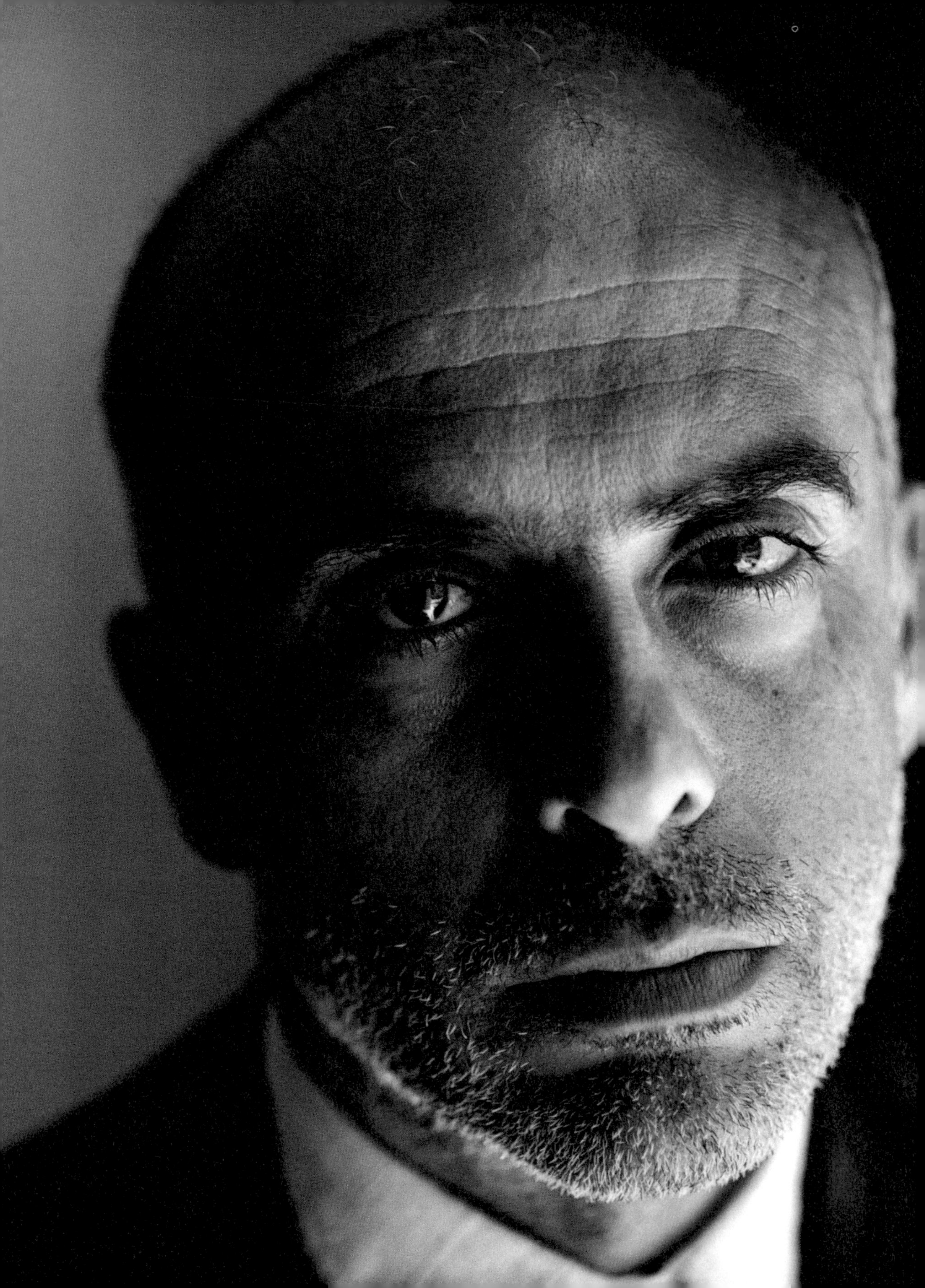

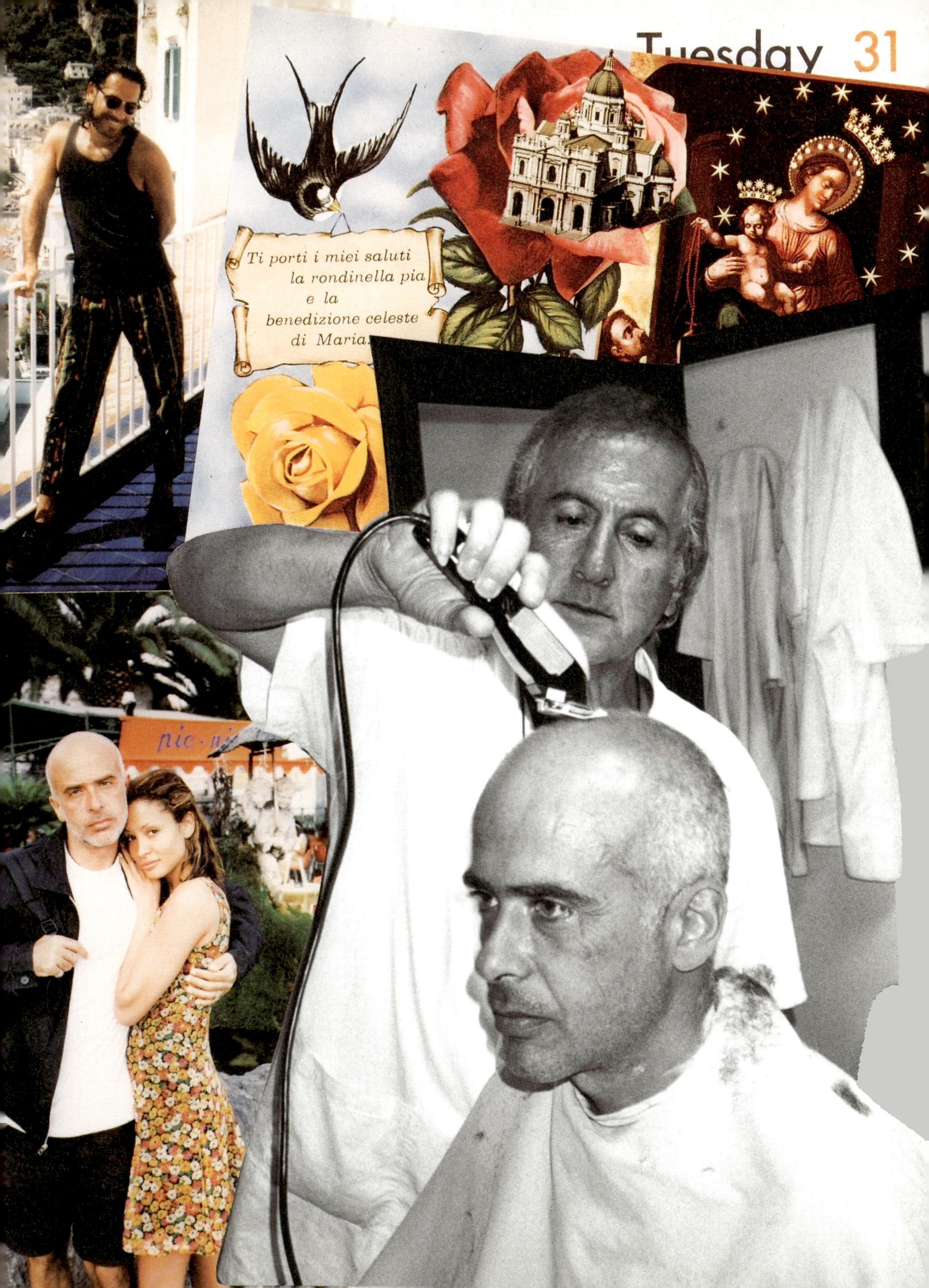

Tuesday 31
Ti porti i miei saluti
la rondinella pia
e la
benedizione celeste
di Maria
pic-nic

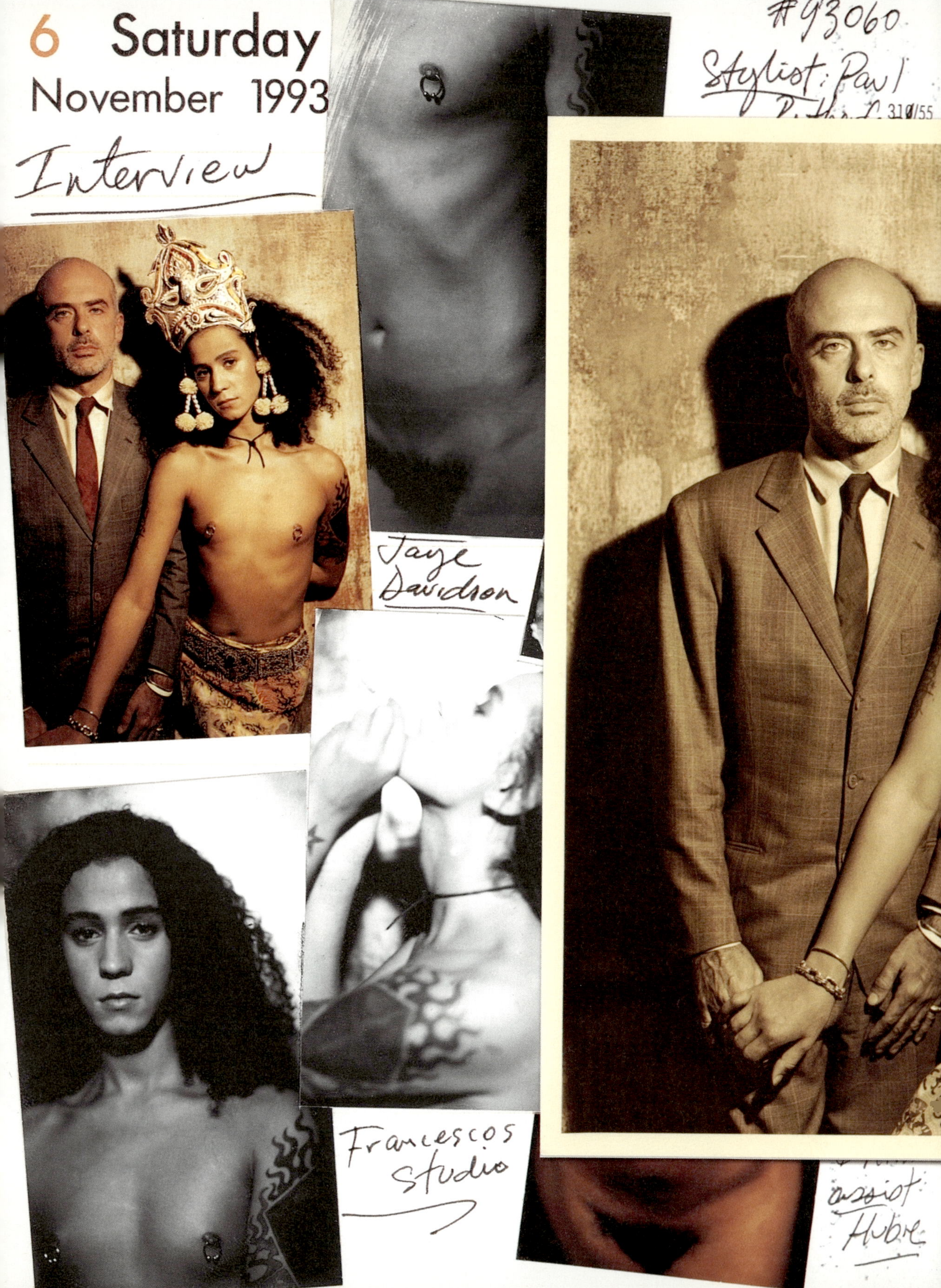
6 Saturday
November 1993
Interview
#93060
Stylist: Paul
Jaye
Davidson
Francescos
Studio

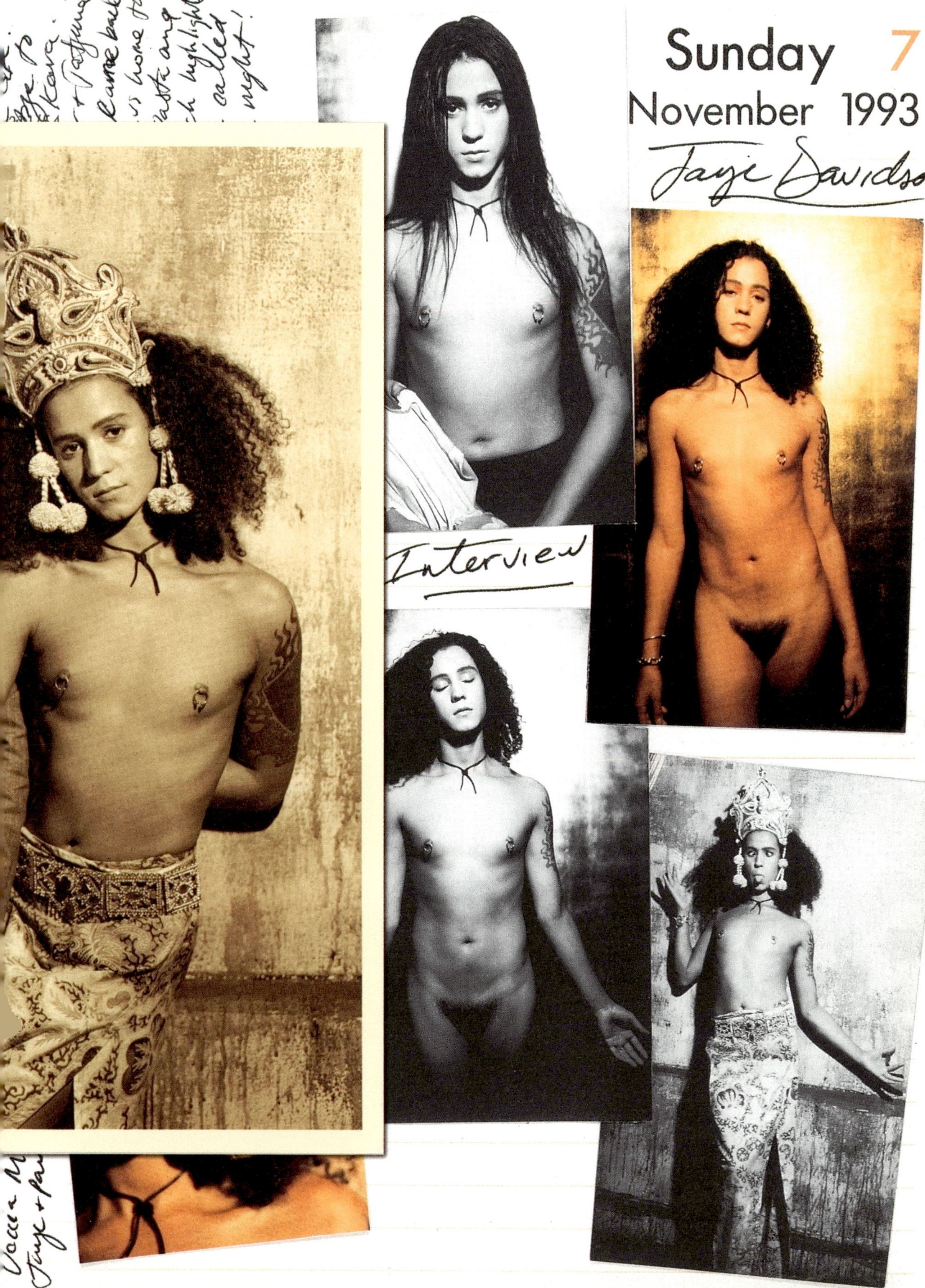

Sunday 7
November 1993
Jaye Davidson
Interview

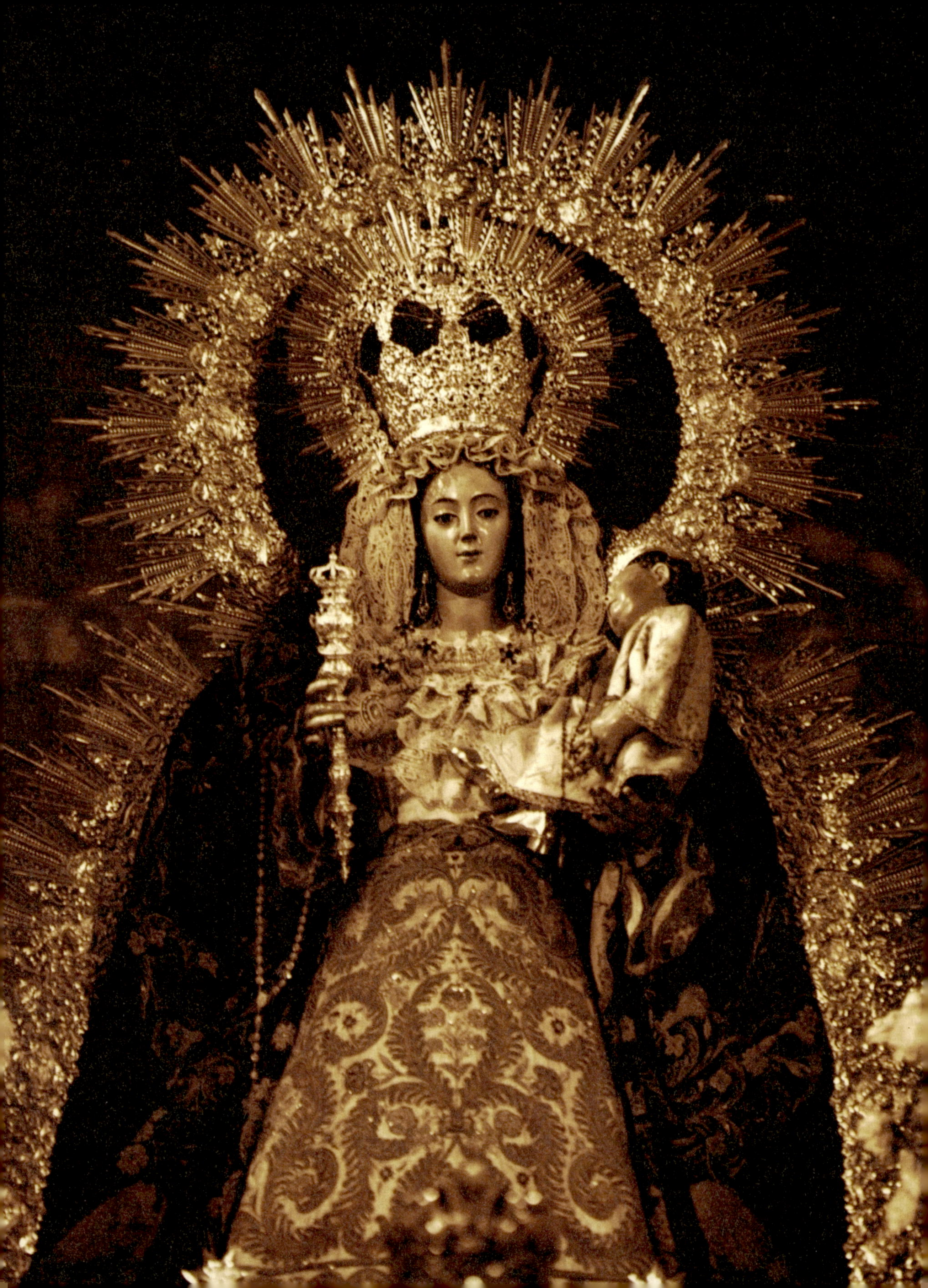

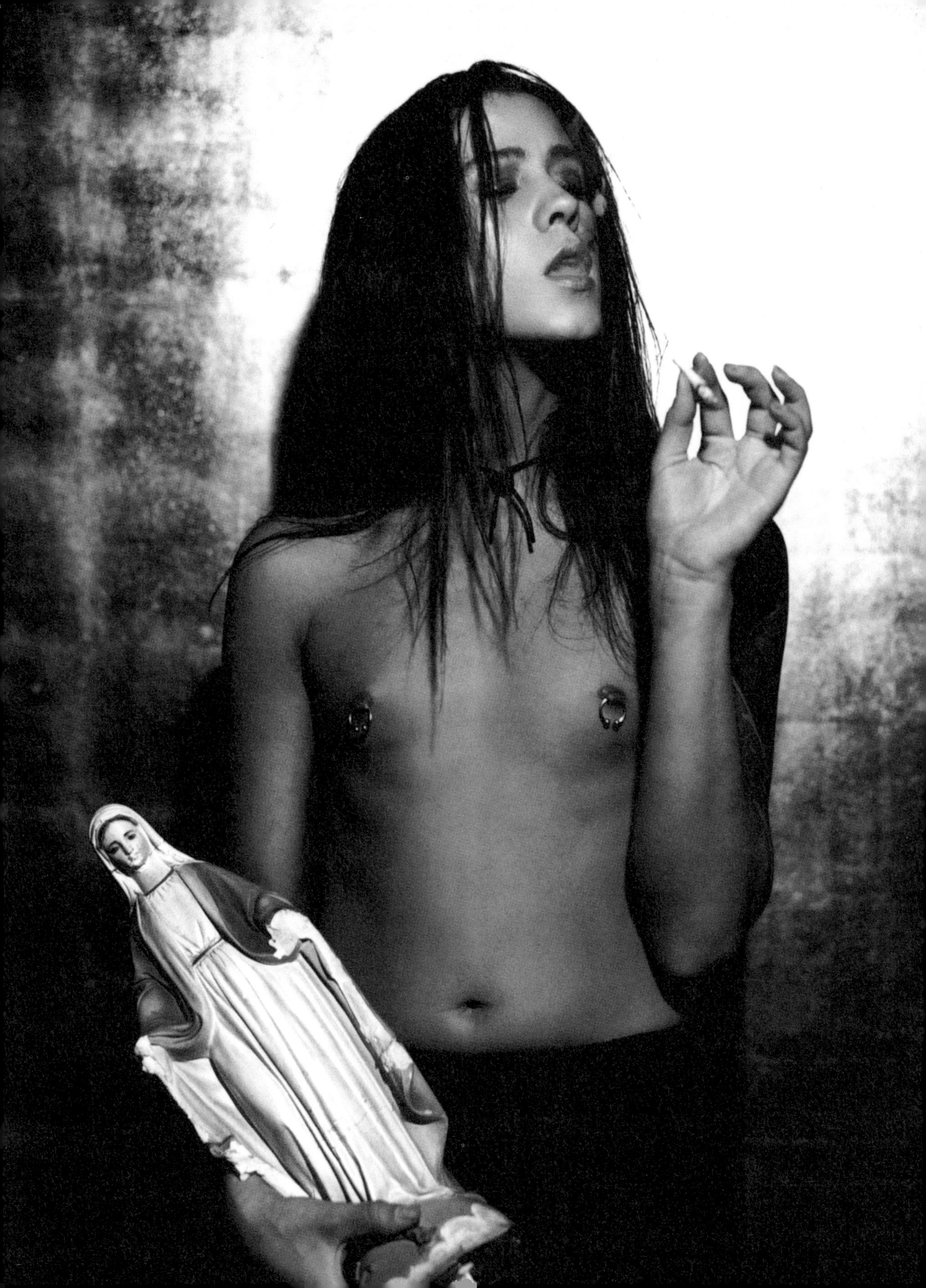

Monday

Kate, Jaye, Paul and me!!

Partied! Went to the shows and had a ball! Cafe Tabac, Jackie60 etc etc..!!

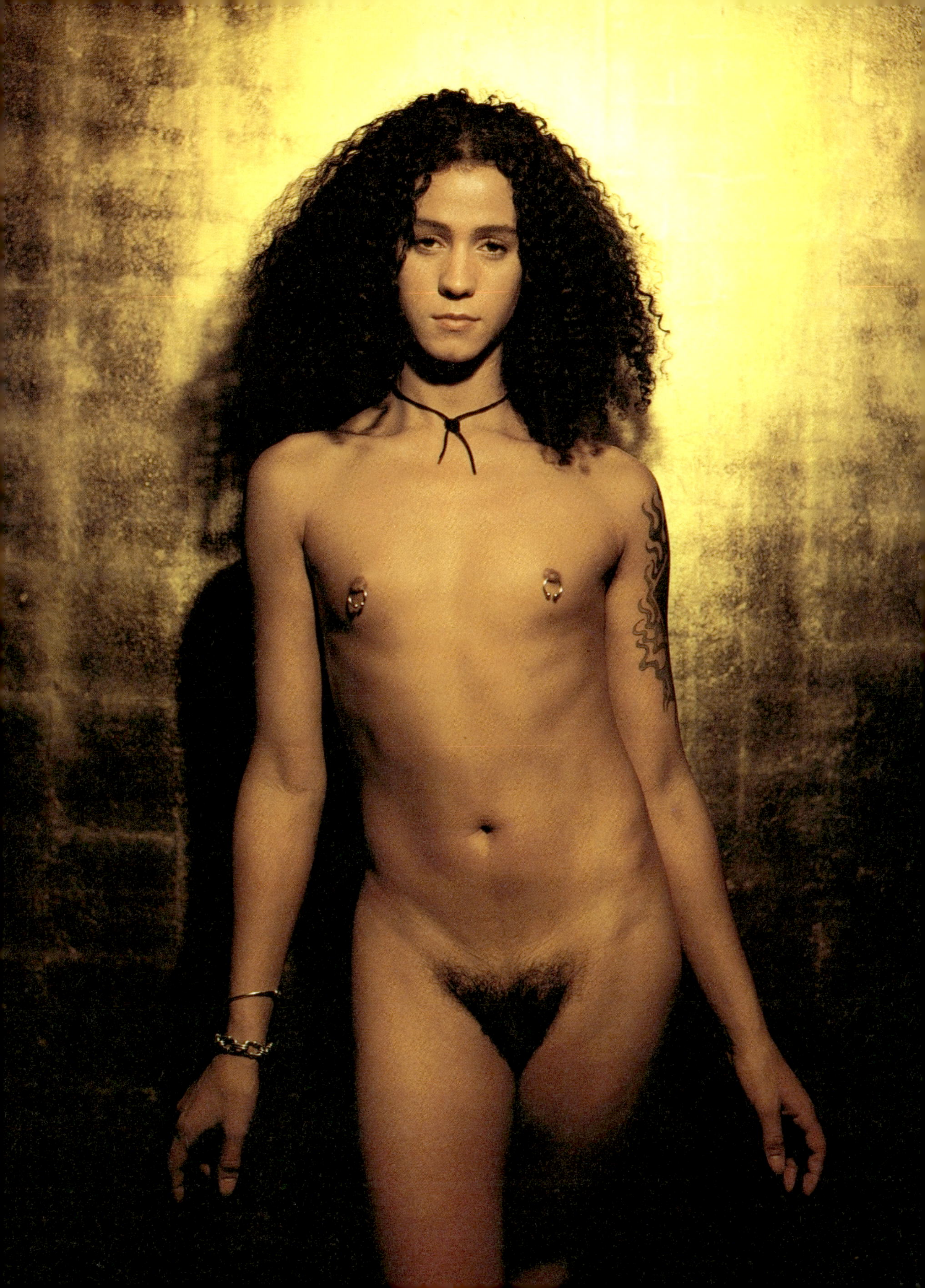

* SAMMY SCREENING
28 Wednesday
October 1992
#9205b
302/
allure
Kate Moss-
Tribeca Films Center Cafe Tabac
Etc: Polly Mellen
Hair: Kevin Mancuso
MK.UP: Sonia Kasuk
Film: 52 Fugi 220
24 clips
10 Pola
14 TX 220
4 TX 135
3 Fugi 135
assist: Hubie + Christiane

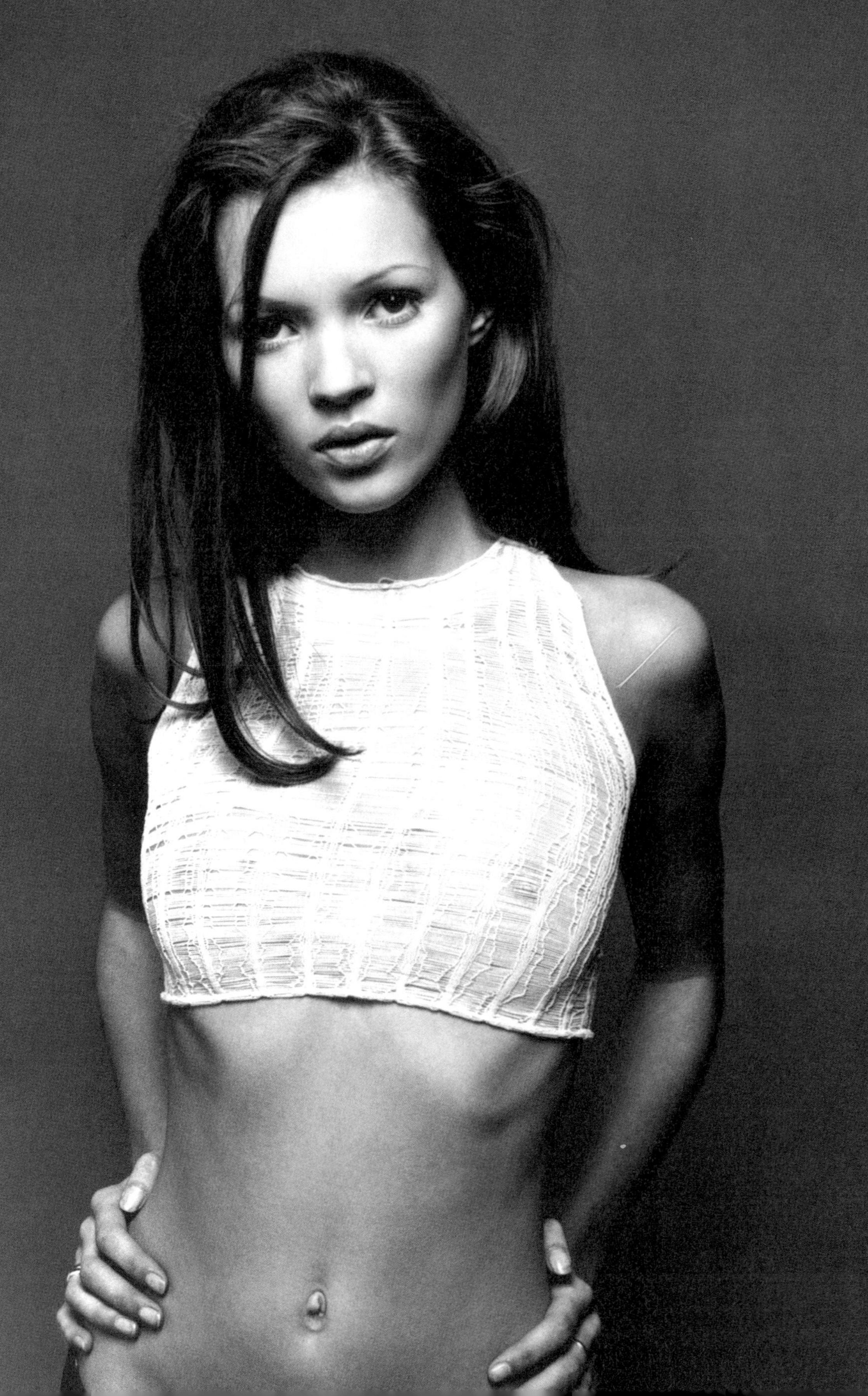

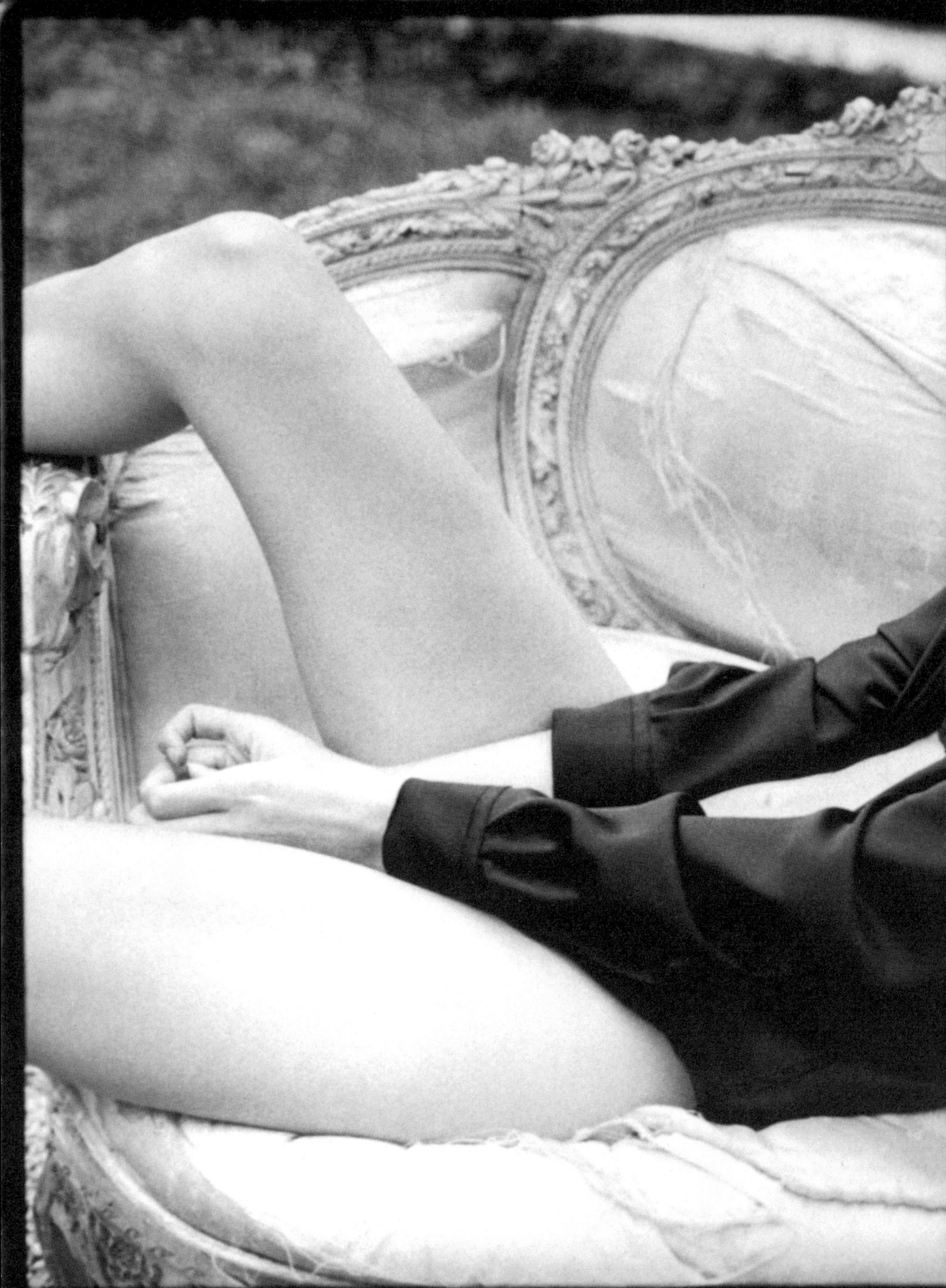

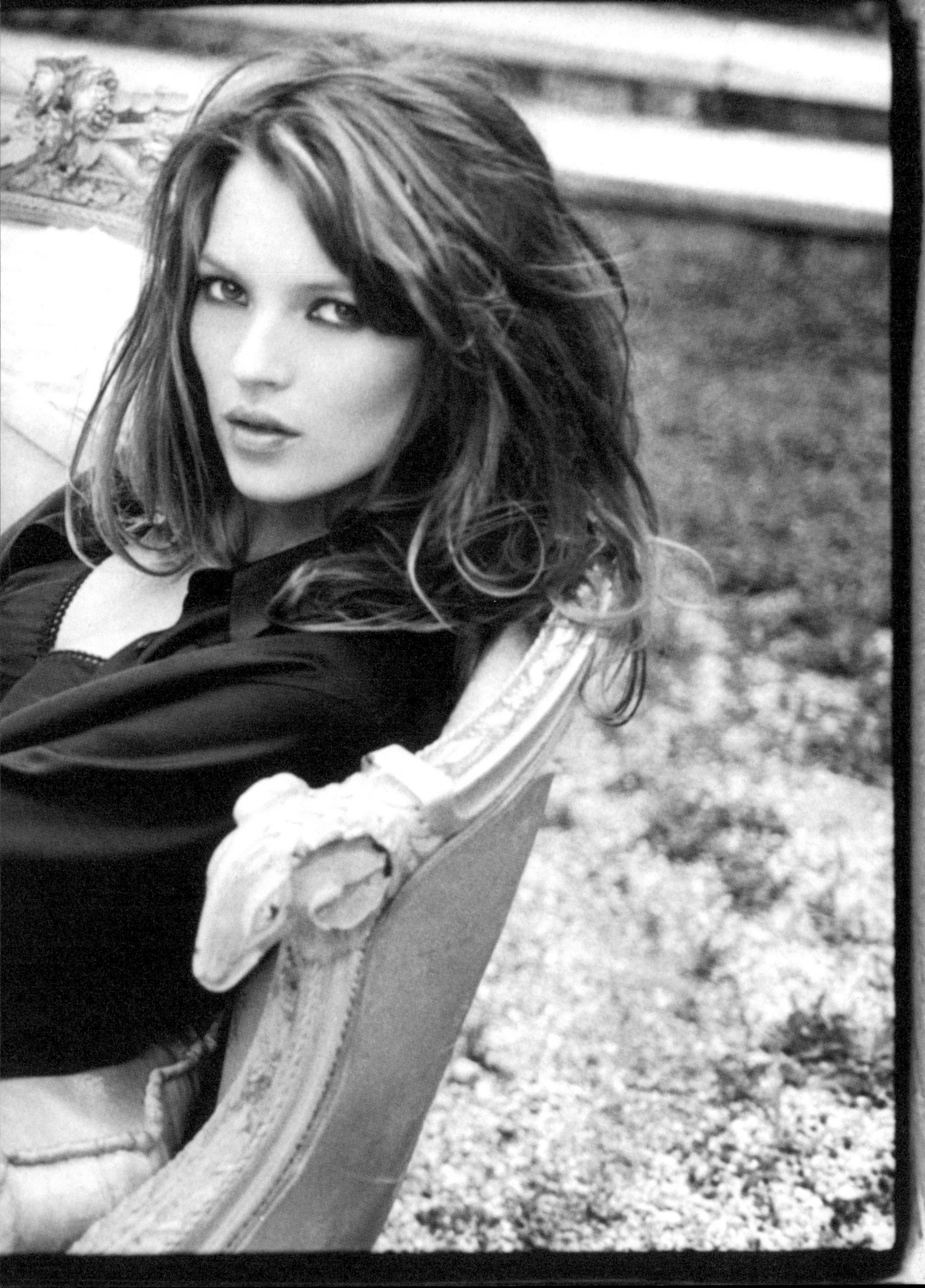

MAY **22** MONDAY

Naomi's birthday!

1:30 apptnt with Dr. Merrill. Went to Barolo afterwards to meet up with Cara, Nick, Edie, Naomi Kate Moss, Linda + Kyle, Sam McKnight + Russell for lunch + Champagne. Came back to the loft for more champagne + we played charades + partied - Naomi's Birthday. After they left got ourselves together for dinner party at Tabac. Faye + Edie came over + we went together, got home by midnight!

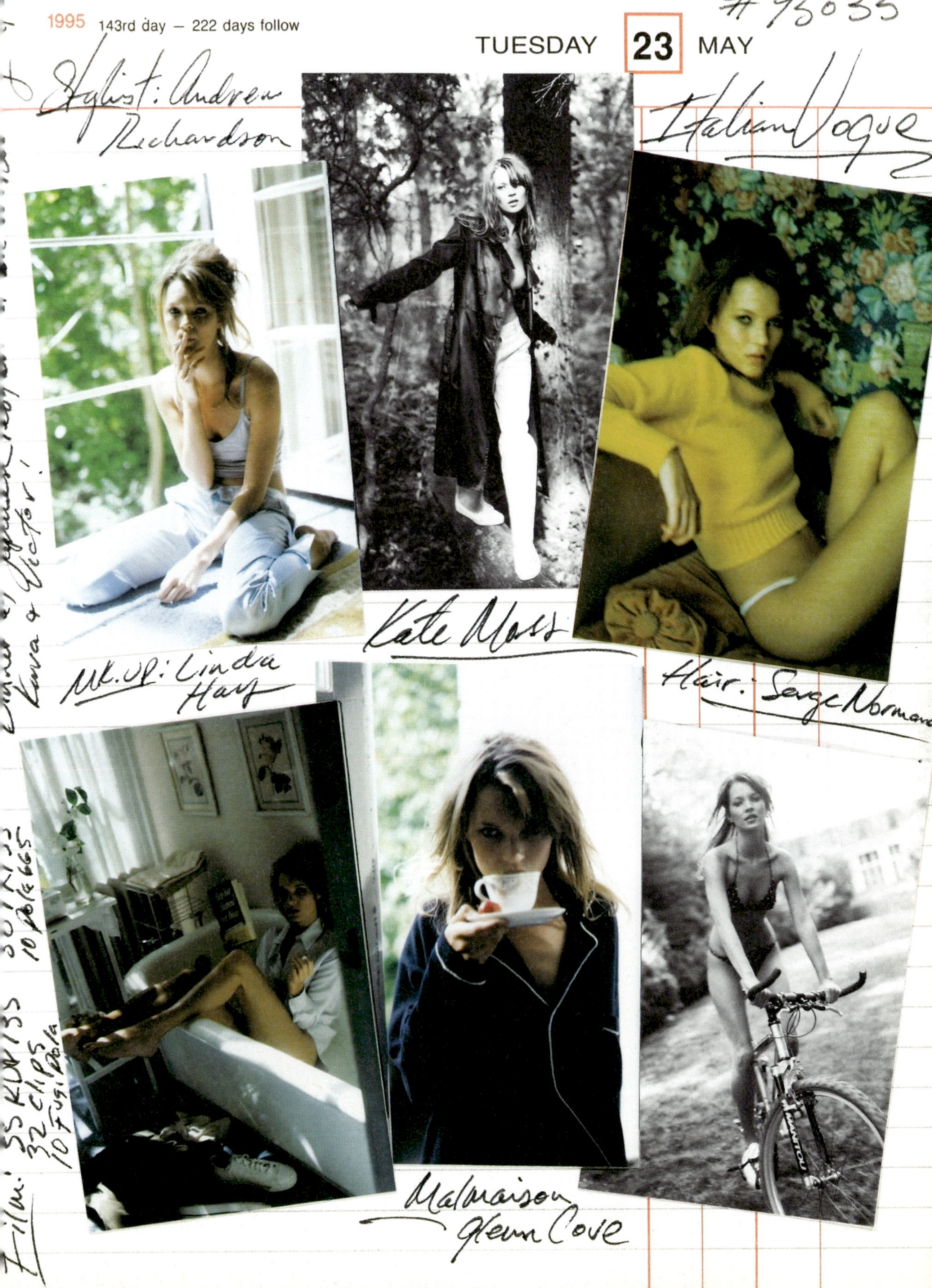

1995 143rd day — 222 days follow
TUESDAY 23 MAY
75035
Stylist: Andrew Richardson
Italian Vogue
Kate Moss
Mk. Up: Linda Hay
Hair: Serge Normant
Malmaison
Glenn Cove

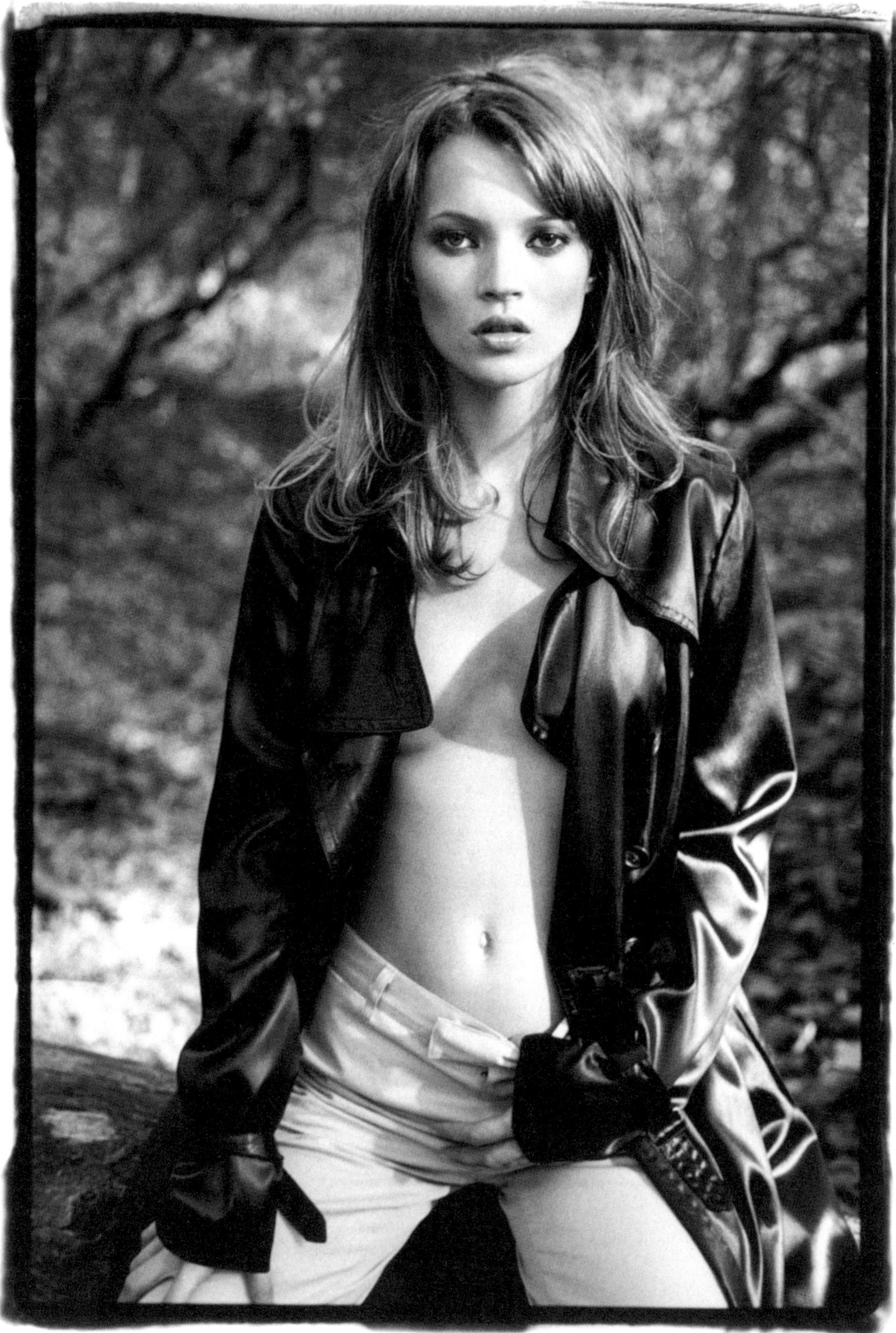

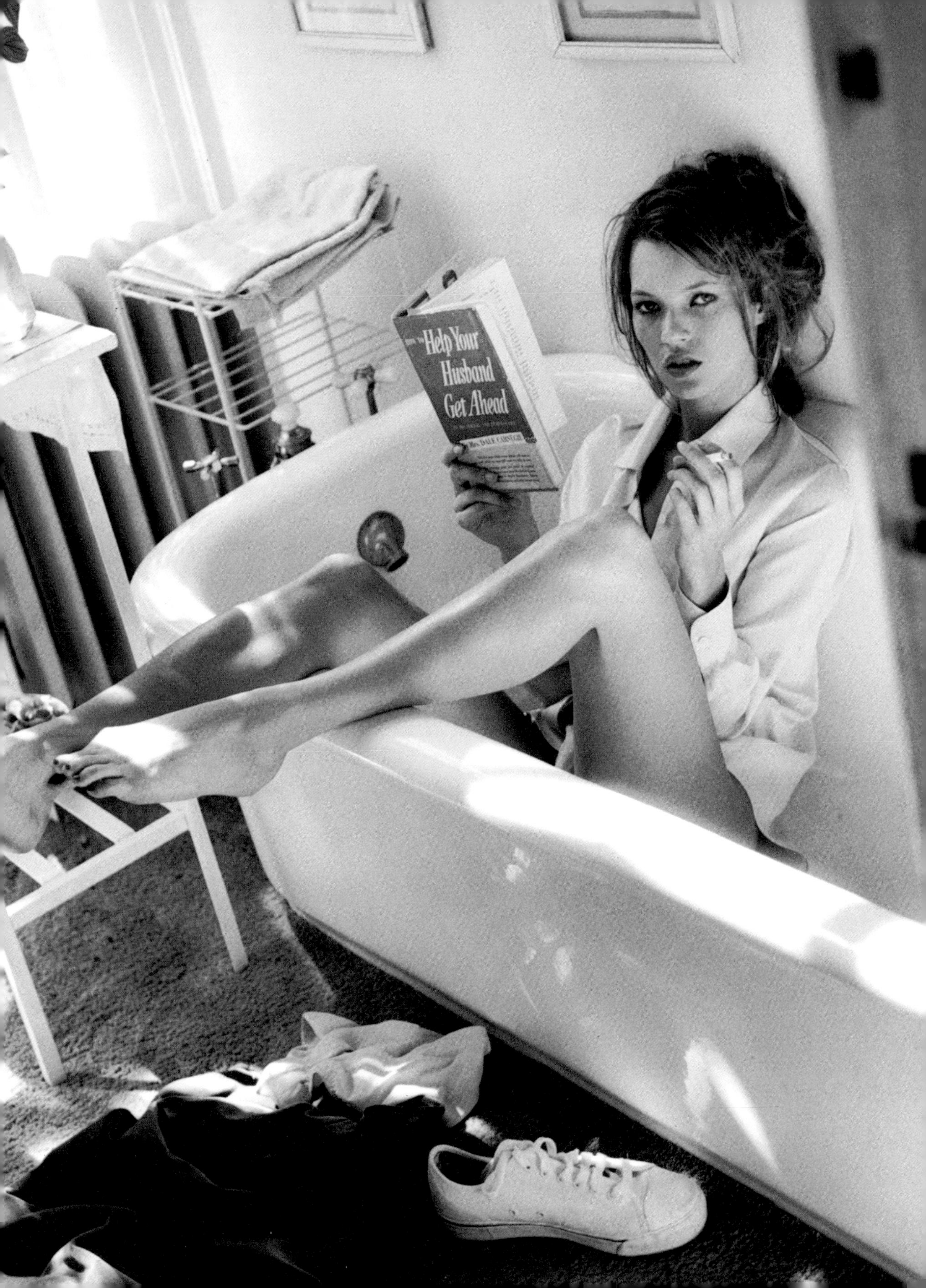
Help Your
Husband
Get Ahead
Mrs. DALE CARNEGIE

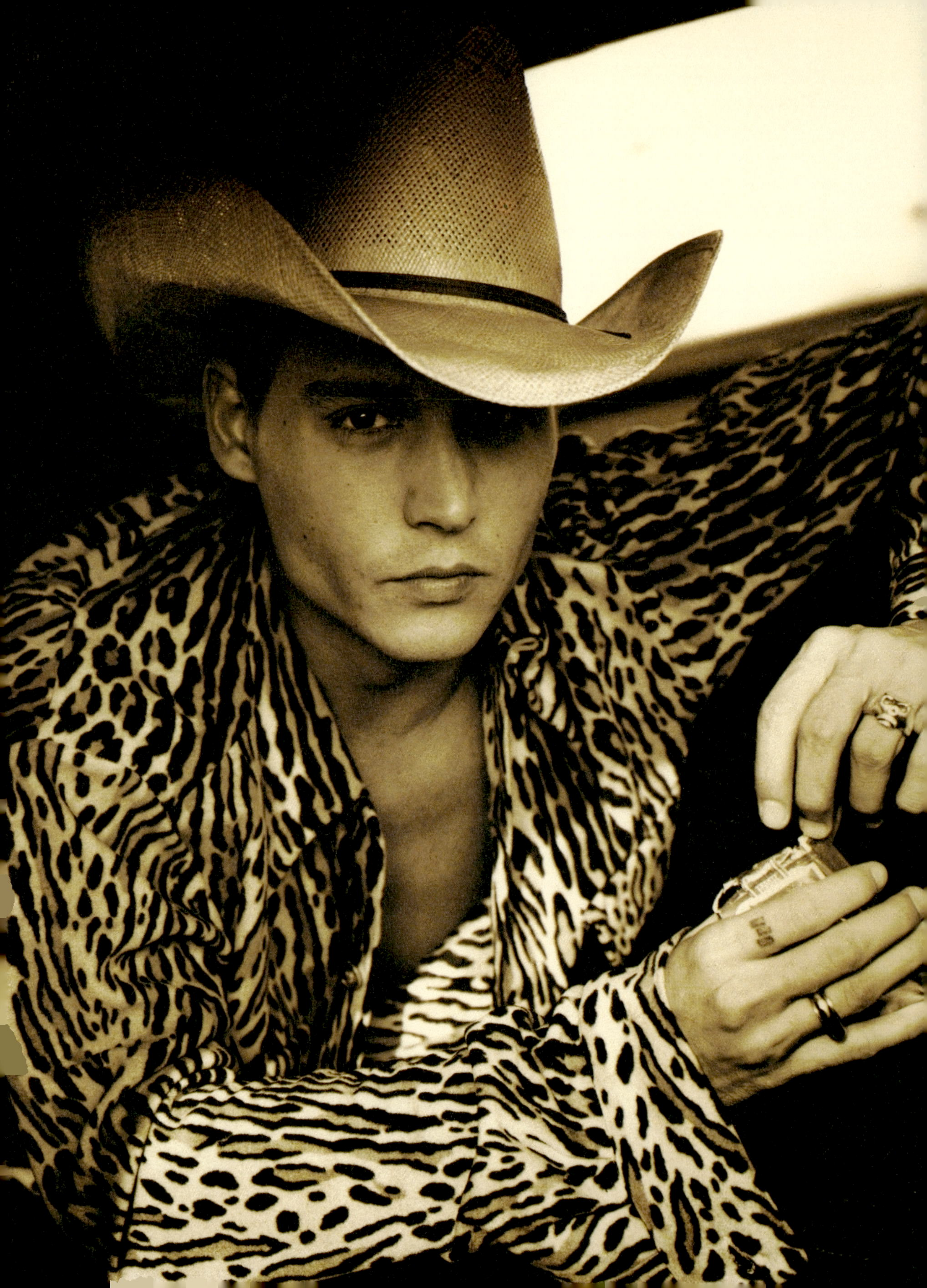

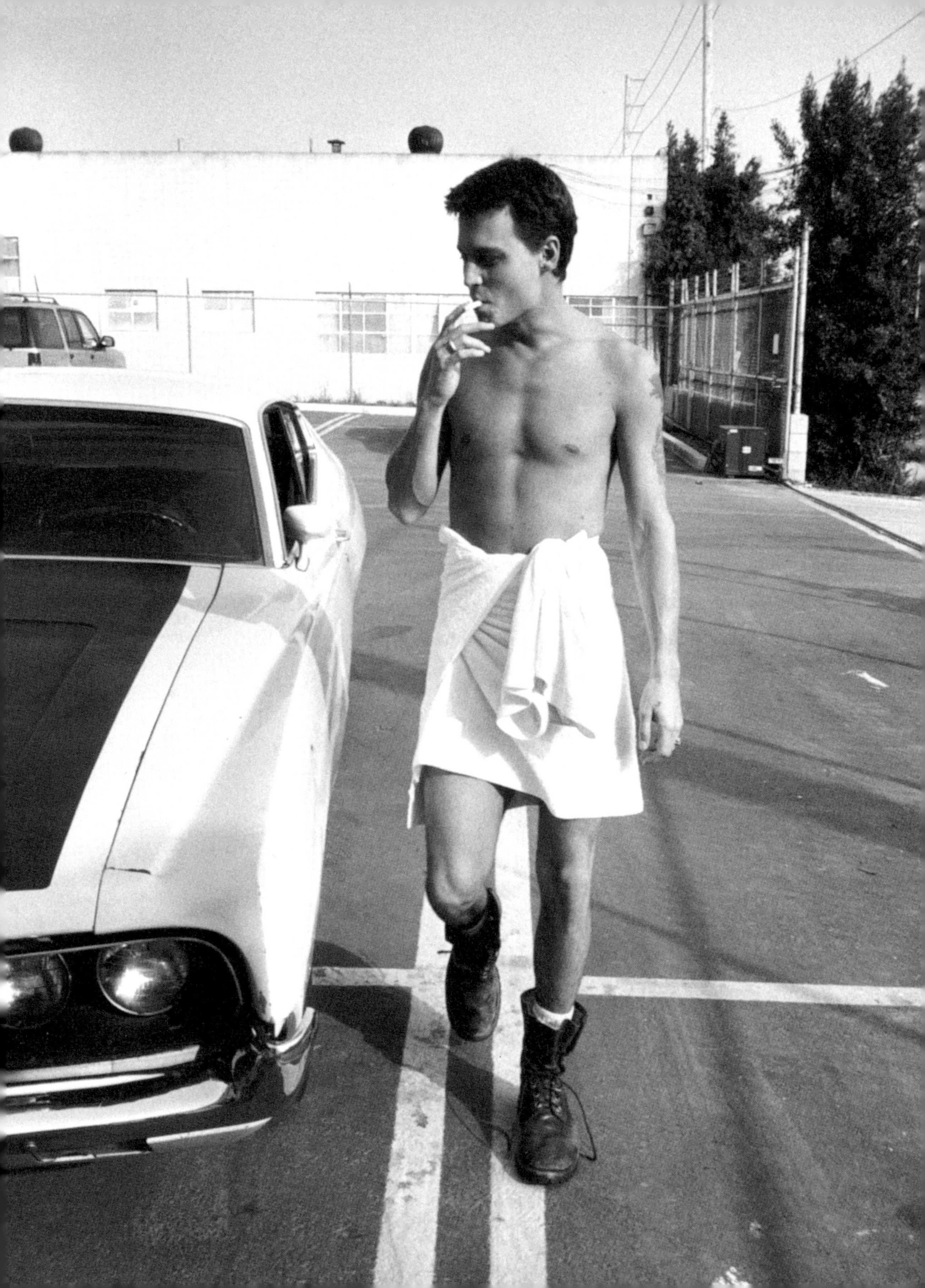

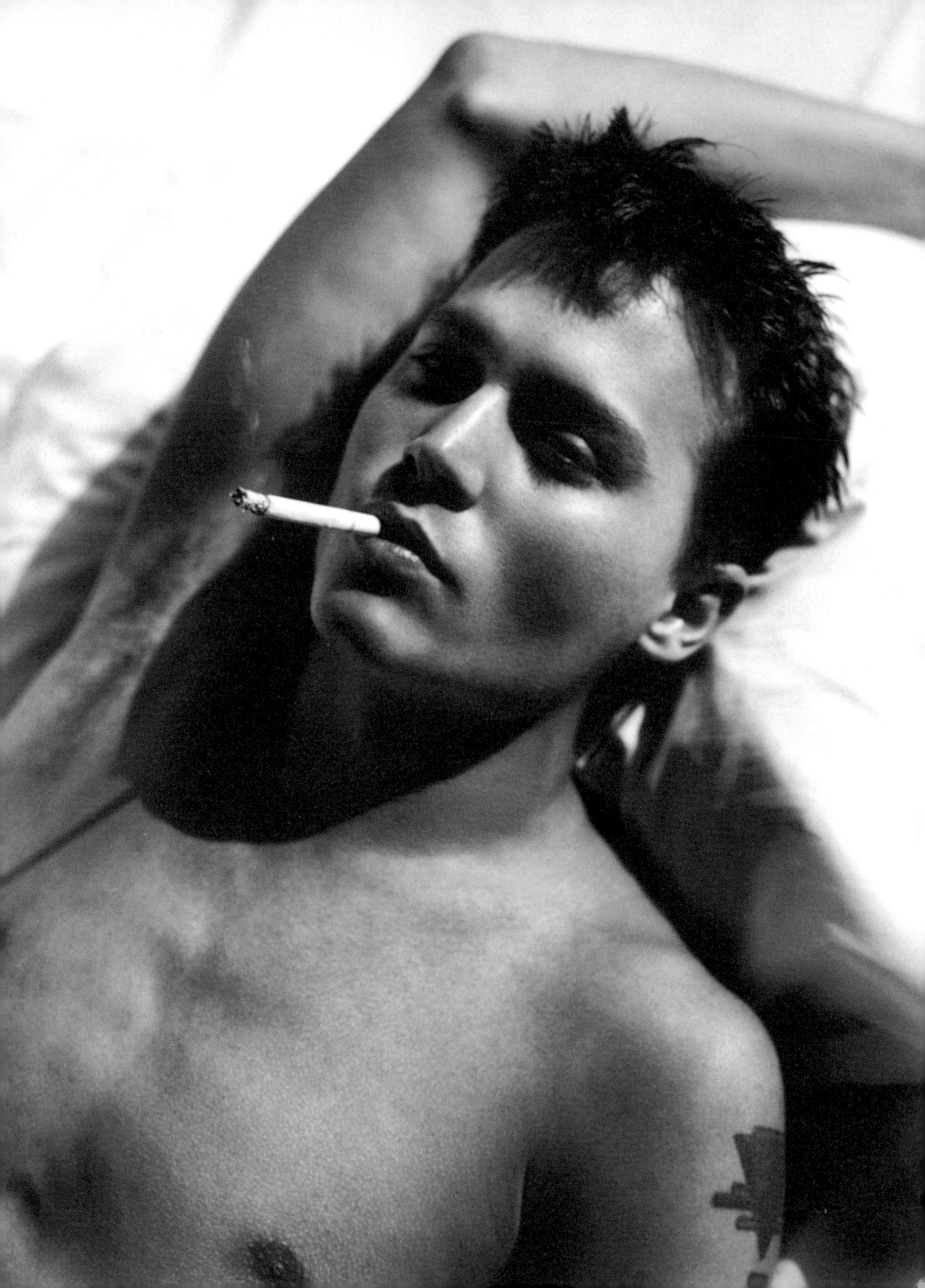

WEDNESDAY 22 FEBRUARY
950014
British
G.Q.
Buffalo Club
Johnny Depp
Stylist:
Stephan Erabino
grooming:
Karen Kawahara
Film:
25 TX 220
6 TX 135
10 Pola 665
30 Fugi 220
10 Fugi Pola

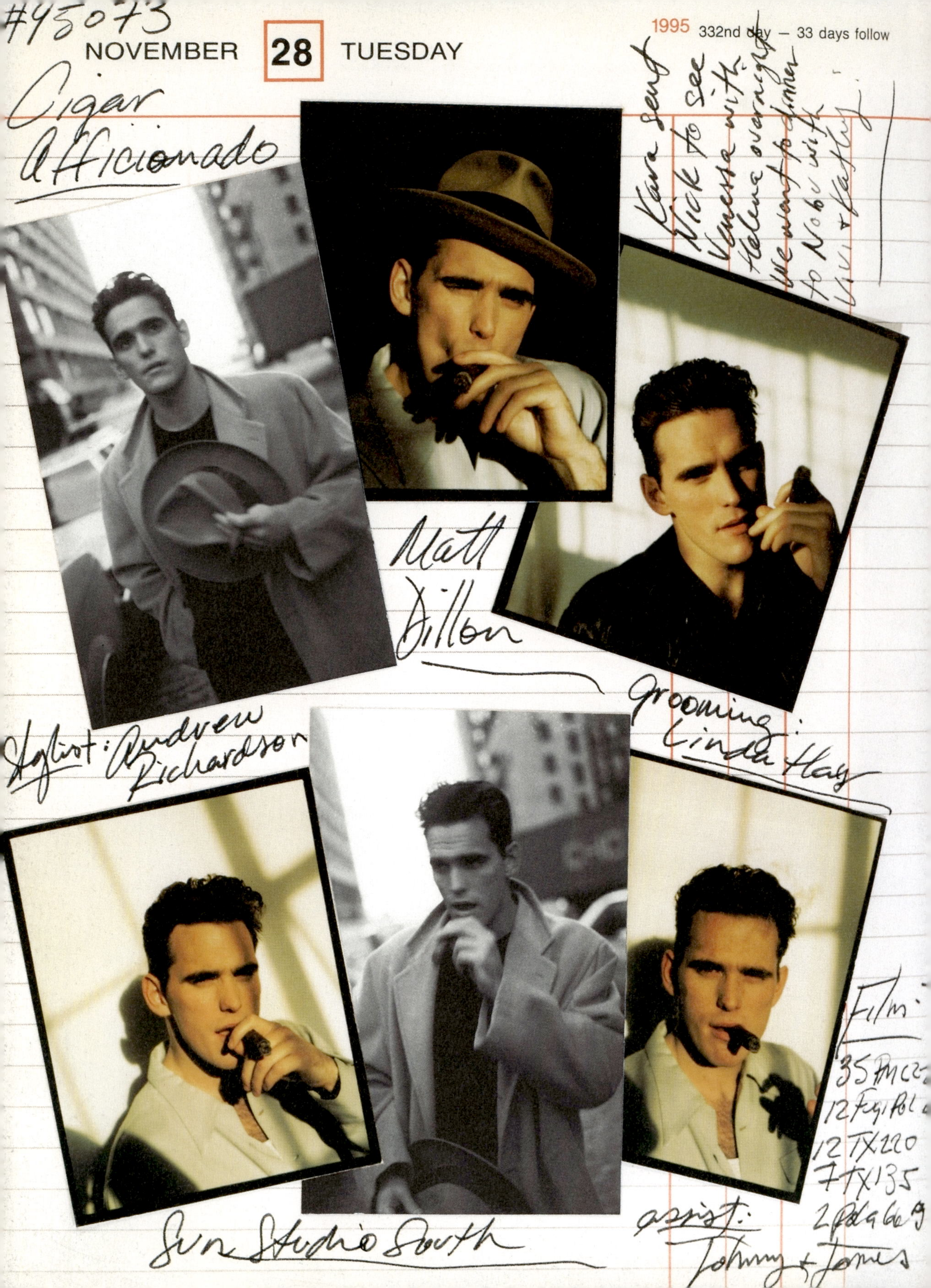
#45073
NOVEMBER 28 TUESDAY
1995 332nd day — 33 days follow
Cigar Afficionado
Kara sent
Nick to see
Venessa with
Helena overnight
We want to dinner
to Nobu with
Livi + Kathy
Matt Dillon
grooming:
Linda Hay
Stylist: Andrew Richardson
Sun Studio South
Film:
35 PMcc
12 Fuji Pol
12 TX 220
7 TX 135
2 Pol 669
assist:
Johnny + James

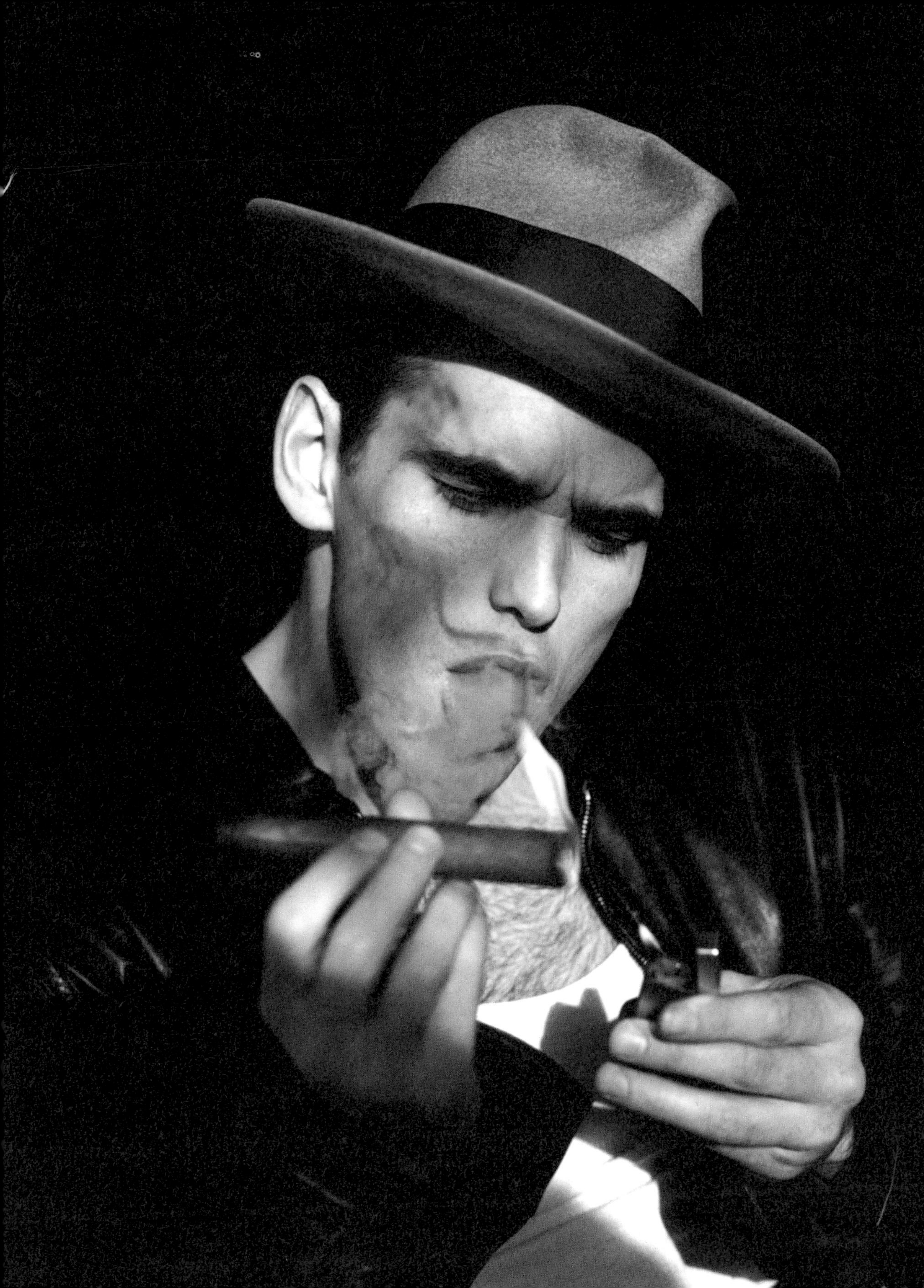

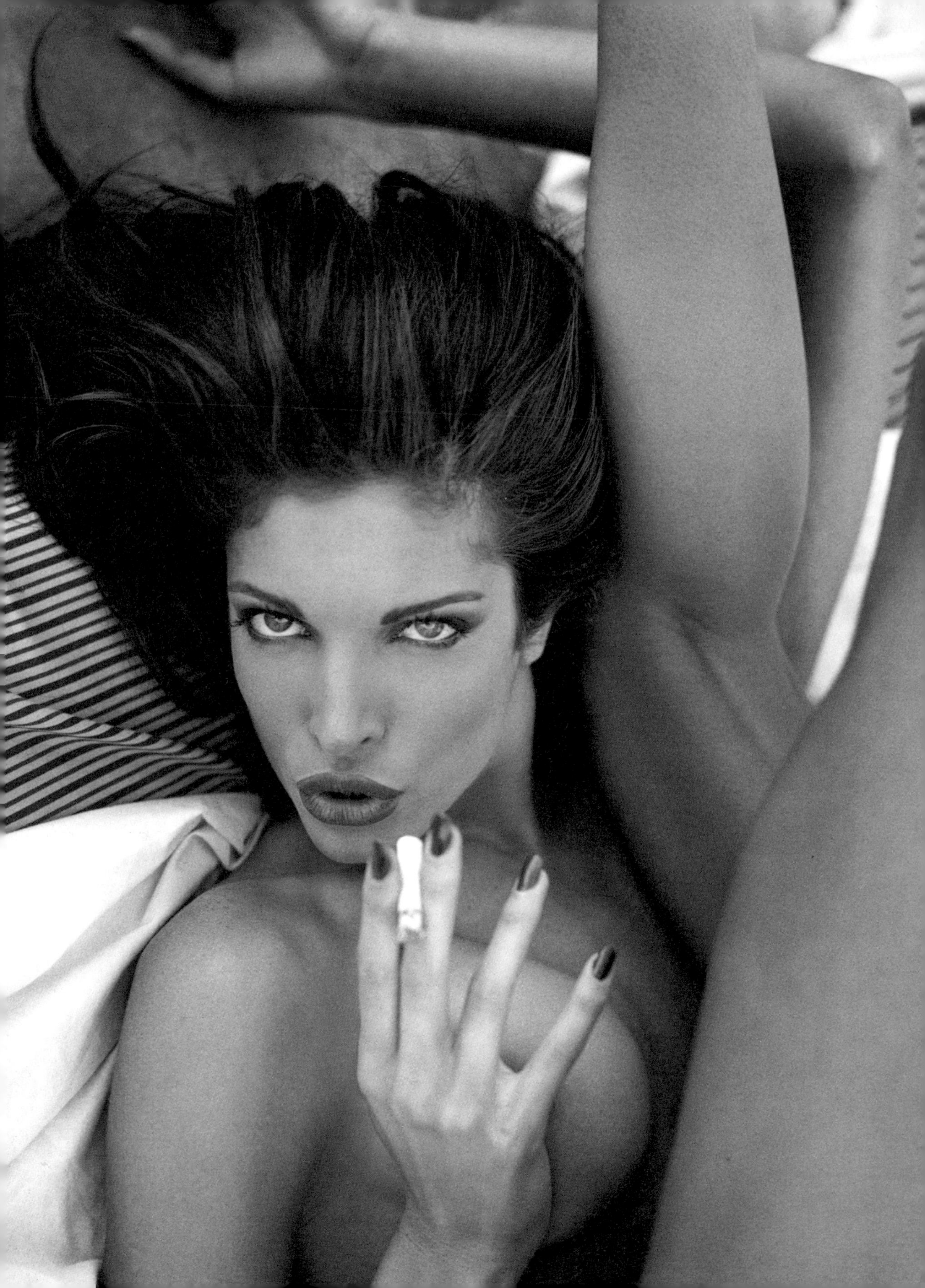

Monday 25
November 1991

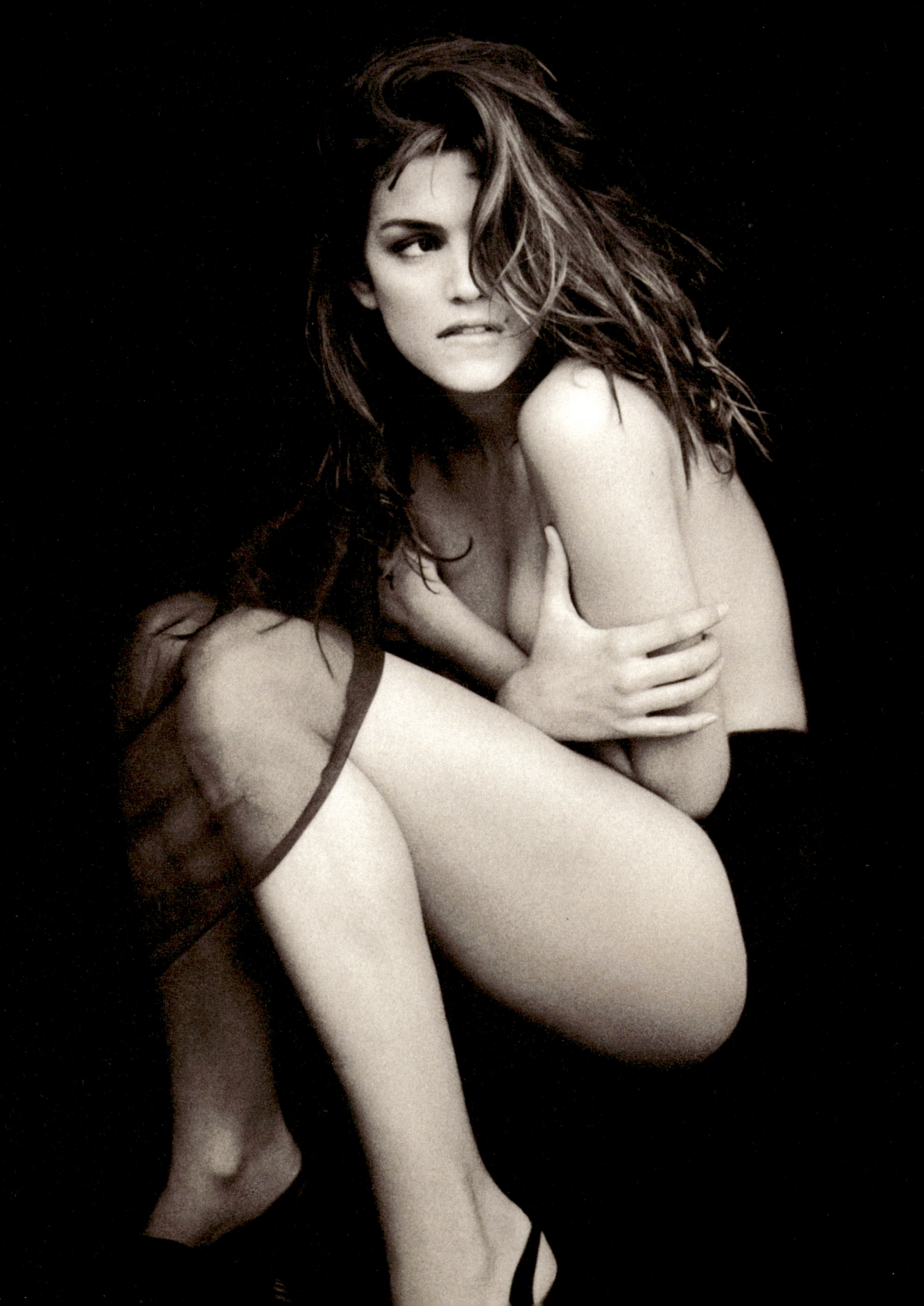

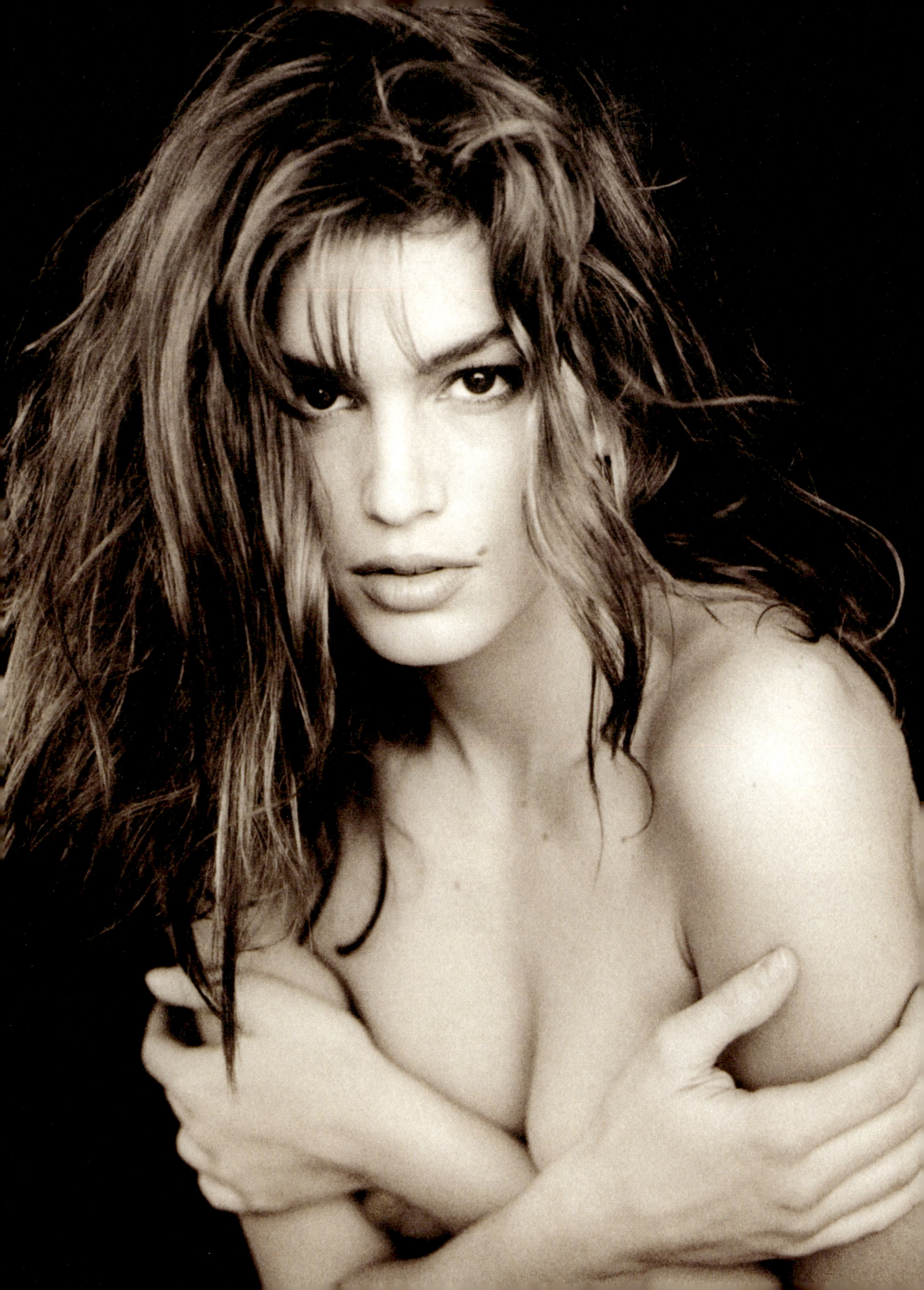

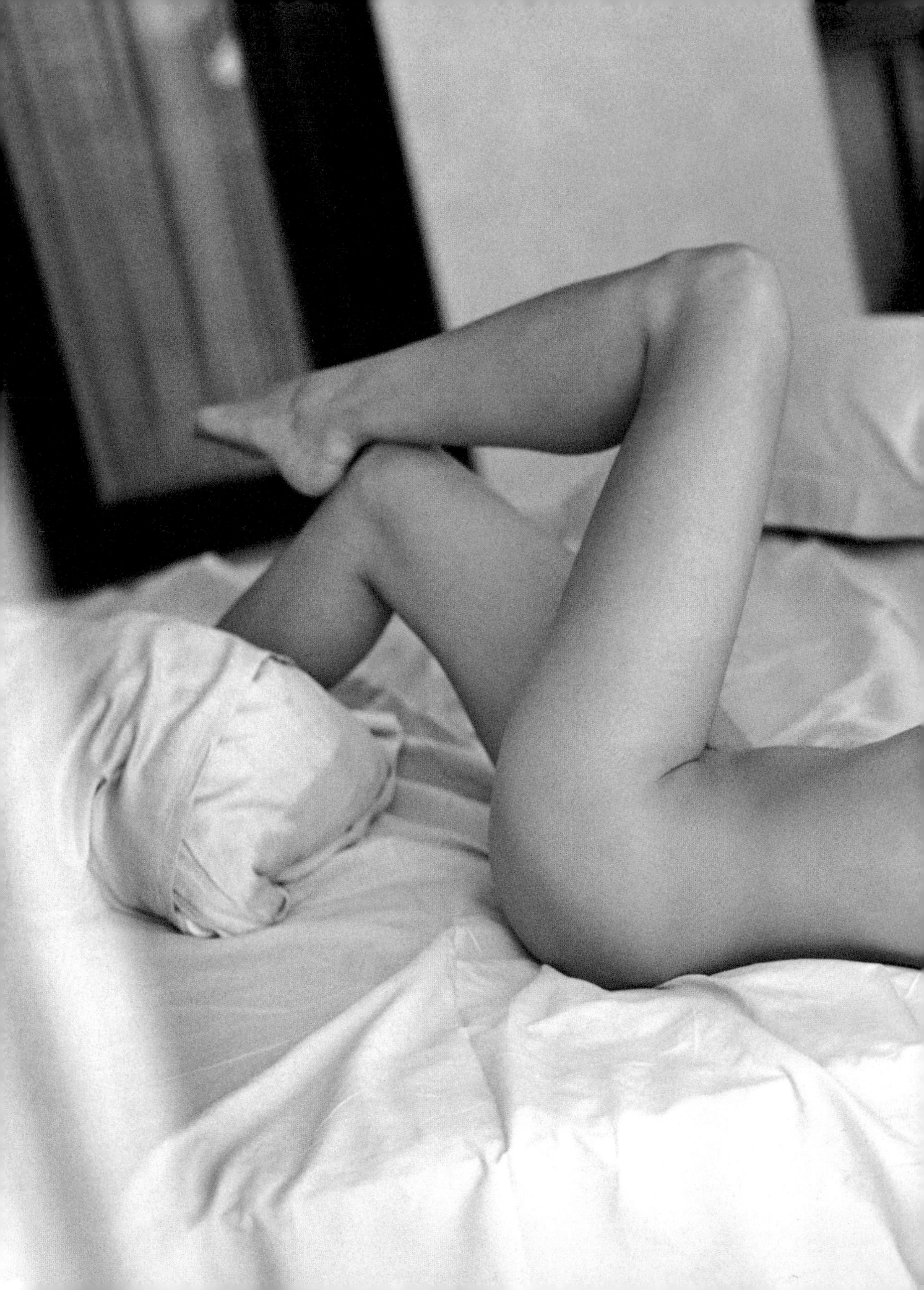

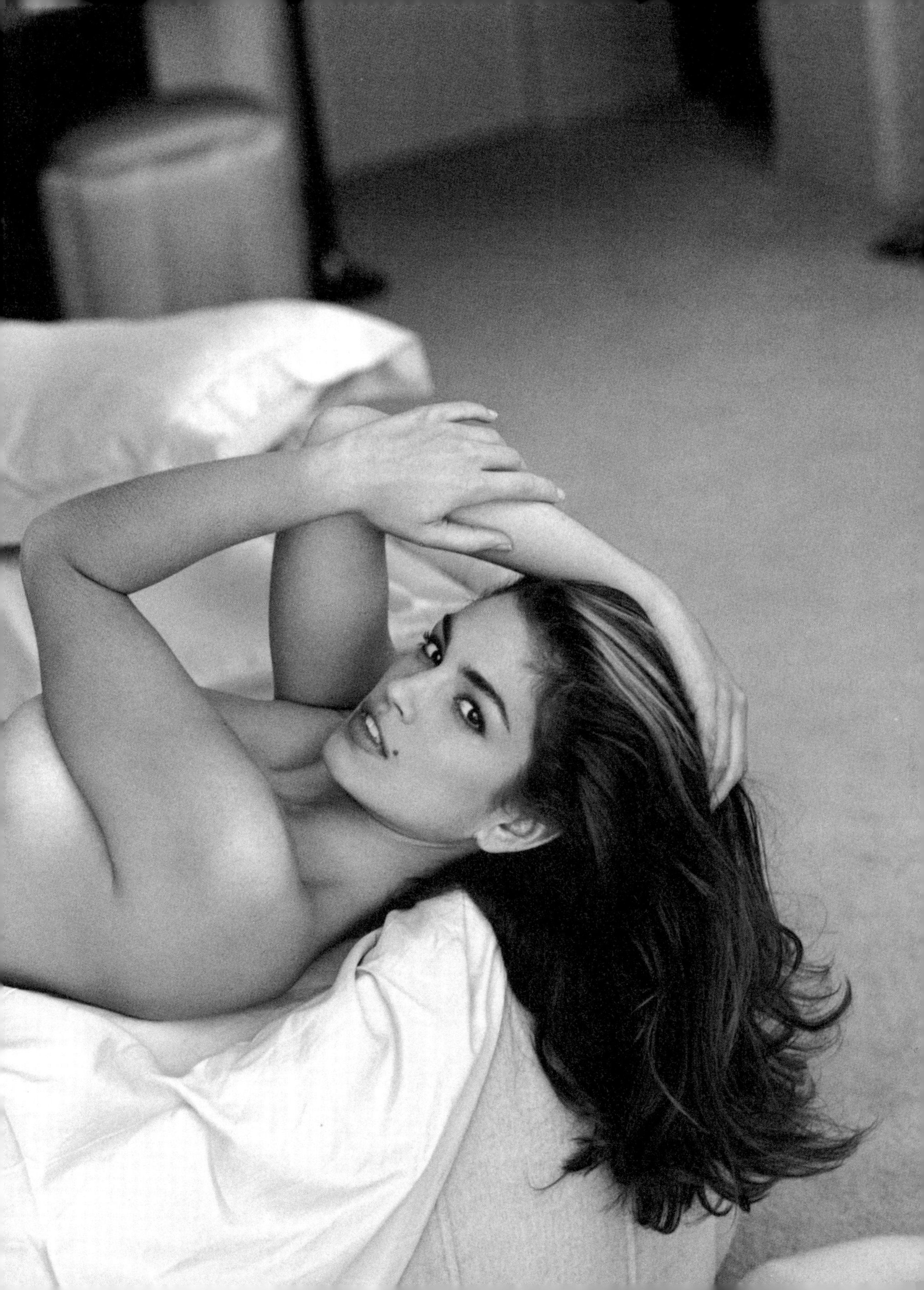

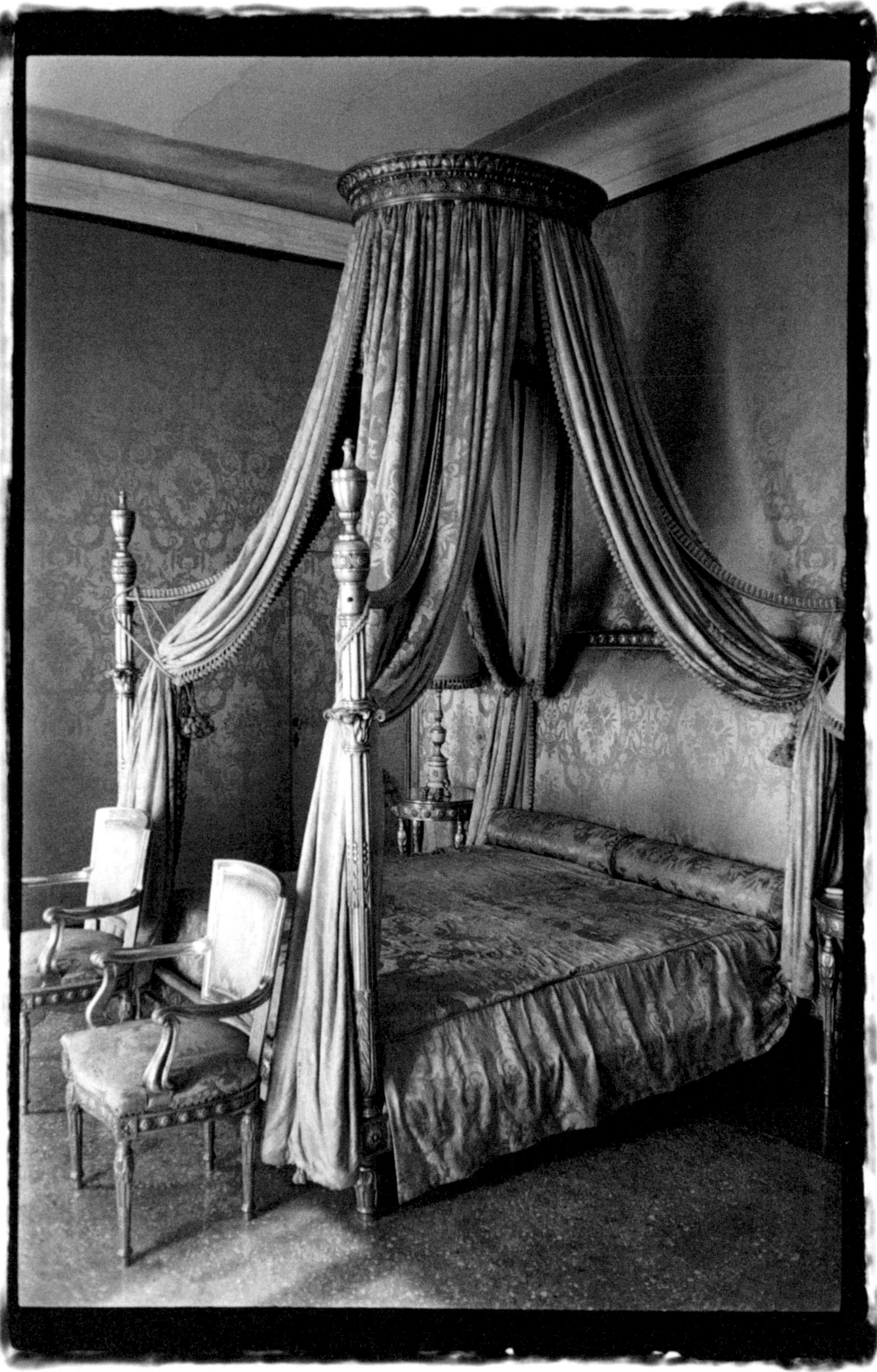

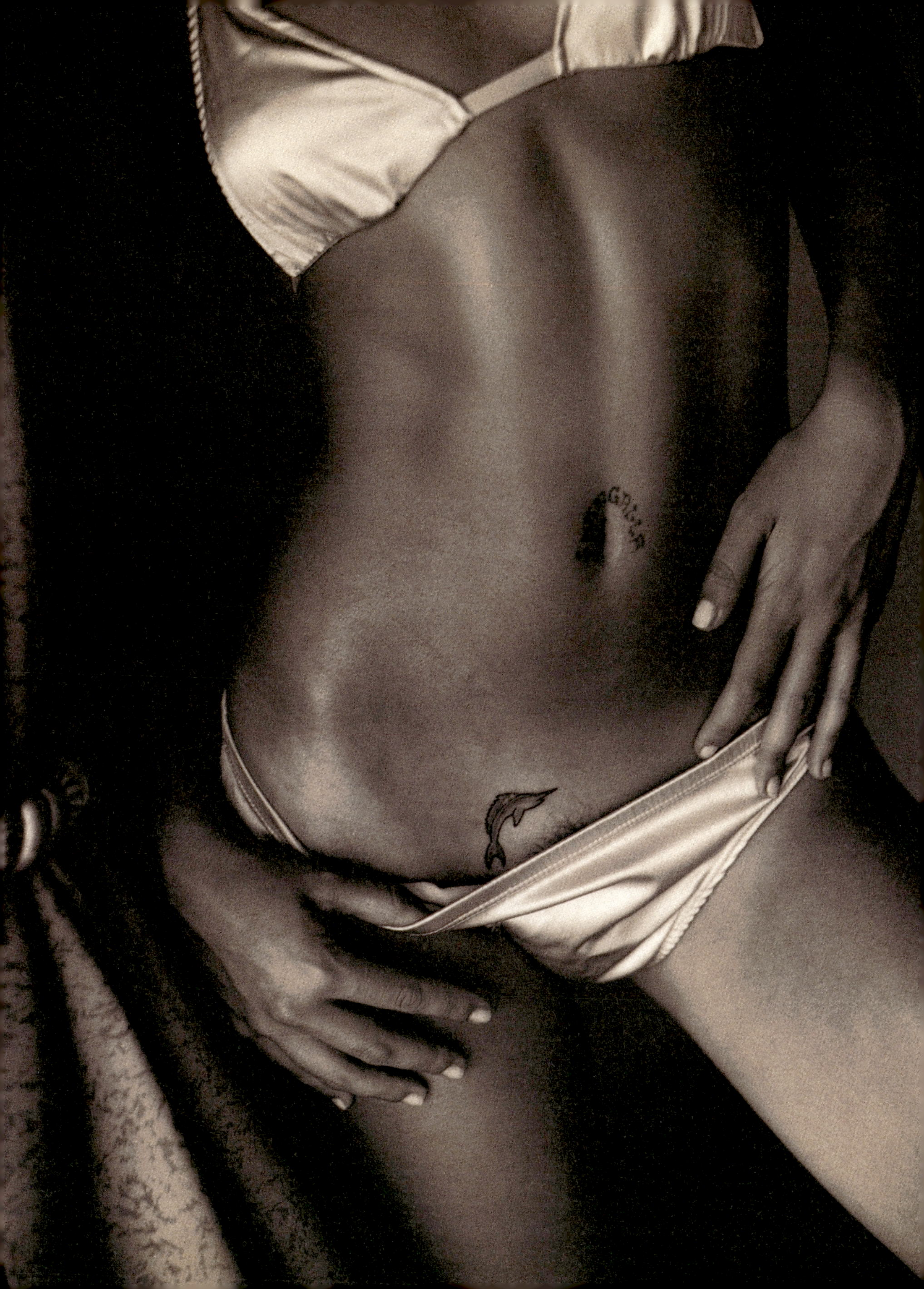

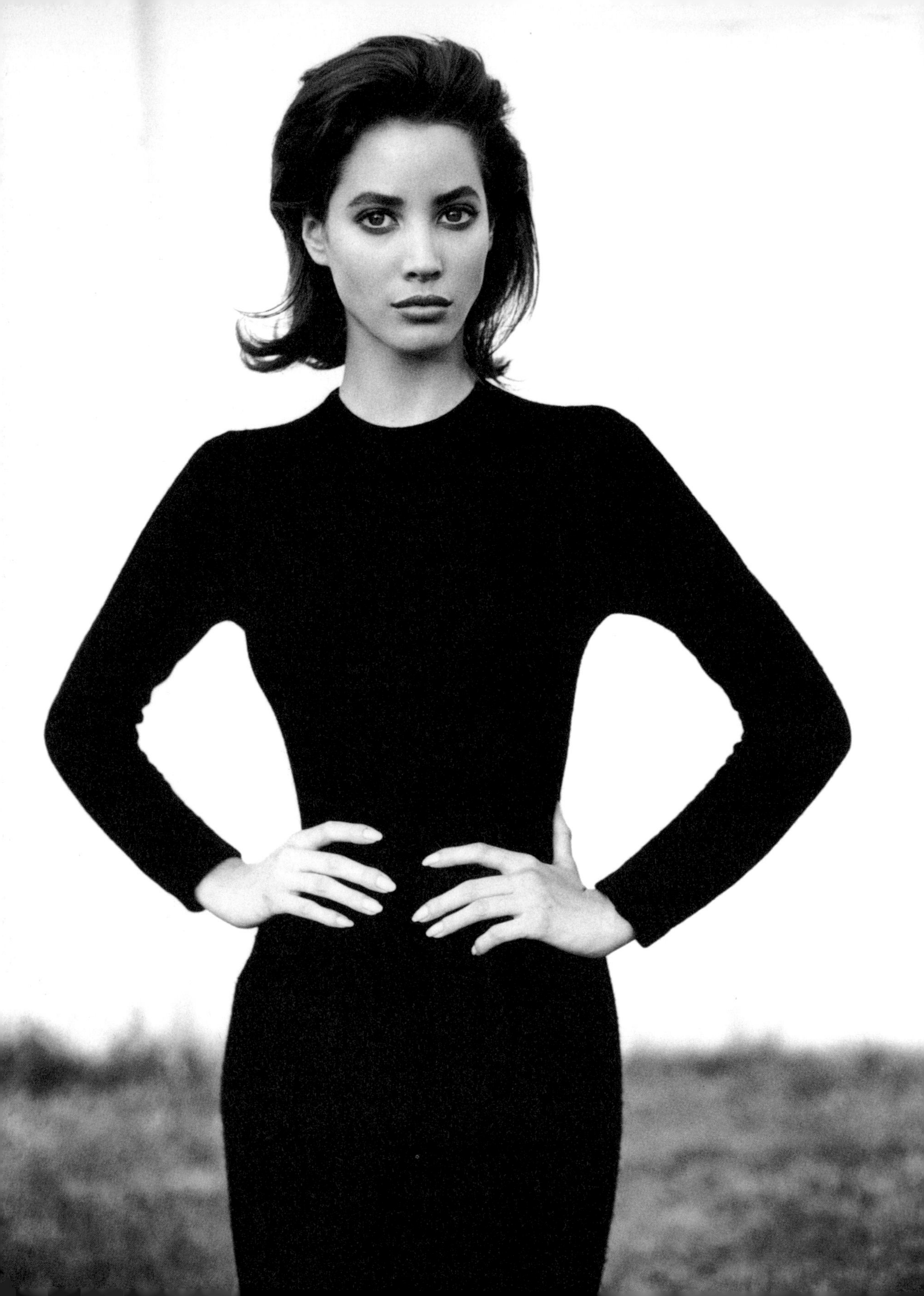

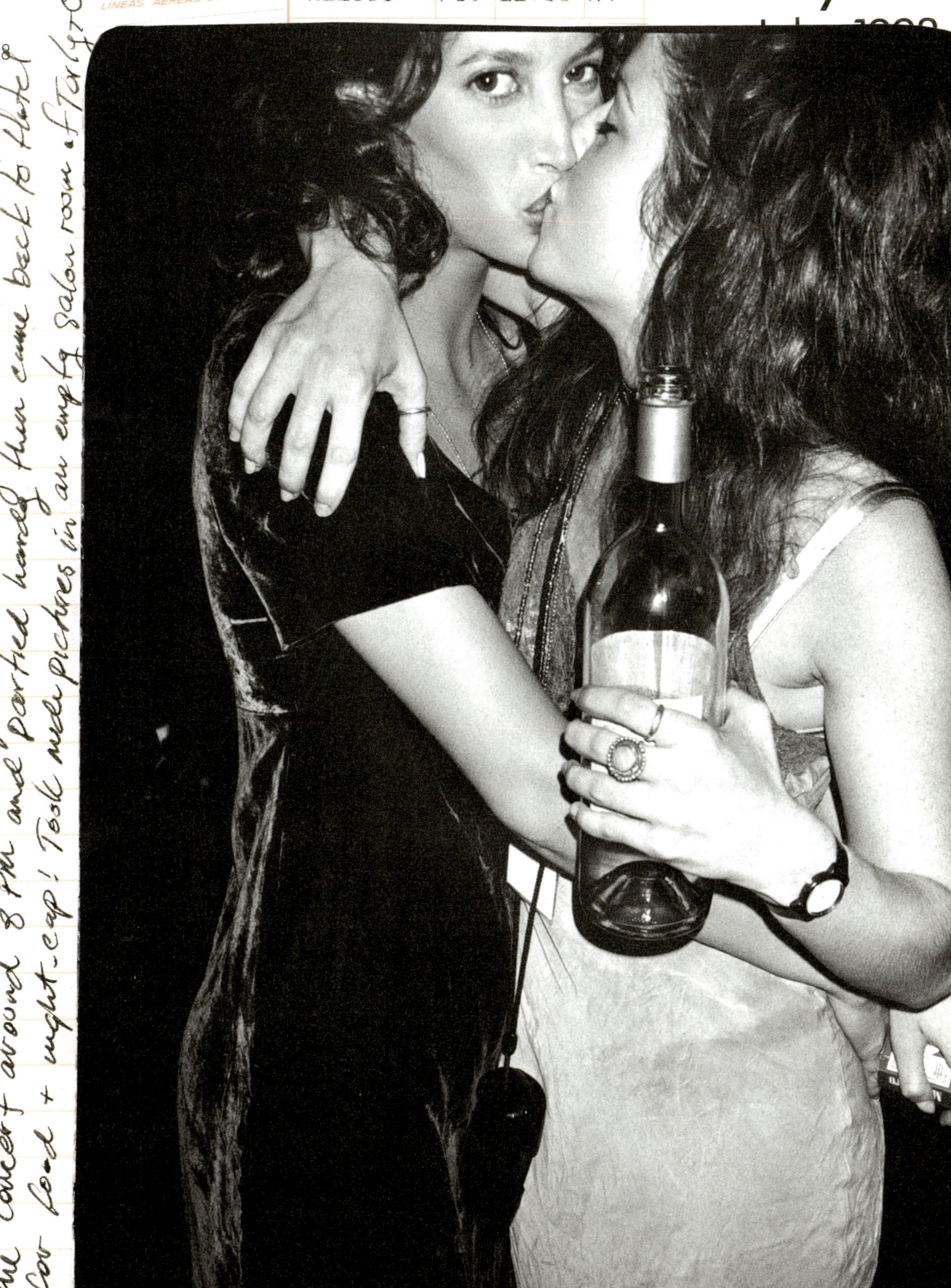

Majestic Hotel. Left Barcelona on noon flight to Rome. Checked into Majestic Hotel. Lunch with Turly, Naomi, Alby me & Kara! Went to the concert around 8PM and partied hard, then came back to Hotel for food + night-cap! Took nice pictures in an empty salon room of Turly, Omi!

23 Tuesday
March 1993
British Vogue
El Mirage
#93021
82/2
MK. UP: Kevin Aucoin
Janet Jackson
Kara arrived from San Francisco
Etr
Isabel
Stenho
Hair:
Janet
Zeitung
assist.
Marco
Bald
Jason
Wilho
Film:
60 Fuji 220
7 Fuji 135
11 Fuji Pola
33 Clips
9 TX 220
7 Pola 665

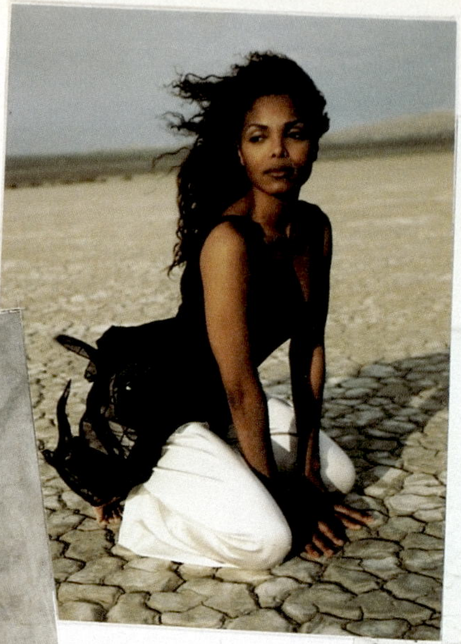

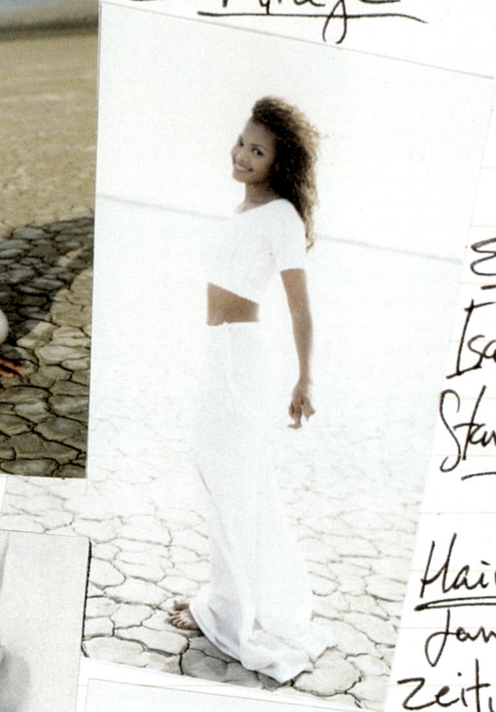

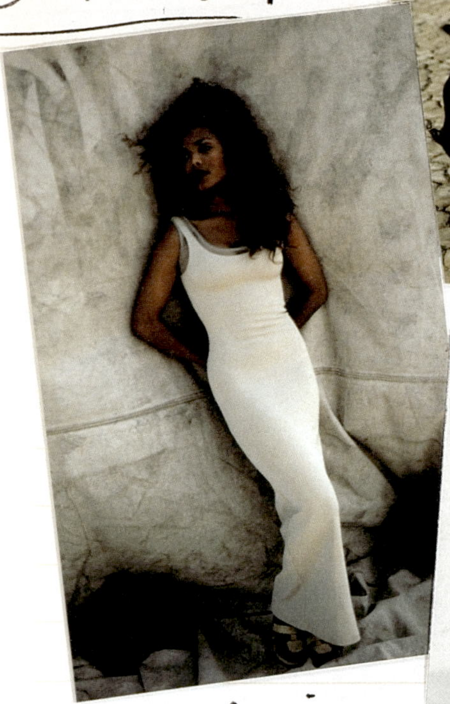

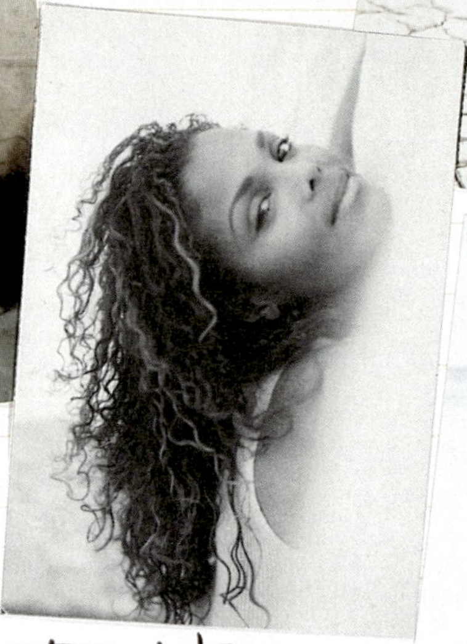

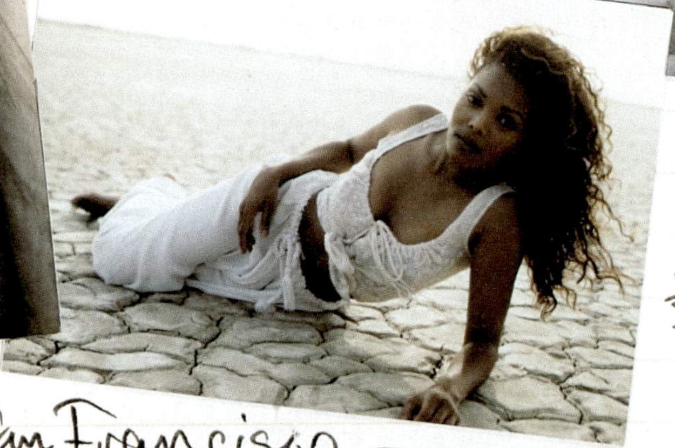

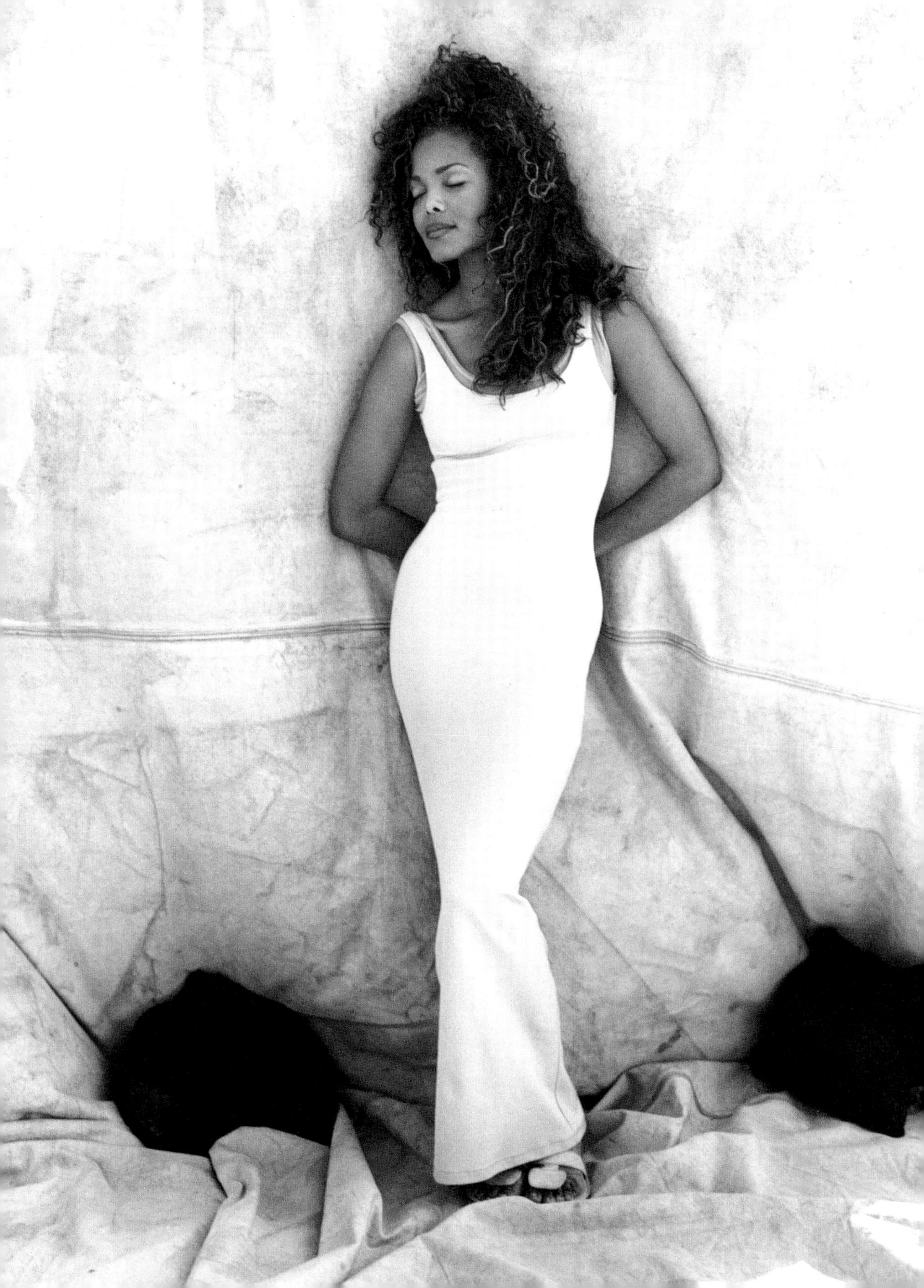

15 Tuesday
June 1993

#93033

Allure

Carla Bruni

Edtr: Polly Mellen

Mark Wilson's House
Long Island.

Mk. Up: Sonia Kashuk
Hair: Garren

assist: Andre & Marco

Film:
20 Fuji 220
18 Fuji 135
21 Clips
10 Fuji Pola

39 TX 220
3 TX 135
10 Pola 665

Dinner with Kate Harrington, Kevin
+ Alexandra at La Frontiera

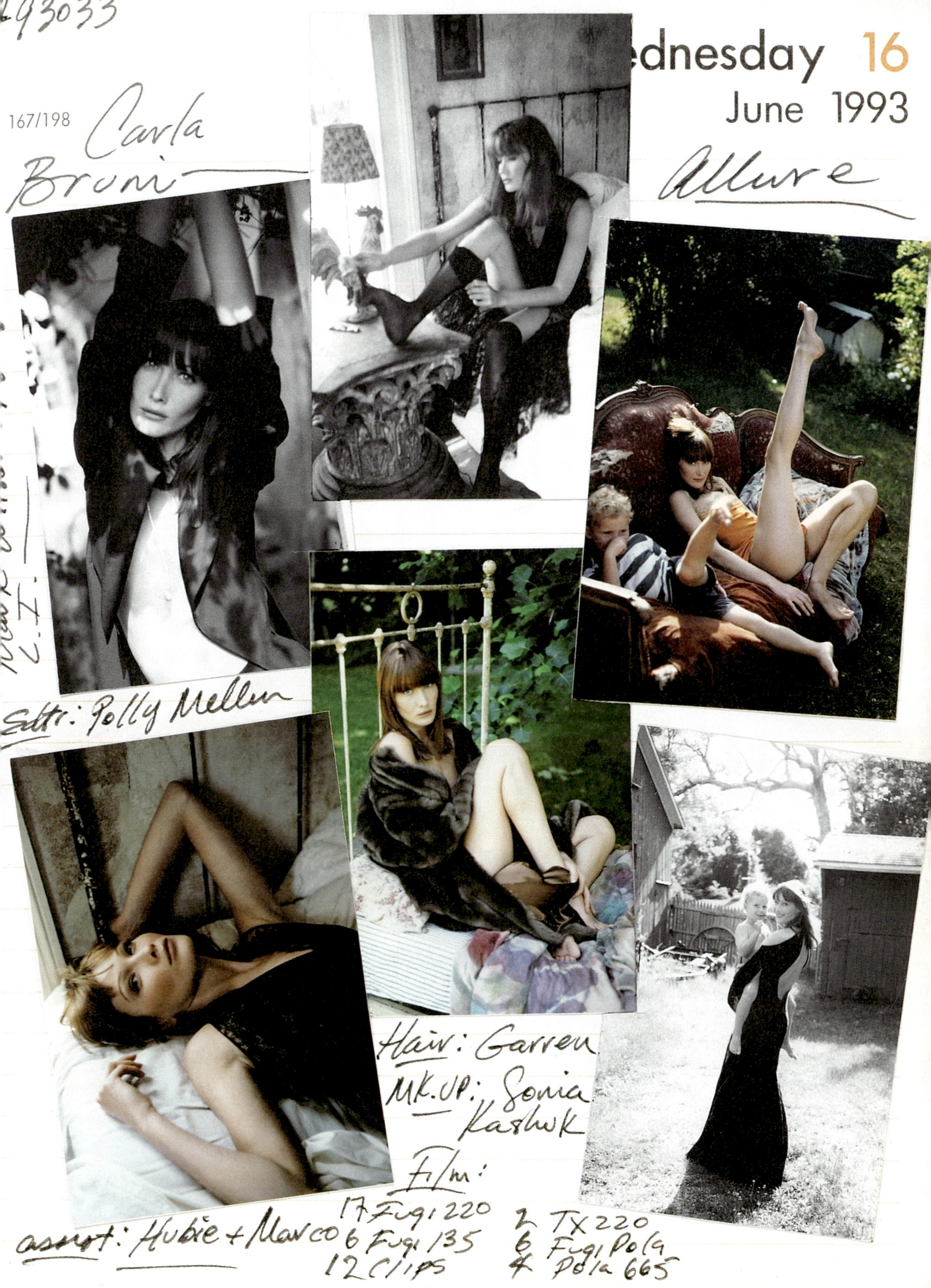
93033
167/198
Carla
Bruni
Wednesday 16
June 1993
Allure
Edtr: Polly Mellen
Hair: Garren
MK.UP: Sonia
Kashuk
Film:
Assrt: Hubie + Marco
17 Fugi 220
6 Fugi 135
12 Clips
2 TX 220
6 Fugi Pola
4 Pola 665

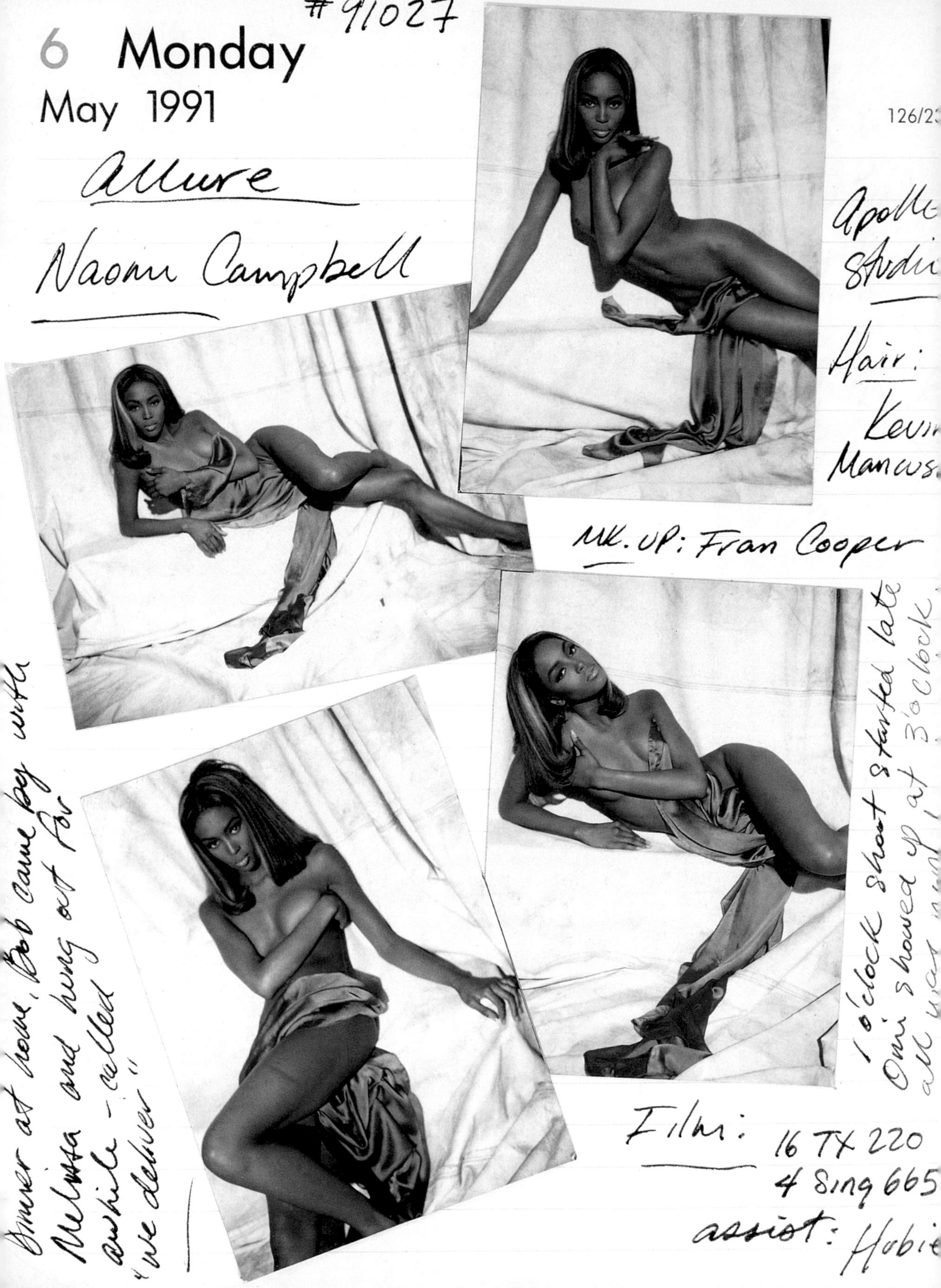
6 Monday
May 1991
#91027
126/2?

Allure

Naomi Campbell

Apollo Studio

Hair:

Kevin Mancuso

MK. UP: Fran Cooper

Film: 16 TX 220
4 8ing 665
assist: Hobie

1 o'clock shoot started late
Omi showed up at 3 o'clock
all was...

Dinner at home. Bob came by with
Melissa and hung out for
awhile - called
"we deliver"

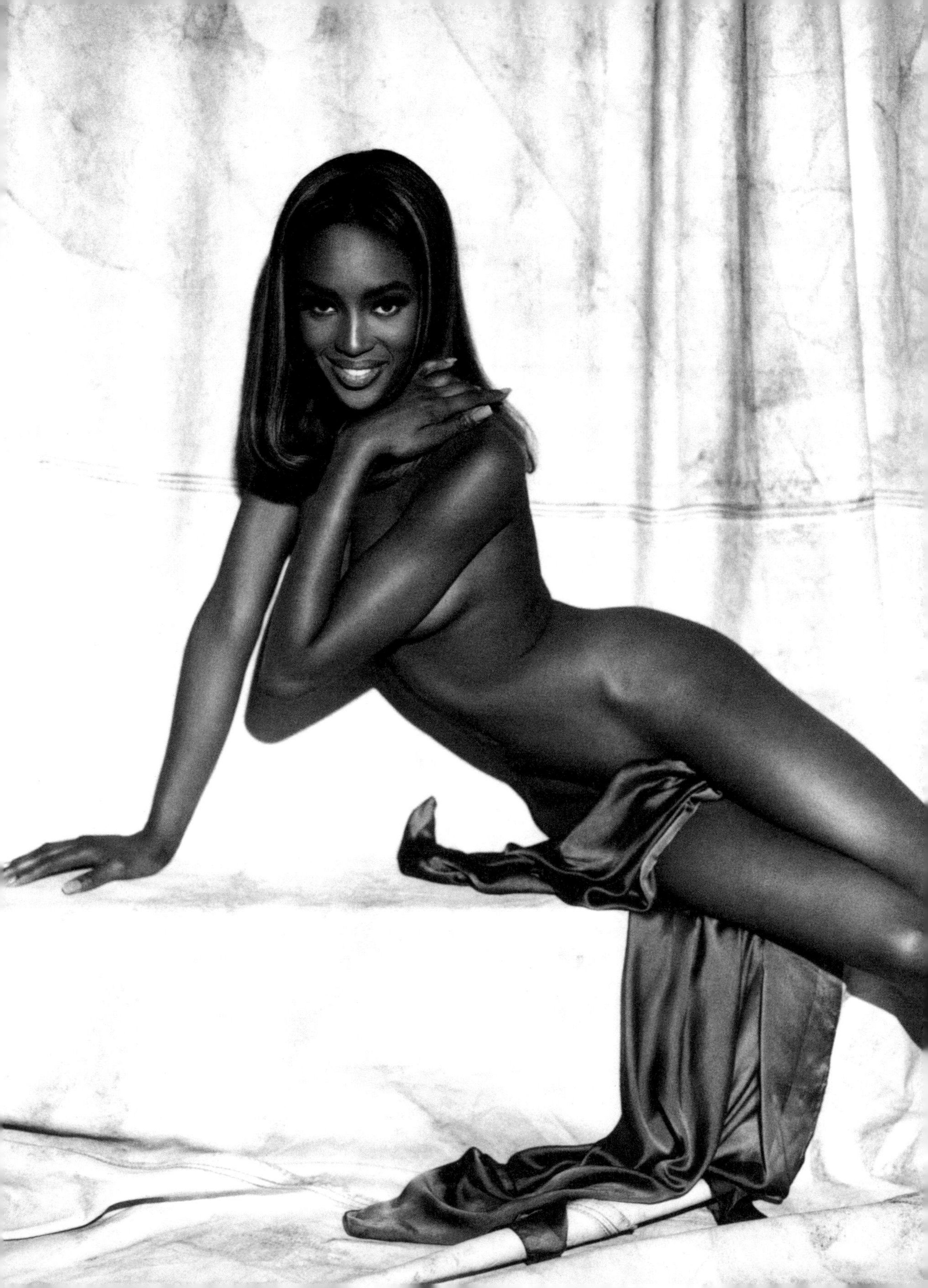

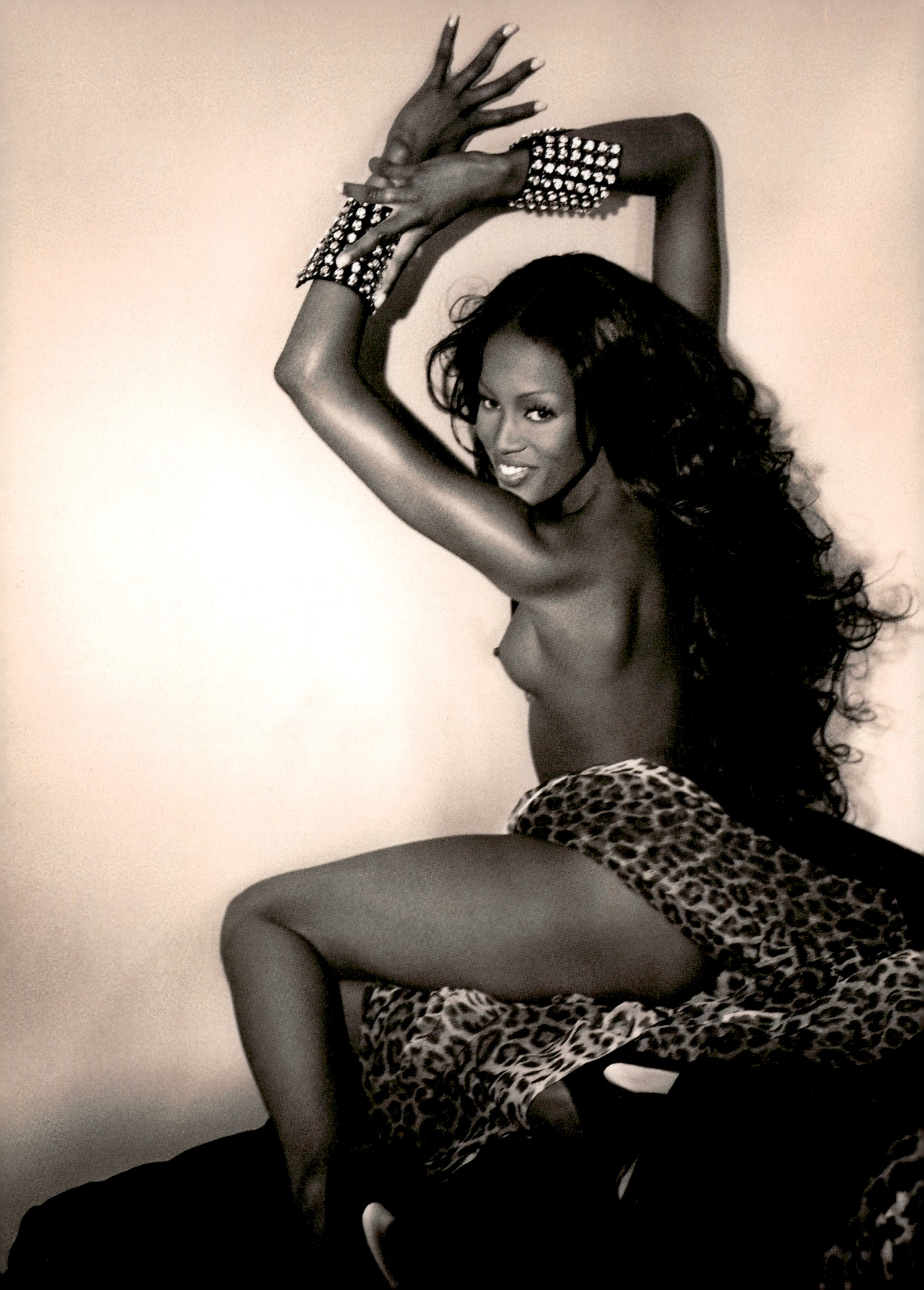

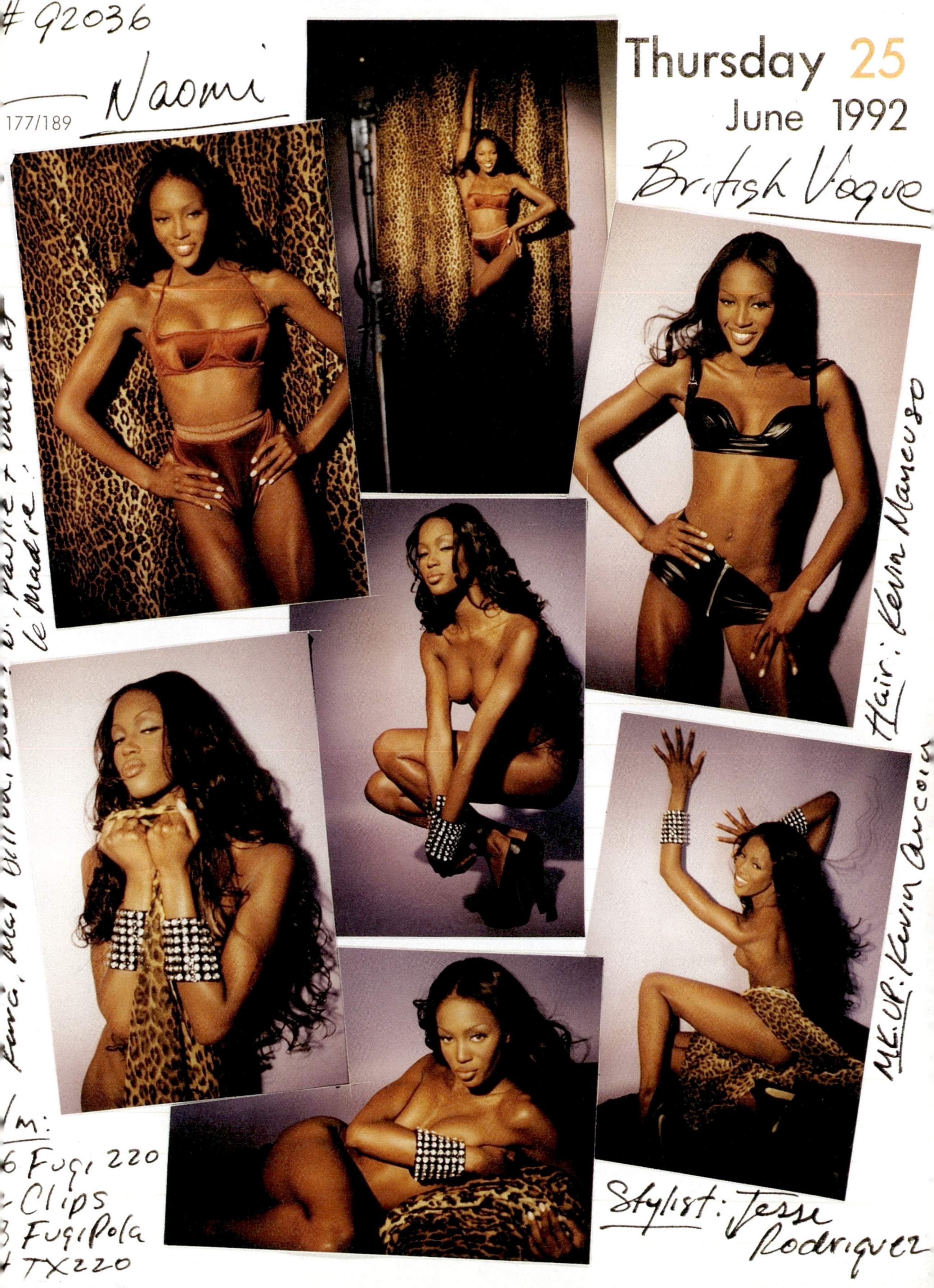

92036
Naomi
177/189
Thursday 25
June 1992
British Vogue
Hair: Kevin Mancuso
MK.UP: Kevin Aucoin
Stylist: Jesse Rodriguez
/m:
6 Fuji 220
Clips
Fujipola
TX220

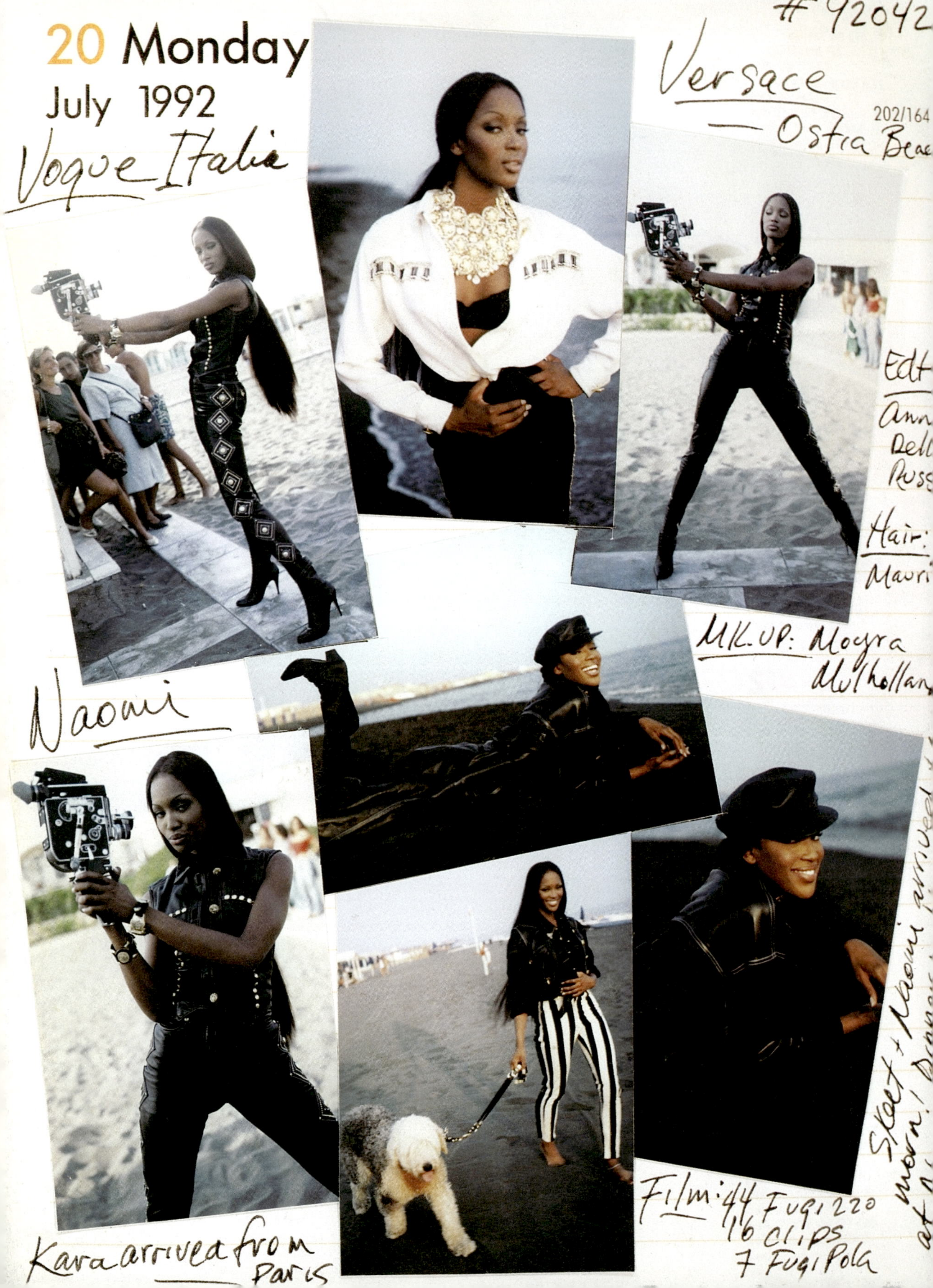

20 Monday
July 1992
Vogue Italia
Naomi
Kava arrived from Paris
#92042
Versace
— Ostra Beac
202/164
Edt
Ann Dell Russ
Hair: Mauri
MK. UP: Moyra Mulhollan
Film: 44 Fugi 220
16 clips
7 Fugi Pola
Stace + Naomi arrived
worn. Dinner arrived
at N

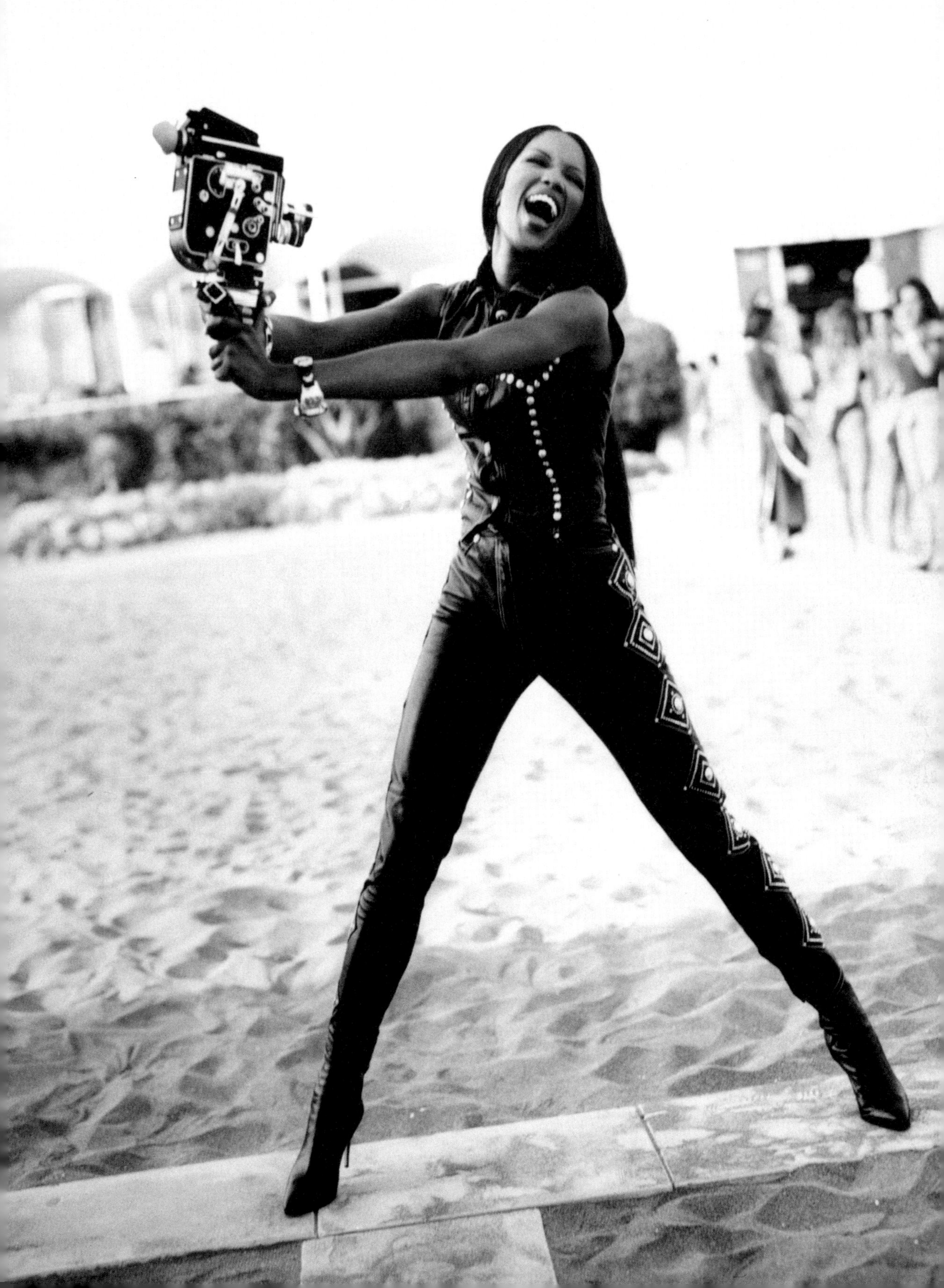

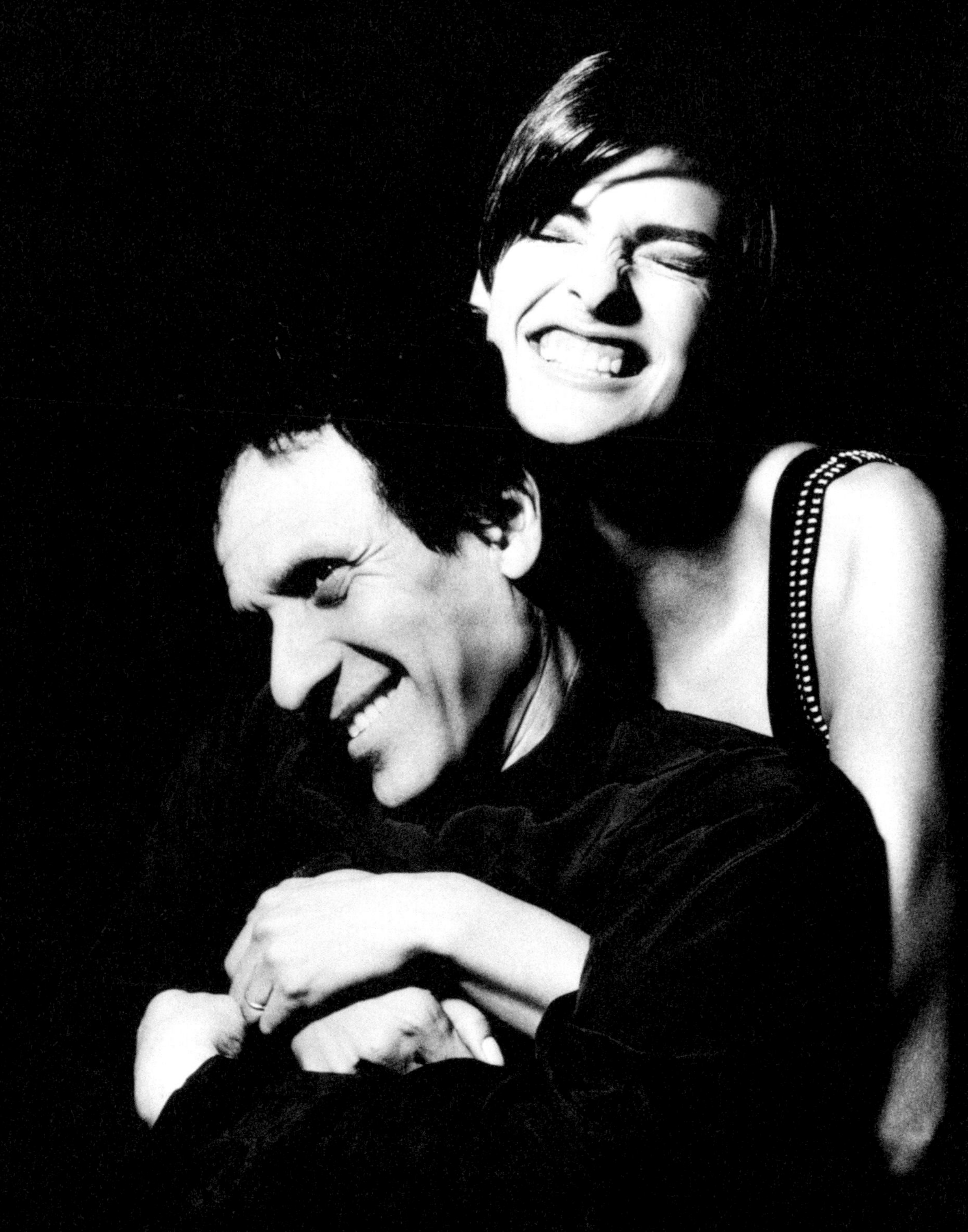

Linda E.

MONDAY **20** FEBRUARY

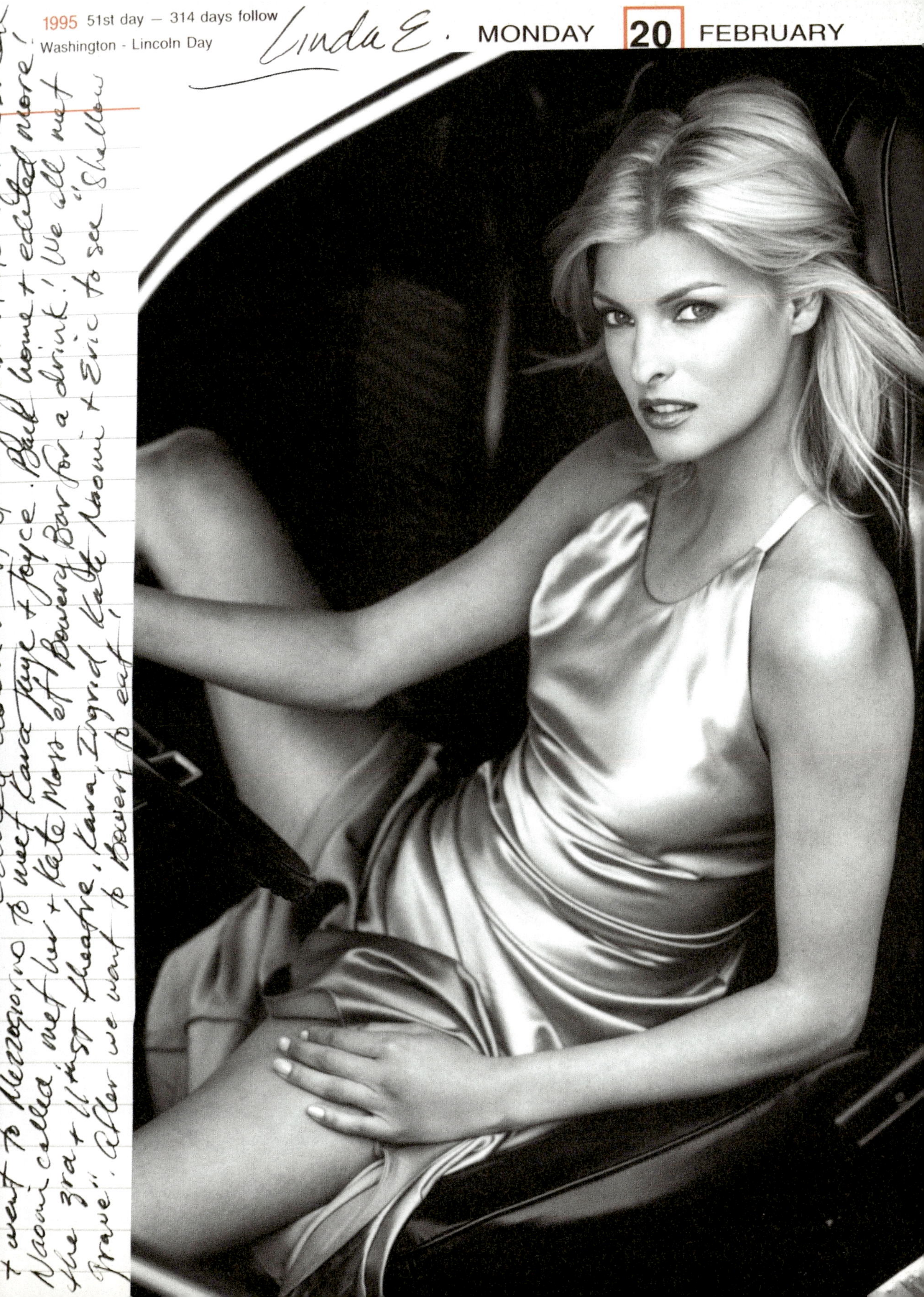

+ went to Mezzogiorno to meet Cara Faye + Joyce. Back home + excited more! Naomi called. Met her + Kate Moss et Bowery Bar for a drink! We all met the 3ra + Whsg theatre. Cara, Zingird, Kate, Naomi + Eric to see "Shallow grave". After we want to Bowery to eat!

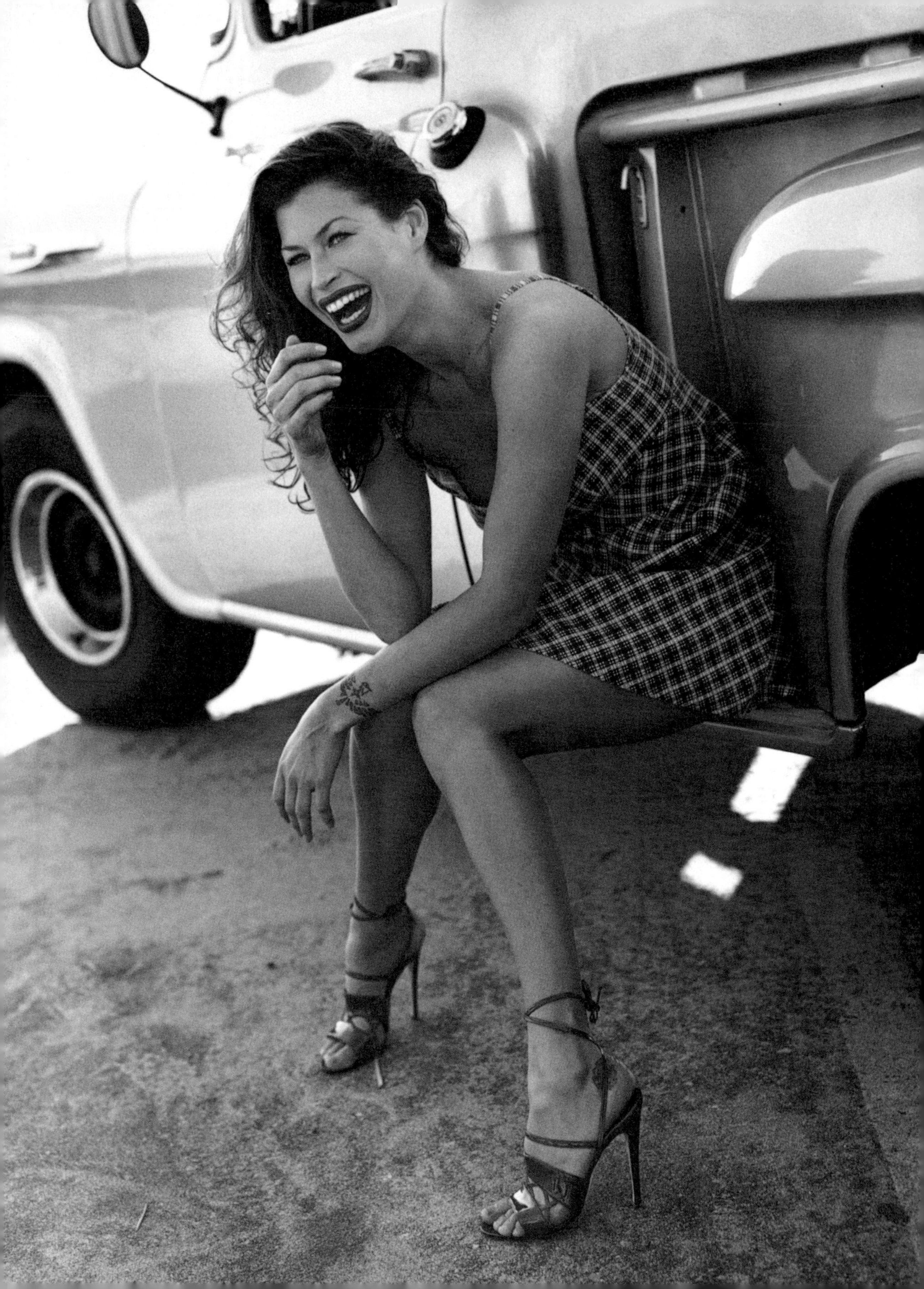

My Anniversary & Carrie's
— Birthday

#95062

edt: Alayne
Patrick

Town &
Country

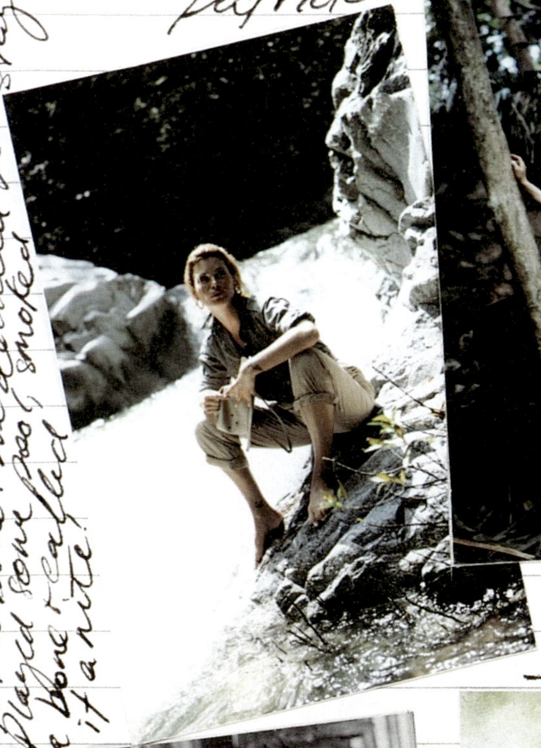

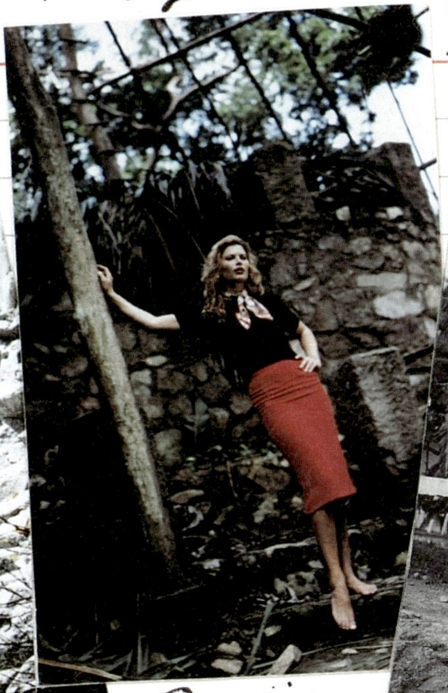

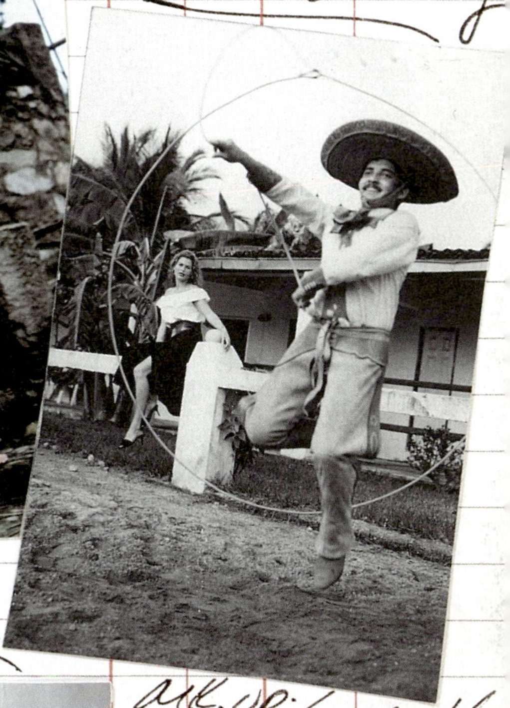

Carrie
Otis

Mk.Up: Linda Hay
Hair: Satoru

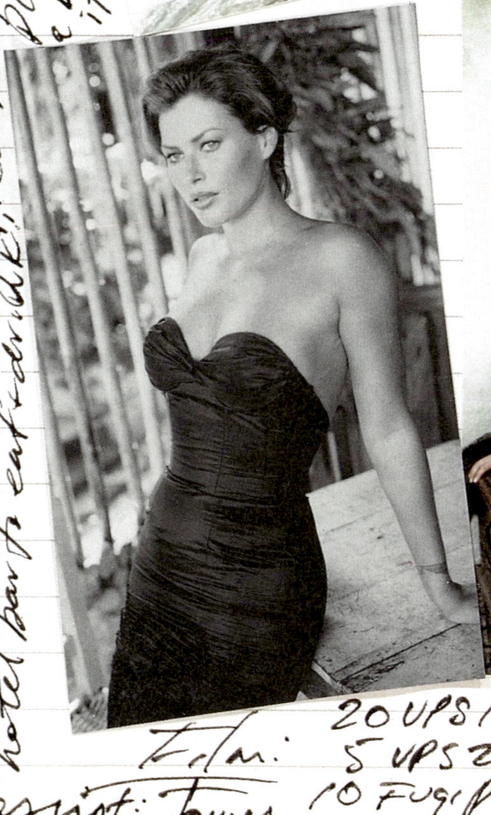

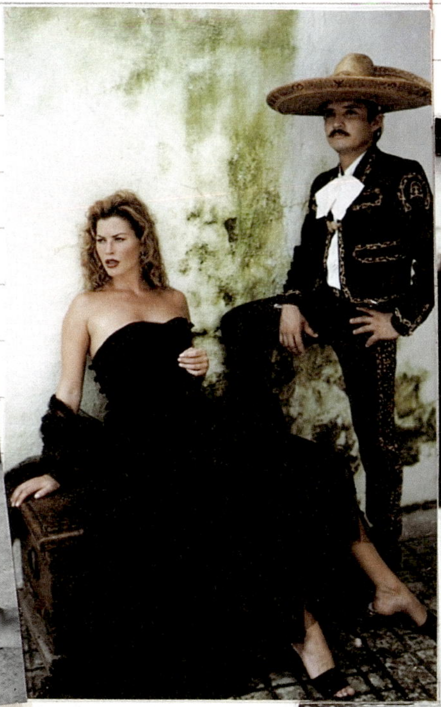

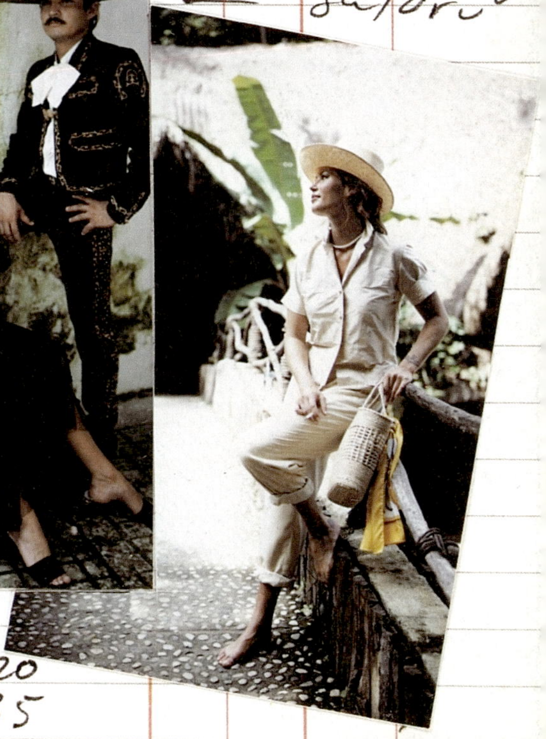

20 UPS 135
5 UPS 220   STX 220
10 Fuji Pola   STX 135
                 5 Pola 665

Eolai:
ssist: James
+ Johnny

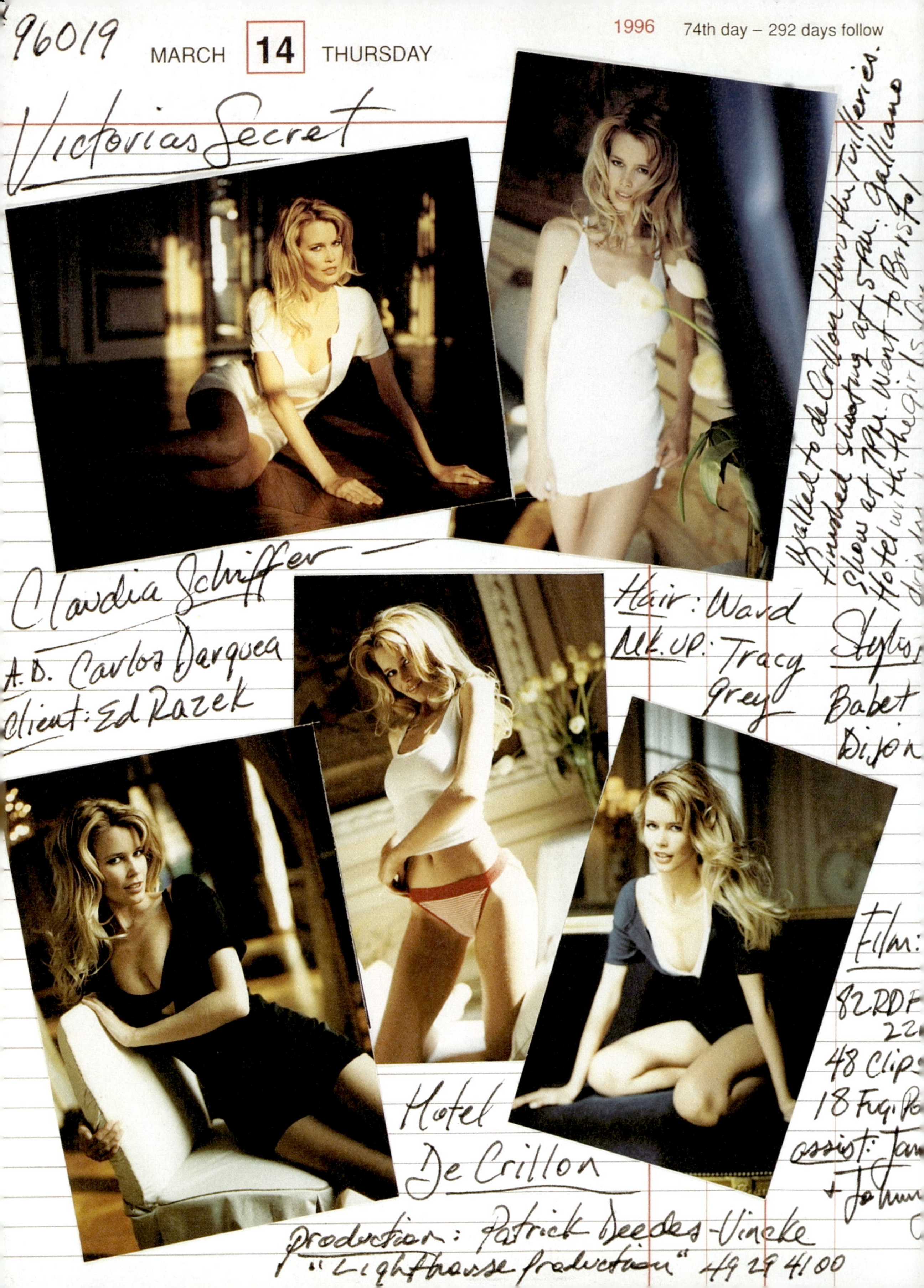

96019
1996   74th day – 292 days follow
MARCH 14 THURSDAY
Victorias Secret
Claudia Schiffer
A.D. Carlos Darquea
Client: Ed Razek
Hair: Ward
Mk. Up: Tracy Grey
Stylist Babet Dijon
Hotel De Crillon
Production: Patrick Deedes-Vincke
"Lighthouse Production" 49 29 41 00
Film:
82 RDP
22
48 Clips
18 Fuji Po
assist: Jan
+ John

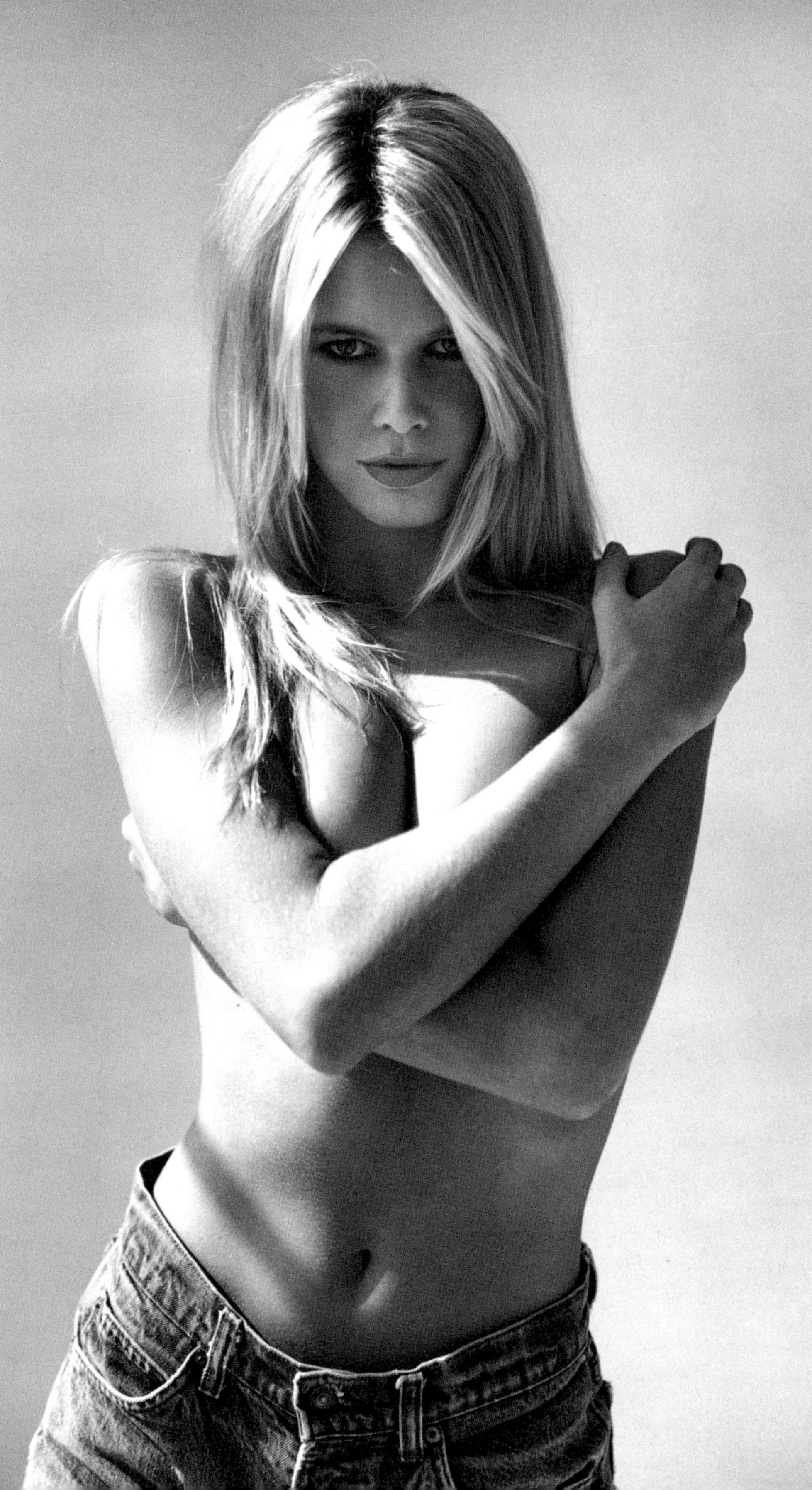

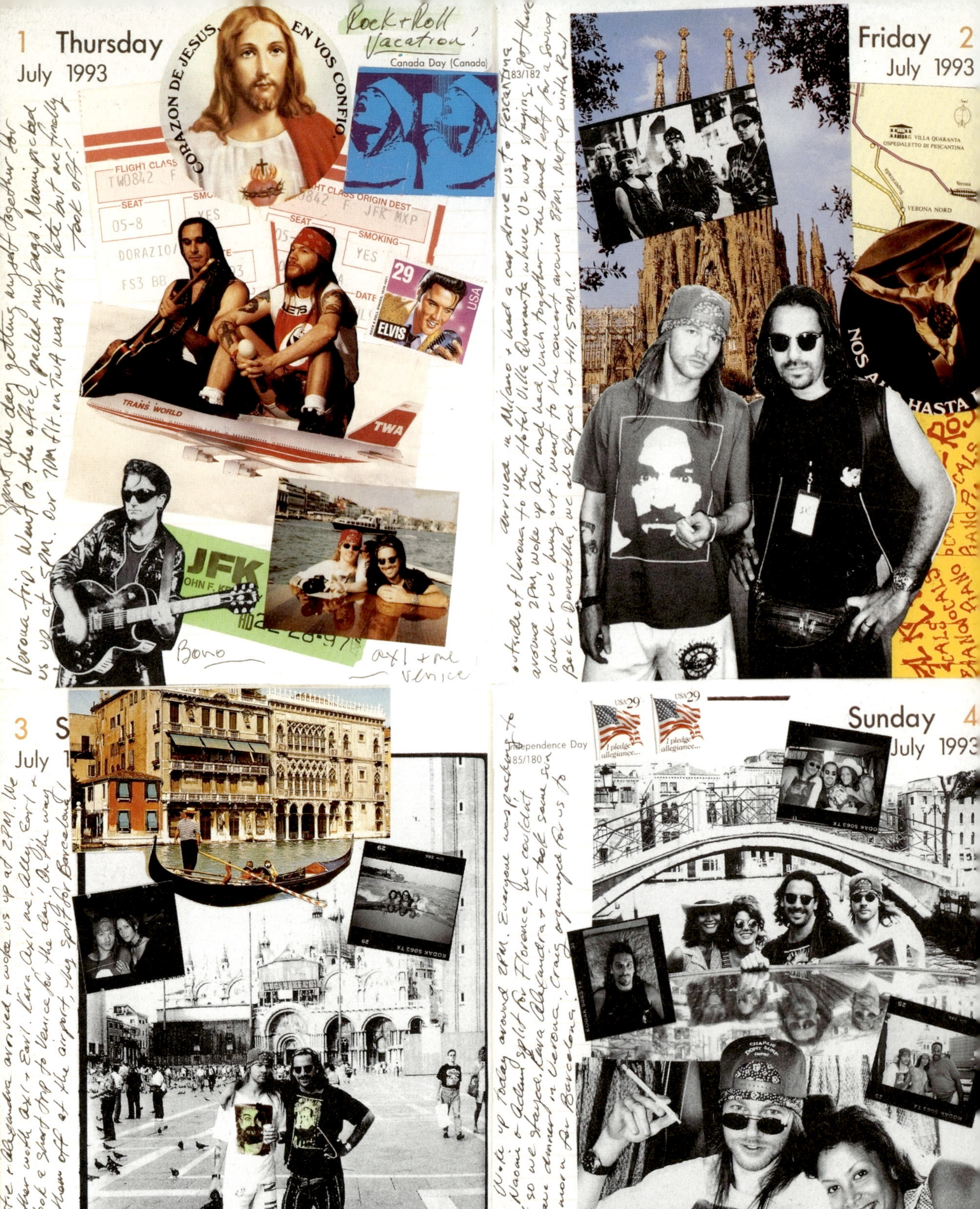

1 Thursday
July 1993

Rock + Roll Vacation!
Canada Day (Canada)

CORAZON DE JESUS, EN VOS CONFIO.

FLIGHT CLASS TWO842 F
SEAT 05-8
DORAZIO/
FS3 BB

FLIGHT CLASS ORIGIN DEST
842 F JFK MXP
SMOKING YES

ELVIS USA 29

TRANS WORLD
TWA

JFK
JOHN F. KENNEDY

Bono

Axl + me
Venice

Friday 2
July 1993

VILLA QUARANTA
OSPEDALETTO DI PESCANTINA
Verona
VERONA NORD

NOS... HASTA

83/182

3 S...
July 1

Sunday 4
July 1993

Independence Day
85/180

USA 29   USA 29
I pledge allegiance...   I pledge allegiance...

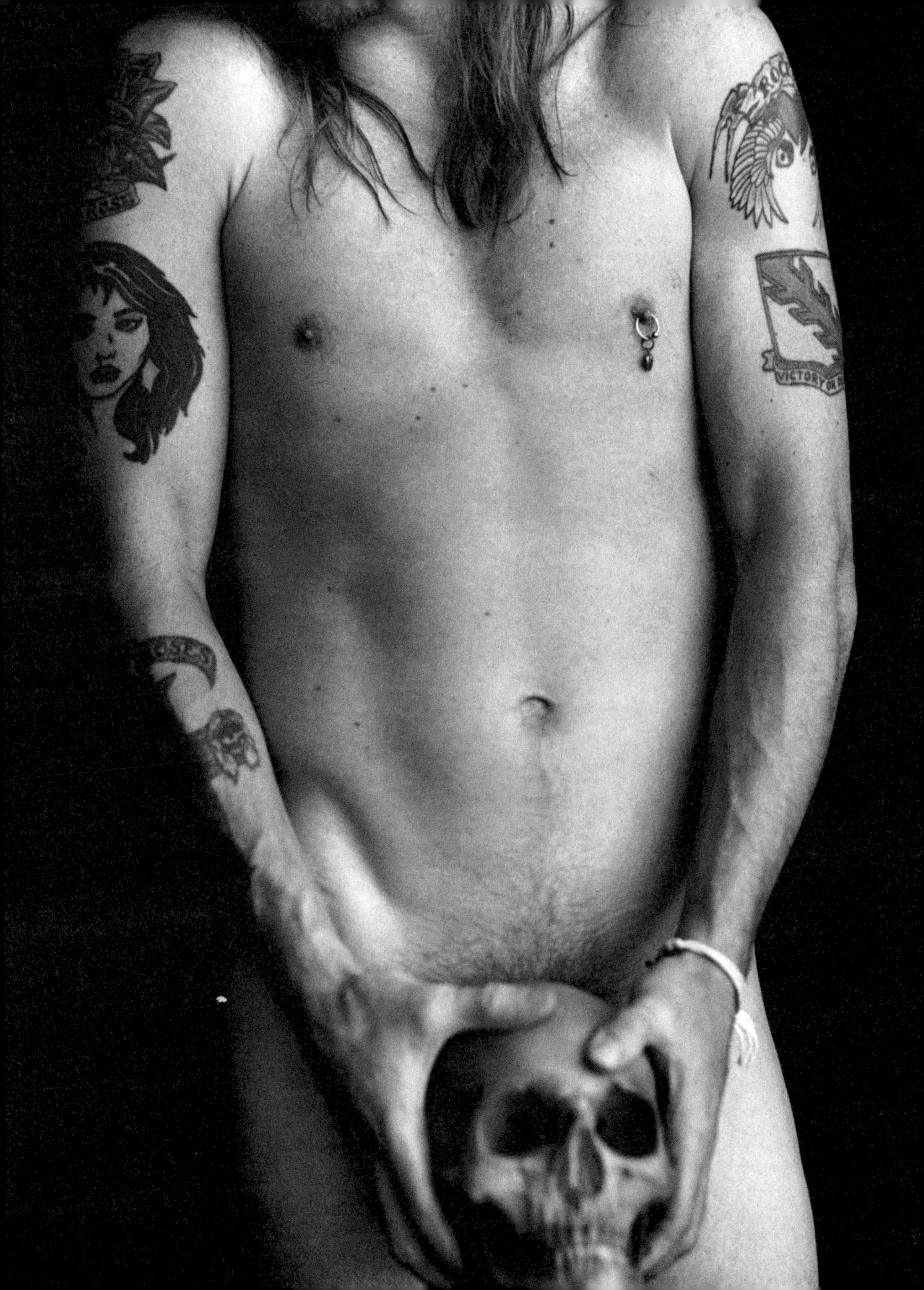

Left Verona early this morn for Milano. Flight to Barcelona, arrived 2PM. Chilled into Hilton. Got some Aquavita for my sinus, then went antique shopping with Axl. Went to the concert around 8PM and saw the best concert ever! The boys left afterwards + we returned to the Hotel!

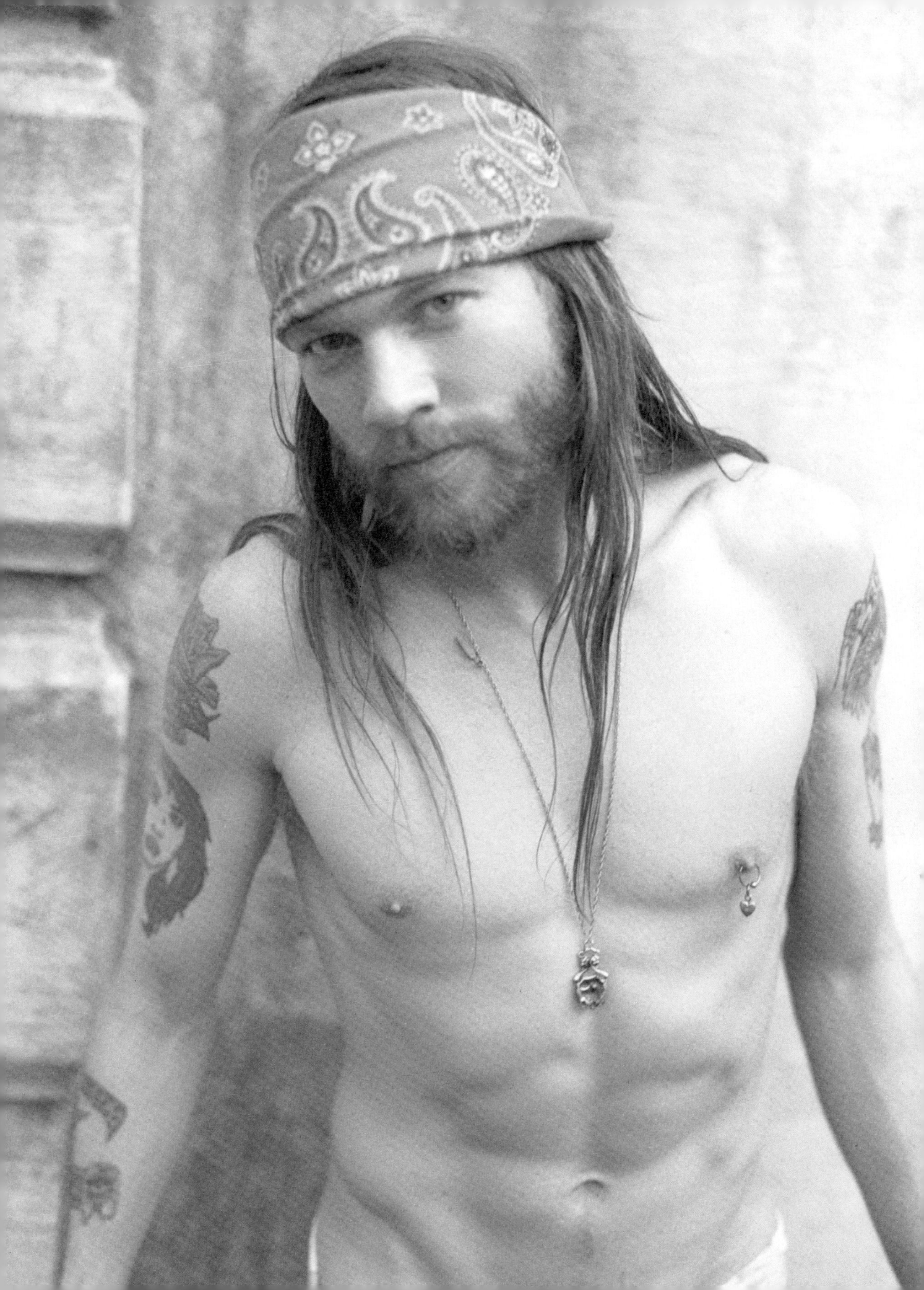

31 Sunday
October 1993

Trick or treat!!
Hallowee[n]
[Daylig]ht Saving Time end[s]
304/6

Woke up late, watched Giants lose 10-6 to Jets! Late lunch at Mezzogiorno with Kara + Naomi. Later we got dressed up + went to Albas Halloween party, me Kara Naomi Kate Christie Christian, Sam etc then we went to the Palladium INXS party + then to Webster Hall! Late night + party party party!!!

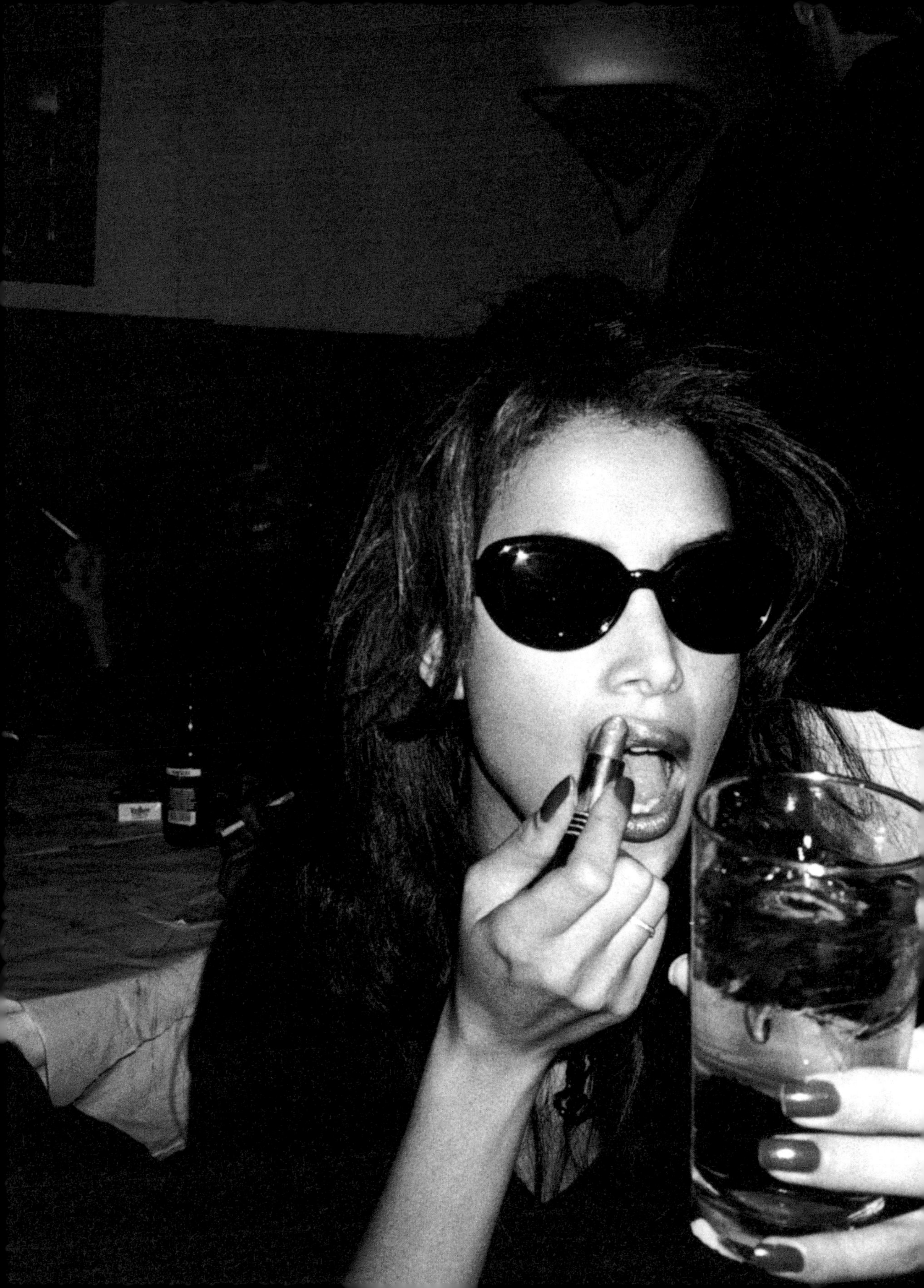

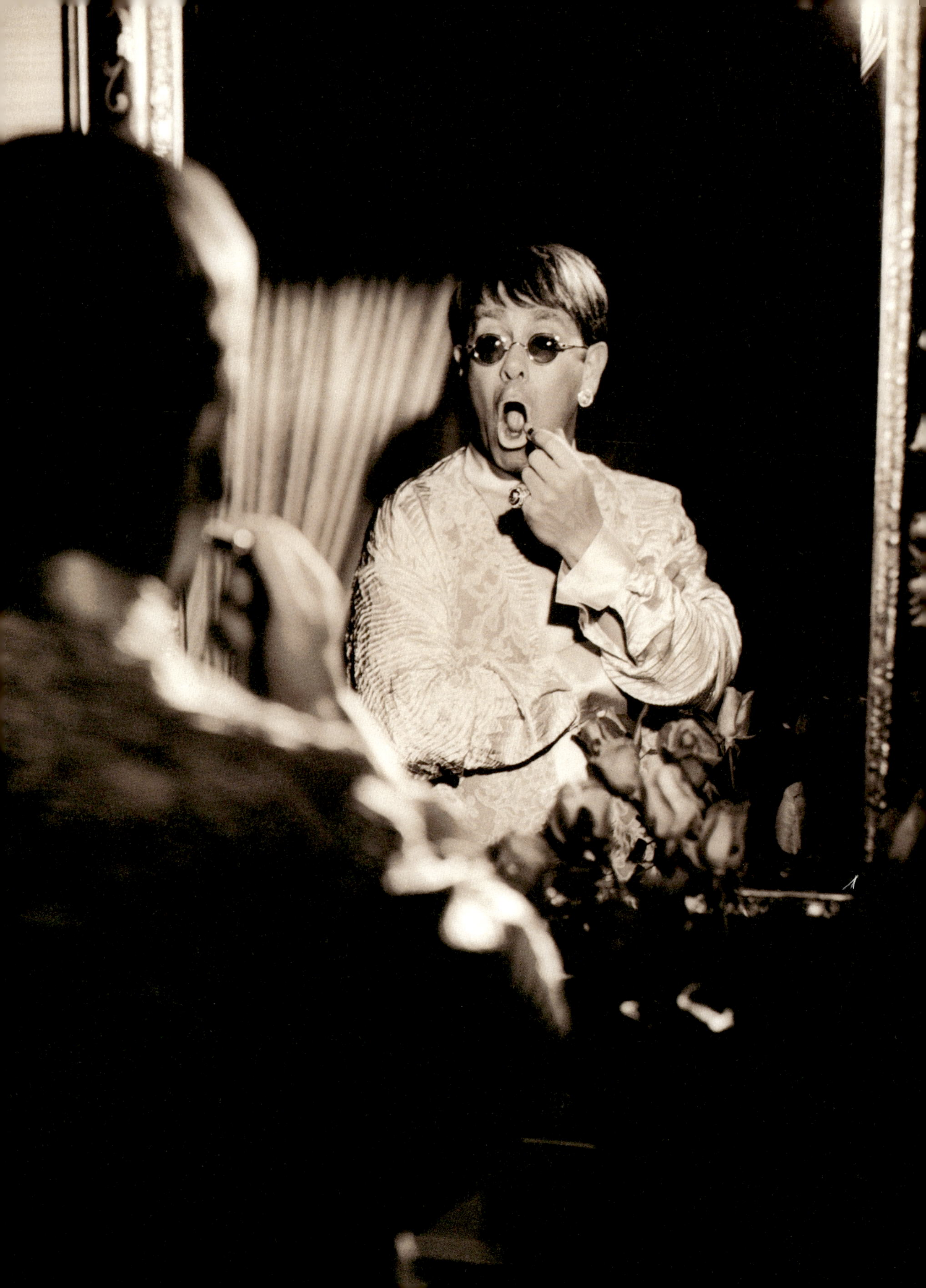

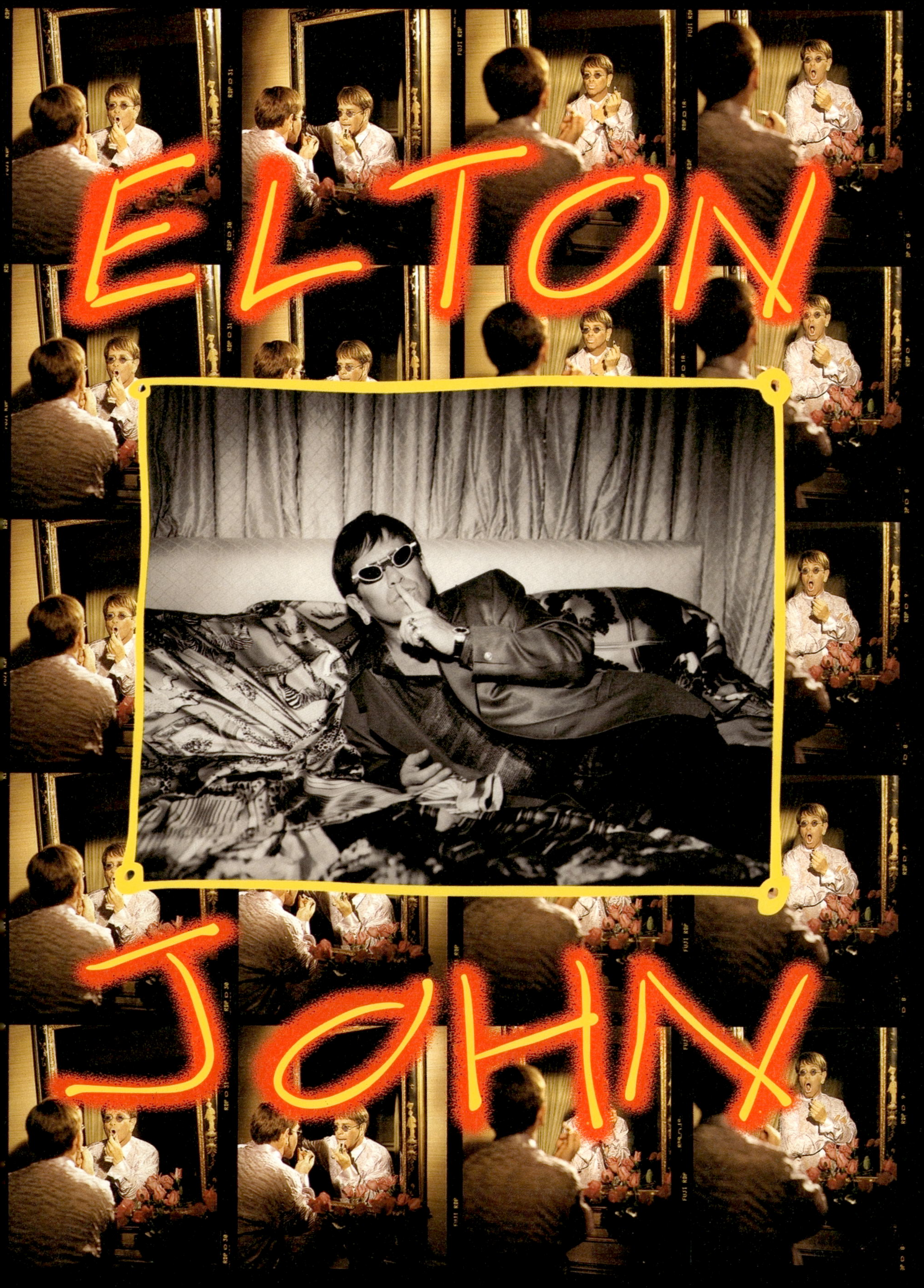

ELTON
JOHN

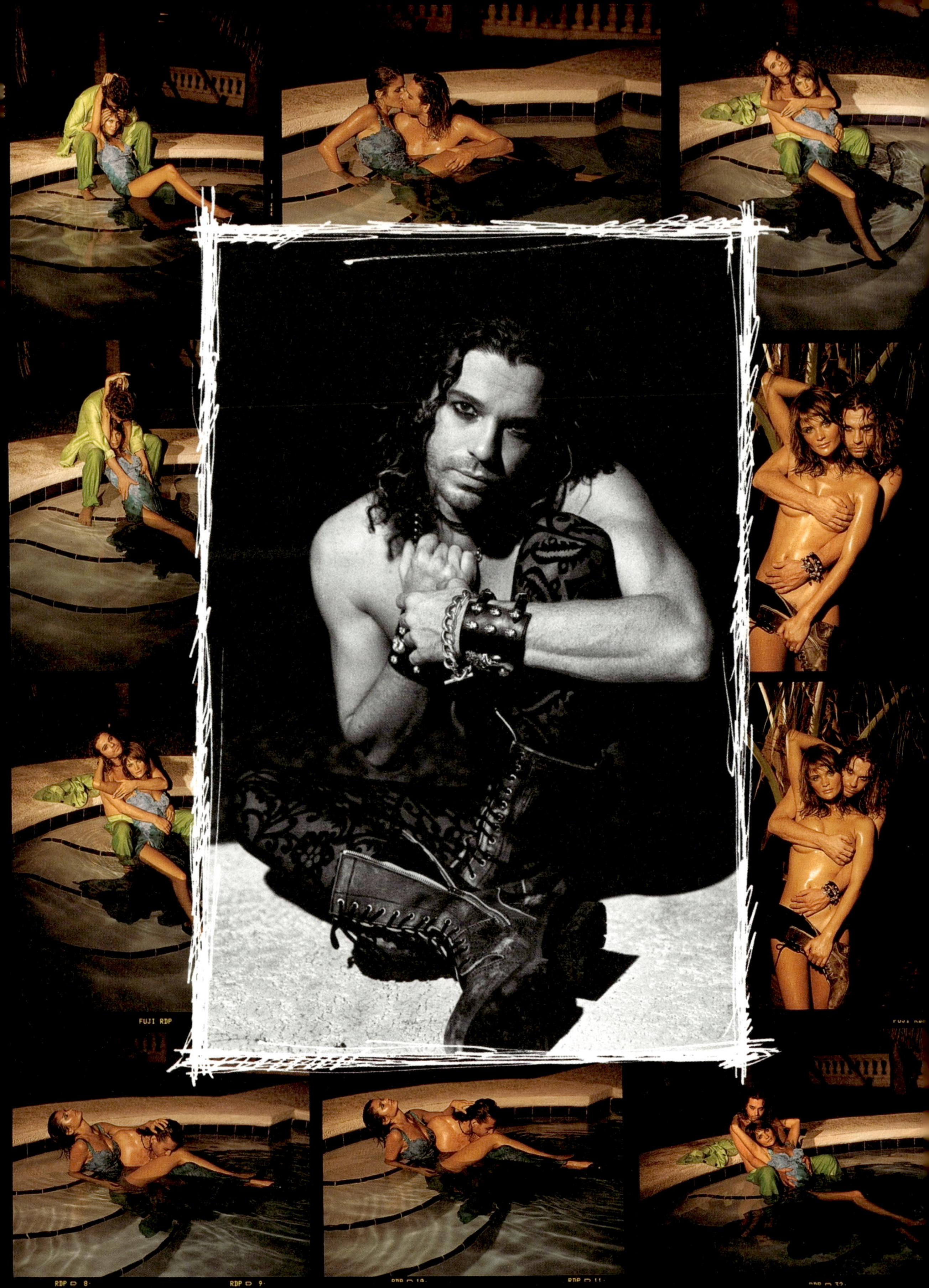

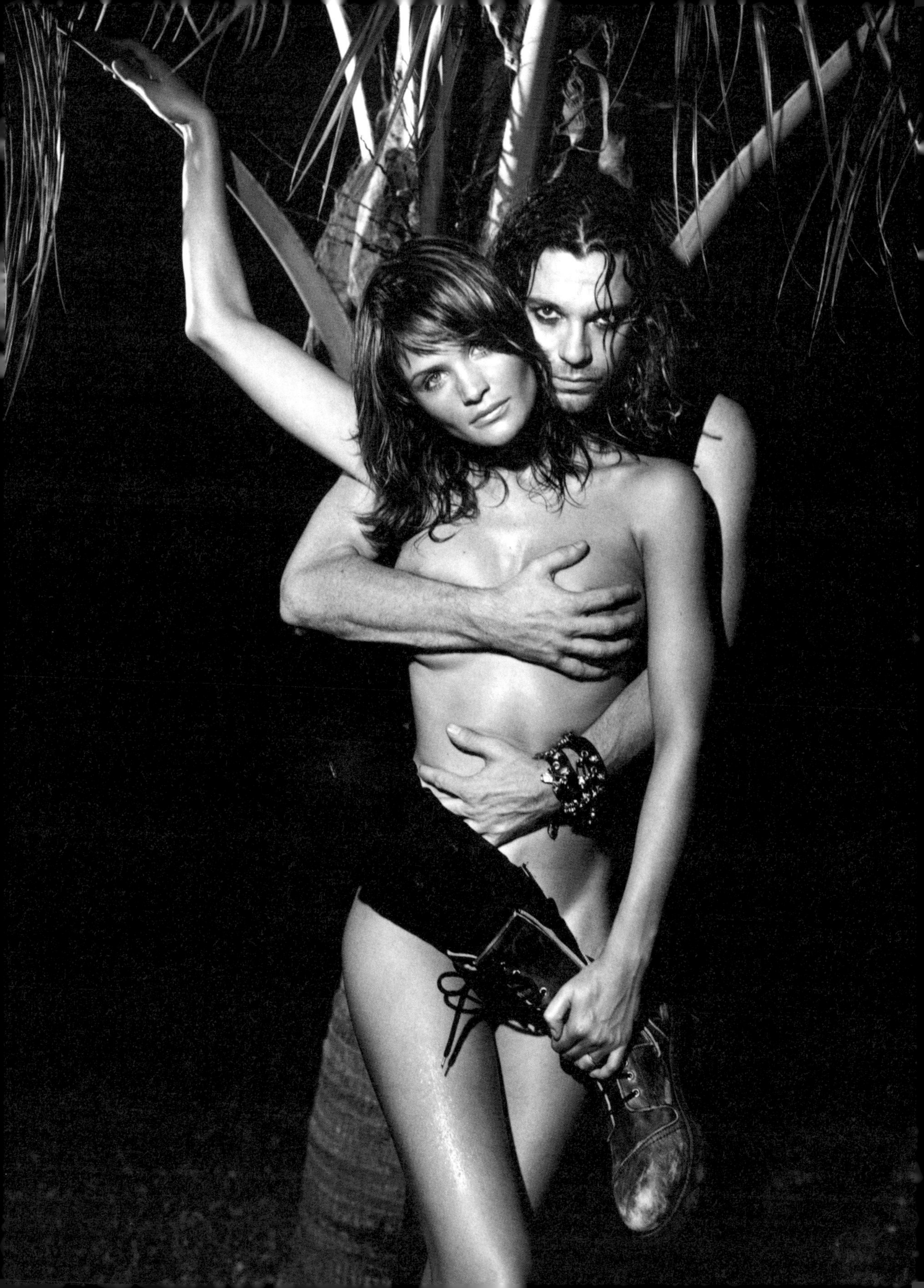

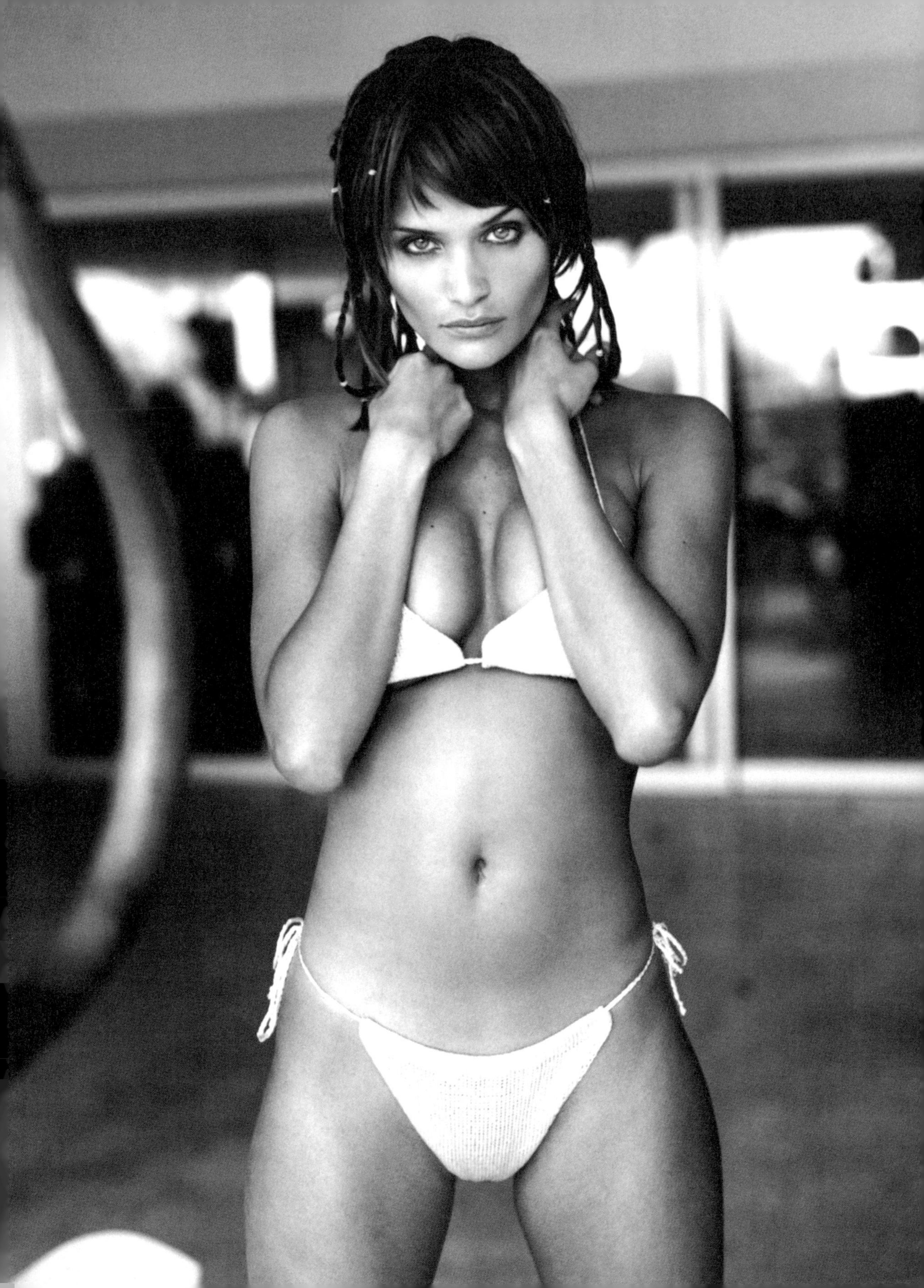

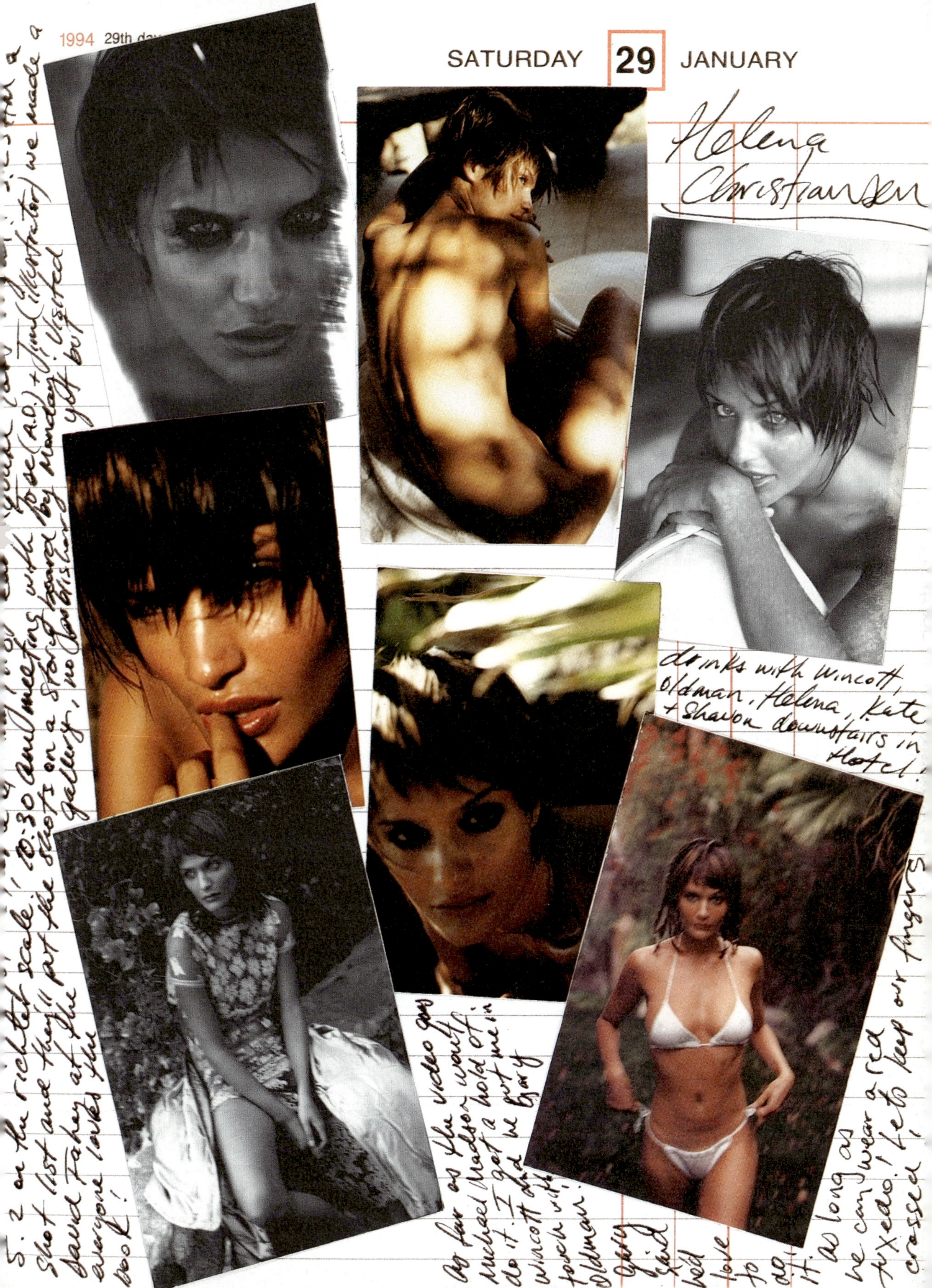

Helena
Christiansen

drinks with Wincott,
Oldman, Helena, Kate
+ Sharon downstairs in
Hotel!

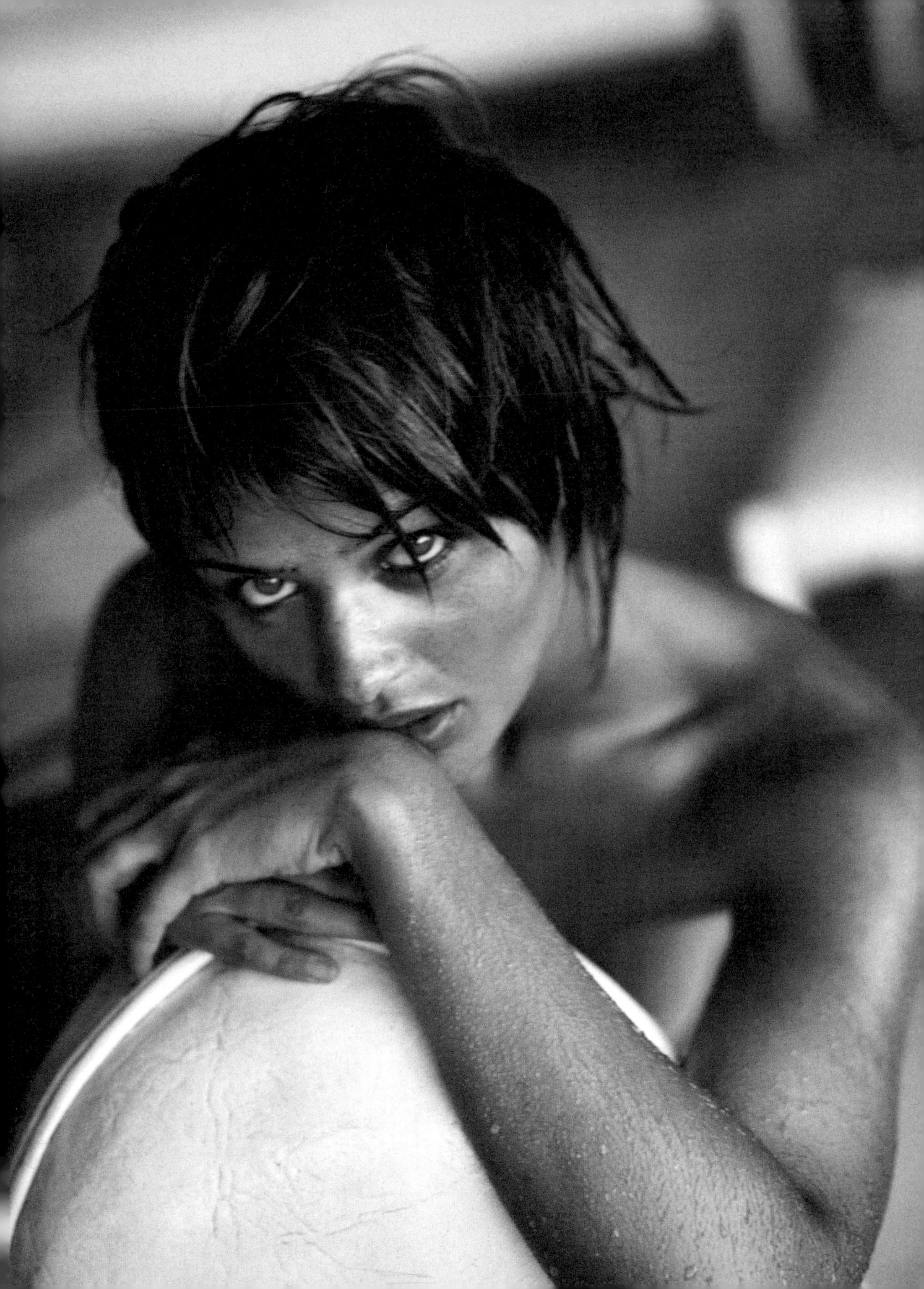

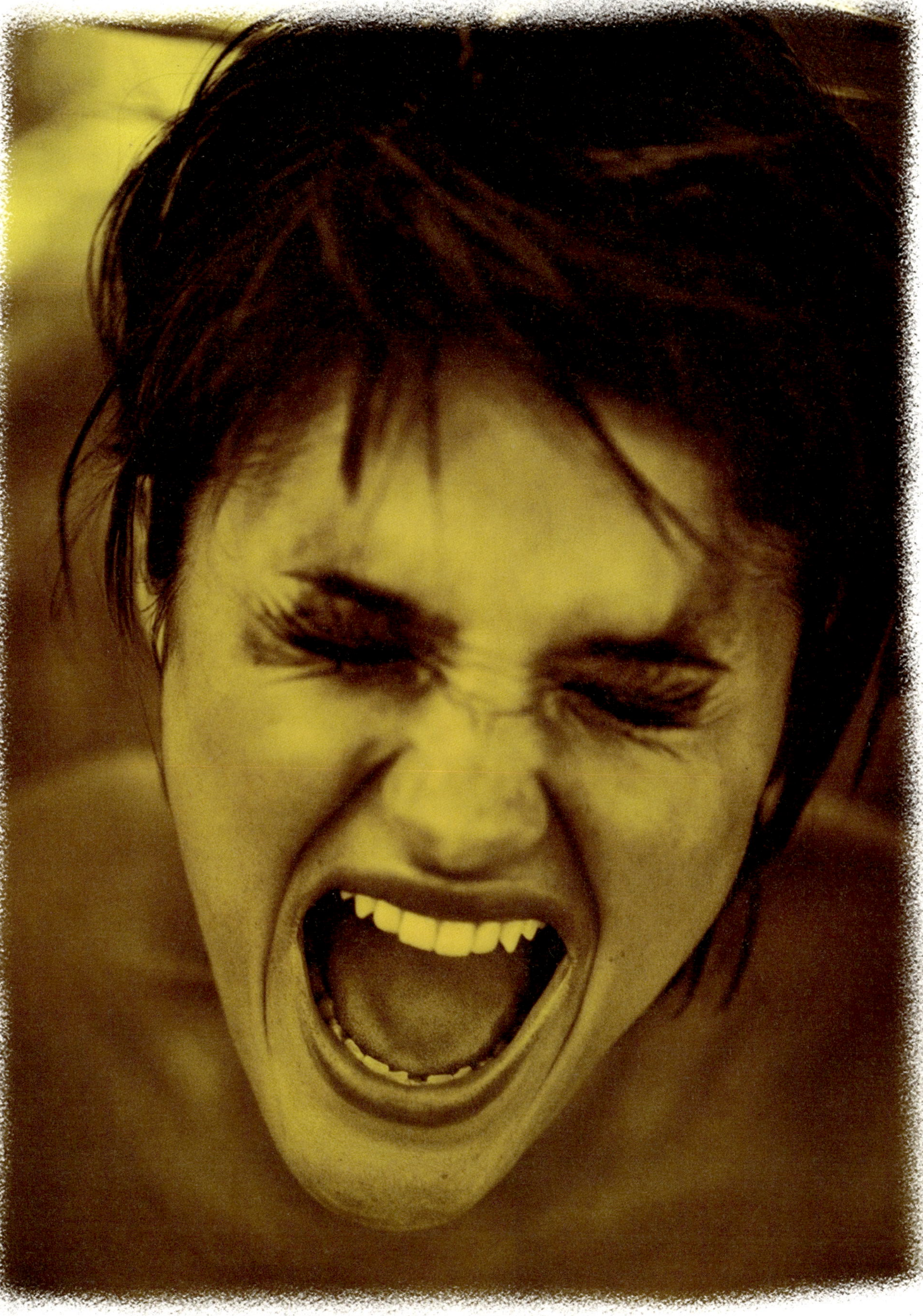

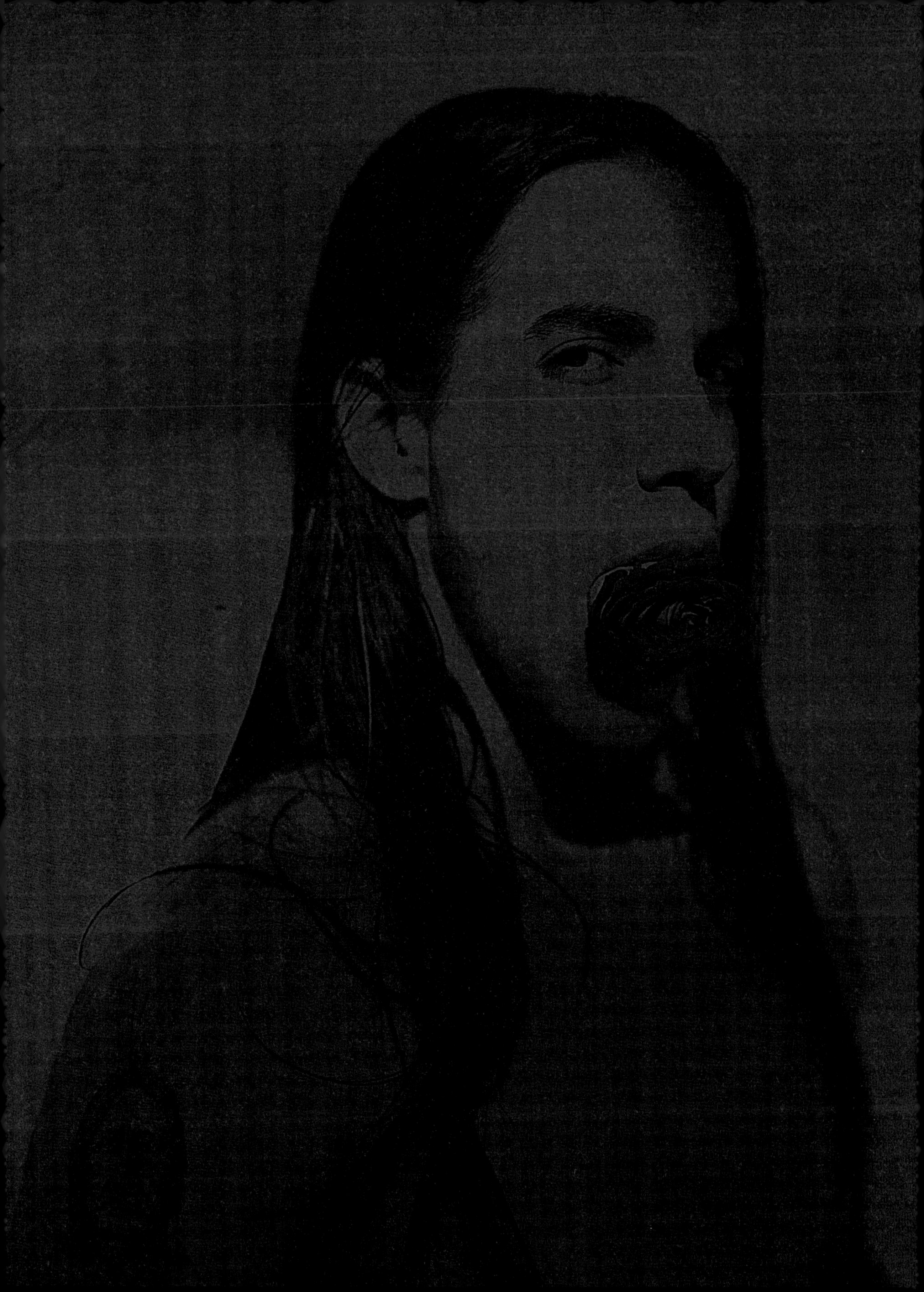

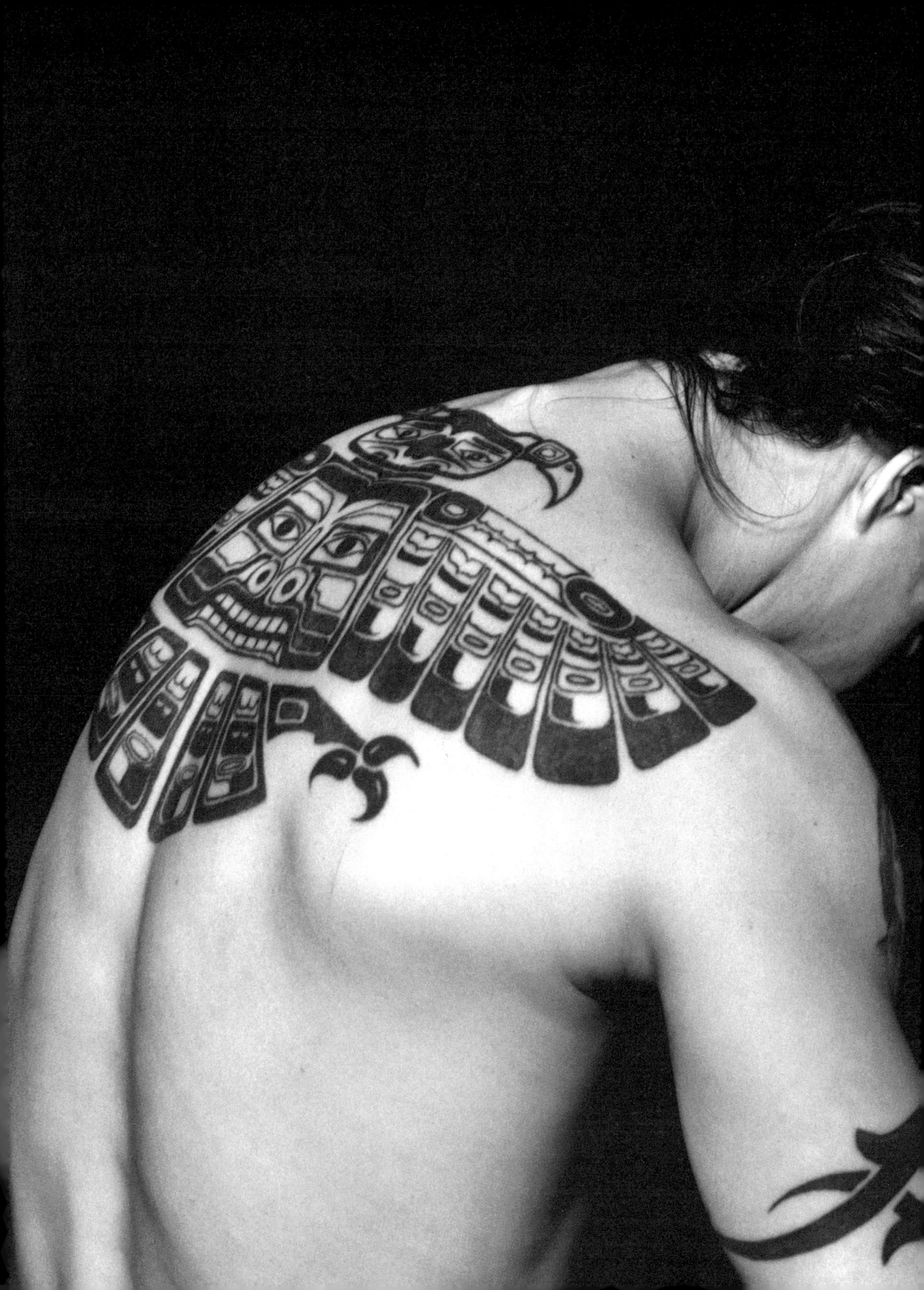

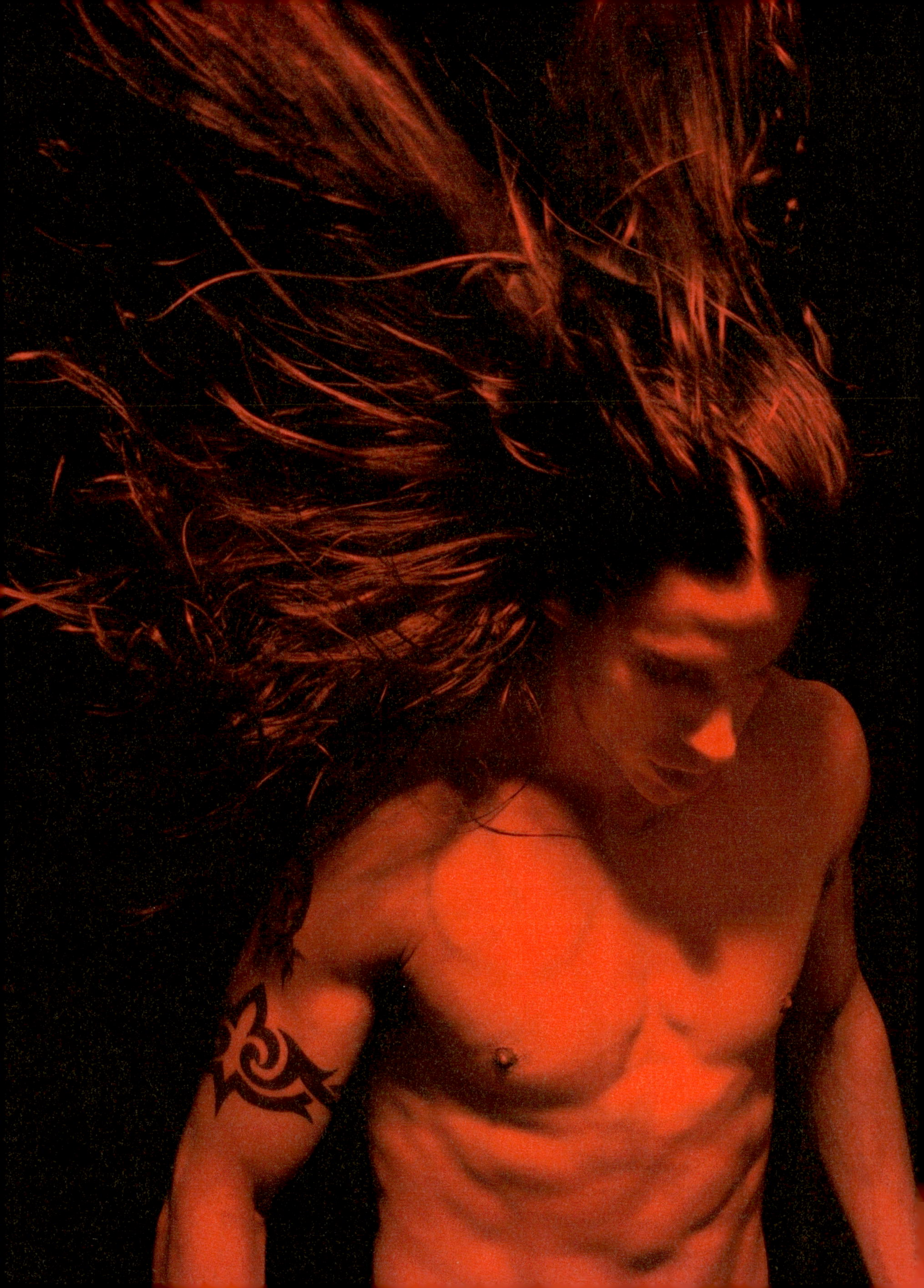

they miss me + love me again.
then came home + edited
then I packed

my pictures were best received
again! Met Kara
B+W

at allure. $550 now.
+ Tahnee for hot chocolate
of Anthony Kiedis,
my bags for tomorrow!

* GNR - ax1
video confirmed

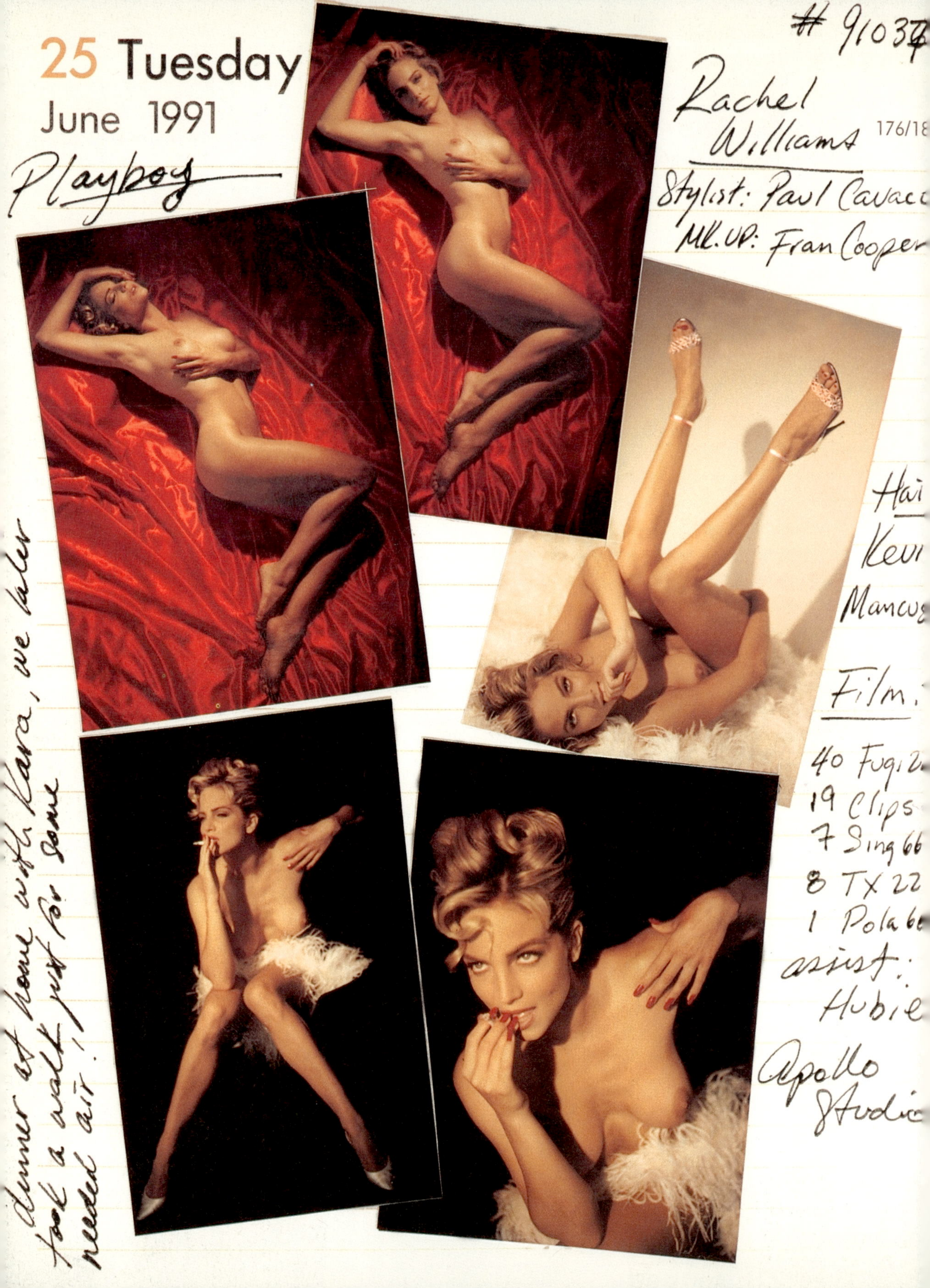
25 Tuesday
June 1991
Playboy
91037
Rachel
Williams
176/18
Stylist: Paul Cavaco
Mk. Up: Fran Cooper
Hai
Kevi
Mancus
Film:
40 Fuji 2
19 Clips
7 Sing 66
8 TX 22
1 Polab
assist:
Hubie
Apollo
Studio
dinner at home with Kara, we later
took a walk just for some
needed air!

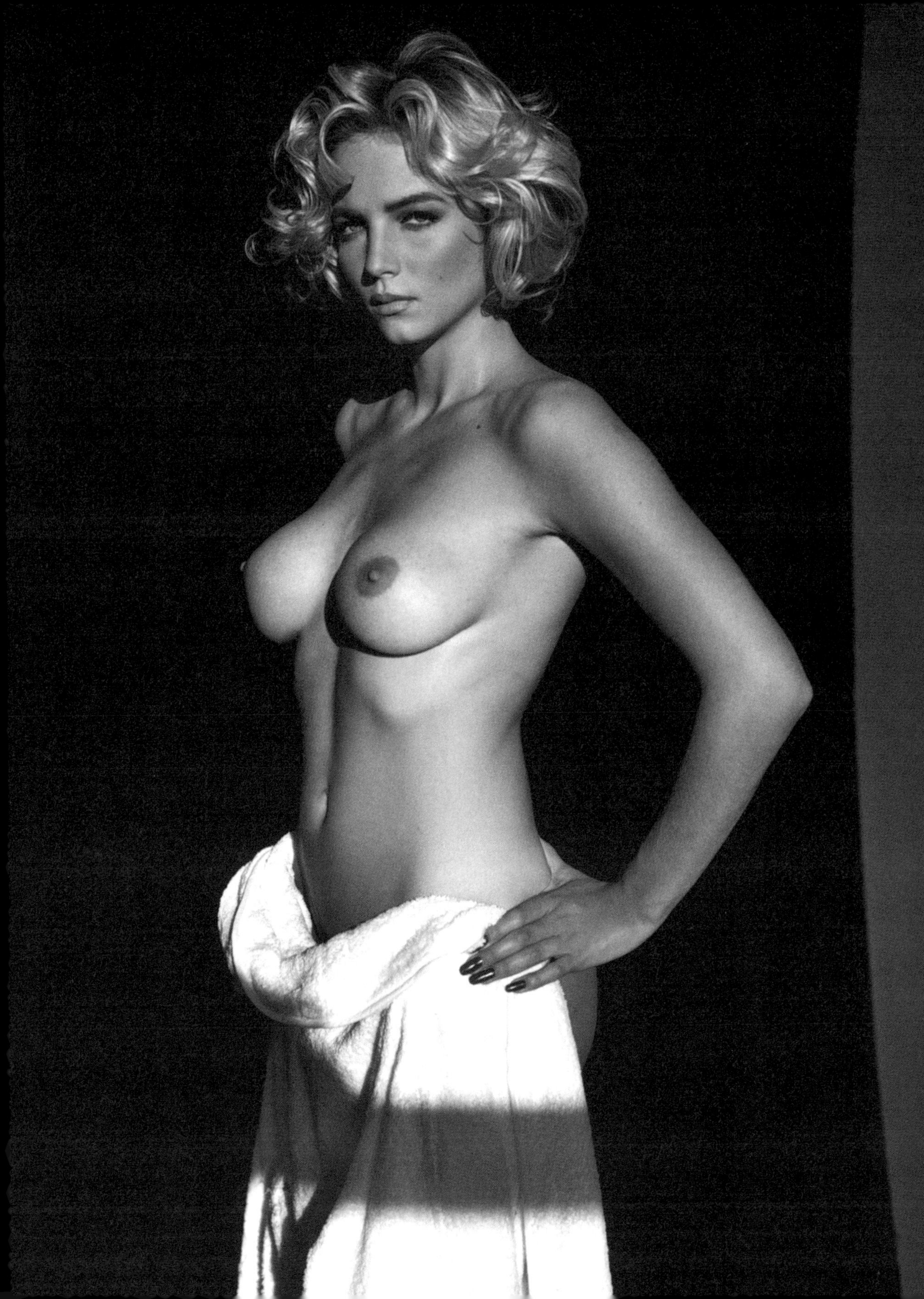

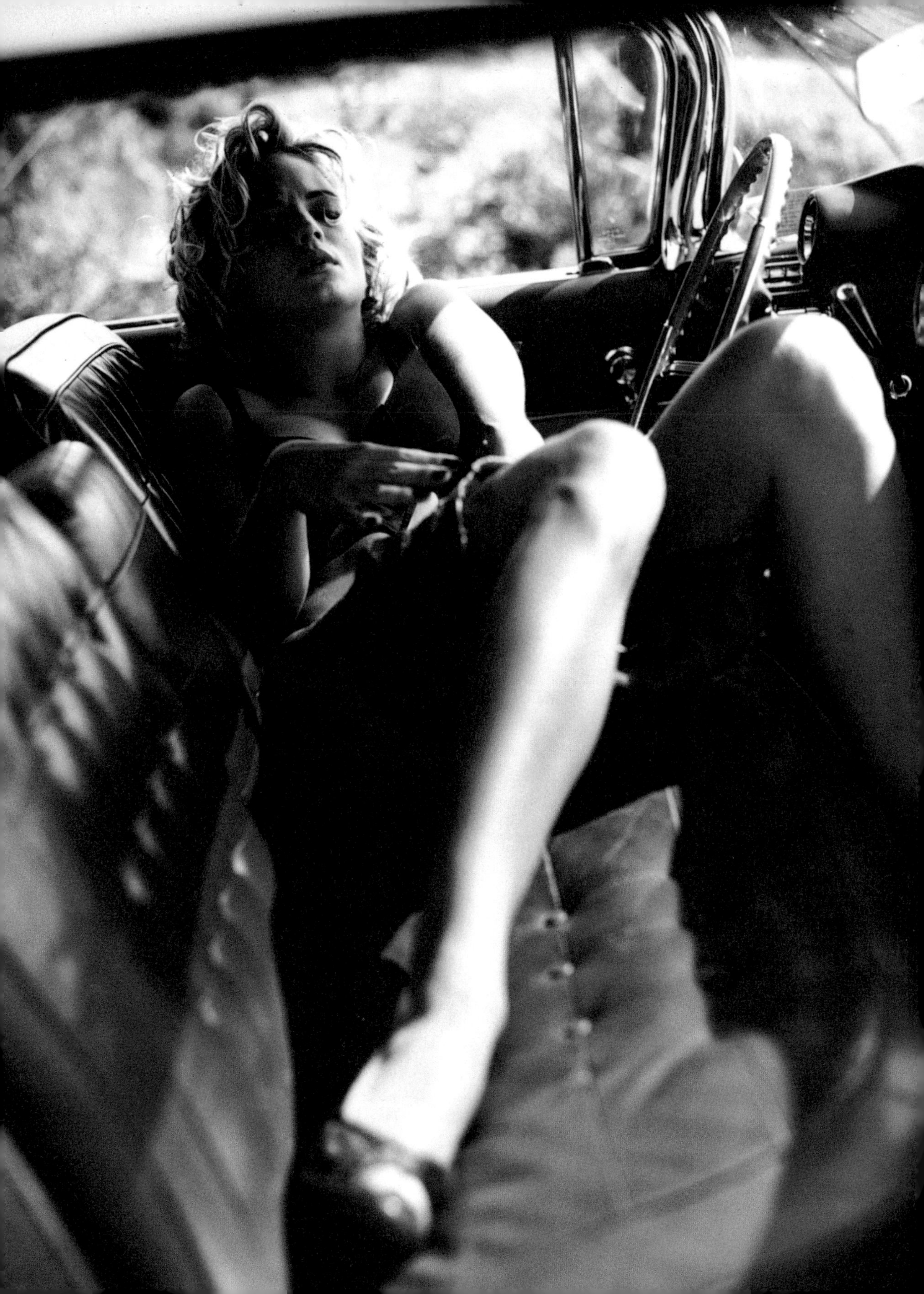

#91037
Montauk
77/188

tylist:
Andrew
om Paul Cavaco
air: Kevin
Mancuso
k.up: Fulvia

shots
dinner at
crew + Jul

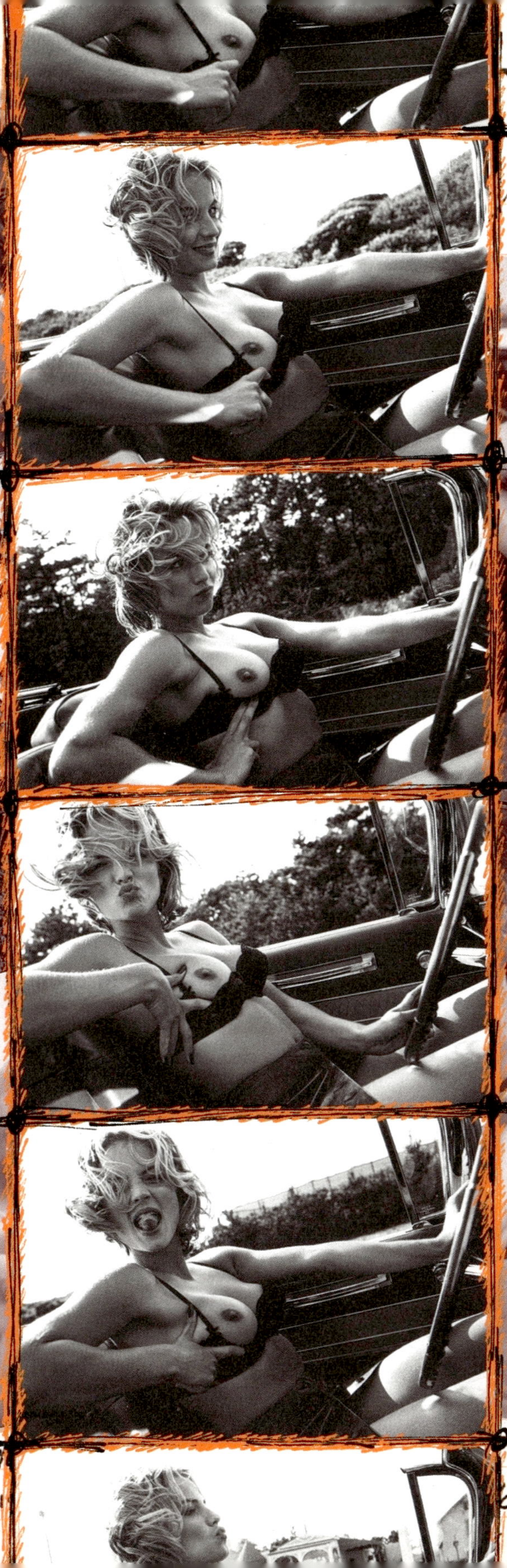

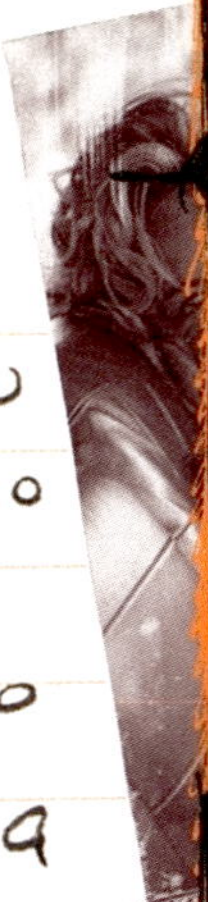

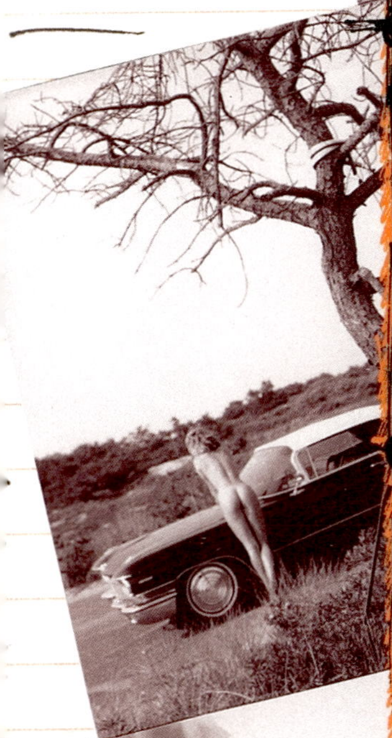

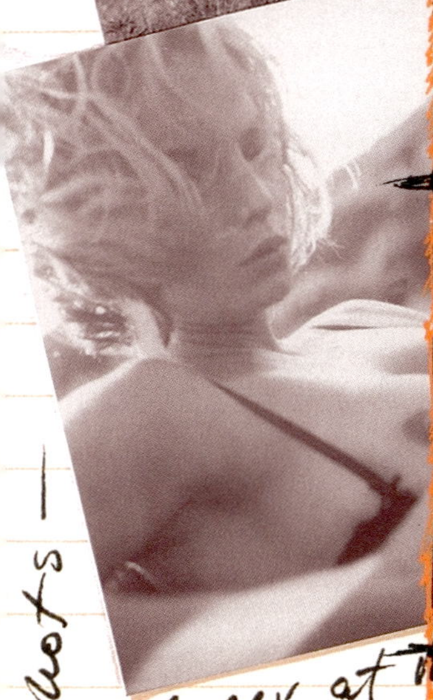

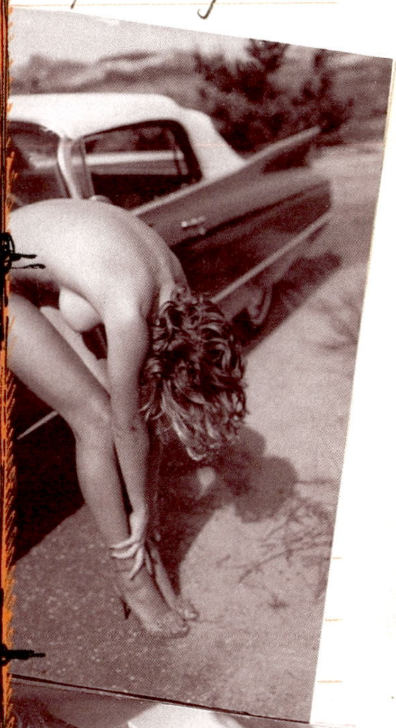

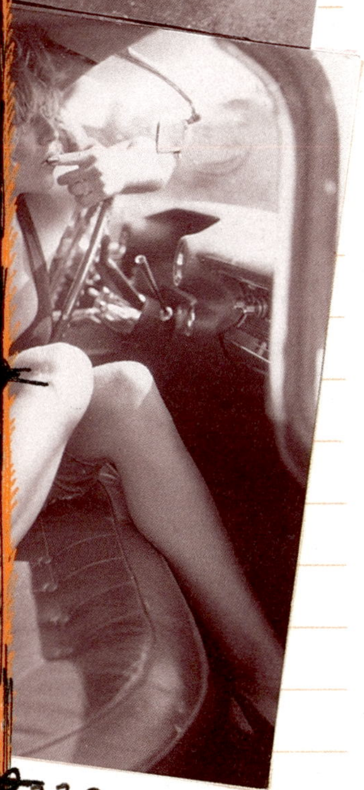

Playboy —

hesday **26**
June. 1991

220
665
135

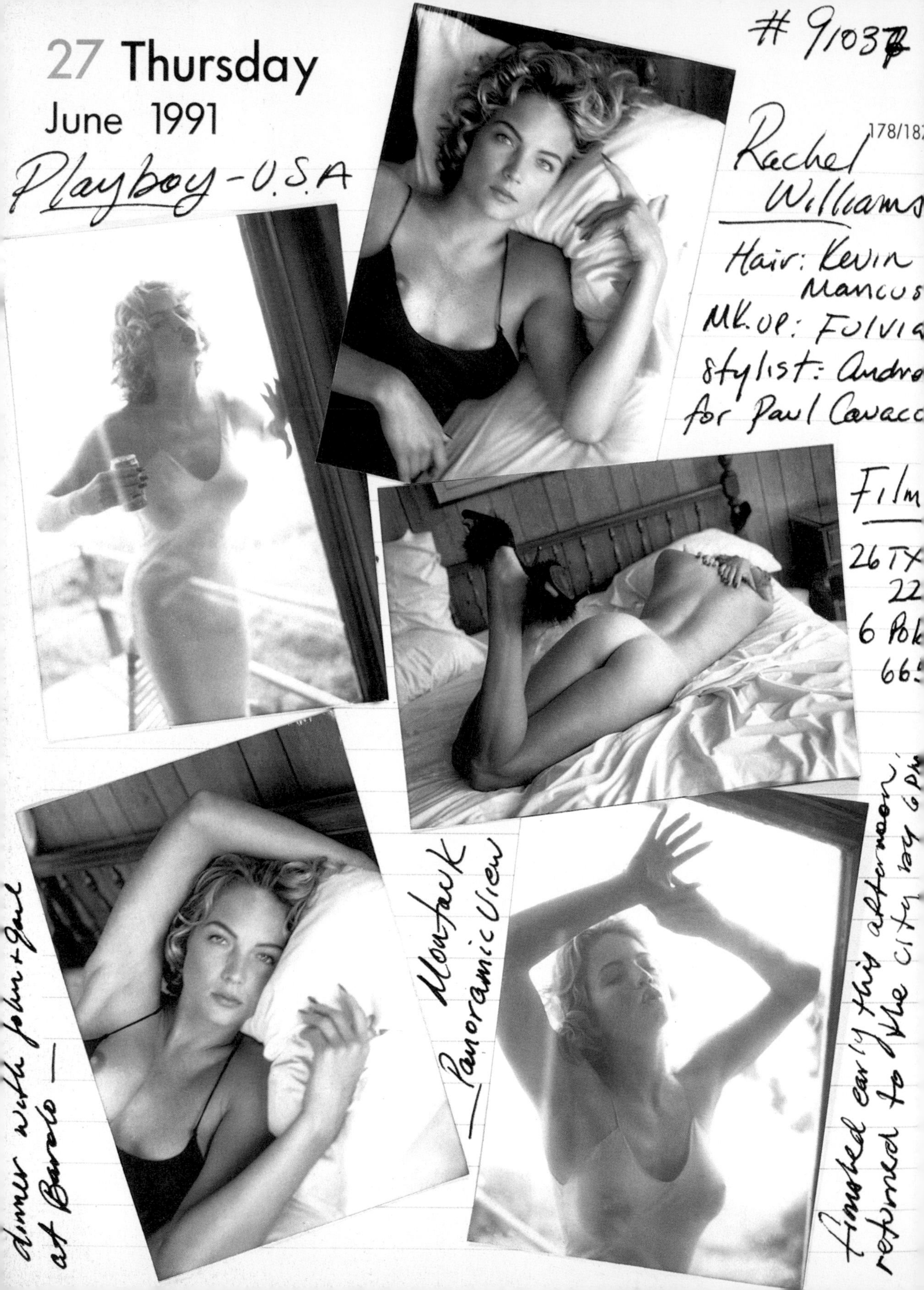
27 Thursday
June 1991
Playboy - U.S.A

91037
178/18?
Rachel
Williams
Hair: Kevin
Mancos
Mk.up: Fulvia
Stylist: Andro
for Paul Cavaco

Film
26 TX
22
6 Pol
66.5

Montauk
— Panoramic View

dinner with John + Gail
at Barolo —

finished early this afternoon,
returned to the city by 6 PM

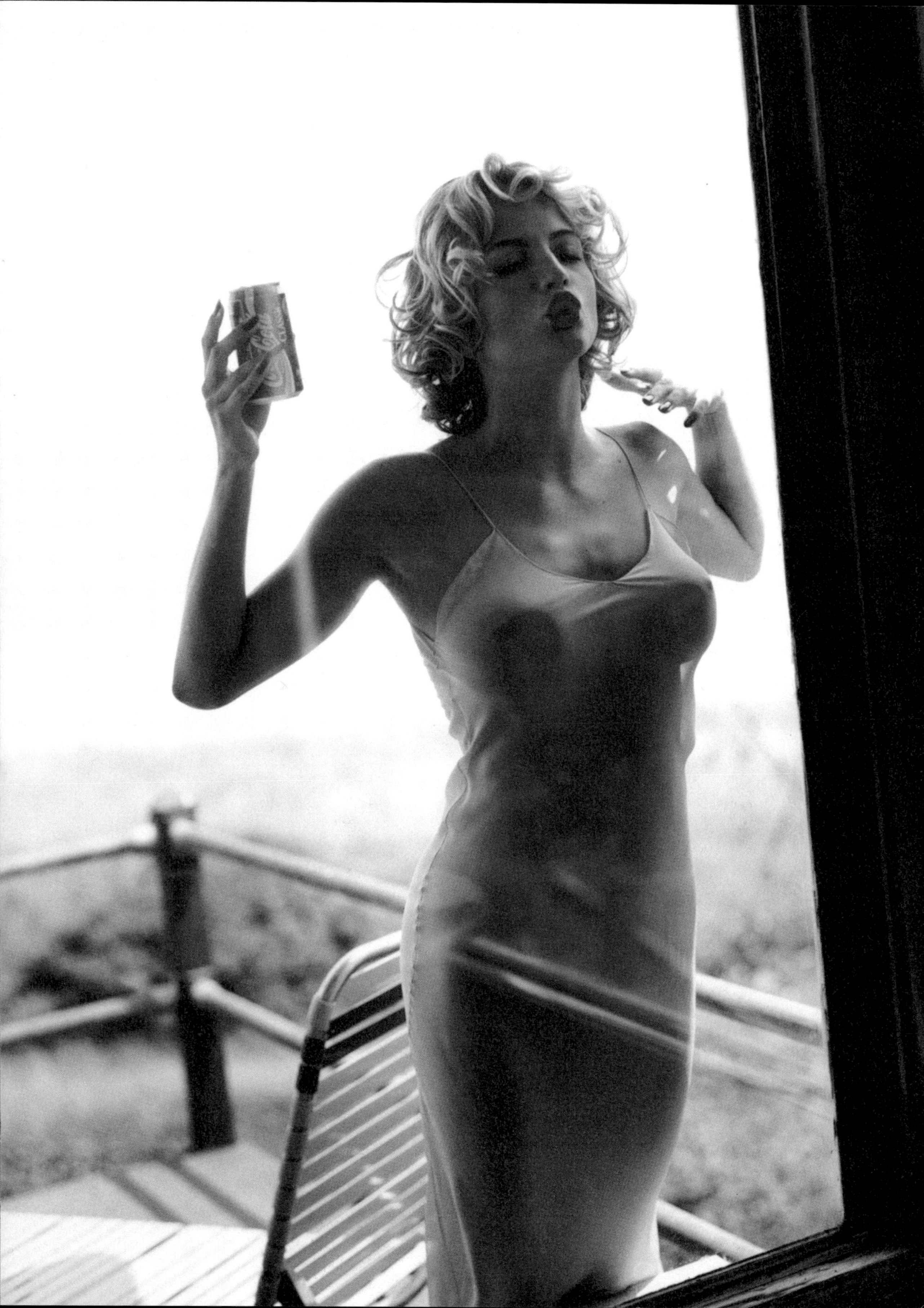

Took a walk this morn to Book Store looking for info on St Francis. Back home went over script! Roy came by + with Kava + Tony went to have lunch at Mezzogiorno! Back home worked on script again the Ilene Silberman (T.V. agent) came over to meet me + we looked at "Sammy" together! Worked more on script. Niki Taylor came over So did Joyce + Ucira with food. Ucira locked her keys in door Kava + girls went to the movies I waited for Mike to come by with keys!

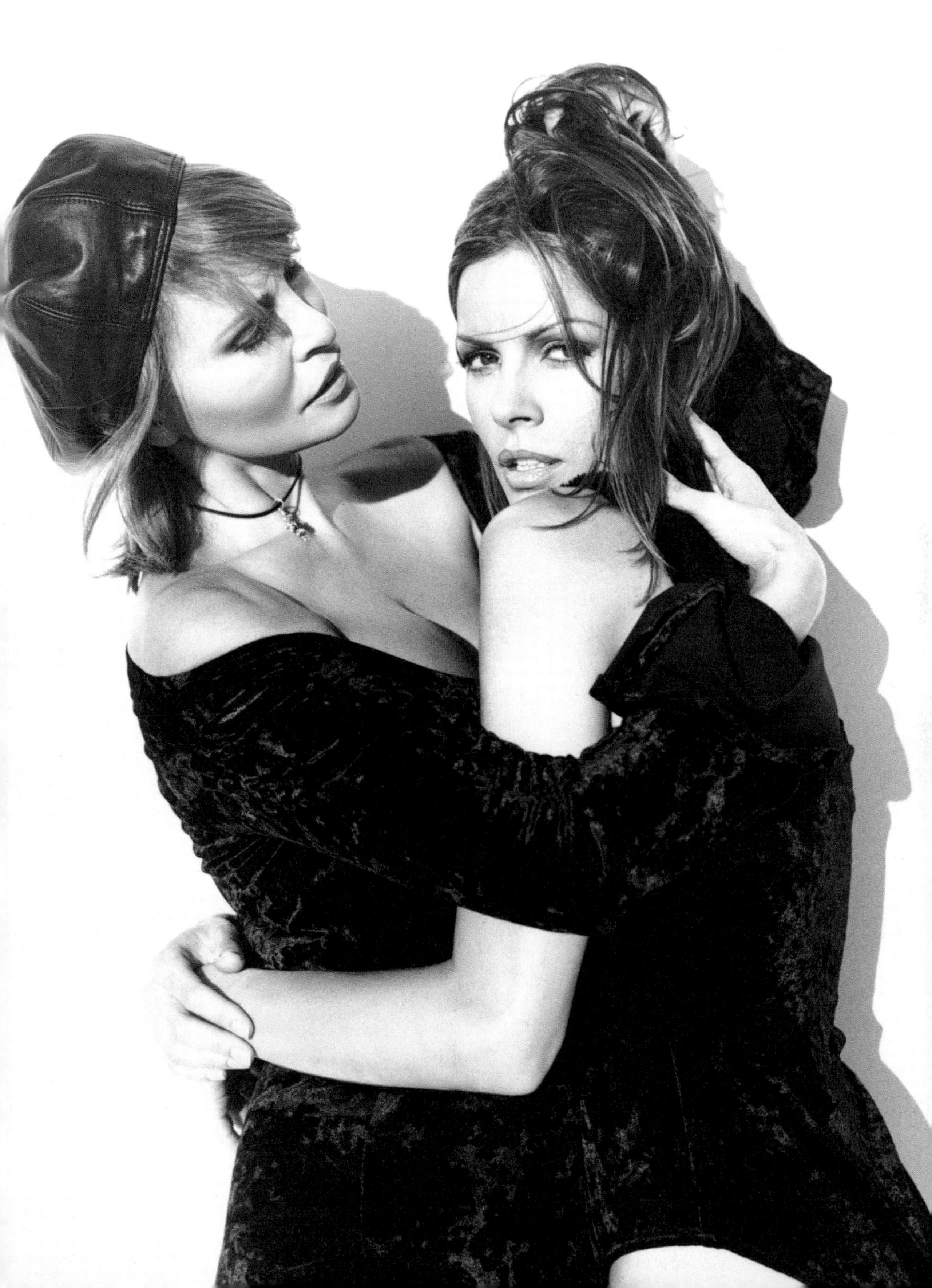

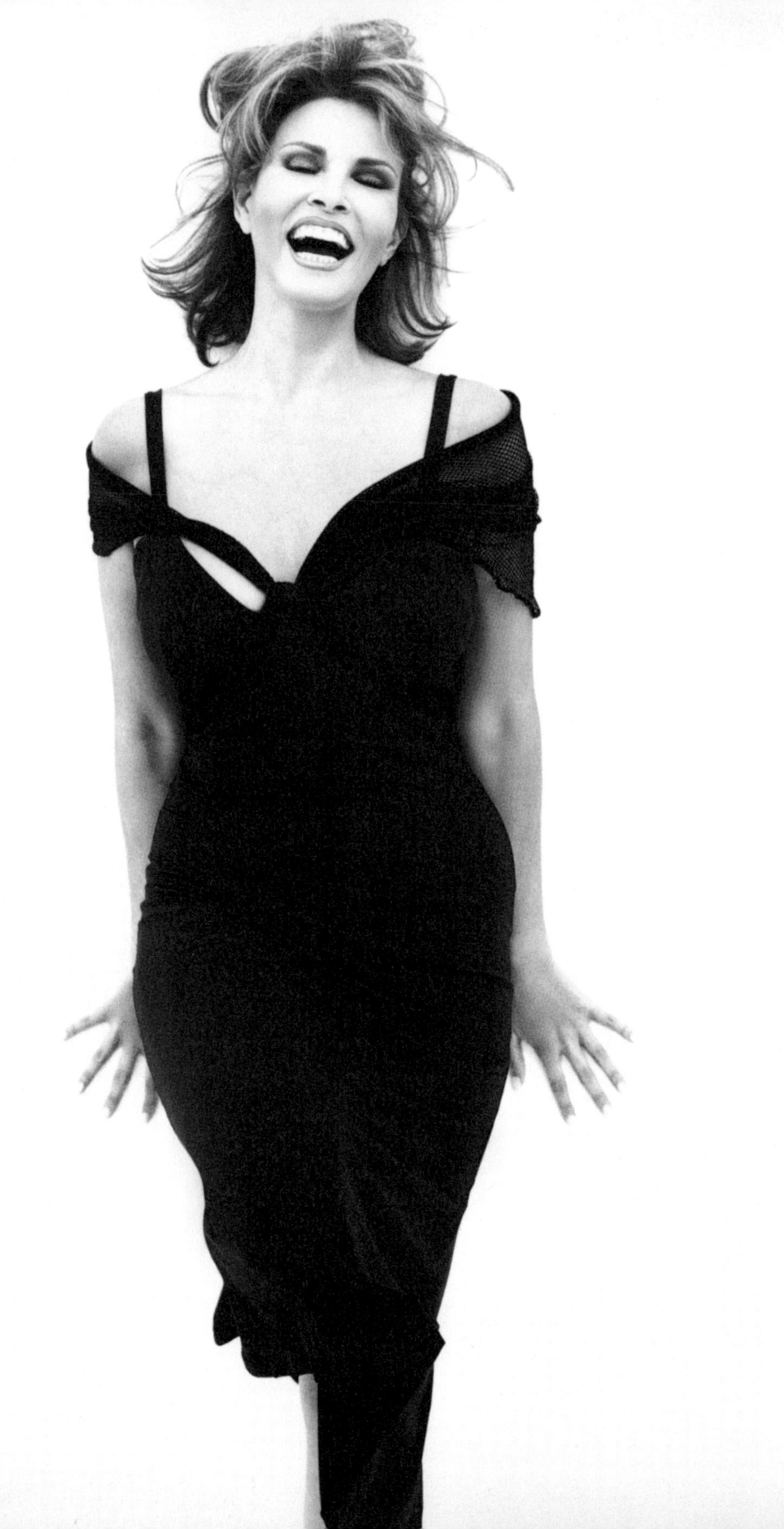

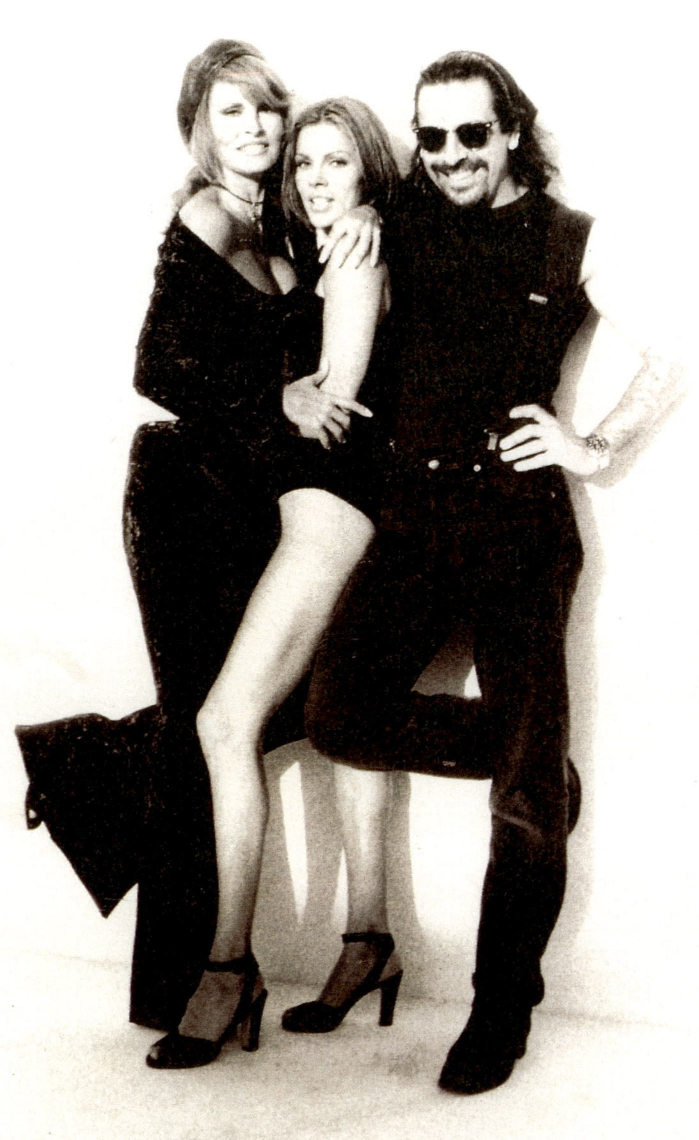

3PM meeting with Lori Kratochvil at Rolling Stone Magazine! Looks like we might do some work together! Spent part of the day on the phone + the other part working on the script! Went to dinner at the Chinese restaurant down on Canal St with Kava + Tahnee then to Tabac for a drink! Back home, Kava + I watched "Mi...

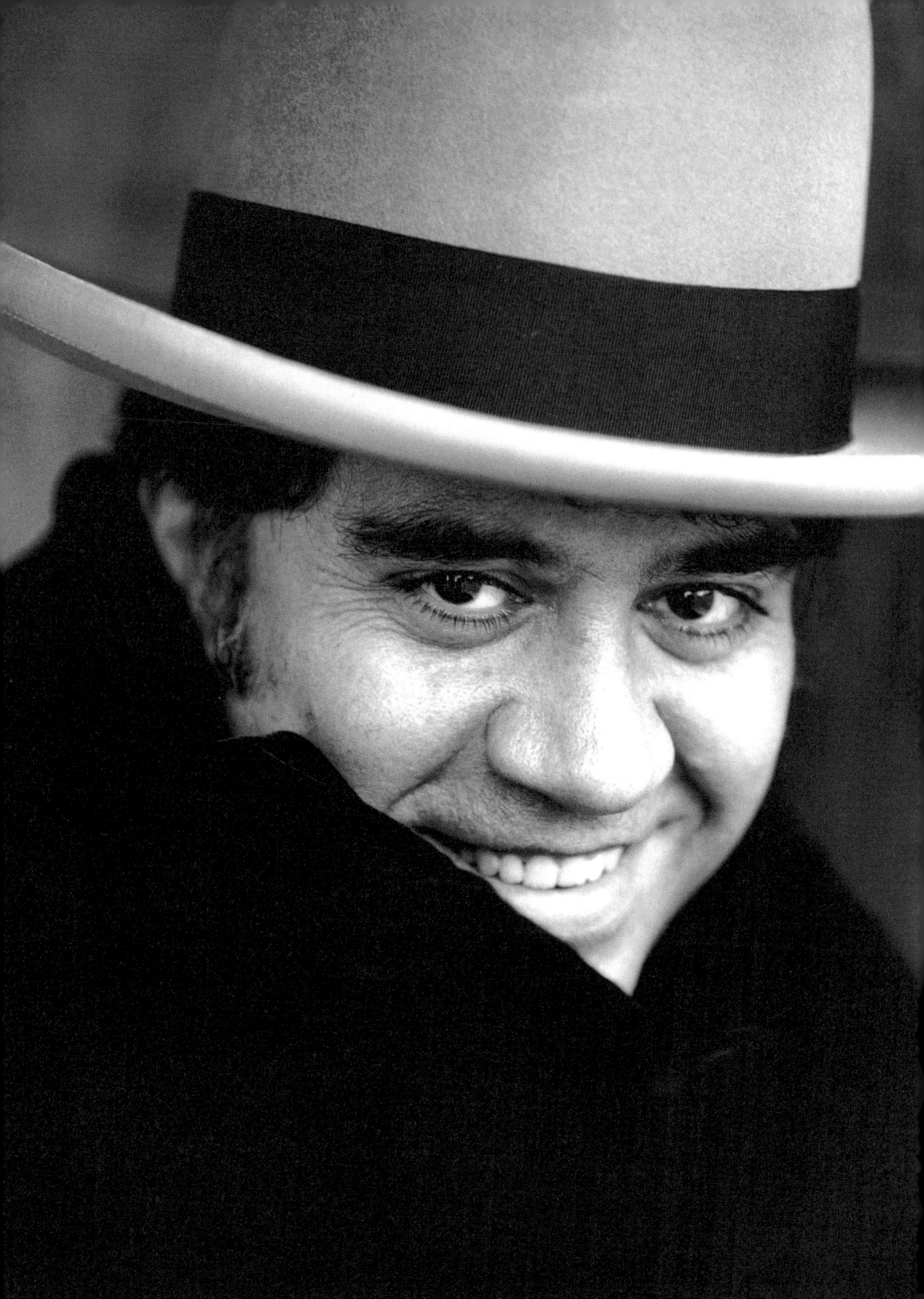

BARCELONA 3ᵉ

B

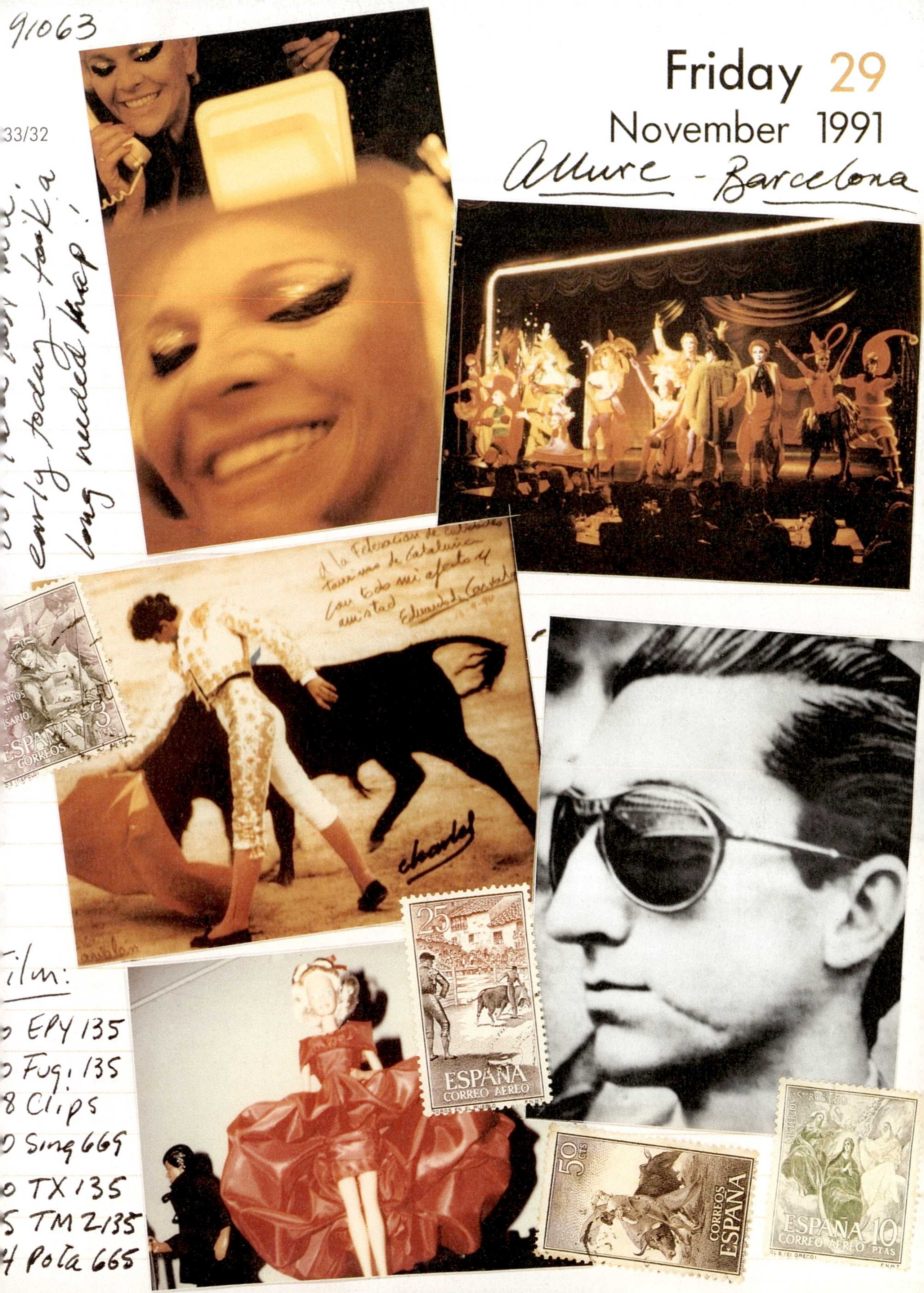
91063
33/32

Friday 29
November 1991
Allure - Barcelona

film:
EPY 135
Fuji 135
8 Clips
Sing 669
TX 135
TM 2 135
Pola 665

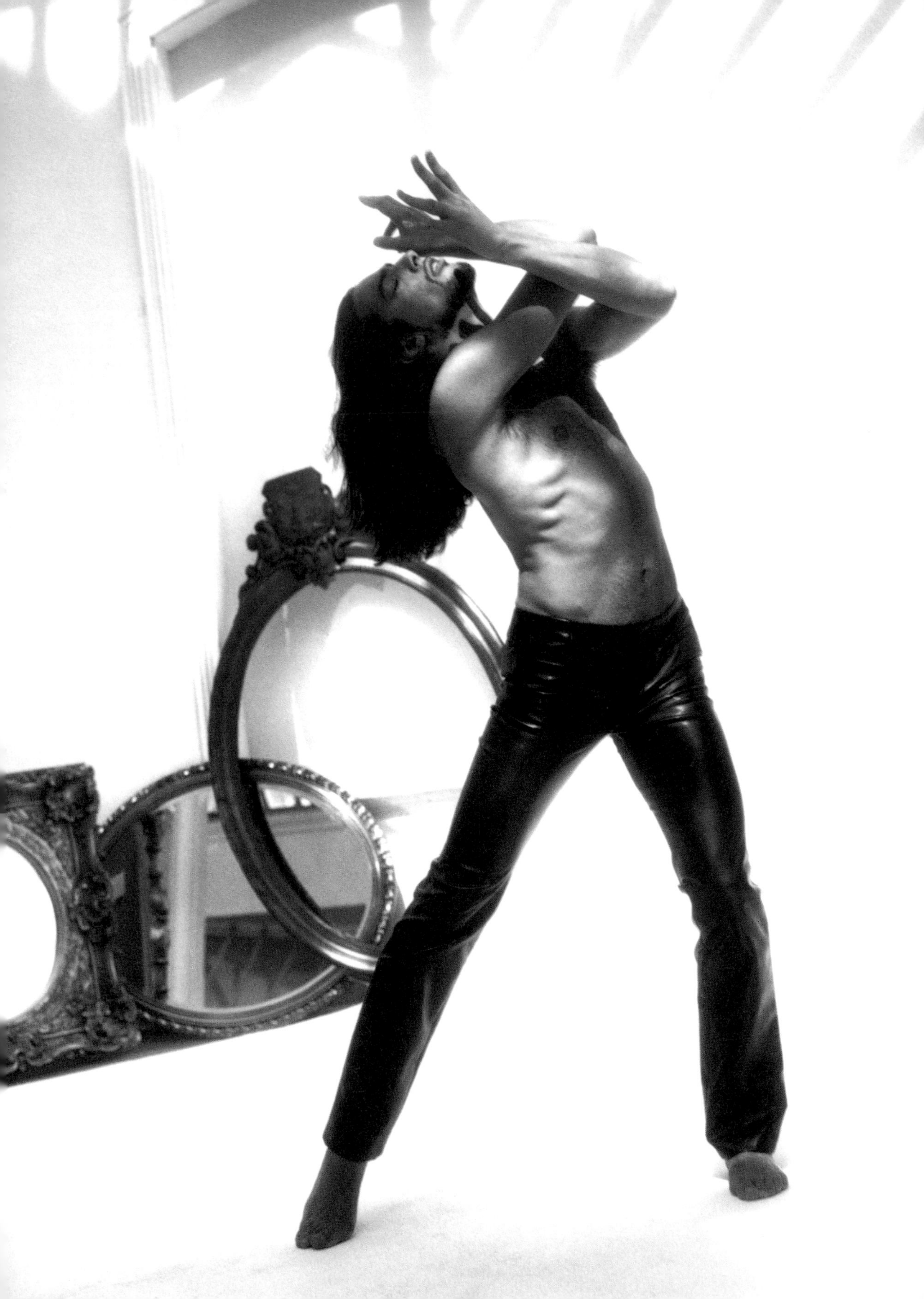

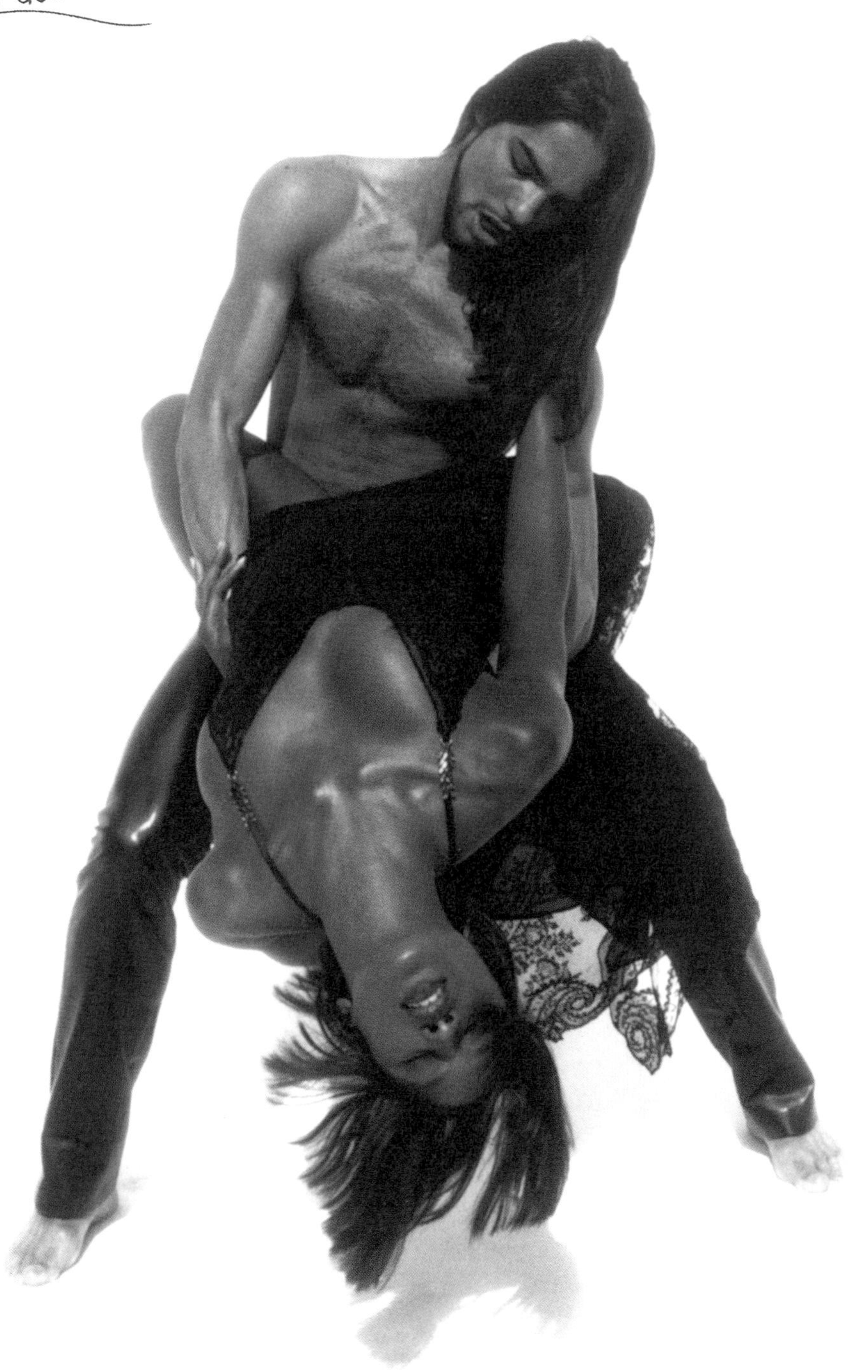

...t at beginnings. He was adorable and played mostly with the trains. I love him! Edited most of today. Went to Valentino party with Bob + Gab at le Colonial. Ran into Sharon Stone + Elisabeth Shue!

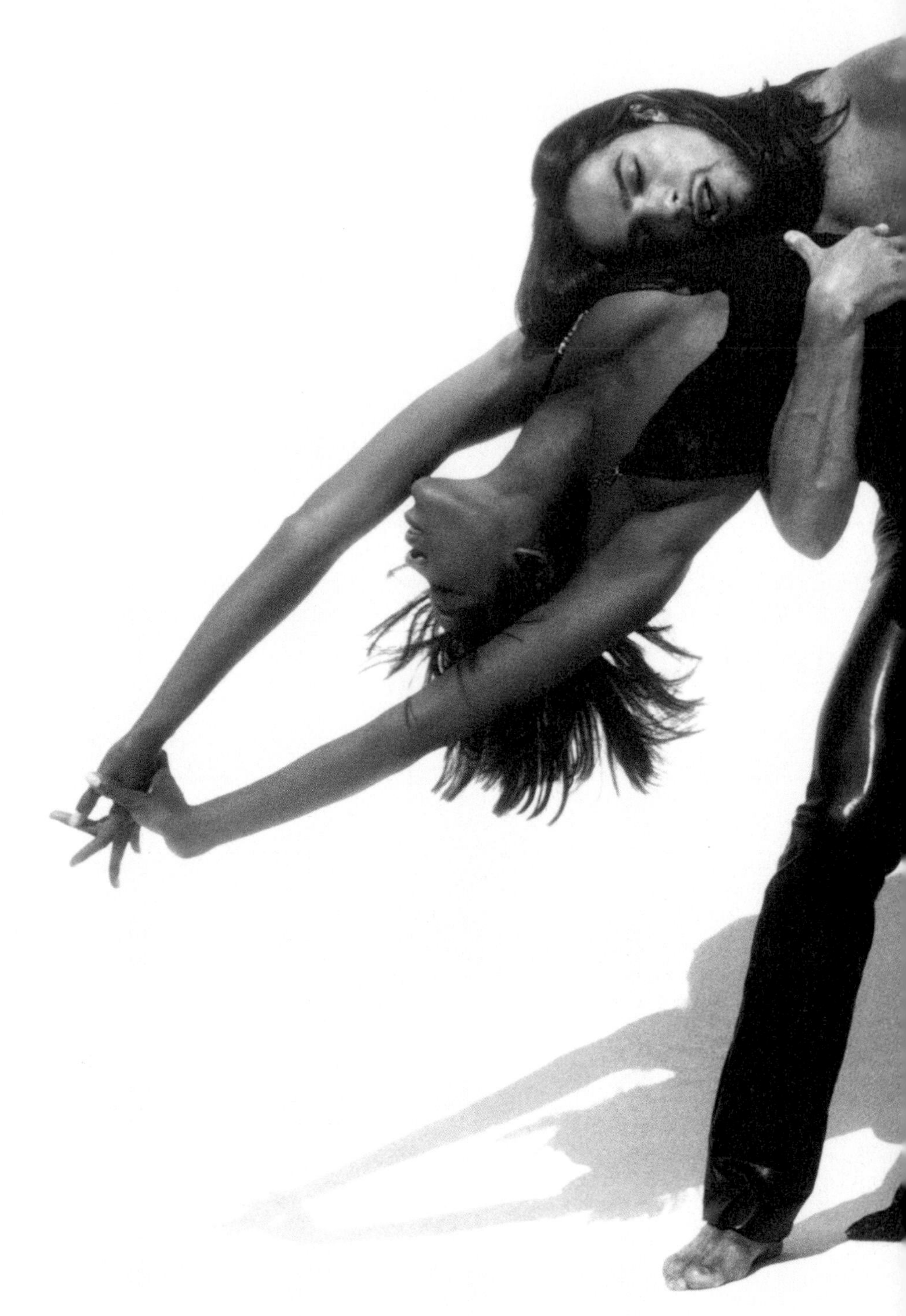

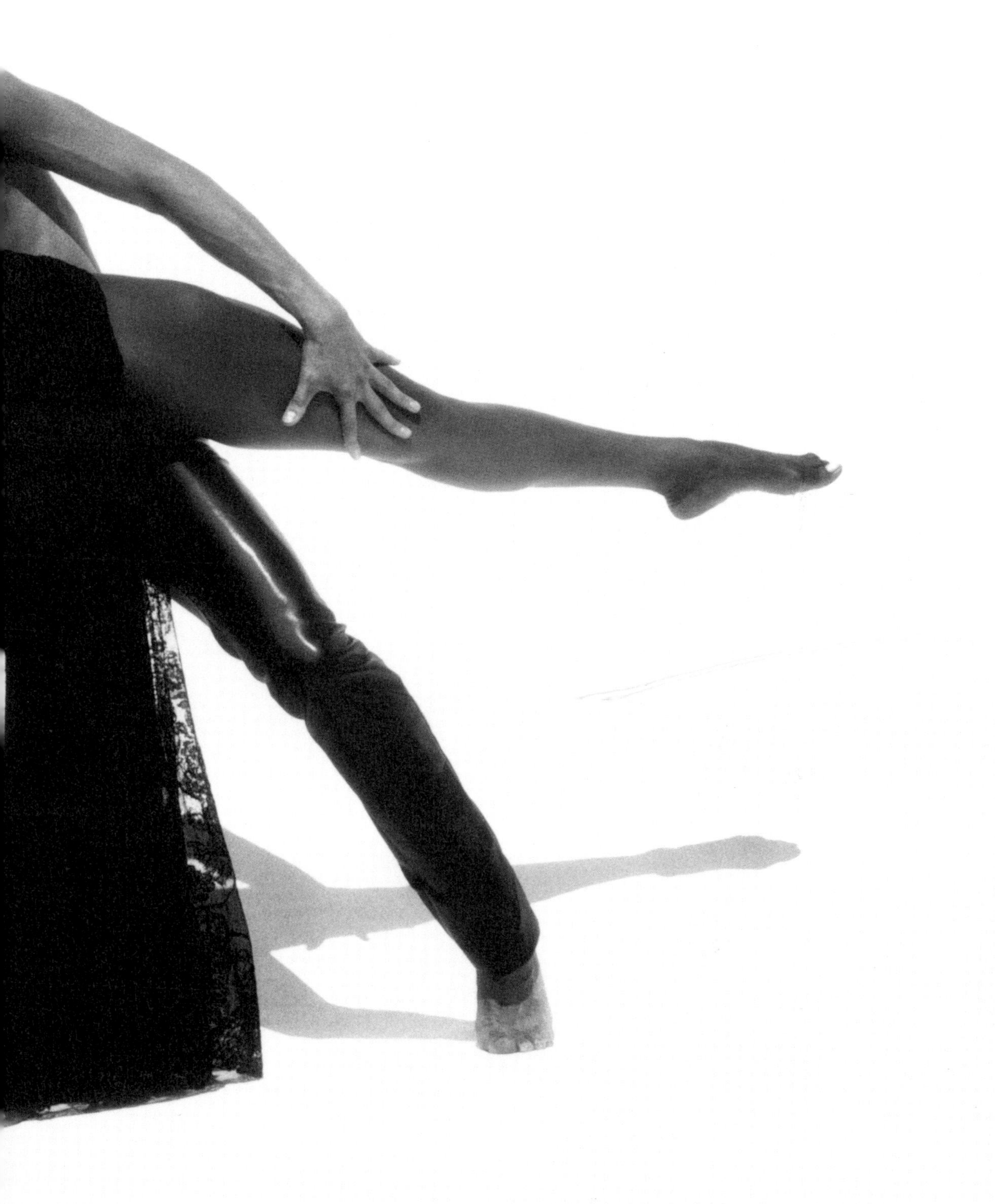

#96059

Joaquin Cortés
& Naomi

Versace

Stylist. Liwren Scott

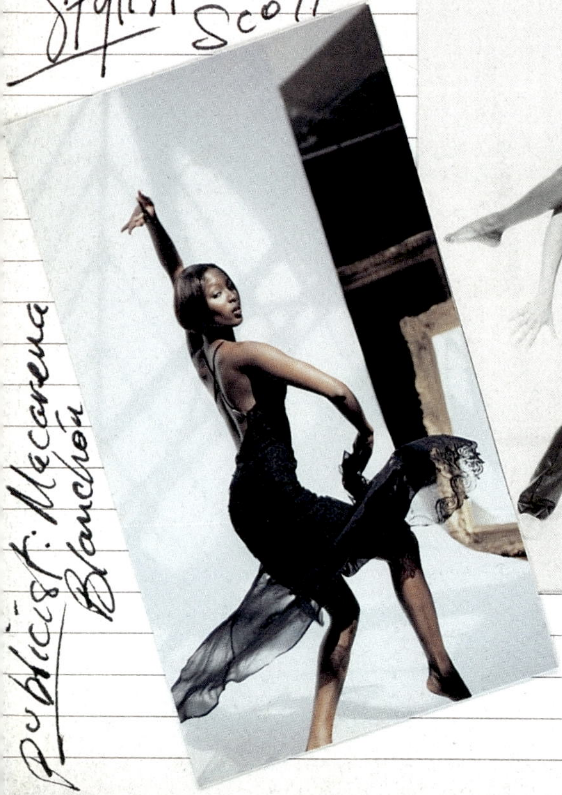

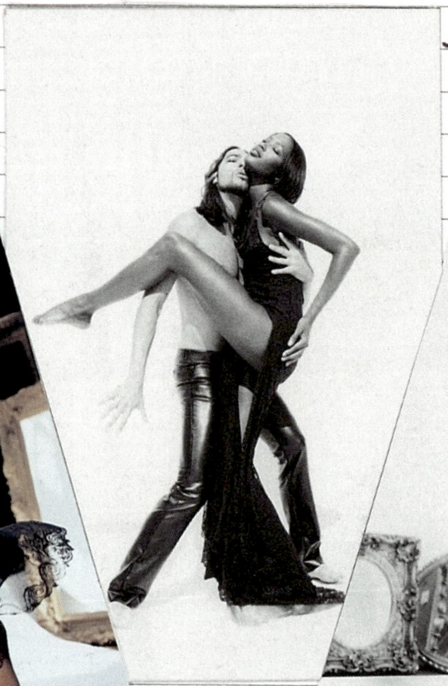

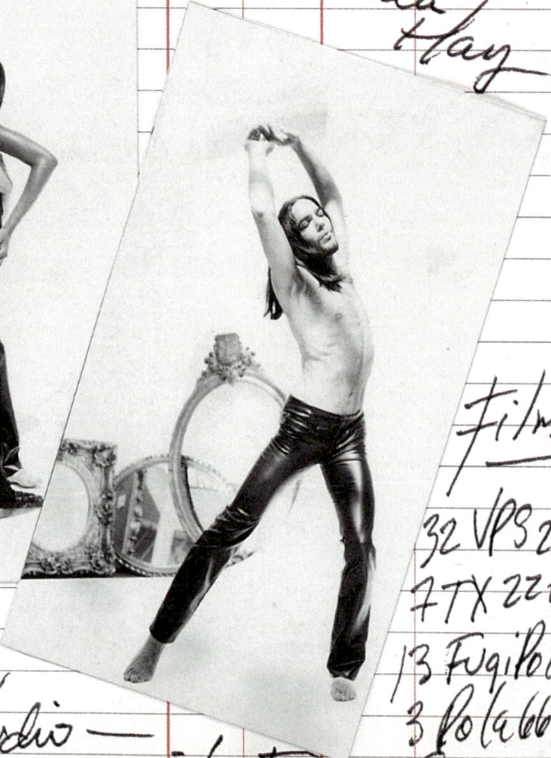

Publicist: Macarena Blanchard

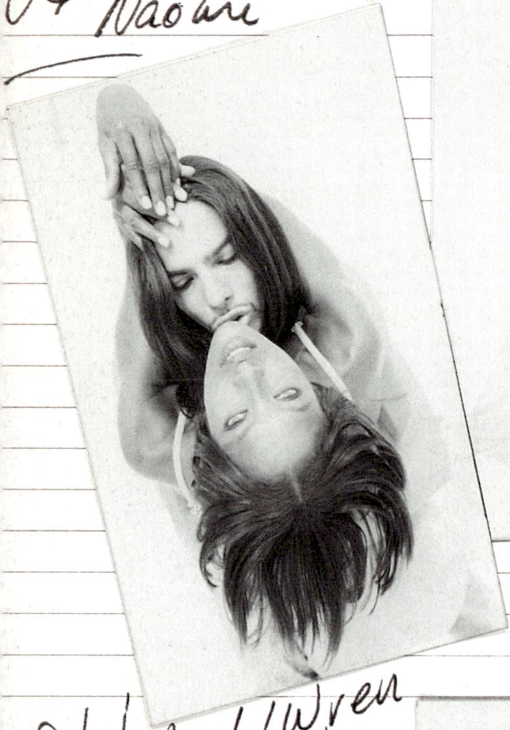

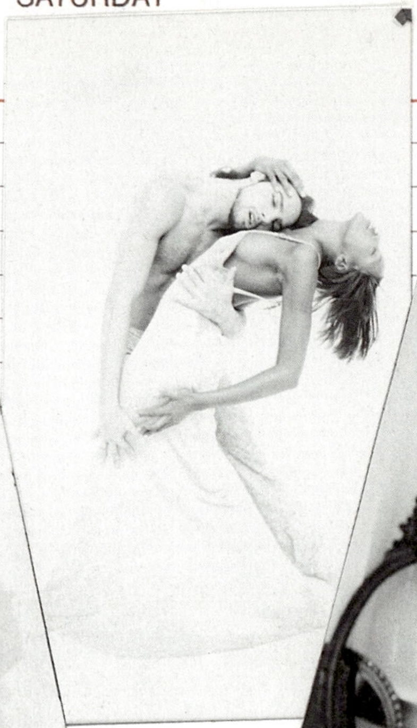

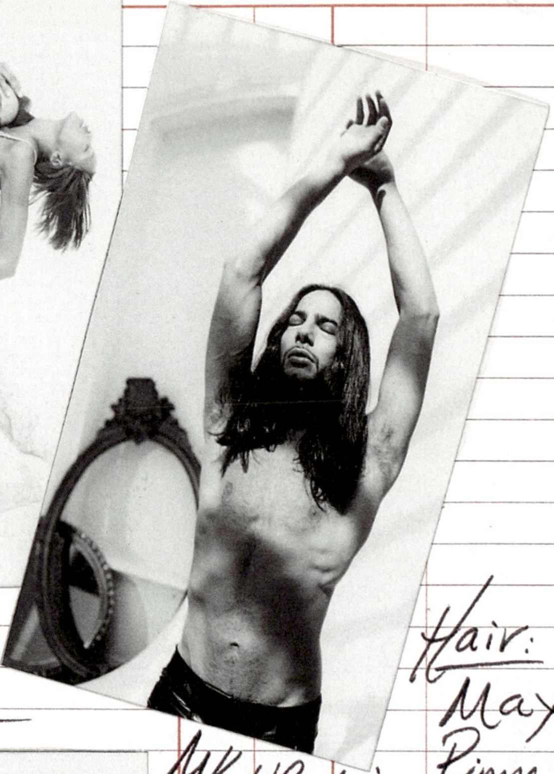

Hair:
Max
Pinnell
Hay

Mk.up. Linda

Films

32 VPS 22
7 TX 220
13 Fujilol
3 Pola 669

Sun Studio —

artist: James + Andrew

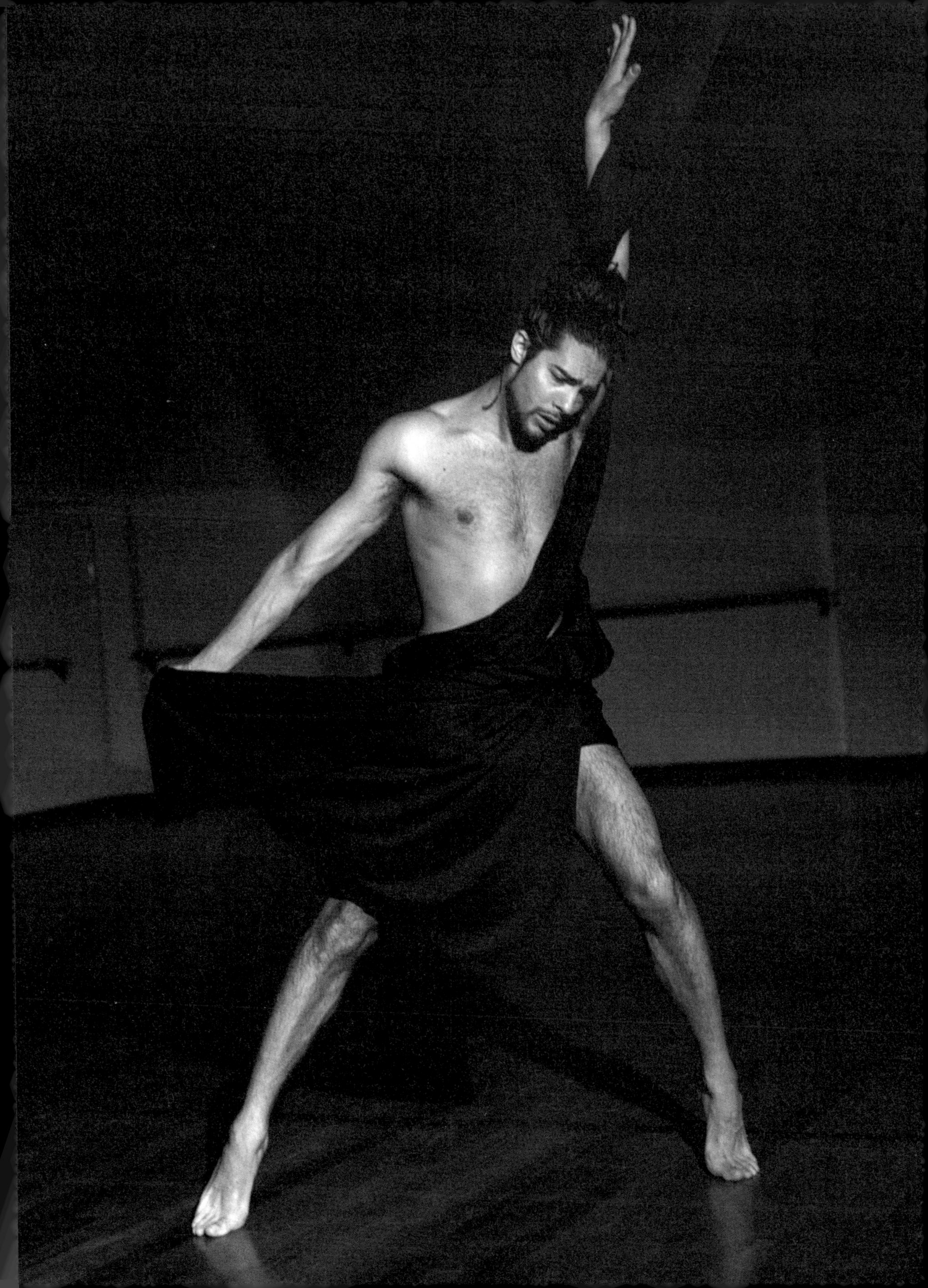

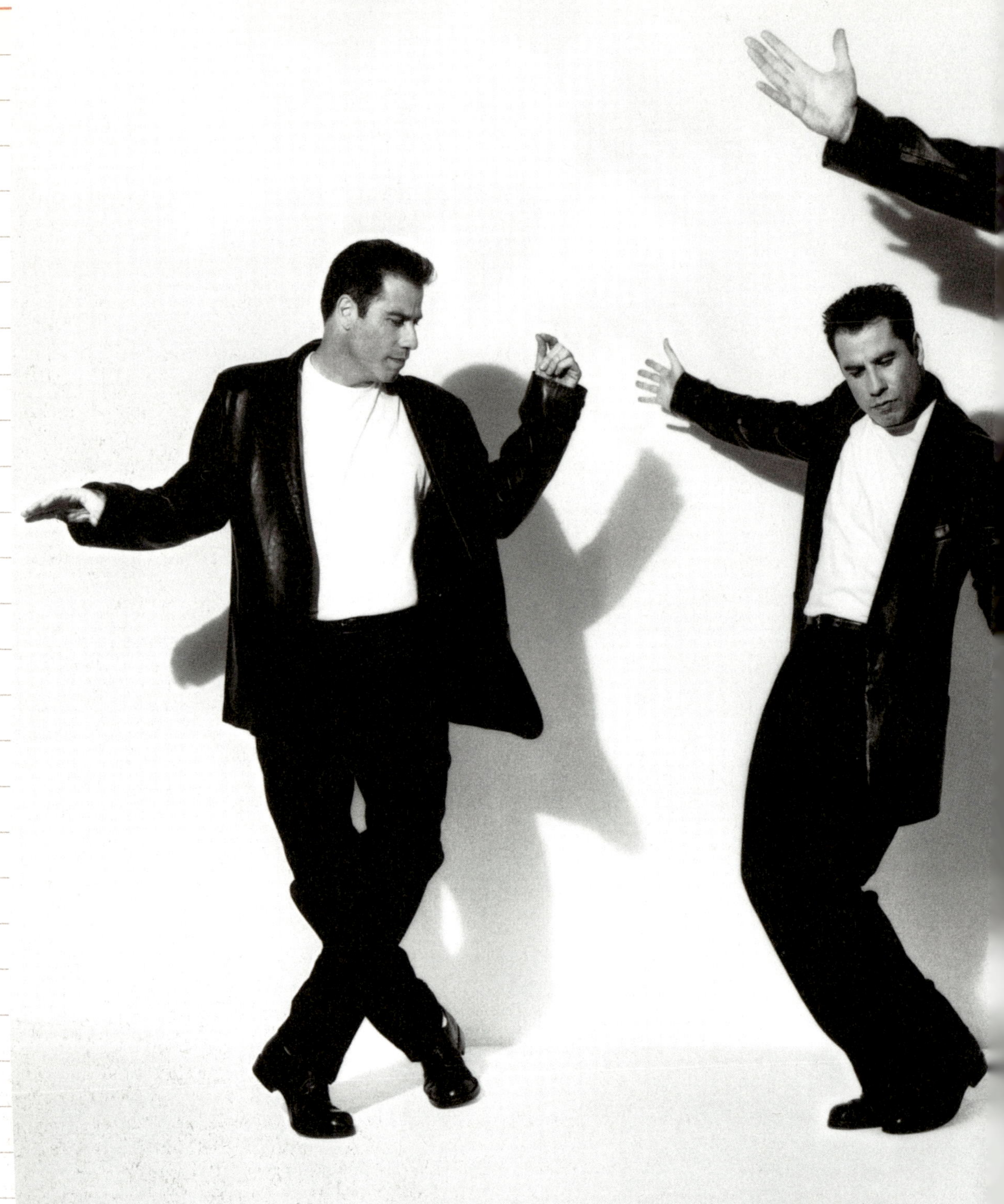

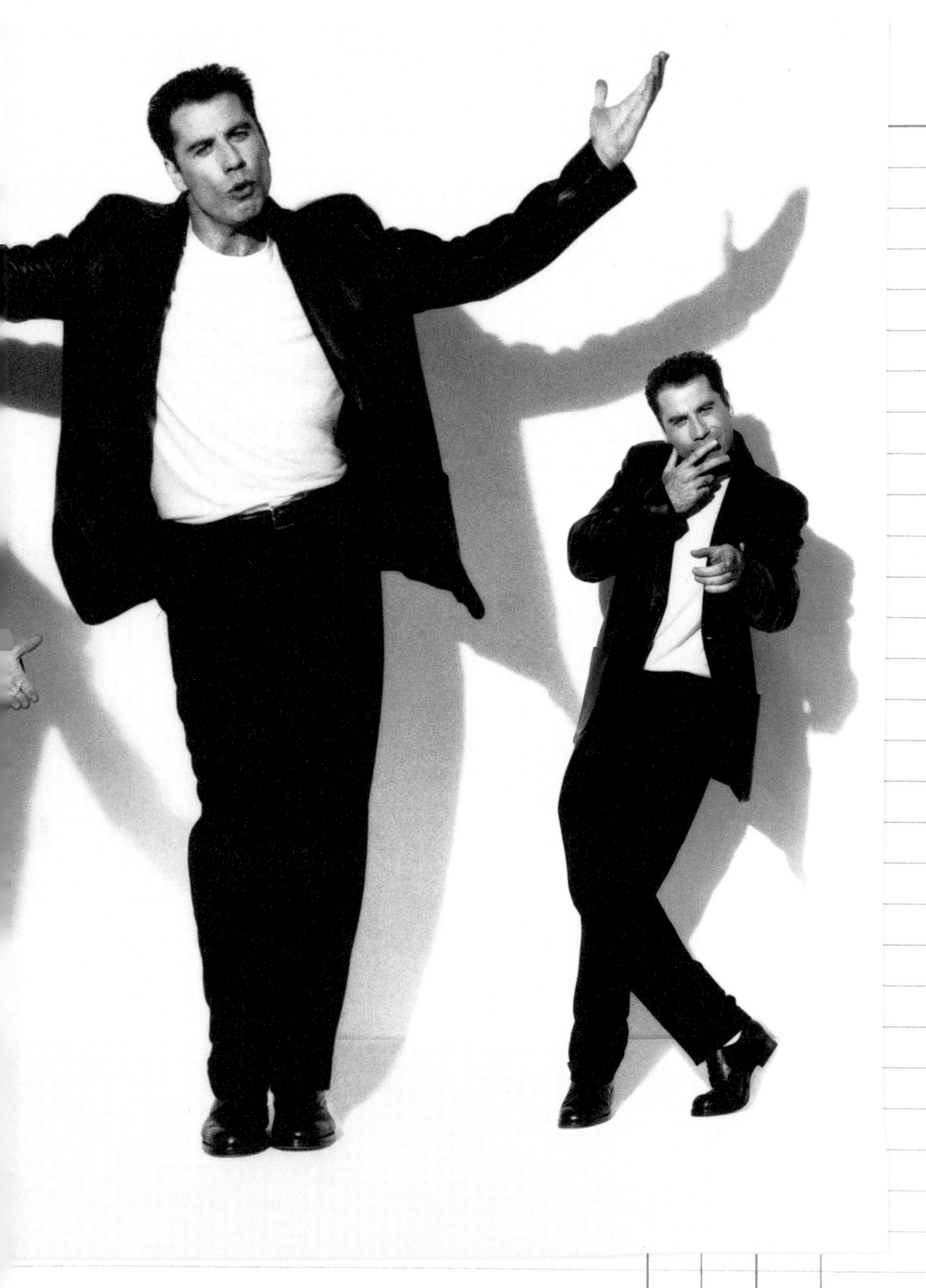

1:30 for lunch meeting with Melissa from Visage. Edited
B&W Travolta film. Victor, Edie + Bill, Bob Mario + Johnny all came
over + we hung out at home. Later went to Tabac for a night cap and
turned it in.

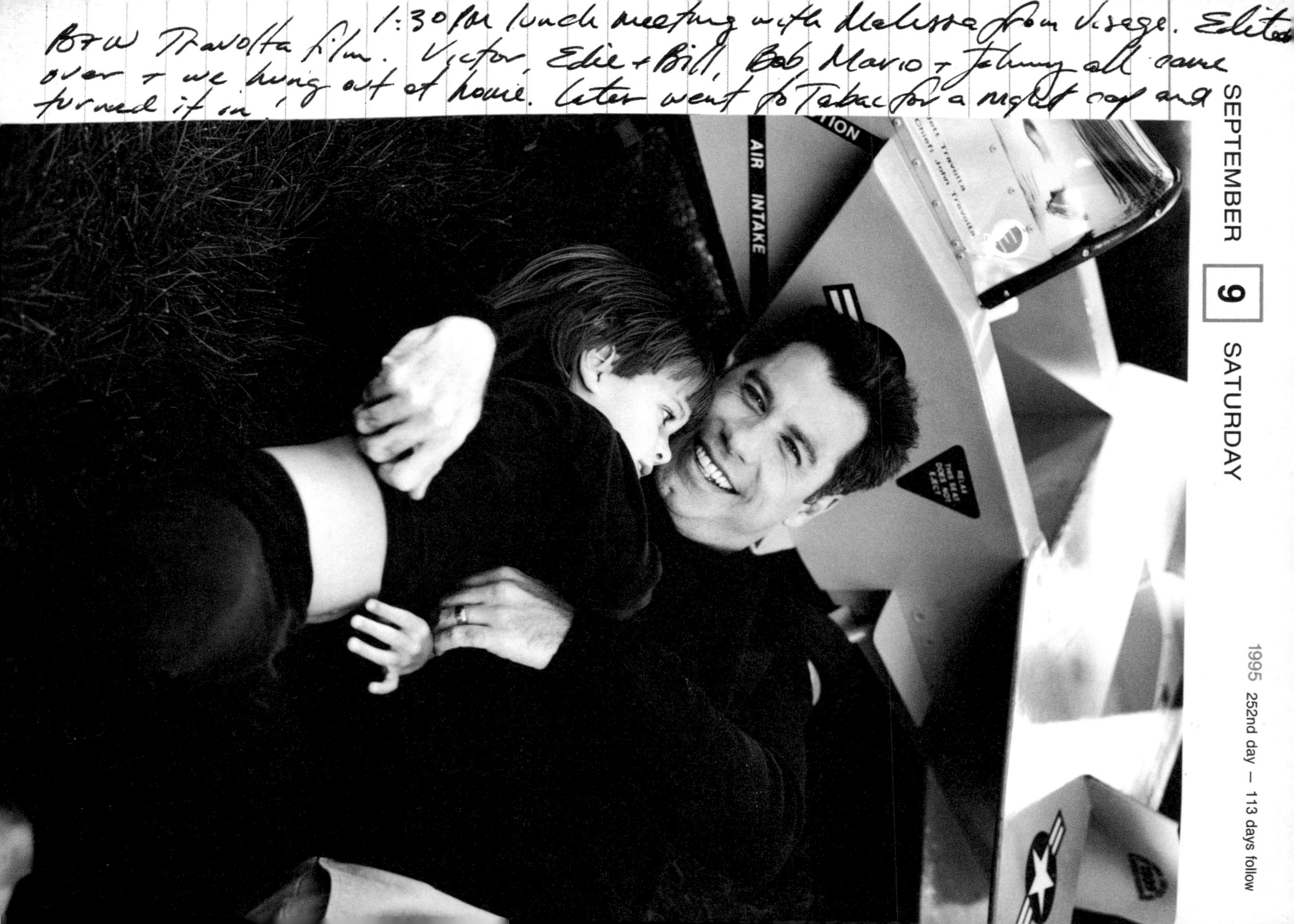

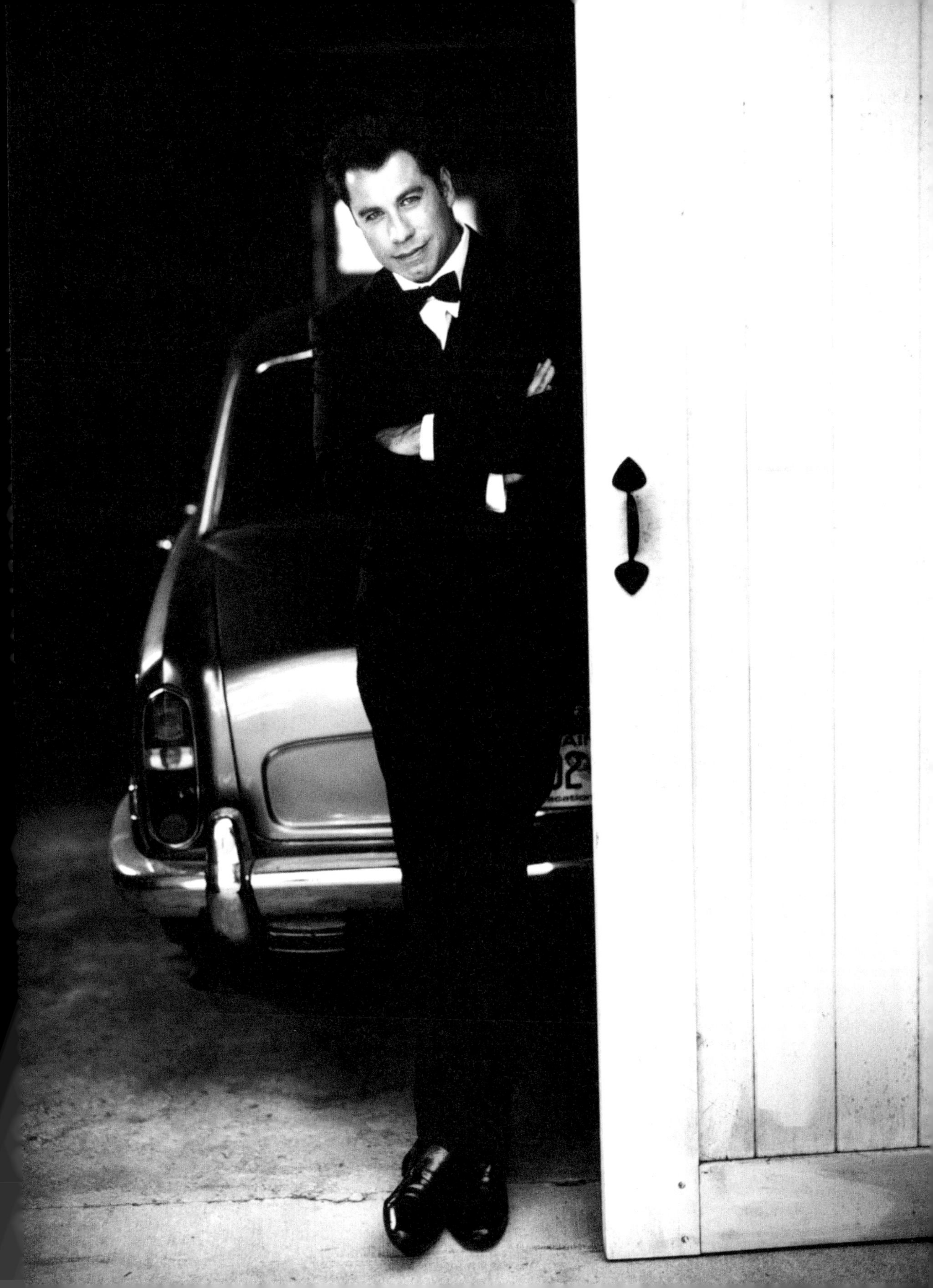

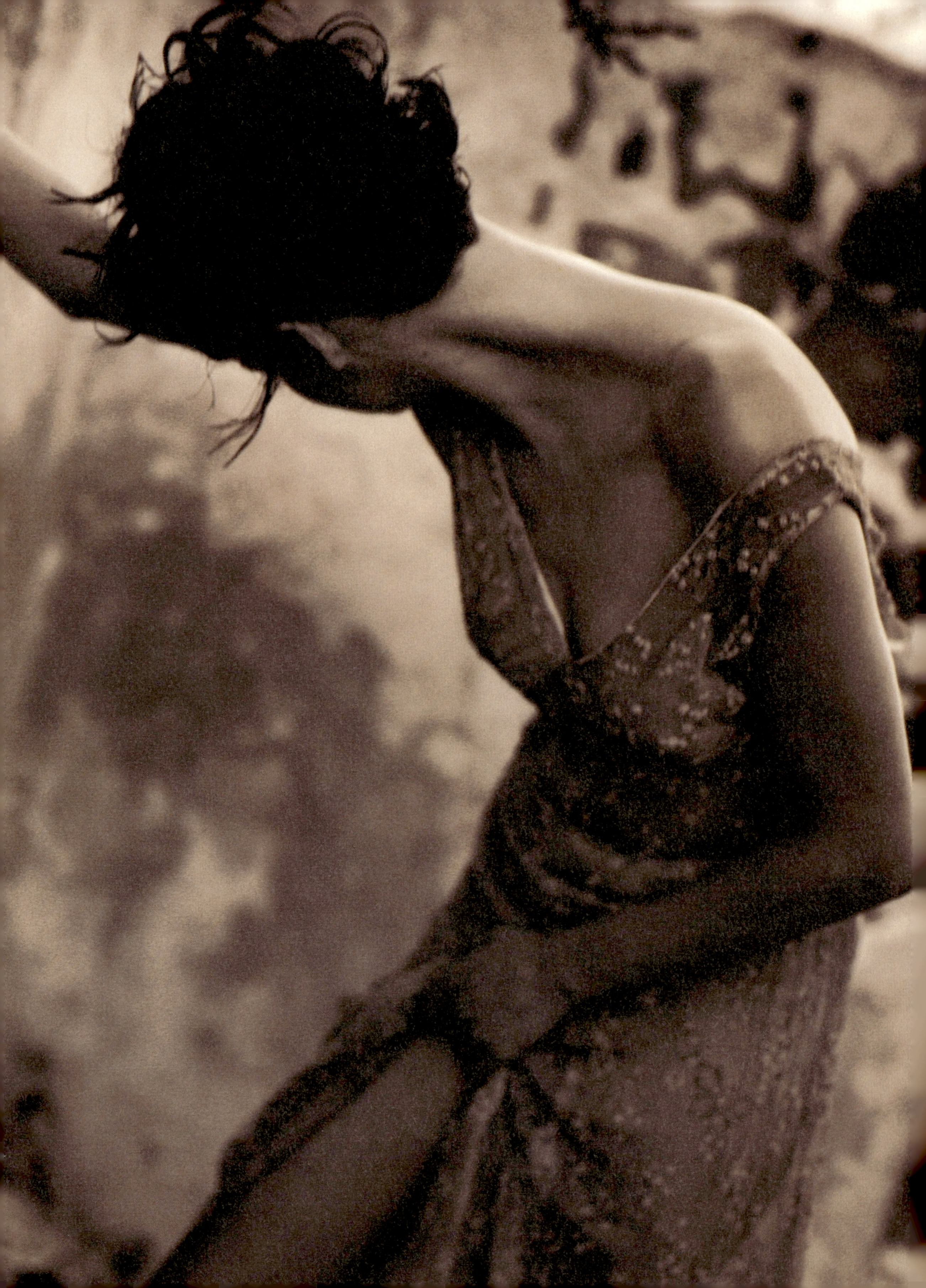

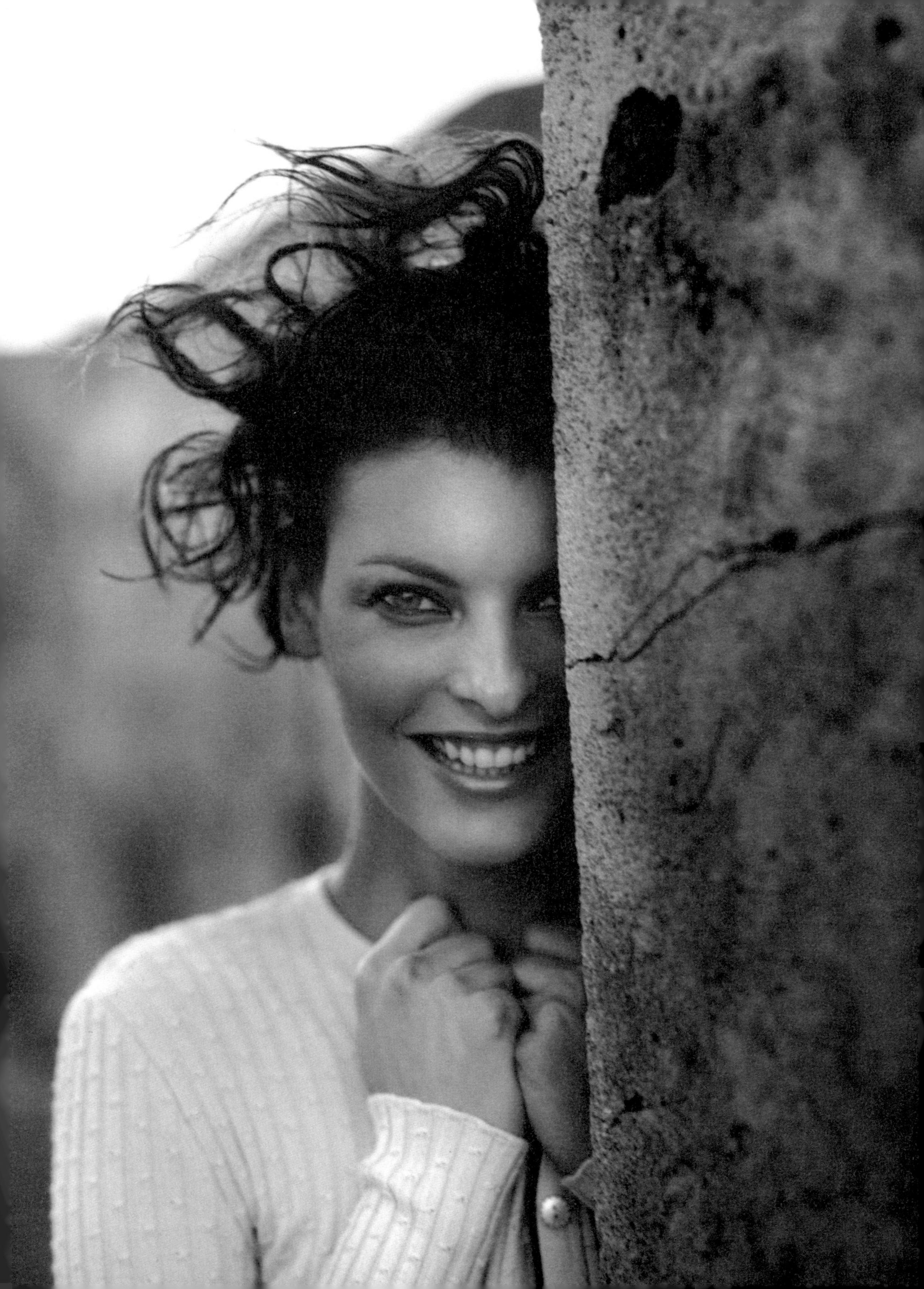

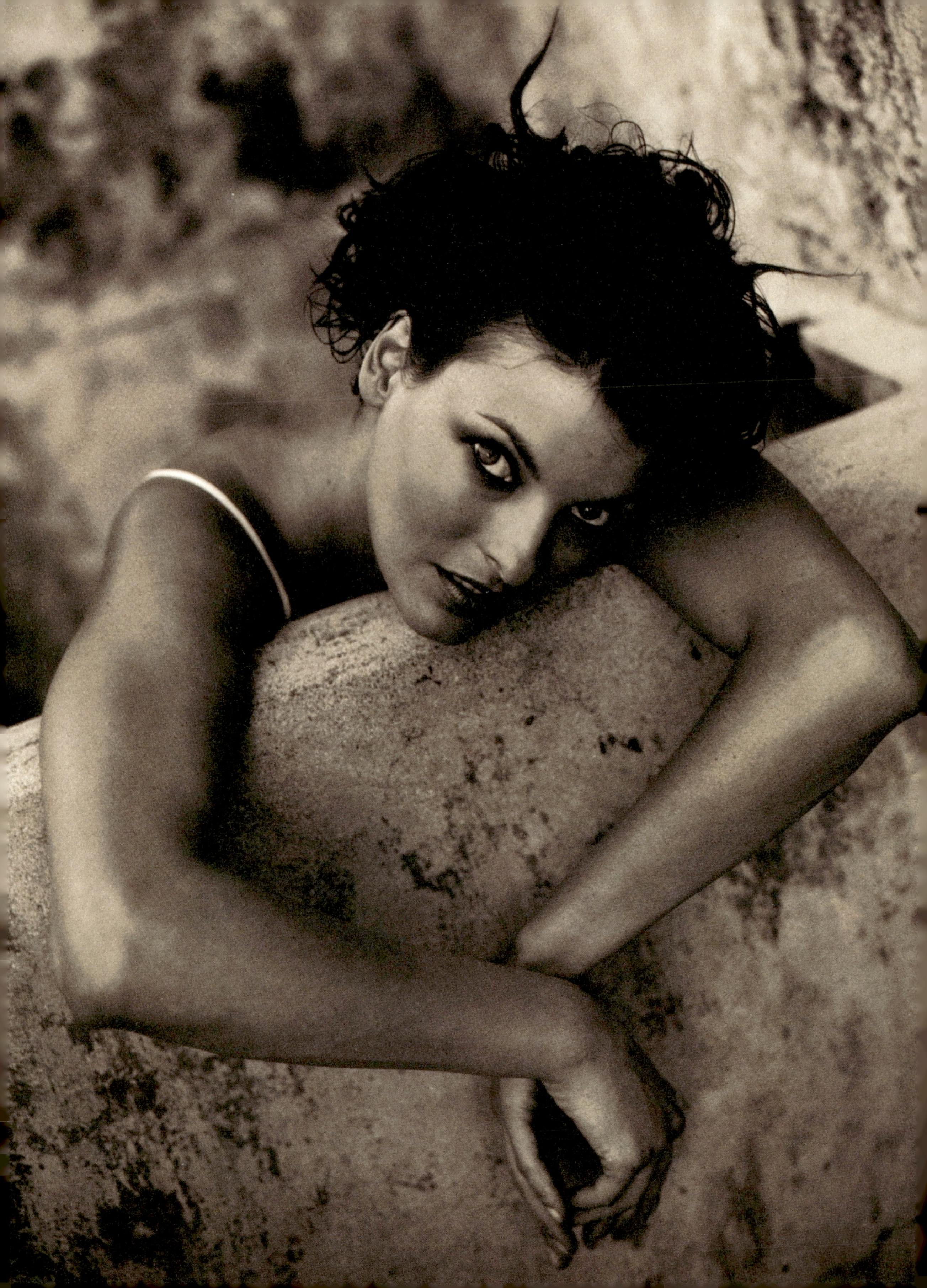

#97002

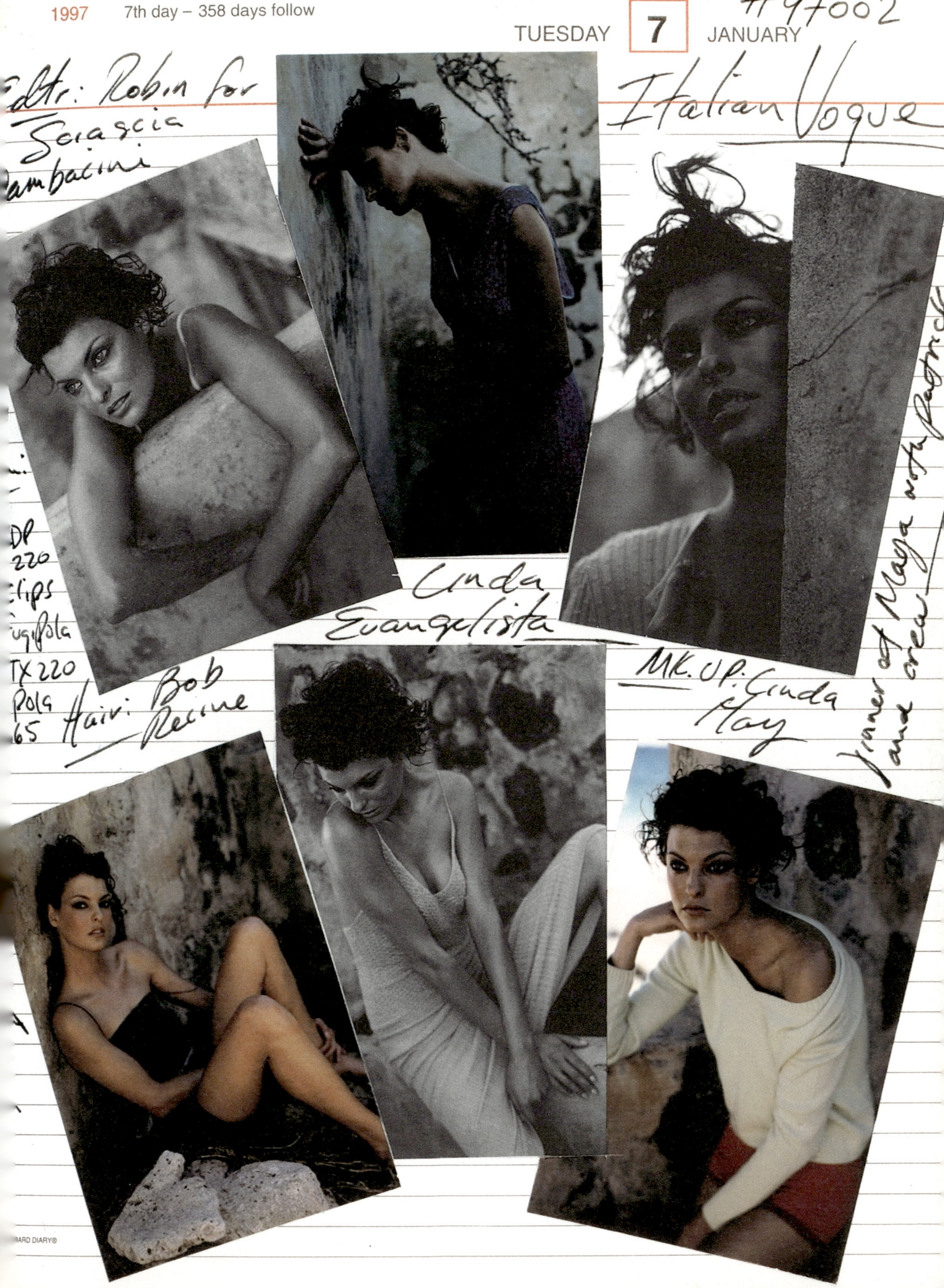

IARD DIARY®

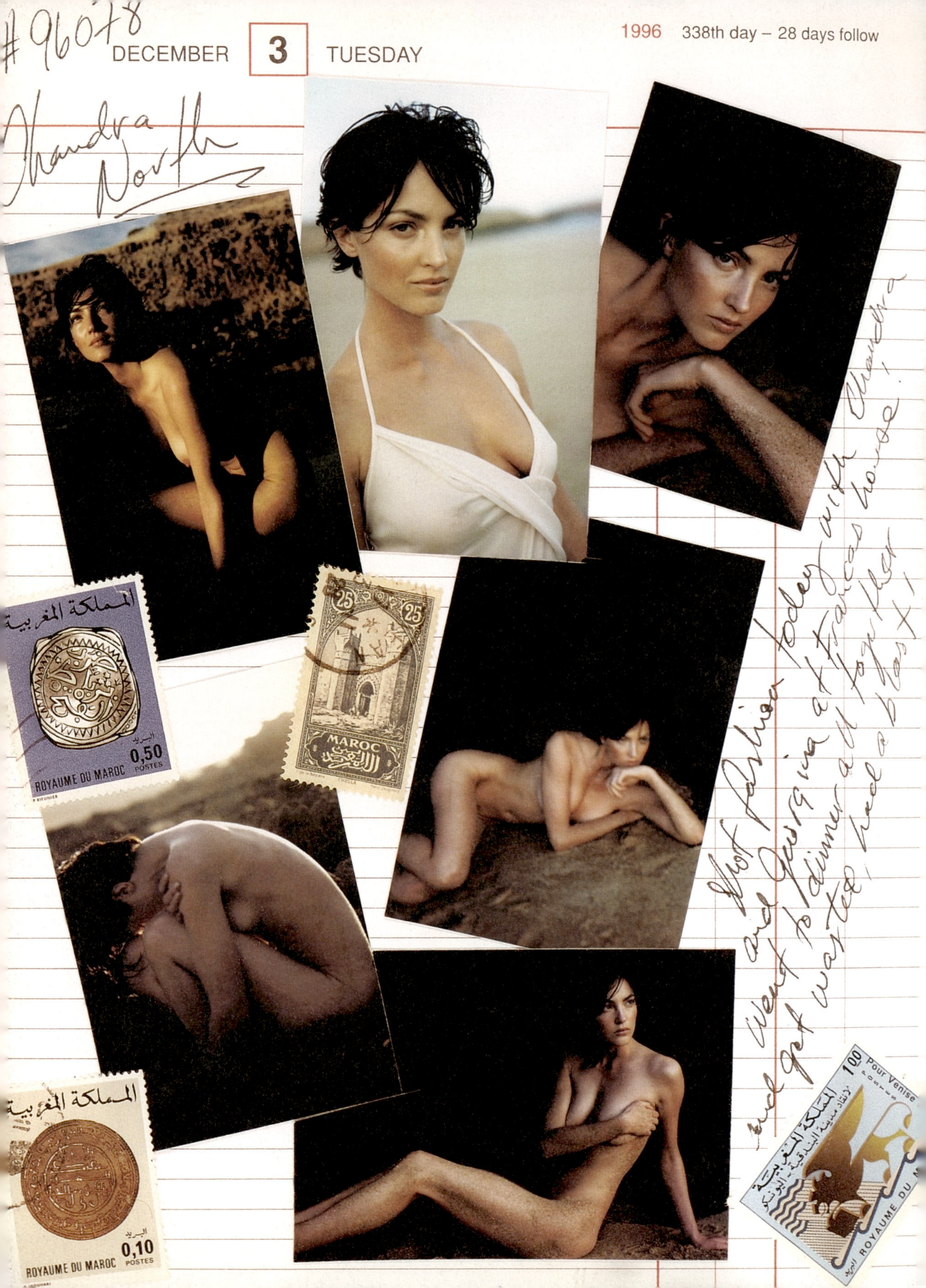

#96078
DECEMBER 3 TUESDAY
1996 338th day – 28 days follow
ROYAUME DU MAROC 0,50 POSTES
25 MAROC 25
ROYAUME DU MAROC 0,10 POSTES
Pour Venise 1,00
ROYAUME DU MAROC

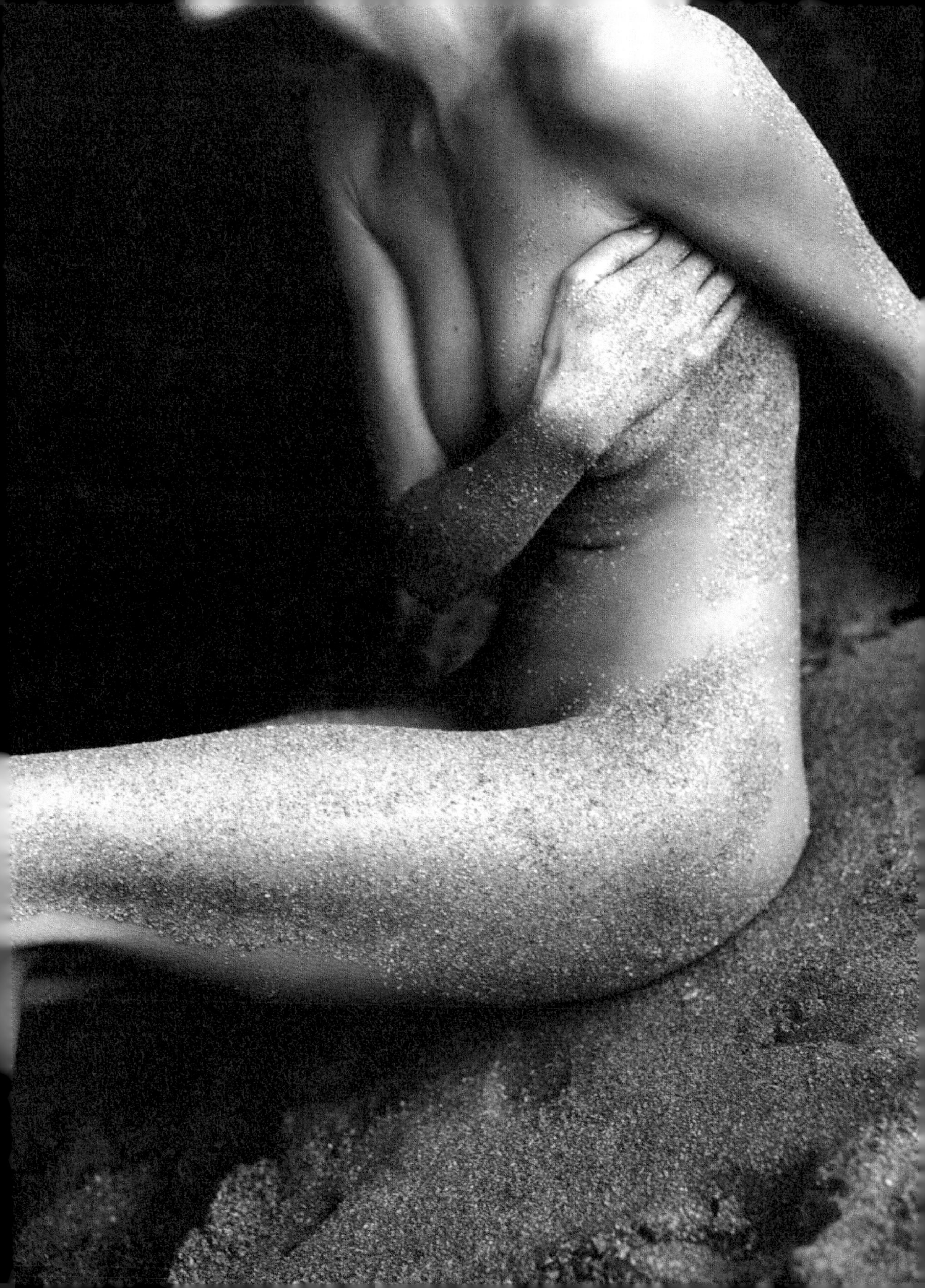

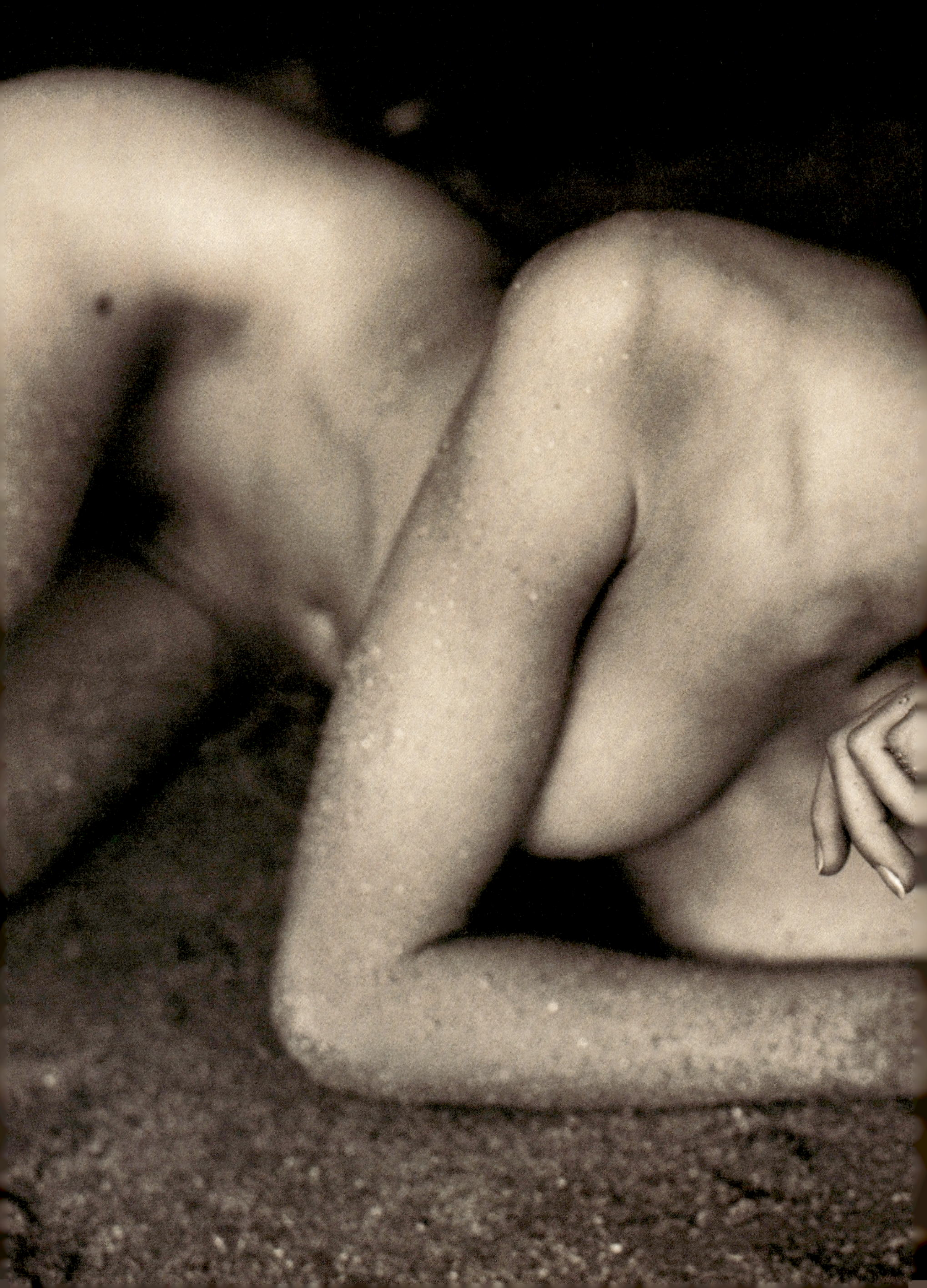

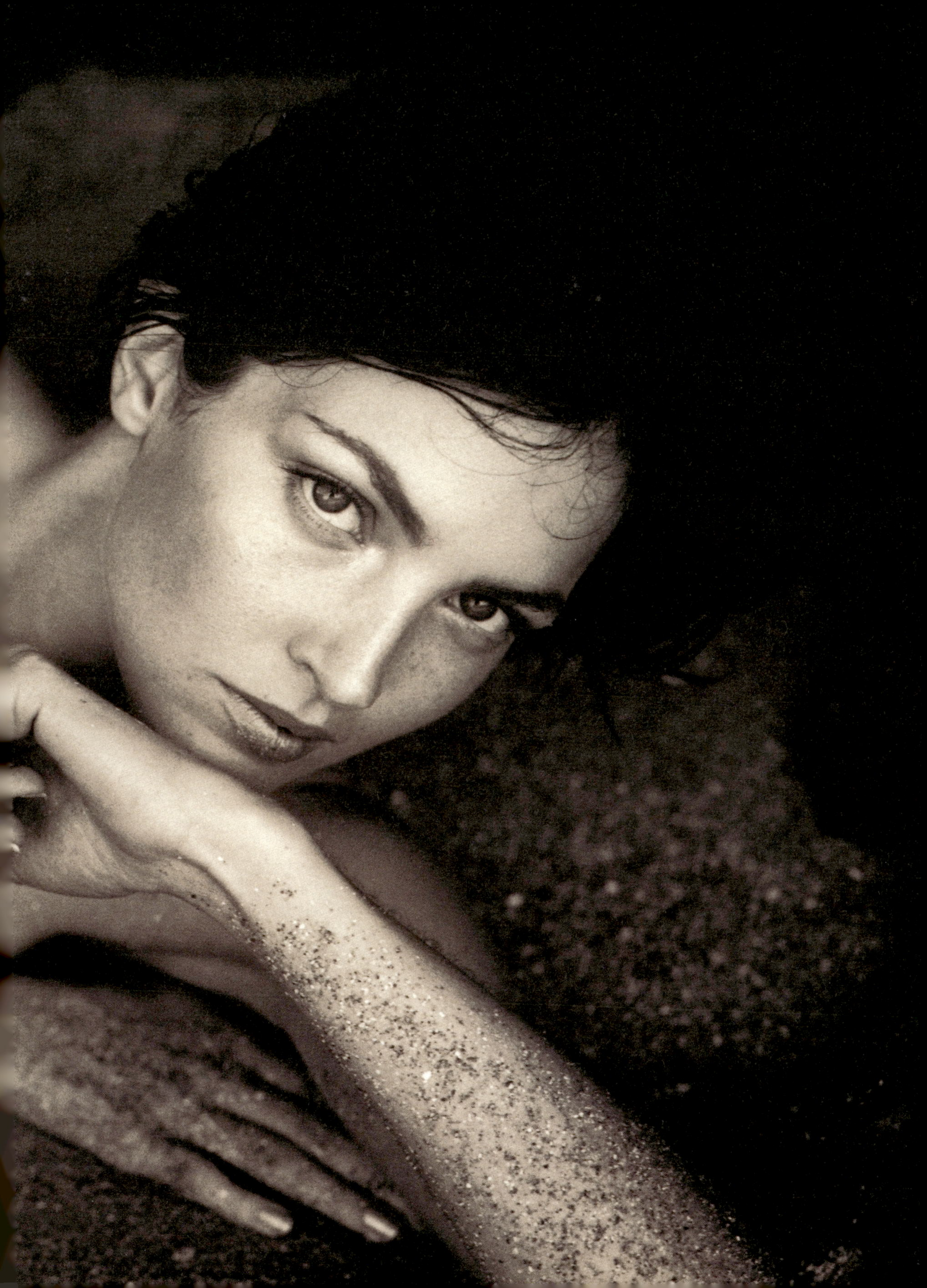

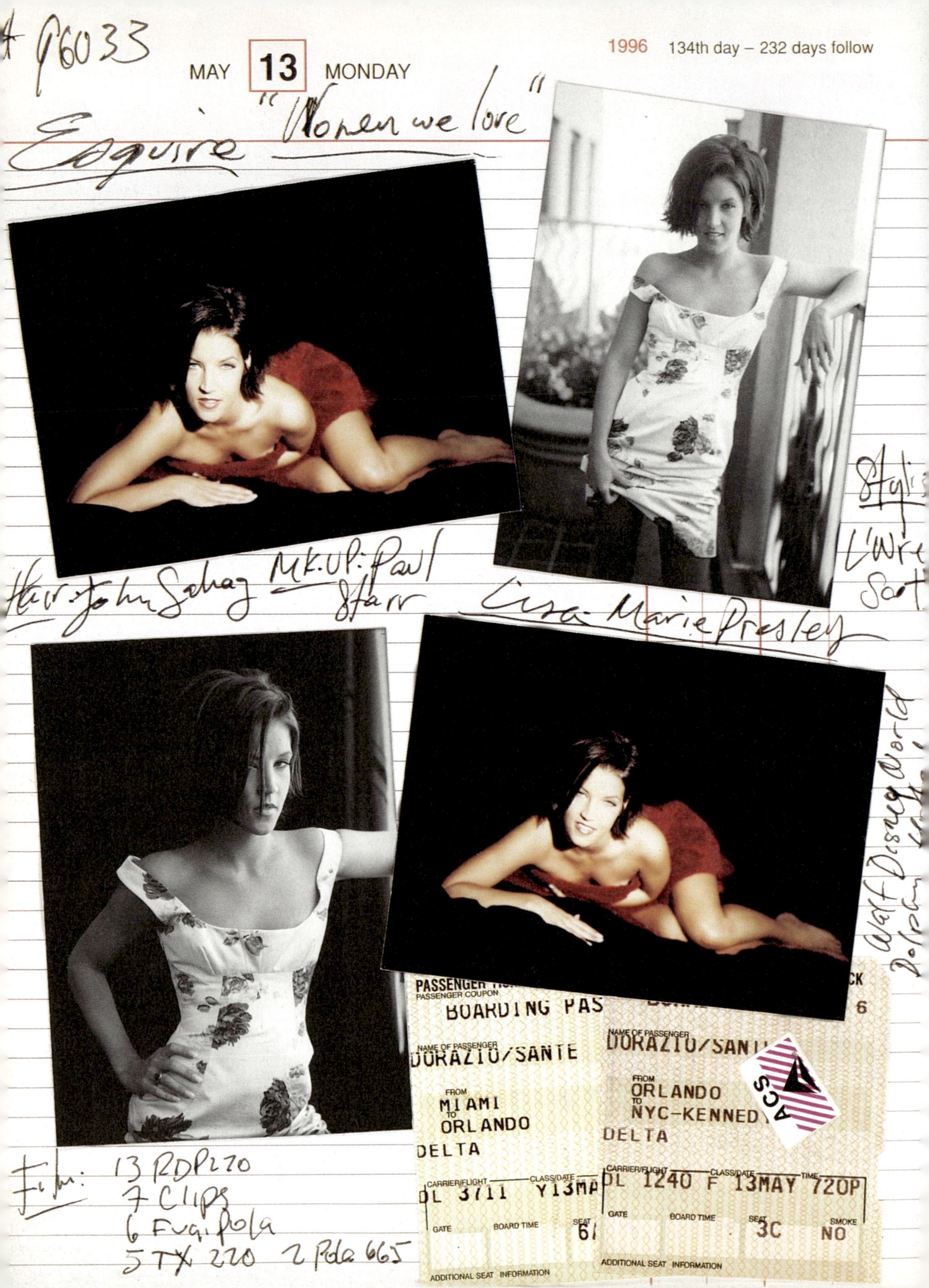
＃ P6033
MAY 13 MONDAY
1996   134th day – 232 days follow
Esquire   "Women we love"
Hair: John Sahag   MK.UP: Paul Starr
Lisa Marie Presley
Styli
L'Wre
Scot
Walt Disney World
Dolphin
Film: 13 RDP270
7 Clips
6 Fuji Pola
5 TX 220   2 Pola 665
PASSENGER COUPON
BOARDING PASS
NAME OF PASSENGER
DORAZIO/SANTE
FROM
MIAMI
TO
ORLANDO
DELTA
CARRIER/FLIGHT   CLASS/DATE
DL 3711   Y13MA
GATE   BOARD TIME   SEAT
6
ADDITIONAL SEAT INFORMATION
NAME OF PASSENGER
DORAZIO/SANTE
FROM
ORLANDO
TO
NYC-KENNED
DELTA
CARRIER/FLIGHT   CLASS/DATE   TIME
DL 1240   F 13MAY   720P
GATE   BOARD TIME   SEAT   SMOKE
3C   NO
ADDITIONAL SEAT INFORMATION
ACS

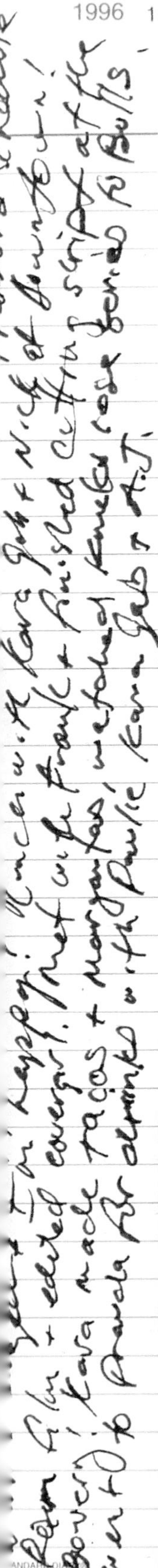

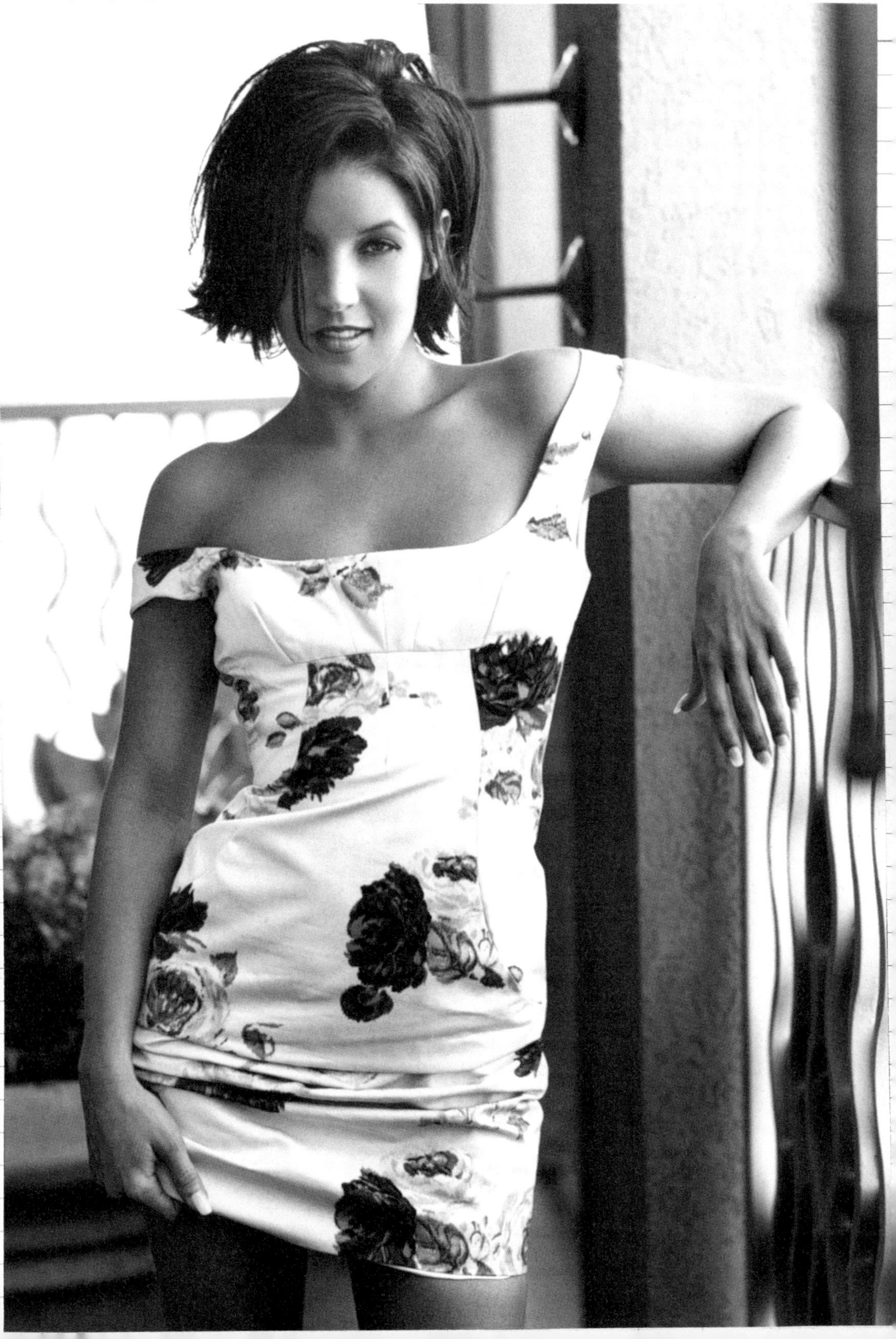

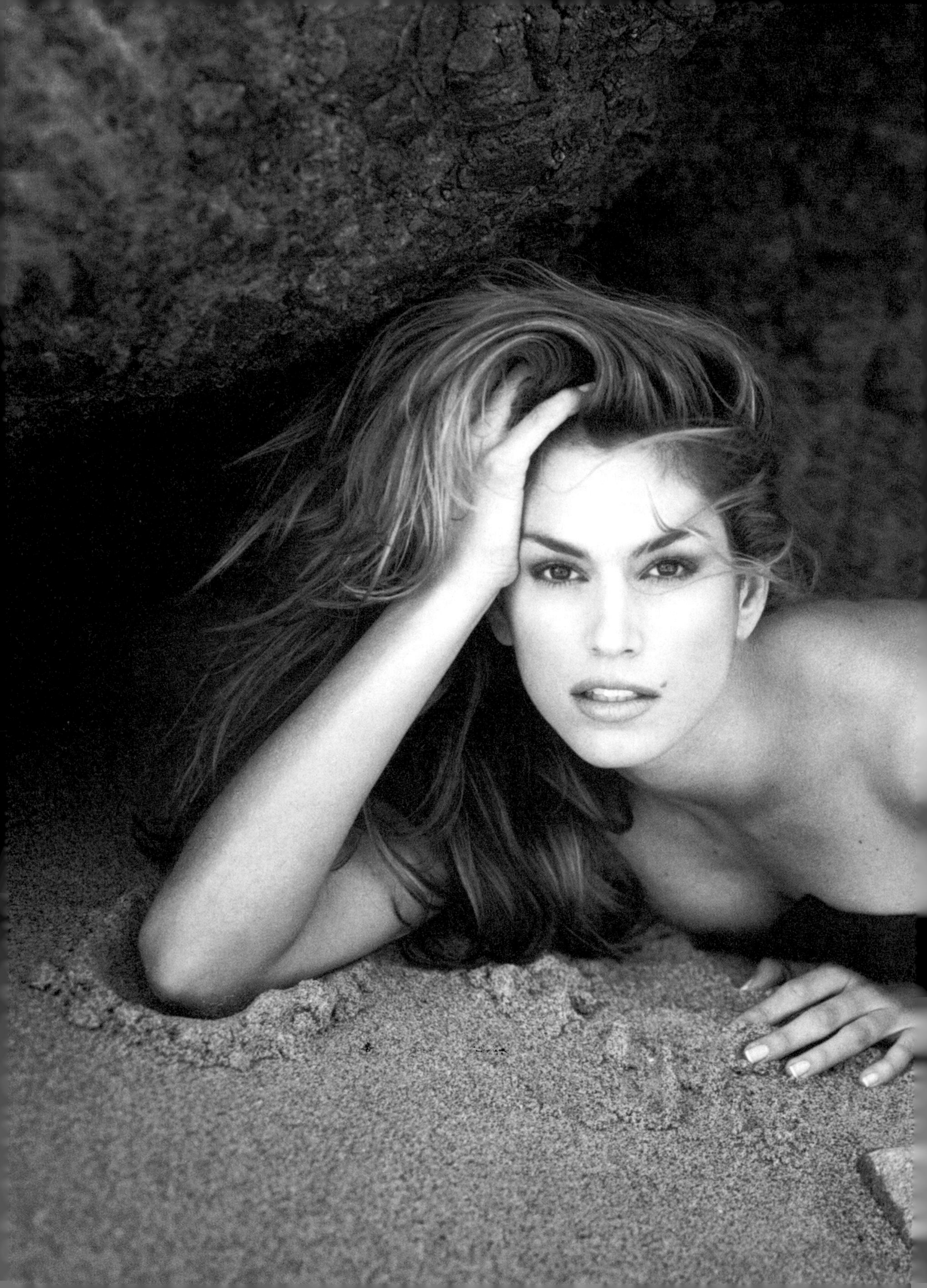

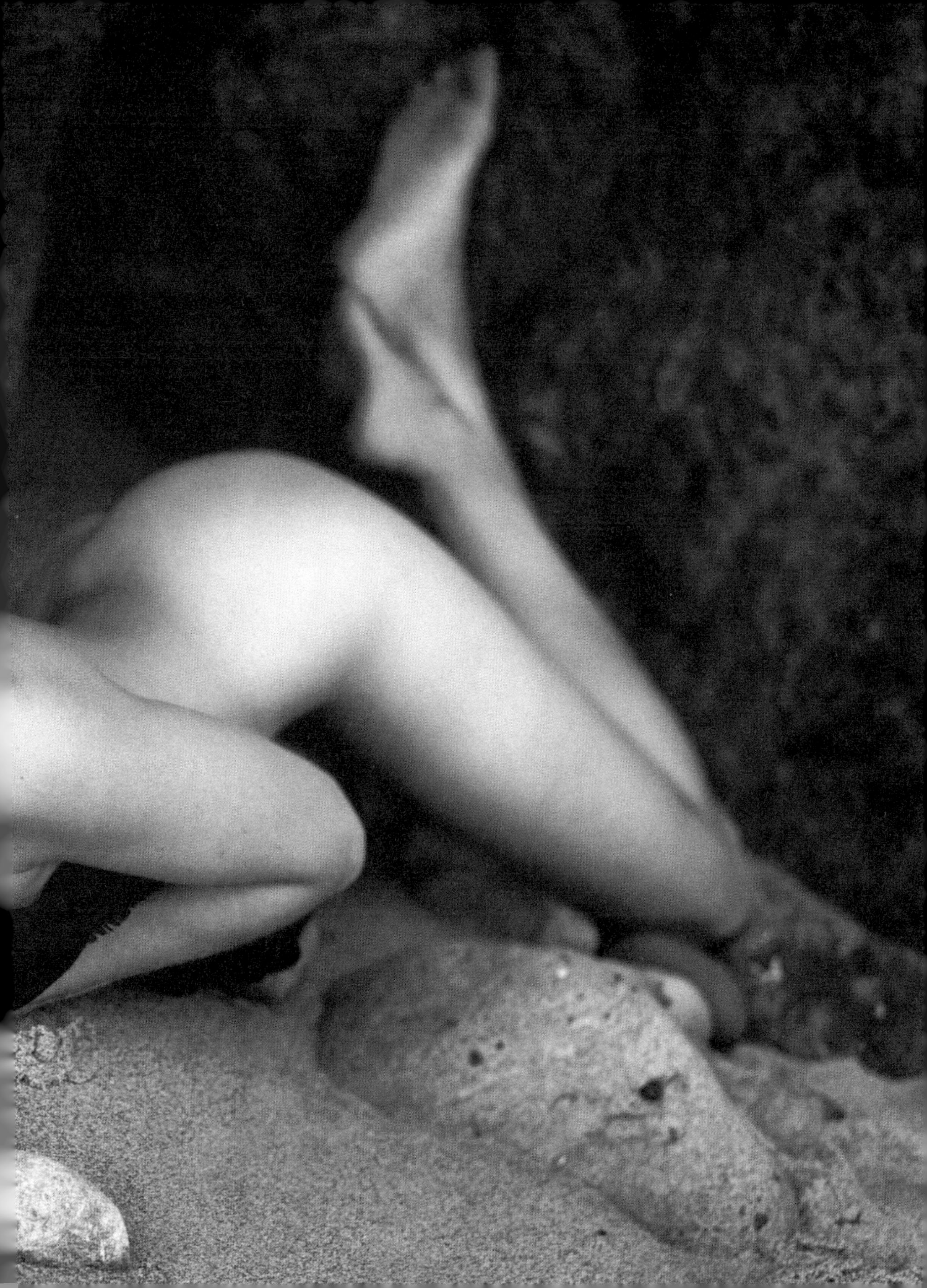

Went to the office to go over things with Joyce. lunch with Kava at Mezzogiorno. Started looking over my script again. Went to Johnny's tonight with Victor Parke Bob + David. Watched 3 basketball games till 11 AM.

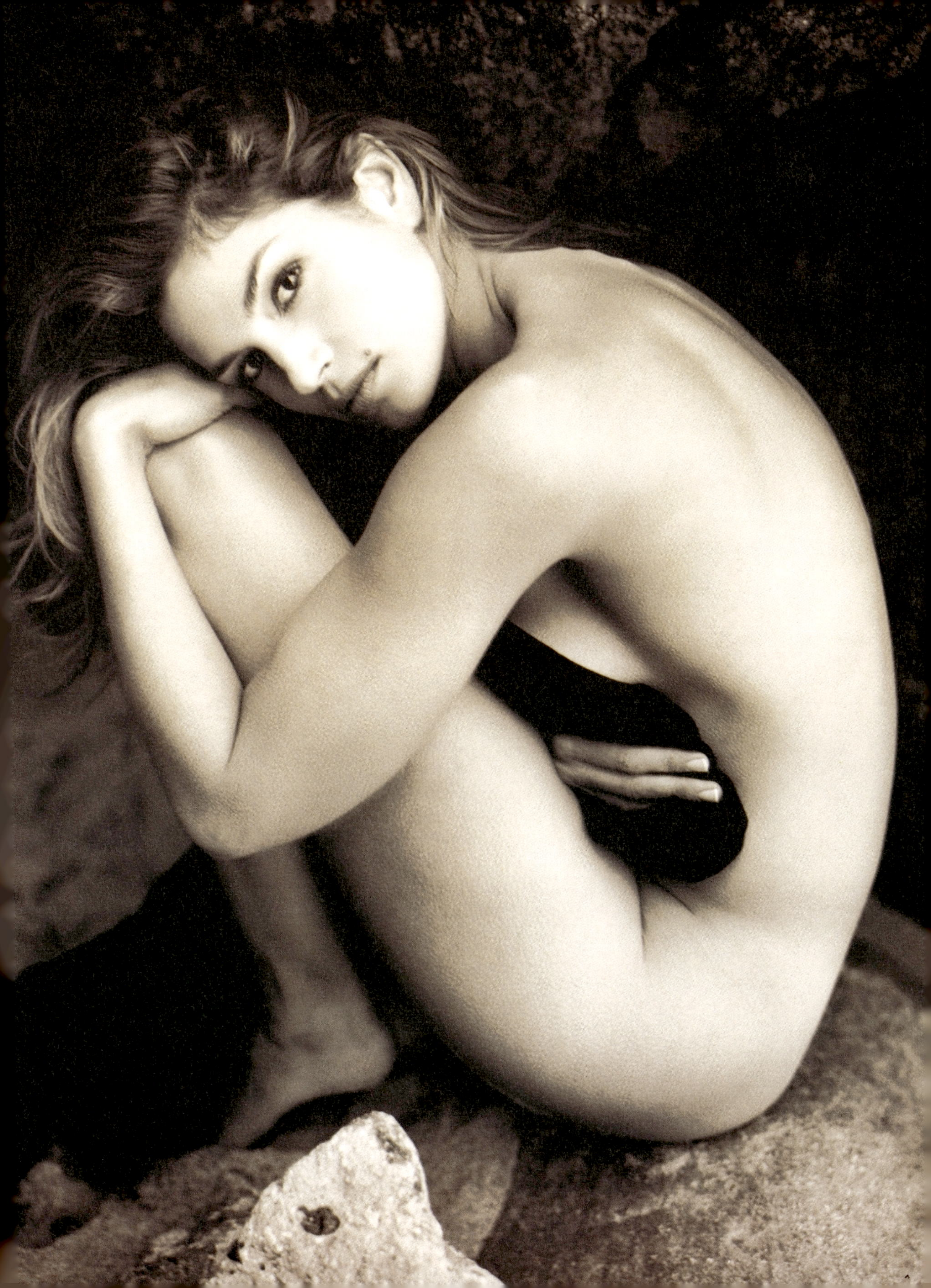

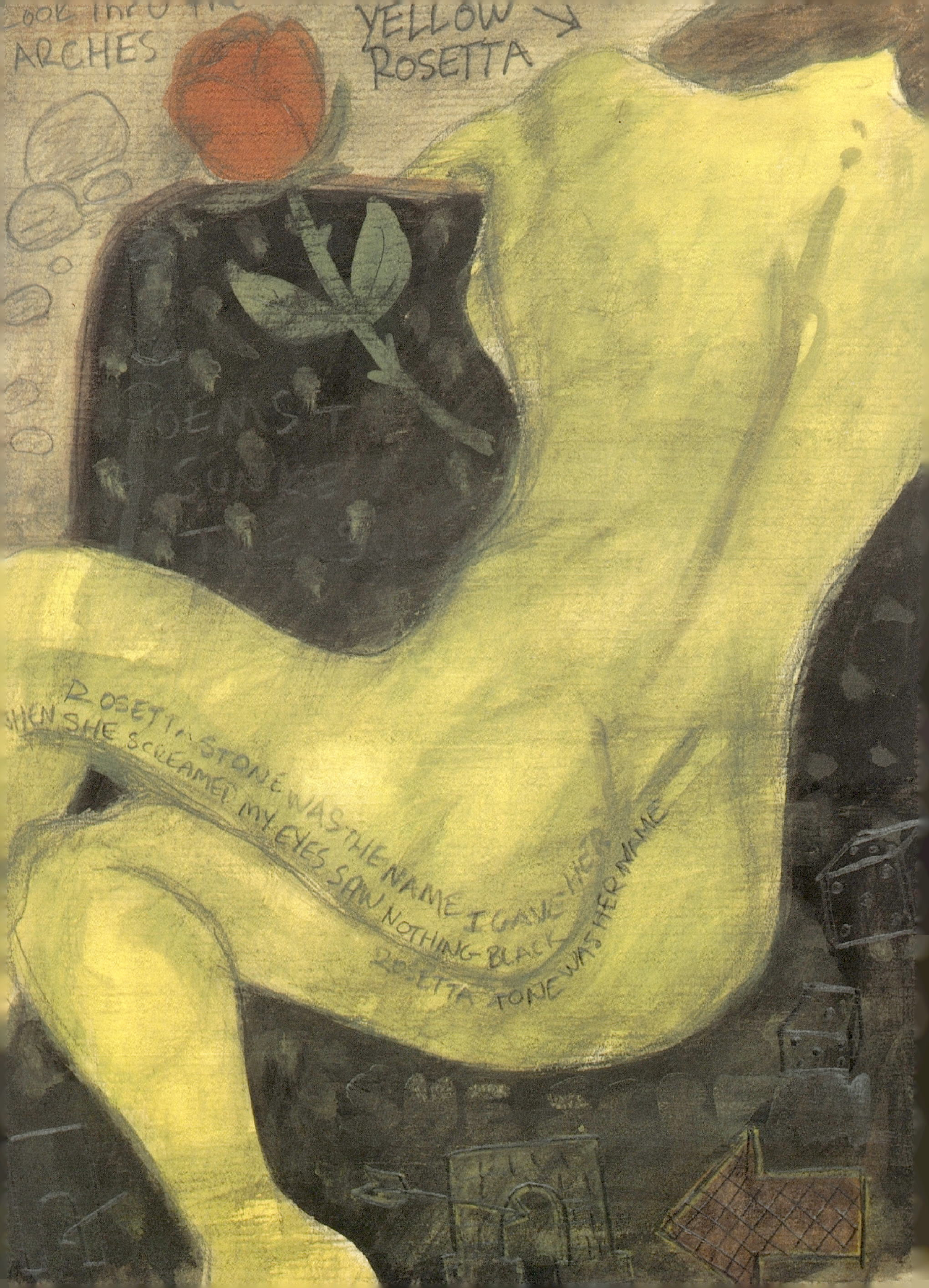

OOK THRU THE
ARCHES

YELLOW
ROSETTA →

POEMS T SQ

ROSETTA STONE WAS THE NAME I GAVE HER
WHEN SHE SCREAMED MY EYES SAW NOTHING BLACK
ROSETTA STONE WAS HER NAME

YELLOW

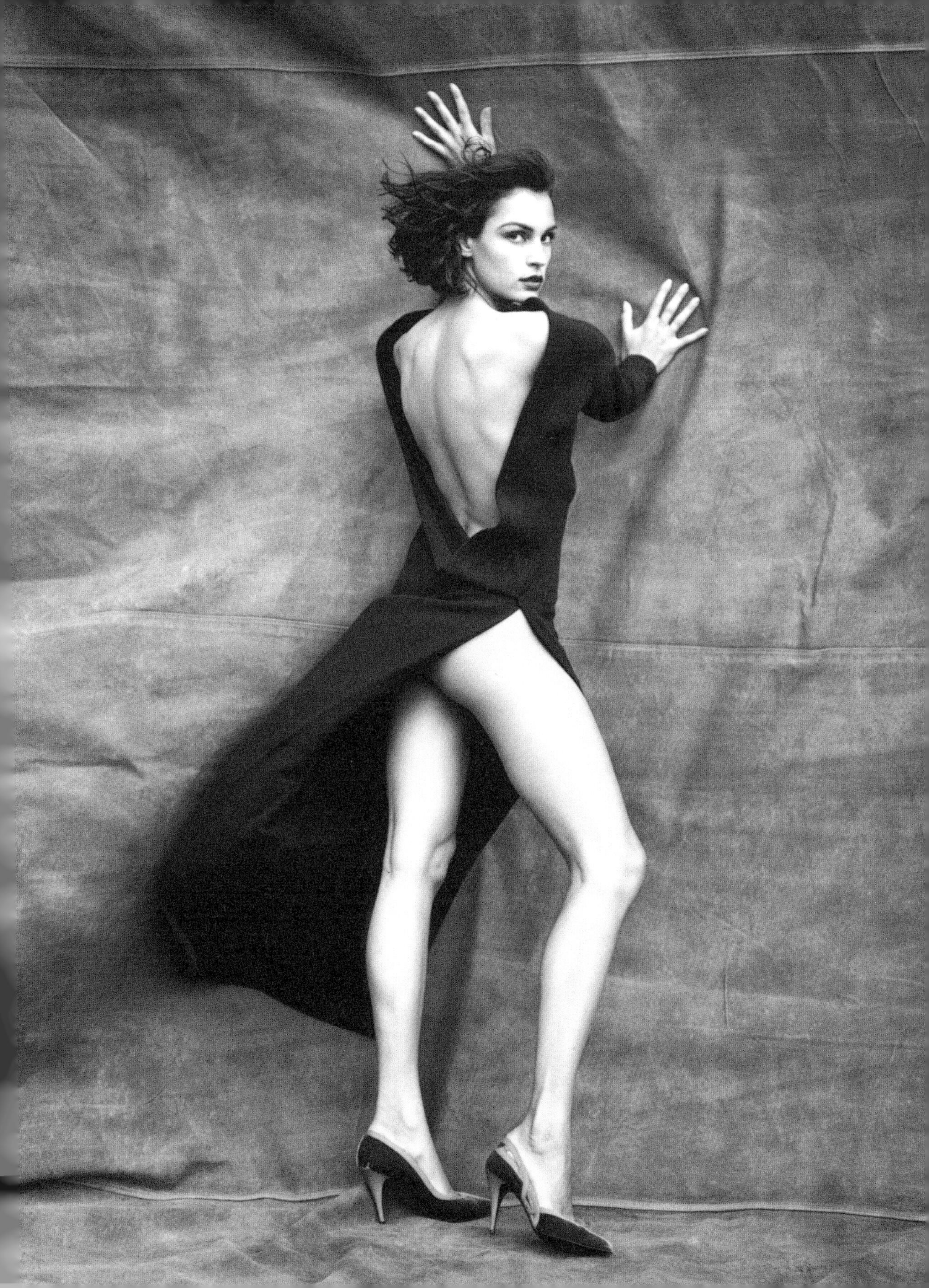

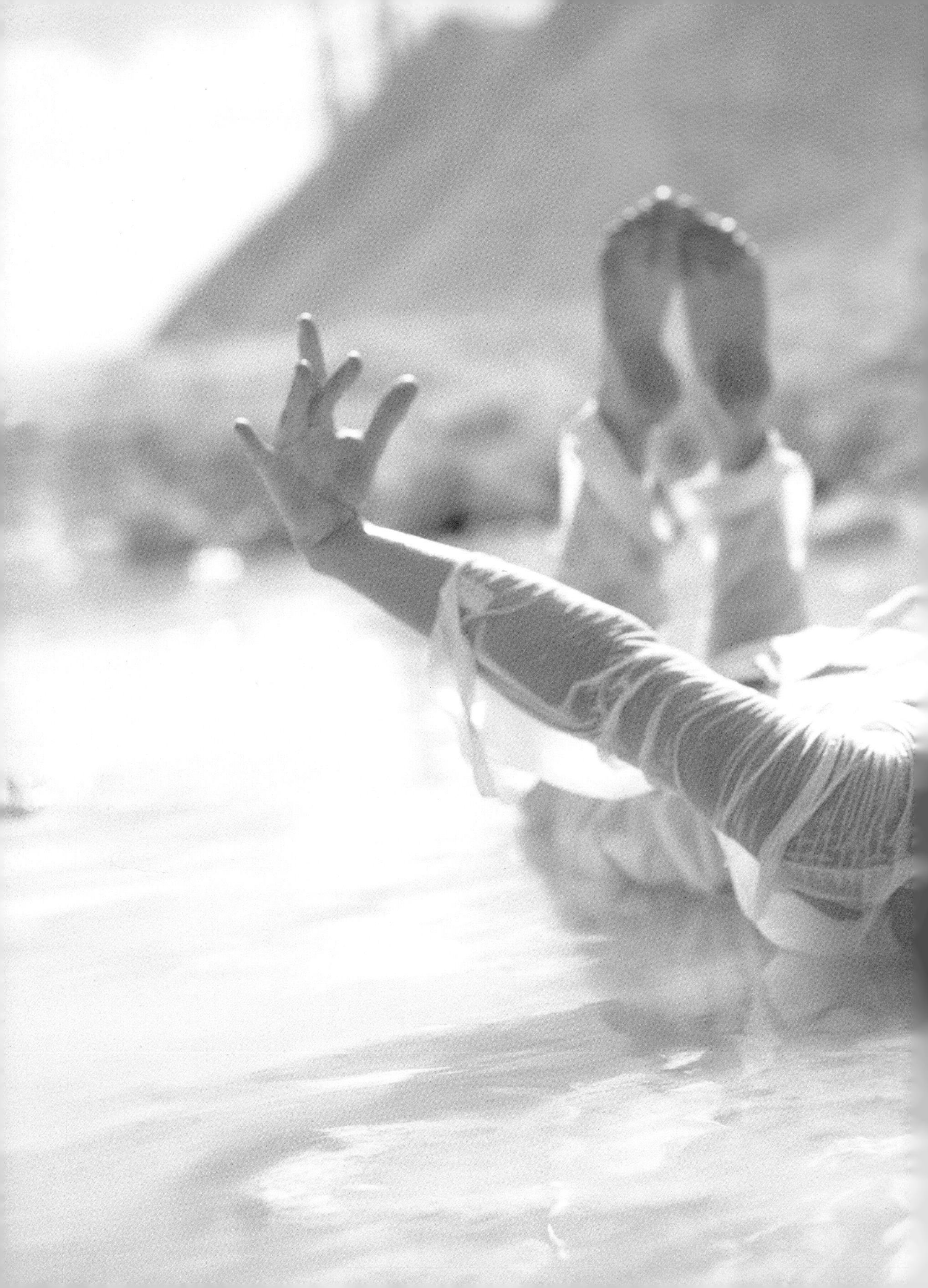

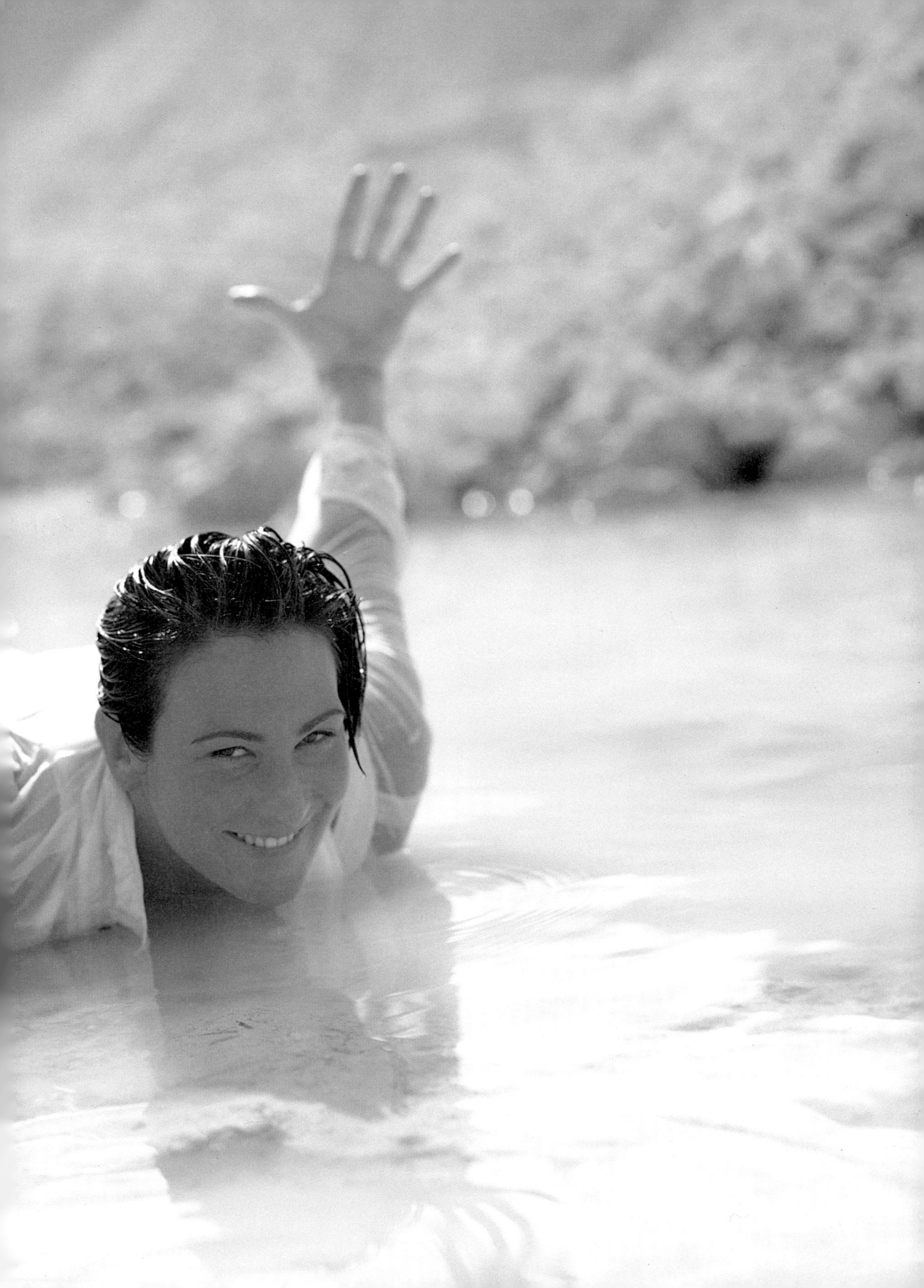

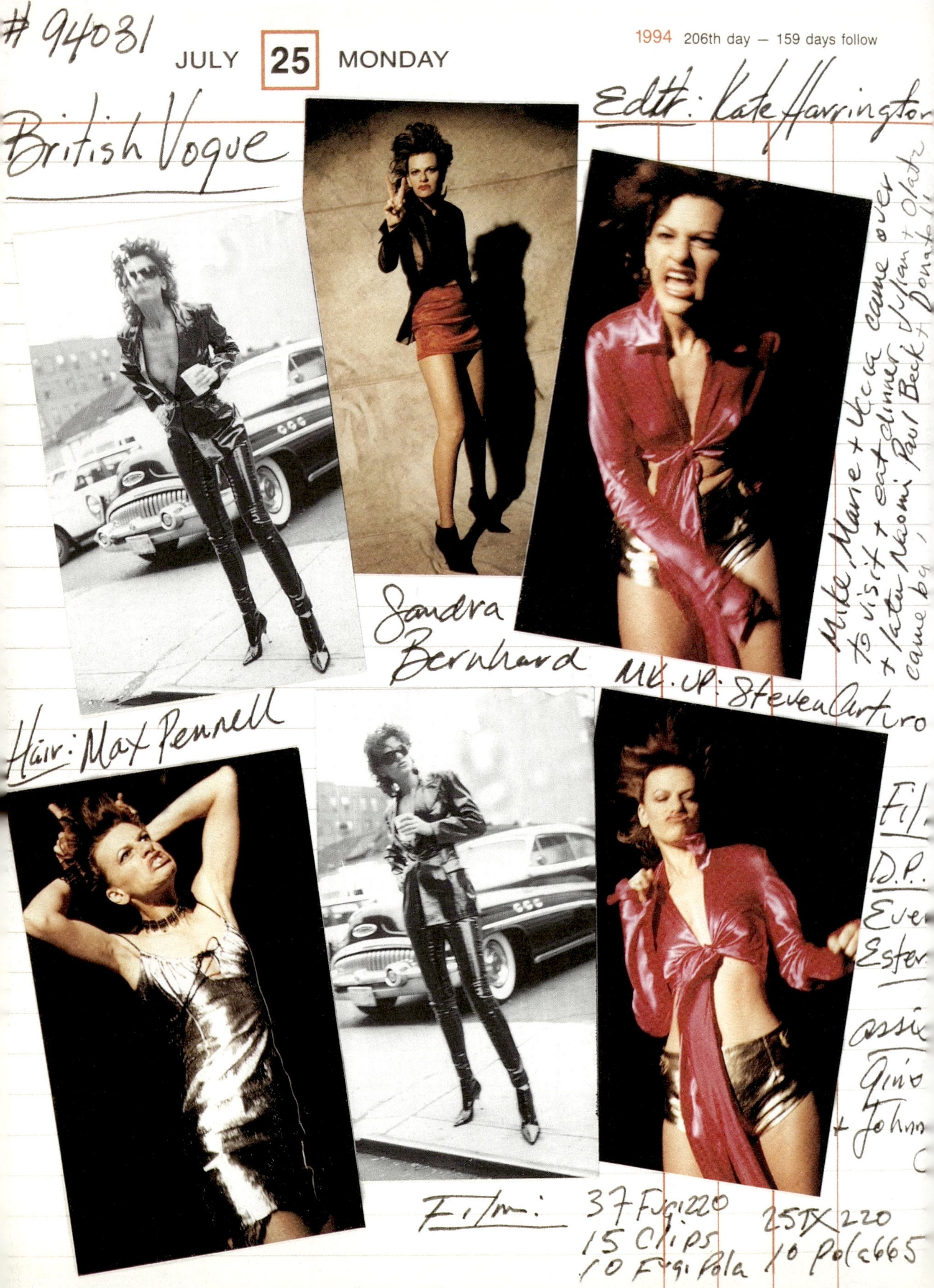

94081
JULY 25 MONDAY
1994 206th day — 159 days follow
British Vogue
Edtr: Kate Harrington
Sandra Bernhard
MK. UP: Steven Arturo
Hair: Max Pennell
Mike Marie + Uccia came over to visit + eat dinner + later Naomi Paul Beck + Clair Donate came by!
Fil D.P. Ever Ester assi Gino + Johns
Film: 37 Fuji 220   25 TX 220
15 Clips   10 Polc 665
10 Fuji Pola

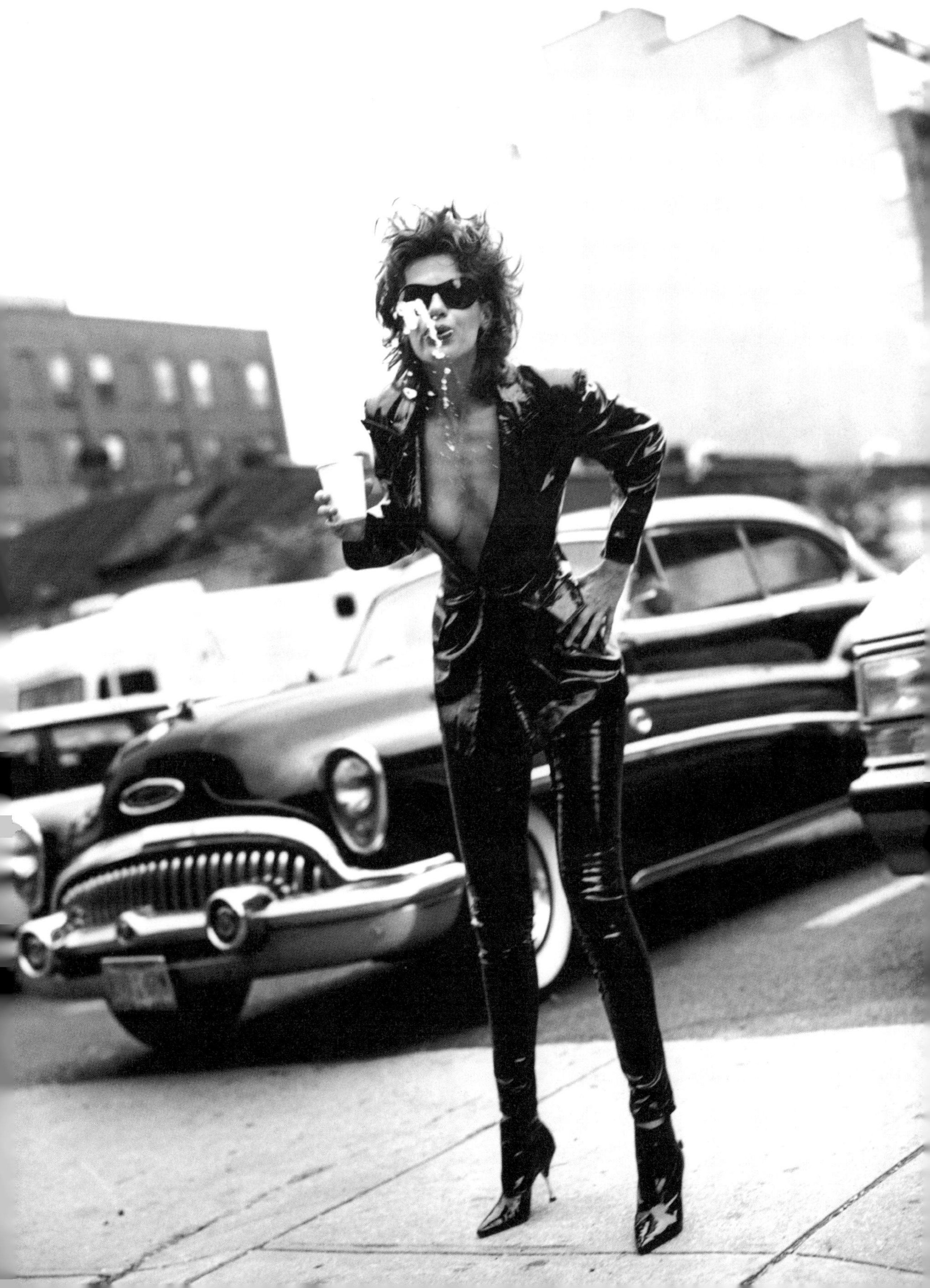

3PM meeting at the office with Vernon and people from Miramax, Pam + James the A.D. Inga Fontaine was also there to style poster shoot for "Fausto". Went with Kara + Tahnee to see Martin Lawrence's Movie.

Vernon came by Friday nite so that we could reschedule another night to shot Charlie with the bags!

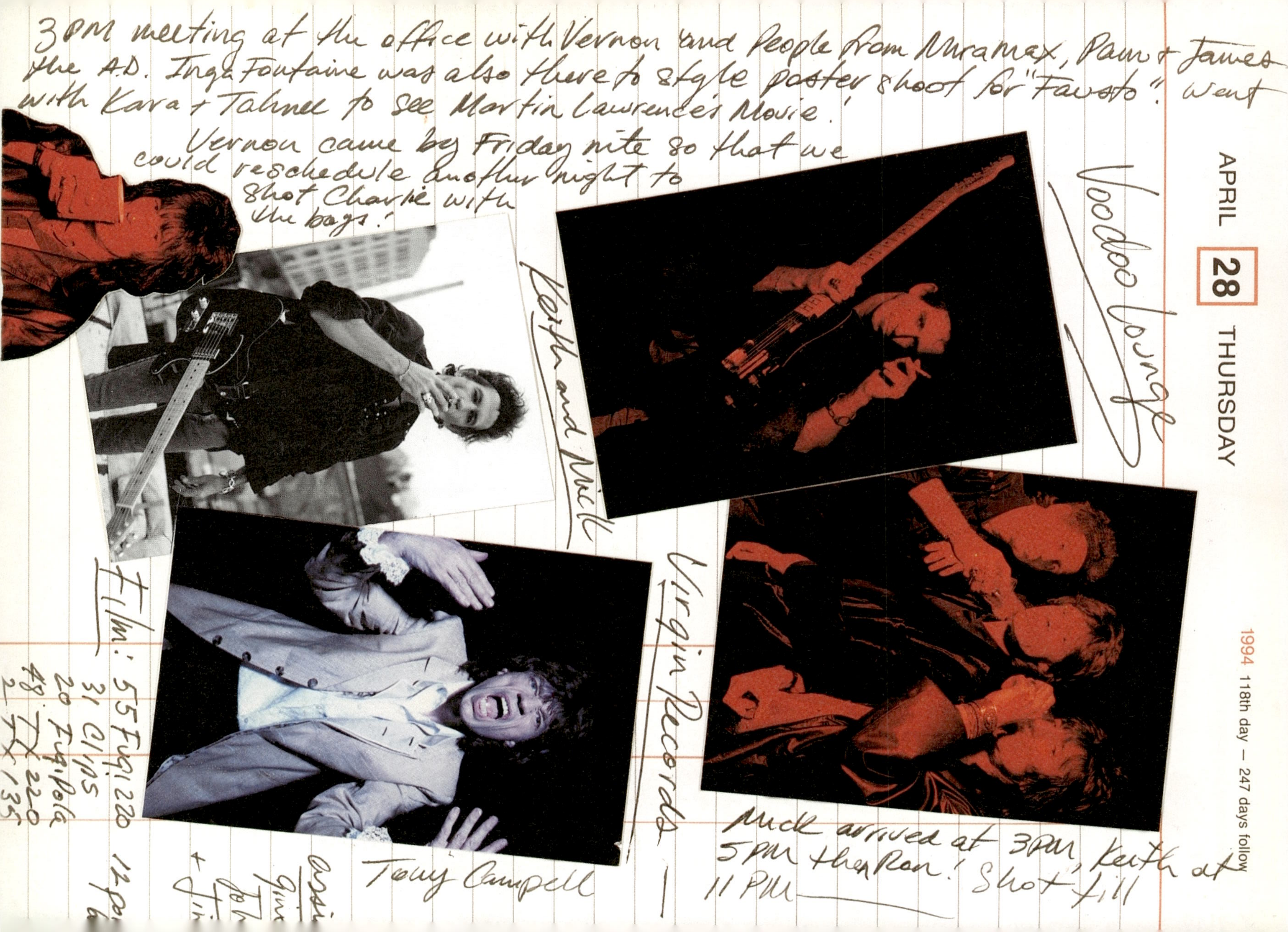

Mick arrived at 3PM, Keith at 5pm then Ron! Shot till 11 PM

Tony Campbell

assi
gin
Joh
+ Jin

Film: 55 Fuqi 220   12 po
31 Clips
20 Fuqi Pola
48 TX 220
2 TX 135

#94014

the Rolling Stones

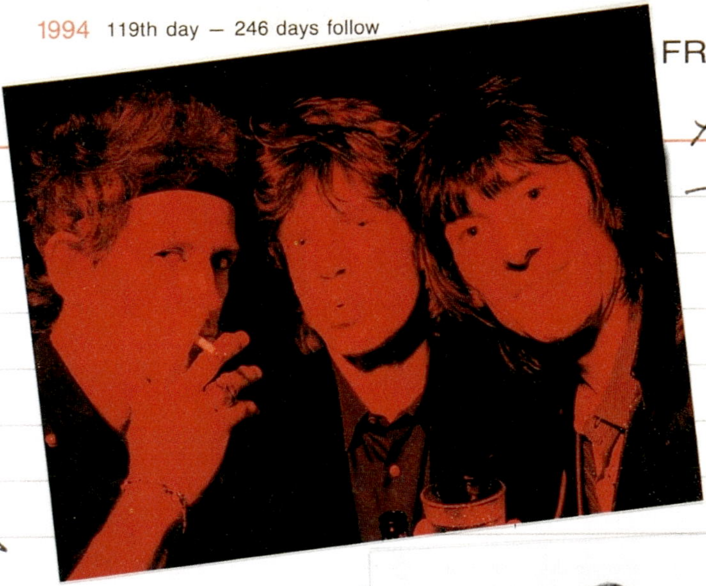

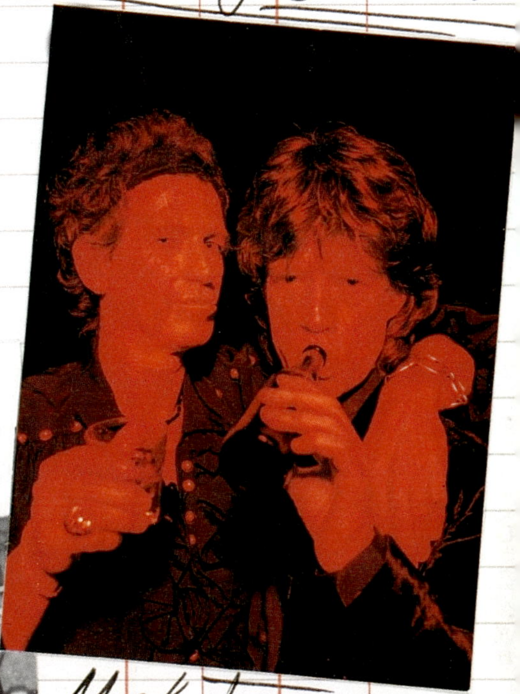

Mick Jagger
Keith Richards —
+ Ron Wood

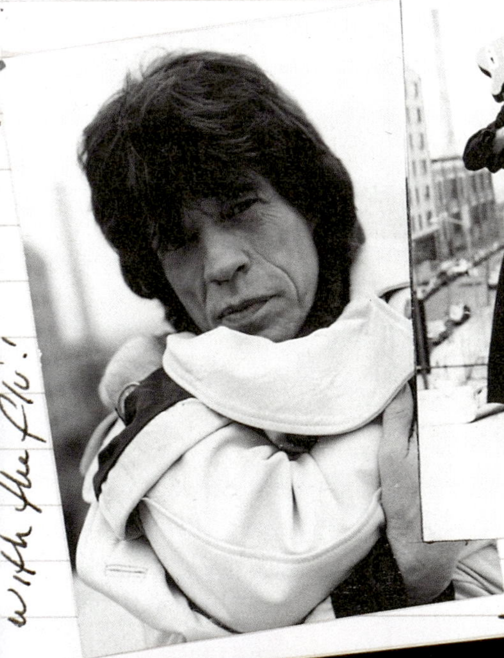

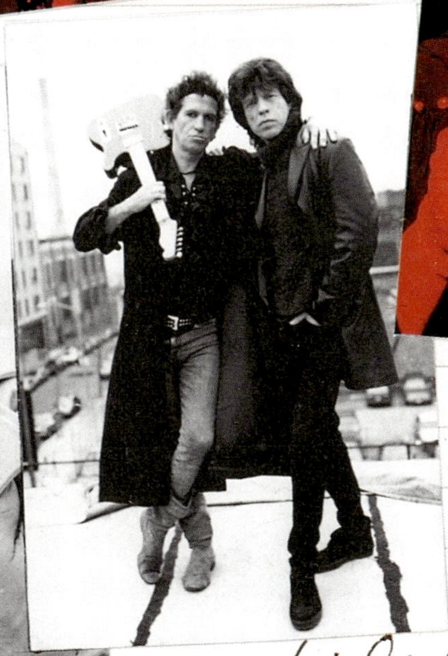

Industria Studio

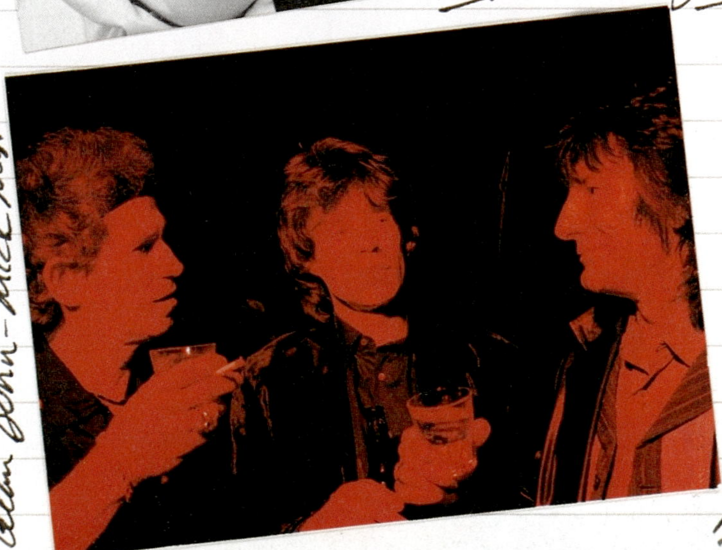

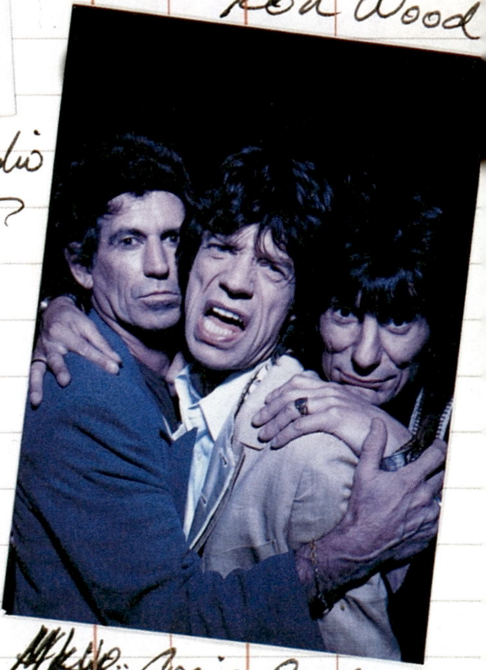

Make-up: Craig Gadson
Hair: Ronnie Stamm

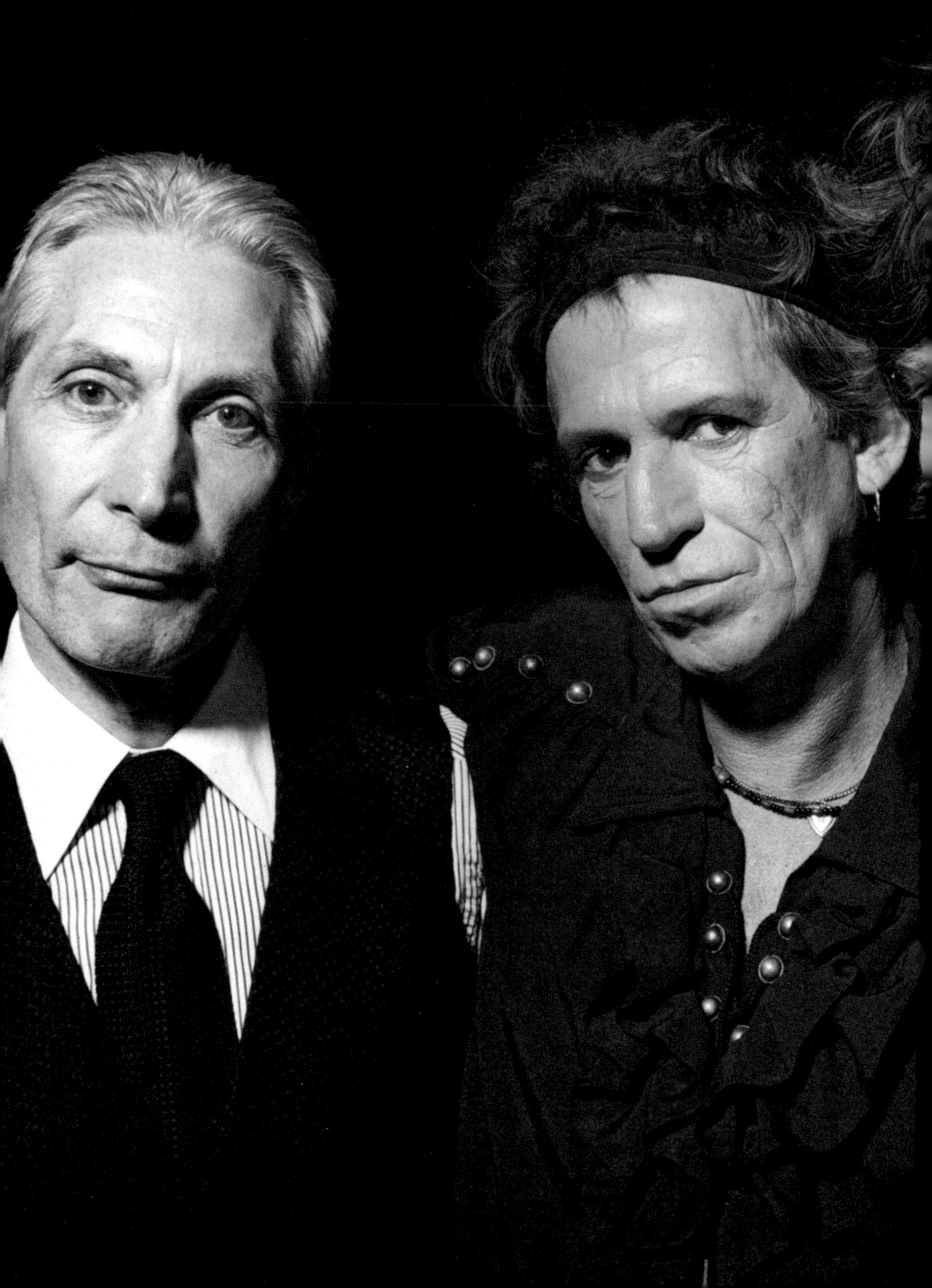

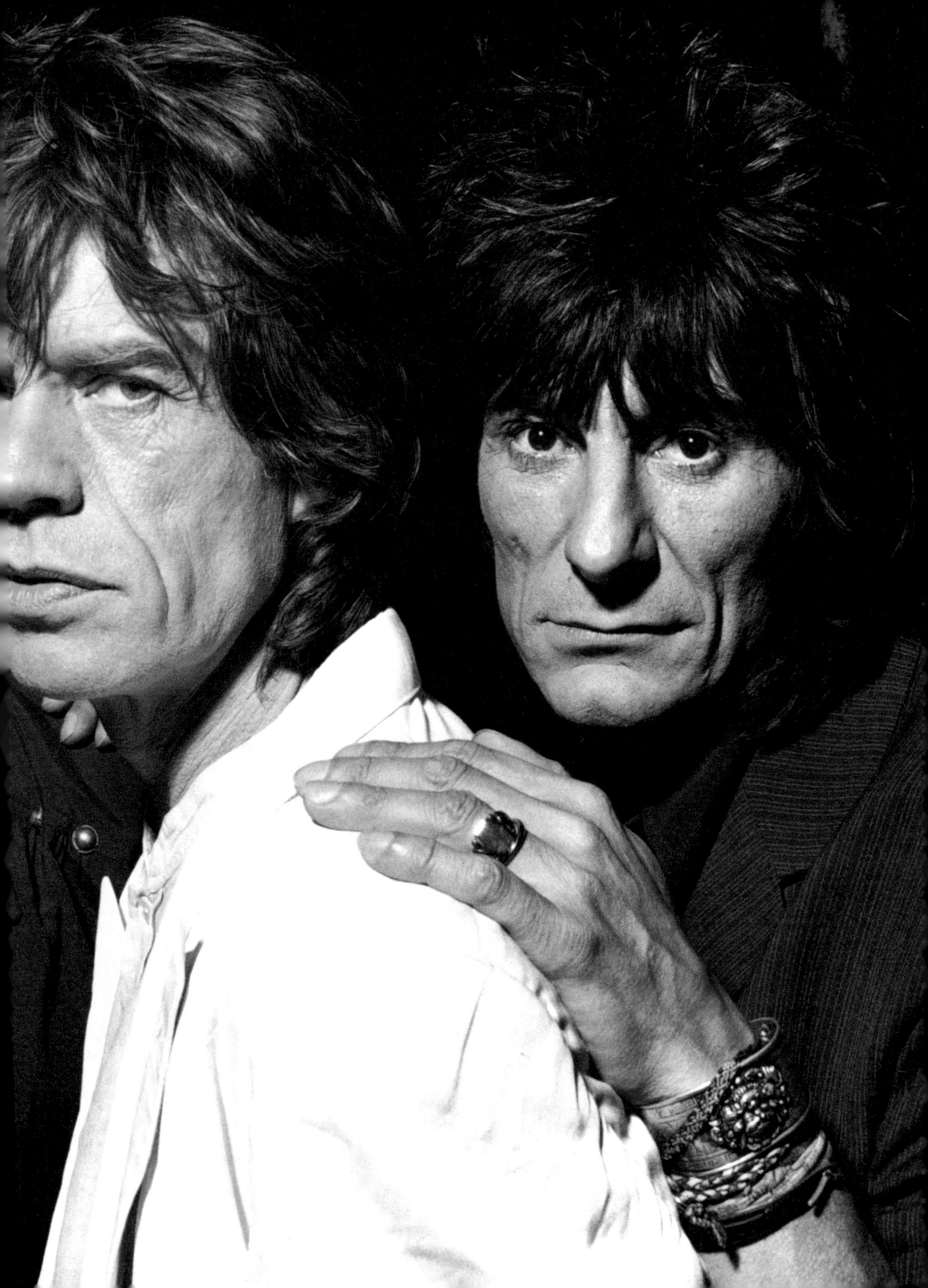

Edited Rolling Stones shoot today. My cugini went to MOMA today. Lunch with Kara. Later I brought my cousins over to Francesco's studio. Ate at home then went to Almodovar "Kika" party with Tahnee, Dukey, Kara + cugini! Tabac after for a drink!

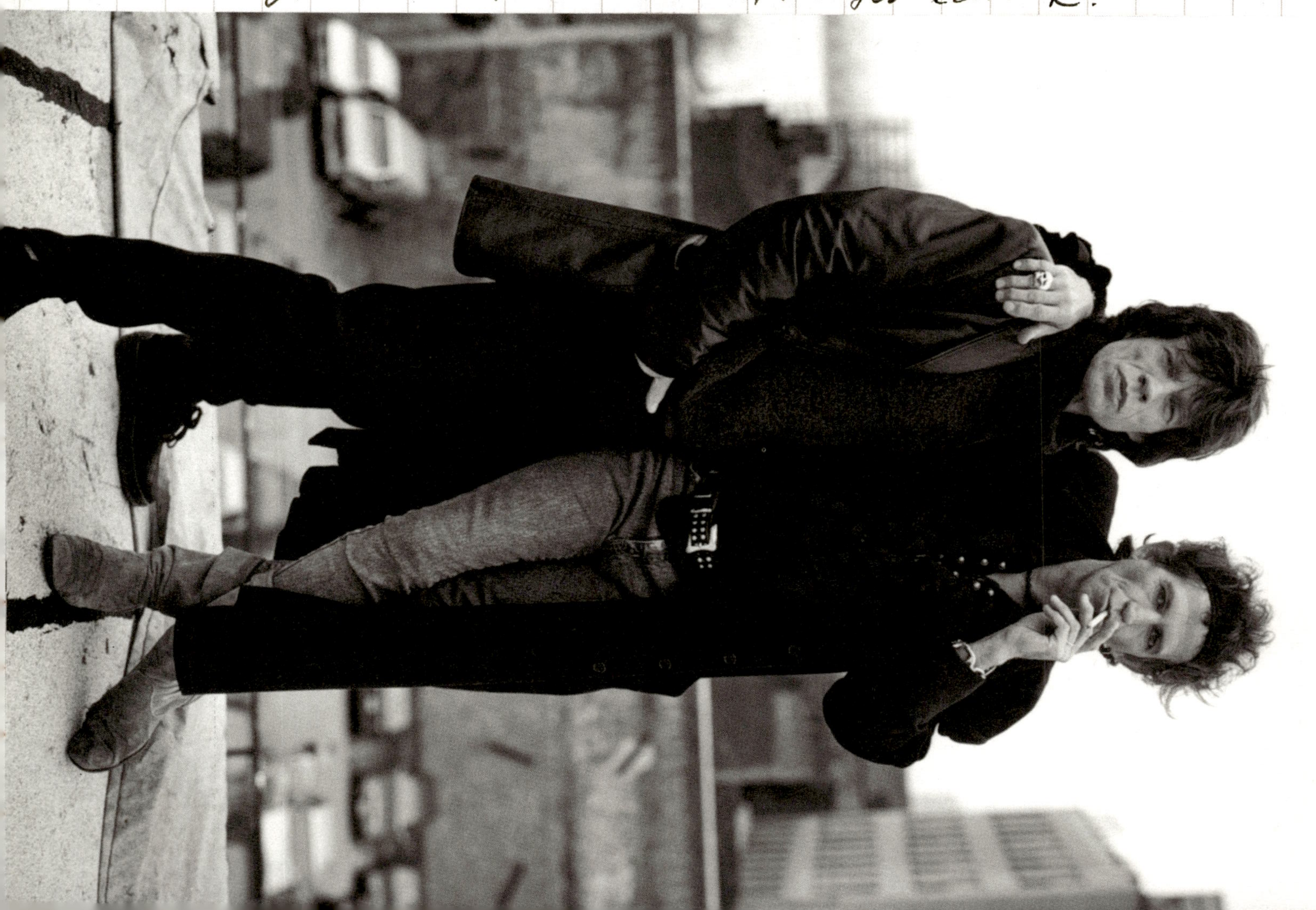

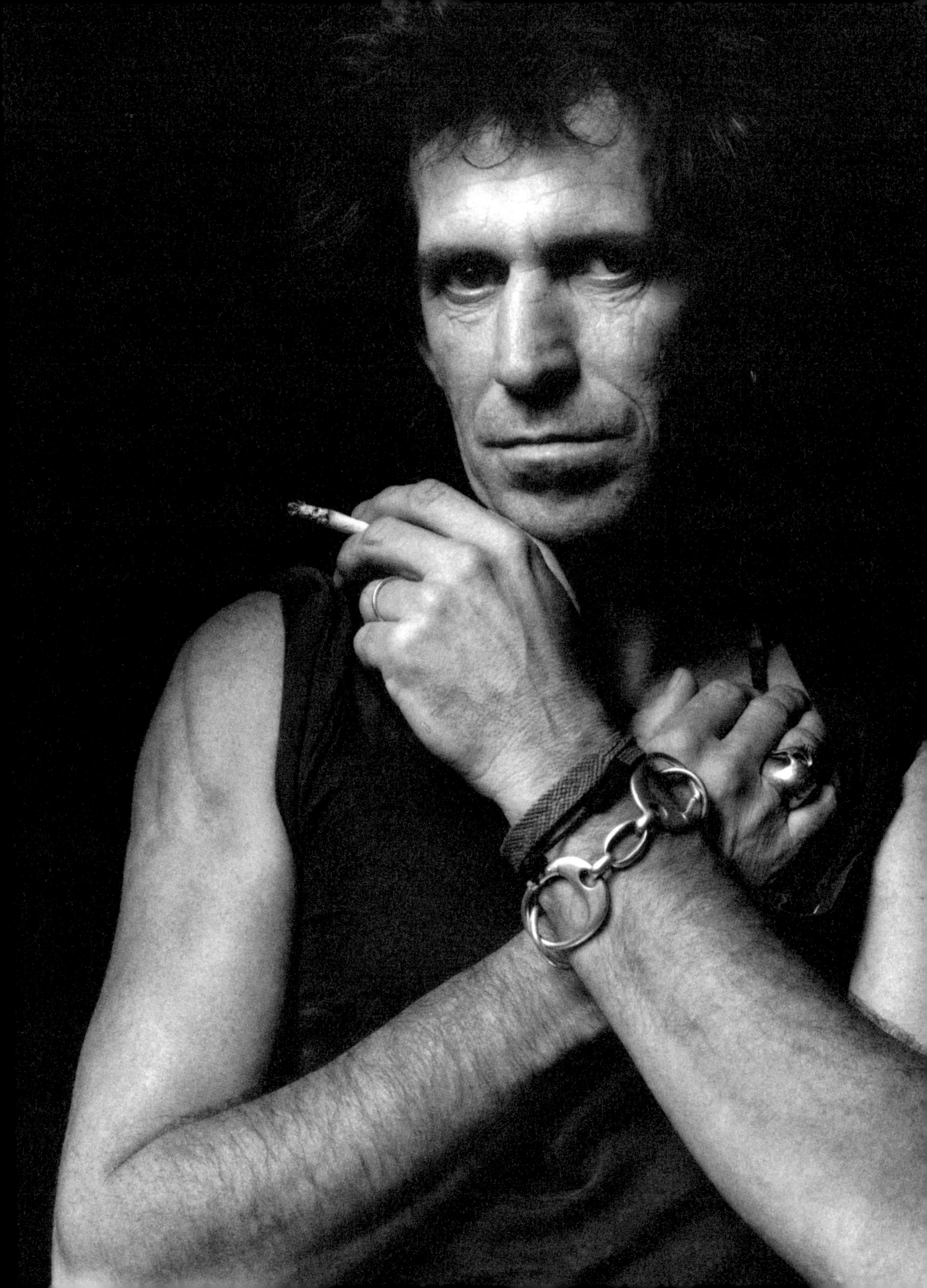

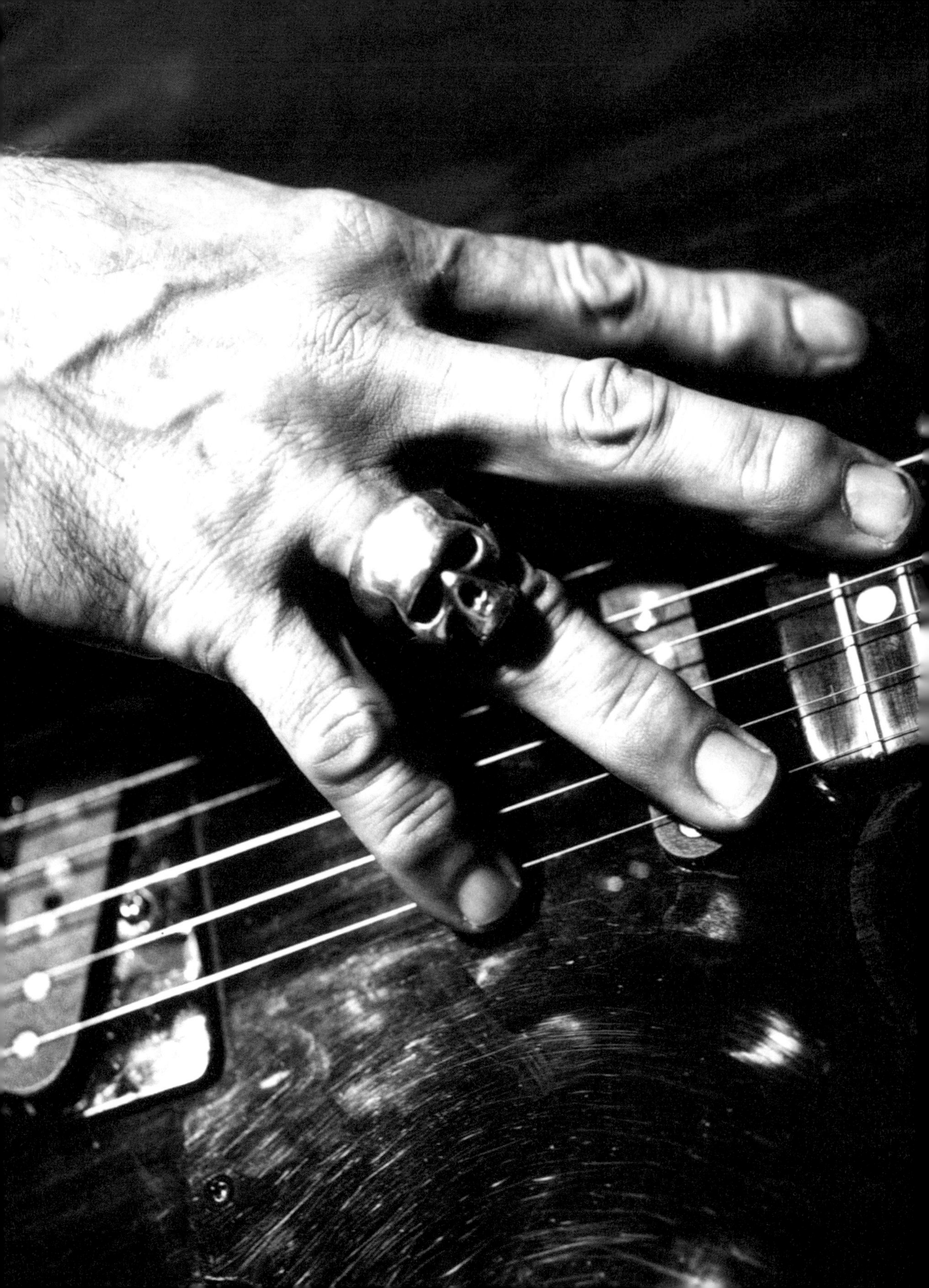

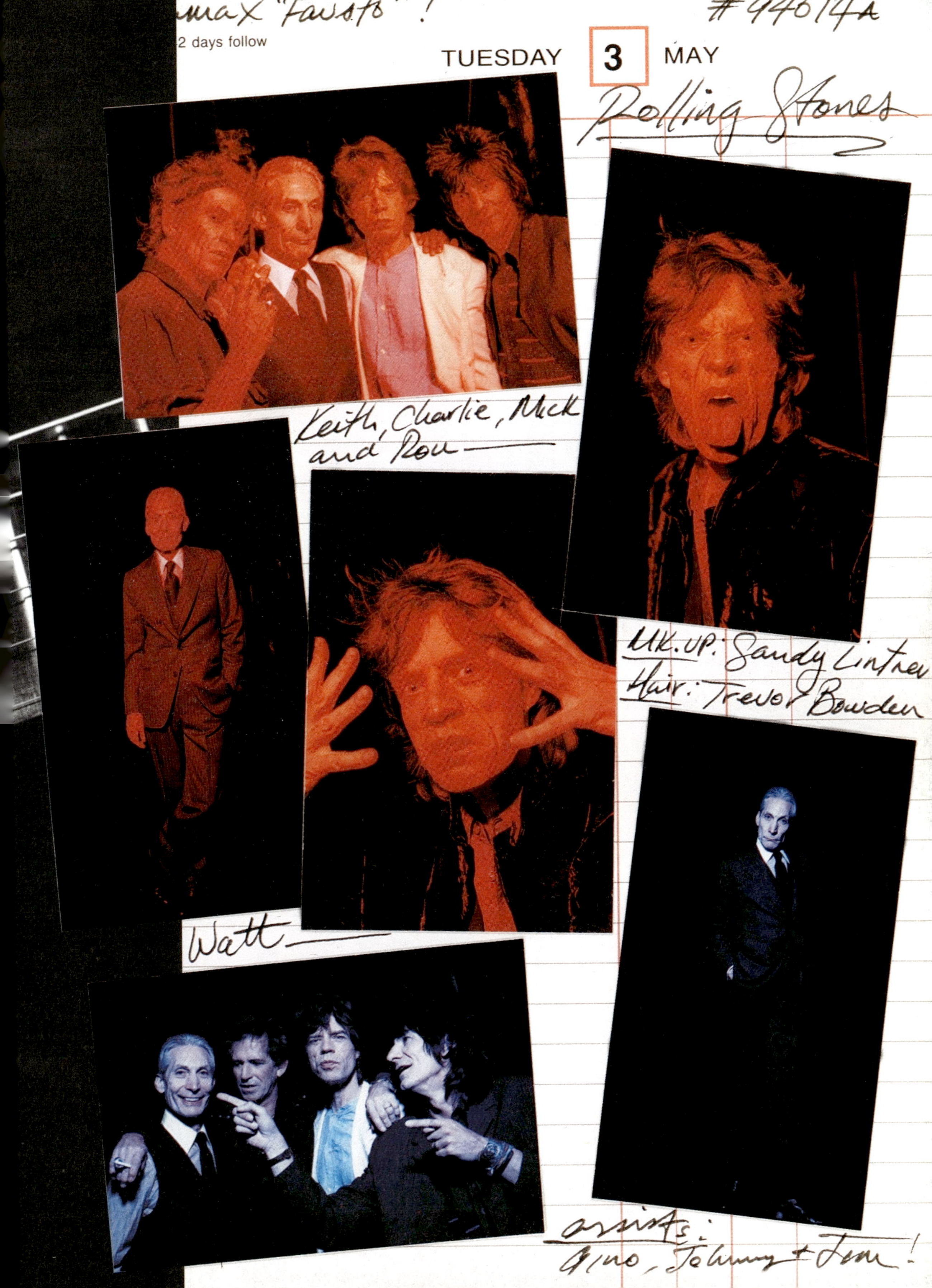
max "Fausto"!
2 days follow
TUESDAY 3 MAY
44014A
Rolling Stones
Keith, Charlie, Mick
and Ron
M.UP. Sandy Lintner
Hair: Trevor Bowden
Watt
artists:
Gino, Johnny + Tom!

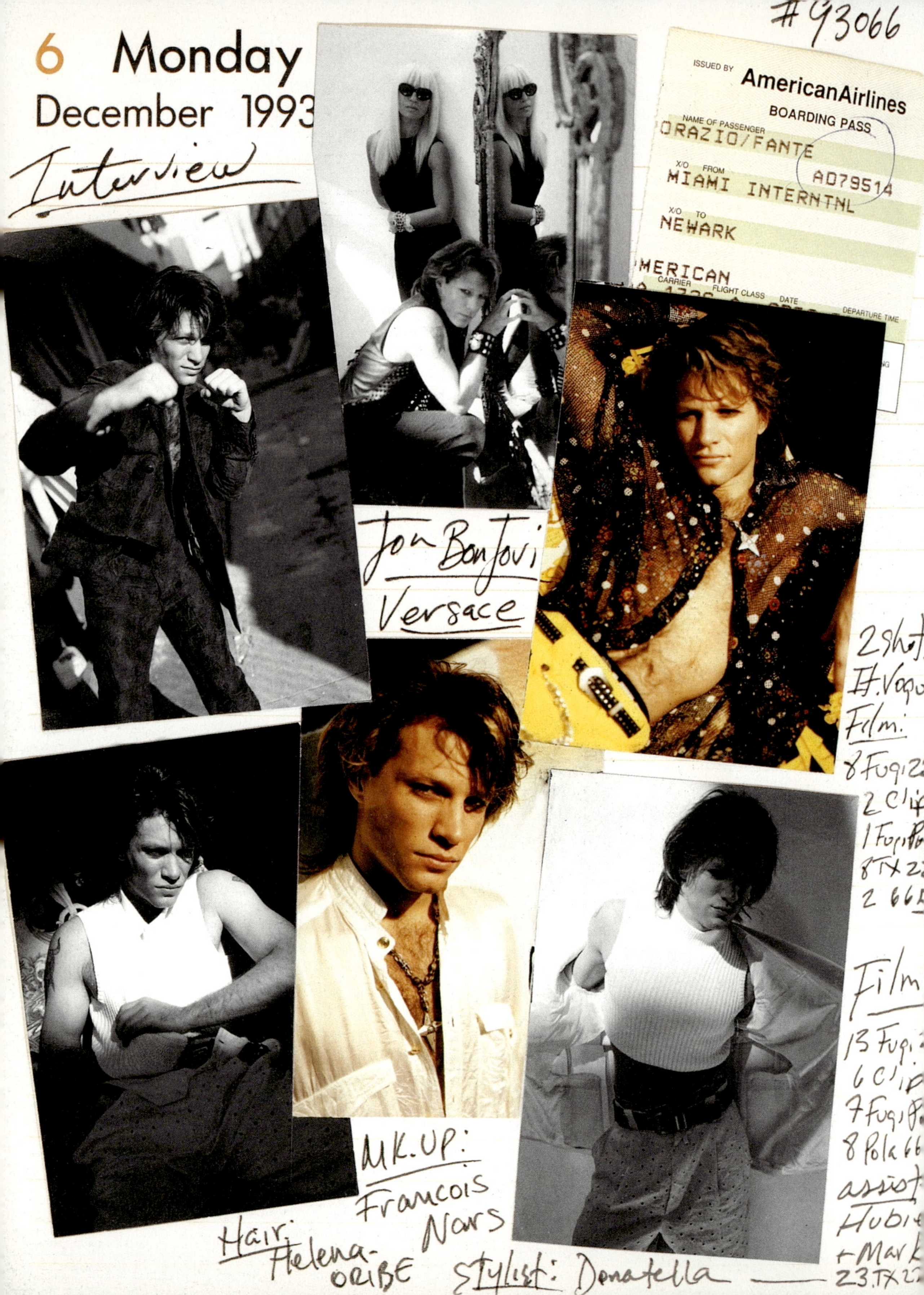
6 Monday
December 1993
Interview
#Y3066
ISSUED BY AmericanAirlines
BOARDING PASS
NAME OF PASSENGER
ORAZIO/FANTE
X/O FROM   A079514
MIAMI INTERNTNL
X/O TO
NEWARK
AMERICAN
CARRIER   FLIGHT CLASS   DATE   DEPARTURE TIME
Jon BonJovi
Versace
2 shots
It. Vogu
Film.
8 Fugi 22
2 Cli4
1 Fugi Po
8 TX 2
2 66E
Film
13 Fugi
6 Cli
7 Fugi P
8 Pola 66
assist
Hubr
+ Mark
23 TX 2
MK.UP:
Francois
Nars
Hair:
Helena-
ORIBE
STYLIST: Donatella

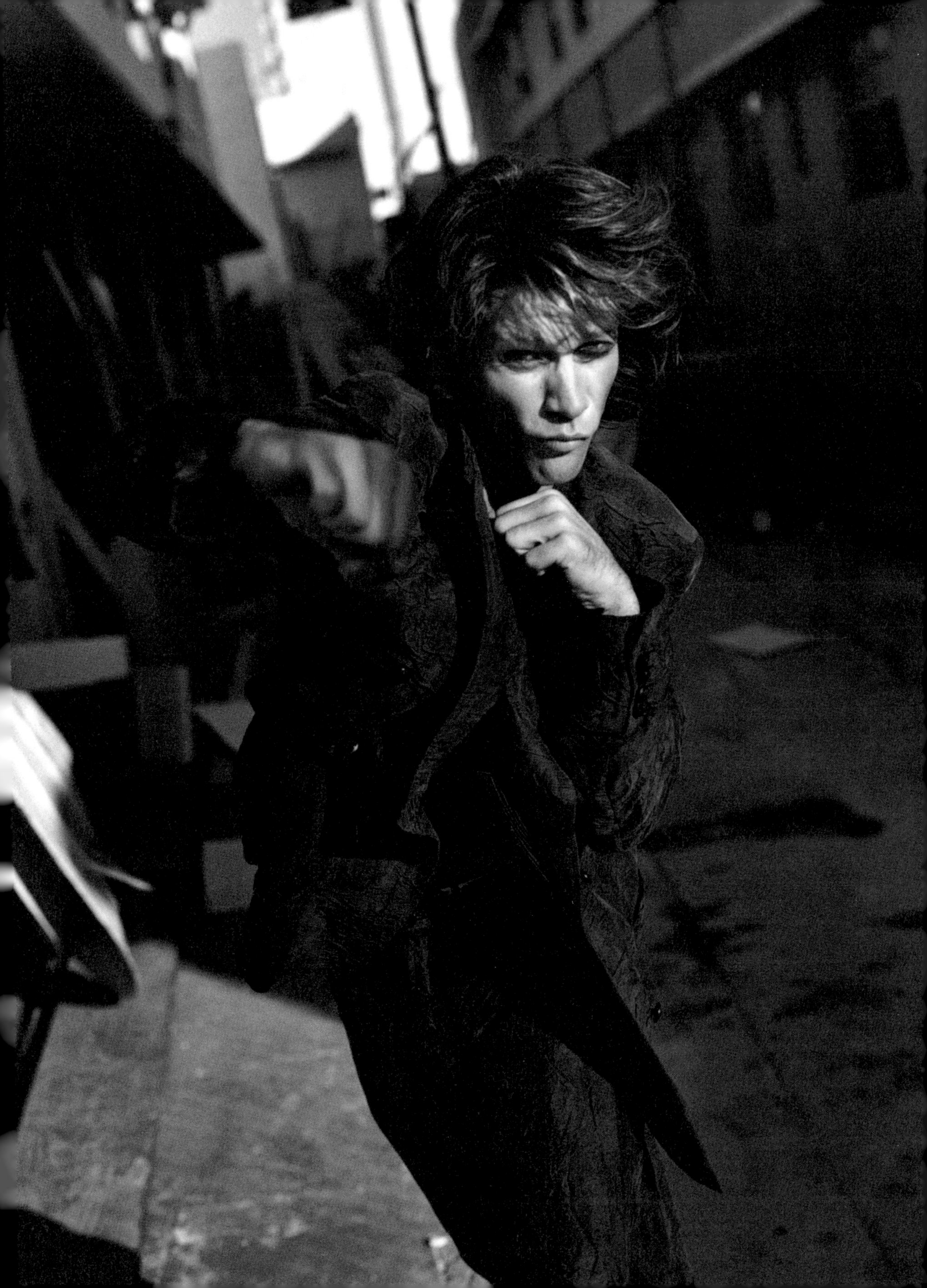

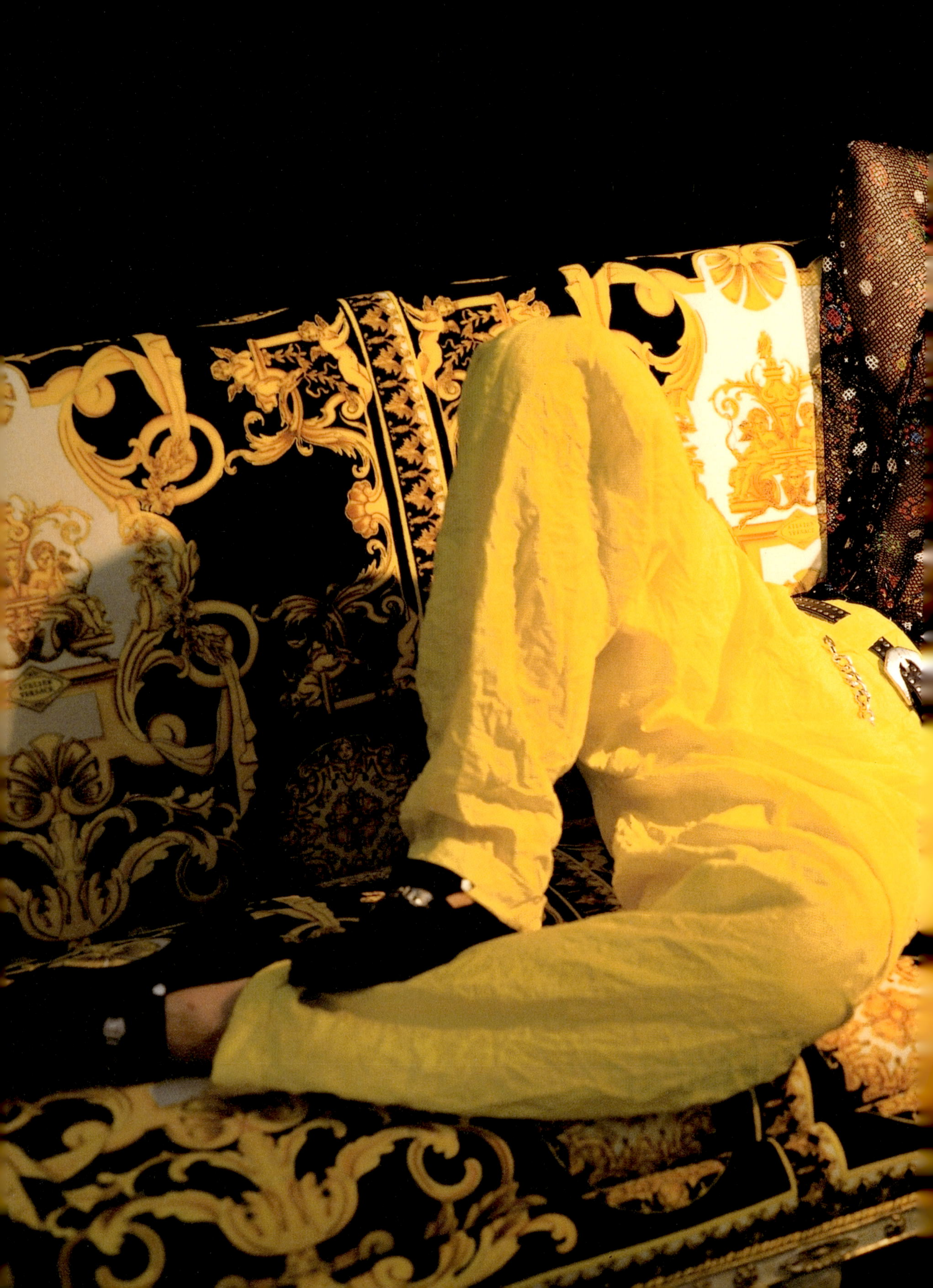

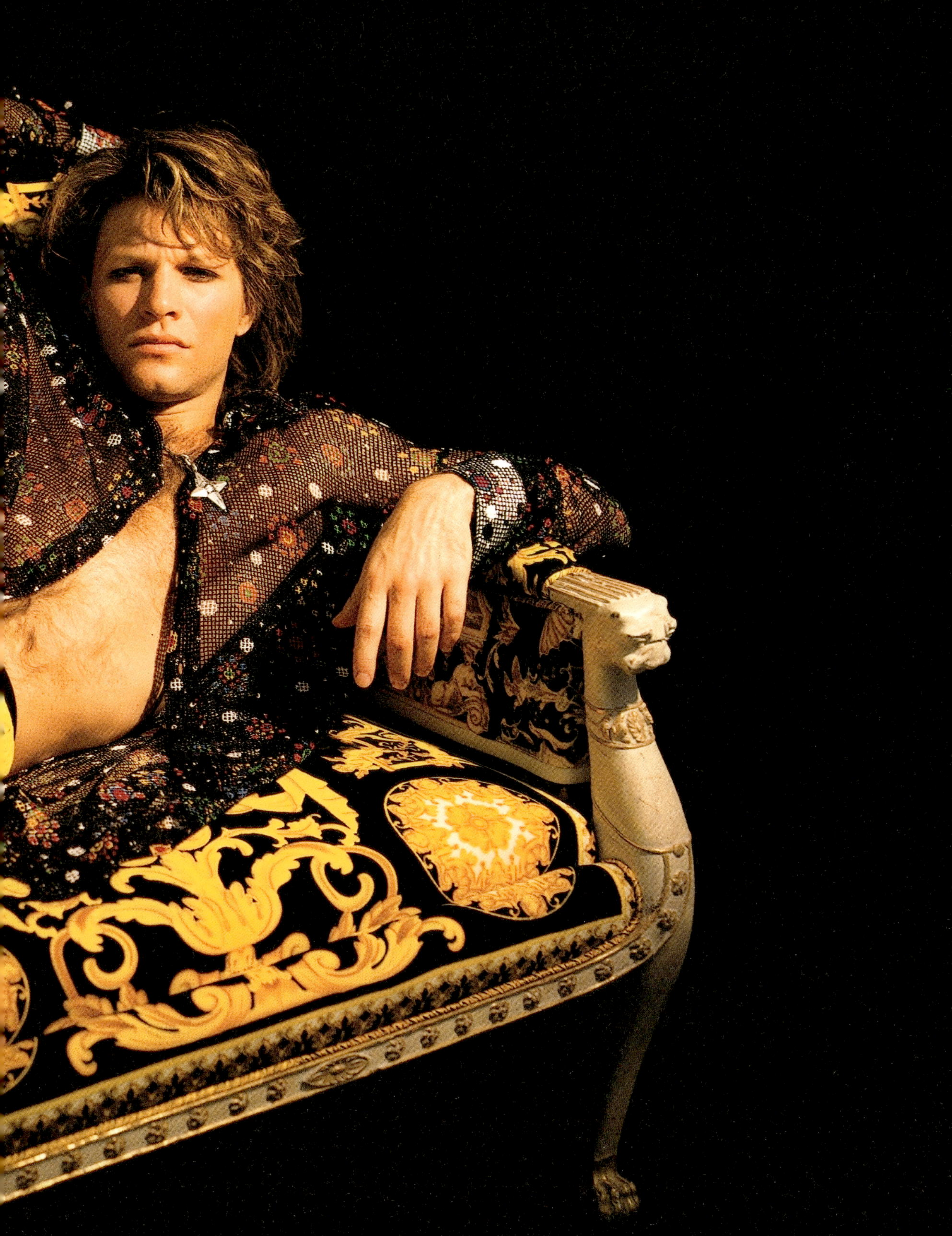

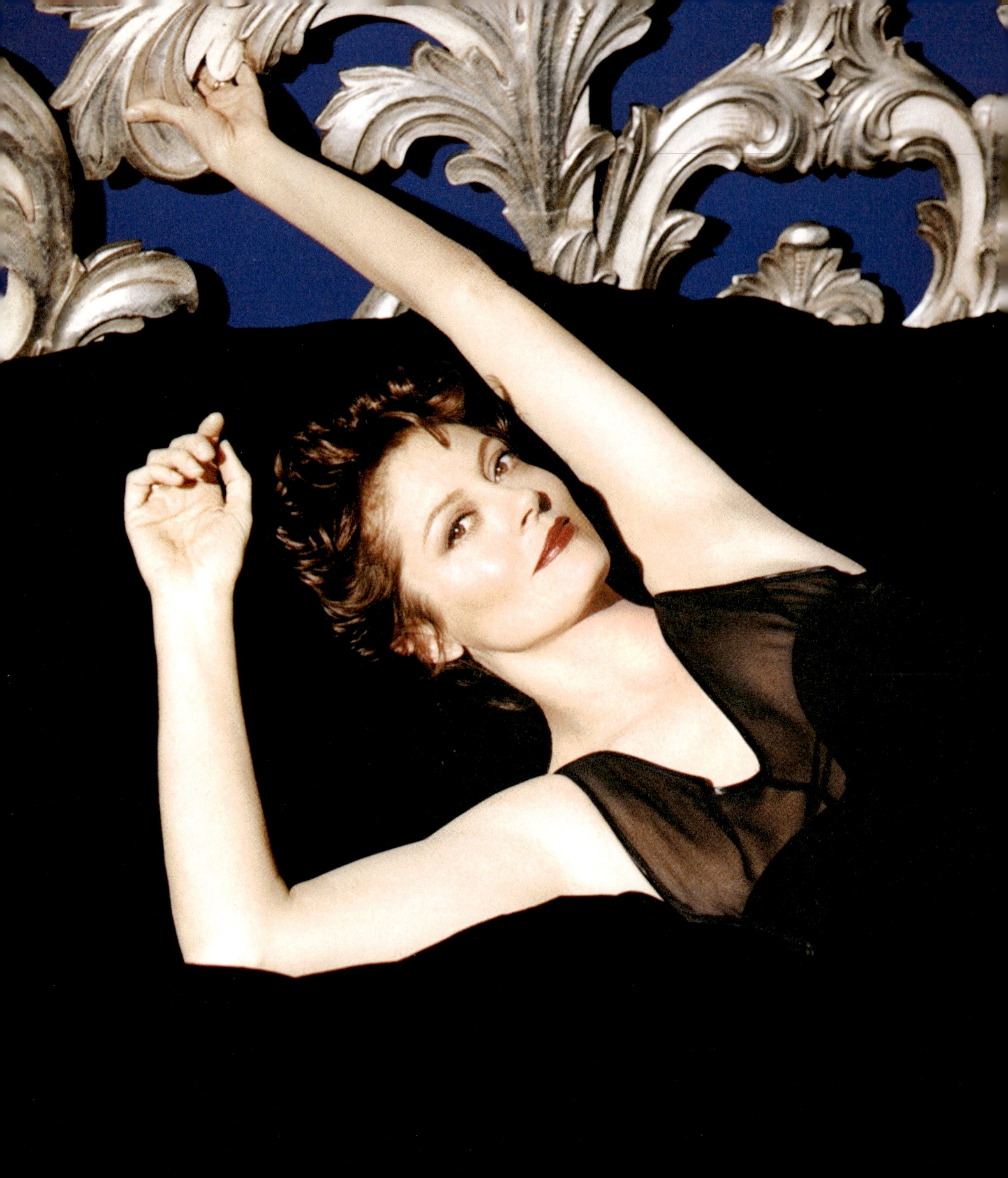

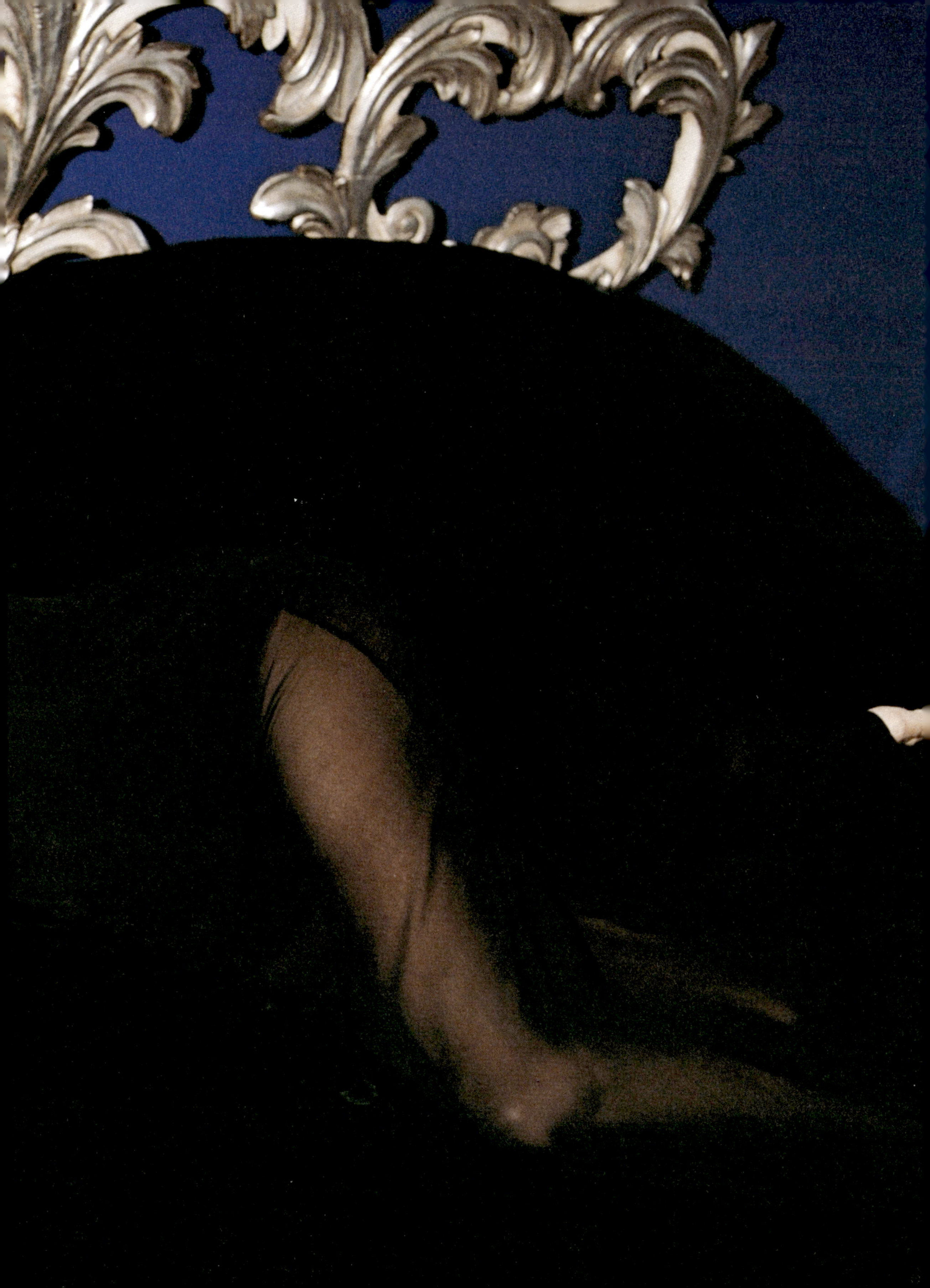

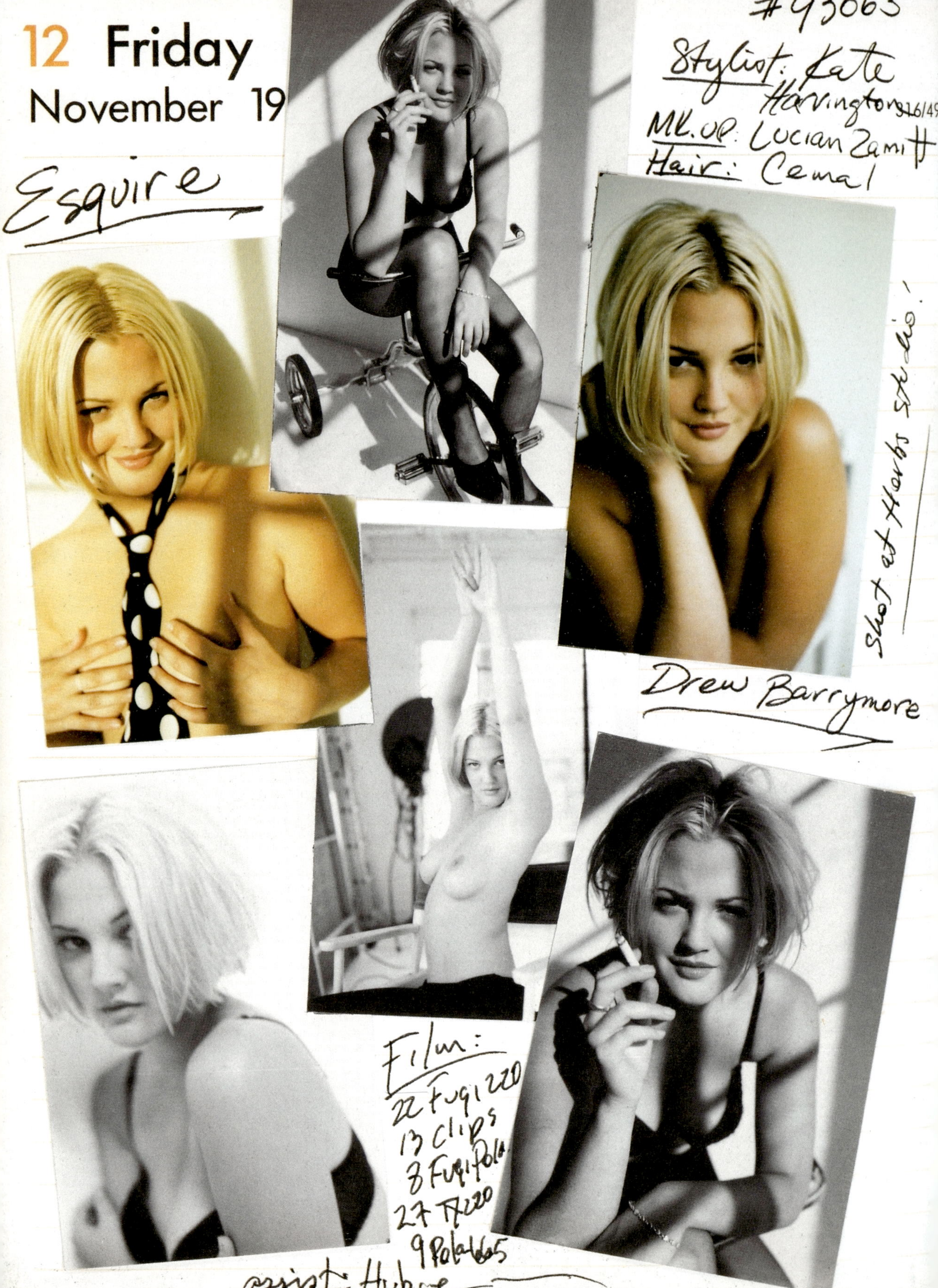

12 Friday
November 19

Esquire

#93063
Stylist: Kate Harrington 316/49
Mk.up: Lucian Zamitt
Hair: Cemal

Shot at Harbs studio!

Drew Barrymore

Film:
22 Fuji 220
13 clips
8 Fuji Pola
27 TX220
9 Pola 665

assist: Hubie

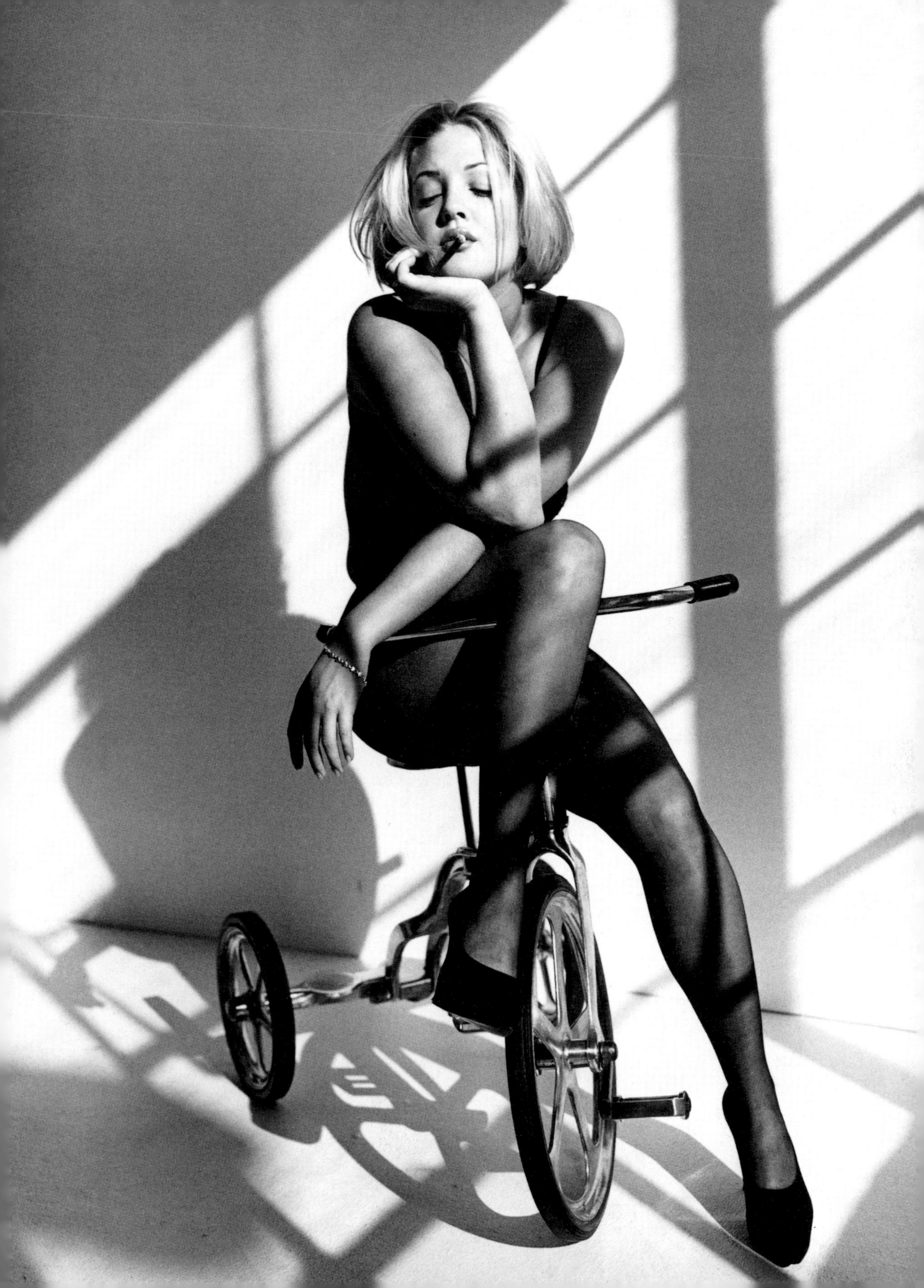

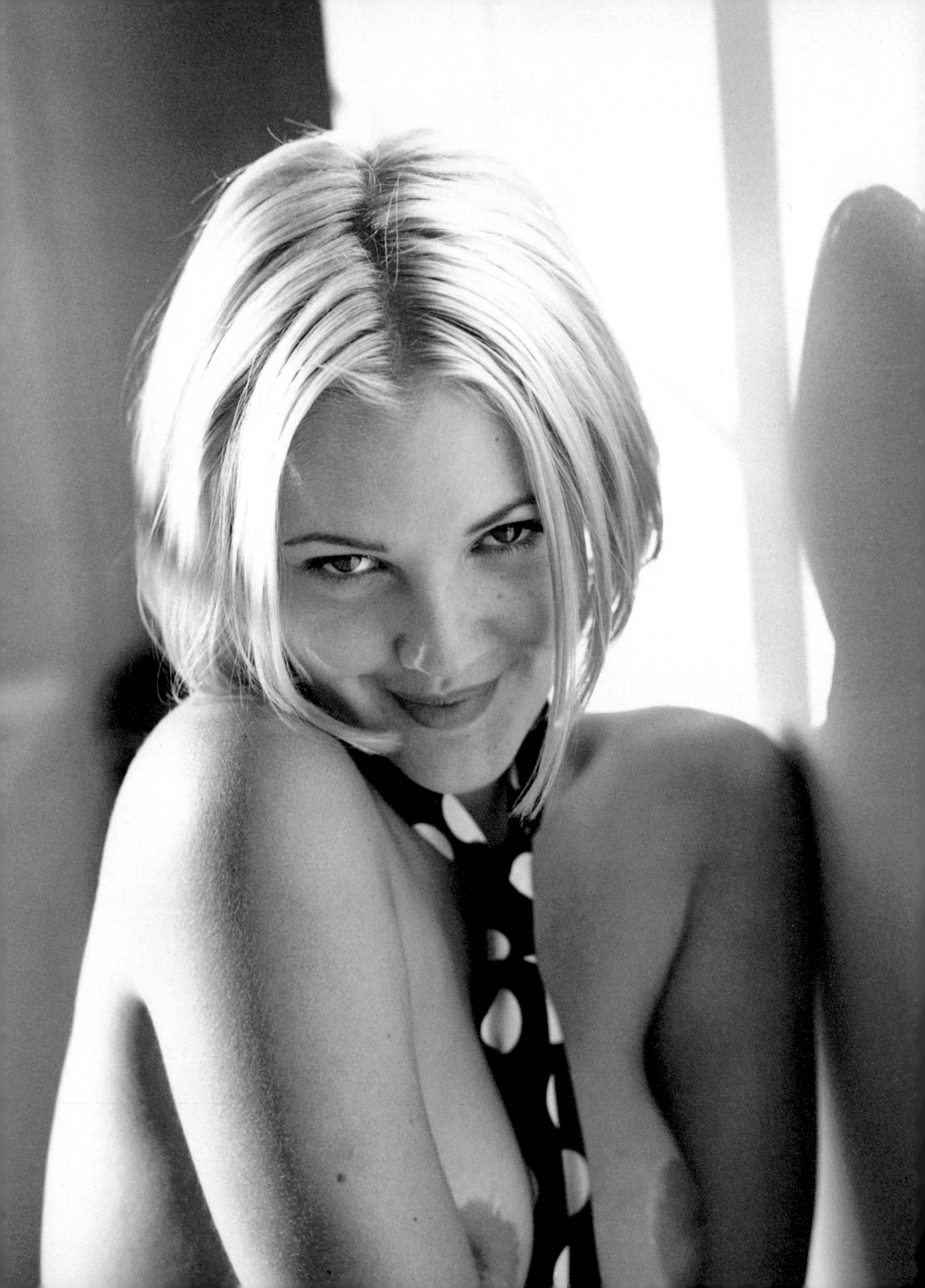

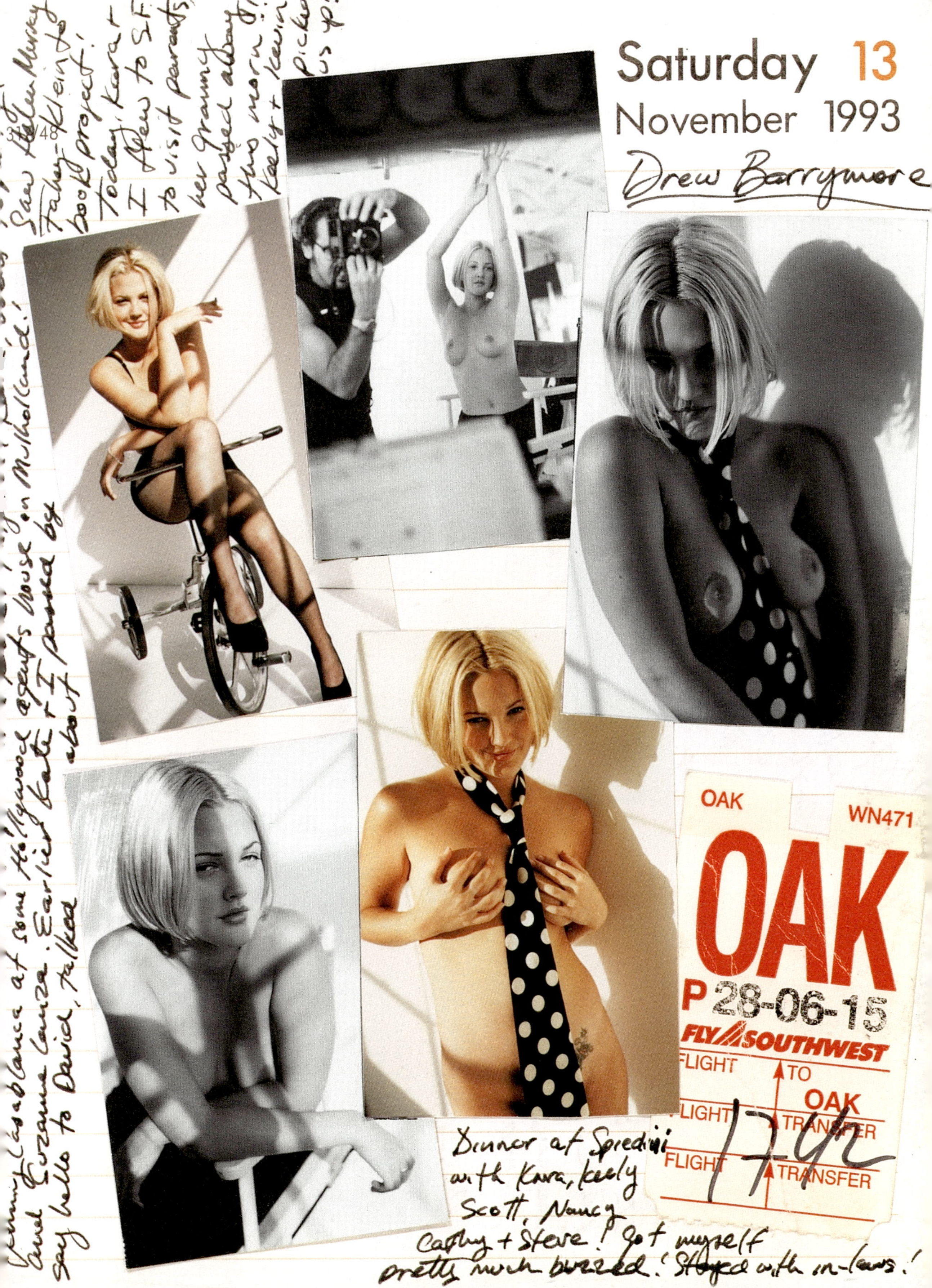

Saturday 13
November 1993
Drew Barrymore
OAK
WN471
OAK
P 28-06-15
FLY SOUTHWEST
FLIGHT TO OAK
FLIGHT TO TRANSFER
FLIGHT TO TRANSFER
Dinner at Spredini
with Kara, Keely
Scott, Nancy
Cathy + Steve! Got myself
pretty much buzzed! Stayed with in-laws!

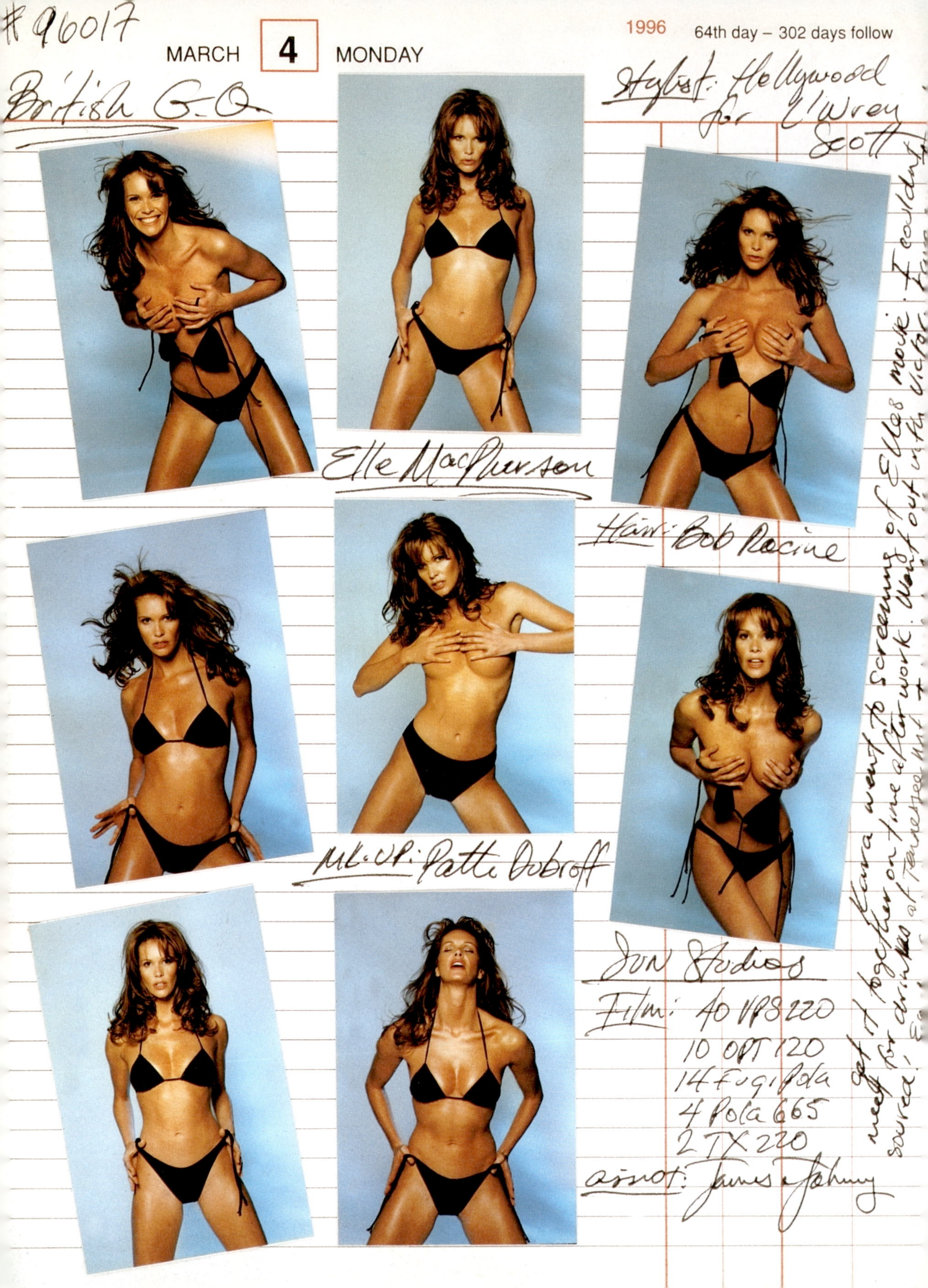

#96017
MARCH 4 MONDAY
1996   64th day – 302 days follow
British G.Q.
Stylist: Hollywood for L'Wren Scott
Elle MacPherson
Hair: Bob Racine
M.U.P: Patti Dobroff
Jon Studios
Film: 40 VPS 220
10 OPT 120
14 Fuji pda
4 Pola 665
2 TX 220
assist: James & Johnny

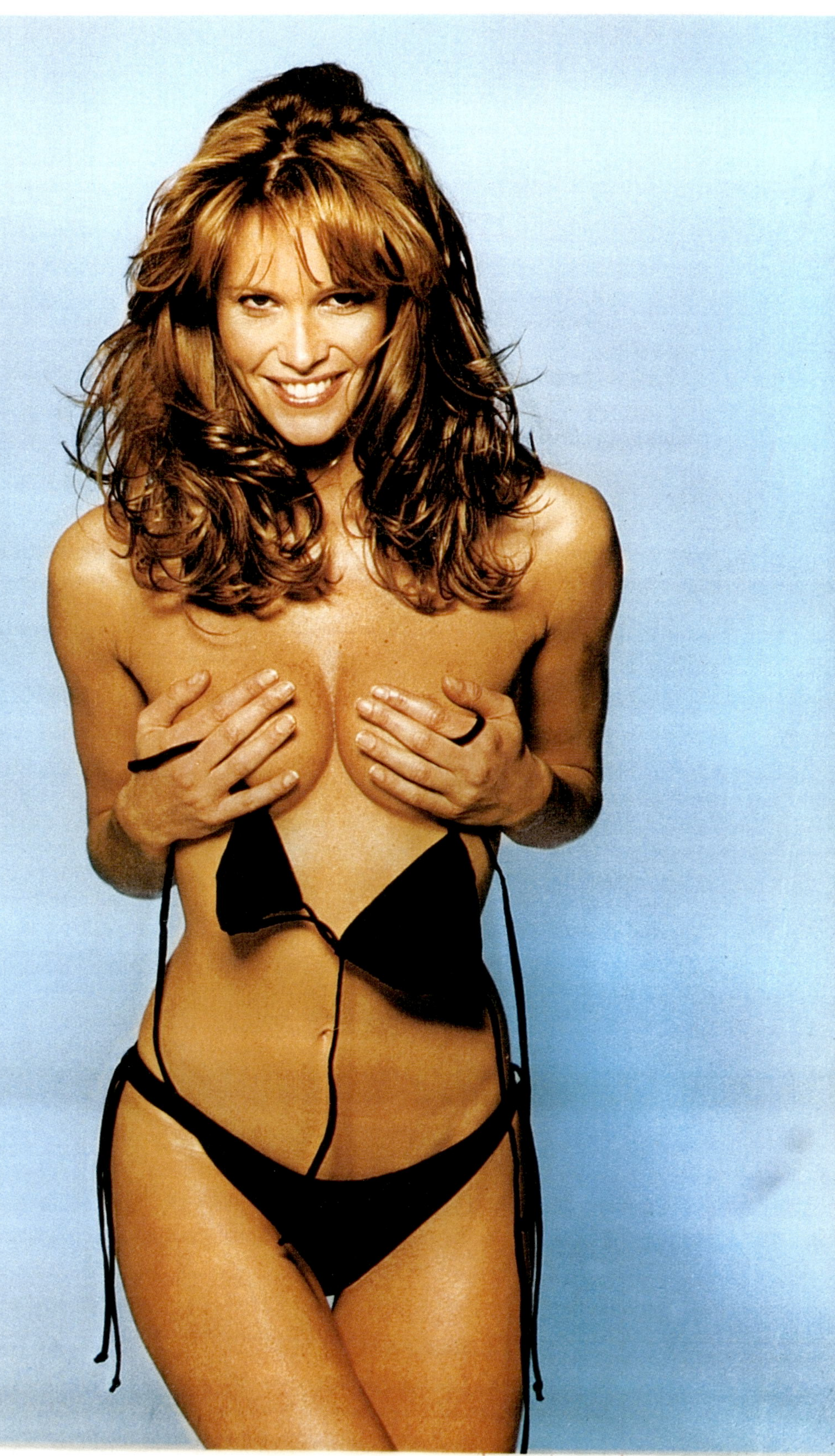

7.00 meeting with Ezra Jones. Lawyer Fernando recommended Me + Rick met him + later had a drink. We both liked him! Came home abit tired and decided to stay in. Started getting a sore throat.

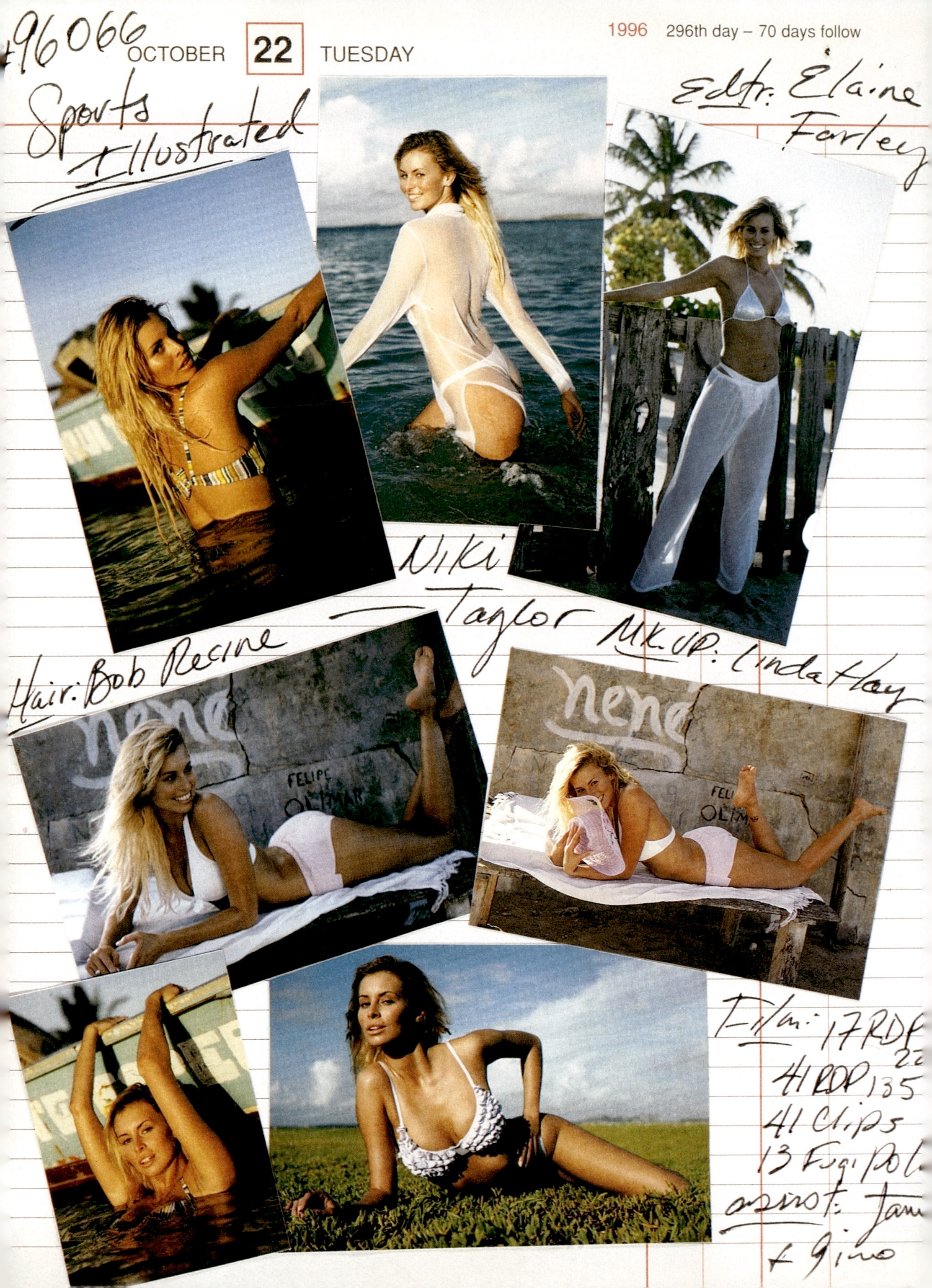

96066
OCTOBER 22 TUESDAY
1996   296th day – 70 days follow
Sports Illustrated
Edtr: Elaine Farley
Niki Taylor
Hair: Bob Recine
MK. UP: Linda Hay
Film: 17 RDF
41 RDP 135
41 Clips
13 Fuji Pol.
assist: Jan
& Gino
nene
FELIPE OLIMAR
nene

Sports Illustrated

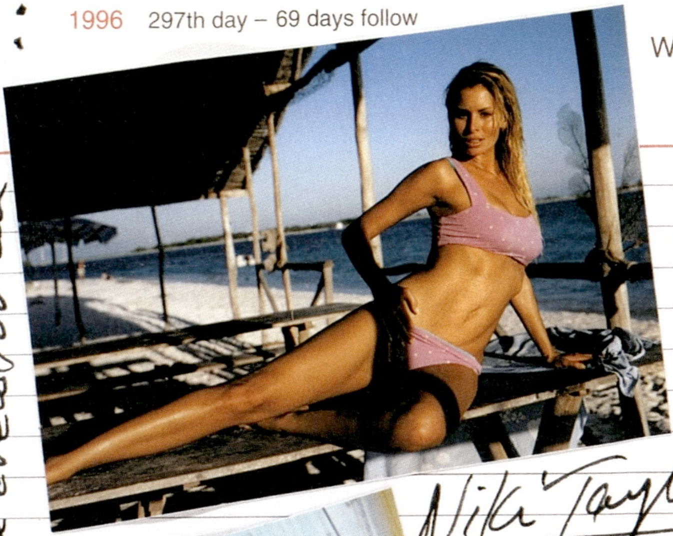

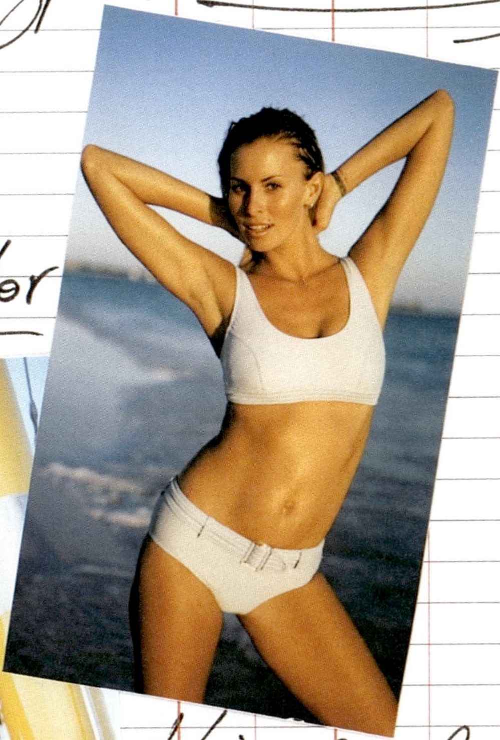

Niki Taylor

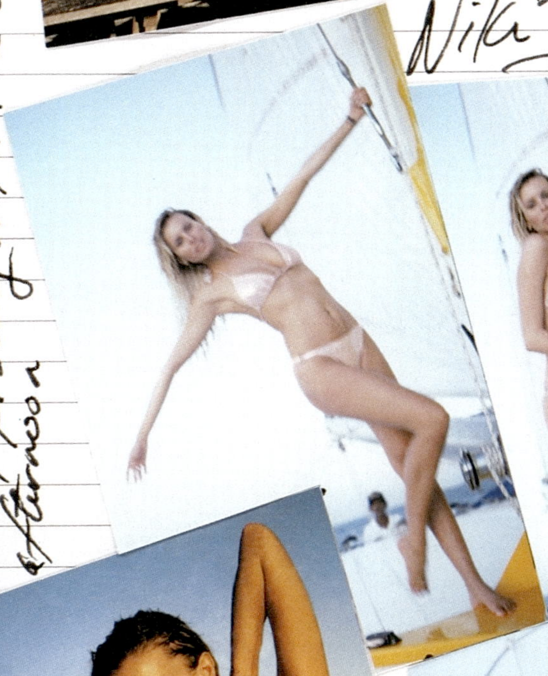

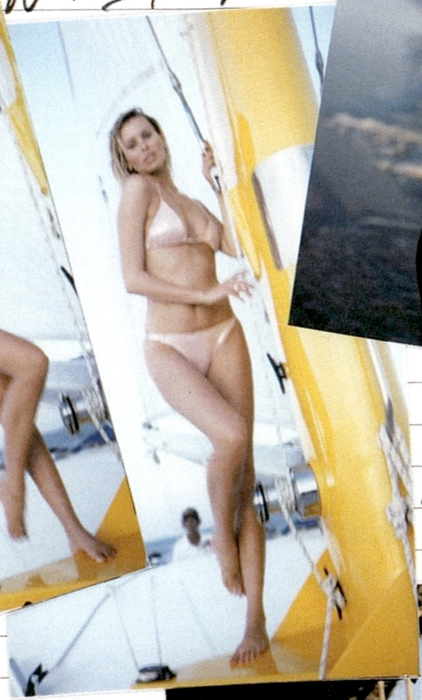

Hair: Bob Recine
Mk.up.: Linda Hay

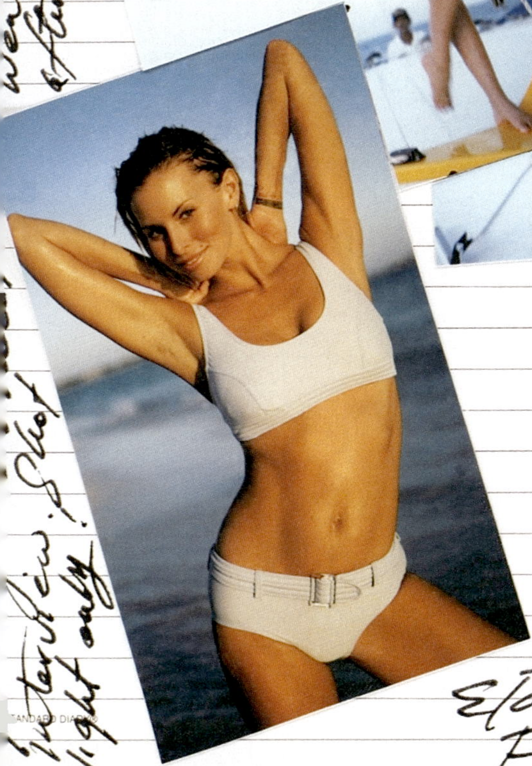

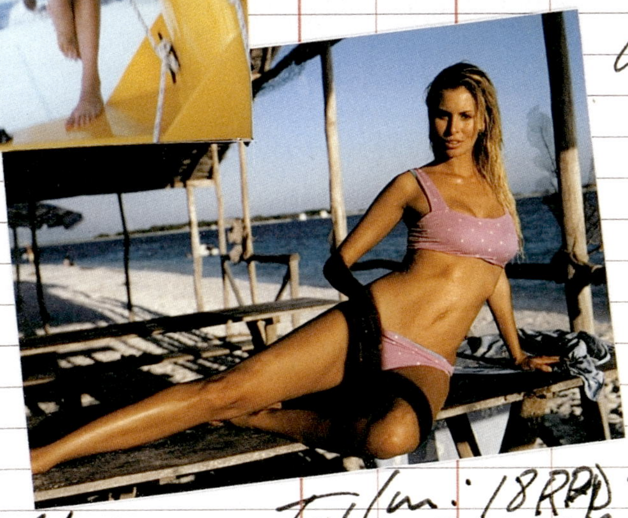

Edtr.:
Elaine
Farley

Film: 18 RDP 220
      6 RDP 135
assist.: 17 Clips
James + Gino   6 Fuji Polo

went to ?hing with the crew or an
afternoon

Interview: Shot
light only.

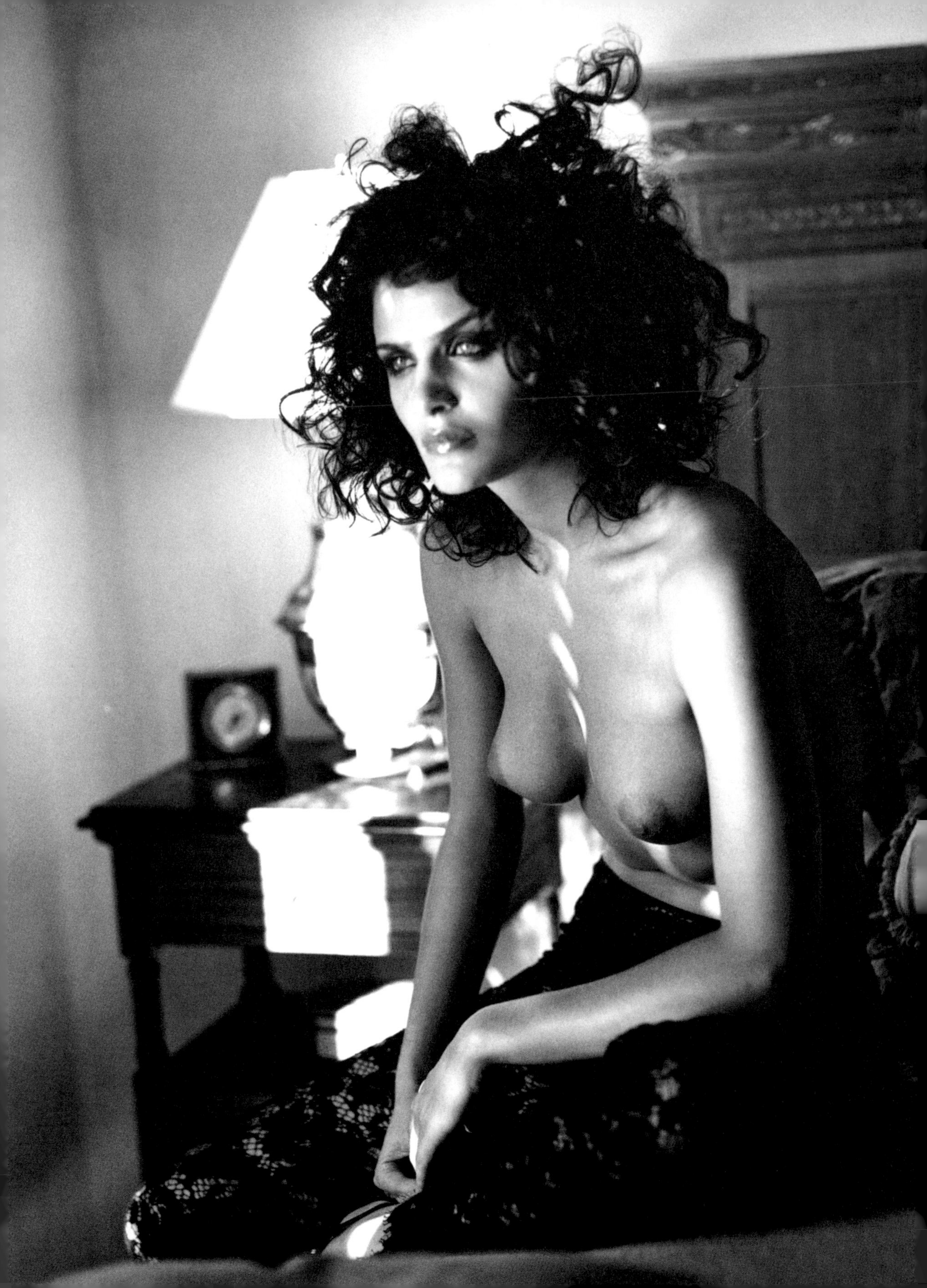

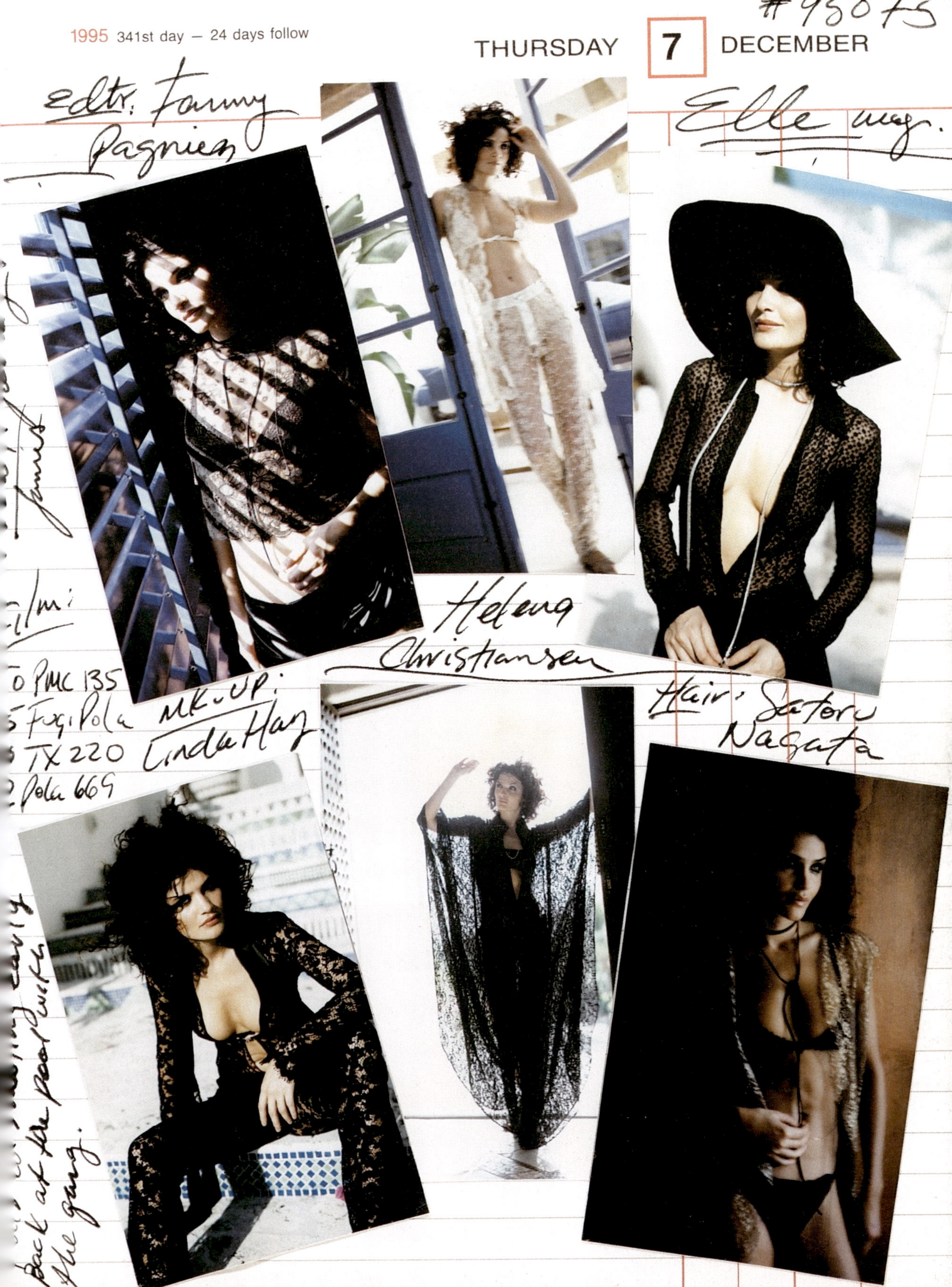

1995 341st day — 24 days follow
THURSDAY 7 DECEMBER
#95075
edtr: Fanny Pagnier
Elle mag.
Helena Christiansen
MK-UP: Linda Hay
Hair: Satoru Nagata
O PMC 135
Fuji Pola
TX 220
Pola 669
back at the pool w/the the gang.

G.Q. - magazine

Edtr: Maria Proroc
Mk. Up: Linda Hay
Hair: Tim Crespin
Prop Stylist

Bradl
Garloc

Sun
Studie

Film:

15 VPS 220
15 Fuji Pola
18 TX 220
8 TX 135
10 pola 665

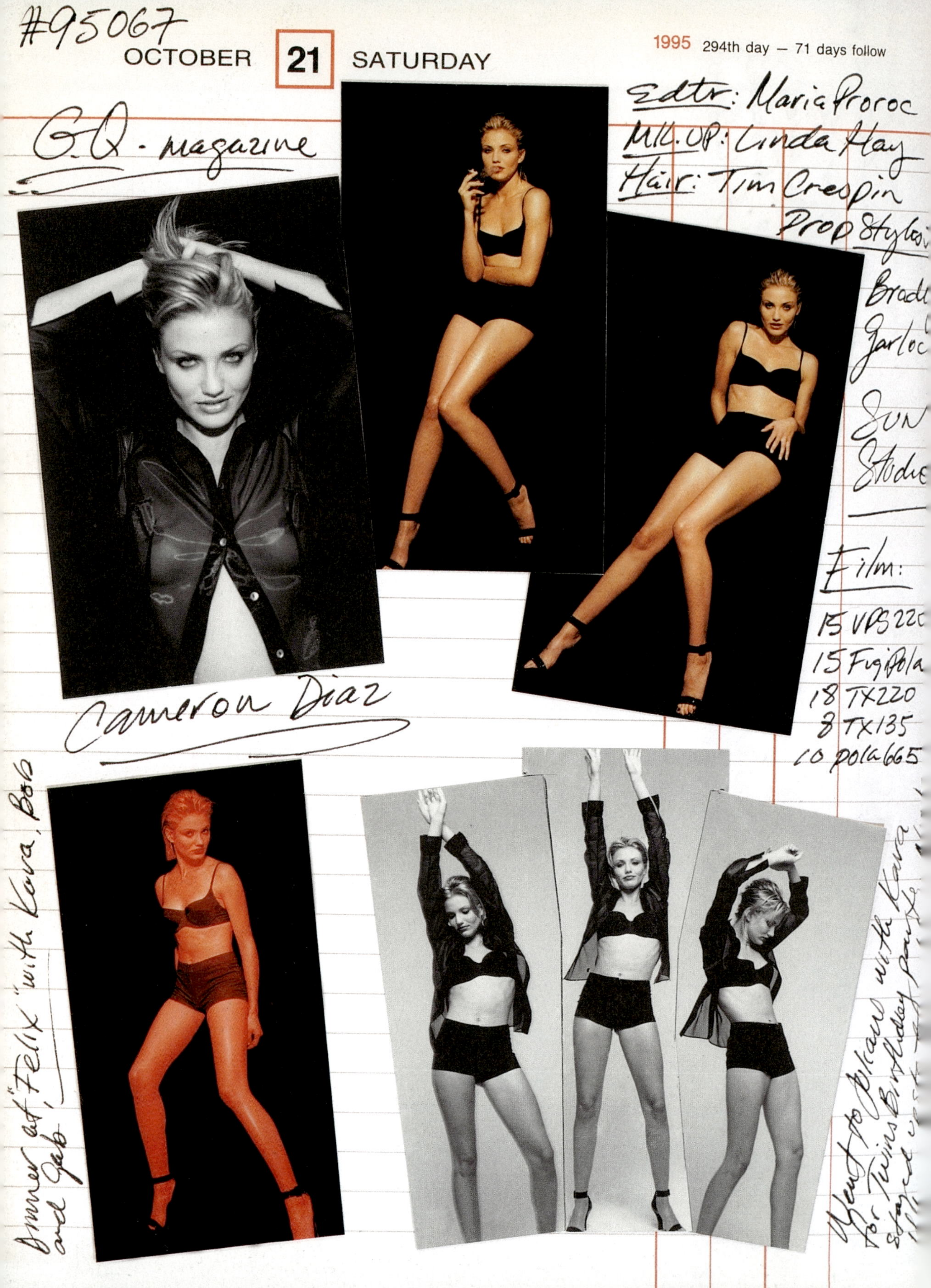

Cameron Diaz

Dinner at "Felix" with Kara, Bob and Seb.

Went to Kara's with Kara after Twin's Birthday Party.

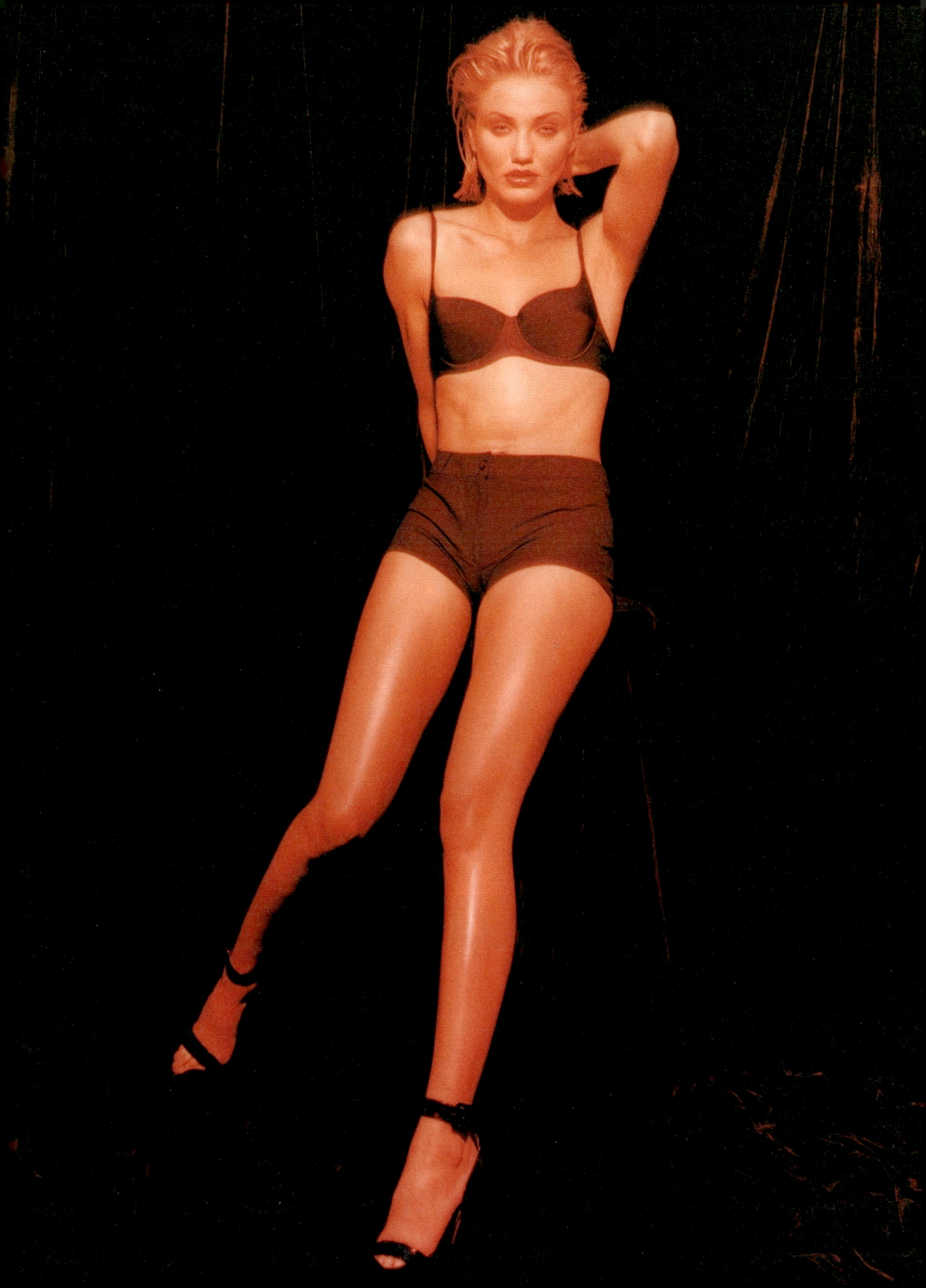

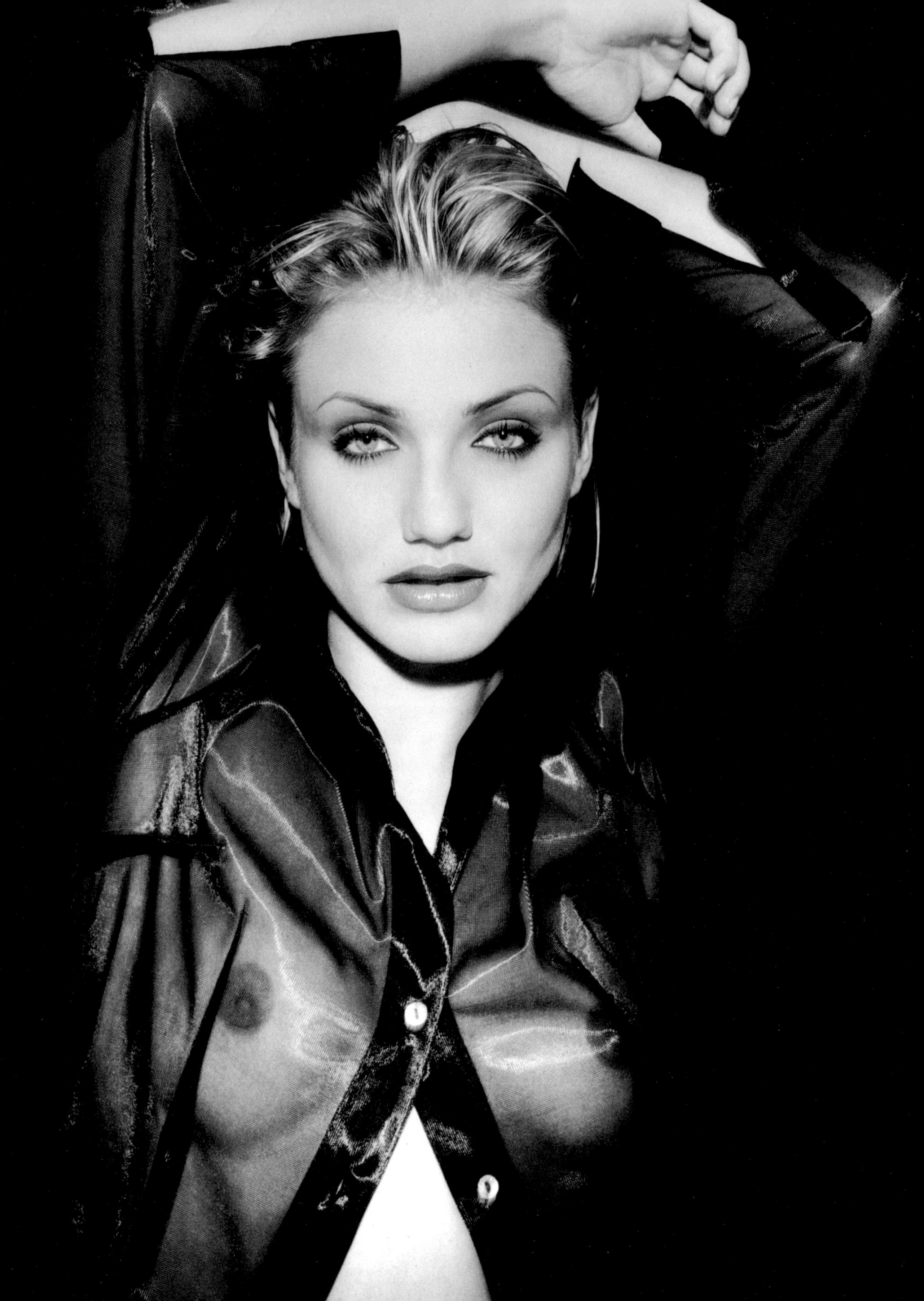

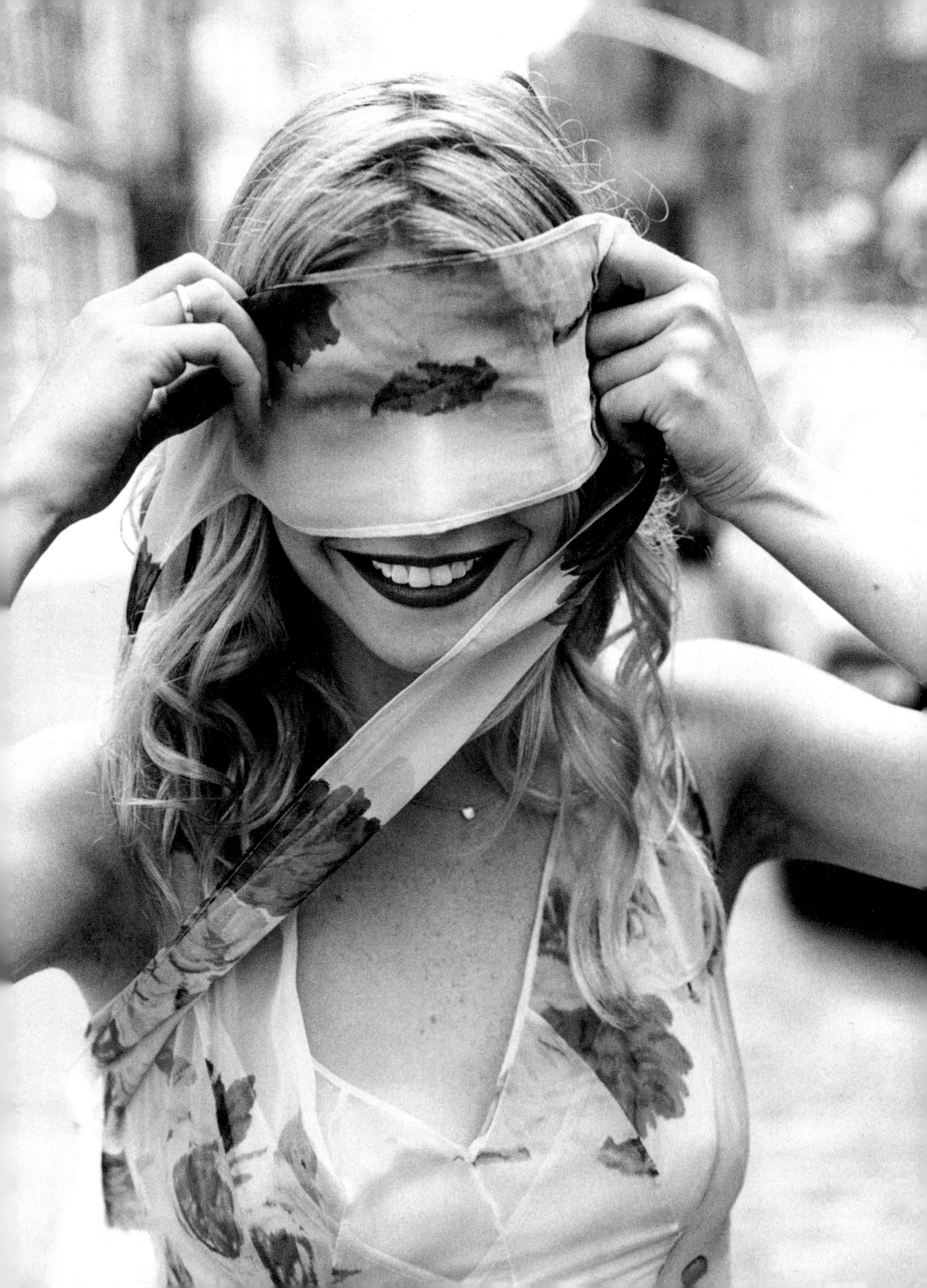

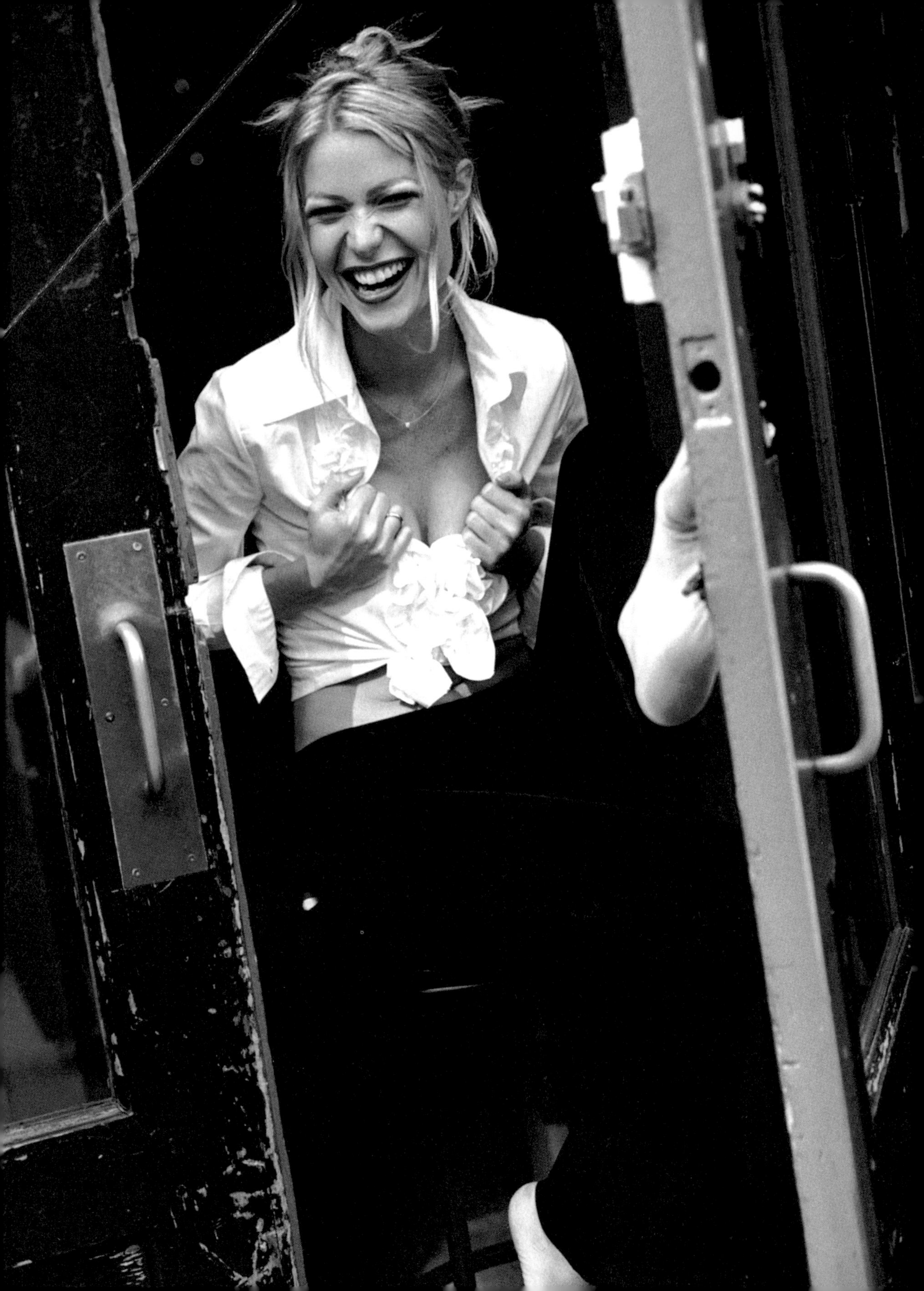

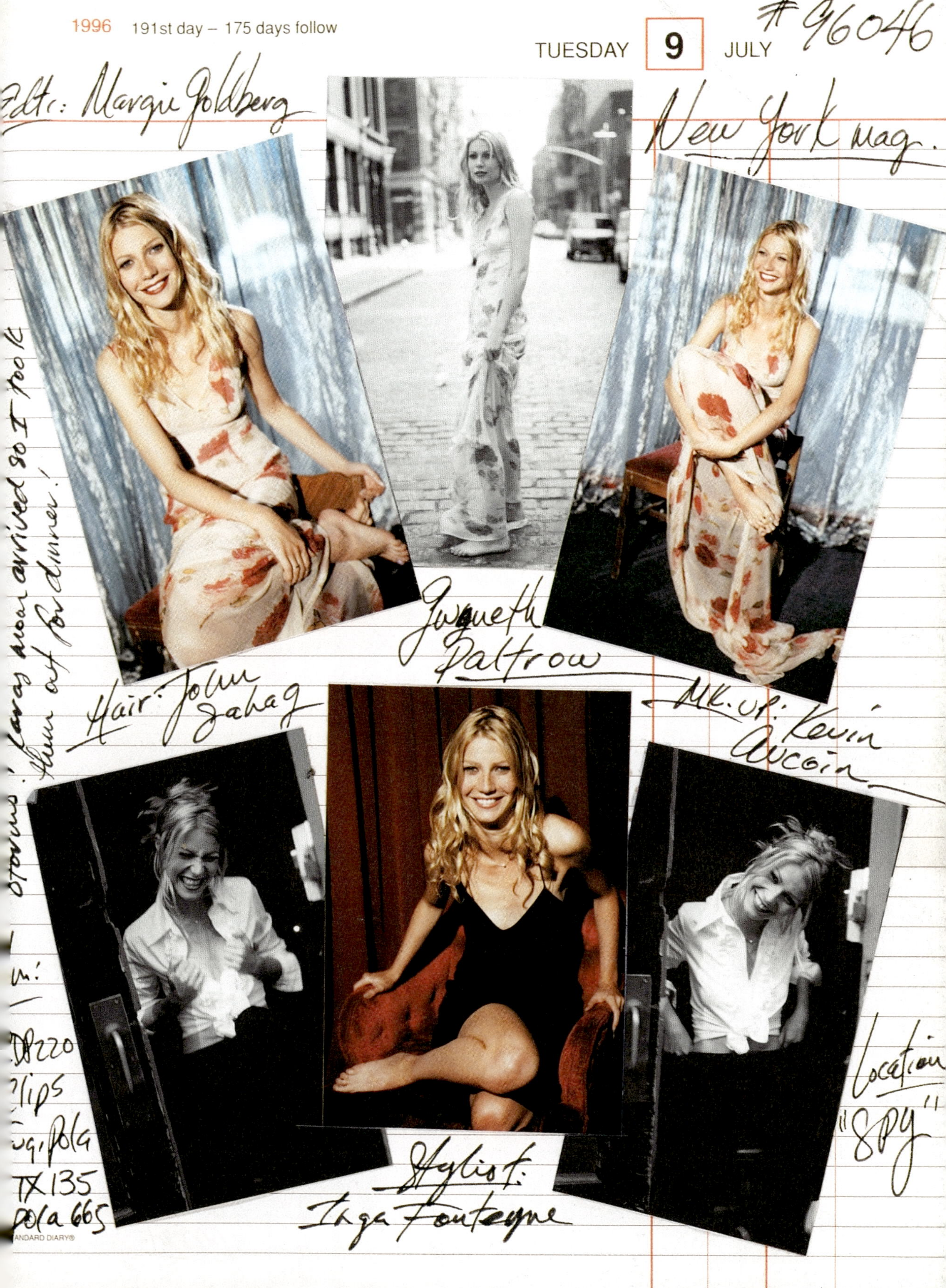

96046
Edtr.: Margie Goldberg
New York mag.
Larry was arrived so I took
them out for dinner!
Gwyneth Paltrow
Hair: John Sahag
Mk. up: Kevin Aucoin
DD220
Flips
Fuji Pola
TX135
Pola 665
Stylist: Inga Fonteyne
Location "SPY"
STANDARD DIARY®

95054

Cosmopolitan

Lucy Sisman —

Location: Sam Green
Oakleyville
Fire Islan

Eva Herzigova

Hair: John Sahag
Mk.Up: Linda Hay

Stylist: Andrew Richardson

Film: 42 RDP135
16 RDP220
45 Chrms
26 TX135
5...

Garbo's old beach house!

Got home around 9:30 —
Jayc went to Bower...
Next morning to Bow...

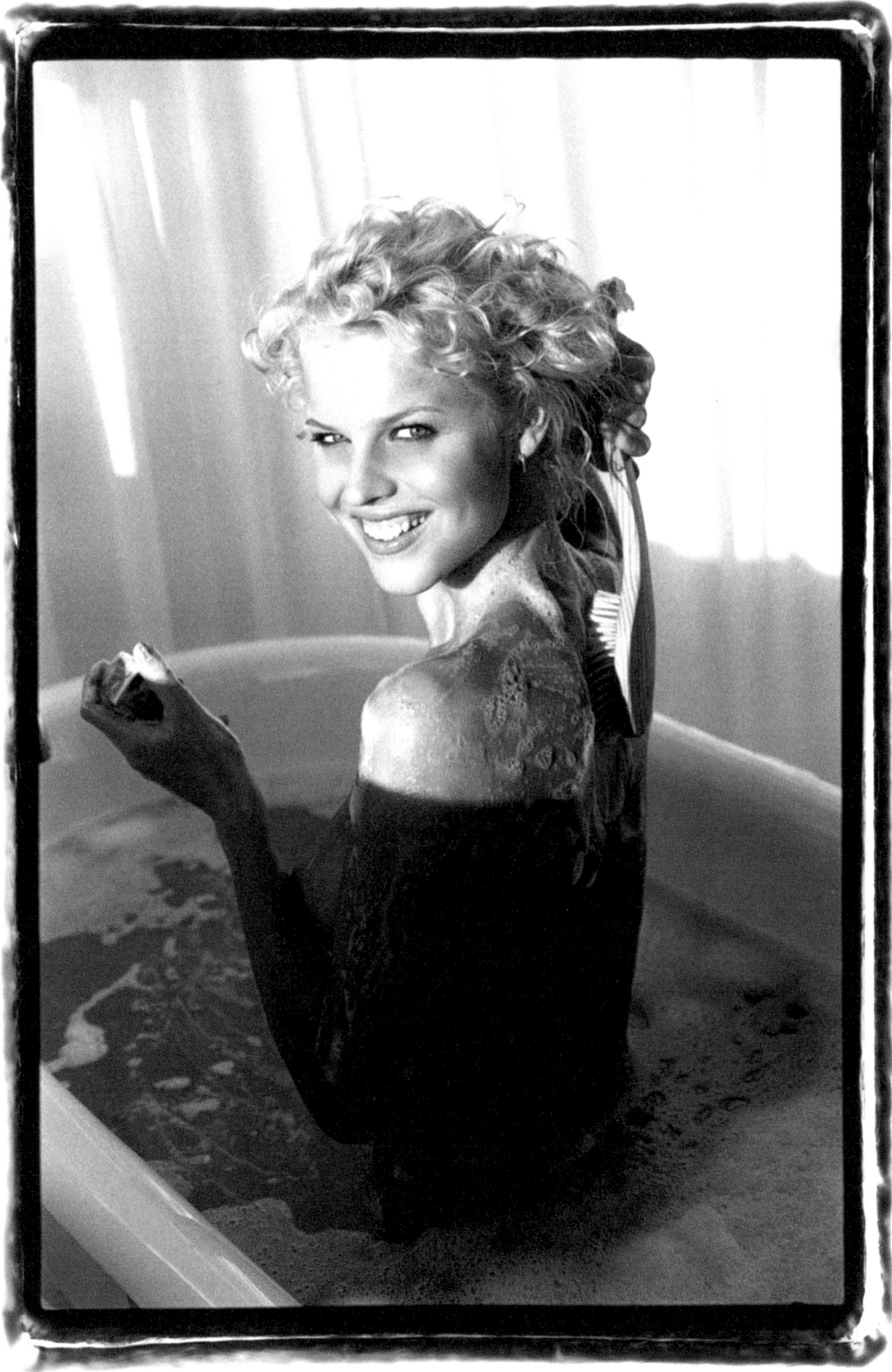

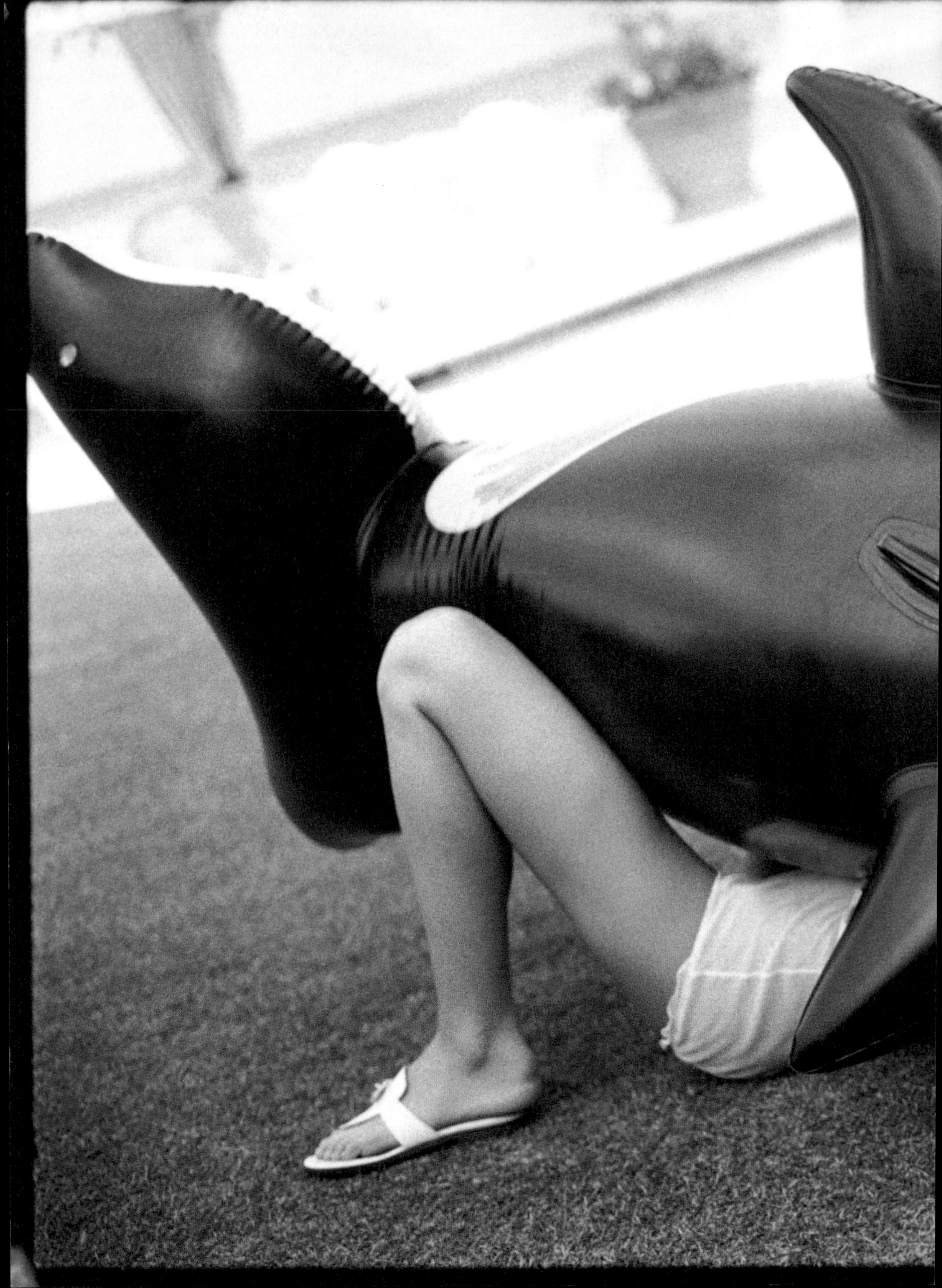

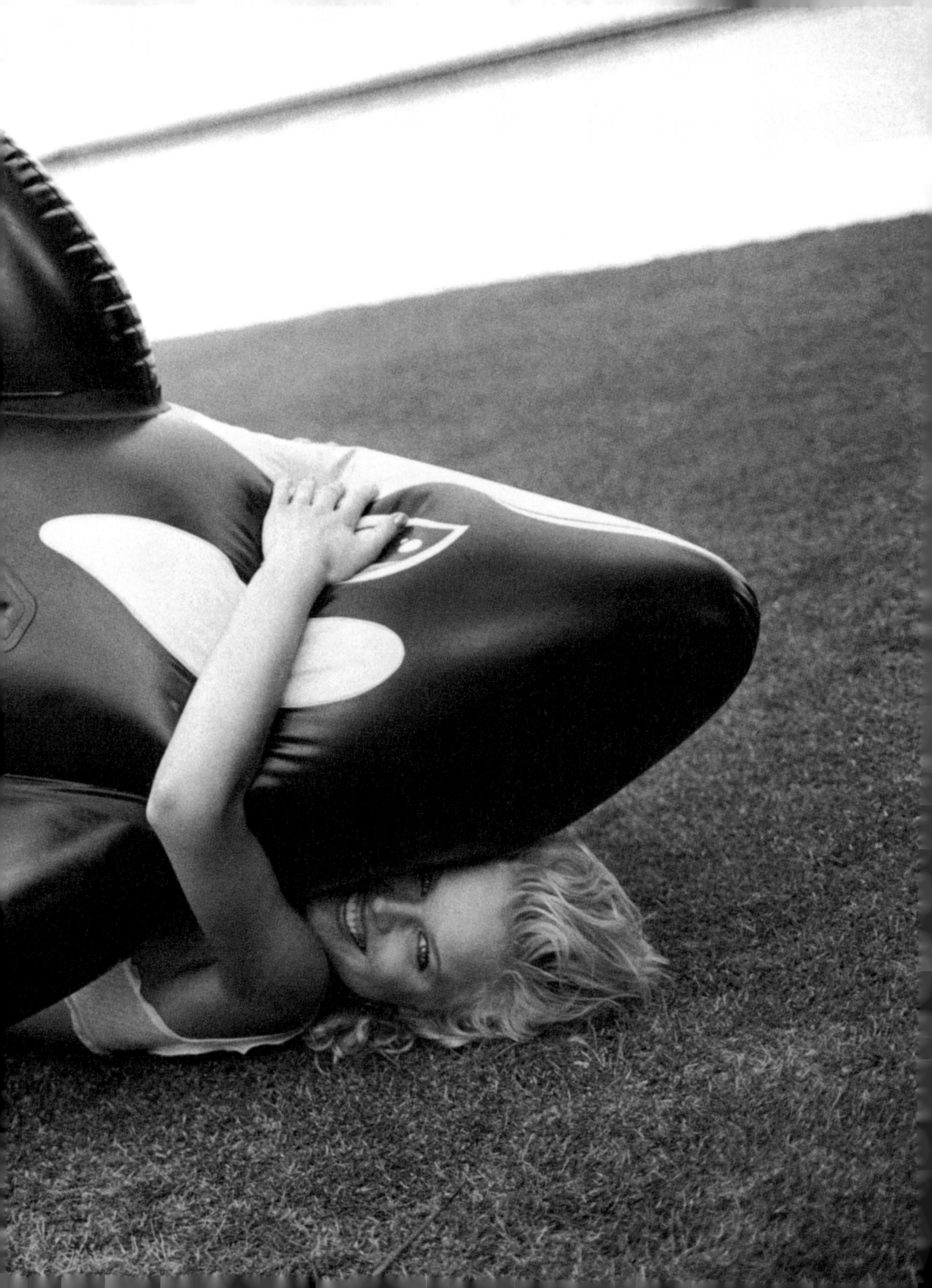

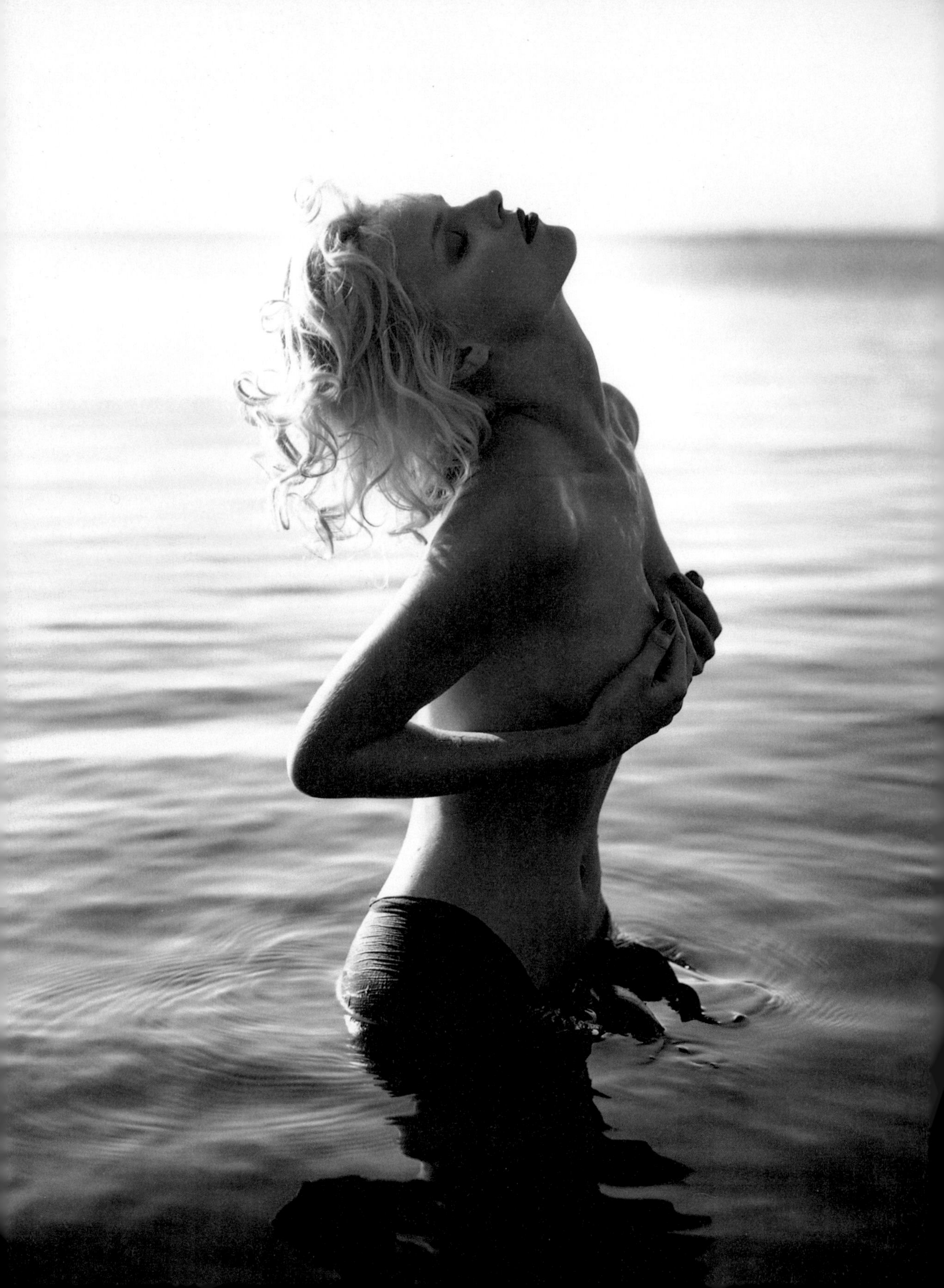

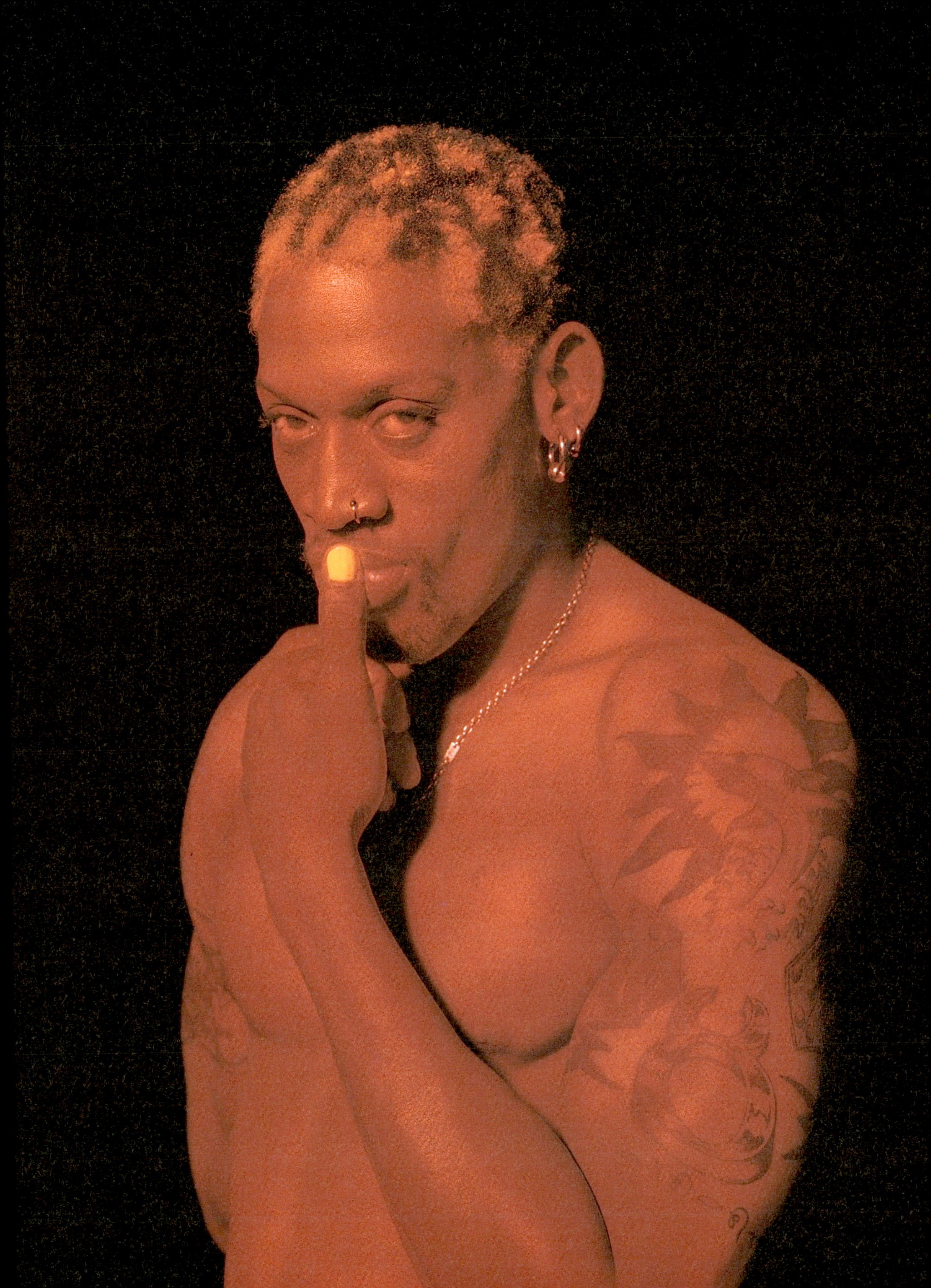

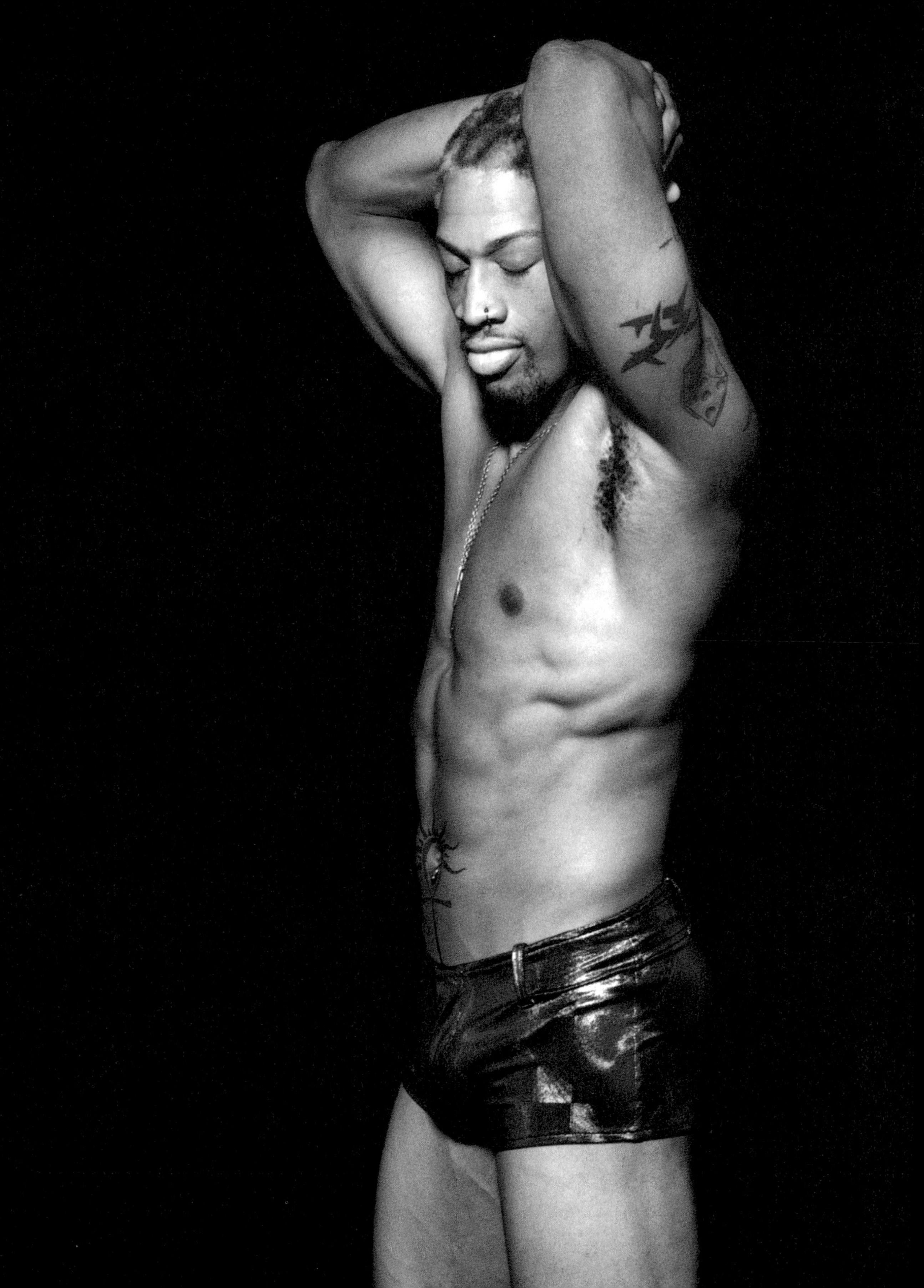

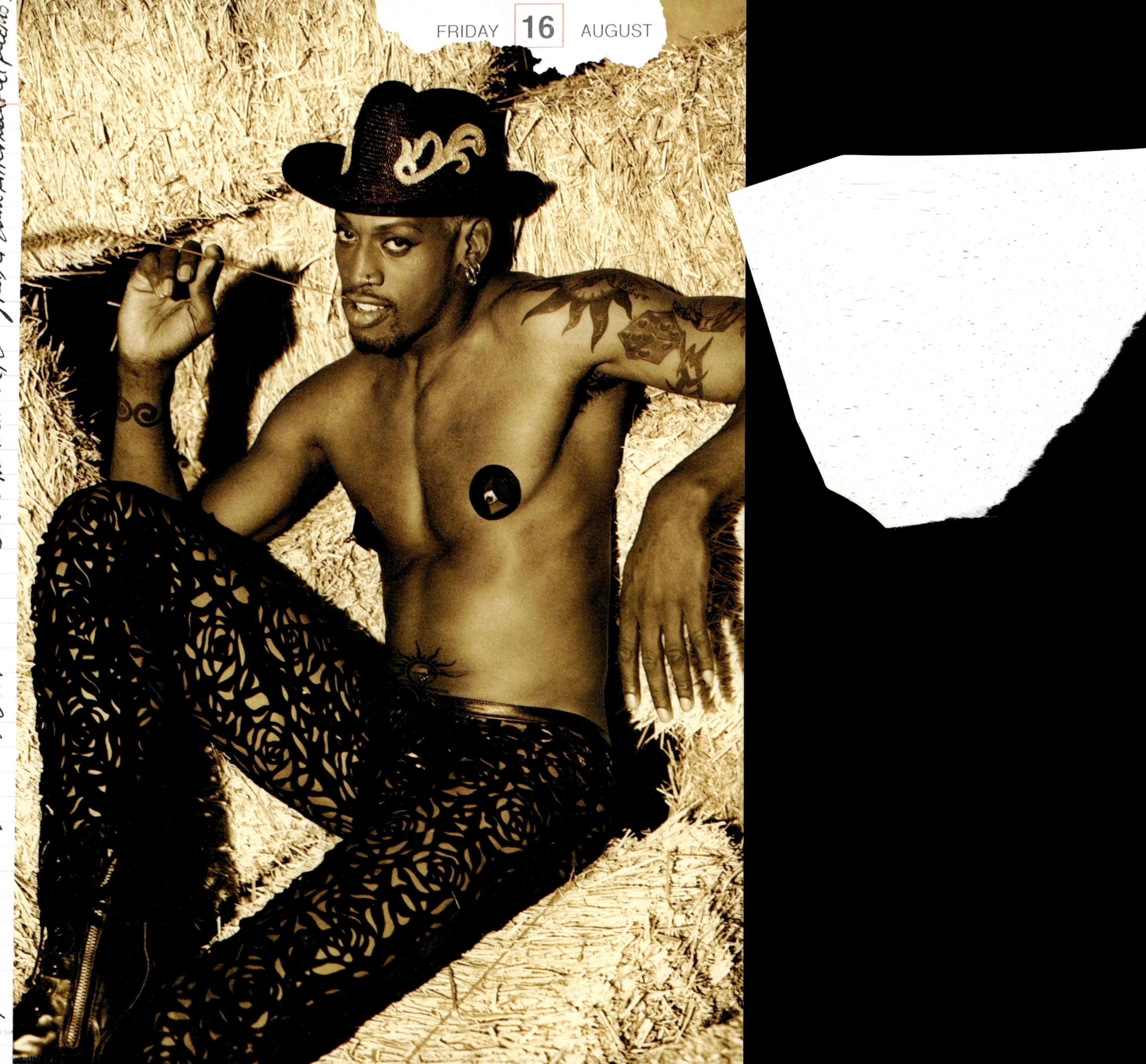

FRIDAY 16 AUGUST
left for L.I. I had Dinner at Da Silvano with Bonnie Timmerman, Honey Kosfes Ann Patterson

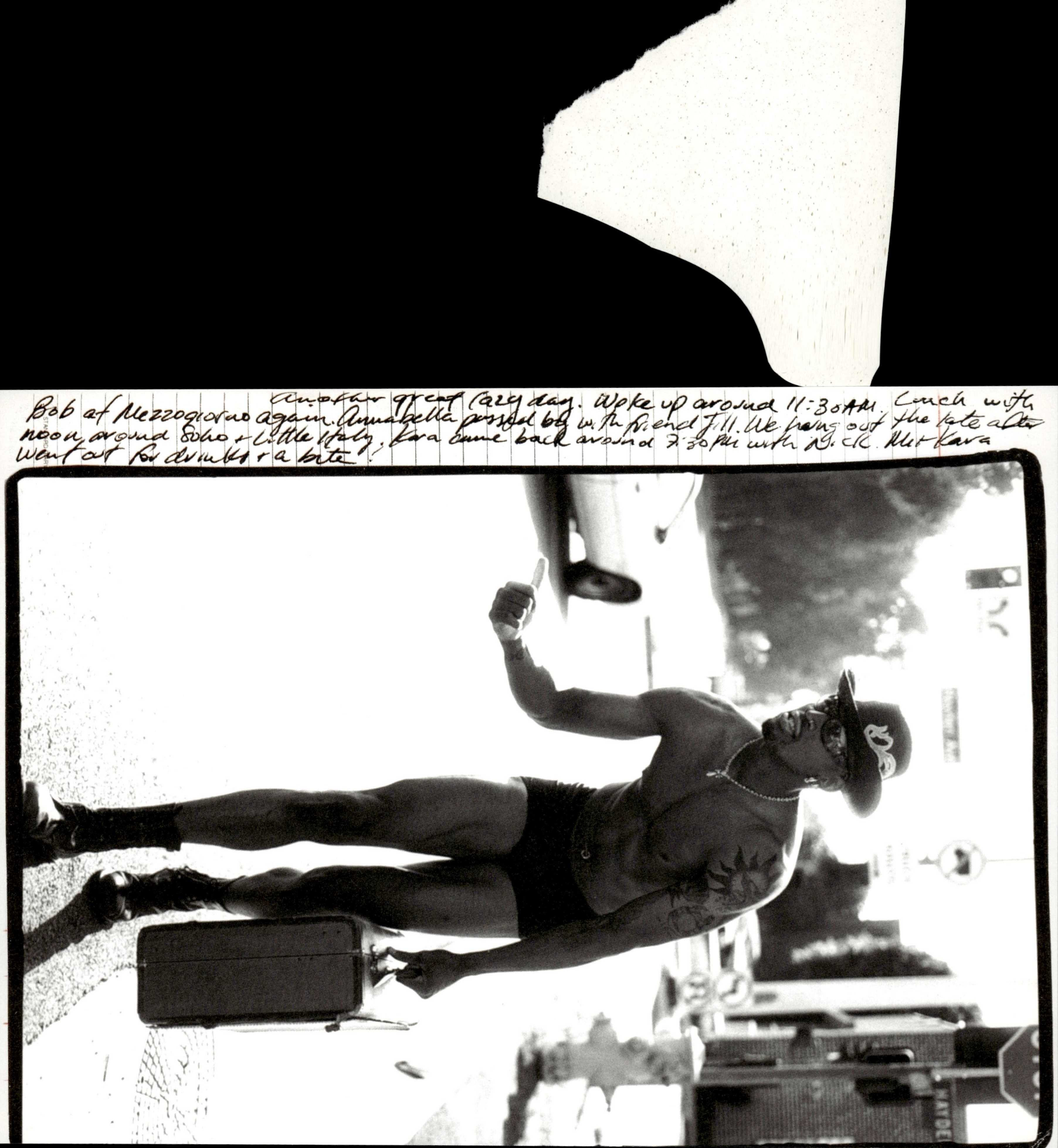

Another great lazy day. Woke up around 11:30AM. Lunch with Bob at Mezzogiorno again. Annabella passed by with friend Jill. We hung out the late afternoon around Soho + Little Italy, Kara came back around 7:30PM with Nick. Me + Kara went out for drinks + a bite!

THURSDAY 21 DECEMBER

[...] wouldn't put his audience through the torture of 3 hrs of film because it was brilliant film making! 10:30AM appt. With Dr. Renda. Went to the office, packed up my tickets + money for St. Barths! Took a bath with Nick, then went to visit Tommy at home. 9PM dinner with Kara, Vivi, Bonnie Timmermann + friend at Lemon on Parkaise South. Bonnie is interested in looking at my script! Packed our bags!

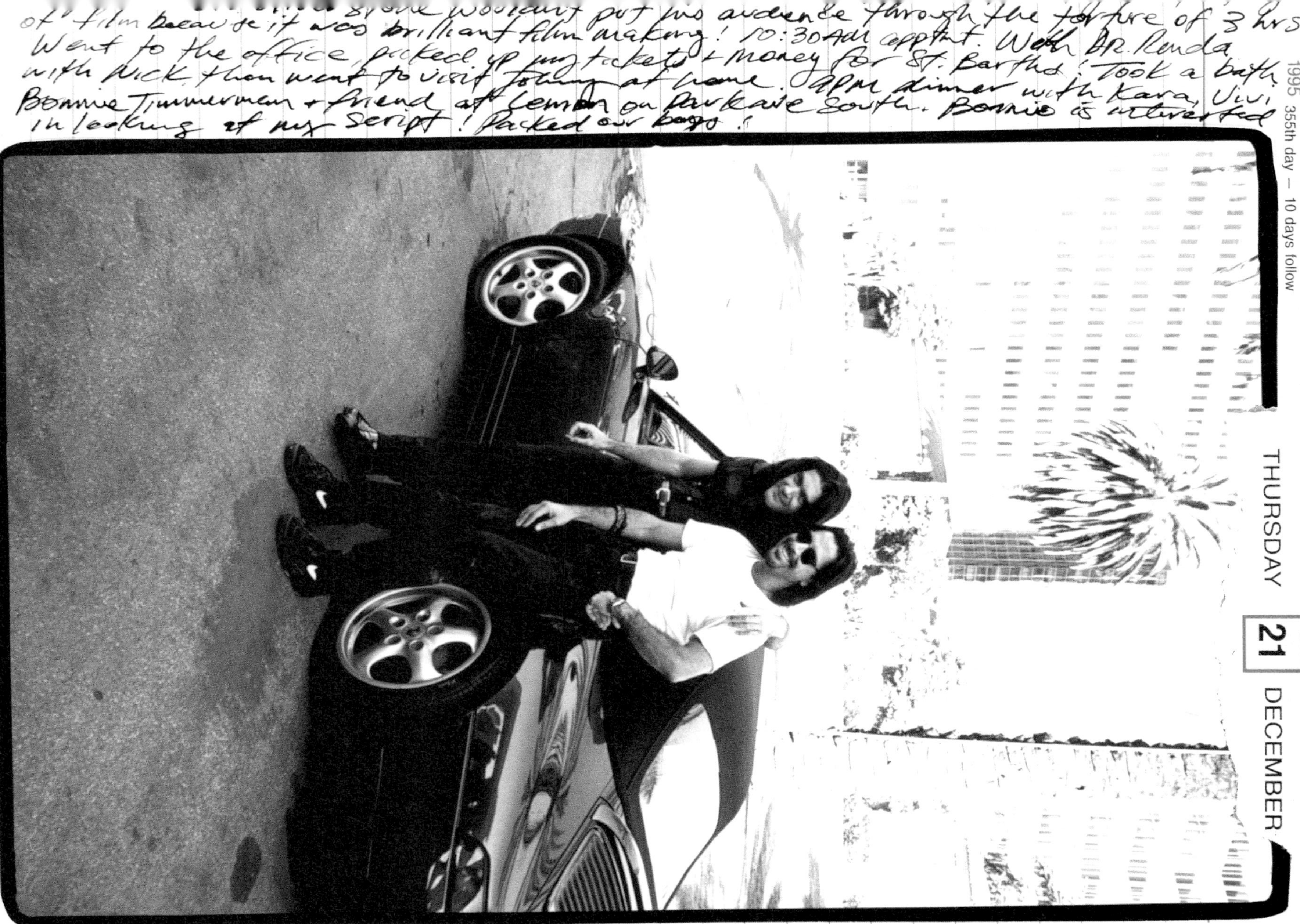

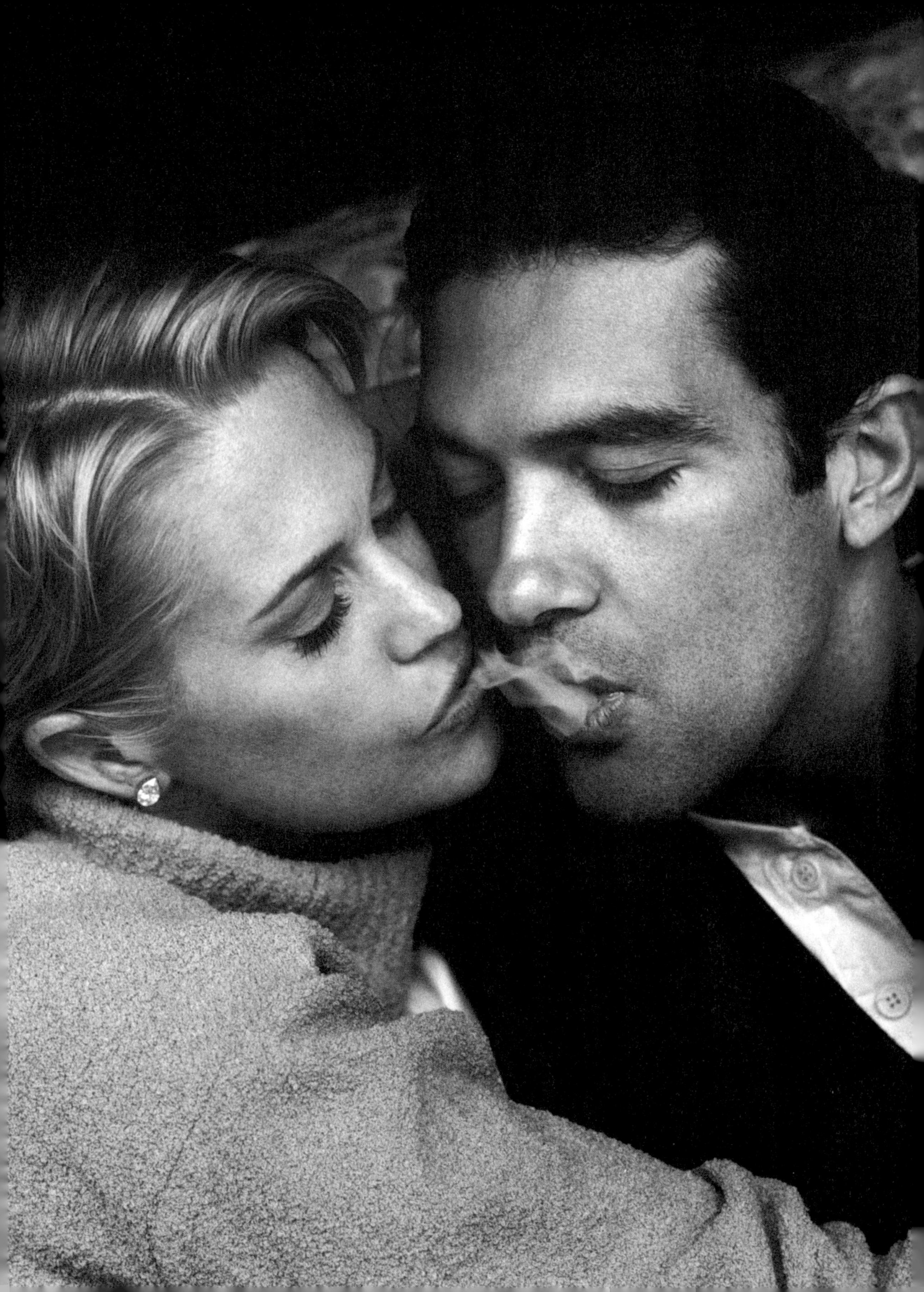

... yes + Kathy ... they're tits cancelled for home. Spent the day in the house. Kara went to Edie's to finish her X-mas video, she took Nick. Gab stayed here + cleaned up. Did more editing

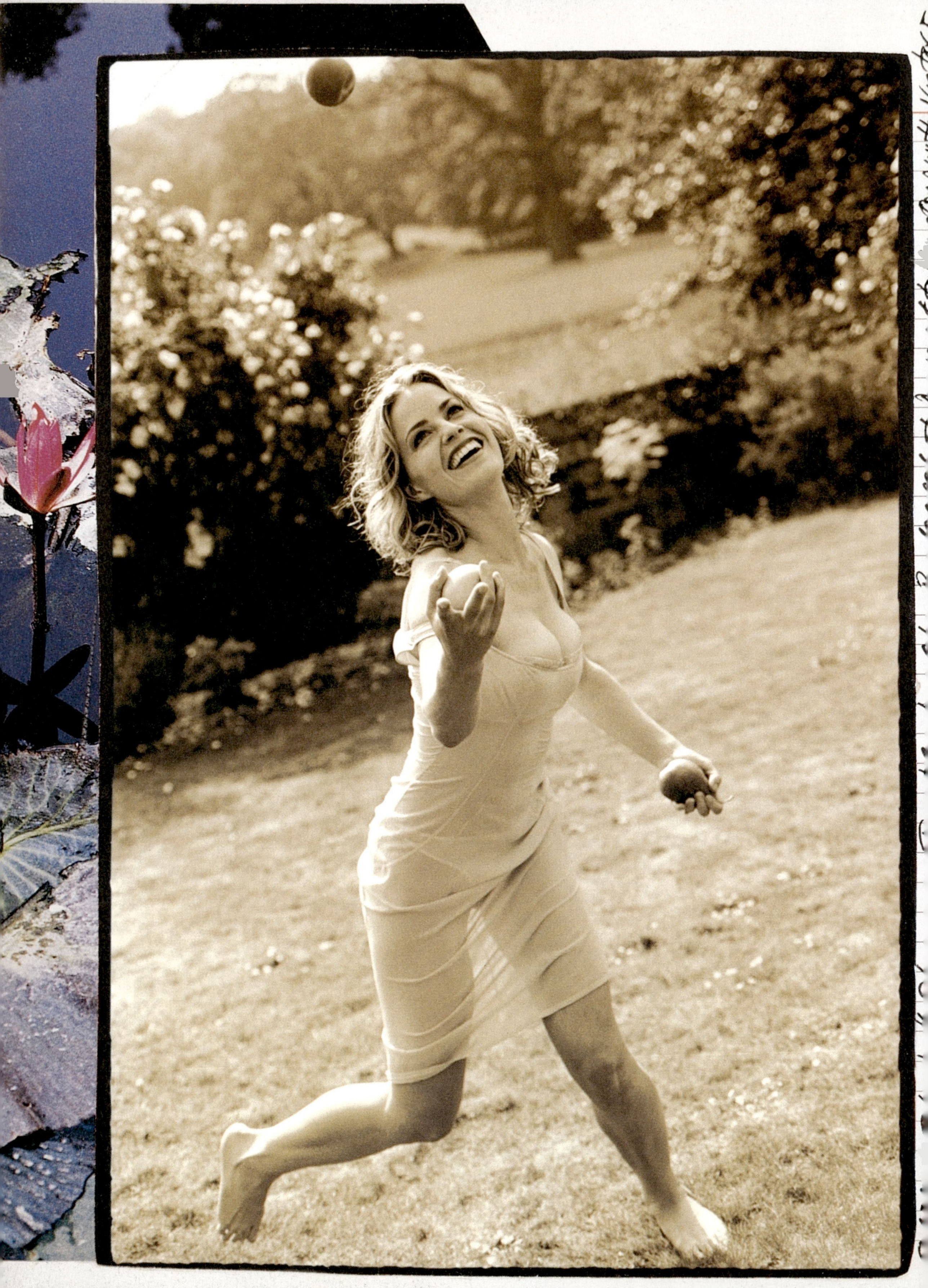

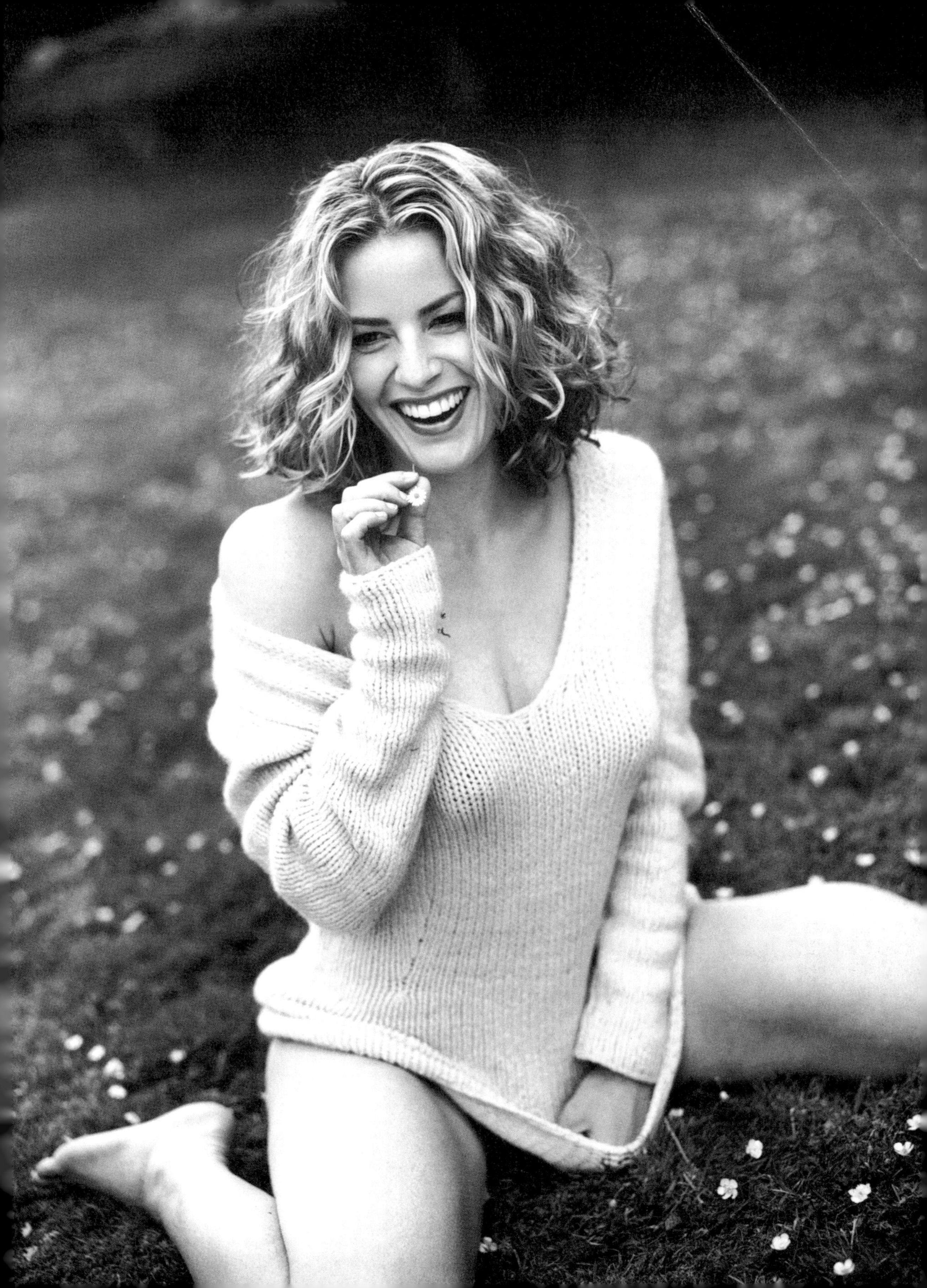

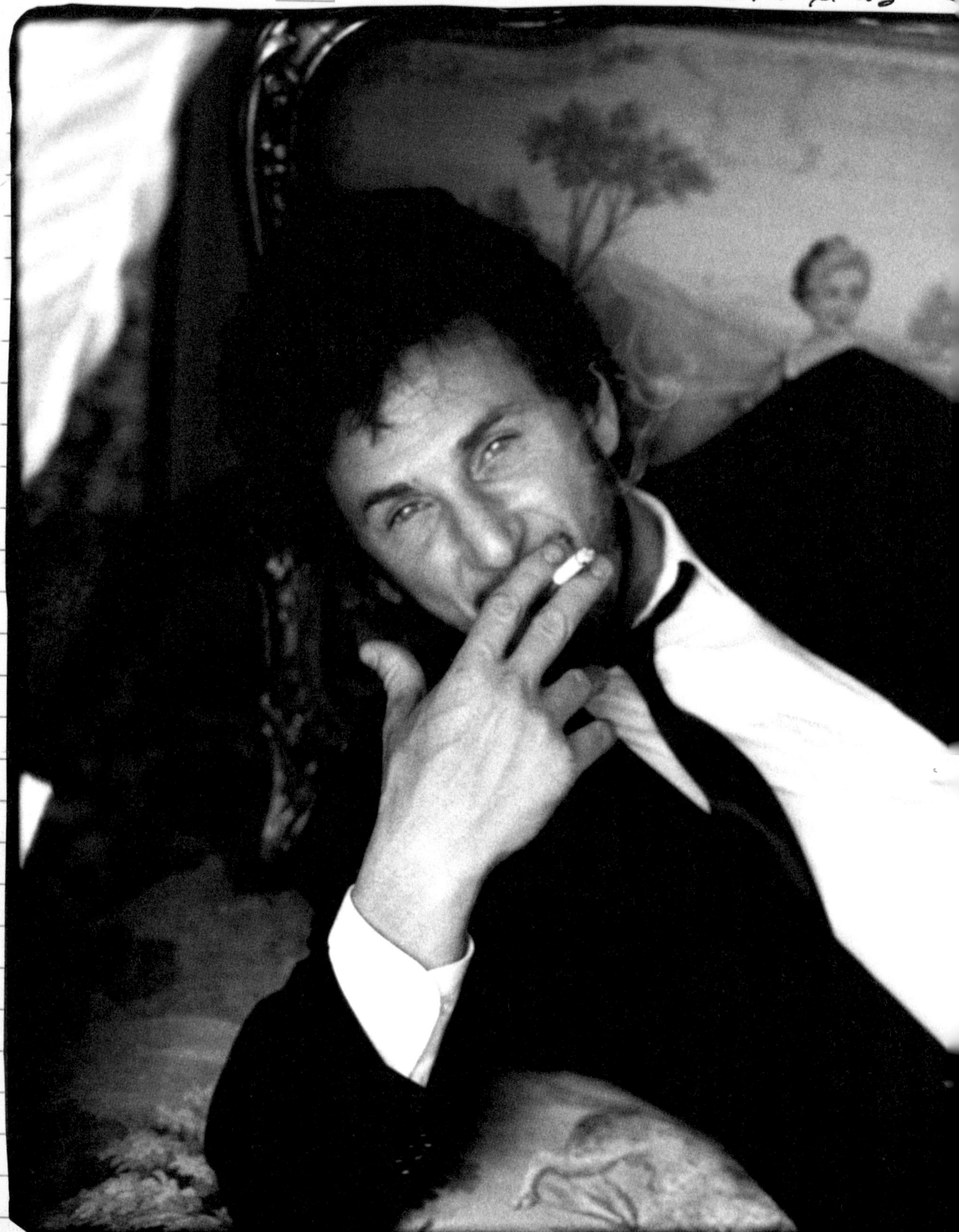

#98016A
MARCH 27 FRIDAY "Sean, Residence Maxims —
1998   86th day – 279 days follow"

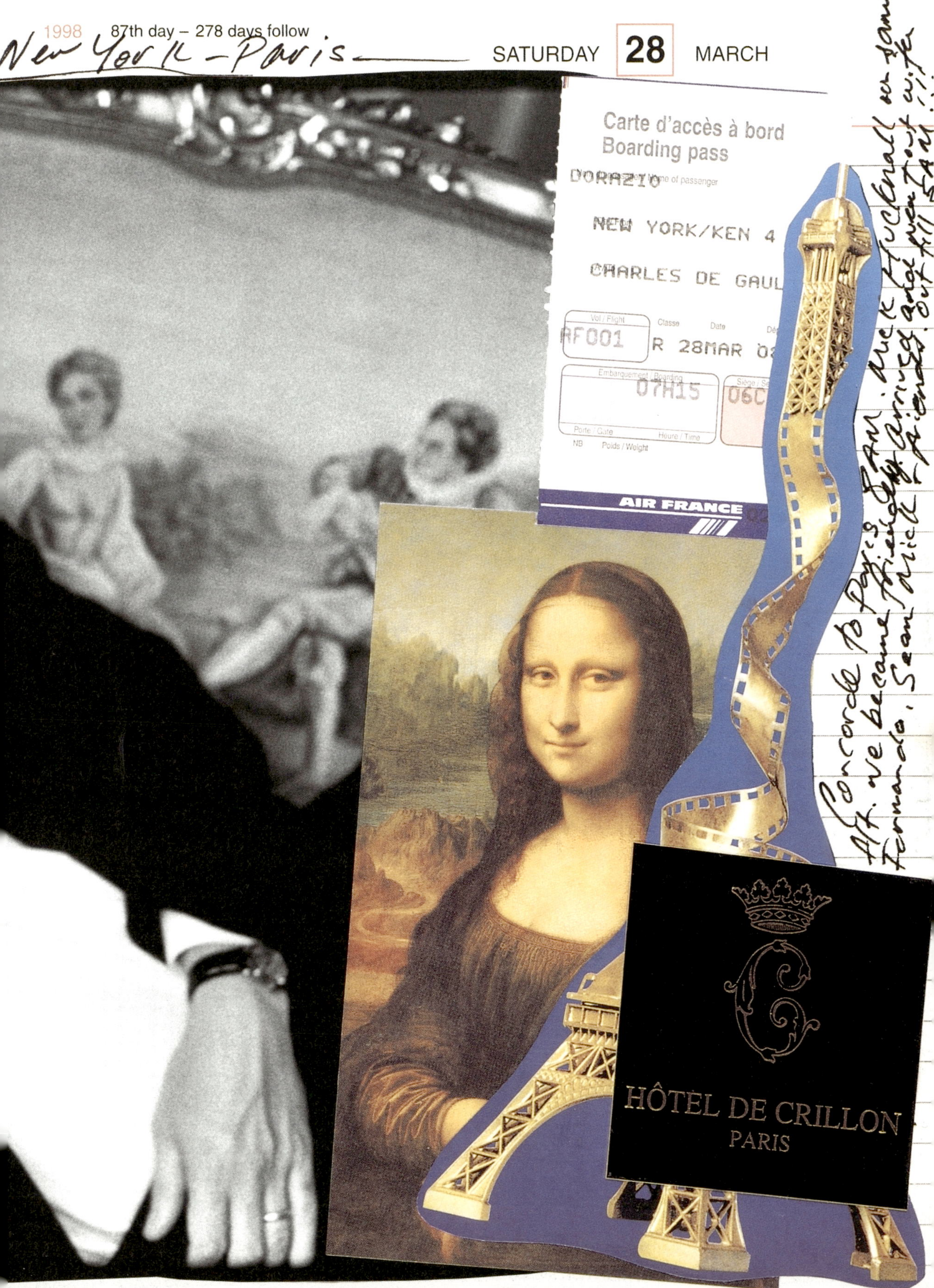
1998
87th day – 278 days follow
New York – Paris
SATURDAY 28 MARCH
Carte d'accès à bord
Boarding pass
Nom du passager / Name of passenger
D'ORAZIO
NEW YORK/KEN 4
CHARLES DE GAUL
Vol / Flight
RF001   R 28MAR 0
Classe   Date   Dé
Embarquement / Boarding
07H15
Siège / S
06C
Porte / Gate   Heure / Time
NB   Poids / Weight
AIR FRANCE
HÔTEL DE CRILLON
PARIS

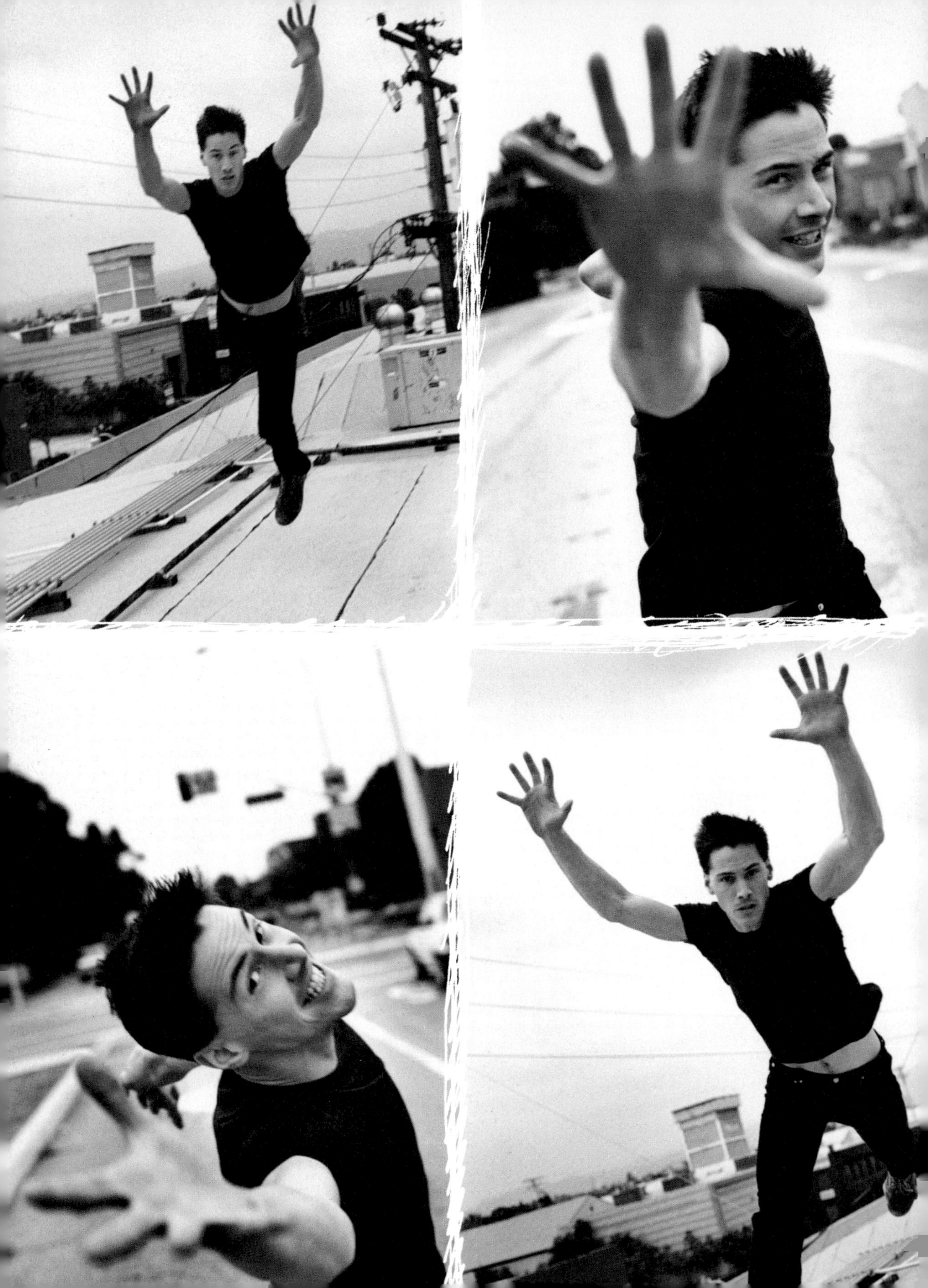

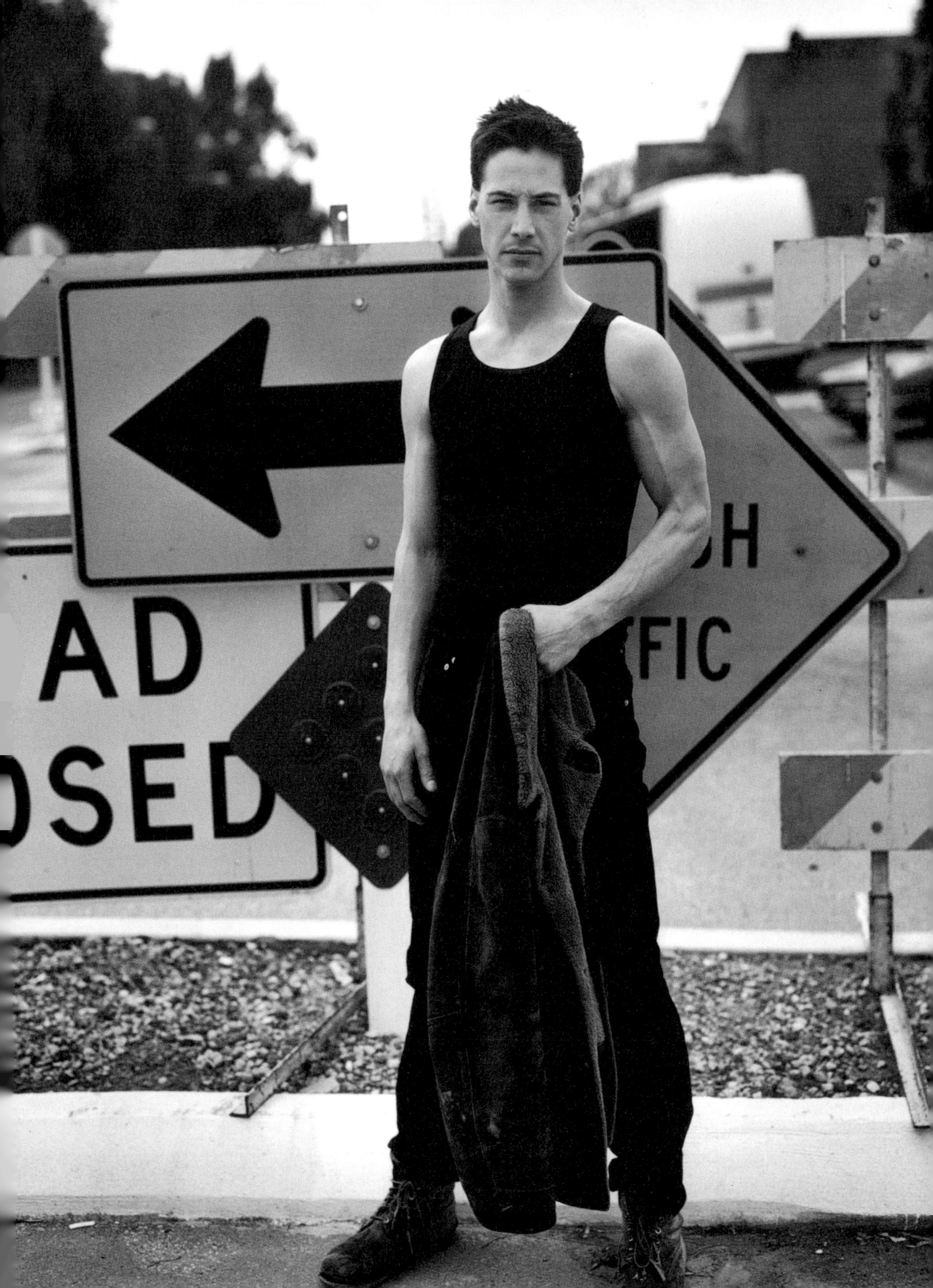

AD
OSED
DH
FIC

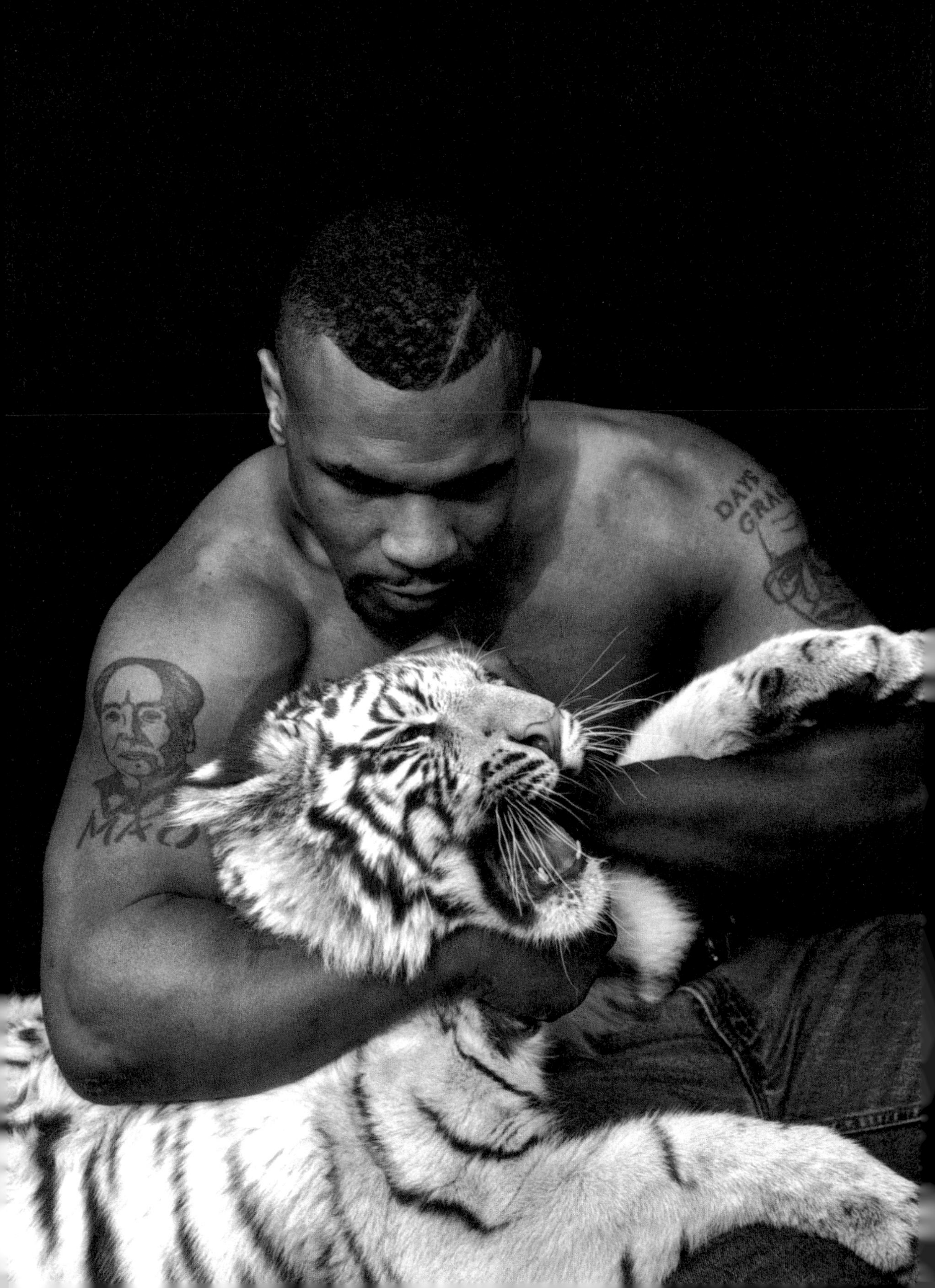

Edited contacts + prints of Mike Tyson in L.A. Did some shopping alone with Kara! Yesterdays shoot ended up happening as an act of God. We parked in front of Mikes House waiting for a call to tell us it's a go. Instead they told us he's not into it. I saw Tysons assistant leave earlier so I waited for him to come back + as he pulled up Russell Simmons called me on my portable I passed the assist the phone + Russell got Mikes phone # + called him! 10 minutes later the gates opened and his security guy waved us in! I did the whole shoot in 20 minutes!

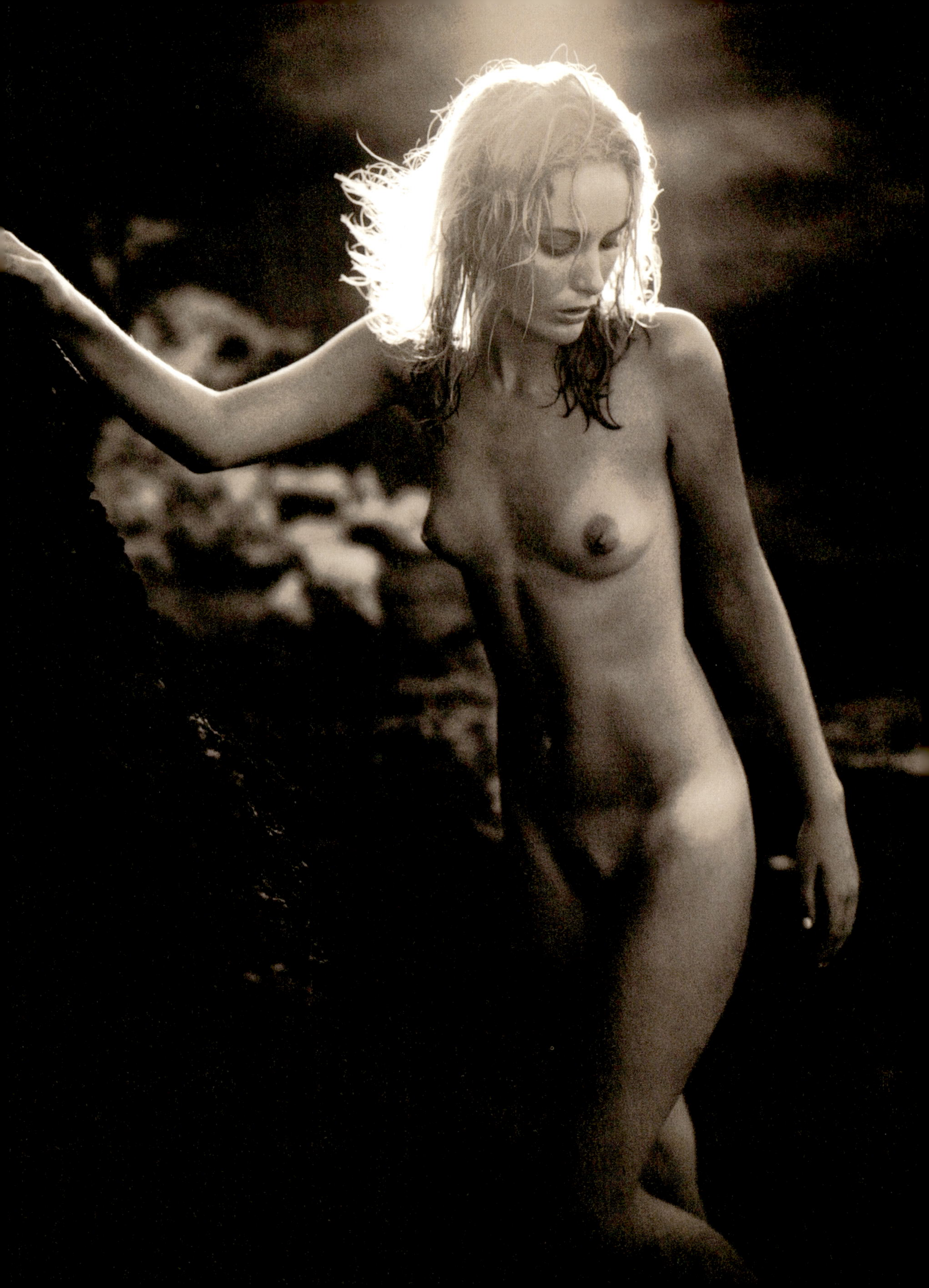

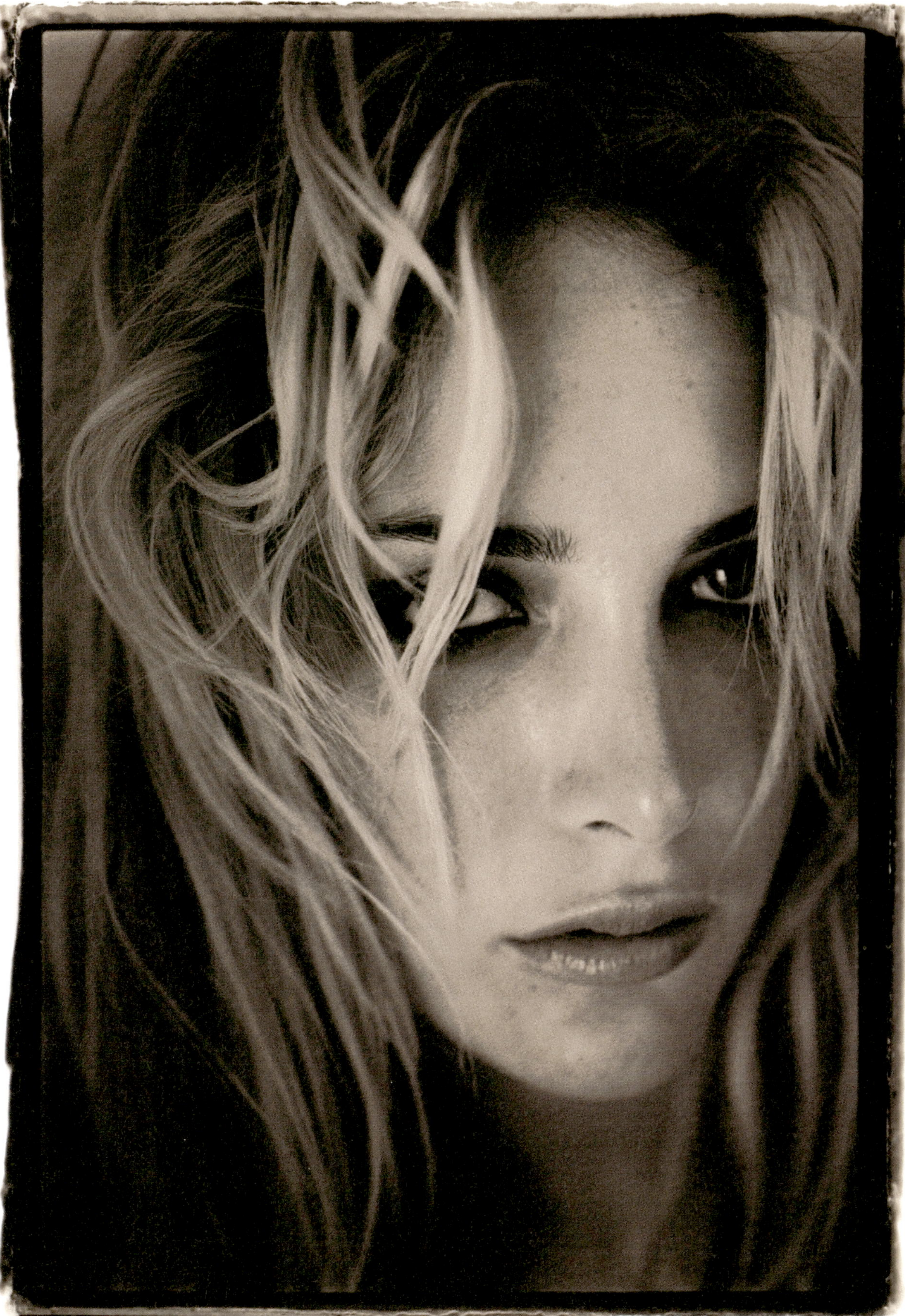

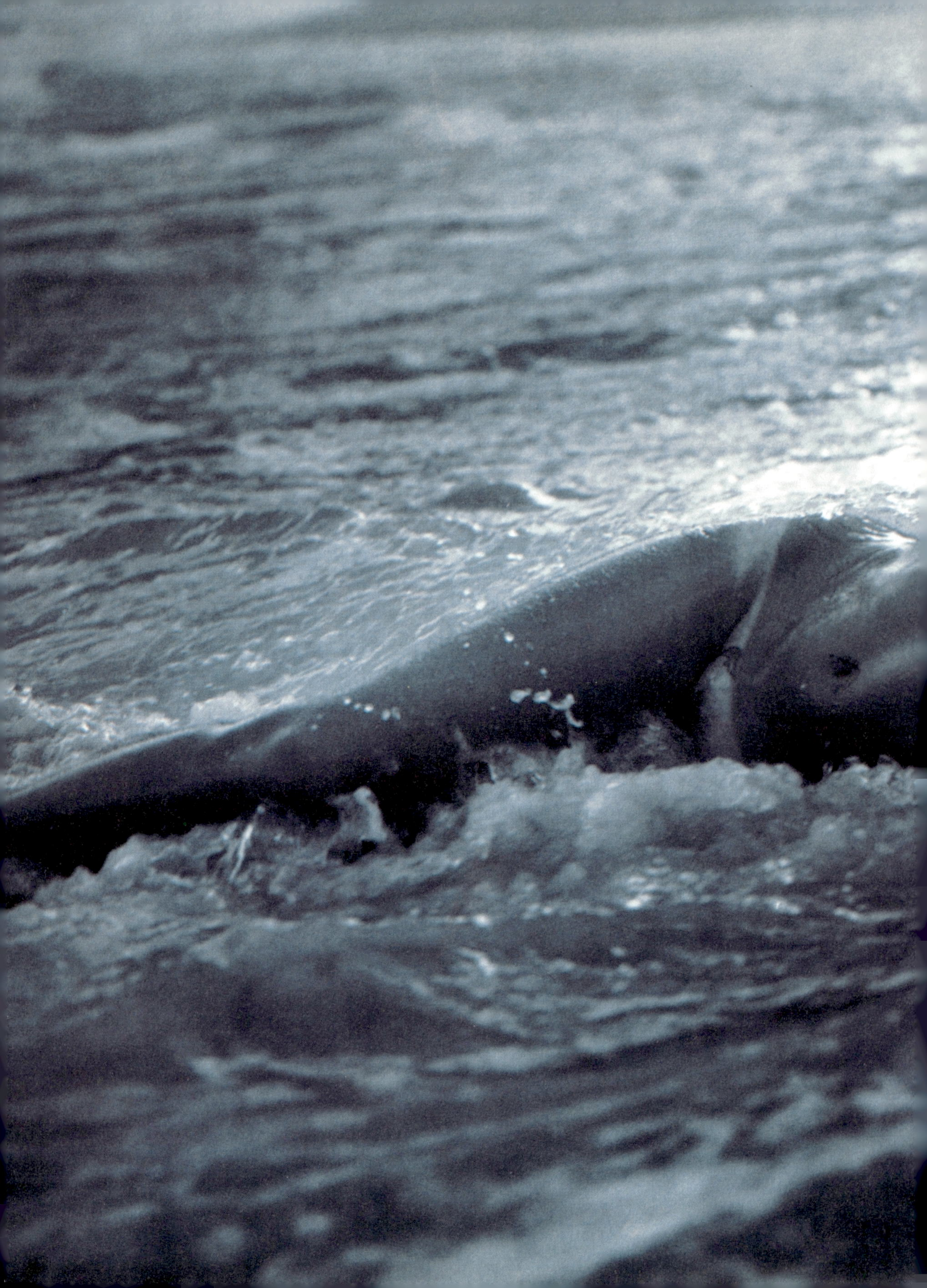

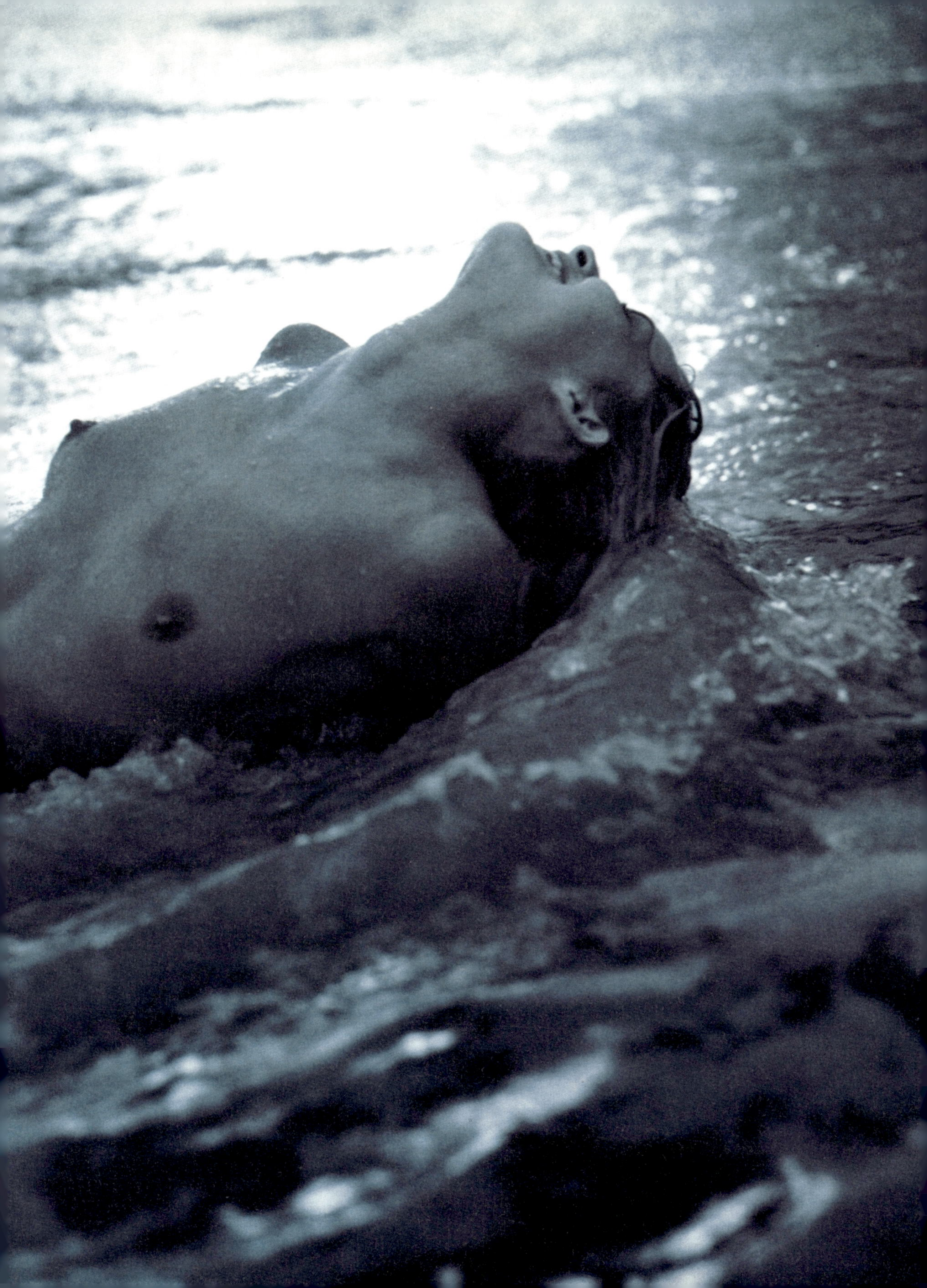

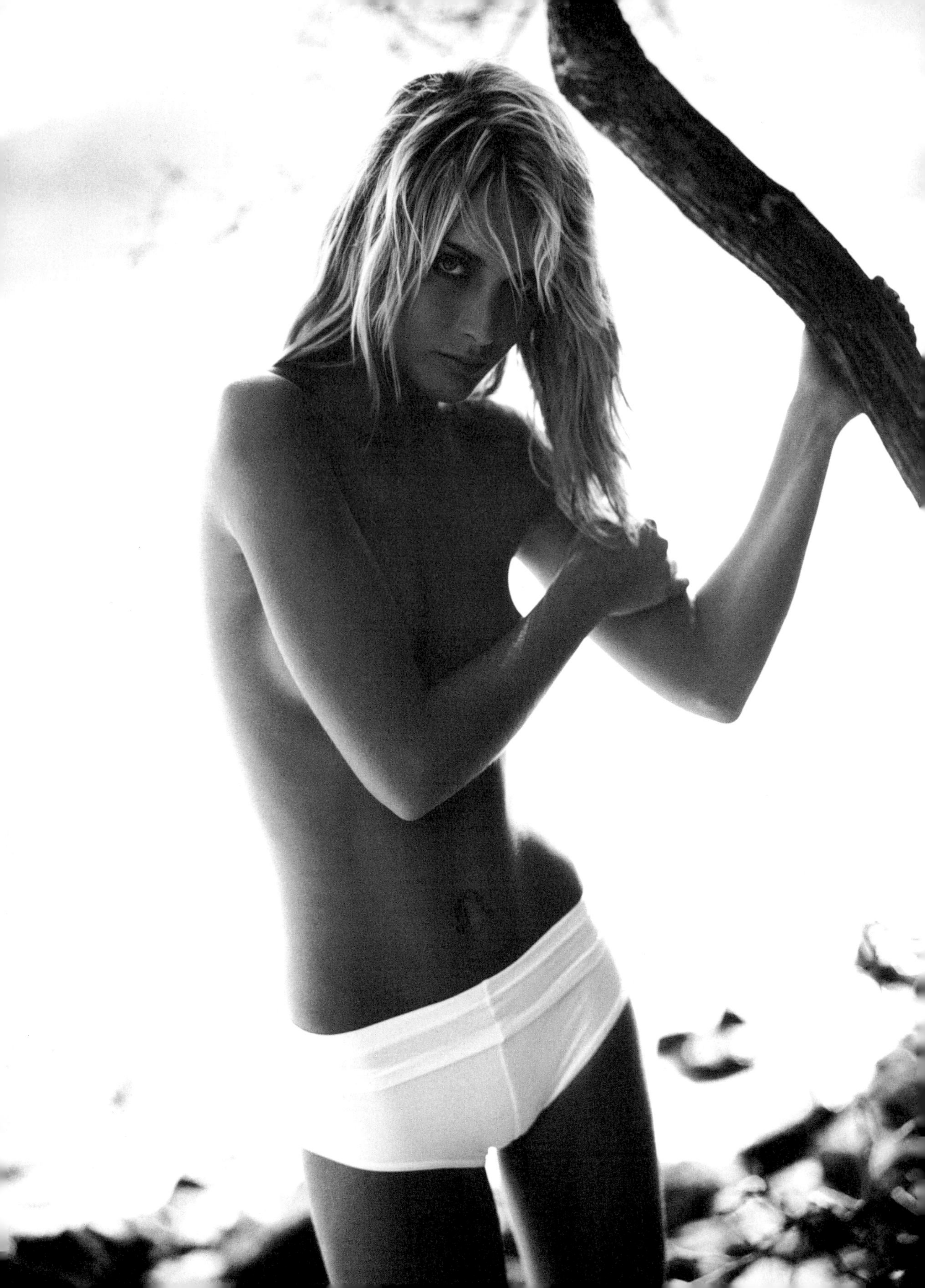

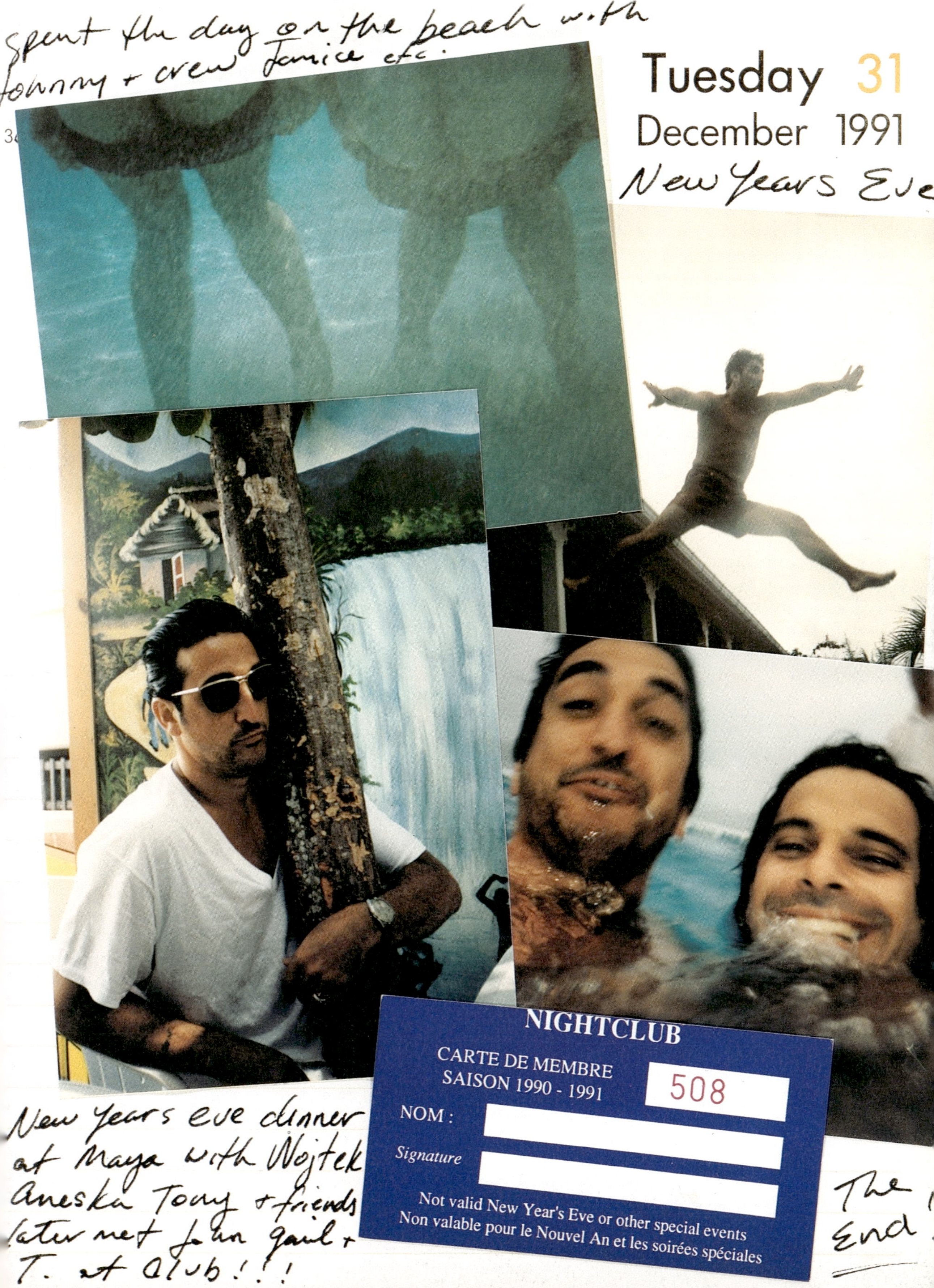
spent the day on the beach with
Johnny + crew Janice etc.
34
Tuesday 31
December 1991
New Years Eve
NIGHTCLUB
CARTE DE MEMBRE
SAISON 1990 - 1991
508
NOM :
Signature
Not valid New Year's Eve or other special events
Non valable pour le Nouvel An et les soirées spéciales
New Years eve dinner
at Maya with Wojtek
Aneska Tony + friends
later met John Gail +
T. at Club!!!
The
End

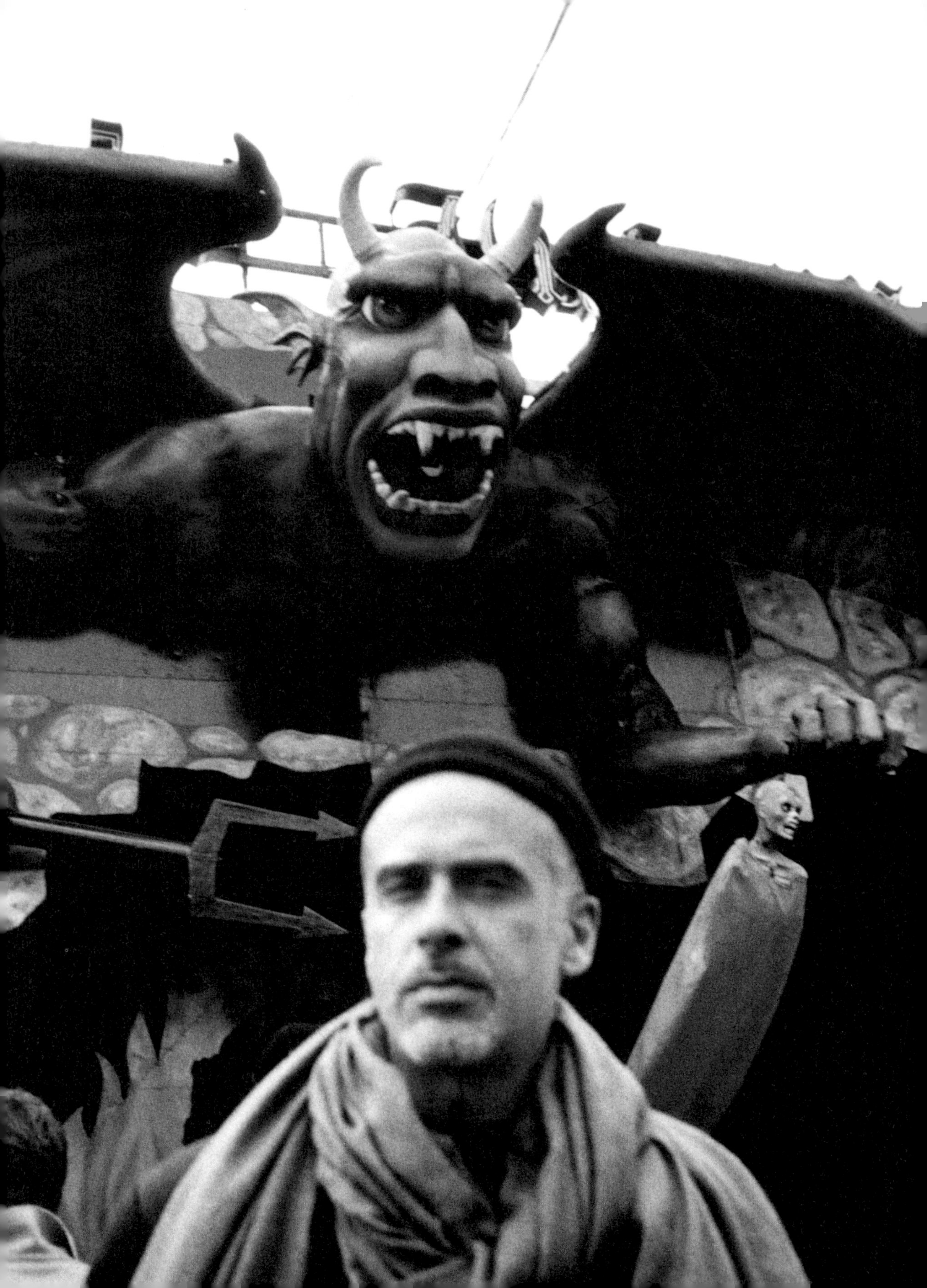

293/72

...spent part of the day in hell! The rest of the day sobering up with some lasagna. Then hung out with Michael Wilcott + Anh the whole evening

Uccia dropped by

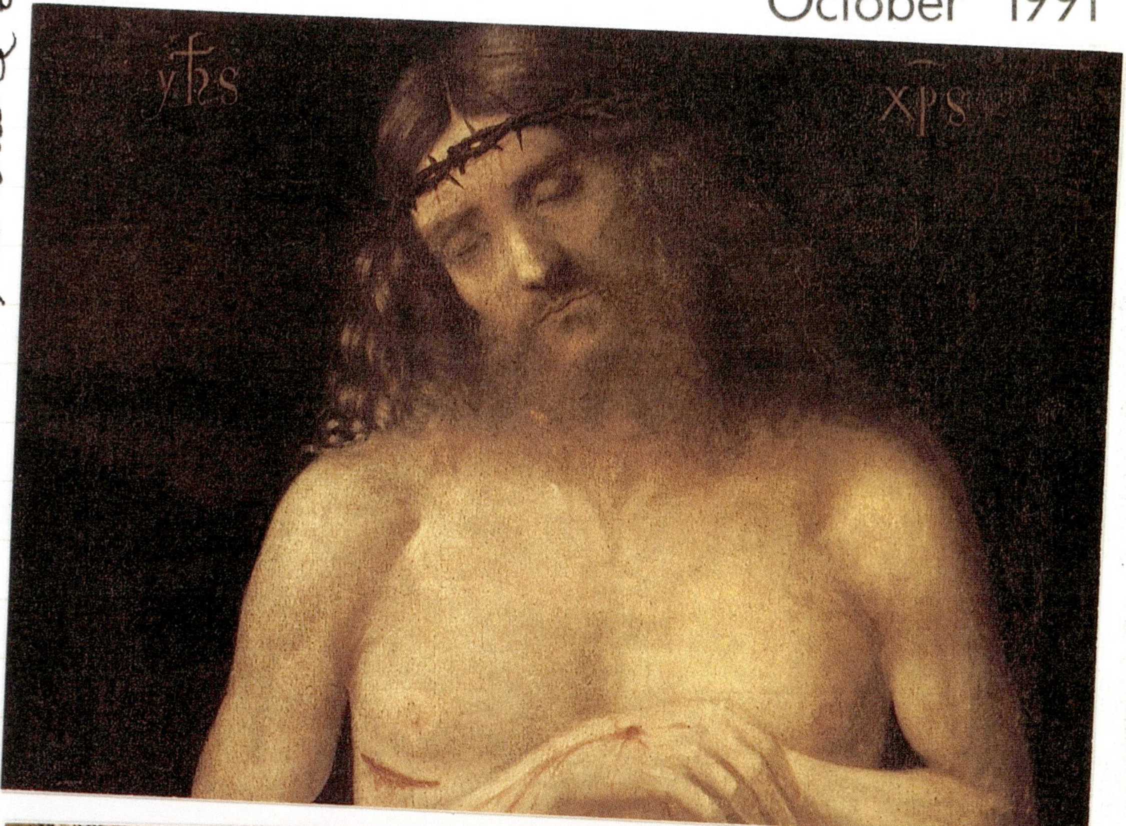

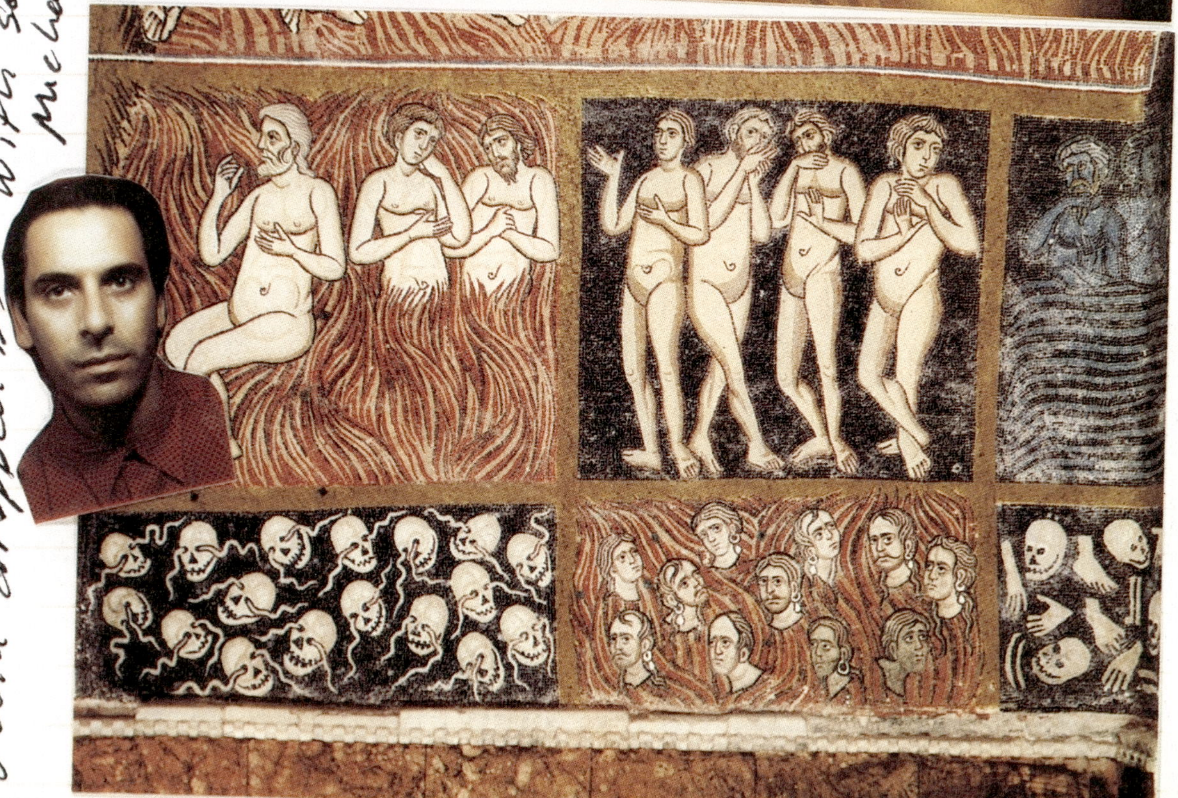

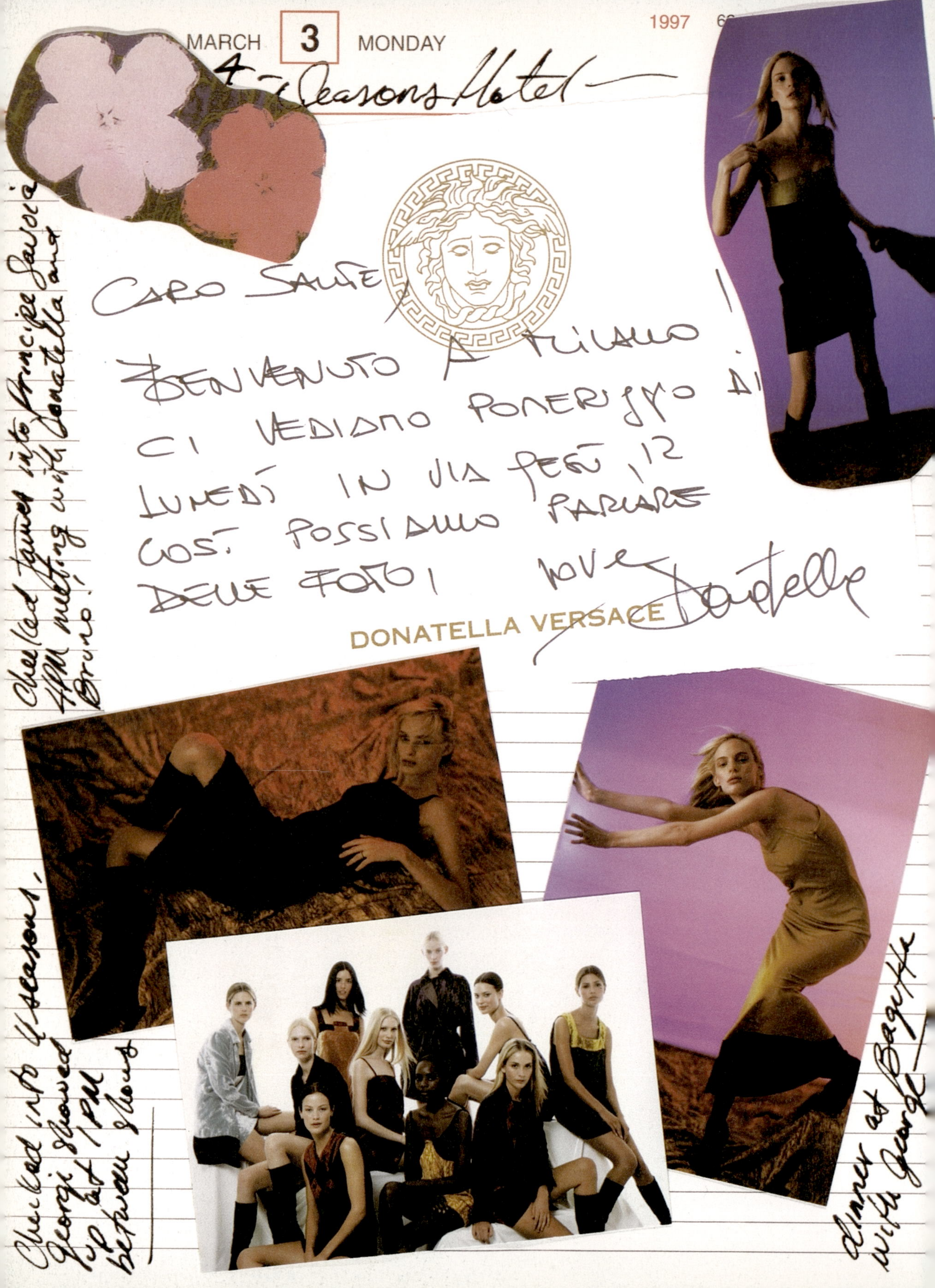

MARCH 3 MONDAY 1997 66

4 Seasons Hotel

CARO SAWE

BENVENUTO A MILANO !
CI VEDIAMO POMERIGGIO DI
LUNEDÍ IN VIA FEG 12
COSÍ POSSIAMO PARLARE
DELLE FOTO! love Donatella

DONATELLA VERSACE

Checked faxes into Principe Savoia
4PM meeting with Donatella and
Bruno!

Checked into 4 Seasons.
Georgi showed up at 1PM
between shows

dinner at Bagatta
with George

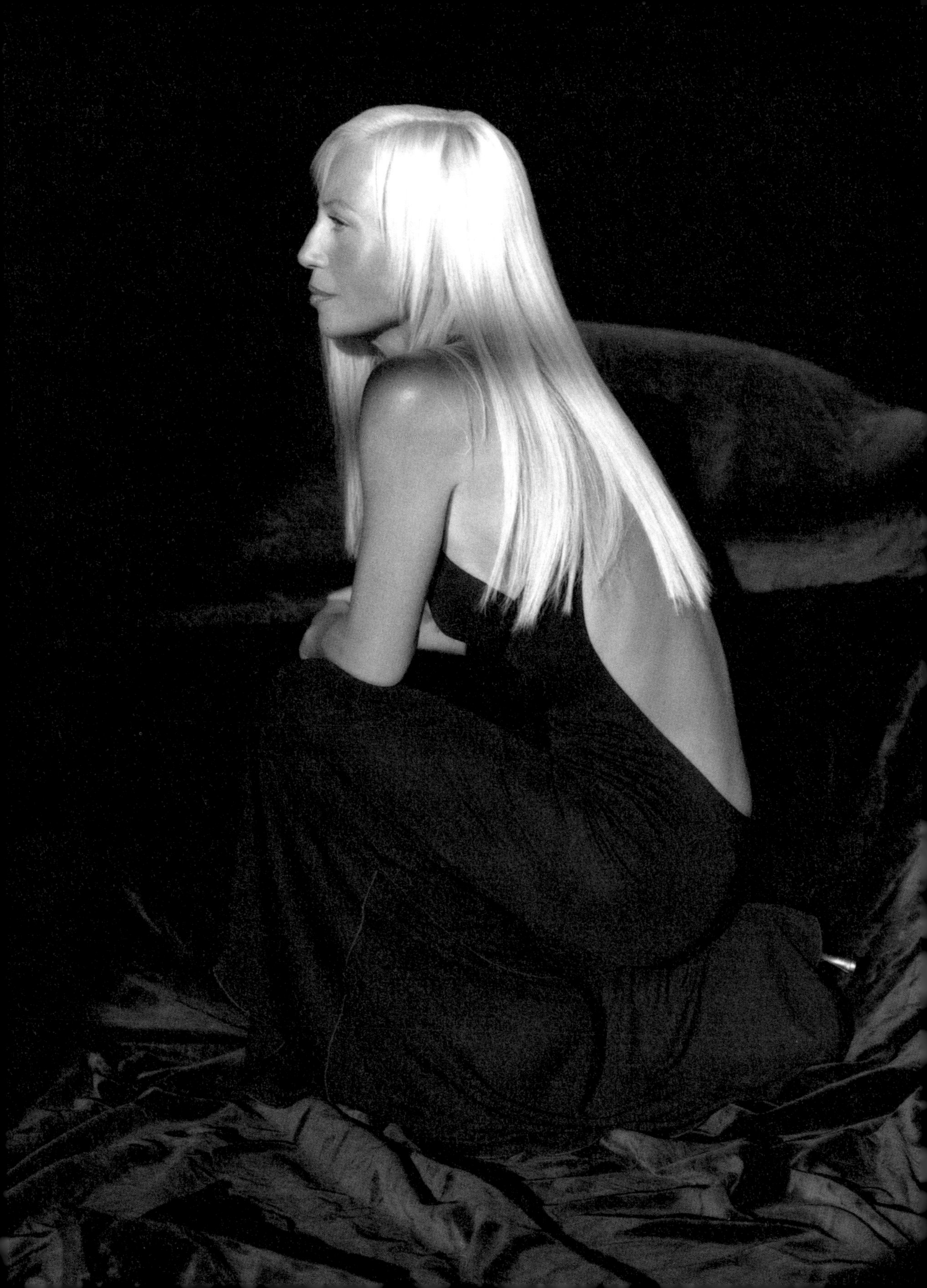

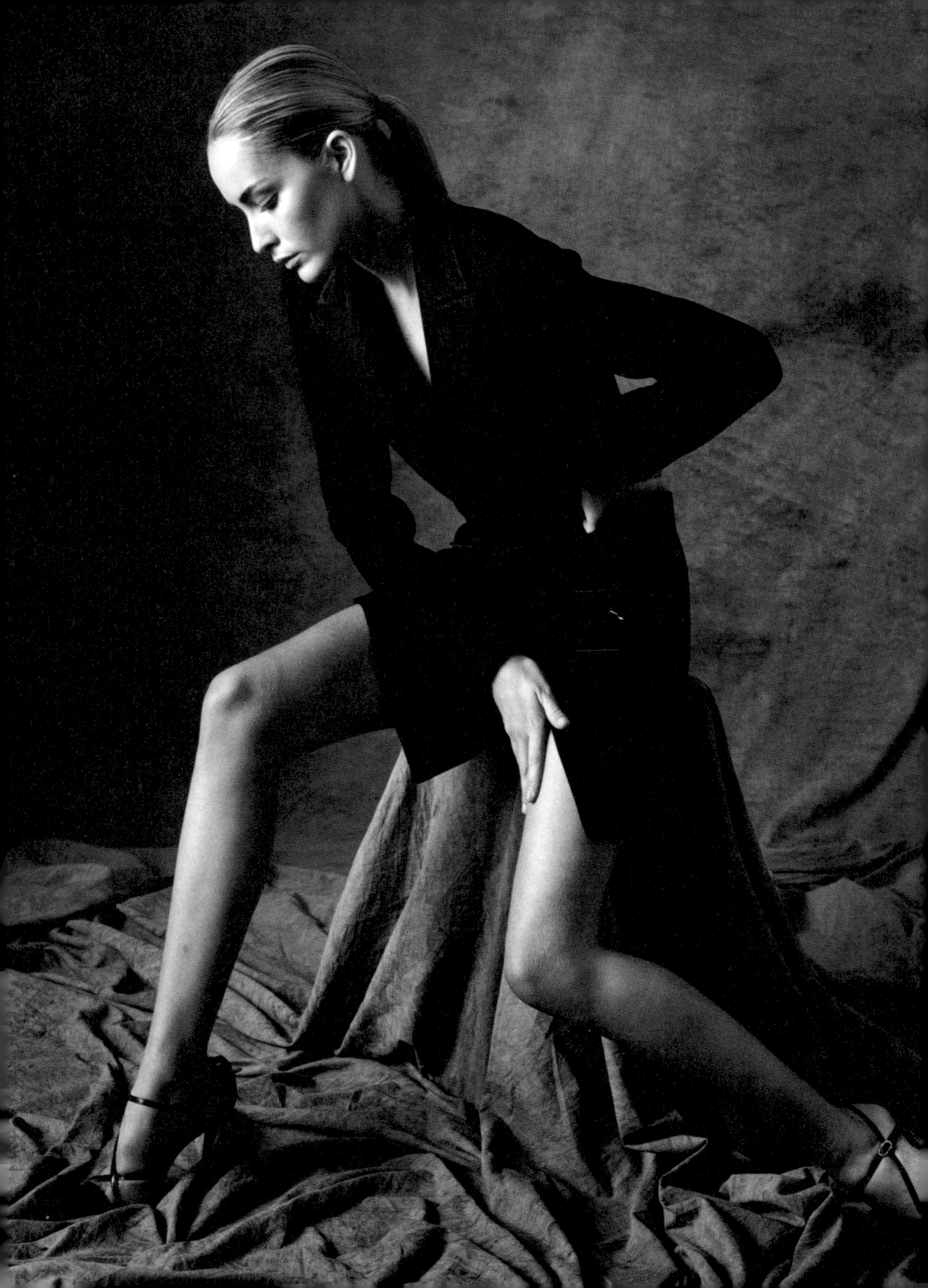

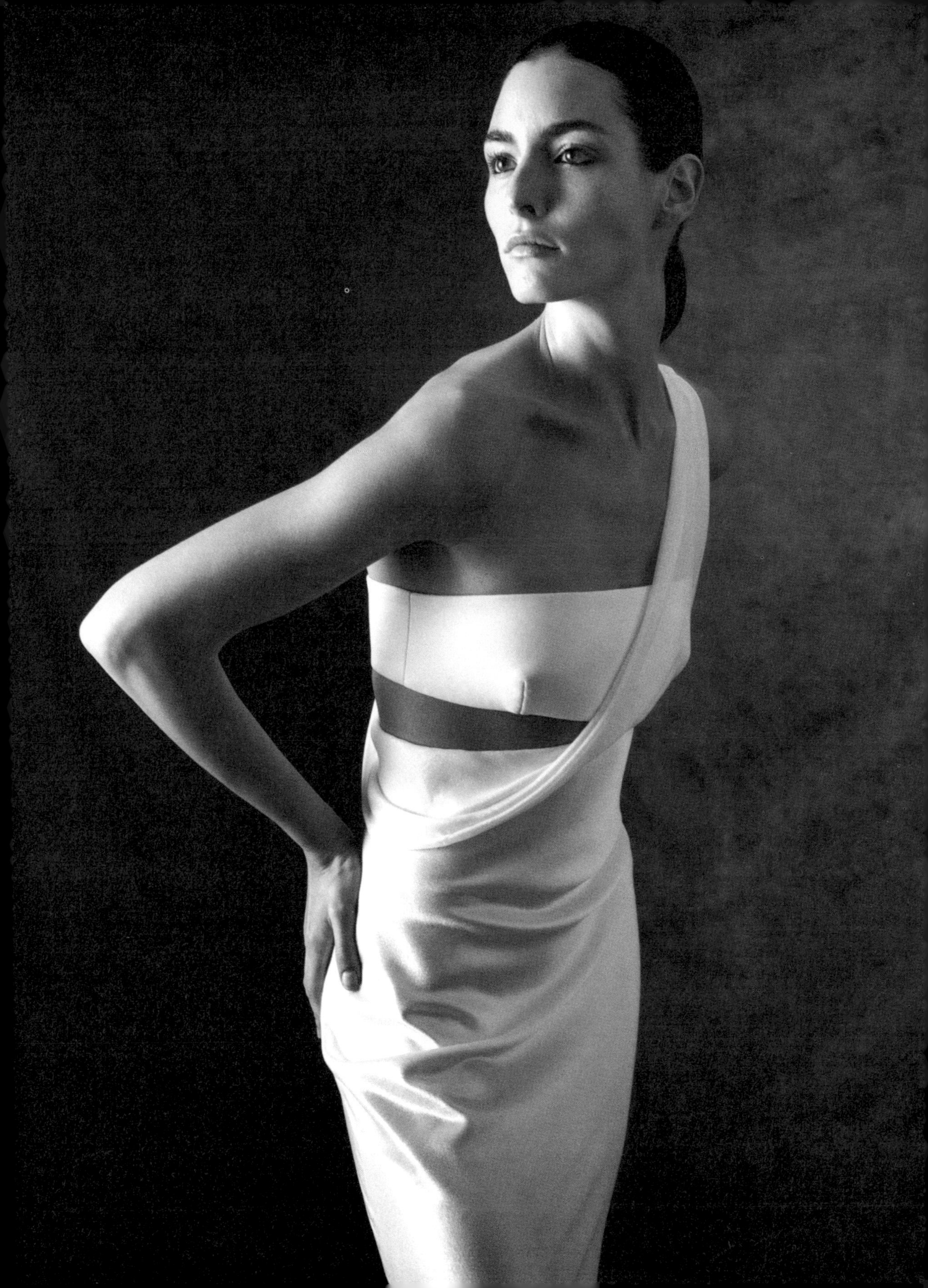

Edited Versace film, got back more black & white. I love this group shot. Looking at it now gives me this feeling of time gone by. It already gives me the sense of an era! I also remember how fun and crazy that week was and I love how enthusiastic Gianni was about the pictures. I love that guy, hes the most gentle and sincere. I get a real sense of family around Donatella and those guys!

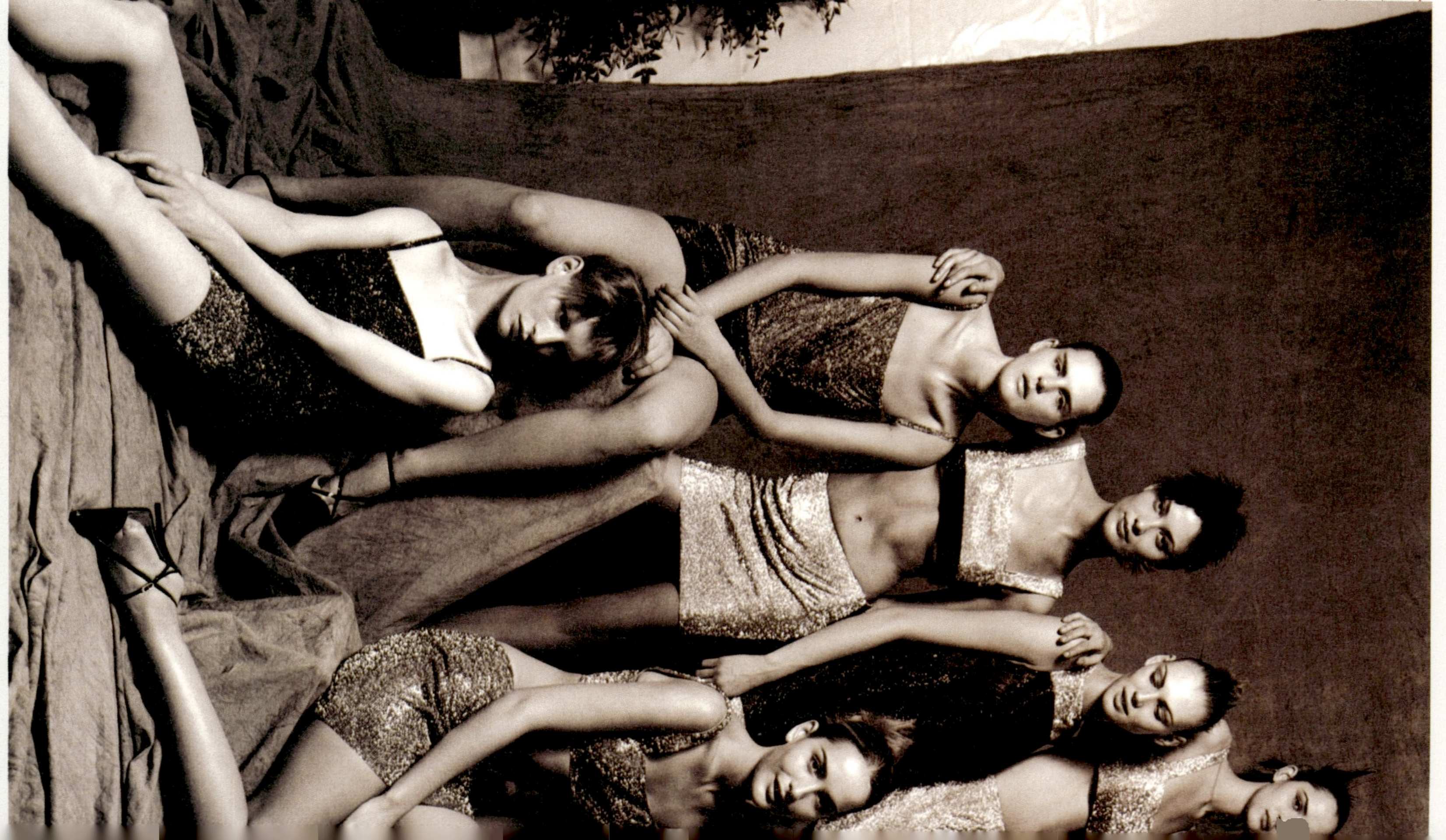

Versace —

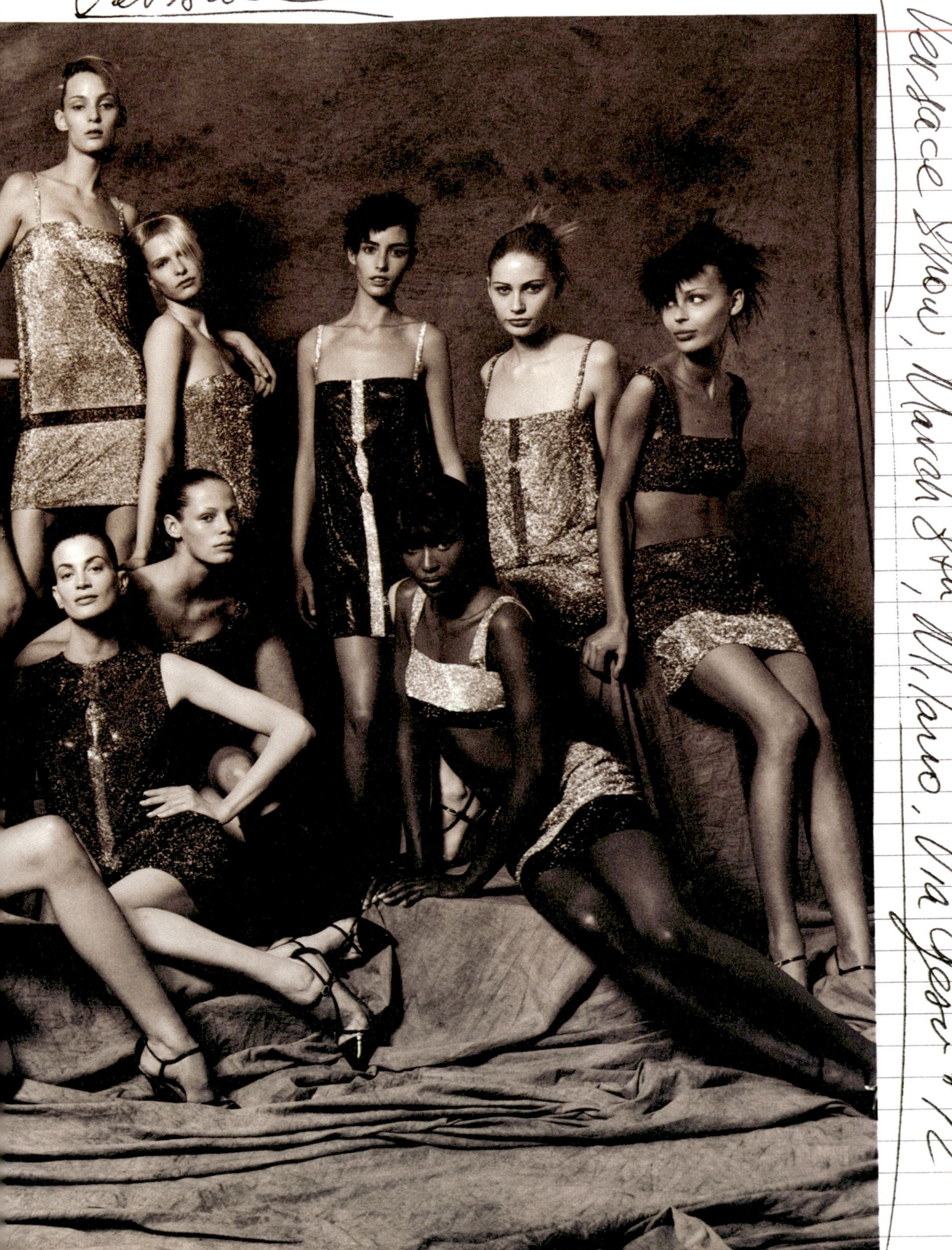

Versace Show, March 8th, Milano, Via Gesu #12

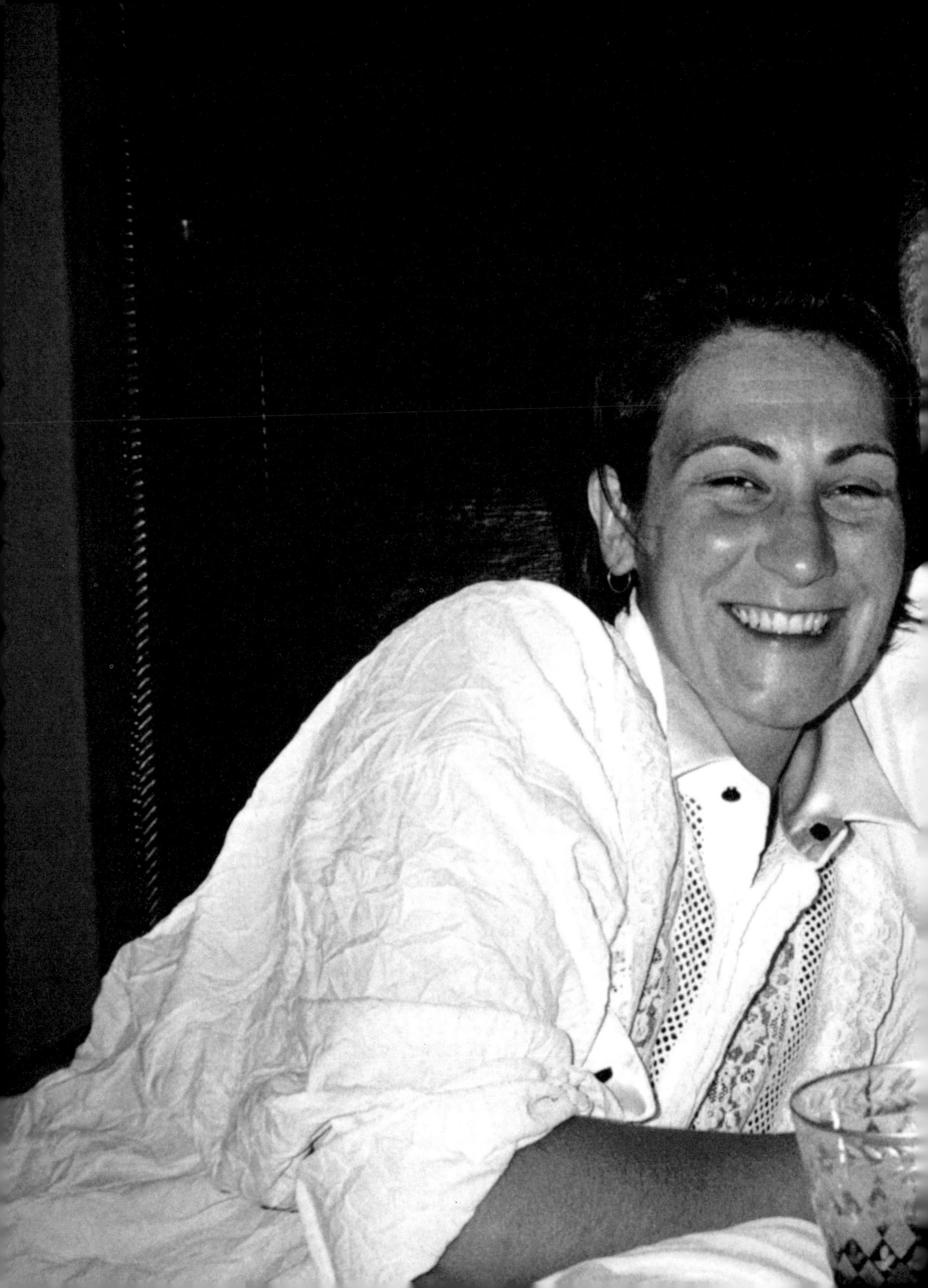

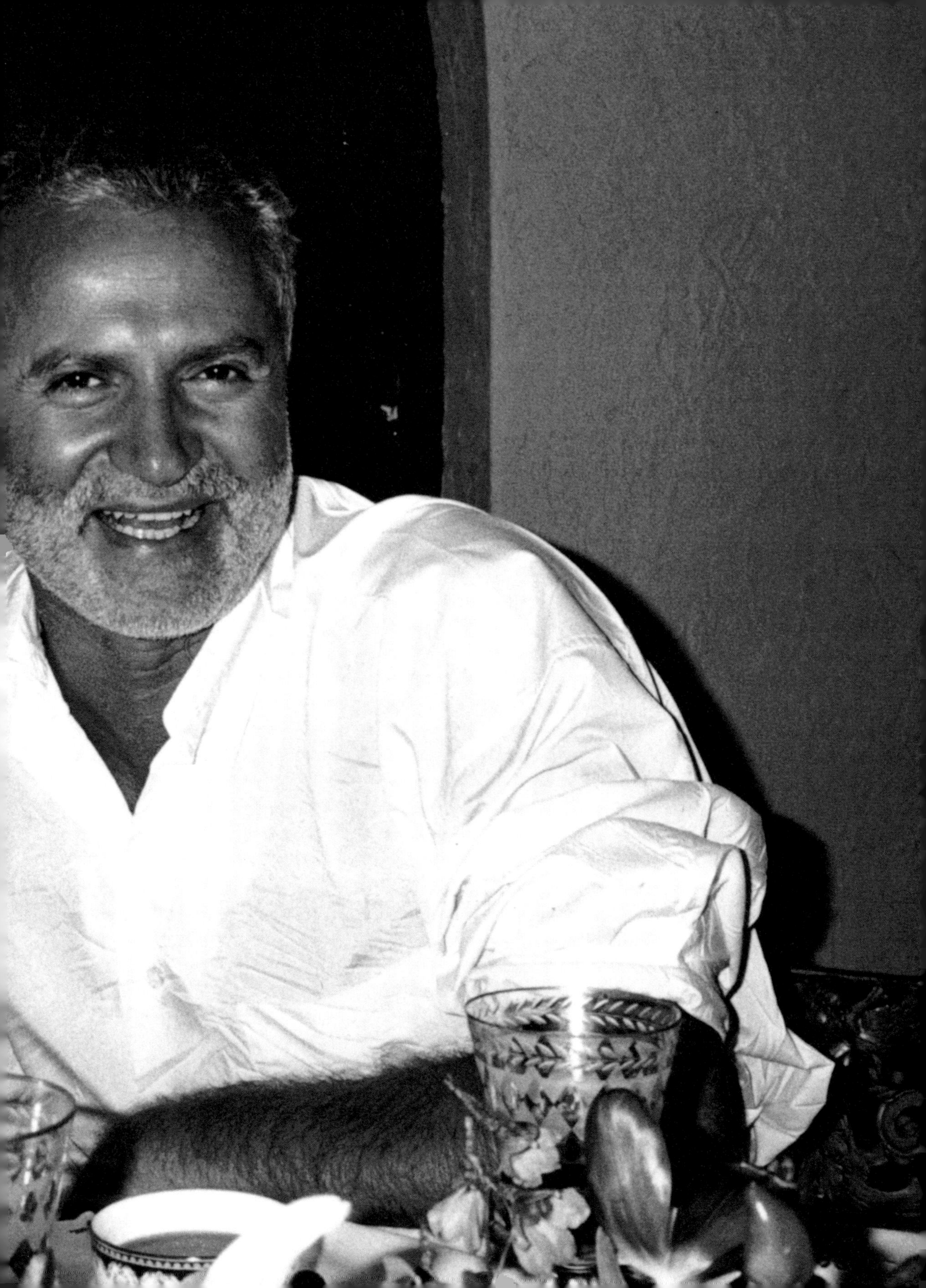

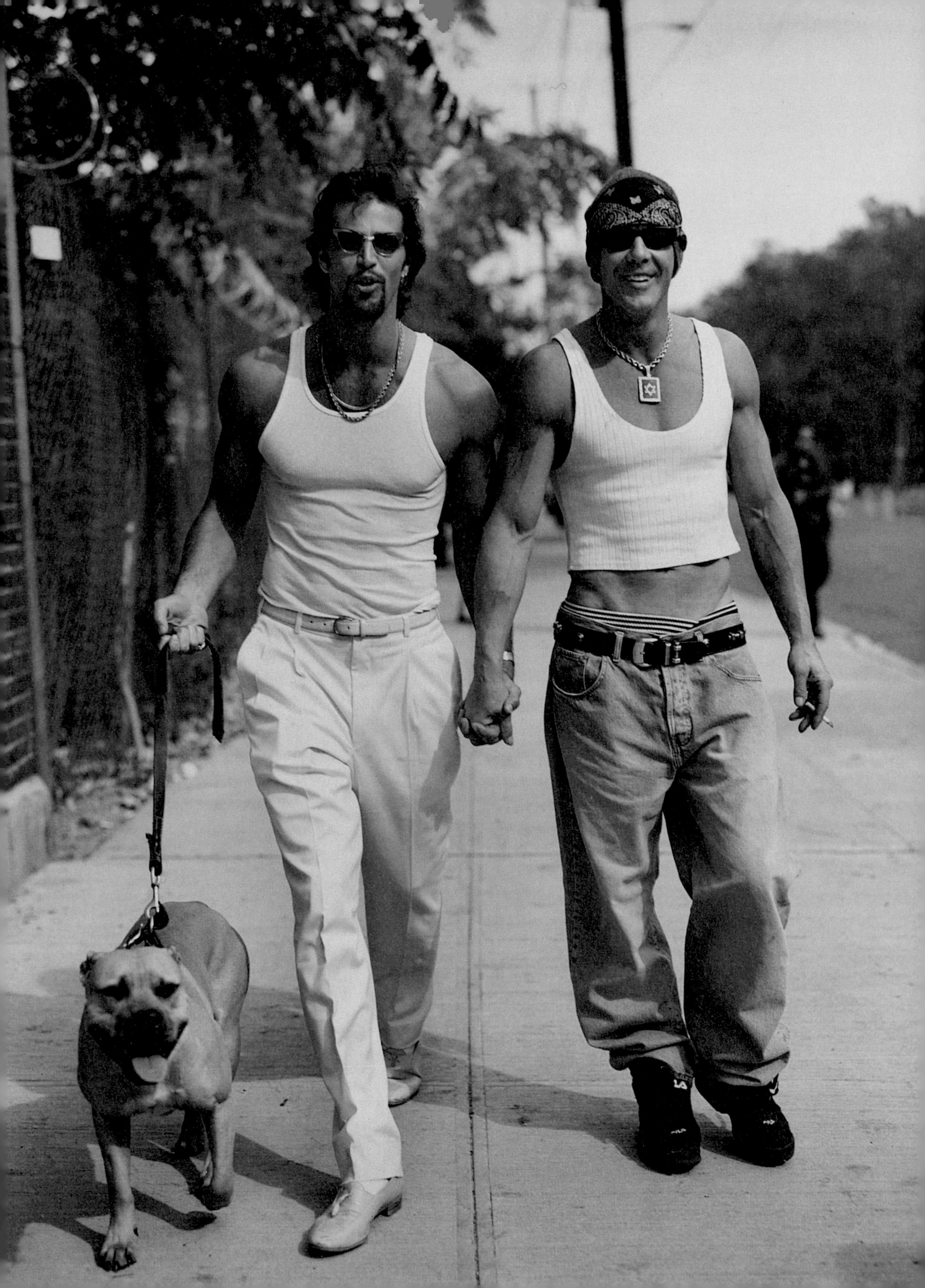

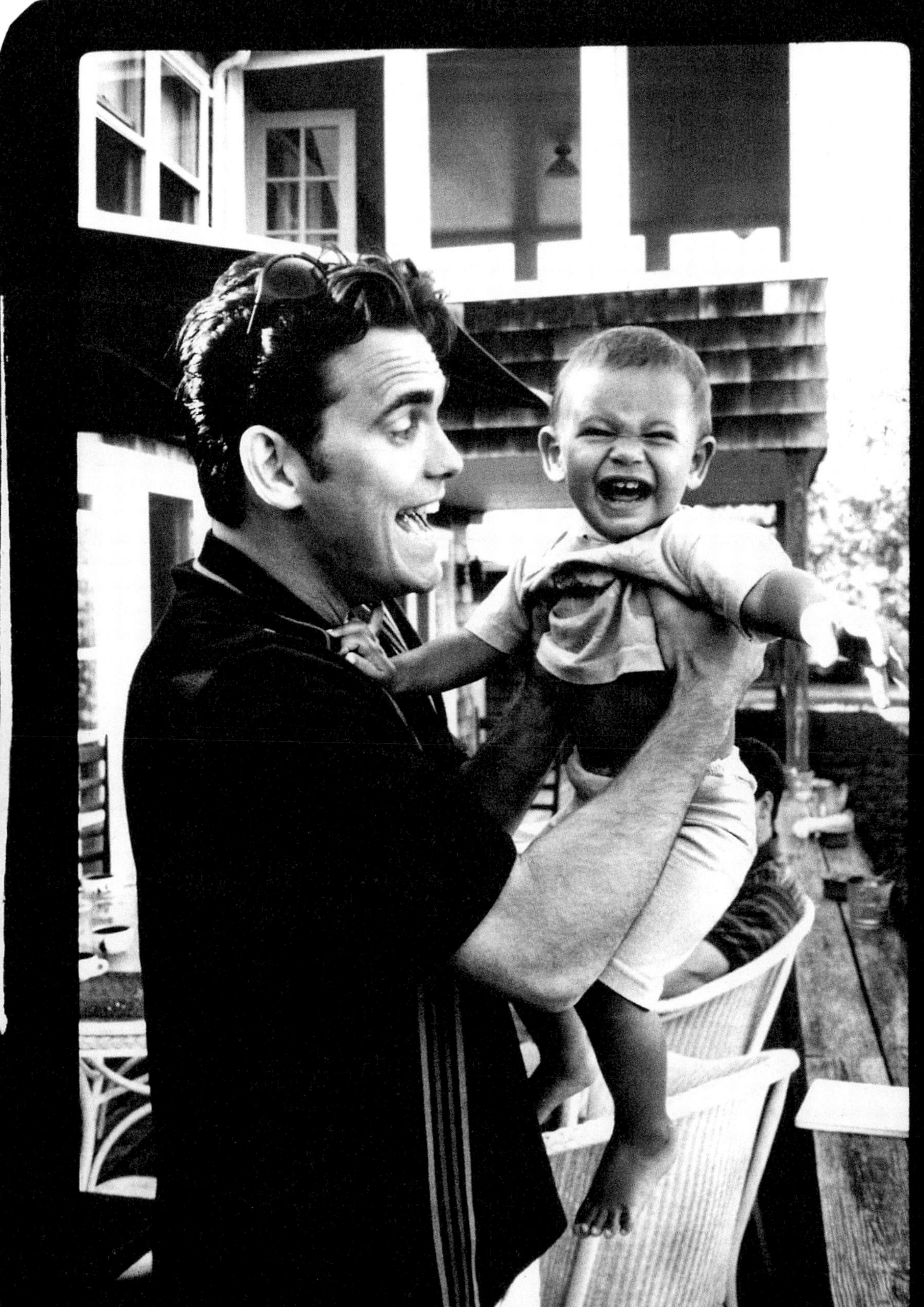

...made ourselves a Barbeque and everyone in the pool! Later we drove by Russells, played some B-ball!

Nick & Sharon Stone – Malibu

Woke up to a dream where Keeley and Al Cowens were after me + looking to kill me, Keeley was foaming at the mouth with anger! Edited Isabel Adjani, Sharon Stone + Tim Roth film, great to get it all behind me. Ischei came over + looked at the pictures, she loved em. Lunch with Kara + Rhea at poolside then back to editing. Dinner at Matsuhisa with Kara + Jab. Ran into Sharon Stone + friend. also Vivi + master. Whiskey for drinks afterwards!

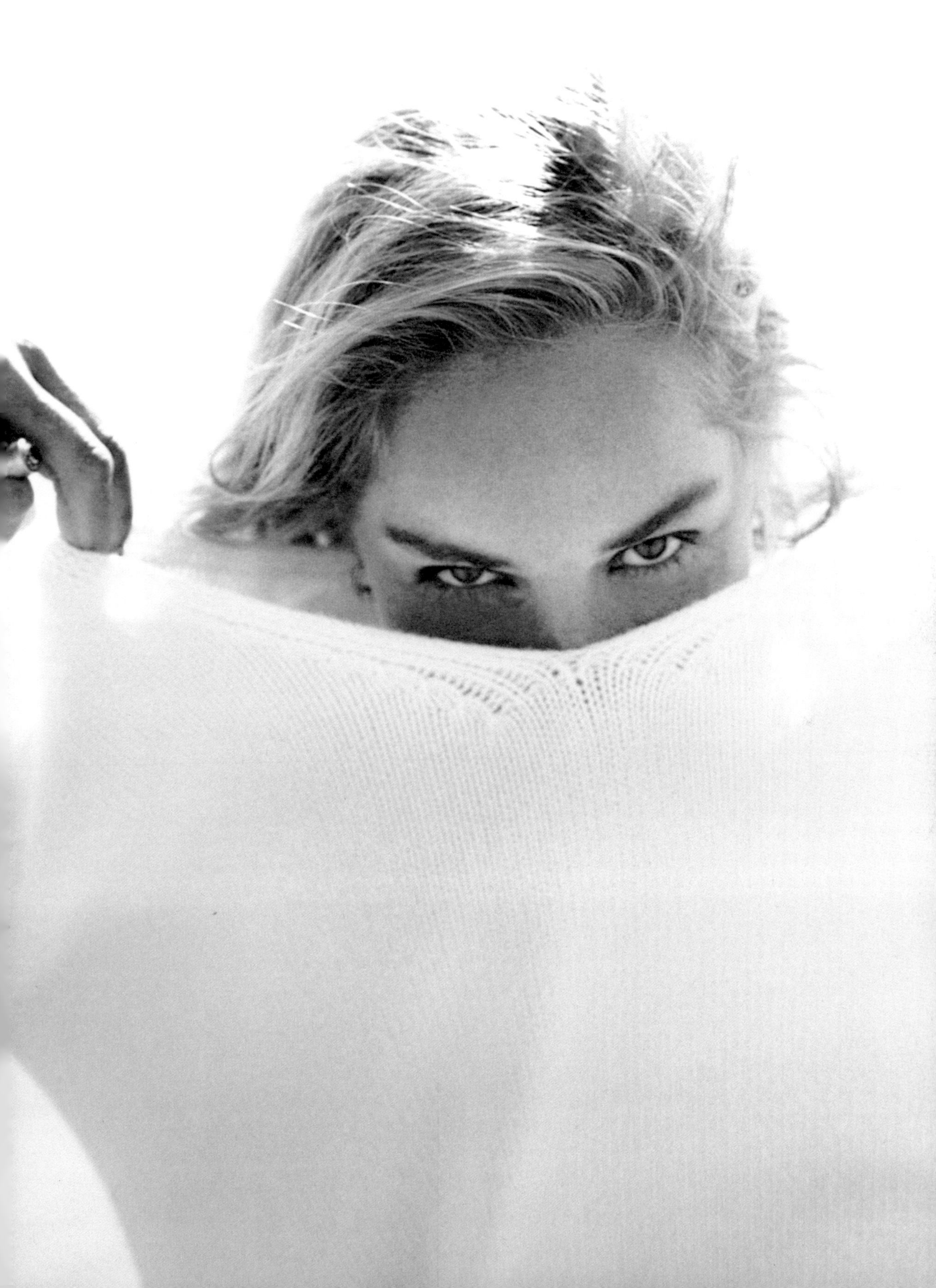

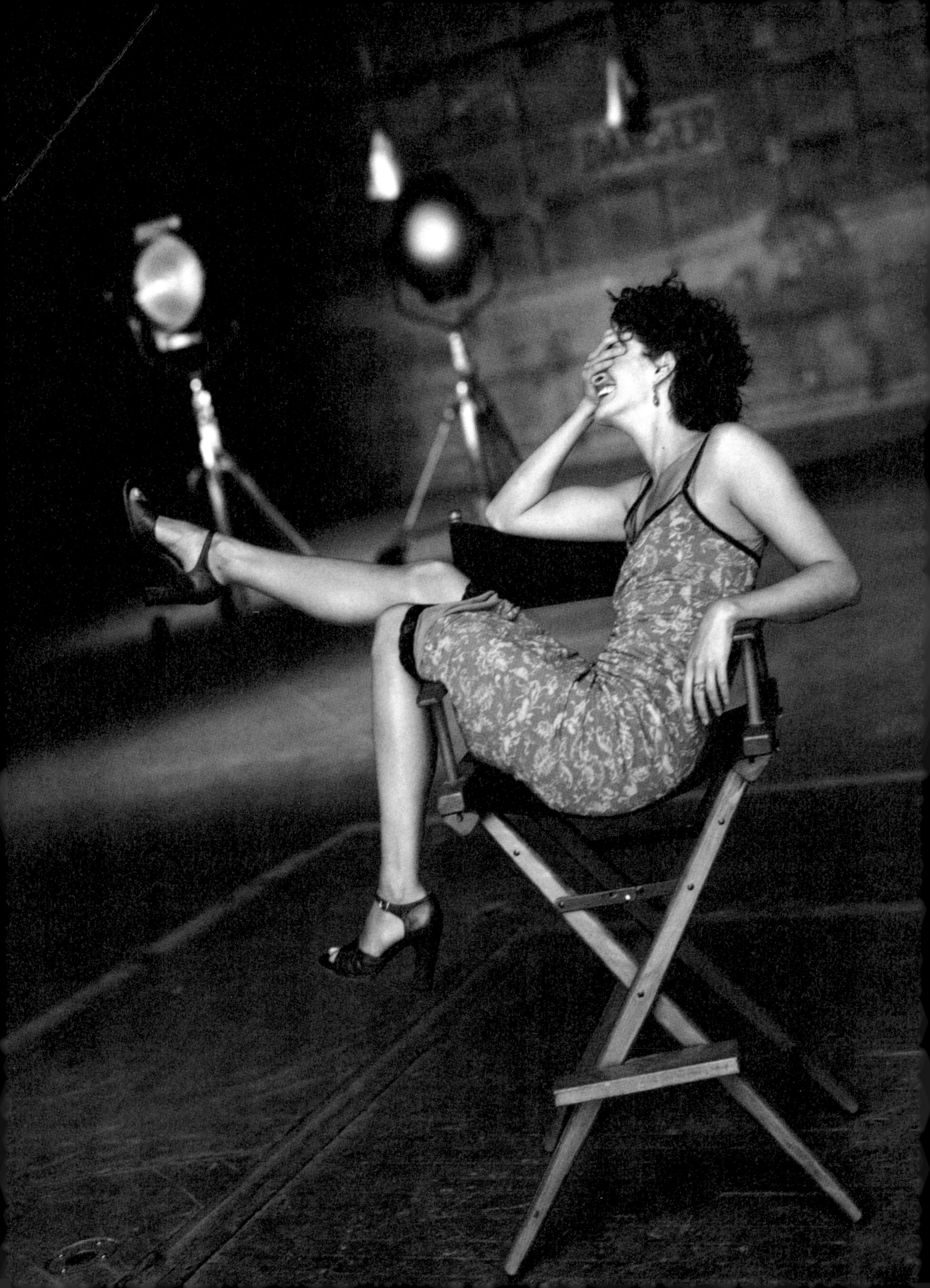

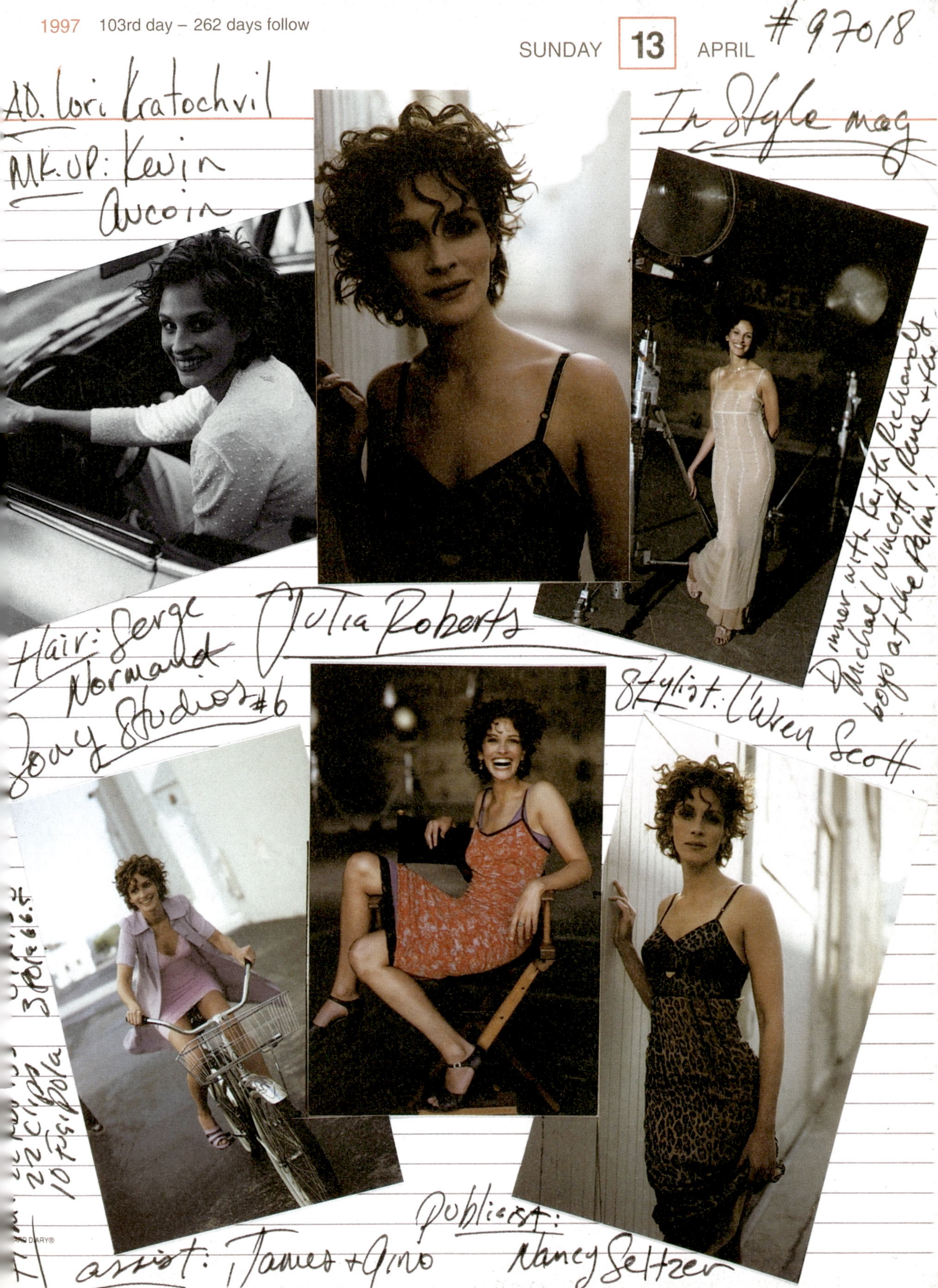
AD. Lori Kratochvil
MK.UP: Kevin
        Aucoin

In Style mag

Hair: Serge
      Normand

Julia Roberts

Sony Studios #6

Stylist: Lauren Scott

Dinner with Keith Richards,
Michael Wincott, Rene + the
boys at the Palm.

Publicist:
assist: James + Gino   Nancy Seltzer

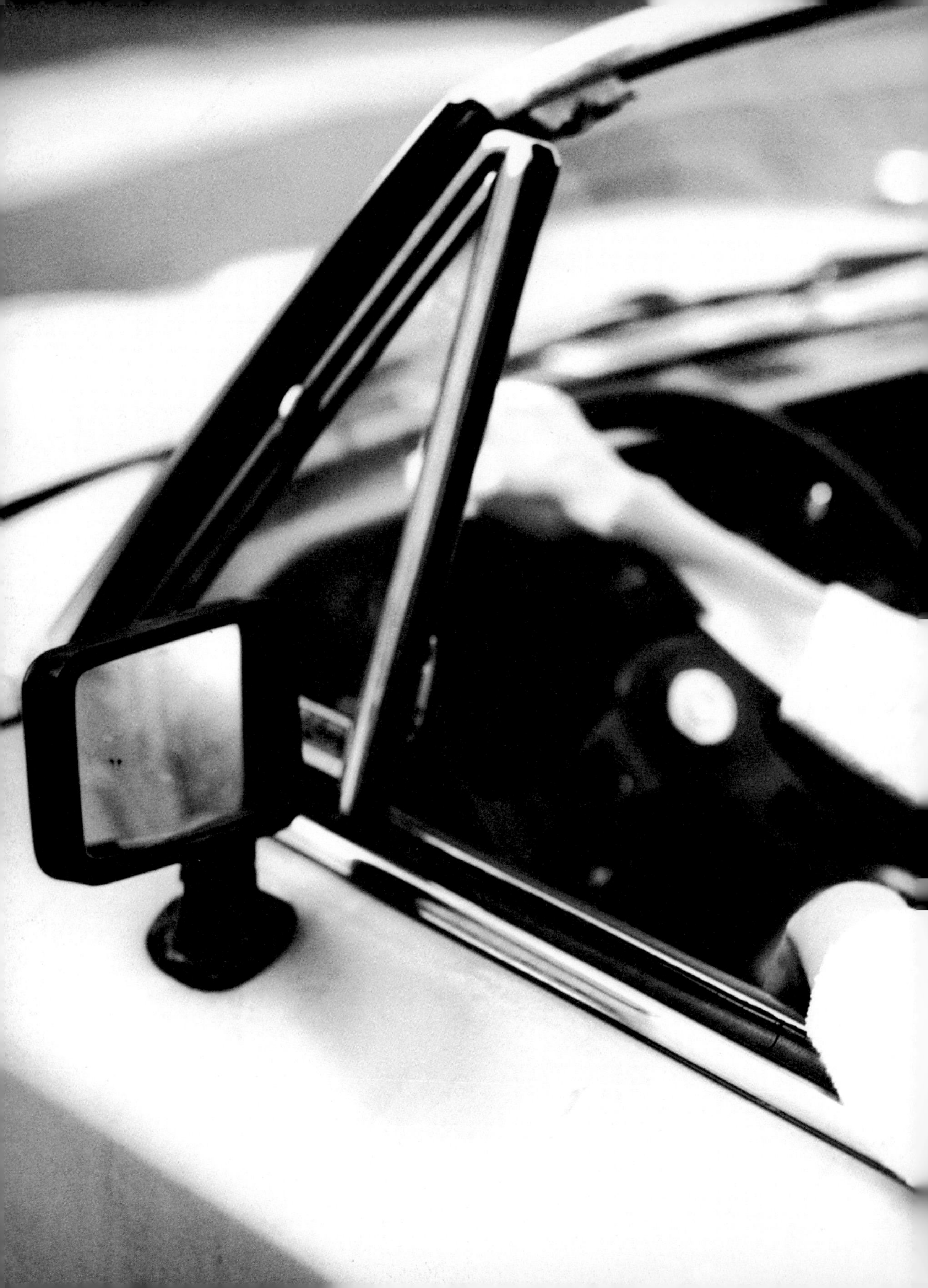

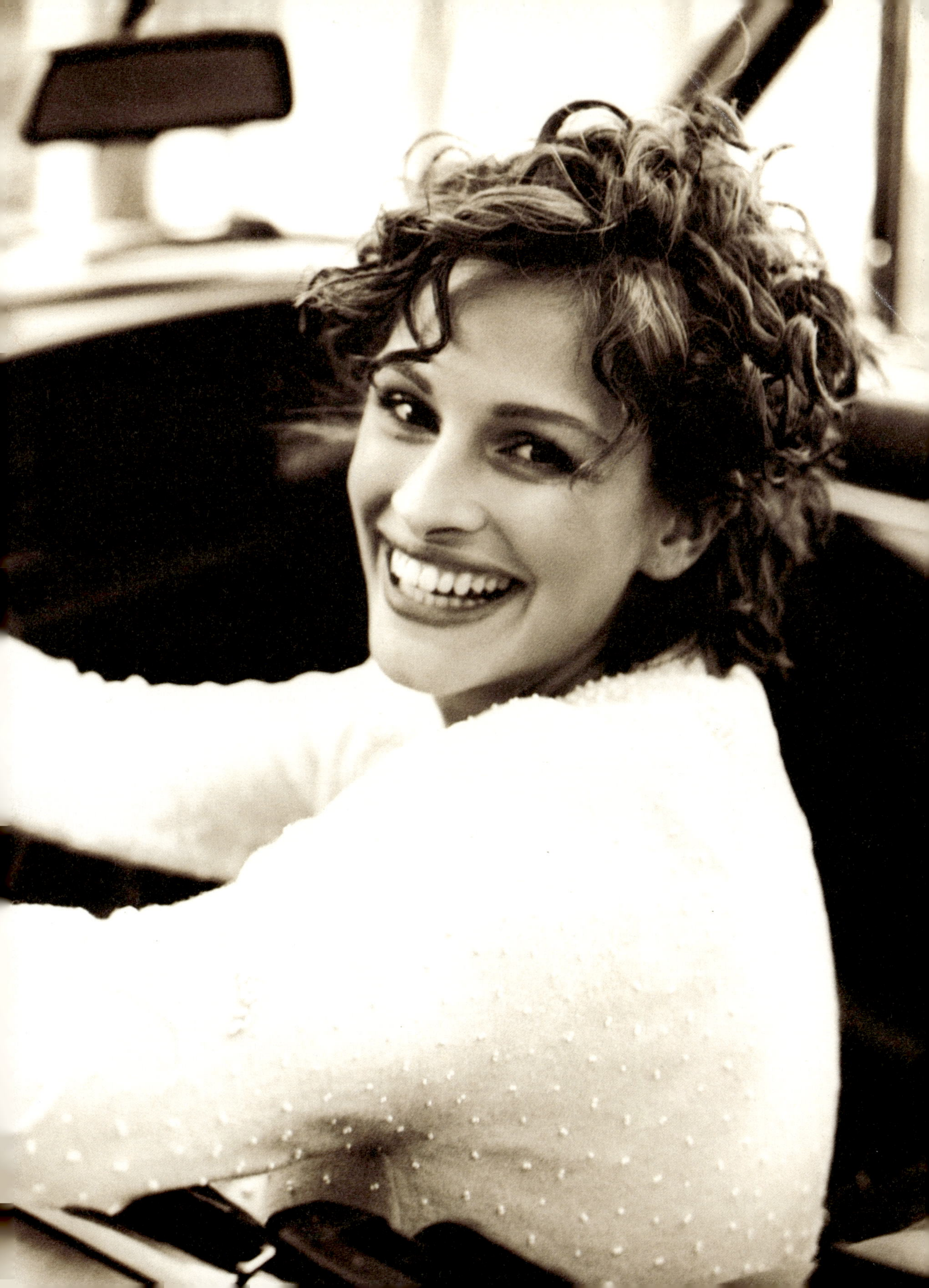

Took Nick out for a stroll met Francesco at his studio then walked him home. Went to Bar Pitti with him + his family and Bill Katz. Michael Wincott met me there + later Lara. Walked around later with Wincott, watched the Bulls beat Orlando. Went to Barbeque at Bowery Bar given by Lisa Cooper, went with Bob + Lara.

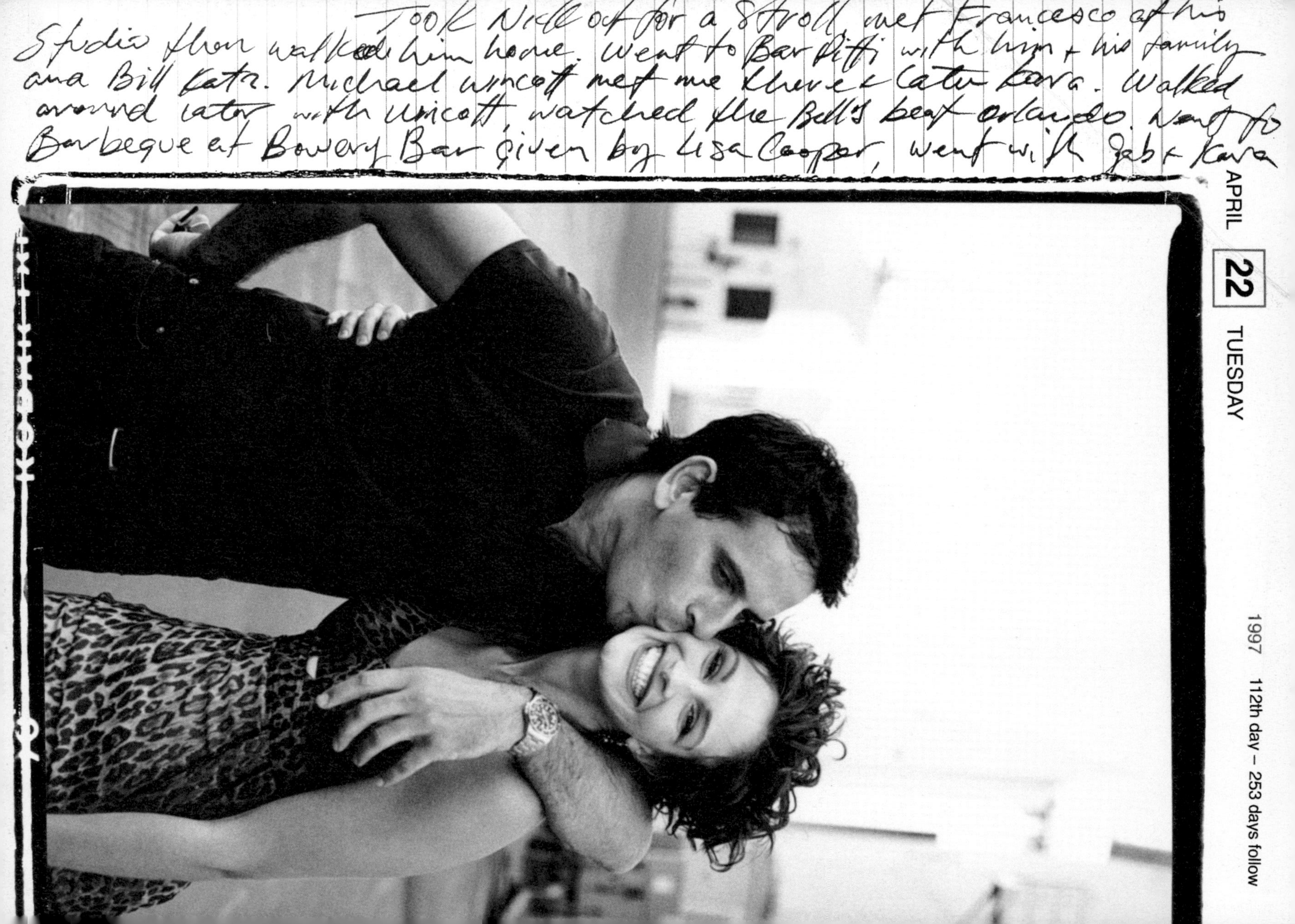

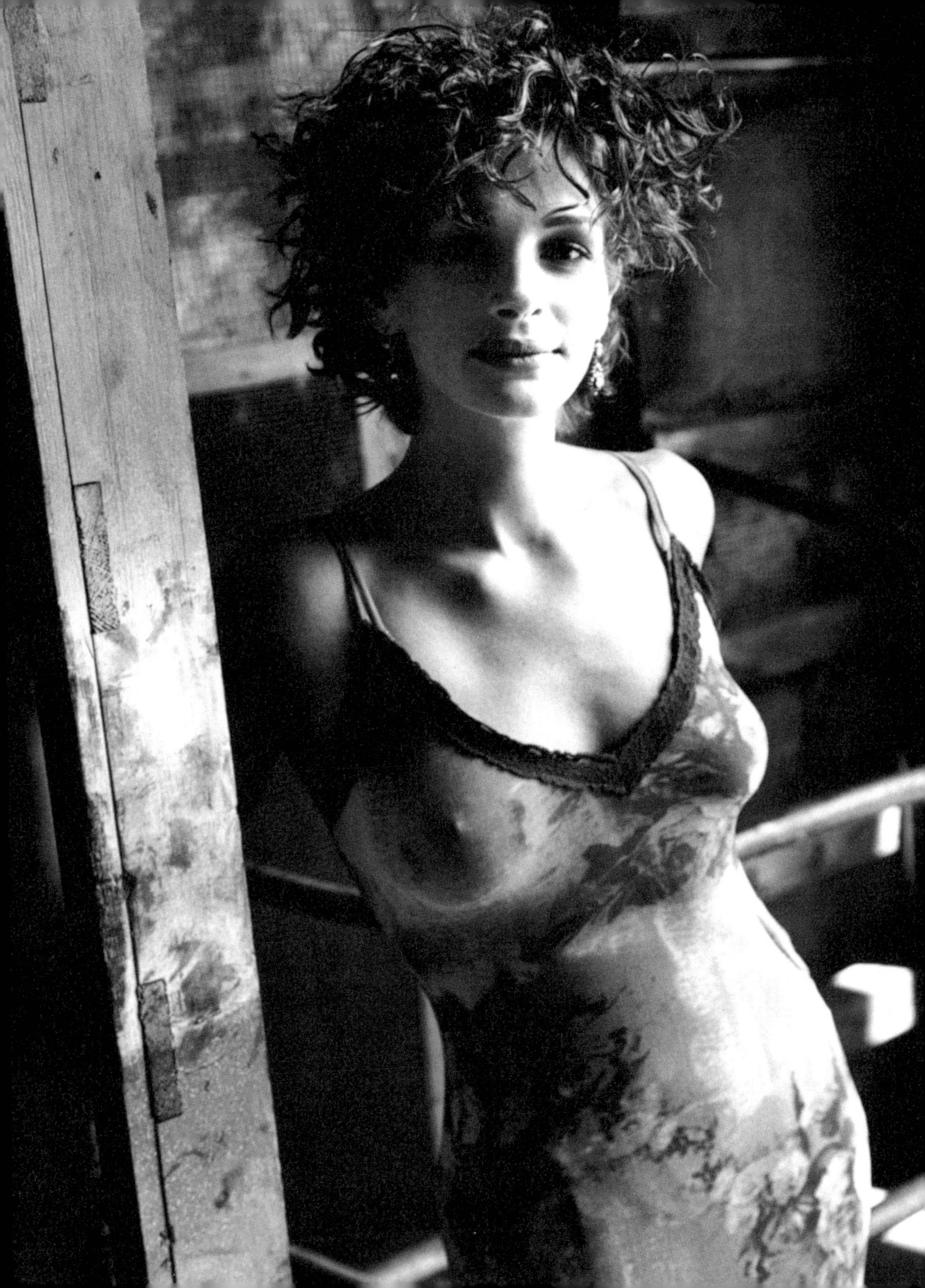

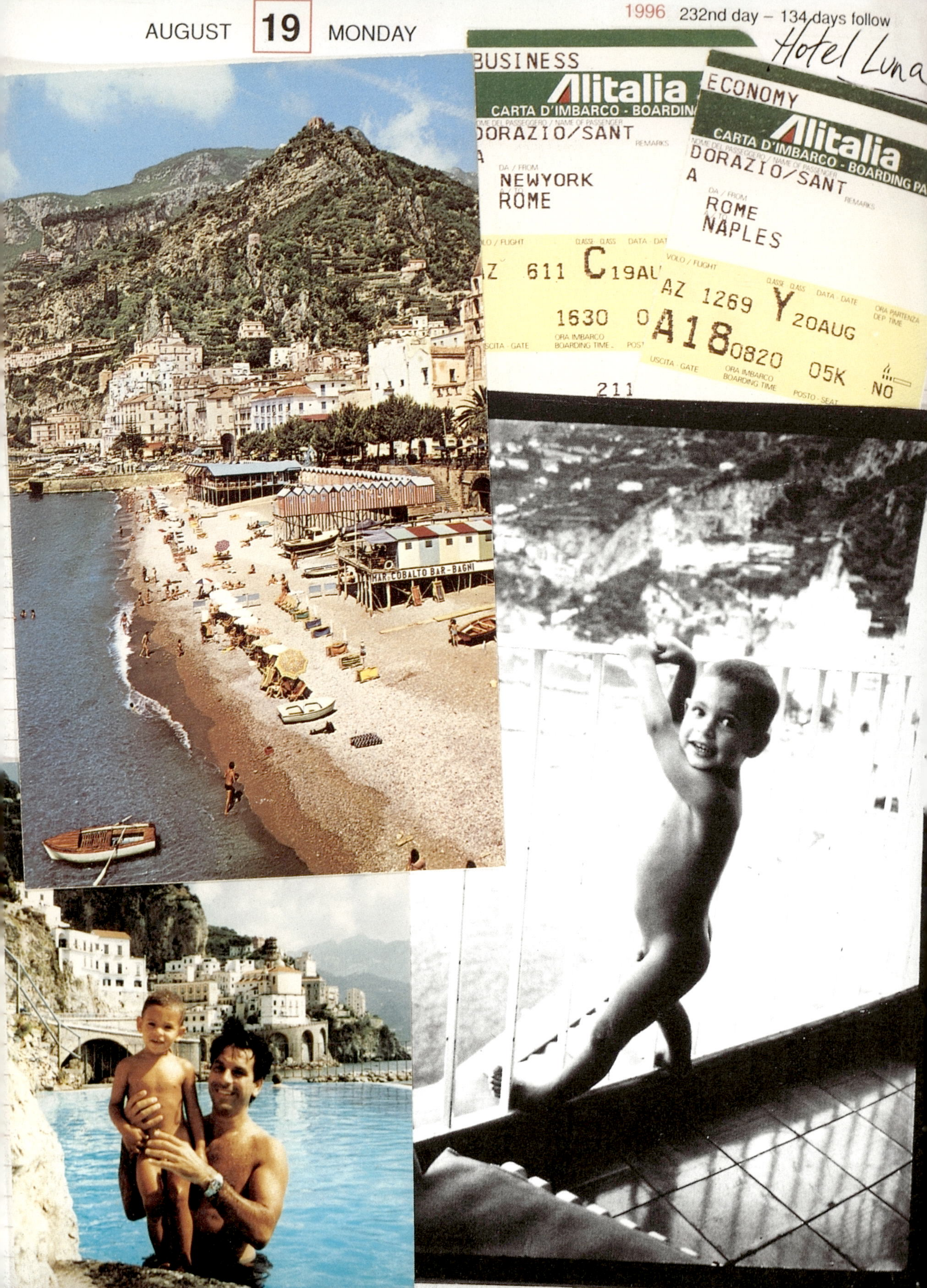

AUGUST 19 MONDAY
1996 232nd day – 134 days follow
Hotel Luna
BUSINESS
ECONOMY
Alitalia
CARTA D'IMBARCO - BOARDING PASS
NOME DEL PASSEGGERO / NAME OF PASSENGER
DORAZIO/SANT
REMARKS
DA / FROM
NEWYORK
A
ROME
VOLO / FLIGHT   CLASSE CLASS   DATA DATE
AZ 611 C 19AUG
1630 0
ORA IMBARCO
BOARDING TIME   POST
211
Alitalia
CARTA D'IMBARCO - BOARDING PASS
NOME DEL PASSEGGERO / NAME OF PASSENGER
DORAZIO/SANT
REMARKS
DA / FROM
ROME
A TO
NAPLES
VOLO / FLIGHT   CLASSE CLASS   DATA - DATE   ORA PARTENZA
AZ 1269 Y 20AUG   DEP TIME
A18 0820 05K
USCITA - GATE   ORA IMBARCO
BOARDING TIME   POSTO - SEAT   NO
BAR COBALTO BAR - BAGNI

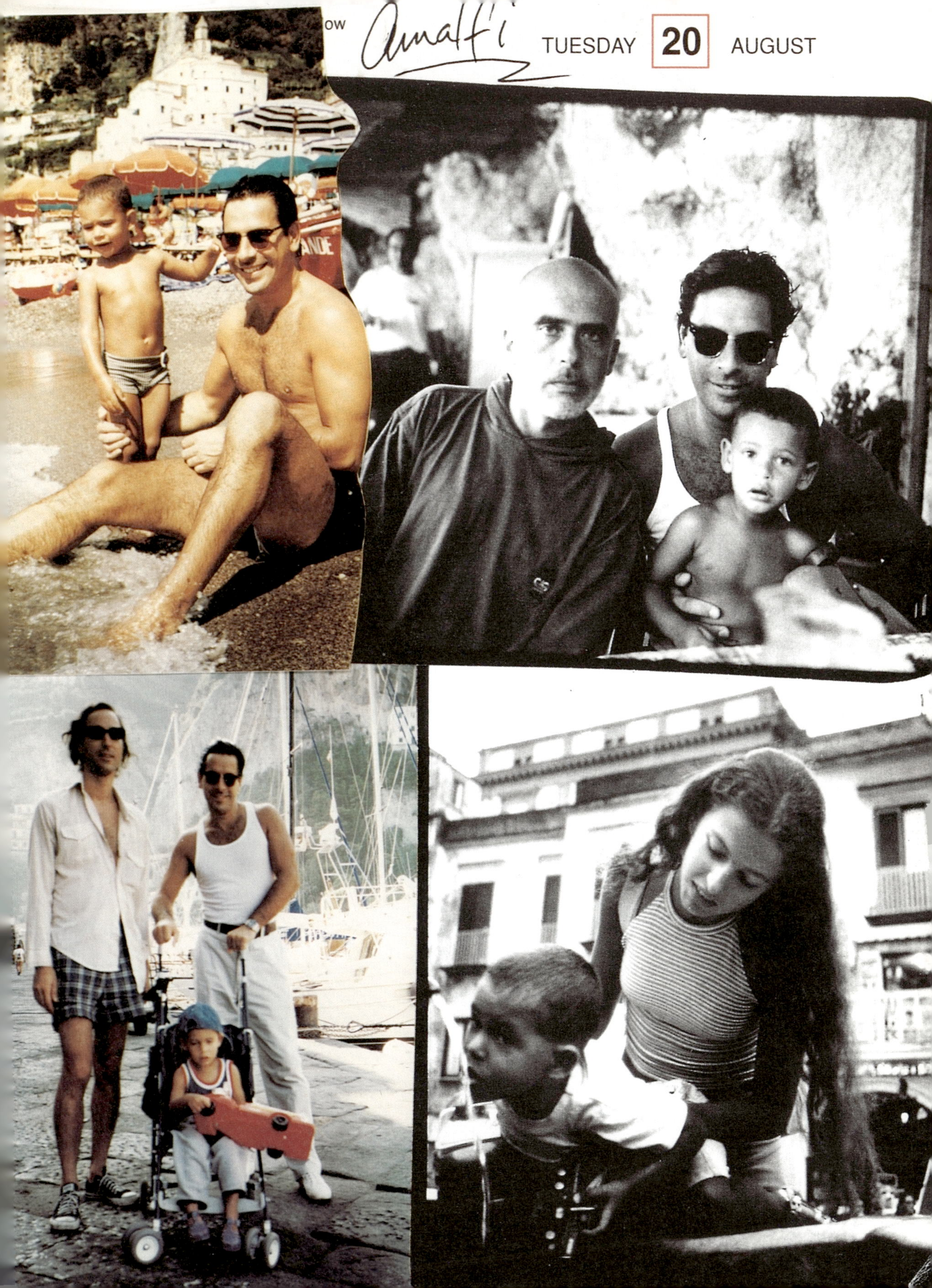

Amalfi
TUESDAY 20 AUGUST

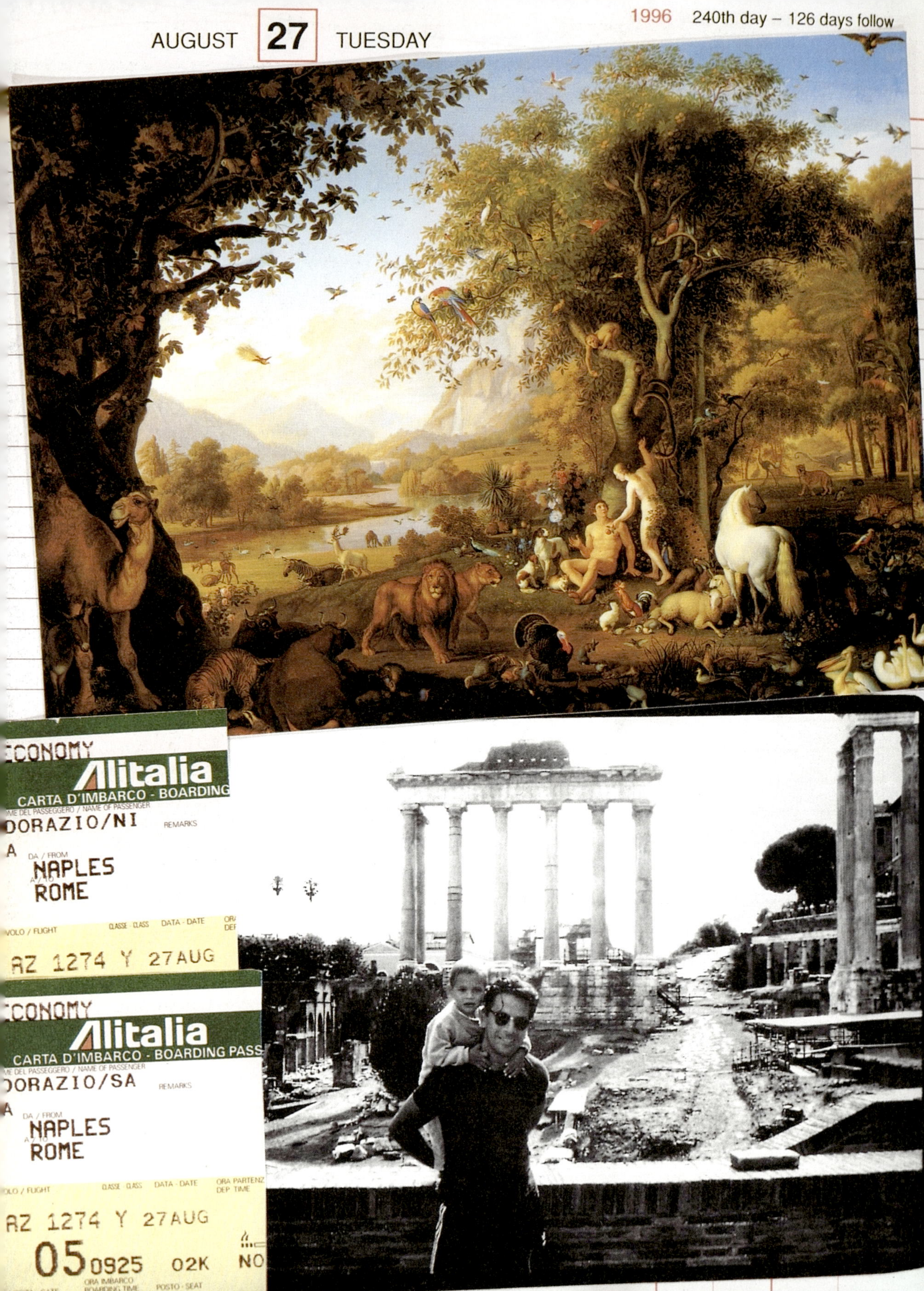
ECONOMY
Alitalia
CARTA D'IMBARCO - BOARDING
NOME DEL PASSEGGERO / NAME OF PASSENGER
DORAZIO/NI   REMARKS
A
DA / FROM
NAPLES
ROME
VOLO / FLIGHT   CLASSE CLASS   DATA - DATE   ORA
DEP
AZ 1274 Y 27AUG

ECONOMY
Alitalia
CARTA D'IMBARCO - BOARDING PASS
NOME DEL PASSEGGERO / NAME OF PASSENGER
DORAZIO/SA   REMARKS
A
DA / FROM
NAPLES
ROME
VOLO / FLIGHT   CLASSE CLASS   DATA - DATE   ORA PARTENZA
DEP TIME
AZ 1274 Y 27AUG
05 0925   02K   NO
ORA IMBARCO
USCITA - GATE   BOARDING TIME   POSTO - SEAT

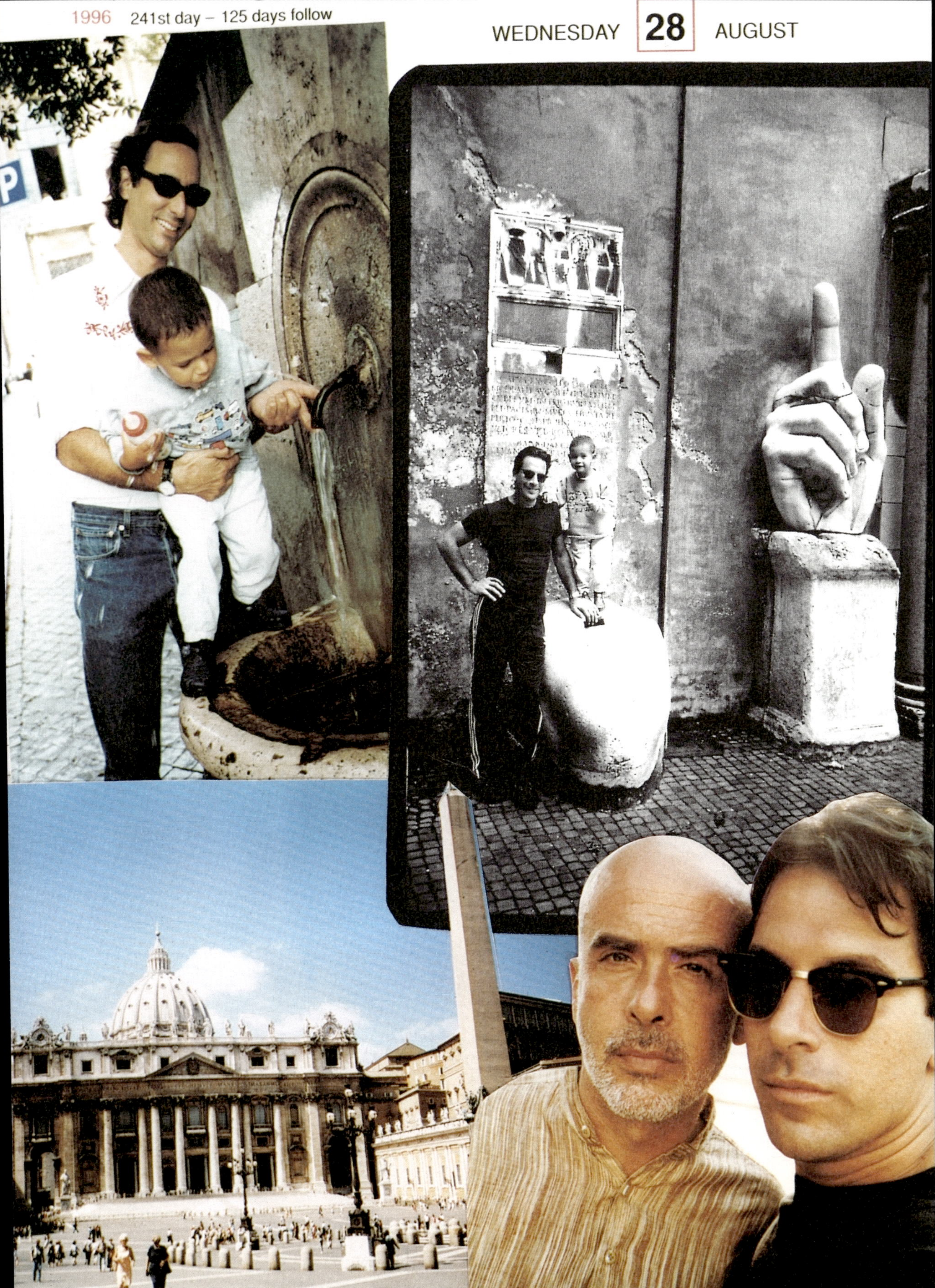

1996   241st day – 125 days follow
WEDNESDAY 28 AUGUST
P

Drove out to the Hamptons with Paulie and Bob

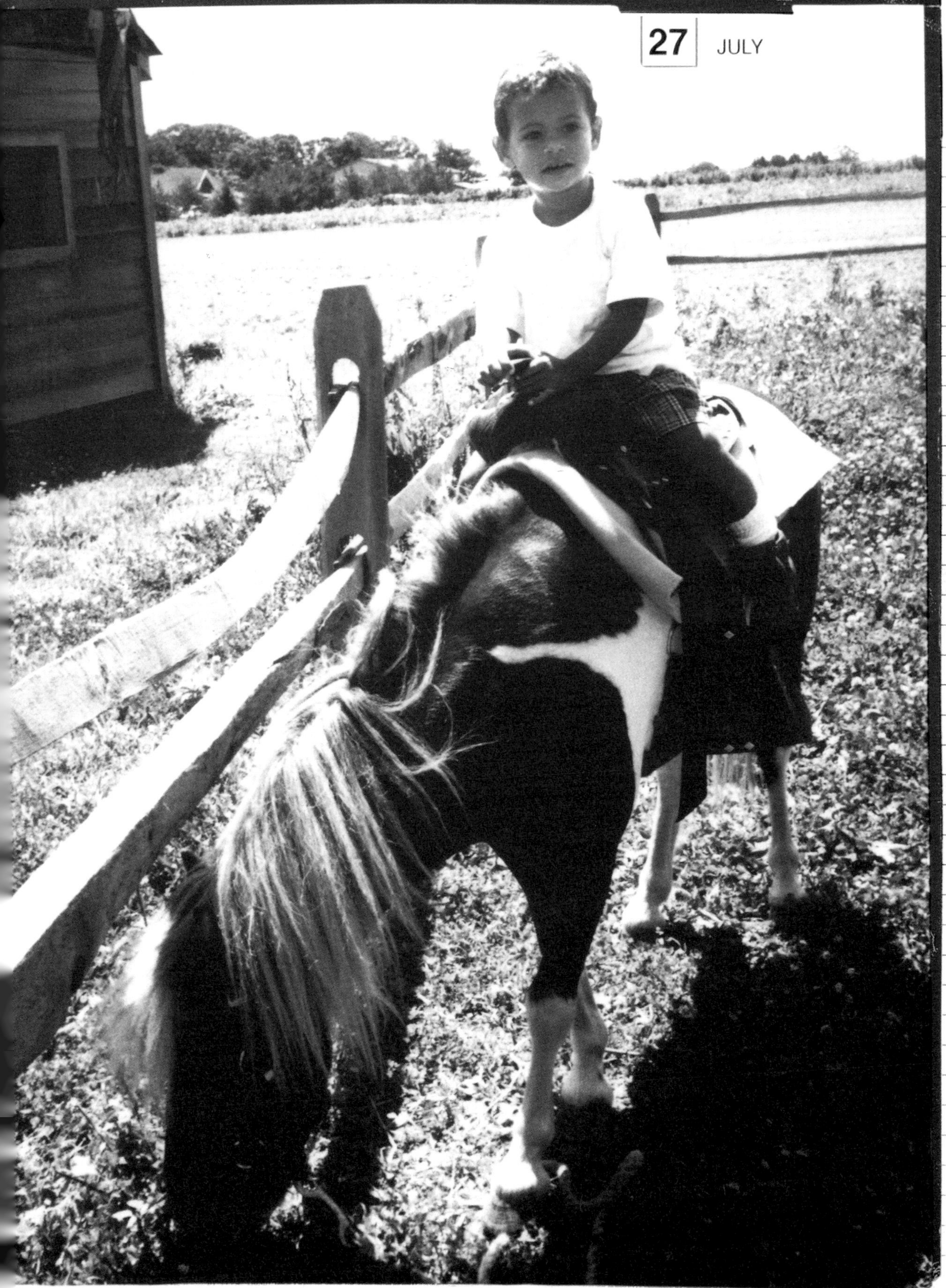

27
JULY

All the author's proceeds
from the publication of this edition will be
donated to the following charities:
The Children's Hope Foundation,
a not-for-profit organization providing
social and medical services
for children with HIV and AIDS,
and the **Elton John Aids Foundation.**

captions

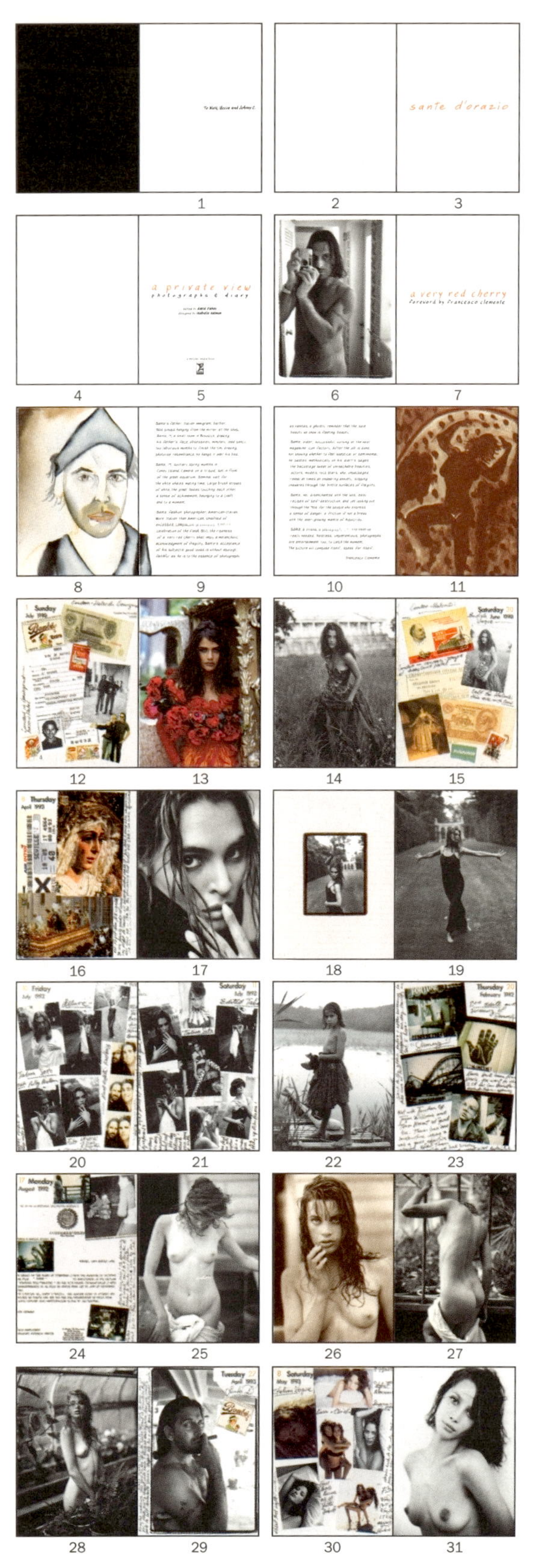

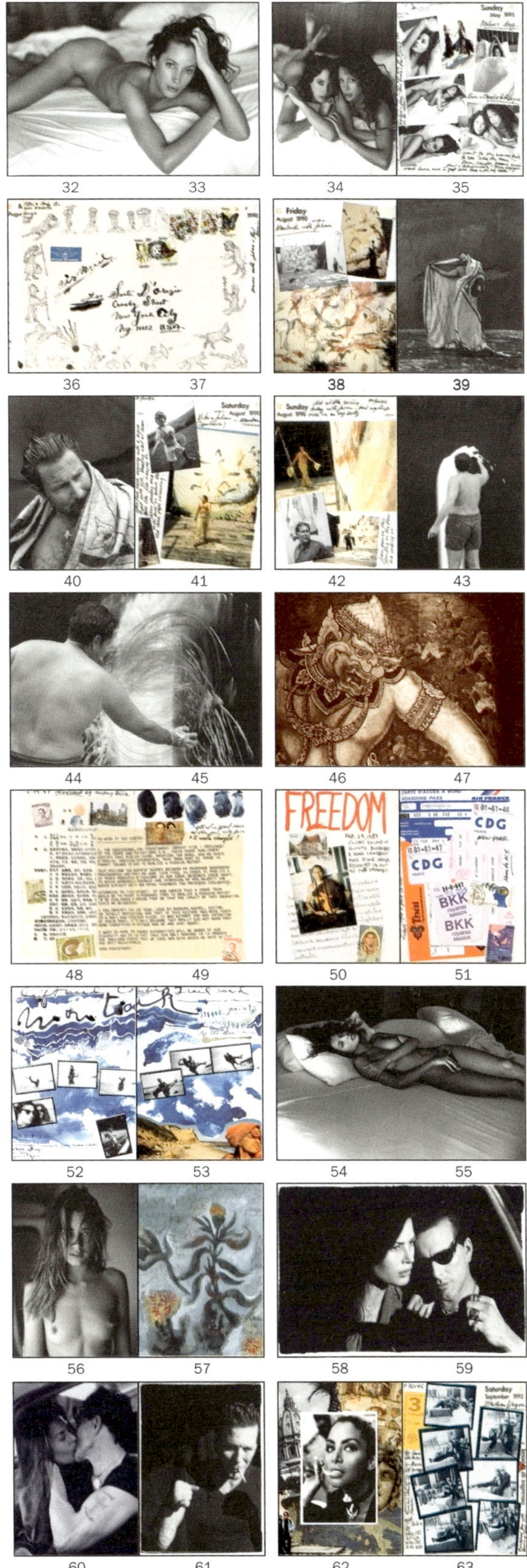

32 33 34 35
36 37 38 39
40 41 42 43
44 45 46 47
48 49 50 51
52 53 54 55
56 57 58 59
60 61 62 63

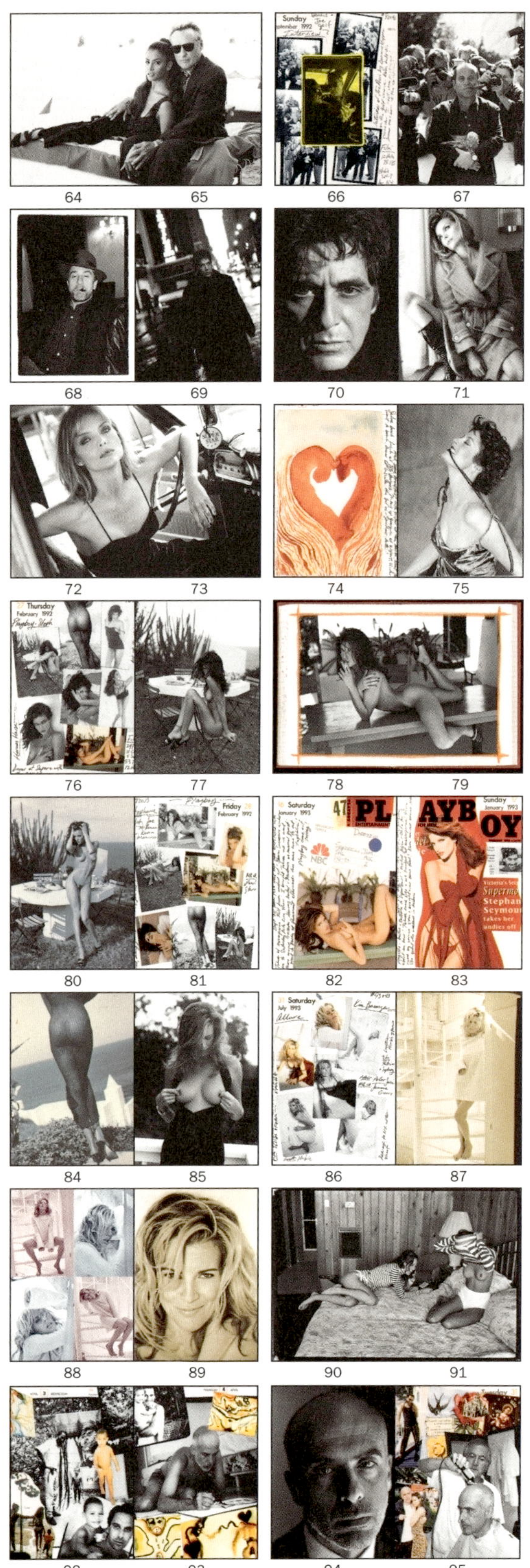

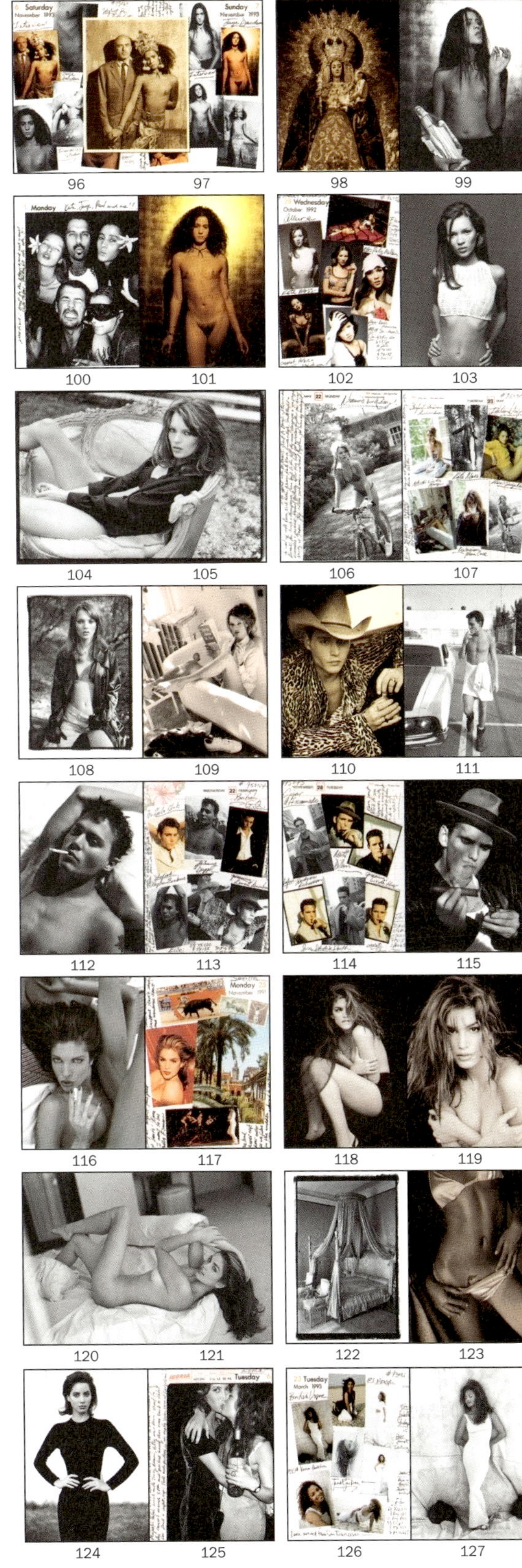

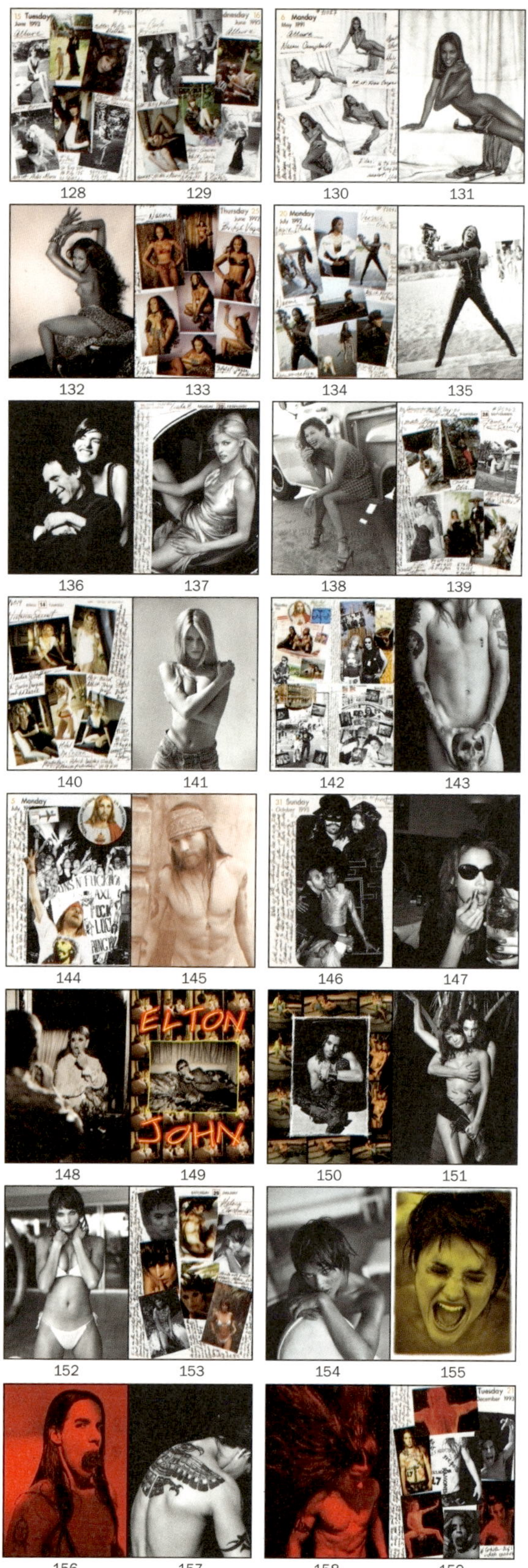

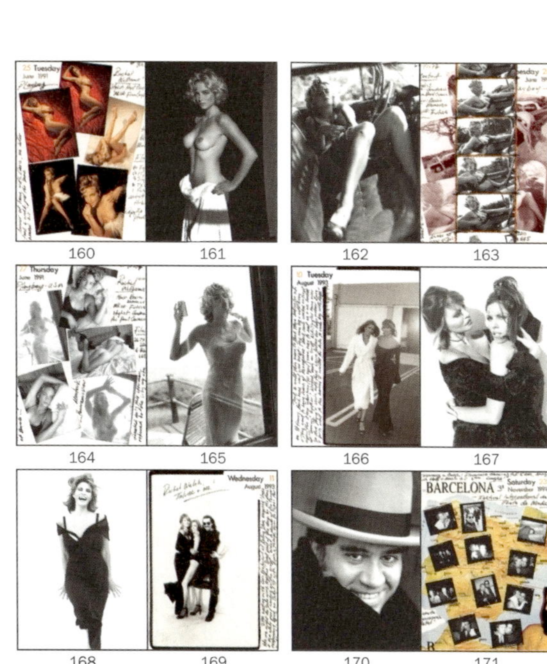

160   161   162   163

164   165   166   167

168   169   170   171

172   173   174   175

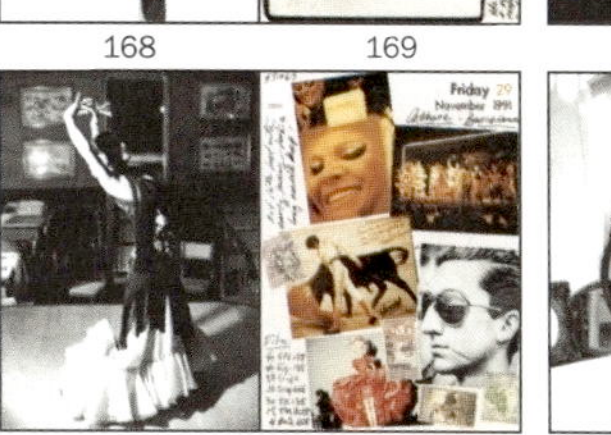
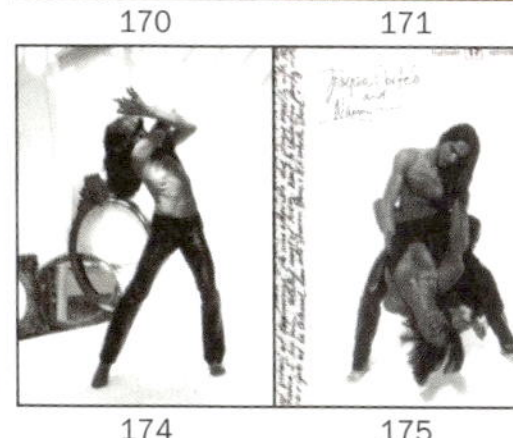
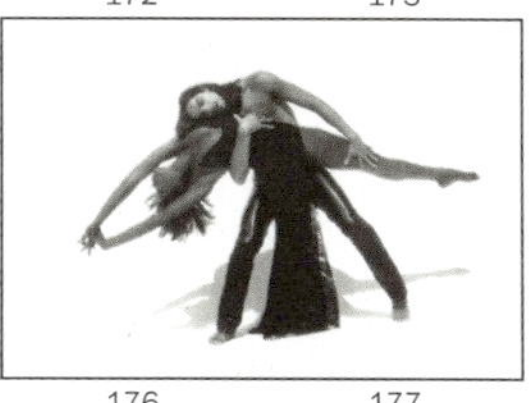
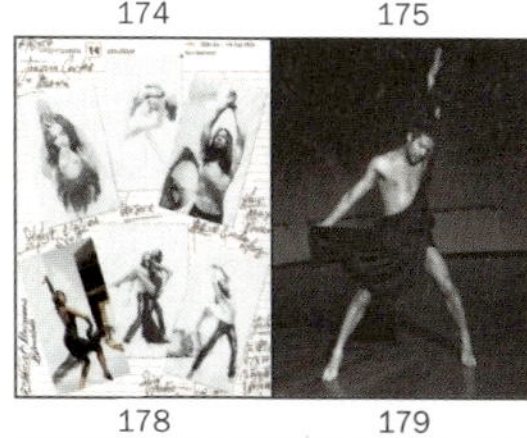
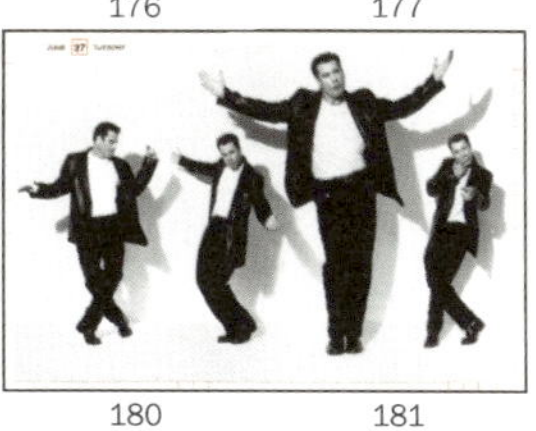
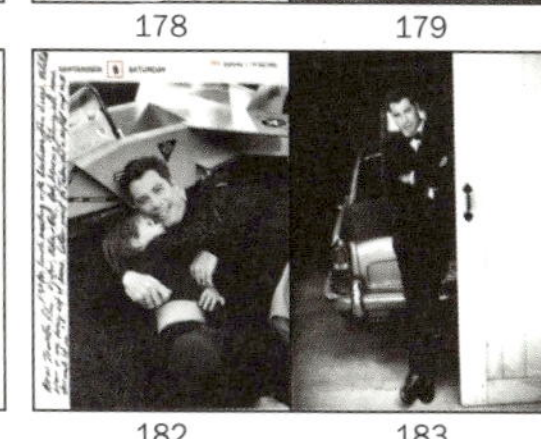

176   177   178   179

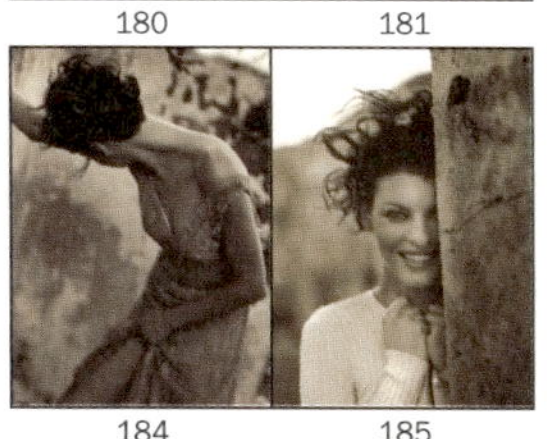
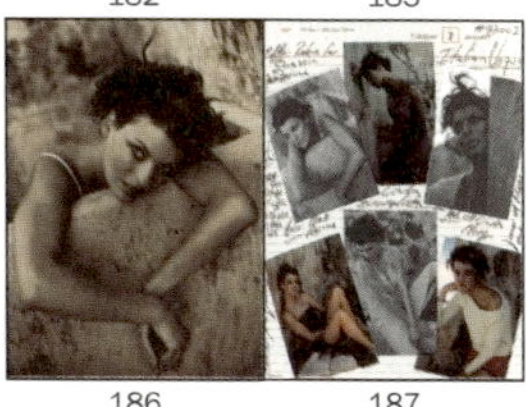

180   181   182   183

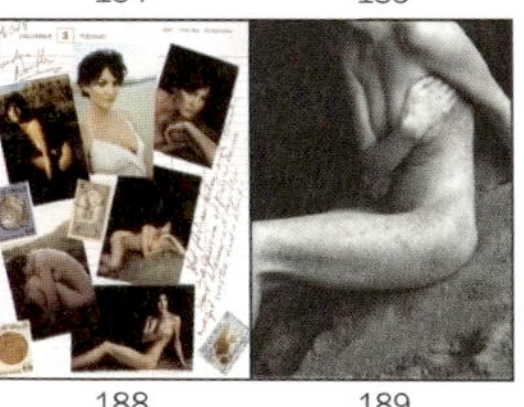
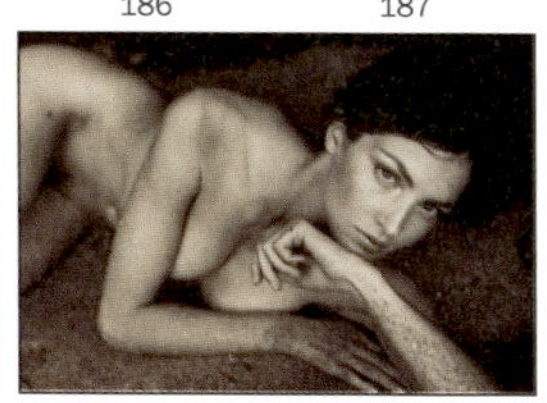

184   185   186   187

188   189   190   191

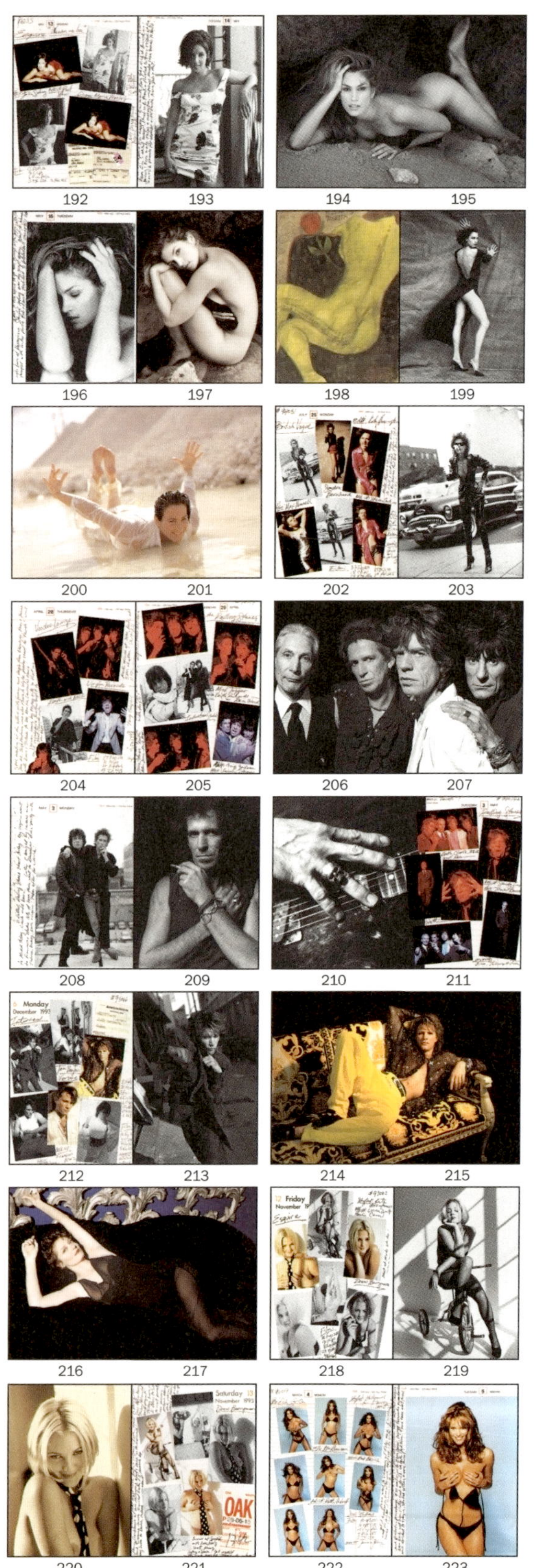

192 193 194 195

196 197 198 199

200 201 202 203

204 205 206 207

208 209 210 211

212 213 214 215

216 217 218 219

220 221 222 223

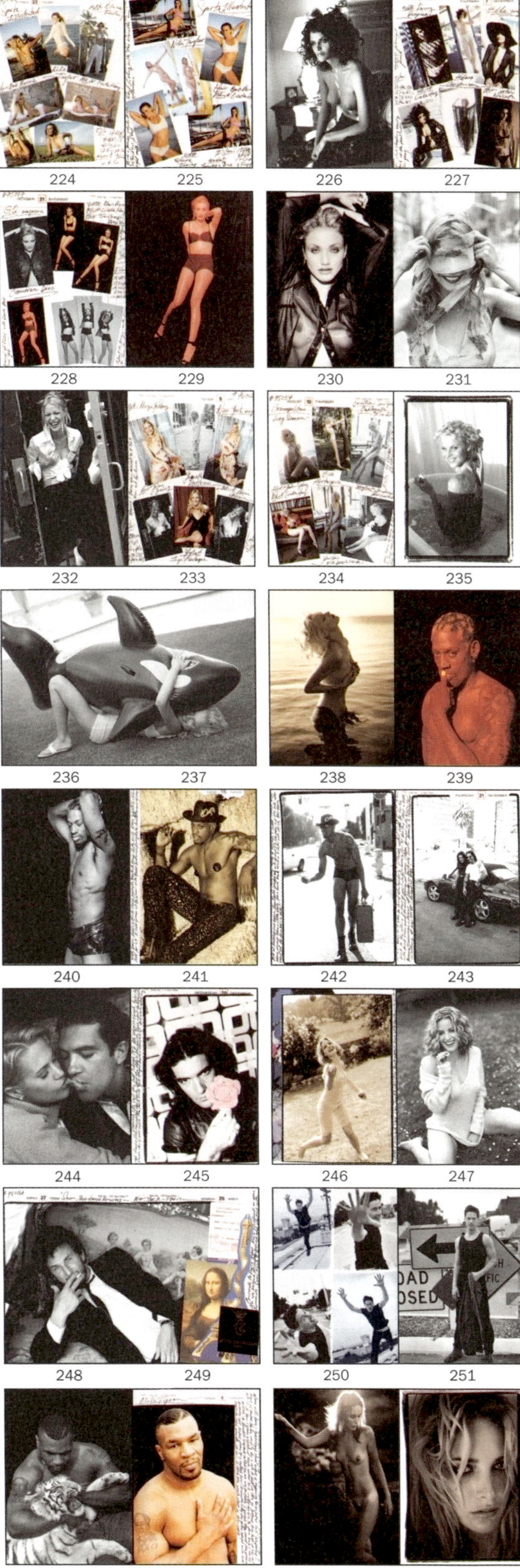

224 225 226 227
228 229 230 231
232 233 234 235
236 237 238 239
240 241 242 243
244 245 246 247
248 249 250 251
252 253 254 255

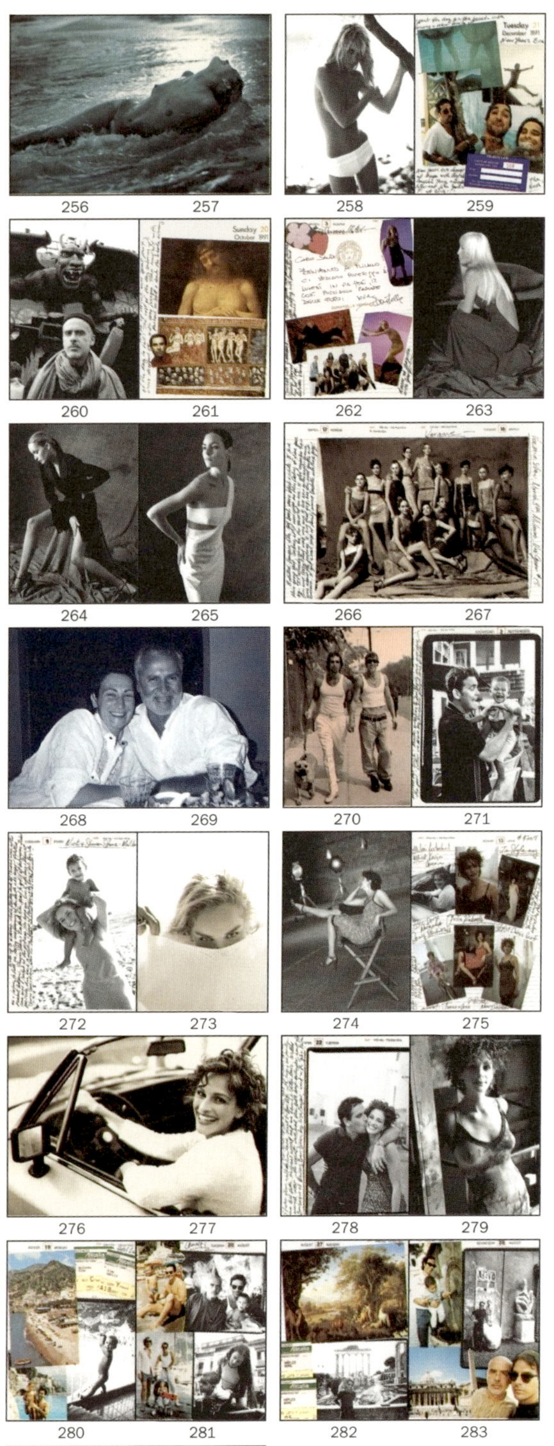

Acknowledgments

I am very grateful for
all the support magazines and
clients have given me over
the years, and I would like to
thank the following:

Condé Nast magazines:
Allure
English Vogue
French Vogue
Italian Vogue
Spanish Vogue
GQ
And the following magazines:
Cigar Aficionado
Cosmopolitan
Detour
Elle
Esquire
German Max
In Style
Interview
Mirabella
New York
Playboy
Premiere
Sports Illustrated
Town & Country

MTV
Victoria's Secret

I would like to thank all
the publicists for making
our lives easier.

Printing and retouching:
Chelsea Black & White Lab,
LTI, Nucleus Imaging
and Chris Bishop.

Very special thanks to my staff
for all their support and hard work:
Joyce Mills, Kate Shela,
Gino Zardo, Ben Hams, James Munoz
and Anna Zantiotis.

Special thanks to David Fahey
and to all my friends, who have made
this book possible.

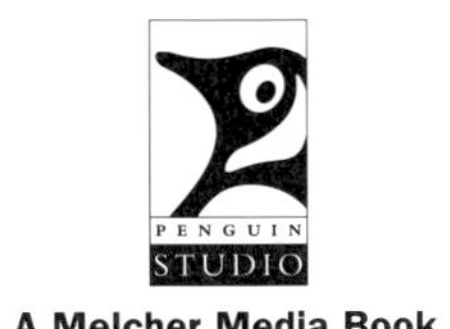

A Melcher Media Book

PENGUIN STUDIO
Published by the Penguin Group
Penguin Putnam Inc.,
375 Hudson Street,
New York, New York 10014, U.S.A.
Penguin Books Ltd,
27 Wrights Lane,
London W8 5TZ, England
Penguin Books Australia Ltd,
Ringwood, Victoria, Australia
Penguin Books Canada Ltd,
10 Alcorn Avenue,
Toronto, Ontario, Canada M4V 3B2
Penguin Books (N.Z.) Ltd,
182-190 Wairau Road,
Auckland 10, New Zealand
Penguin India,
210 Chiranjiv Tower, 43 Nehru Place,
New Delhi 11009, India

Penguin Books Ltd, Registered Offices:
Harmondsworth, Middlesex, England

First published in 1998 by Penguin Studio,
a member of Penguin Putnam Inc.

10 9 8 7 6 5 4 3 2 1

This book has been produced by
Editions du Collectionneur,
13, rue du Cherche-Midi,
75006 Paris, France
under the editorial direction of
Isabelle Salmon, Designer
Dorothee Walliser, Editorial Director
Gilles Tarral, Director of Production

ISBN 0-670-88251-8

About the Author

Born in 1956, Sante D'Orazio grew up in
Brooklyn, New York, and studied fine arts at
Brooklyn College. His photography has appeared
in **Vogue, Allure, Elle, GQ, Playboy, Interview** and
many other publications, and his commercial
clients include **L'Oréal** and **Victoria's Secret**.
D'Orazio's film documentary, **Sammy**, was shown
at the 49th Venice Film Festival. He won Grand
Prize at the International Festival of Fashion
Photography in 1994 and was named one of the 100
most important people in photography by
American Photo in 1998. He lives in
New York City.

Gallery representation:
Fahey/Klein Gallery
148 N. La Brea Avenue,
Los Angeles, CA 90036
Tel: 213.934.2250
Fax: 213.934.4243